THE
WAY
THINGS
WORK
NOW

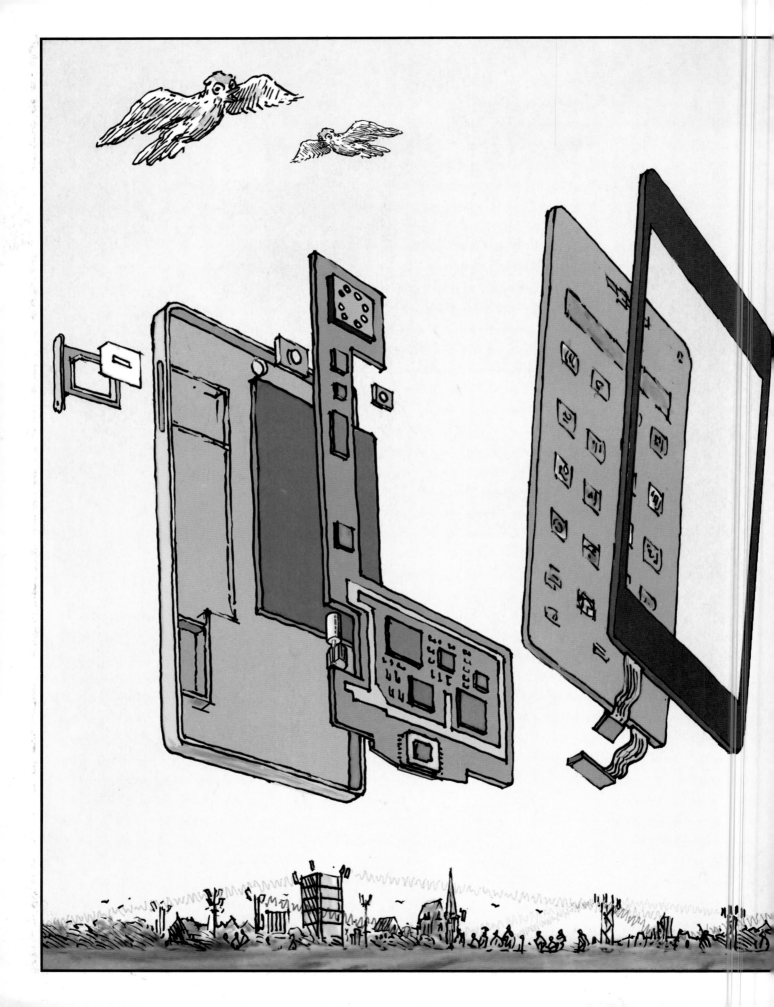

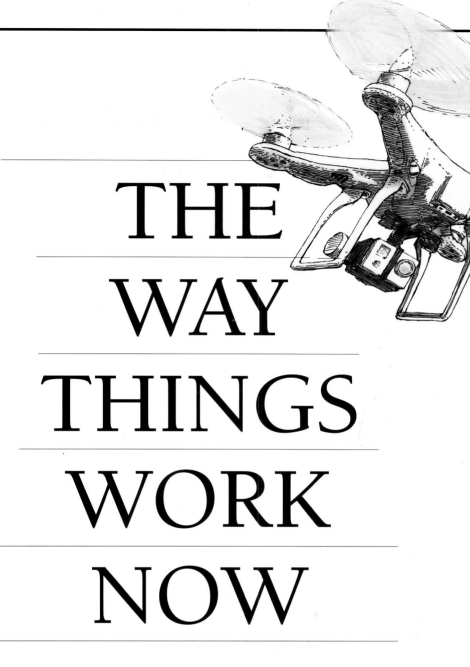

THE WAY THINGS WORK NOW

FROM **LEVERS** TO **LASERS**, **WINDMILLS** TO **WI-FI**, A **VISUAL GUIDE** TO THE **WORLD** OF **MACHINES**

DAVID MACAULAY

WITH NEIL ARDLEY

HOUGHTON MIFFLIN HARCOURT
Boston   New York

Revised text provided by Jack Challoner
Consultants Jack Challoner and Chris Woodford

Compilation copyright © 1988, 1998, 2016 Dorling Kindersley Limited, London
Text copyright © 1988, 1998, 2016 by David Macaulay, Neil Ardley
Illustrations copyright © 1988, 1998, 2016 by David Macaulay
Originally published as *The New Way Things Work*

www.hmhco.com
Library of Congress Cataloging-in-Publication Data is on file.
ISBN 978-0-544-82438-6

Manufactured in China
SCP 10 9 8 7 6 5 4 3 2 1
4500599743

CONTENTS

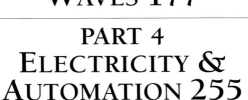

PART 1
THE MECHANICS OF MOVEMENT

INTRODUCTION

Everything a machine does is in accordance with a set of principles or **scientific laws**. To see the way a machine works, you can take the covers off and look inside. But to understand what goes on, you need to get to know the principles that govern its actions. The machines in this and the following parts of this book are therefore grouped by their principles rather than by their uses. This produces some interesting neighbors: the plow rubs shoulders with the zipper, for example, and the hydroelectric power station with the dentist's drill. They may be vastly different in scale and have different purposes, but when seen in terms of principles, *they work in the same way.*

MACHINERY IN MOTION

Mechanical machines work with parts that move, including **levers, gears, belts, wheels, cams, cranks, and springs**. These moving parts are often interconnected in complex linkages, some large enough to move mountains and others almost invisible. Their movement can be so fast that it disappears in a blur of spinning axles and whirling gears, or it can be so slow that nothing seems to be moving at all. But whatever their nature, all machines that use mechanical parts are built with the same single aim: *to change the size or direction of a force.*

MOVEMENT AND FORCE

Many machines convert one form of movement into another. Often linear movement is converted into circular or rotary movement, and vice versa, because the power source driving the machine moves in one way and the machine in another. But whether direction is altered or not, the mechanical parts change the force applied into one—either larger or smaller—that is appropriate for the task to be tackled. A force may be the push of a motor, or the pull of muscle or **gravity**, for example. A machine changes the size of this force and conveys it to the right place to do a job. When you squeeze and twist the handles of a can opener, the blade cuts easily through the lid of the can. This makes light work of something that would otherwise be impossible. The can opener *increases the force* that your wrist produces and applies it where it is needed.

THE CONSERVATION OF ENERGY

Underlying the actions of all machines is one principle that encompasses all the others—the conservation of energy. This principle says that *you can only get as much energy out of a machine as you put into it in the first place*—no more and no less. Energy takes different forms. Movement is a form of energy called **kinetic energy**. It is produced by converting other forms of energy, such as the **potential energy** stored in a spring, the heat in a gasoline engine, the **electric energy** in an electric motor, or the **chemical energy** in muscles. A machine can expend only the same amount of energy as that which is put into it to get things moving. If the force the machine applies is to be greater, then the movement produced must be correspondingly smaller, and vice versa. Overall, *the total energy always remains the same*. The principle of conservation of energy governs all actions. Springs may store energy, and **friction** *will convert energy to* **heat**, but when everything is taken into account, no energy is created and none destroyed. If the principle of conservation of energy were to vanish, then nothing would work. If energy were destroyed as machines worked, then, no matter how powerful they might be, they would all slow down and stop. And if the workings of machines created energy, then all machines would get faster and faster in an energy build-up of titanic proportions. Either way, the world would end—with a whimper in one case and a bang in the other. But the principle of conservation of energy holds good and all machines obey: *energy cannot be created or destroyed, only* **converted** *into different forms*.

THE INCLINED PLANE

ON CAPTURING A MAMMOTH

*I*n the spring of that year, I was invited to the land of the much sought-after wooly mammoth, a land dotted by the now familiar high wooden towers of the mammoth captors. In ancient times the mammoth had been hunted simply for its meat. But its subsequent usefulness in industry and growing popularity as a pet had brought about the development of a more sophisticated and less terminal means of apprehension.

Each unsuspecting beast was lured to the base of a tower from which a boulder of reasonable dimensions was then dropped from a humanitarian height onto its thick skull. Once stunned, a mammoth could easily be led to the paddock, where an ice pack and fresh swamp grass would quickly overcome hurt feelings and innate distrust.

THE PRINCIPLE OF THE INCLINED PLANE

The laws of physics decree that raising an object, such as a mammoth-stunning boulder, to a particular height requires a certain amount of work. Those same laws also decree that no way can ever be found to reduce that amount. The ramp makes life easier not by altering the amount of work that is needed, but by altering the *way* in which the work is done.

Work has two aspects to it: the effort that you put in, and the distance over which you maintain the effort. If the effort increases, the distance must decrease, and vice versa.

This is easiest to understand by looking at two extremes. Climbing a hill by the steepest route requires the most effort, but the distance that you have to cover is shortest. Climbing up the gentlest slope requires the least effort, but the

distance is greatest. The work you do is the same in either case, and equals the effort (the force you exert) multiplied by the distance over which you maintain the effort.

So what you gain in effort, you pay in distance. This is a basic rule that is obeyed by many mechanical devices, and it is the reason why the ramp works: it reduces the effort needed to raise an object by increasing the distance that it moves.

The ramp is an example of an inclined plane. The principle behind the inclined plane was made use of in ancient times. Ramps enabled the Egyptians to build their pyramids and temples. Since then, the inclined plane has been put to work in a whole host of devices from locks and cutters to plows and zippers, as well as in all the many machines that make use of the screw.

While the process was more or less successful, it had a couple of major drawbacks. The biggest problem was that of simply getting a heavy boulder to the right height. This required an almost Herculean effort, and Hercules was not due to be born for several centuries yet. The second problem was that the mammoth, once hit, would invariably crash into the tower, either hurling his captors to the ground, or at least seriously damaging the structure.

After making a few calculations, I informed my hosts that both problems could be solved simultaneously by building earth ramps rather than wooden towers. The inherent sturdiness of the ramp would make it virtually indestructible should a mammoth fall against it. And now, rather than trying to hoist the boulder straight up, it could be rolled gradually to the required height, therefore necessitating far less effort.

At first, the simplicity of my solution was greeted with understandable skepticism. "What do we do with the towers?" they asked. I made a few more calculations and then suggested commercial and retail development on the lower levels and luxury apartments above.

HOW EFFORT AND DISTANCE ARE LINKED

The sloping face of this ramp is twice as long as its vertical face. The effort that is needed to move a load up the sloping face is therefore half that needed to raise it up the vertical face.

HALF EFFORT

FULL EFFORT

SLOPING FACE

VERTICAL FACE

THE WEDGE

In most of the machines that make use of the inclined plane, it appears in the form of a wedge. A door wedge is a simple application; you push the sharp end of the wedge under the door and it moves in to jam the door open.

The wedge acts as a moving inclined plane. Instead of having an object move up an inclined plane, the plane itself can move to raise the object. As the plane moves a greater distance than the object, it raises the object with a greater force. The door wedge works in this way. As it jams under the door, the wedge raises the door slightly and exerts a strong force on it. The door in turn forces the wedge hard against the floor, and friction (see pp. 82-83) with the floor makes the wedge grip the floor so that it holds the door open.

LOCKS AND KEYS

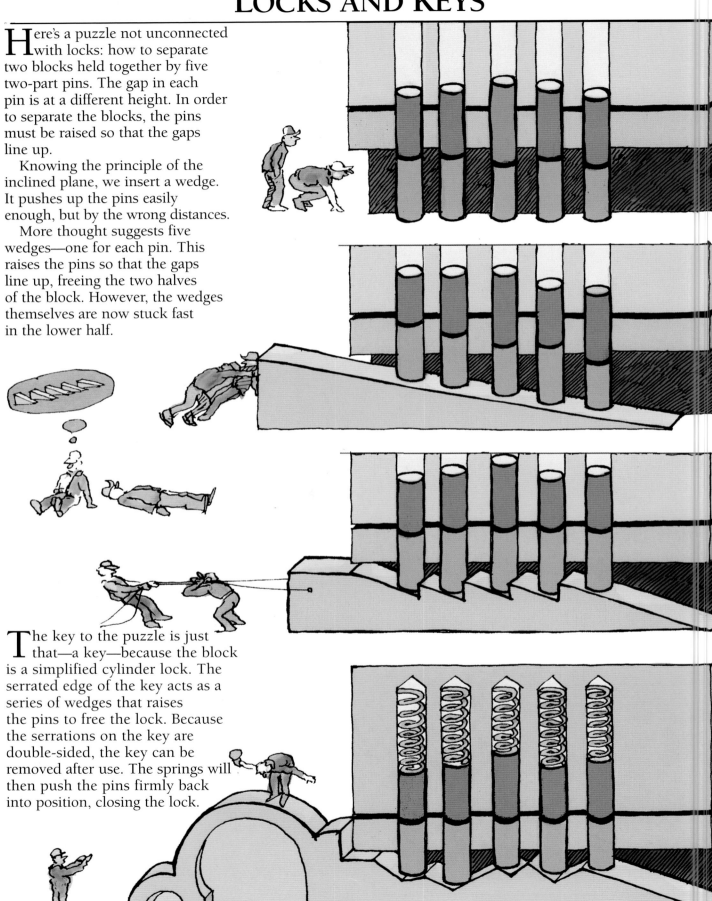

Here's a puzzle not unconnected with locks: how to separate two blocks held together by five two-part pins. The gap in each pin is at a different height. In order to separate the blocks, the pins must be raised so that the gaps line up.

Knowing the principle of the inclined plane, we insert a wedge. It pushes up the pins easily enough, but by the wrong distances.

More thought suggests five wedges—one for each pin. This raises the pins so that the gaps line up, freeing the two halves of the block. However, the wedges themselves are now stuck fast in the lower half.

The key to the puzzle is just that—a key—because the block is a simplified cylinder lock. The serrated edge of the key acts as a series of wedges that raises the pins to free the lock. Because the serrations on the key are double-sided, the key can be removed after use. The springs will then push the pins firmly back into position, closing the lock.

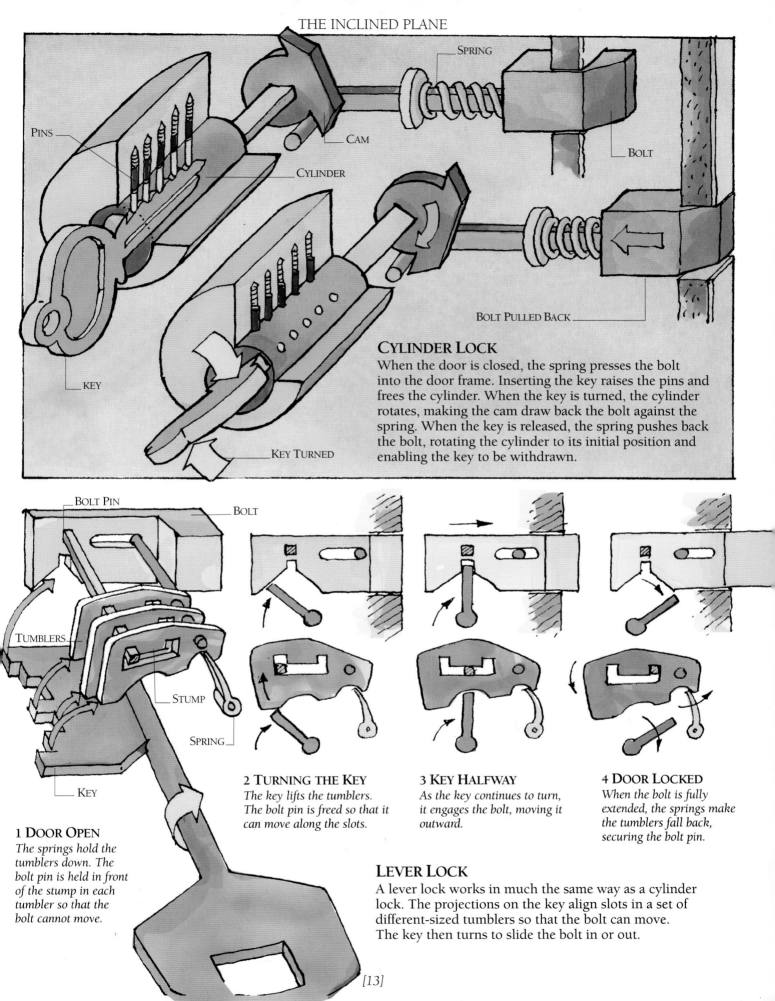

PINS

CYLINDER

CAM

SPRING

BOLT

KEY

BOLT PULLED BACK

KEY TURNED

CYLINDER LOCK

When the door is closed, the spring presses the bolt into the door frame. Inserting the key raises the pins and frees the cylinder. When the key is turned, the cylinder rotates, making the cam draw back the bolt against the spring. When the key is released, the spring pushes back the bolt, rotating the cylinder to its initial position and enabling the key to be withdrawn.

BOLT PIN

BOLT

TUMBLERS

STUMP

SPRING

KEY

2 TURNING THE KEY
The key lifts the tumblers. The bolt pin is freed so that it can move along the slots.

3 KEY HALFWAY
As the key continues to turn, it engages the bolt, moving it outward.

4 DOOR LOCKED
When the bolt is fully extended, the springs make the tumblers fall back, securing the bolt pin.

1 DOOR OPEN
The springs hold the tumblers down. The bolt pin is held in front of the stump in each tumbler so that the bolt cannot move.

LEVER LOCK

A lever lock works in much the same way as a cylinder lock. The projections on the key align slots in a set of different-sized tumblers so that the bolt can move. The key then turns to slide the bolt in or out.

[13]

CUTTING MACHINES

Nearly all cutting machines make use of the wedge, a form of inclined plane. A wedge-shaped blade converts a forward movement into a parting movement that acts at right angles to the blade.

MOVEMENT DOWNWARD

MOVEMENT SIDEWAYS

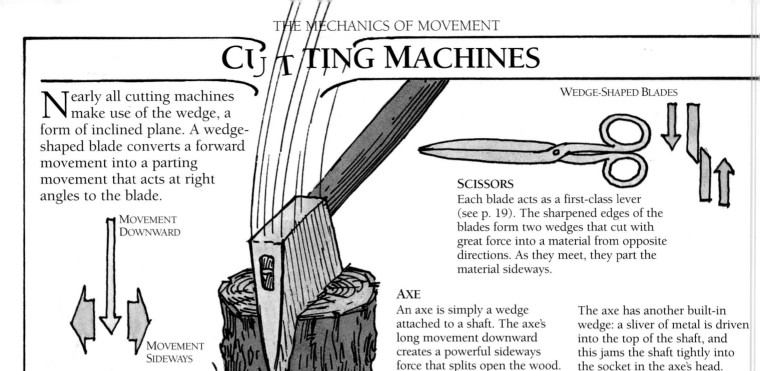

WEDGE-SHAPED BLADES

SCISSORS

Each blade acts as a first-class lever (see p. 19). The sharpened edges of the blades form two wedges that cut with great force into a material from opposite directions. As they meet, they part the material sideways.

AXE

An axe is simply a wedge attached to a shaft. The axe's long movement downward creates a powerful sideways force that splits open the wood.

The axe has another built-in wedge: a sliver of metal is driven into the top of the shaft, and this jams the shaft tightly into the socket in the axe's head.

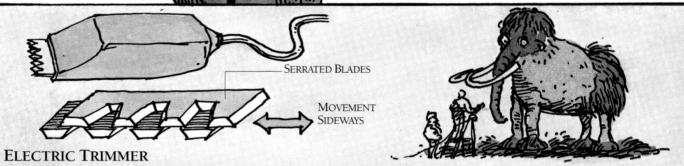

SERRATED BLADES

MOVEMENT SIDEWAYS

ELECTRIC TRIMMER

An electric trimmer contains two serrated blades driven by a crank mechanism (see pp. 48-49). The blades move to and fro over each other. As gaps open between the serrations, stems or hairs enter to be trapped and then sliced as the blades cross. The trimmer's blades act as paired wedges like the blades of scissors.

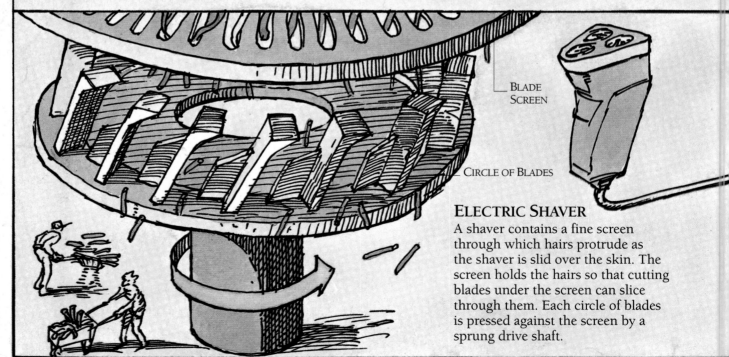

BLADE SCREEN

CIRCLE OF BLADES

ELECTRIC SHAVER

A shaver contains a fine screen through which hairs protrude as the shaver is slid over the skin. The screen holds the hairs so that cutting blades under the screen can slice through them. Each circle of blades is pressed against the screen by a sprung drive shaft.

THE CAN OPENER

HANDLE

CUTTING WHEEL

SPUR GEARS

TOOTHED WHEEL

A can opener has a sharp-edged cutting blade or wheel that slices into the lid. A toothed wheel fits beneath the lip of the can, and rotates the can so that the cutting wheel is forced into the lid. Two further toothed wheels—one above the other—form a pair of spur gears (see p. 37) to transmit the turning force from the handle.

THE PLOW

A plow is a wedge that is dragged through the ground either by a draft animal or a tractor. It cuts away the top layer of soil, and then lifts and turns over the layer. In this way, the soil is broken up for planting crops. In addition, vegetation growing in or lying on the soil is buried so that it rots and provides nutrients for the crops. The plow is one of our oldest machines. Wooden plows have been in use for about five thousand years, although steel plows date back less than two centuries.

THE MAIN PARTS OF A PLOW

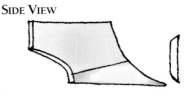

SIDE VIEW

A plow has four main parts, which are all made of steel. The coulter precedes the main body of the plow, which consists of the share, moldboard and landside. The coulter, share, and moldboard all act as wedges, and can exert great force to plow hard and heavy soil.

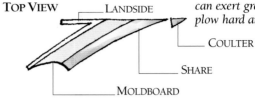

TOP VIEW — LANDSIDE

COULTER

SHARE

MOLDBOARD

THE PLOWING SEQUENCE

THE COULTER *slices a furrow in the soil.*

The coulter creates a furrow by making a vertical cut in the soil. With animal plows, the coulter is a knife-like blade. Tractor-drawn plows normally have disk coulters, which are sharp-edged wheels that spin freely as the plow is drawn forward.

The share follows the coulter, making a horizontal cut and freeing the top layer of soil. Attached to the share is the moldboard, which lifts and turns the layer. The landside is fixed to the side of the moldboard and slides along the vertical wall of the furrow. It thrusts the moldboard outward to move the layer of soil.

THE SHARE *cuts loose the top layer of soil.*

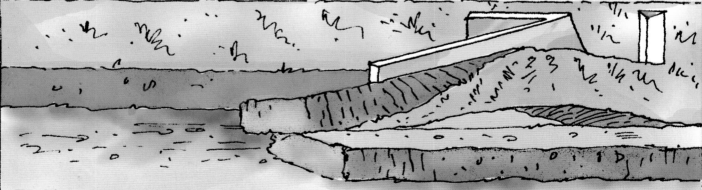

THE MOLDBOARD *lifts and turns the layer of soil.*

THE ZIP

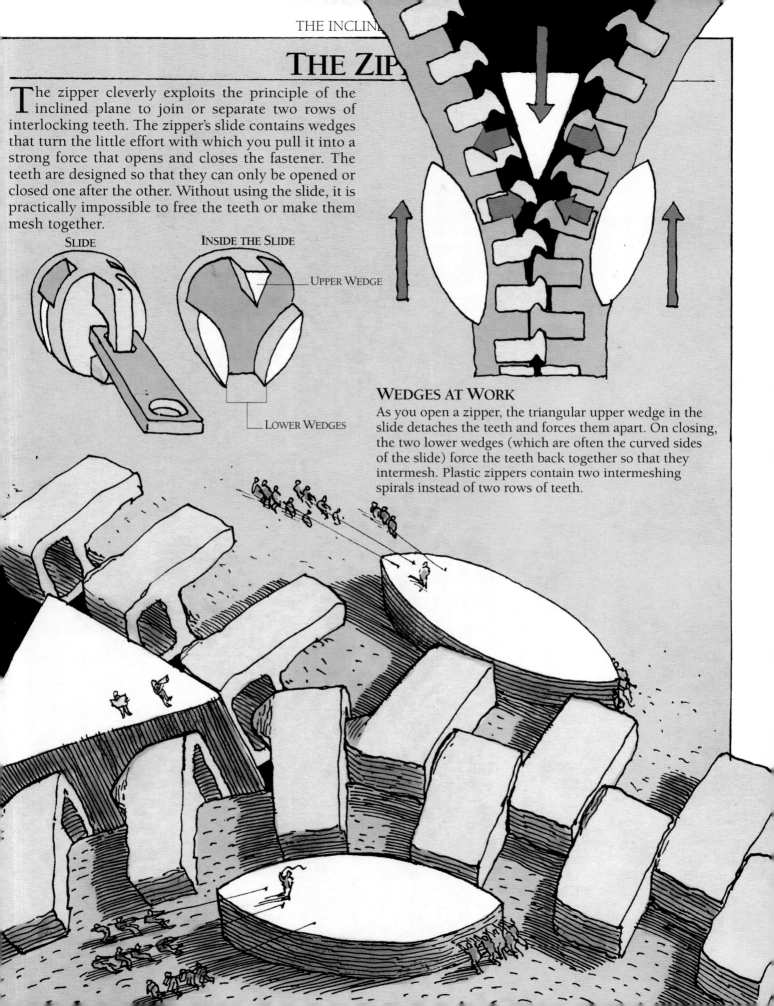

The zipper cleverly exploits the principle of the inclined plane to join or separate two rows of interlocking teeth. The zipper's slide contains wedges that turn the little effort with which you pull it into a strong force that opens and closes the fastener. The teeth are designed so that they can only be opened or closed one after the other. Without using the slide, it is practically impossible to free the teeth or make them mesh together.

SLIDE

INSIDE THE SLIDE

UPPER WEDGE

LOWER WEDGES

WEDGES AT WORK

As you open a zipper, the triangular upper wedge in the slide detaches the teeth and forces them apart. On closing, the two lower wedges (which are often the curved sides of the slide) force the teeth back together so that they intermesh. Plastic zippers contain two intermeshing spirals instead of two rows of teeth.

LEVERS

ON WEIGHING A MAMMOTH

*B*efore being shipped to its final destination, a mammoth must be weighed. I was fortunate enough in one village to witness the procedure at first hand. The center of a tree trunk was placed directly on a boulder. One end of the trunk was then pulled down and the mammoth encouraged to sit on it. No sooner did the beast seem reasonably comfortable than a number of villagers scrambled onto the other end of the trunk. Slowly their end sank and, as it did, the startled mammoth rose into the air. I was told that when the trunk reached a horizontal position, the combined weight of the people would equal that of the mammoth. This seemed reasonable enough.

THE PRINCIPLE OF LEVERS

The tree trunk is acting as a lever, which is simply a bar or rod that tilts on a pivot, or fulcrum. If you apply a force by pushing or pulling on one part of the lever, the lever swings about the fulcrum to produce a useful action at another point. The force that you apply is called the *effort*, and the lever moves at another point to raise a weight or overcome a resistance, both of which are called the *load*.

Where you move a lever is just as important as the amount of effort you apply to it. Less effort can move the same load, provided that it is applied further from the fulcrum; however, the effort has to move a greater distance to shift the load. As with the inclined plane, you gain in force what you pay in distance. Some levers reverse this effect to produce a gain in distance moved at the expense of force.

With levers, the distances moved by the effort and load depend on how far they are from the fulcrum. The principle of levers, which relates the effort and load, states that the effort times its distance from the fulcrum equals the load times its distance from the fulcrum.

FULCRUM IN CENTER

The effort and load are the same distance from the fulcrum. In this situation, the load and effort are equal, and both move the same distance up or down as the lever balances.

LOAD
Weight of mammoth.

EFFORT
Weight of ten people.

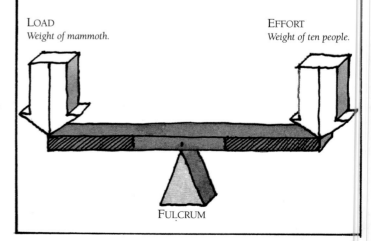

FULCRUM

It was then that I noticed across the square a second equally large mammoth about to be weighed, this time using far fewer people as a counterbalance. As I watched, anticipating disaster, the boulder was rolled closer to what would be the mammoth's end of the tree trunk. Once the mammoth was in place, a mere handful of people climbed onto the other end. To my amazement the tree trunk gently assumed a horizontal position. I was then informed that the length of the tree trunk from the people to the boulder multiplied by their combined weight would equal the length of the trunk from the boulder to the mammoth multiplied by its weight.

I was in the midst of calculations to verify this most unlikely theory when I heard a scream. Apparently, all the villagers had not disembarked from the trunk simultaneously, thereby causing a lad to be dramatically launched. I made a note, thinking that one day this might be useful.

FIRST-CLASS LEVERS

There are three different basic kinds of levers. All the levers on these two pages are first-class levers. First-class levers aren't superior to other-class levers; they are just levers in which the fulcrum is always placed between the effort and the load.

If the fulcrum is placed in the center—as in the diagram on the left—the effort and load are at the same distance from it and are equal. The weight of the people is the same as the weight of the mammoth.

However, if the people are placed twice as far from the fulcrum as the mammoth—as in the diagram on the right—only half the number of people is needed to raise the mammoth. And if the people were three times as far from the fulcrum than the mammoth, only a third would be needed, and so on, because the lever magnifies the force applied to it.

These mammoth-weighing levers balance in order to measure weight, which is why this kind of weighing machine is called a balance. When the lever comes to rest, the force of the effort balances the force of the load, which is its weight. Many other kinds of levers work to produce movement.

FULCRUM OFF-CENTER
The effort is twice as far from the fulcrum as the load. Here, the effort moves twice as far as the load, but is only half its amount.

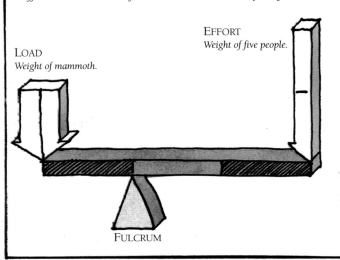

EFFORT
Weight of five people.

LOAD
Weight of mammoth.

FULCRUM

ON MAMMOTH HYGIENE

*E*arly in my researches I discovered that mammoths smell and so unavoidably do their immediate surroundings. I was therefore gratified to observe that in order to minimize any unpleasant odor, the staff of the mammoth paddock train their animals to sit on mats. These they change with some regularity.

Since mammoths often refuse to budge once settled, the keepers have learned how to remove mats while in use. One end of a trimmed tree trunk is carefully slipped under the mammoth. By raising the other end a fair distance the mammoth is lifted just enough to release the fetid fabric.

I found the ease with which the keepers could raise their oversize charges quite astounding. I also noted that wheelbarrows are an invaluable asset during clean-up sessions.

SECOND-CLASS LEVERS

Both the mammoth-lifter and the wheelbarrow are examples of second-class levers. Here, the fulcrum is at one end of the bar or rod and the effort is applied to the other end. The load to be raised or overcome lies between them.

With this kind of lever, the effort is always further from the fulcrum than the load. As a result, the load cannot move as far as the effort, but the force with which it moves is always greater than the effort. The closer the load is to the fulcrum, the more the force is increased, and the easier it becomes to raise the load. A second-class lever always magnifies force but decreases the distance moved.

A wheelbarrow works in the same way as the mammoth-lifter, allowing one to lift and shift a heavy load with the wheel as a fulcrum. Levers can also act to press on objects with great force rather than to lift them. In this case, the load is the resistance that the object makes to the pressing force. Scissors and nutcrackers (see p. 22) are first-class and second-class examples. These devices are compound levers, which are pairs of levers hinged at the fulcrum.

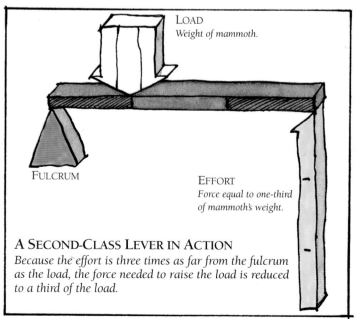

LOAD
Weight of mammoth.

FULCRUM

EFFORT
Force equal to one-third of mammoth's weight.

A SECOND-CLASS LEVER IN ACTION
Because the effort is three times as far from the fulcrum as the load, the force needed to raise the load is reduced to a third of the load.

ON TUSK TRIMMING AND ATTENDANT PROBLEMS

I *watched with great curiosity a mammoth that was having its tusks trimmed as a precaution prior to being shipped. The beast was clearly not happy as the workers sawed, chipped, and filed away. No sooner had I recalled the old adage that second only to the fury of a woman scorned is the wrath of a disgruntled mammoth, when suddenly the enraged creature wrapped its trunk around the end of a nearby weighing log and began swinging it from side to side.*

I was able to note during the ensuing collapse of the trimming stand that although the mammoth's head pivoted only a short distance, the free end of the log was swinging much further, thereby achieving a stunning velocity.

THIRD-CLASS LEVERS

In extending its trunk with that of a tree, the mammoth now has something in common with such innocuous devices as a fishing rod and a pair of tweezers. It has become a giant-sized third-class lever.

Here, the fulcrum is again at one end of the lever but this time the positions of the load and effort are reversed. The load to be raised or overcome is furthest away from the fulcrum, while the effort is applied between the fulcrum and the load. As the load is furthest out, it always moves with less force than the effort, but it travels a proportionately greater distance. A third-class lever therefore always magnifies the distance moved but reduces the force.

The mammoth's neck is the fulcrum, and the end of the log moves a greater distance than the trunk gripping it. The force with which the log strikes the people is less than the effort of the trunk, but still enough to overcome their weight and scatter them far and wide. The end of the log moves faster than the trunk and builds up quite a speed to get the people moving quickly.

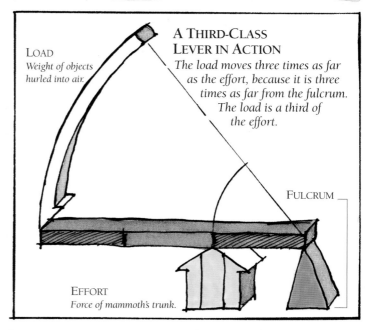

LOAD
Weight of objects hurled into air.

A THIRD-CLASS LEVER IN ACTION
The load moves three times as far as the effort, because it is three times as far from the fulcrum. The load is a third of the effort.

FULCRUM

EFFORT
Force of mammoth's trunk.

LEVERS IN ACTION

Oh, Lever! How do I use thee?
Why not count the ways?...

FULCRUM   LOAD   EFFORT

FIRST-CLASS LEVERS

BALANCE
The object to be weighed is the load and the weights make up the effort. The two are equal, being at the same distance from the fulcrum.

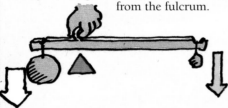

BEAM SCALE
The fulcrum is off-center, and the weight is moved along the bar until it balances the object being weighed.

NAIL EXTRACTOR

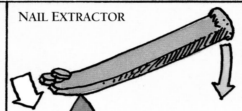

The effort of the hand is magnified to pull out a nail. The load is the resistance of a nail to extraction.

HAND CART

Tipping the handle of the hand cart with a light effort raises a heavy load.

PLIERS

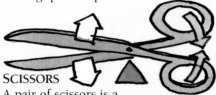

A pair of pliers is a compound lever (a pair of levers hinged at the fulcrum). The load is the resistance of an object to the grip of the pliers.

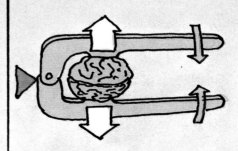

SCISSORS
A pair of scissors is a compound first-class lever. It produces a strong cutting action very near the hinge. The load is the resistance of the fabric to the cutting blades.

SECOND-CLASS LEVERS

WHEELBARROW
Lifting the handles with a light effort raises a heavy load nearer the wheel.

BOTTLE OPENER
Pushing up the handle overcomes the strong resistance of a bottle cap.

NUTCRACKERS
A pair of nutcrackers is a compound second-class lever. The load is the resistance of a shell to cracking.

THIRD-CLASS LEVERS

HAMMER

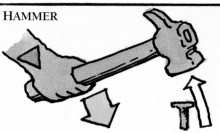

A hammer acts as a third-class lever when it is used to drive in a nail. The fulcrum is the wrist, and the load is the resistance of the wood. The hammer head moves faster than the hand to strike the nail.

FISHING ROD

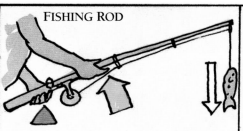

One hand supplies the effort to move the rod, while the other hand acts as the fulcrum. The load is the weight of the fish, which is raised a long distance with a short movement of the hand.

TWEEZERS

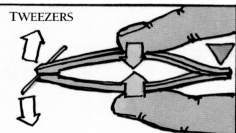

A pair of tweezers is a compound third-class lever. The effort exerted by the fingers is reduced at the tweezer tips, so that delicate objects can be gripped. The load is the resistance of the hair.

MULTIPLE LEVERS

EXCAVATOR

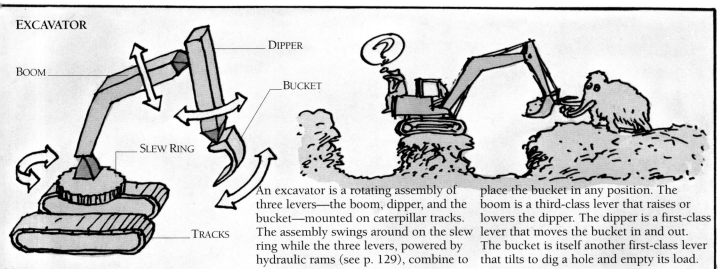

BOOM

DIPPER

BUCKET

SLEW RING

TRACKS

An excavator is a rotating assembly of three levers—the boom, dipper, and the bucket—mounted on caterpillar tracks. The assembly swings around on the slew ring while the three levers, powered by hydraulic rams (see p. 129), combine to place the bucket in any position. The boom is a third-class lever that raises or lowers the dipper. The dipper is a first-class lever that moves the bucket in and out. The bucket is itself another first-class lever that tilts to dig a hole and empty its load.

NAIL CLIPPERS

Nail clippers are a neat combination of two levers that produce a strong cutting action while at the same time being easy to control. The handle is a second-class lever that presses the cutting blades together. It produces a strong effort on the blades, which form a compound third-class lever. The cutting edges move a short distance to overcome the tough resistance of the nail as they slice through it.

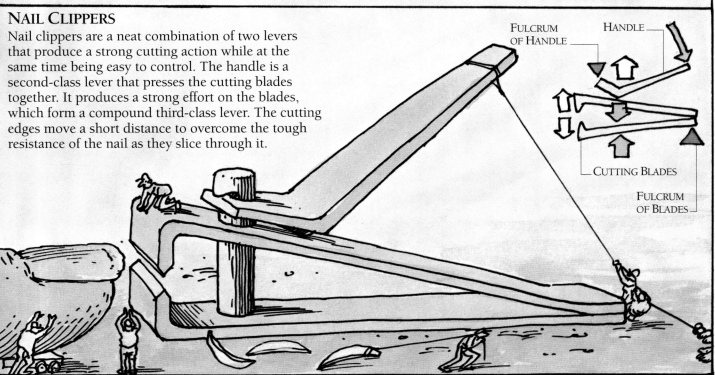

FULCRUM OF HANDLE

HANDLE

CUTTING BLADES

FULCRUM OF BLADES

WEIGHING MACHINES

THE ROBERVAL ENIGMA

This simple kitchen balance or scale is based on the Roberval enigma, a linkage of parallel levers devised by the French mathematician Roberval in 1669. This allows the pans to remain horizontal, and also allows objects and weights to be placed at any position in the pans without affecting the accuracy of the scale.

At first sight, this seems to defy the principle of levers – hence the enigma. But their weight acts at the support of each pan, and not at its position on the pan.

A balance is a first-class lever. As the centers of the two pans are the same distance from the central pivot, they balance when the weight on one pan equals that on the other. Balances with suspended pans work in the same way.

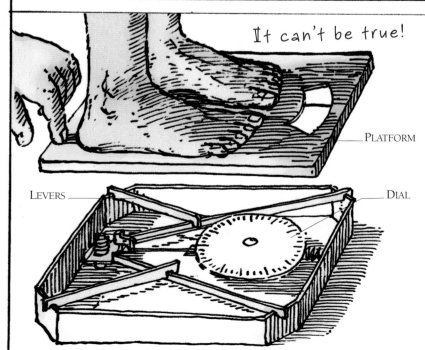

It can't be true!

PLATFORM

LEVERS

DIAL

BATHROOM SCALE

For safety, your bathroom scale will barely move as you step onto the platform, no matter how heavy you are. The mechanism inside magnifies this tiny movement considerably, turning the dial sufficiently to register your weight.

A system of third-class levers pivoting on the case beneath the platform transmits its movement to the calibrating plate, which is attached to the powerful main spring. The levers force the plate down, extending the spring by an amount in exact proportion to your weight, one of the key properties of springs (see pp. 78-79). The crank—a first-class lever—turns, pulled by another spring attached to the dial mechanism. This contains a rack and pinion gear (see p. 37) which turns the dial, showing your weight through a window in the platform.

On your stepping off the platform, the main spring retracts. It raises the platform and turns the crank to return the dial to zero.

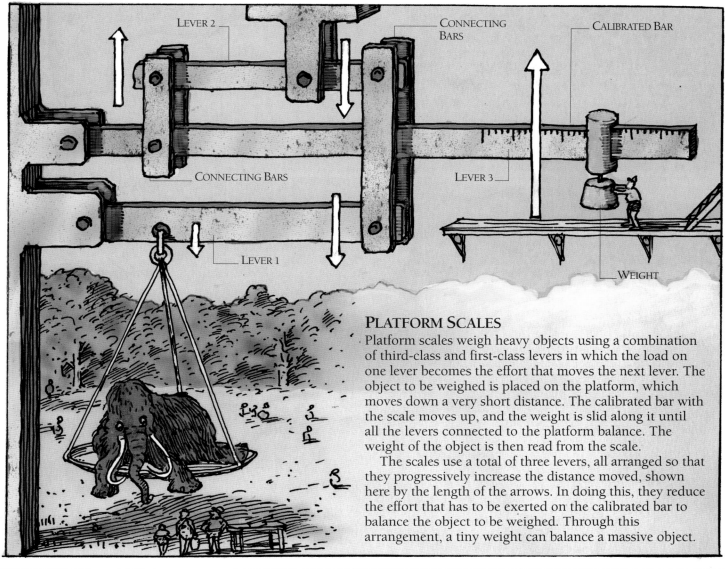

LEVER 2

CONNECTING BARS

CALIBRATED BAR

CONNECTING BARS

LEVER 3

LEVER 1

WEIGHT

PLATFORM SCALES

Platform scales weigh heavy objects using a combination of third-class and first-class levers in which the load on one lever becomes the effort that moves the next lever. The object to be weighed is placed on the platform, which moves down a very short distance. The calibrated bar with the scale moves up, and the weight is slid along it until all the levers connected to the platform balance. The weight of the object is then read from the scale.

The scales use a total of three levers, all arranged so that they progressively increase the distance moved, shown here by the length of the arrows. In doing this, they reduce the effort that has to be exerted on the calibrated bar to balance the object to be weighed. Through this arrangement, a tiny weight can balance a massive object.

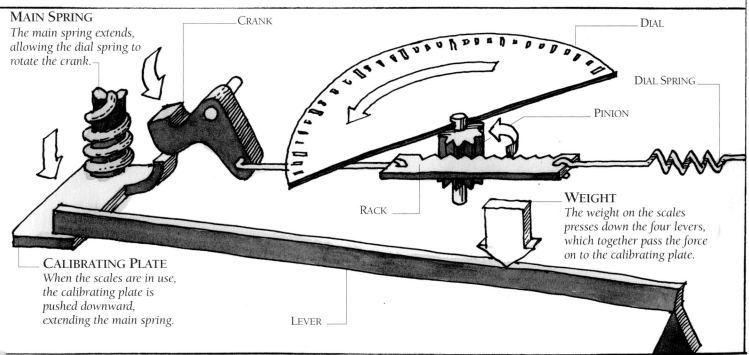

MAIN SPRING
The main spring extends, allowing the dial spring to rotate the crank.

CRANK

DIAL

DIAL SPRING

PINION

RACK

WEIGHT
The weight on the scales presses down the four levers, which together pass the force on to the calibrating plate.

CALIBRATING PLATE
When the scales are in use, the calibrating plate is pushed downward, extending the main spring.

LEVER

GRAND PIANO

Each key of a piano is linked to a complex system of levers called the action. Overall, the levers transmit the movement of the fingertip to the felt-tipped hammer that strikes the taut piano wire and sounds a note. The action magnifies movement so that the hammer moves a greater distance than the player's fingertip. The system of levers is very responsive, allowing the pianist to play quickly and produce a wide range of volume.

THE ACTION IN ACTION

The key raises the wippen, which forces up the jack against the hammer roller and lifts the lever carrying the hammer. The key also raises the damper and immediately *after striking the wire, the hammer drops back, allowing the wire to sound. On releasing the key, the damper drops back onto the wire, cutting off the sound.*

PARTS OF THE ACTION
1 KEY
2 WIPPEN
3 JACK
4 HAMMER ROLLER
5 REPETITION LEVER
6 HAMMER
7 WIRE
8 DAMPER
9 CHECK

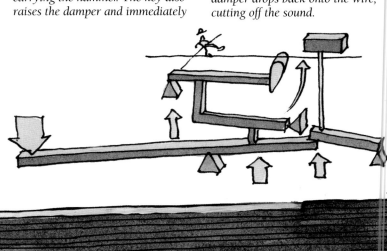

PEDAL POWER

A piano's pedals change the sound the piano makes.
The pedals are first-class levers (see p. 19), which transmit the force applied by the player's foot to various parts inside the piano. Because the fulcrum is halfway along the length of a pedal, pressing it does not change the strength of the force applied; it simply changes its direction: one end of the lever pushes a rod upward whenever the player pushes down on the other end.

SOFT PEDAL

Most keys have two or three strings, which are struck together to sound the note. The soft pedal moves the hammer sideways so that it strikes only one or two of the three strings, producing a quieter sound.

SOSTENUTO PEDAL

The central pedal keeps up any dampers that have already been lifted off the strings. This means that certain notes can be sustained while others are played normally.

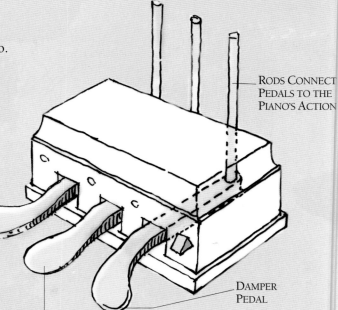

RODS CONNECT PEDALS TO THE PIANO'S ACTION

DAMPER PEDAL

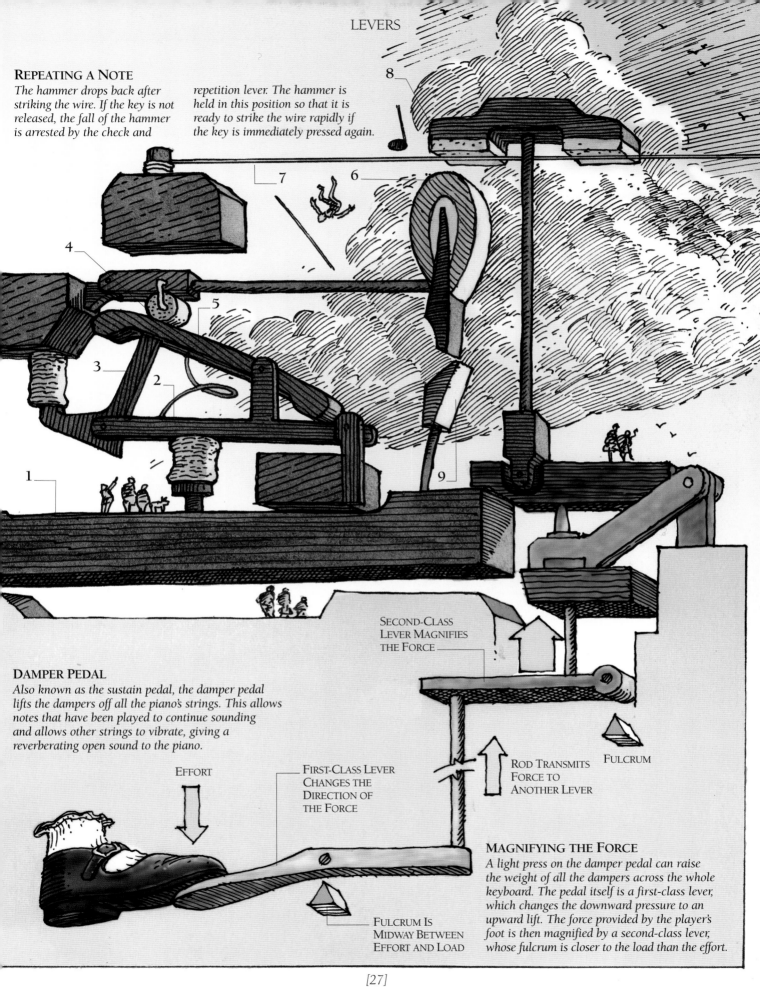

REPEATING A NOTE

The hammer drops back after striking the wire. If the key is not released, the fall of the hammer is arrested by the check and repetition lever. The hammer is held in this position so that it is ready to strike the wire rapidly if the key is immediately pressed again.

8

7

6

4

5

3

2

9

1

DAMPER PEDAL

Also known as the sustain pedal, the damper pedal lifts the dampers off all the piano's strings. This allows notes that have been played to continue sounding and allows other strings to vibrate, giving a reverberating open sound to the piano.

EFFORT

FIRST-CLASS LEVER CHANGES THE DIRECTION OF THE FORCE

FULCRUM IS MIDWAY BETWEEN EFFORT AND LOAD

SECOND-CLASS LEVER MAGNIFIES THE FORCE

ROD TRANSMITS FORCE TO ANOTHER LEVER

FULCRUM

MAGNIFYING THE FORCE

A light press on the damper pedal can raise the weight of all the dampers across the whole keyboard. The pedal itself is a first-class lever, which changes the downward pressure to an upward lift. The force provided by the player's foot is then magnified by a second-class lever, whose fulcrum is closer to the load than the effort.

BICYCLE BRAKE

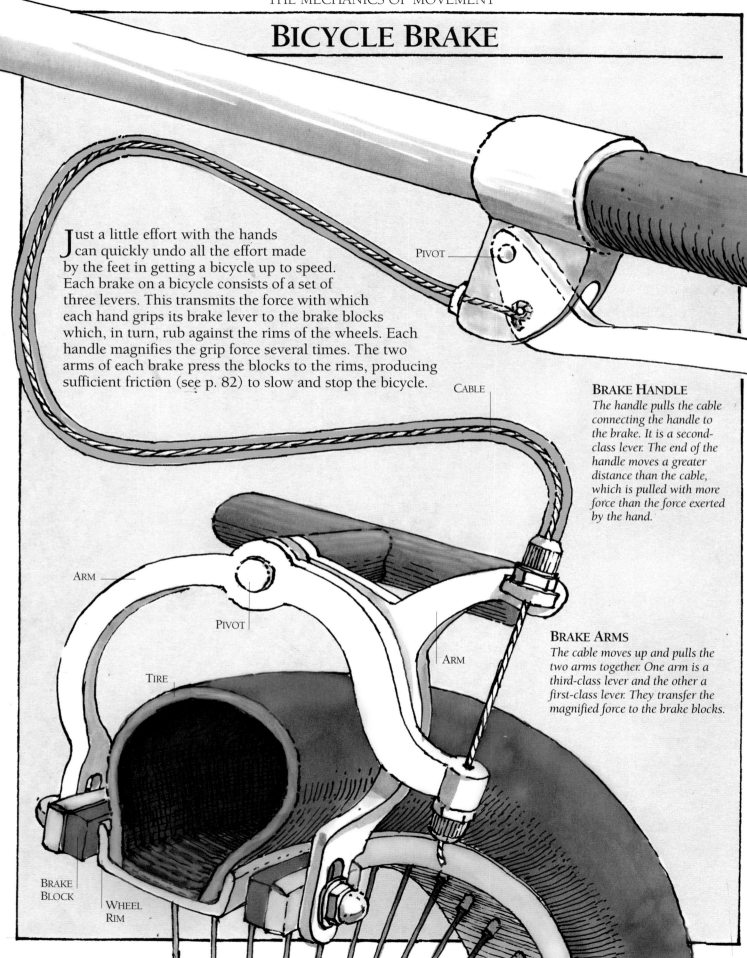

PIVOT

Just a little effort with the hands can quickly undo all the effort made by the feet in getting a bicycle up to speed. Each brake on a bicycle consists of a set of three levers. This transmits the force with which each hand grips its brake lever to the brake blocks which, in turn, rub against the rims of the wheels. Each handle magnifies the grip force several times. The two arms of each brake press the blocks to the rims, producing sufficient friction (see p. 82) to slow and stop the bicycle.

CABLE

BRAKE HANDLE

The handle pulls the cable connecting the handle to the brake. It is a second-class lever. The end of the handle moves a greater distance than the cable, which is pulled with more force than the force exerted by the hand.

ARM

PIVOT

ARM

TIRE

BRAKE ARMS

The cable moves up and pulls the two arms together. One arm is a third-class lever and the other a first-class lever. They transfer the magnified force to the brake blocks.

BRAKE
BLOCK

WHEEL
RIM

HYDRAULIC PLATFORM

CAGE

UPPER BOOM
A ram mounted on the lower boom retracts to pull up the base of the upper boom. This effort raises the end of the upper boom to lift the cage and firefighter into position.

Firefighters may have to tackle a fire in the upper floors of a tall building and possibly rescue people. They use a hydraulic platform that can raise them high in the air. It consists of a cage on the end of a pair of long booms that are hinged together. The vehicle carrying the platform first lowers stabilizers to secure it firmly to the ground. Hydraulic rams (see p. 129) then push and pull on the booms, which are both third-class levers. The upper ends move up a greater distance than the rams, so that the booms can be extended to reach the fire or people.

UPPER-BOOM RAM

EXTENDING SECTIONS

EFFORT (PULL OF CABLE)

FULCRUM

ARM (FIRST-CLASS LEVER)

LOAD (RESISTANCE OF RIM)

FULCRUM

ARM (THIRD-CLASS LEVER)

EFFORT (PULL OF CABLE)

LOAD (RESISTANCE OF RIM)

FULCRUM

EFFORT (PULL OF HAND)

LOAD (RESISTANCE OF BOTH RIMS)

HANDLE (SECOND-CLASS LEVER)

LOWER BOOM
A pair of powerful rams pushes up the base of the boom. The lower boom contains several sections that extend to raise the upper boom.

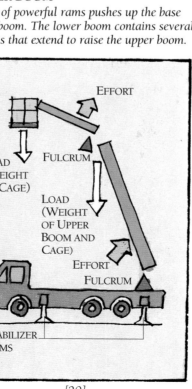

EFFORT

LOAD (WEIGHT OF CAGE)

FULCRUM

LOAD (WEIGHT OF UPPER BOOM AND CAGE)

EFFORT

FULCRUM

STABILIZER RAMS

LOWER-BOOM RAMS

THE WHEEL AND AXLE

ON THE GROOMING OF MAMMOTHS

*T*he problem with washing a mammoth, assuming that you can get close enough with the water (a point I will address further on), is the length of time it takes for the creature's hair to dry. The problem is greatly aggravated when steady sunshine is unavailable.

Recalling the incident between the mammoth and the tusk trimmers, and particularly the motion of the free end of the log, I invented a mechanical drier. It was composed of feathers secured to the ends of long spokes that radiated from one end of a sturdy shaft. At the other end of the shaft radiated a set of short boards. The entire machine was powered by a continuous line of sprightly workers who leaped one by one from a raised platform onto the projecting boards. Their weight against the boards turned the shaft. Because the spokes at the opposite end of the shaft were considerably longer than the boards, their feathered ends naturally turned much faster thereby producing the steady wind required for speedy drying.

A colleague once suggested I replace manpower with a constant stream of water. I left him in no doubt as to my views on this ludicrous proposal.

In the very same village where I built my first feather drier there began the strange—albeit fashionable—practice of tusk modification. A blindfolded mammoth was drawn up against a fixed post or tree by ropes secured to its tusks. The other ends of the ropes were fastened around the drum of a powerful winch—a most ingenious device. As workers turned the drum with handles that projected from it, they were able to straighten the tusks.

Keeping the tusks straight would of course require frequent visits and have been quite lucrative. However, since the process not only made movement through doors impossible, but also affected a mammoth's breathing, it had to be abandoned.

WHEELS AS LEVERS

While many machines work with parts that move up and down or in and out, most depend on rotary motion. These machines contain wheels, but not only wheels that roll on roads. Just as important are a class of devices known as the wheel and axle, which are used to transmit force. Some of these devices look like wheels with axles, while others do not. However, they all rotate around a fixed point to act as a rotating lever.

The center of the wheel and axle is the fulcrum of the rotating lever. The wheel is the outer part of the lever, and the axle is the inner part near the center. In the mammoth drier, the feathers form the wheel and the boards are the axle. In the winch, the drum is the axle and the handles form the wheel.

As the device rotates, the wheel moves a greater distance than the axle but turns with less force. Effort applied to the wheel, as in the winch, causes the axle to turn with a greater force than the wheel. Many machines use the wheel and axle to increase force in this way. Turning the axle, as in the mammoth drier, makes the wheel move at a greater speed than the axle.

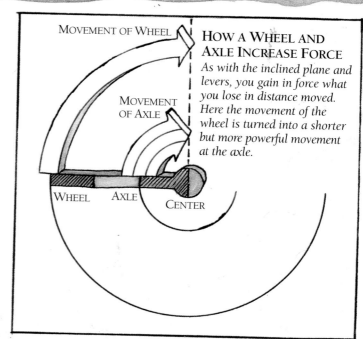

HOW A WHEEL AND AXLE INCREASE FORCE

As with the inclined plane and levers, you gain in force what you lose in distance moved. Here the movement of the wheel is turned into a shorter but more powerful movement at the axle.

MOVEMENT OF WHEEL

MOVEMENT OF AXLE

WHEEL   AXLE   CENTER

THE WHEEL AND AXLE AT WORK

SCREWDRIVER

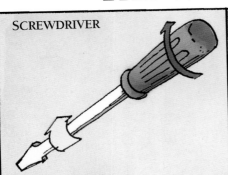

The handle of a screwdriver does more than enable you to hold it. It amplifies the force with which you turn it to drive the screw home.

SARDINE CAN

The key of a sardine can exerts a strong force to pull the metal sealing band away from the can.

STEERING WHEEL

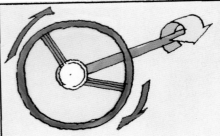

The force of the driver's hands is magnified to turn the shaft, producing sufficient force to operate the steering mechanism.

BRACE AND BIT

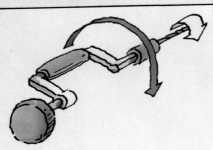

The handle of the brace moves a greater distance than the drill bit at the center, so the bit turns with a stronger force than the handle.

WRENCH

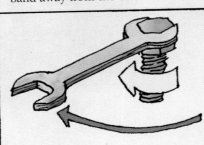

Pulling one end of the wrench exerts a powerful force on the bolt at the other end, screwing it tight.

FAUCET

The handle of a faucet magnifies the force of the hand to screw down the washer inside firmly and prevent the faucet from dripping.

WATERWHEEL

The earliest waterwheel—the Greek mill of the first century BC—had a horizontal wheel. It was superseded by vertical wheels, which could be built to a larger size and thus developed greater power. Waterwheels obey the principle of the wheel and axle, with the force of the water on the paddles at the rim producing a strong driving force at the central shaft.

OVERSHOT WATERWHEEL

GREEK MILL

AXLE

CHUTE

PADDLES

HYDROELECTRIC TURBINE

Hydroelectric power stations contain water turbines that are direct descendants of waterwheels. An efficient turbine extracts as much energy from the water as possible, reducing a powerful intake flow to a relatively weak outlet flow. Modern turbines, such as the Francis turbine shown here, are carefully designed so that the water is guided onto the blades with the minimum of energy-wasting turbulence.

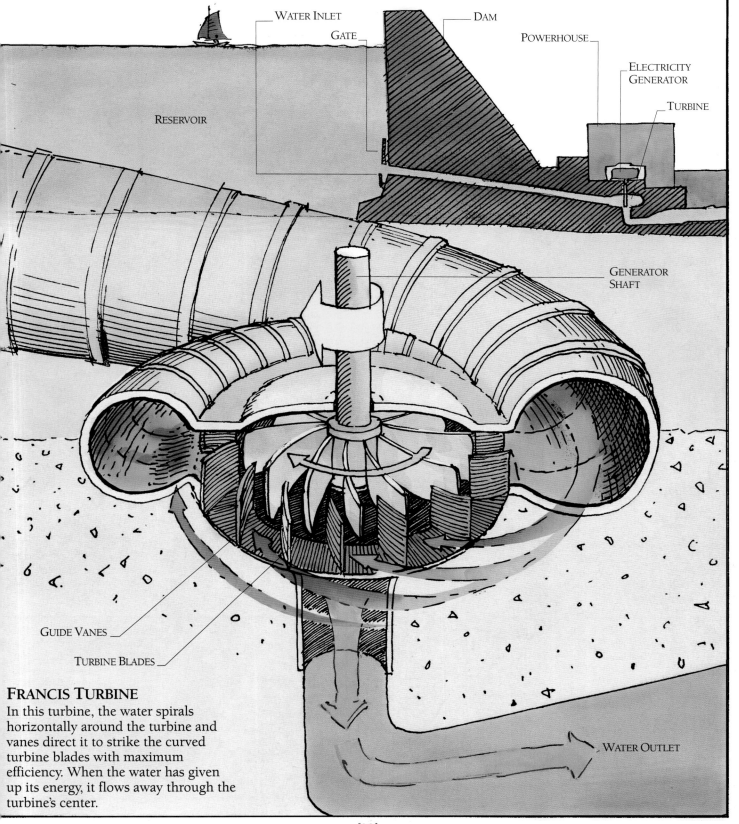

WATER INLET

GATE

DAM

POWERHOUSE

ELECTRICITY GENERATOR

TURBINE

RESERVOIR

GENERATOR SHAFT

GUIDE VANES

TURBINE BLADES

WATER OUTLET

FRANCIS TURBINE

In this turbine, the water spirals horizontally around the turbine and vanes direct it to strike the curved turbine blades with maximum efficiency. When the water has given up its energy, it flows away through the turbine's center.

THE WINDMILL

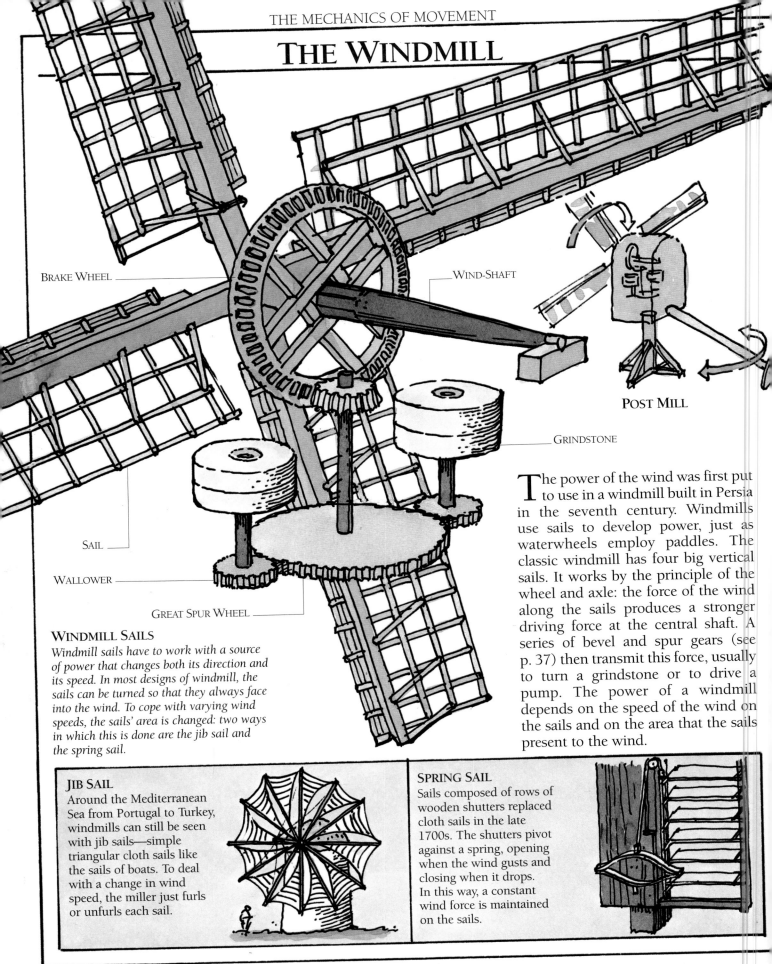

BRAKE WHEEL

WIND-SHAFT

POST MILL

GRINDSTONE

SAIL

WALLOWER

GREAT SPUR WHEEL

WINDMILL SAILS

Windmill sails have to work with a source of power that changes both its direction and its speed. In most designs of windmill, the sails can be turned so that they always face into the wind. To cope with varying wind speeds, the sails' area is changed: two ways in which this is done are the jib sail and the spring sail.

The power of the wind was first put to use in a windmill built in Persia in the seventh century. Windmills use sails to develop power, just as waterwheels employ paddles. The classic windmill has four big vertical sails. It works by the principle of the wheel and axle: the force of the wind along the sails produces a stronger driving force at the central shaft. A series of bevel and spur gears (see p. 37) then transmit this force, usually to turn a grindstone or to drive a pump. The power of a windmill depends on the speed of the wind on the sails and on the area that the sails present to the wind.

JIB SAIL
Around the Mediterranean Sea from Portugal to Turkey, windmills can still be seen with jib sails—simple triangular cloth sails like the sails of boats. To deal with a change in wind speed, the miller just furls or unfurls each sail.

SPRING SAIL
Sails composed of rows of wooden shutters replaced cloth sails in the late 1700s. The shutters pivot against a spring, opening when the wind gusts and closing when it drops. In this way, a constant wind force is maintained on the sails.

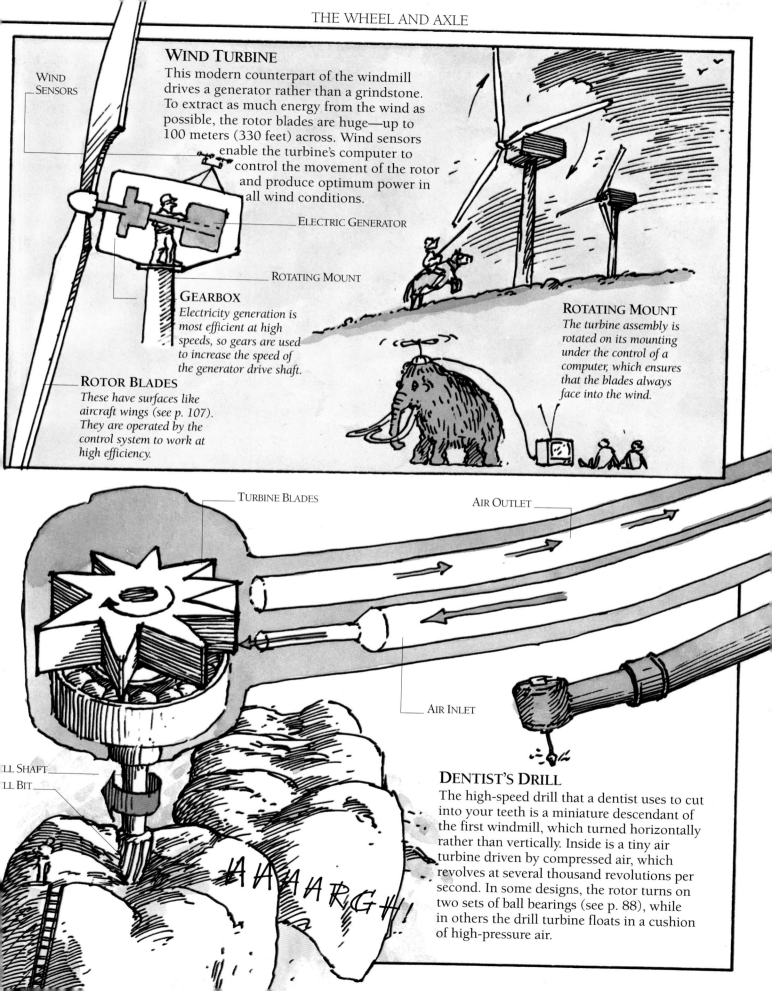

WIND SENSORS

WIND TURBINE
This modern counterpart of the windmill drives a generator rather than a grindstone. To extract as much energy from the wind as possible, the rotor blades are huge—up to 100 meters (330 feet) across. Wind sensors enable the turbine's computer to control the movement of the rotor and produce optimum power in all wind conditions.

ELECTRIC GENERATOR

ROTATING MOUNT

GEARBOX
Electricity generation is most efficient at high speeds, so gears are used to increase the speed of the generator drive shaft.

ROTOR BLADES
These have surfaces like aircraft wings (see p. 107). They are operated by the control system to work at high efficiency.

ROTATING MOUNT
The turbine assembly is rotated on its mounting under the control of a computer, which ensures that the blades always face into the wind.

TURBINE BLADES

AIR OUTLET

AIR INLET

LL SHAFT
LL BIT

DENTIST'S DRILL
The high-speed drill that a dentist uses to cut into your teeth is a miniature descendant of the first windmill, which turned horizontally rather than vertically. Inside is a tiny air turbine driven by compressed air, which revolves at several thousand revolutions per second. In some designs, the rotor turns on two sets of ball bearings (see p. 88), while in others the drill turbine floats in a cushion of high-pressure air.

GEARS AND BELTS

ON EARLY MAMMOTH POWER

As far as I can ascertain, the first use of mammoths in industry was to provide power for the famous merry-go-round experiment. The equipment consisted of two wheels, one large and one small, placed edge to edge so that when the mammoths turned one wheel, the other would turn automatically. At first seats were hung from the small wheel that was driven by the large wheel. The result was a hair-raising ride. When the wheels were reversed, the ride was far too sedate. Eventually belts connected to drive wheels of different sizes operated two rides simultaneously, one fast and one gentle. Carrot consumption during the experiment was astronomical.

fig.1.

fig.2.

fig.3

TYPES OF GEARS

Gears come in a variety of sizes with their teeth straight or curved and inclined at a variety of angles. They are connected together in various ways to transmit motion and force in machines. However, there are only four basic types of gears. They all act so that one gear wheel turns faster or slower than the other, or moves in a different direction. A difference in speed between two gears produces a change in the force transmitted.

SPUR GEARS
Two gear wheels intermesh in the same plane, regulating the speed or force of motion and reversing its direction.

RACK AND PINION GEARS
One wheel, the pinion, meshes with a sliding toothed rack, converting rotary motion to reciprocating (to-and-fro) motion and vice versa.

BEVEL GEARS
Two wheels intermesh at an angle to change the direction of rotation, also altering speed and force if necessary. These are sometimes known as a pinion and crown wheel, or pinion and ring gear.

WORM GEARS
A shaft with a screw thread meshes with a toothed wheel to alter the direction of motion, and change the speed and force.

HOW GEARS AND BELTS WORK

The way gears and belts control movement depends entirely on the sizes of the two connecting wheels. In any pair of wheels, the larger wheel will rotate more slowly than the smaller wheel, but it will rotate with greater force. The bigger the difference in size between the two wheels, the bigger the difference in speed and force.

Wheels connected by belts or chains work in just the same way as gears, with the only difference being in the direction that the wheels rotate.

GEARS
The big wheel has twice the number of teeth, and twice the circumference, of the small wheel. It rotates with twice the force and half the speed in the opposite direction.

FORCE

BELTS
The big wheel has twice the circumference of the small wheel. It also rotates with twice the force and half the speed, but in the same direction.

SPEED

FORCE

SPEED

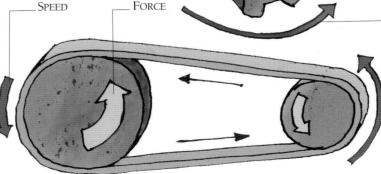

SPUR GEARS

DERAILLEUR GEARS

The chain connecting the pedals of a bicycle to the rear wheel acts as a belt to make the wheel turn faster than the feet. To ride on the level or downhill, the rear-wheel sprocket needs to be small for high speed. But to climb hills, it needs to be large so that the rear wheel turns with less speed but more force.

Derailleur gears solve the problem by having rear-wheel sprockets of different sizes. A gear-changing mechanism transfers the chain from one sprocket to the next.

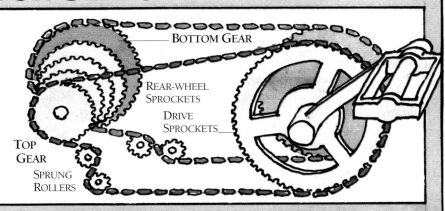

BOTTOM GEAR

REAR-WHEEL SPROCKETS

DRIVE SPROCKETS

TOP GEAR

SPRUNG ROLLERS

DRIVING GEAR

The driving gear is turned by one tooth every time the wheel rotates. The counter records how many revolutions take place, converting this figure into the distance traveled.

DRUMS

The drums bear twenty teeth—two for each numeral—on their right sides. On the left side of each drum is a gap by the numeral 2 and two projections on either side of the gap.

BICYCLE DISTANCE COUNTER

The counter is mounted on the front axle, and driven by a small peg fixed to a front wheel spoke. A reduction gear makes the right-hand numbered drum revolve once every kilometer or mile. As it makes a complete revolution, it makes the next drum to the left move by one-tenth of a revolution, and so on. The movement of the drums is produced by the row of small gear wheels beneath the drums. The wheels have teeth that are alternately wide and narrow, a feature that enables them to lock adjoining drums together when one drum completes a revolution.

GEAR WHEELS

The wheels intermesh with each drum except the one at the right-hand end.

REDUCTION GEAR

PROJECTION

DRUM TOOTH

WIDE TOOTH

NARROW TOOTH

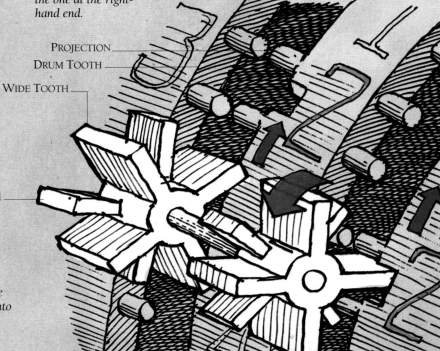

HOW ADJOINING DRUMS LOCK

Normally, a narrow wheel tooth fits between two drum teeth and the drums do not move. When a 9 moves up into the viewing window at the top of the drums, the projection on that drum catches the narrow tooth on the gear wheel, making it rotate. The next wide tooth fits into the gap by the 2 and locks the drum and the next left drum together. As the 9 changes to 0, the gear wheel rotates and the next drum also moves up one numeral.

CAR WINDOW WINDER

Most cars have windows that can be opened and closed at the touch of a button. An electric motor turns a small cog that moves a toothed quadrant (a section of a large spur gear), which in turn raises or lowers levers supporting the car window. There are gears inside the motor housing that enable the motor to provide a small but powerful movement.

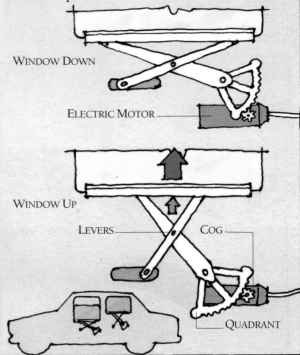

WINDOW DOWN

ELECTRIC MOTOR

WINDOW UP

LEVERS

COG

QUADRANT

SALAD SPINNER

A salad spinner rotates at high speed, throwing off water by centrifugal force (see p. 71). The drive mechanism consists of an epicyclic or planetary gear—a system of spur gears in which an outer gear ring turns an inner planet gear that drives a small central sun gear. Epicyclic gears can achieve a high speed magnification yet are simple and compact.

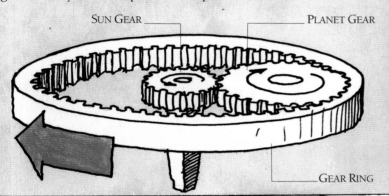

SUN GEAR

PLANET GEAR

GEAR RING

ᴸAWN MOWER

A push-mower contains an internal pinion turned by a gear ᵣⁱng inside the wheel. The pinion turns the cylinder of ᶜᵘtting blades as the wheels move, and the grass is trapped ᵇᵉtween the spinning blades and a fixed cutting blade. The ᵇˡades spin much faster than the wheels so that each blade ˢˡices only a small amount of grass, mowing the lawn neatly ⁱn a single pass.

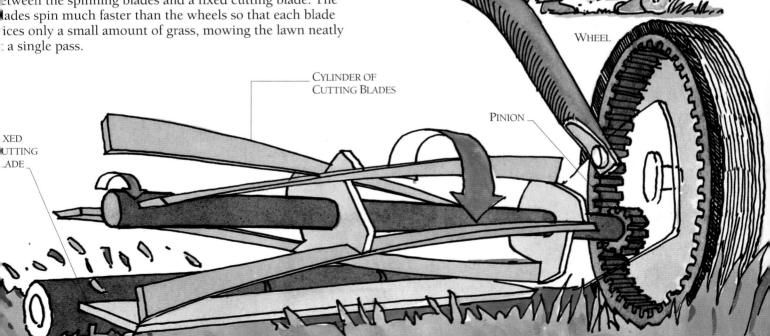

CYLINDER OF
CUTTING BLADES

PINION

WHEEL

ᶠIXED
ᶜUTTING
ᴮᴸADE

THE GEARBOX

All gasoline and diesel engines work best if they run at a high but limited rate of revolutions. The job of the gearbox is to keep the engine running at its most efficient rate while allowing the car to travel at a large range of speed.

The speed rotation of the engine's crankshaft (see p. 51) is reduced by the gearbox, and by the differential (see p. 45) on the back axle. The crankshaft first turns a shaft in the clutch (see p. 84). Disengaging the clutch stops the crankshaft from turning the gearbox, allowing the driver to select between the different gears.

When the clutch is engaged, the rotation is passed on to gear wheels on the transmission shaft—one gear wheel for each of the car's gear speeds. All of the gear wheels on the transmission shaft turn, each one at a different speed. But only one actually turns the transmission shaft at any time.

The different ratios of teeth in the gear chain between clutch and transmission shaft determine the speed at which the transmission shaft turns. Selecting reverse gear introduces an extra gear wheel, which reverses the rotation of the transmission shaft.

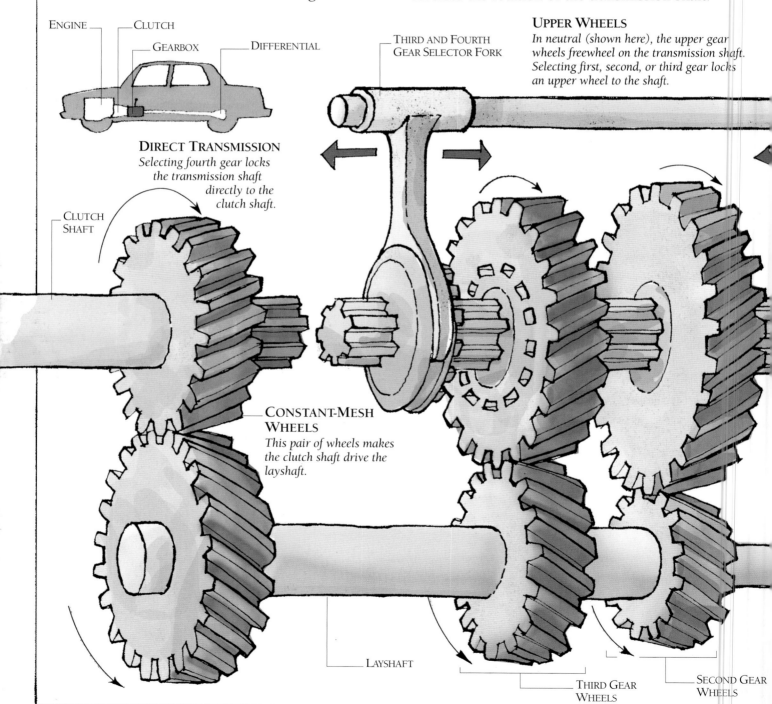

ENGINE

CLUTCH

GEARBOX

DIFFERENTIAL

THIRD AND FOURTH
GEAR SELECTOR FORK

UPPER WHEELS
In neutral (shown here), the upper gear wheels freewheel on the transmission shaft. Selecting first, second, or third gear locks an upper wheel to the shaft.

DIRECT TRANSMISSION
Selecting fourth gear locks the transmission shaft directly to the clutch shaft.

CLUTCH
SHAFT

CONSTANT-MESH WHEELS
This pair of wheels makes the clutch shaft drive the layshaft.

LAYSHAFT

THIRD GEAR
WHEELS

SECOND GEAR
WHEELS

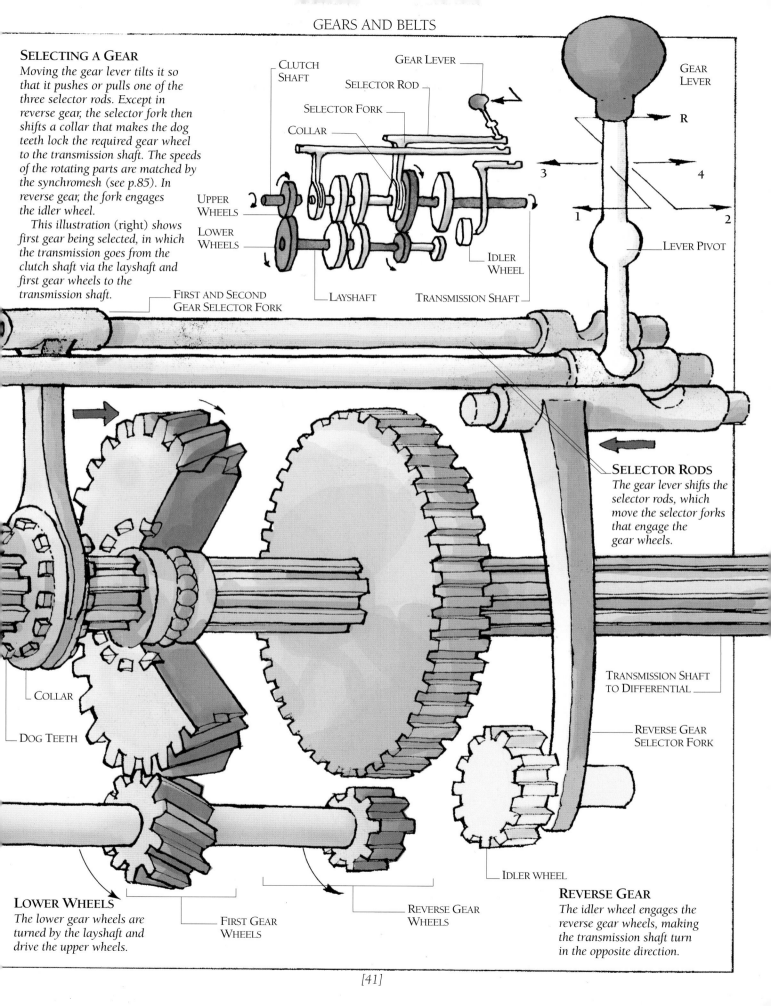

SELECTING A GEAR

Moving the gear lever tilts it so that it pushes or pulls one of the three selector rods. Except in reverse gear, the selector fork then shifts a collar that makes the dog teeth lock the required gear wheel to the transmission shaft. The speeds of the rotating parts are matched by the synchromesh (see p.85). In reverse gear, the fork engages the idler wheel.

This illustration (right) shows first gear being selected, in which the transmission goes from the clutch shaft via the layshaft and first gear wheels to the transmission shaft.

CLUTCH SHAFT
GEAR LEVER
SELECTOR ROD
SELECTOR FORK
COLLAR
UPPER WHEELS
LOWER WHEELS
IDLER WHEEL
FIRST AND SECOND GEAR SELECTOR FORK
LAYSHAFT
TRANSMISSION SHAFT

GEAR LEVER
R
3
1
4
2
LEVER PIVOT

SELECTOR RODS

The gear lever shifts the selector rods, which move the selector forks that engage the gear wheels.

COLLAR
DOG TEETH

TRANSMISSION SHAFT TO DIFFERENTIAL

REVERSE GEAR SELECTOR FORK

IDLER WHEEL

LOWER WHEELS

The lower gear wheels are turned by the layshaft and drive the upper wheels.

FIRST GEAR WHEELS

REVERSE GEAR WHEELS

REVERSE GEAR

The idler wheel engages the reverse gear wheels, making the transmission shaft turn in the opposite direction.

MECHANICAL CLOCKS AND WATCHES

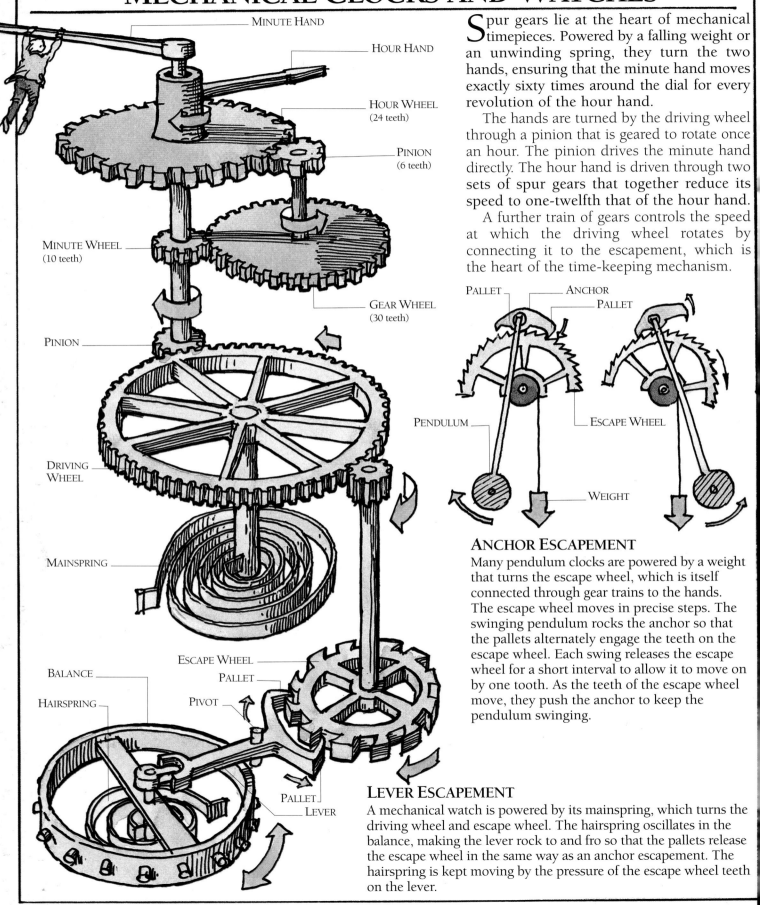

MINUTE HAND

HOUR HAND

HOUR WHEEL
(24 teeth)

PINION
(6 teeth)

MINUTE WHEEL
(10 teeth)

GEAR WHEEL
(30 teeth)

PINION

DRIVING
WHEEL

MAINSPRING

ESCAPE WHEEL

BALANCE

PALLET

HAIRSPRING

PIVOT

PALLET

LEVER

Spur gears lie at the heart of mechanical timepieces. Powered by a falling weight or an unwinding spring, they turn the two hands, ensuring that the minute hand moves exactly sixty times around the dial for every revolution of the hour hand.

The hands are turned by the driving wheel through a pinion that is geared to rotate once an hour. The pinion drives the minute hand directly. The hour hand is driven through two sets of spur gears that together reduce its speed to one-twelfth that of the hour hand.

A further train of gears controls the speed at which the driving wheel rotates by connecting it to the escapement, which is the heart of the time-keeping mechanism.

PALLET

ANCHOR

PALLET

PENDULUM

ESCAPE WHEEL

WEIGHT

ANCHOR ESCAPEMENT

Many pendulum clocks are powered by a weight that turns the escape wheel, which is itself connected through gear trains to the hands. The escape wheel moves in precise steps. The swinging pendulum rocks the anchor so that the pallets alternately engage the teeth on the escape wheel. Each swing releases the escape wheel for a short interval to allow it to move on by one tooth. As the teeth of the escape wheel move, they push the anchor to keep the pendulum swinging.

LEVER ESCAPEMENT

A mechanical watch is powered by its mainspring, which turns the driving wheel and escape wheel. The hairspring oscillates in the balance, making the lever rock to and fro so that the pallets release the escape wheel in the same way as an anchor escapement. The hairspring is kept moving by the pressure of the escape wheel teeth on the lever.

THE RACK AND PINION

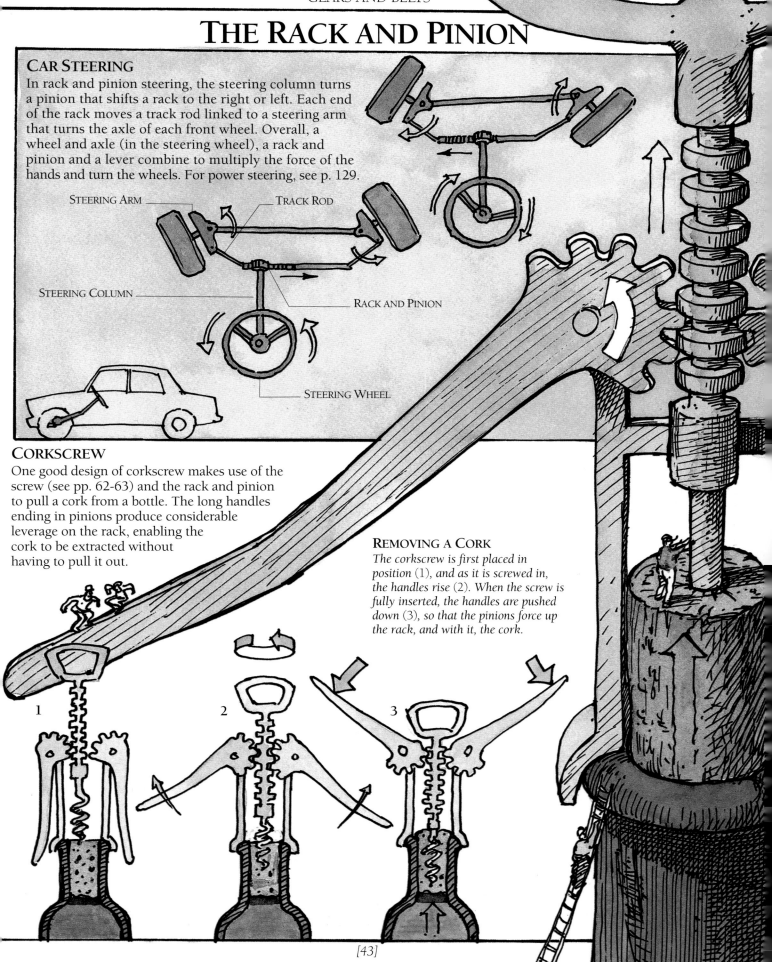

CAR STEERING

In rack and pinion steering, the steering column turns a pinion that shifts a rack to the right or left. Each end of the rack moves a track rod linked to a steering arm that turns the axle of each front wheel. Overall, a wheel and axle (in the steering wheel), a rack and pinion and a lever combine to multiply the force of the hands and turn the wheels. For power steering, see p. 129.

STEERING ARM

TRACK ROD

STEERING COLUMN

RACK AND PINION

STEERING WHEEL

CORKSCREW

One good design of corkscrew makes use of the screw (see pp. 62-63) and the rack and pinion to pull a cork from a bottle. The long handles ending in pinions produce considerable leverage on the rack, enabling the cork to be extracted without having to pull it out.

REMOVING A CORK

The corkscrew is first placed in position (1), and as it is screwed in, the handles rise (2). When the screw is fully inserted, the handles are pushed down (3), so that the pinions force up the rack, and with it, the cork.

1

2

3

BEVEL GEARS

EGG WHISK

In bevel gears, the gear wheels are often of very different sizes. This difference serves to change either the force that is applied to one of the gears, or to increase or decrease the speed of motion. An egg whisk converts a slow rotation into two much faster rotations that work in opposite directions. Its handle turns a large double-sided crown wheel, which in turn drives two bevel pinions to spin the beaters. The great increase in speed is produced by the much larger diameter of the crown wheel compared to the bevel pinions.

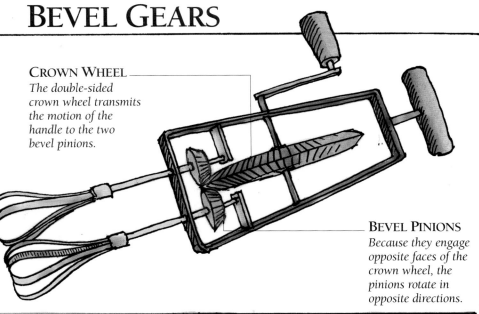

CROWN WHEEL
The double-sided crown wheel transmits the motion of the handle to the two bevel pinions.

BEVEL PINIONS
Because they engage opposite faces of the crown wheel, the pinions rotate in opposite directions.

DRILL CHUCK

The chuck of a power drill has to grip very strongly as it rotates the drill, yet it must be possible to loosen or tighten the chuck by hand. A compact arrangement of bevel gears and levers does the trick.

The key pinion is turned to rotate the collar of the chuck, which turns the screw inside the chuck to move the jaws in or out. The screw is set at an angle so that the jaws open as they withdraw into the chuck, and close to grip the drill bit as they protrude from the chuck.

THE DIFFERENTIAL

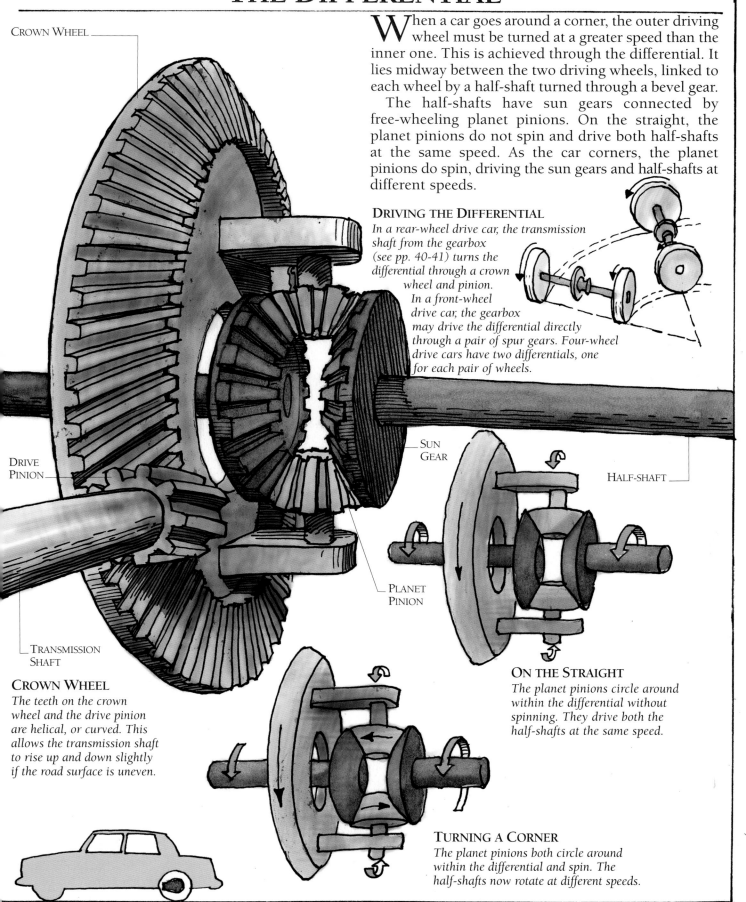

When a car goes around a corner, the outer driving wheel must be turned at a greater speed than the inner one. This is achieved through the differential. It lies midway between the two driving wheels, linked to each wheel by a half-shaft turned through a bevel gear.

The half-shafts have sun gears connected by free-wheeling planet pinions. On the straight, the planet pinions do not spin and drive both half-shafts at the same speed. As the car corners, the planet pinions do spin, driving the sun gears and half-shafts at different speeds.

CROWN WHEEL

DRIVING THE DIFFERENTIAL

In a rear-wheel drive car, the transmission shaft from the gearbox (see pp. 40-41) turns the differential through a crown wheel and pinion. In a front-wheel drive car, the gearbox may drive the differential directly through a pair of spur gears. Four-wheel drive cars have two differentials, one for each pair of wheels.

DRIVE PINION

SUN GEAR

HALF-SHAFT

TRANSMISSION SHAFT

PLANET PINION

CROWN WHEEL

The teeth on the crown wheel and the drive pinion are helical, or curved. This allows the transmission shaft to rise up and down slightly if the road surface is uneven.

ON THE STRAIGHT

The planet pinions circle around within the differential without spinning. They drive both the half-shafts at the same speed.

TURNING A CORNER

The planet pinions both circle around within the differential and spin. The half-shafts now rotate at different speeds.

WORM GEARS

ELECTRIC MIXER

An electric mixer has a pair of contra-rotating beaters, just like an egg whisk. However, electric motors rotate at very high speeds and develop heat. The speed therefore has to be reduced when the motor is put to work, rather than increased as in the hand-powered egg whisk. A worm gear is used to drive the beater shafts, and a fan attached to the motor shaft blows air over the motor to cool it.

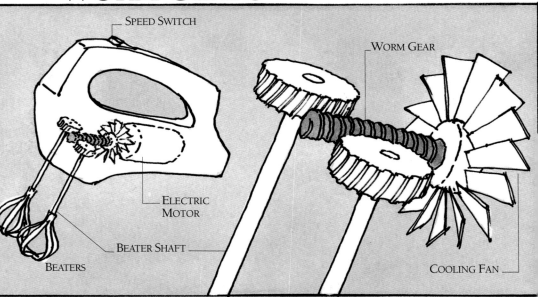

SPEED SWITCH

WORM GEAR

ELECTRIC MOTOR

BEATER SHAFT

BEATERS

COOLING FAN

SPEEDOMETER

A car's speedometer uses worm gears to produce an enormous reduction in speed. The final drum of numbers in the distance counter turns just once every hundred thousand miles or kilometers, while the transmission shaft that drives it turns several hundred million times.

The speedometer is driven by a flexible cable. This contains a rotating wire connected to a small drive wheel that is rotated by a large worm on a shaft that drives the wheels. Inside the speedometer, the wire drives the speed indicator through magnetic induction (see p. 276). Its speed is further reduced by another worm gear to turn the distance counter, which itself contains reducing gears so that each numeral drum rotates at a tenth the speed of its neighbor.

CABLE CONNECTION

The speedometer cable is attached to the gearbox output shaft, transmission shaft, or differential, all of which rotate at a speed that depends on the road speed.

SPEED INDICATOR

The shaft rotates a magnet inside a drag cup.

DRAG CUP

DIAL

POINTER

HAIRSPRING

NUMERAL DRUMS

MAGNET

WORM GEAR

RATCHET

DRIVE ARM

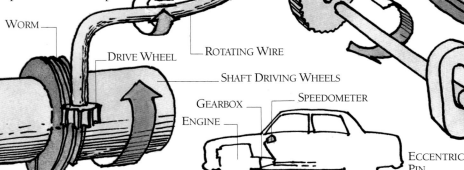

WORM

DRIVE WHEEL

ROTATING WIRE

SHAFT DRIVING WHEELS

GEARBOX

ENGINE

SPEEDOMETER

ECCENTRIC PIN

DISTANCE COUNTER

An eccentric pin, driven by a worm gear, pushes the drive arm backward and forward to operate the counter.

LAWN SPRINKLER

A good sprinkler not only produces a fine spray of water but also swings the spray to and fro to water a wide area of grass. No extra source of power is needed, because the mechanism is driven by the movement of the water through the sprinkler, using a system of worm gears.

As the water enters the sprinkler, it drives a turbine at high speed and then rushes to the spray tube. The turbine drives two worm gears that reduce the speed of the turbine to turn a crank at low speed. The crank moves the spray tube slowly to and fro.

SPRAY TUBE

TURBINE

CRANK

WATER HOSE

CAMS AND CRANKS

ON AN ANCIENT MACHINE

I have recently come across the remains of an extraordinary machine, the operation of which is here depicted. I believe that the machine was designed to crack the eggs of some huge and now extinct beast. Each egg was shattered by a mammoth-powered hammer, and the broken shell pushed out of the way by a shovel. My discovery prompts two observations: (a) the mammoth merry-go-round may not have been the first industrial use of mammoths after all, and (b) there must have been considerable demand for omelettes of prodigious proportions.

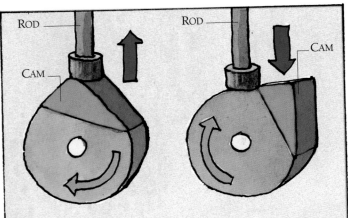

THE CAM

The egg-cracker uses a cam, a device that in its most basic form is simply a fixed wheel with one or more projections. A rod is pressed against the wheel, and as the wheel rotates, the rod moves out and in as the projection passes.

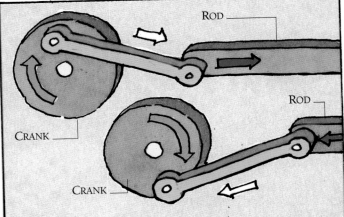

THE CRANK

The shovel is moved by a crank. This is a wheel with a pivot to which a rod is attached. The other end of the rod is hinged so that the rod moves backward and forward as the wheel rotates. Unlike cams, cranks may work in reverse, with the rod making the wheel rotate.

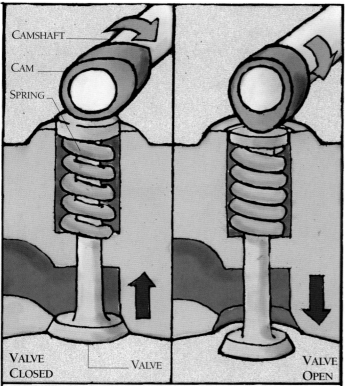

CAMSHAFT

CAM

SPRING

VALVE CLOSED — VALVE — VALVE OPEN

CAR ENGINE CAMSHAFT

Each cylinder of a car engine contains valves that admit the fuel or expel the exhaust gases. Each valve is operated by a cam attached to a rotating camshaft. The cam opens the valve by forcing it down against a spring. The spring then closes the valve until the cam comes around again. The cam may operate the valve directly, as here, or through levers, as shown on the next page.

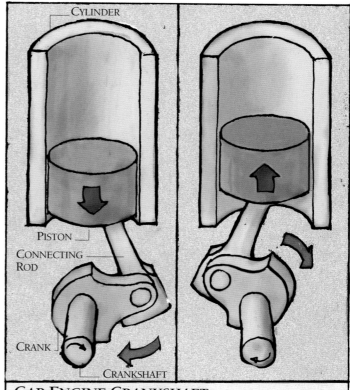

CYLINDER

PISTON

CONNECTING ROD

CRANK

CRANKSHAFT

CAR ENGINE CRANKSHAFT

Powered by the explosion of the fuel, a piston moves down inside each cylinder of a car engine. A connecting rod links the piston to a crank on the crankshaft. The rod turns the crank, which then continues to rotate and drives the piston back up the cylinder. In this way, the crankshaft converts the movement of the pistons into rotary power.

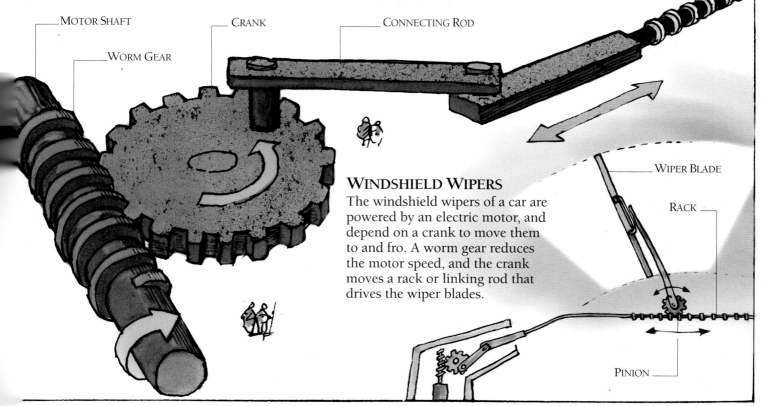

MOTOR SHAFT

WORM GEAR

CRANK

CONNECTING ROD

WIPER BLADE

RACK

WINDSHIELD WIPERS

The windshield wipers of a car are powered by an electric motor, and depend on a crank to move them to and fro. A worm gear reduces the motor speed, and the crank moves a rack or linking rod that drives the wiper blades.

PINION

CAMS AND CRANKS IN THE CAR

Split-second timing is essential for smooth and powerful running in a car engine. It is achieved by the engine's camshaft and crankshaft working in concert.

As the pistons move up and down in the cylinders, they drive the crankshaft, which turns the flywheel and, ultimately, the wheels. But, through a chain linkage, the crankshaft also turns the camshaft. As the camshaft rotates, the cams operate the cylinder valves. In an overhead camshaft engine, the cams lie over the valves and move the valves directly. Here, the camshaft is to one side, and it operates the valves through push-rods and rockers. The cams and cranks involved open and close the valves in step with the movements of the pistons to follow the four-stroke cycle (see pp. 156-57).

The camshaft and crankshaft may also drive other parts of the engine. A gear wheel on the camshaft, for example, drives the oil pump (see p. 124) and the distributor.

THE SEWING MACHINE

The sewing machine is a marvel of mechanical ingenuity. Its source of power is the simple rotary movement of an electric motor. The machine converts this into a complex sequence of movements that makes each stitch and shifts the fabric between stitches. Cams and cranks play an important part in the mechanism. A crank drives the needle up and down, while two trains of cams and cranks move the serrated feed-dog that shifts the fabric.

In order to make a stitch, the sewing machine has to loop one thread around another. The first thread passes through the eye of the needle and the second thread is beneath the fabric. As the needle moves up and down, a curved hook rotates to loop the thread and form a stitch. When a stitch has been completed, the feed-dog repositions the fabric so that the next can be made. The amount of fabric moved by the feed-dog can be altered to produce long or short stitches.

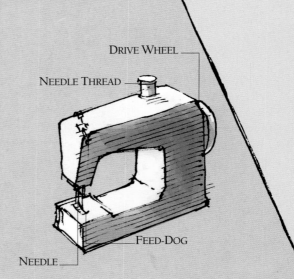

DRIVE WHEEL

NEEDLE THREAD

FEED-DOG

NEEDLE

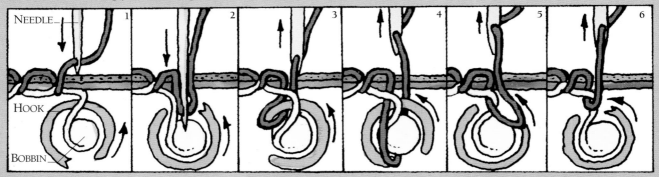

NEEDLE

1 2 3 4 5 6

HOOK

BOBBIN

FORMING THE LOOP

The needle, carrying one thread, moves down (1). The other thread is wound on the bobbin in the rotary shuttle below the fabric. The needle pierces the fabric and then moves up, leaving a loop of thread beneath the fabric (2).

HOOKING THE LOOP

The hook on the shuttle catches the loop of needle thread (3). It then pulls the loop around the bobbin and around the bobbin thread (4). The bobbin thread is effectively put through the loop of needle thread.

COMPLETING THE STITCH

The hook continues to turn (5). The loop then slips off the hook as the needle rises above the fabric (6). The needle thread is then pulled tight by a lever on the sewing machine to form the stitch.

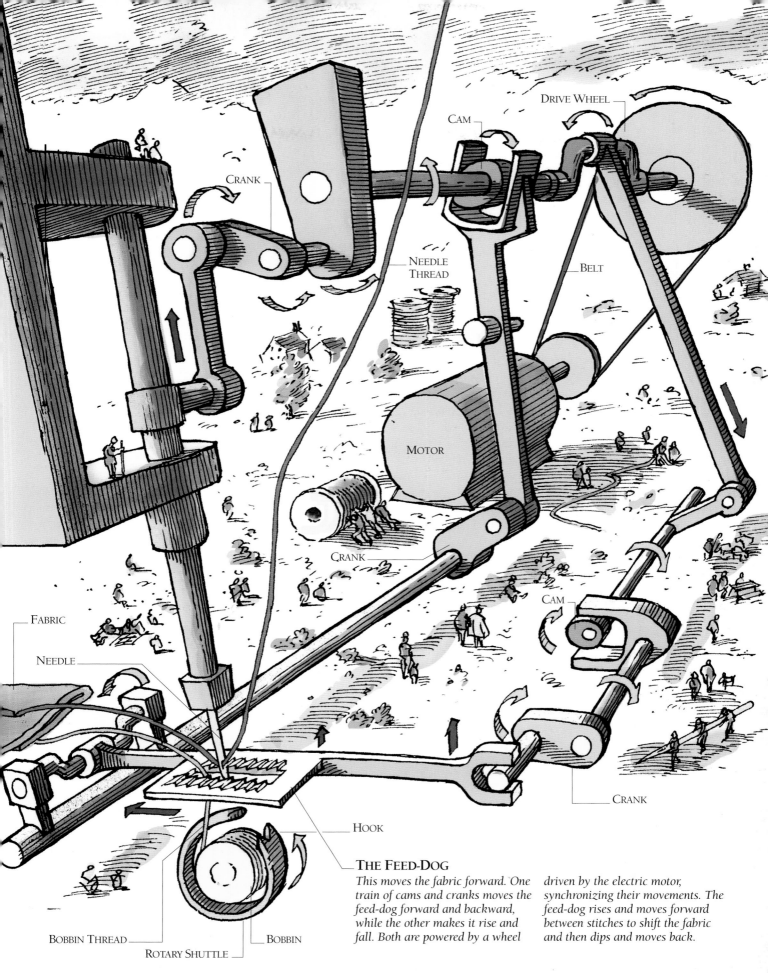

CRANK

CAM

DRIVE WHEEL

NEEDLE
THREAD

BELT

MOTOR

CRANK

CAM

FABRIC

NEEDLE

CRANK

HOOK

THE FEED-DOG

This moves the fabric forward. One
train of cams and cranks moves the
feed-dog forward and backward,
while the other makes it rise and
fall. Both are powered by a wheel

driven by the electric motor,
synchronizing their movements. The
feed-dog rises and moves forward
between stitches to shift the fabric
and then dips and moves back.

BOBBIN THREAD

BOBBIN

ROTARY SHUTTLE

PULLEYS

ON MILKING A MAMMOTH

*A*lthough it has a rather strong flavor, mammoth milk is rich in minerals and vitamins. I have passed through countless villages of white-toothed, strong-boned folk all of whom attribute their remarkable health to a life of drinking this exceptionally nutritious fluid. The only problem in milking these creatures, besides obtaining enough buckets (they produce an unbelievable amount of milk), is the animals' great reluctance to be touched. It is necessary therefore to raise the mammoth

far enough above the ground to deny it any traction. The milker is only safe when the milkee is dangling helplessly.

In many villages, I observed mammoths being lifted in a harness using a number of wheels. These wheels, around which a strong rope traveled, were hung in a given order from a very stout framework. Although the weight to be lifted was often tremendous, a system of wheels greatly reduced the effort required. I noticed that the more wheels the villagers used, the easier it was to lift the weight, but by the same token, it was also necessary to pull in much more rope to get the mammoth up to a sufficient height.

PULLEY POWER

For some, lifting a heavy weight while climbing a ladder poses no problems. For most of us, however, pulling something down is a lot easier than lifting it up.

This change of direction can be arranged with no more than a wheel and a rope. The wheel is fixed to a support and the rope is run over the wheel to the load. A pull downward on the rope can lift the load as high as the support. And because the puller's body weight works downward, it now becomes a help rather than a hindrance. A wheel used in this way is a pulley, and the lifting system it makes up is a simple crane.

Single pulleys are used in machines where the direction of a movement must be changed, as for example in an elevator (see p. 61), where the upward movement of the elevator must be linked to the downward movement of a counterweight.

In an ideal pulley, the effort with which the rope is pulled is equal to the weight of the load. In practice, the effort is always slightly more than the load, because it has to overcome the force of friction (see pp. 82-83) in the pulley wheel as well as raise the load. Friction reduces the efficiency of all machines in this way.

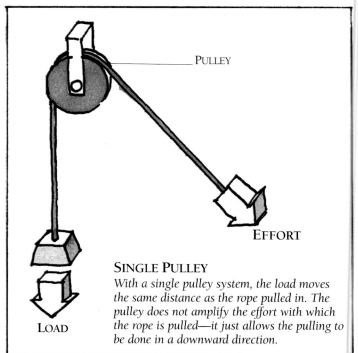

PULLEY

EFFORT

LOAD

SINGLE PULLEY

With a single pulley system, the load moves the same distance as the rope pulled in. The pulley does not amplify the effort with which the rope is pulled—it just allows the pulling to be done in a downward direction.

One wise old milker informed me that to avoid unnecessary delay and expenditure of energy, the sex of the mammoth should be checked before attaching the harness.

CONNECTED PULLEYS

As well as changing a pulling force's direction, pulleys can also be used to amplify it, just like levers. Connecting pulley wheels together to make a compound pulley enables one person to raise loads many times their own weight.

In a system with two pulleys, one pulley is attached to the load and the other to the support. The rope runs over the upper pulley, down and around the lower pulley and back up to the upper pulley, where it is fixed. The lower pulley is free to move and as the rope is pulled, it raises the load. This arrangement of pulleys causes the load to move only half as far as the free end of the rope. But in return, the force raising the load is doubled. As with levers, the distance moved is traded off against force—much to the puller's advantage.

The amount by which a compound pulley amplifies the pull or effort to raise a load depends on how many wheels it has. Ideally, the amplification is equal to the number of sections of rope that raise the lower set of pulleys attached to the load. In practice, the effort has to overcome friction in all the pulleys and raise the weight of the lower set of pulleys as well as the load. This reduces the amplification of the effort.

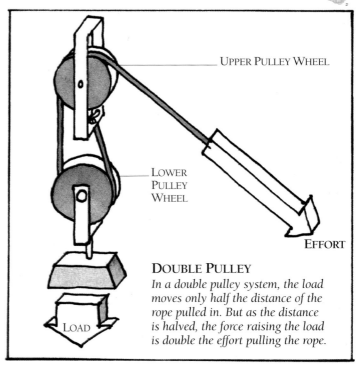

UPPER PULLEY WHEEL

LOWER PULLEY WHEEL

EFFORT

DOUBLE PULLEY

In a double pulley system, the load moves only half the distance of the rope pulled in. But as the distance is halved, the force raising the load is double the effort pulling the rope.

LOAD

CHAIN HOIST

The chain hoist consists of an endless chain looped around three pulleys. The upper two pulleys are fixed together, while the load hangs from a lower pulley, which is supported by a loop of chain. The load remains still unless the chain is moved. Just how much effort is needed to move the load depends on the difference in diameter between the two upper pulleys.

RAISING AND LOWERING THE HOIST

When the chain is pulled so that the paired pulleys rotate counterclockwise (left), the larger wheel pulls in more chain than the smaller wheel lets out, magnifying the pull exerted and raising the load a shorter distance. When the chain moves in the reverse direction (below), the load is lowered.

EFFORT

LOAD

LOAD

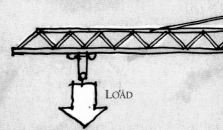

LOAD

TOWER CRANE

The tower crane is a modern equivalent of the shadoof, using a counterweight to balance its load in the same way.

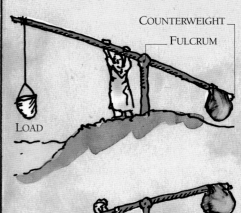

COUNTERWEIGHT

FULCRUM

LOAD

SHADOOF

This water-raising machine, invented in antiquity, has a counterweight at one end of a pivoted beam that balances a container of water at the other end. When full, the container can be raised with little more than a light touch.

COUNTER-WEIGHT

LOAD

FORKLIFT TRUCK

The heavy counterweight at the rear of a forklift truck helps raise a load high into the air by preventing the truck from toppling forward.

BLOCK AND TACKLE

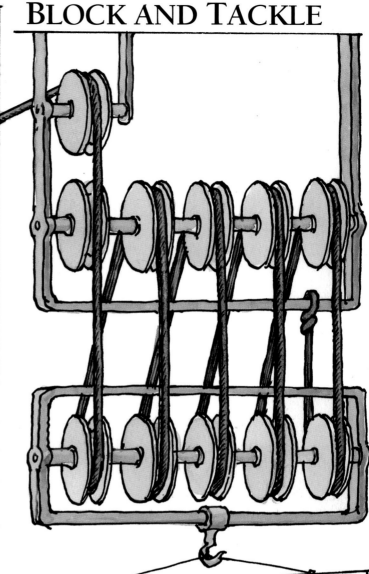

COUNTERWEIGHTS

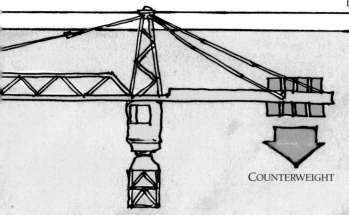

COUNTERWEIGHT

Cranes and other lifting machines often make use of counterweights in raising loads. The counterweight balances the weight of the load so that the machine's motor has only to move the load and not to support it. The counterweight may also stop the machine from tipping over as the load leaves the ground. In accordance with the principle of levers (see p. 18) a heavy counterweight placed near the fulcrum of a machine such as a crane has the same effect as a lighter counterweight positioned farther away.

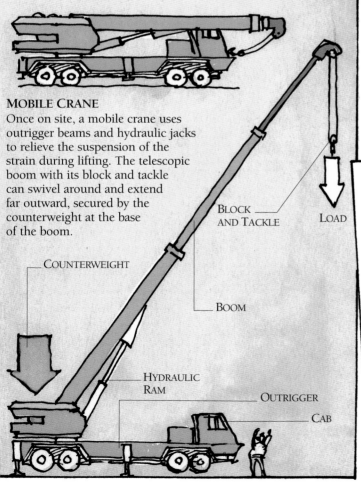

MOBILE CRANE
Once on site, a mobile crane uses outrigger beams and hydraulic jacks to relieve the suspension of the strain during lifting. The telescopic boom with its block and tackle can swivel around and extend far outward, secured by the counterweight at the base of the boom.

BLOCK AND TACKLE

LOAD

COUNTERWEIGHT

BOOM

HYDRAULIC RAM

OUTRIGGER

CAB

The block and tackle is a system of pulleys that is compact yet able to raise substantial loads. It is commonly used at the end of the boom of a crane to increase the force of the crane's motor in lifting a load.

The system contains one rope wound around two separate sets of pulleys. The pulleys in each set are free to rotate independently on the same axle. The upper set is fixed to a support such as a boom, while the lower set is attached to the load. Pulling the rope raises the lower set of pulleys. The magnification of the force that the block and tackle produces is equal to the number of pulley wheels it contains.

This block and tackle contains five pulleys in each set plus a guide wheel above. The load is raised by ten pulleys, so the block and tackle increases the force applied to it by ten times.

TOWER CRANE

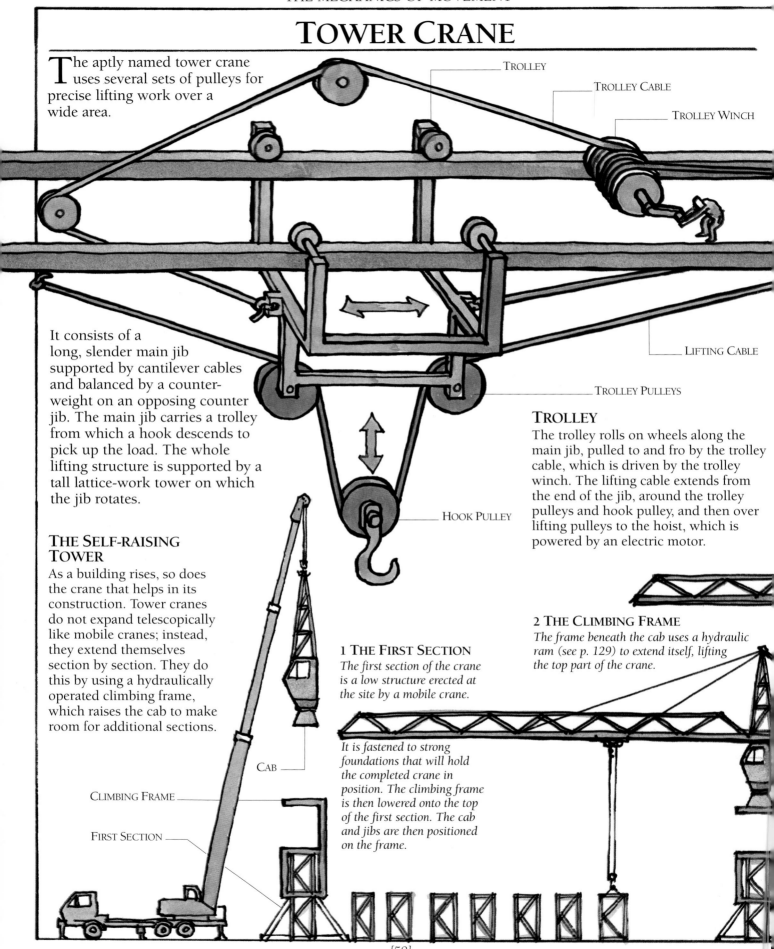

The aptly named tower crane uses several sets of pulleys for precise lifting work over a wide area.

TROLLEY

TROLLEY CABLE

TROLLEY WINCH

LIFTING CABLE

It consists of a long, slender main jib supported by cantilever cables and balanced by a counterweight on an opposing counter jib. The main jib carries a trolley from which a hook descends to pick up the load. The whole lifting structure is supported by a tall lattice-work tower on which the jib rotates.

TROLLEY PULLEYS

TROLLEY

The trolley rolls on wheels along the main jib, pulled to and fro by the trolley cable, which is driven by the trolley winch. The lifting cable extends from the end of the jib, around the trolley pulleys and hook pulley, and then over lifting pulleys to the hoist, which is powered by an electric motor.

HOOK PULLEY

THE SELF-RAISING TOWER

As a building rises, so does the crane that helps in its construction. Tower cranes do not expand telescopically like mobile cranes; instead, they extend themselves section by section. They do this by using a hydraulically operated climbing frame, which raises the cab to make room for additional sections.

CAB

CLIMBING FRAME

FIRST SECTION

1 THE FIRST SECTION

The first section of the crane is a low structure erected at the site by a mobile crane.

It is fastened to strong foundations that will hold the completed crane in position. The climbing frame is then lowered onto the top of the first section. The cab and jibs are then positioned on the frame.

2 THE CLIMBING FRAME

The frame beneath the cab uses a hydraulic ram (see p. 129) to extend itself, lifting the top part of the crane.

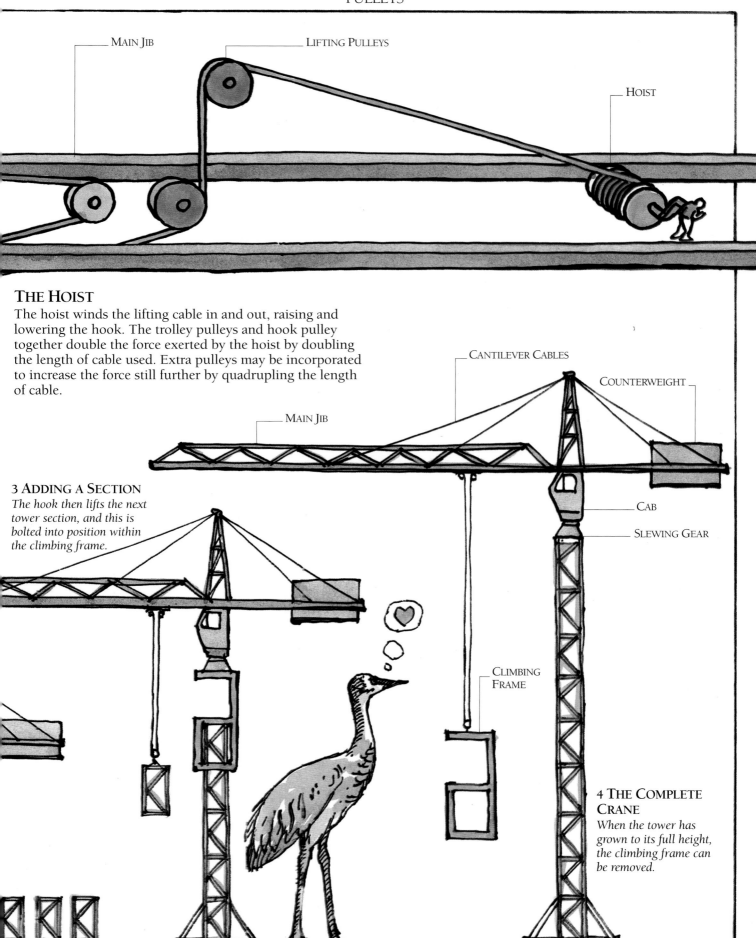

MAIN JIB

LIFTING PULLEYS

HOIST

THE HOIST

The hoist winds the lifting cable in and out, raising and lowering the hook. The trolley pulleys and hook pulley together double the force exerted by the hoist by doubling the length of cable used. Extra pulleys may be incorporated to increase the force still further by quadrupling the length of cable.

CANTILEVER CABLES

COUNTERWEIGHT

MAIN JIB

3 ADDING A SECTION
The hook then lifts the next tower section, and this is bolted into position within the climbing frame.

CAB

SLEWING GEAR

CLIMBING FRAME

4 THE COMPLETE CRANE
When the tower has grown to its full height, the climbing frame can be removed.

ESCALATOR AND ELEVATOR

Escalators and elevators are both lifting machines that make use of pulleys and counterweights. This is obvious in the elevator, where the cable supporting the elevator runs over a pulley to a counterweight. The pulley also drives the cable. Although it is not so immediately apparent, the escalator works in a similar way. A drive wheel moves a chain attached to the stairs, while the returning stairs act as a counterweight.

ESCALATOR

Escalator stairs are connected to an endless chain that runs around a drive wheel. The wheel is powered by an electric motor at the top of the escalator. The descending half of the stairs acts as a counterweight to the ascending half, so that the motor moves only the weight of the people riding. Every stair has a pair of wheels on each side and each pair runs on two rails beneath the stair. The rails are in line except at the top and the bottom of the escalator. Here, the inner rail goes beneath the outer rail so that each stair moves to the level of the next stair. In this way, the stairs fold flat for people to get on and off.

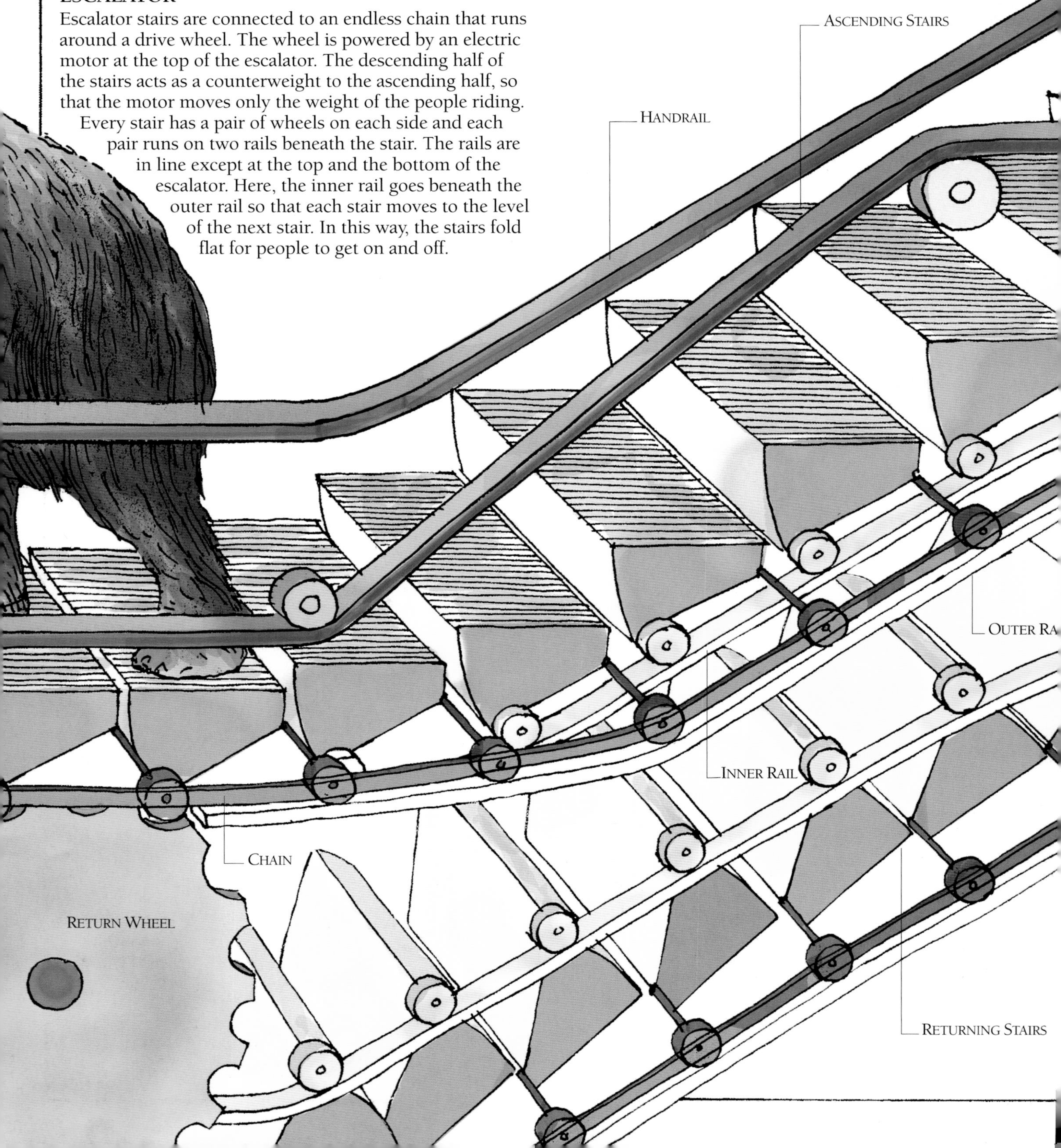

ASCENDING STAIRS

HANDRAIL

OUTER RA

INNER RAIL

CHAIN

RETURN WHEEL

RETURNING STAIRS

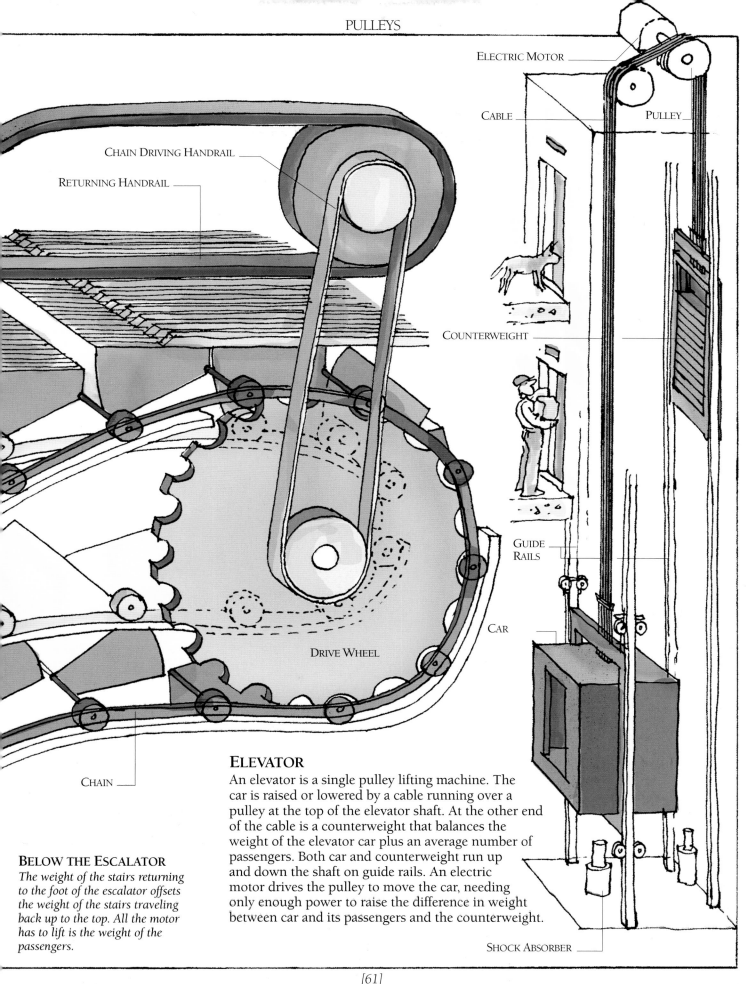

ELECTRIC MOTOR

CABLE

PULLEY

CHAIN DRIVING HANDRAIL

RETURNING HANDRAIL

COUNTERWEIGHT

GUIDE RAILS

CAR

DRIVE WHEEL

CHAIN

ELEVATOR

An elevator is a single pulley lifting machine. The car is raised or lowered by a cable running over a pulley at the top of the elevator shaft. At the other end of the cable is a counterweight that balances the weight of the elevator car plus an average number of passengers. Both car and counterweight run up and down the shaft on guide rails. An electric motor drives the pulley to move the car, needing only enough power to raise the difference in weight between car and its passengers and the counterweight.

BELOW THE ESCALATOR

The weight of the stairs returning to the foot of the escalator offsets the weight of the stairs traveling back up to the top. All the motor has to lift is the weight of the passengers.

SHOCK ABSORBER

SCREWS

ON THE INTELLIGENCE OF MAMMOTHS

I have recently unearthed a document that, I believe, proves beyond doubt the much-debated intellectual capacity of mammoths. One day, the document records, while seeking some good to do, a knight and his mammoth came upon a damsel imprisoned at the top of a stone tower. The tower contained no doors and only tiny windows. The knight attempted to rescue the damsel with a short ladder, but his armor was so heavy that he found the climb impossible. Next it appears that he built a long ramp by tying several planks together. Unfortunately, the knight was no good at tying knots.

NUTS AND BOLTS

The screw is a heavily disguised form of inclined plane, one that is wrapped around a cylinder—just as the knight's ramp encircles the tower. As we have already seen on p. 10, inclined planes alter force and distance. When something moves along a screw thread, like a nut on a bolt, it has to turn several times to move forward a short distance. As in a linear inclined plane, when distance decreases, force increases. A nut therefore moves along the bolt with a much greater force than the effort used to turn it.

A nut and bolt hold objects together because they grip the object with great force. Friction (see pp. 82-83) stops the nut from working loose.

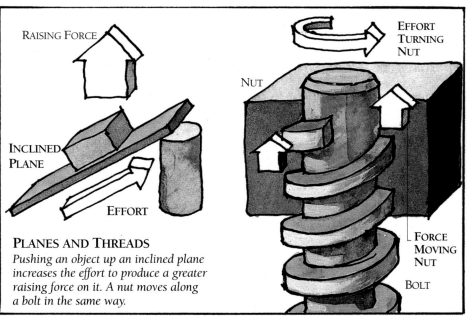

RAISING FORCE

INCLINED PLANE

EFFORT

EFFORT TURNING NUT

NUT

FORCE MOVING NUT

BOLT

PLANES AND THREADS

Pushing an object up an inclined plane increases the effort to produce a greater raising force on it. A nut moves along a bolt in the same way.

*T*he knight's next idea was to assemble the planks into another ramp, and to fix it in a spiral around the tower. But the ramp was not long enough to reach the damsel.

At this point, the trusty mammoth acted. He picked up a nearby tree trunk, inserted it into one of the windows, and turned the entire tower. Uncertain of what was going on, the knight joined in. To his amazement, the end of the ramp started to dig into the soil. By turning the tower many times they slowly screwed it into the ground. Soon the top of the tower was within easy reach of the ladder, and the dizzy damsel skipped to freedom.

SCREWS

Straight inclined planes are often used as wedges, in which the plane moves to force a load upward. Spiral inclined planes can work like wedges too. In most kinds of screws, the screw turns and moves itself into the material—like the damsel's tower. As with the nut and bolt, the turning effort is magnified so that the screw moves forward with an increased force. The force acts on the material to drive the screw into it.

As in the case of the nut and bolt, friction acts to hold the screw in the material. The friction occurs between the spiral thread and the material around it. It is strong because the spiral thread is long and the force between the thread and material is powerful.

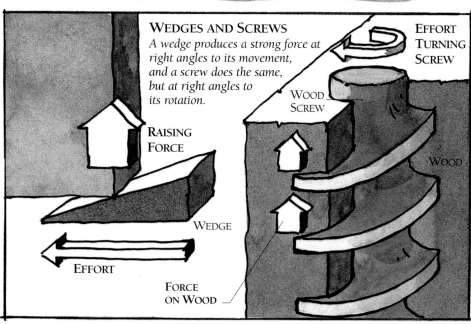

WEDGES AND SCREWS
A wedge produces a strong force at right angles to its movement, and a screw does the same, but at right angles to its rotation.

RAISING FORCE

WEDGE

EFFORT

FORCE ON WOOD

EFFORT TURNING SCREW

WOOD SCREW

WOOD

THE SCREW AT WORK

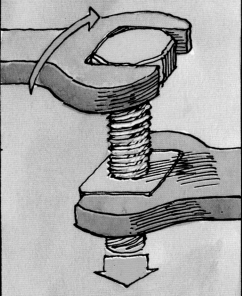

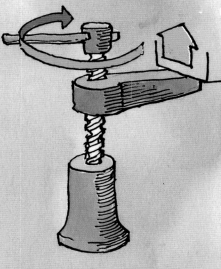

WOOD SCREW

The thread of a wood screw pulls strongly against the wood as it turns and drives itself into the wood. The screwdriver helps to increase the driving force even more.

NUT AND BOLT

The thread forces a nut and bolt together. The turning force is increased by the leverage of a wrench.

SCREW JACK

A screw jack uses a screw mechanism to lift a car. The handle may move fifty times further than the car, so the force on the car is fifty times greater than the effort on the handle.

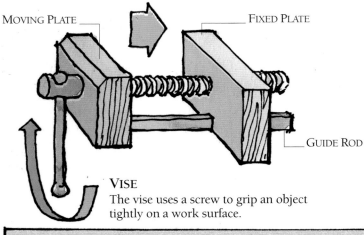

MOVING PLATE

FIXED PLATE

GUIDE ROD

VISE

The vise uses a screw to grip an object tightly on a work surface.

CORKSCREW

The corkscrew works like a wood screw, but is shaped in a helix to stop the cork splitting when it is pulled from the bottle. The handle increases the turning force applied, and provides a good grip for extracting the cork.

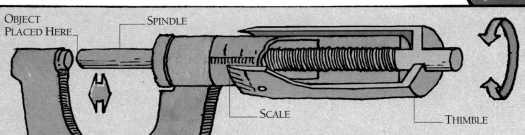

OBJECT PLACED HERE

SPINDLE

SCALE

THIMBLE

THIMBLE

The thimble turns on a ratchet mechanism. The ratchet stops the spindle moving forward when it touches the object.

MICROMETER

This instrument measures the width of objects with great precision. The object is placed in the micrometer and the thimble turned until the spindle touches the object. The spindle and thimble gradually move along a screw thread. The movement of the spindle is read on a scale, while the graduations on the thimble itself show small fractions of a revolution. Added together, the two figures give a highly accurate measurement.

THE FAUCET

If you've ever tried to stop water flowing from a faucet with a finger, you'll know just how much pressure the water can exert. But a faucet controls the flow with little effort, using a screw (aided by the use of the wheel and axle in the handle) to drive the washer down against the water flow with great force. Once tightened, friction (see pp. 82-83) acts on a screw thread to prevent the screw from working loose. A steep pitch on the screw thread minimizes the turning needed to work the faucet.

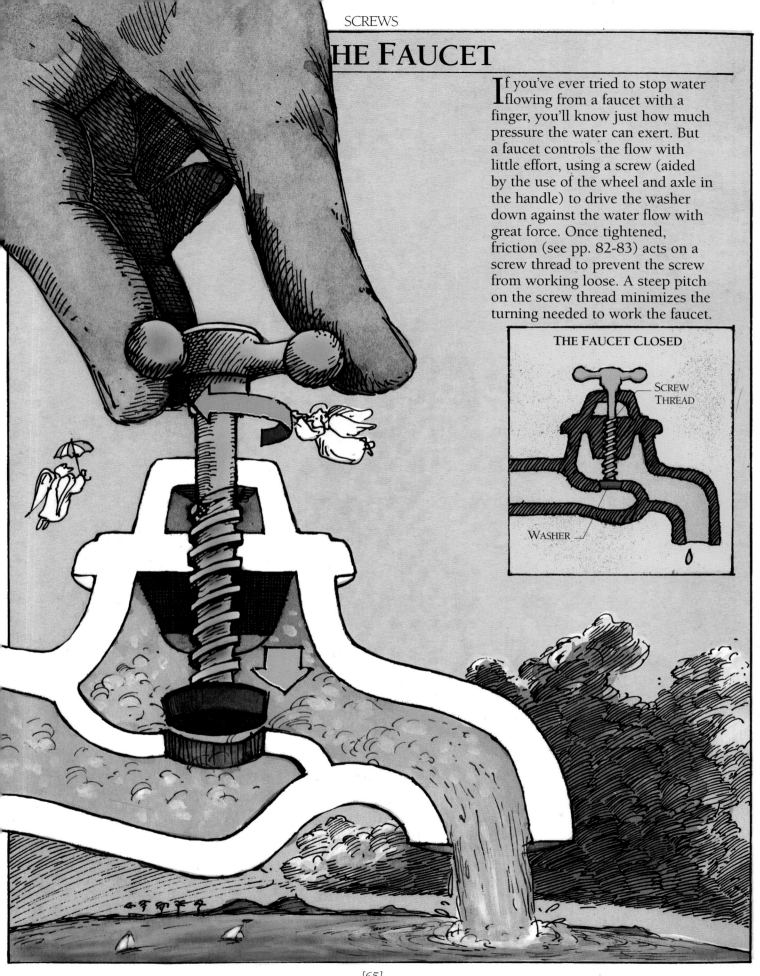

THE FAUCET CLOSED

SCREW
THREAD

WASHER

DRILLS AND AUGERS

In drills and augers, the screw is used as a means of carrying loose material. As a drill cuts forward into a material with its sharp point, it also channels waste away backward along its screw-shaped grooves. In large-diameter drills, the grooves that remove waste material are more pronounced and these give the drill a corkscrew shape.

BRACE AND BIT

When a lot of force is needed—for example, in drilling a wide-diameter hole—an ordinary hand drill will grind to a halt. The answer is a brace and bit. The bowed handle enables the bit to be turned with great leverage.

HAND DRILL

A hand drill uses a bevel gear (see p. 37) to step up the speed at which the bit rotates. One bevel gear transmits the turning force, while the other freewheels. Hand drills are fast, but not very powerful.

POWER DRILL

An electric power drill has gears to drive the bit at high speed. It may also have an impact mechanism that hammers the drill bit through a tough material.

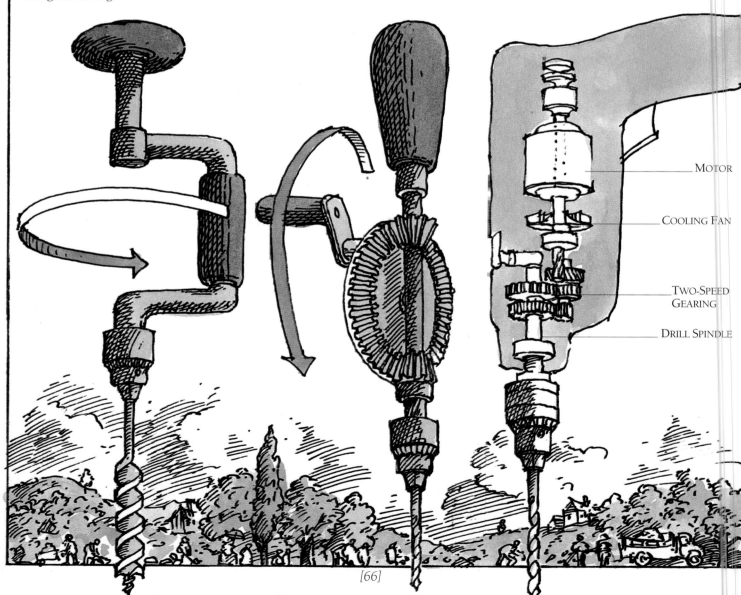

MOTOR

COOLING FAN

TWO-SPEED GEARING

DRILL SPINDLE

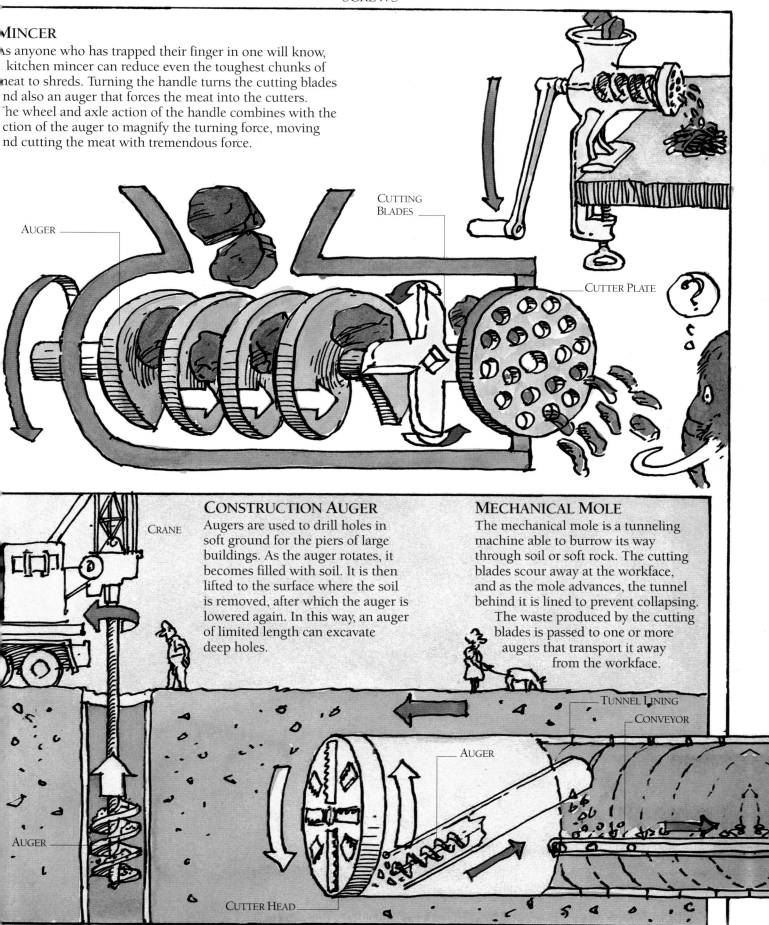

MINCER

As anyone who has trapped their finger in one will know, a kitchen mincer can reduce even the toughest chunks of meat to shreds. Turning the handle turns the cutting blades and also an auger that forces the meat into the cutters. The wheel and axle action of the handle combines with the action of the auger to magnify the turning force, moving and cutting the meat with tremendous force.

AUGER

CUTTING BLADES

CUTTER PLATE

CONSTRUCTION AUGER

CRANE

Augers are used to drill holes in soft ground for the piers of large buildings. As the auger rotates, it becomes filled with soil. It is then lifted to the surface where the soil is removed, after which the auger is lowered again. In this way, an auger of limited length can excavate deep holes.

AUGER

MECHANICAL MOLE

The mechanical mole is a tunneling machine able to burrow its way through soil or soft rock. The cutting blades scour away at the workface, and as the mole advances, the tunnel behind it is lined to prevent collapsing.

The waste produced by the cutting blades is passed to one or more augers that transport it away from the workface.

TUNNEL LINING

CONVEYOR

AUGER

CUTTER HEAD

THE COMBINE HARVESTER

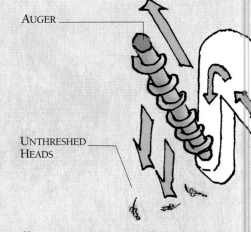

The combine harvester gets its name because it combines the two basic harvesting activities of reaping (cutting the crop) and threshing (separating out the grain). It may also bale the straw so that large fields can be harvested and cleared in one quick and tidy operation. Combine harvesters feature a number of screw mechanisms to transport the grain within the machine. Harvesters for seed crops other than grain work in similar ways.

KEY TO PARTS

1 REEL
The reel sweeps the stalks of the crop into the cutter bar.

2 CUTTER BAR
The bar contains a knife that moves to and fro between the prongs, slicing the stalks near ground level.

3 STALK AUGER
This transports the stalks to the elevator.

4 ELEVATOR
The elevator carries the stalks up to the threshing cylinder.

5 THRESHING CYLINDER
This contains a set of bars that rotates at high speed. The grain is separated from the heads and falls through the concave to the grain pan.

6 REAR BEATER
As this rotates, the straw (the threshed stalks) is moved to the straw walkers.

7 STRAW WALKERS
These carry the straw to the rear of the harvester, where it drops to the ground or is packed into bales.

8 GRAIN PAN
The vibrating surface of the pan transports the grain to the sieves.

9 SIEVES
The grain, unthreshed heads and chaff fall onto vibrating sieves. Air blows the chaff out of the rear of the harvester, while the sieves retain the unthreshed heads. The grain falls through the sieves to the base of the harvester.

10 TAILINGS ELEVATOR
This returns the unthreshed heads blown from the sieves to the threshing cylinder.

11 GRAIN AUGER AND ELEVATOR
The grain is carried by the auger and elevator to the grain tank.

12 UNLOADING AUGER
This transports the grain from the tank to a trailer or into bags.

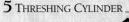

AUGER

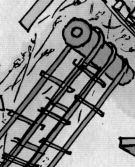

UNTHRESHED HEADS

5 THRESHING CYLINDER

CONCAVE

1 REEL

4 ELEVATOR

8 GRAIN PAN

TINES

3 STALK AUGER

2 CUTTER BAR

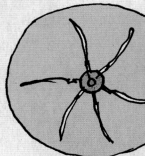

FAN

AIR BLAST

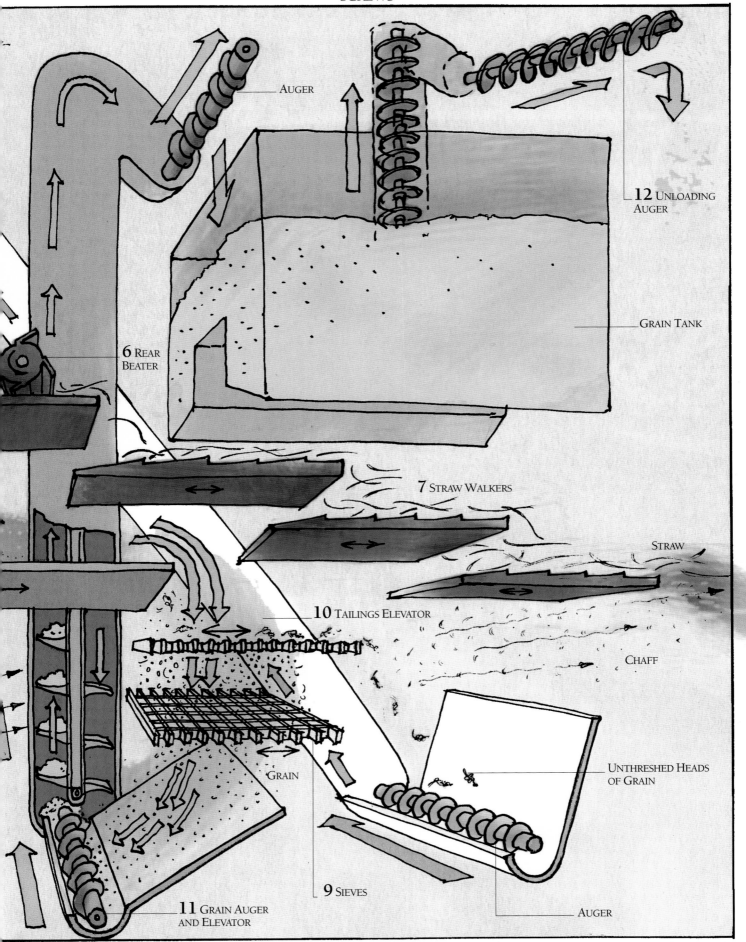

AUGER

12 UNLOADING AUGER

GRAIN TANK

6 REAR BEATER

7 STRAW WALKERS

STRAW

10 TAILINGS ELEVATOR

CHAFF

GRAIN

UNTHRESHED HEADS OF GRAIN

11 GRAIN AUGER AND ELEVATOR

9 SIEVES

AUGER

ROTATING WHEELS

ON LEARNING FROM MAMMOTH ADVERSITY

I once made the mistake of leaving my unicycle unattended in the presence of a young mammoth. Being innately curious, the mischievous creature promptly took to the road. Even as I shouted, I could not help noting the extraordinary stability of the rotating wheel that allowed the novice cyclist to make good its escape.

Although the mammoth soon lost interest in the undertaking, the wheel—now rolling along at full tilt—seemed reluctant to stop. By the time the unicycle had reached the top of a small hill, its terrified rider was being carried helplessly forward. Everything in their path was promptly and unceremoniously flattened.

PRECESSION

Precession is a strange kind of motion that occurs in wheels and other rotating objects. You can feel its effects for yourself if you hold a spinning bicycle wheel by its axle. When you try to turn it, you will find that the wheel won't turn in the way you intend it to. Instead, it will "precess," so that the axle actually turns at right angles to the direction you expect.

Precession makes a wheel rolling on its own stay upright, and it enables a cyclist (or unicyclist) to ride. We use precession instinctively by slightly swiveling the front wheel. Each swivel brings precession into play to correct tilting, helping us to keep the bicycle upright.

The force of precession increases with speed. Conversely, it decreases as a wheel slows down. This is why it is difficult to ride a bicycle that is moving slowly. Remaining upright on a stationary cycle is purely a feat of balance, and does not involve precession.

INERTIA

You'll have experienced the effects of inertia if you've ever had to push a car in order to start it. It takes a lot of effort to get a car moving, but once it is going, it will carry on for some distance without further pushing and, with luck, will start itself.

Inertia accounts for all the pushing and shoving. It is the resistance of objects to any change in their speed, even if the speed is zero. Everything has inertia, and the amount depends on mass. The greater an object's mass, the more inertia it has.

In a rotating wheel, inertia also depends on how the mass is distributed. A wheel has more inertia if its mass is concentrated near the rim than if it is concentrated around the center. This means that two wheels of the same mass can have different inertia. Wheels designed to exploit inertia in machines often have heavy or thickened rims to provide the maximum resistance to any change in speed.

As I raced down the hill and over the wreckage, I wondered about my insurance coverage. Then I noticed the pond and its stunned occupant. The mammoth's little adventure had ended, but it was several minutes before I could approach my vehicle. Although upside down in the mud, the wheel was spinning rapidly and as it did, it flung everything attached to it a considerable distance.

CENTRIFUGAL FORCE

When an object moves in a circle, it is also always changing direction. Its inertia resists any change in direction as well as speed, and will make the object move straight on if it is free to leave the circle.

So, relative to the circle, the object is always trying to move away from the center under an apparent outward-acting force. This is known as centrifugal force, and anything moving in a circle—like the mud on the unicycle—experiences it. The faster an object is traveling, the stronger the force is.

Centrifugal force is used in machines to throw something outward. The simplest example is probably the spin drier, in which a spinning drum holds clothes while the water in them is forced outward through holes in the drum. Other machines use the centrifugal force that is generated by a sudden movement to activate catches and ratchets.

INERTIA AT WORK

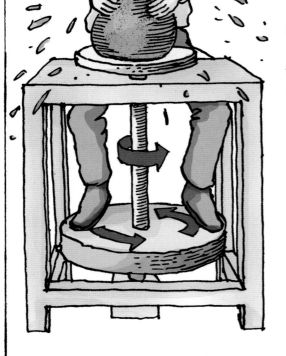

POTTER'S WHEEL

The potter's wheel is a heavy disk with an axle.
It is usually turned either by kicking the axle around or
by operating a treadle. The wheel has considerable inertia,
and this keeps it turning between kicks or presses of
the treadle.

Centrifugal Force!

FRICTION-DRIVE TOY

Friction-drive toys store up energy in
a flywheel. When you push the toy
along the floor, the flywheel is set
spinning by the wheels. Its inertia
keeps it spinning so that
when the toy is put
down, it scoots
across the
floor.

TURNTABLE

The turntable of a record player has to rotate at a very
constant speed. To do this, it has a heavy rim so that
most of its mass is concentrated in the part that moves
fastest, thereby raising its inertia. The inertia of the
turntable cancels out any slight variation in speed that
occurs in the turntable motor.

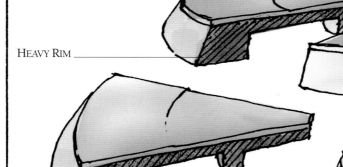

HEAVY RIM

PLAYING ARM

SPINDLE

STARTER MOT

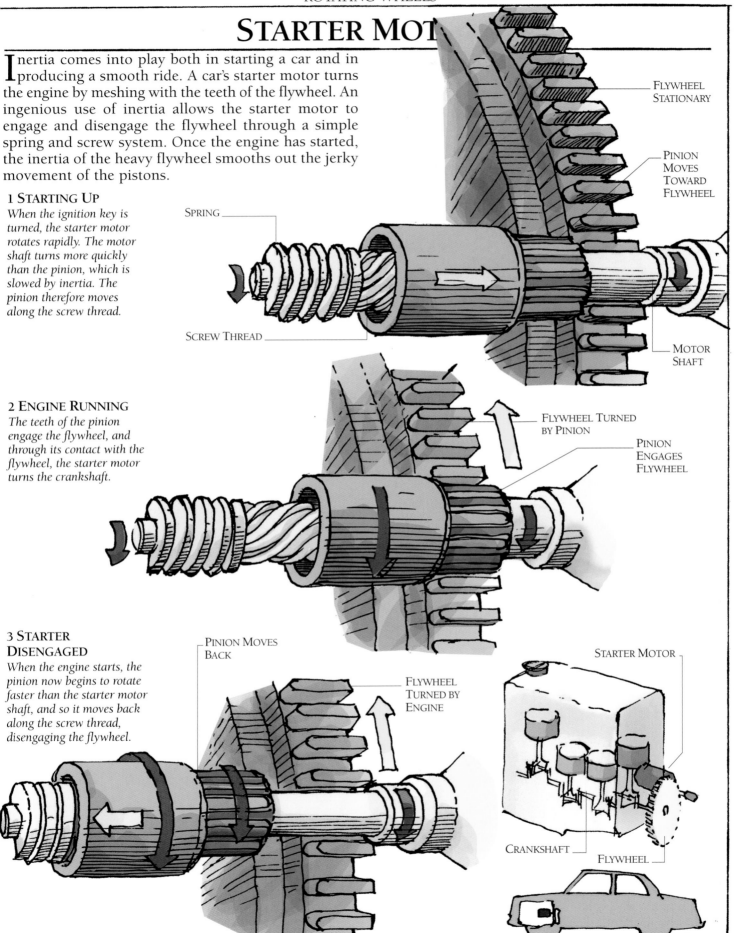

Inertia comes into play both in starting a car and in producing a smooth ride. A car's starter motor turns the engine by meshing with the teeth of the flywheel. An ingenious use of inertia allows the starter motor to engage and disengage the flywheel through a simple spring and screw system. Once the engine has started, the inertia of the heavy flywheel smooths out the jerky movement of the pistons.

1 STARTING UP
When the ignition key is turned, the starter motor rotates rapidly. The motor shaft turns more quickly than the pinion, which is slowed by inertia. The pinion therefore moves along the screw thread.

SPRING

SCREW THREAD

FLYWHEEL STATIONARY

PINION MOVES TOWARD FLYWHEEL

MOTOR SHAFT

2 ENGINE RUNNING
The teeth of the pinion engage the flywheel, and through its contact with the flywheel, the starter motor turns the crankshaft.

FLYWHEEL TURNED BY PINION

PINION ENGAGES FLYWHEEL

3 STARTER DISENGAGED
When the engine starts, the pinion now begins to rotate faster than the starter motor shaft, and so it moves back along the screw thread, disengaging the flywheel.

PINION MOVES BACK

FLYWHEEL TURNED BY ENGINE

STARTER MOTOR

CRANKSHAFT

FLYWHEEL

WINDOW SHADE

A window shade is lowered simply by pulling it down; the shade unrolls and remains in any position. To raise the shade, all that is needed is a sharp tug and the whole shade will roll up. But how can it tell a gentle pull from a sharp tug?

The shaft on which the shade is rolled contains a powerful spring. This winds up as the shade is lowered.

A locking mechanism—a simple ratchet—prevents the spring unwinding if it is released gently. But when the shade is pulled suddenly, the ratchet no longer holds the shade in position. The motion makes a centrifugal device in the locking mechanism release the spring: the spring unwinds, releasing the energy that it has stored, and up goes the shade.

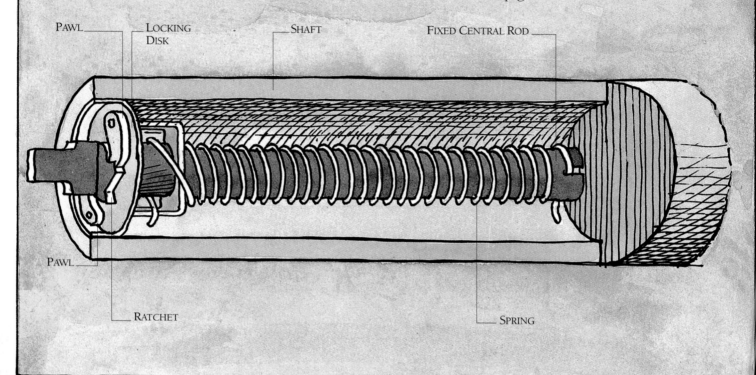

PAWL   LOCKING DISK   SHAFT   FIXED CENTRAL ROD

PAWL

RATCHET   SPRING

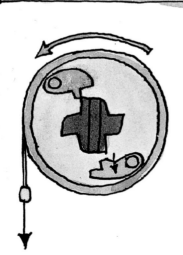

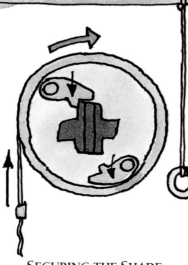

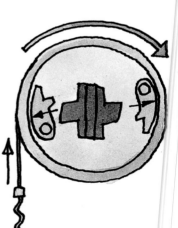

LOWERING THE SHADE

As the shaft rotates, it turns the locking disk to wind up the spring. The pawls are hinged and move over the ratchet, which is fixed to the central rod and does not move.

SECURING THE SHADE

When the shaft stops, the spring pulls the locking disk back slightly. One of the pawls falls to engage the ratchet, securing the locking disk.

FREEING THE SHADE

A tug on the shade rotates the shaft sharply, making the locking pawl move back and disengage the ratchet. The locking disk is now free to move.

RAISING THE SHADE

The spring unwinds, rotating the locking disk rapidly. Centrifugal force holds the pawls away from the ratchet, and the shade rolls up.

CAR SEAT BELT

A car seat belt works in the reverse way to the window shade. Instead of locking when the belt is pulled gently, it locks when the belt is given a sharp tug of the kind that would occur in a crash, and so secures the driver or passenger. The belt remains unlocked when pulled slowly, allowing normal movement in the seat. At the heart of the seat belt is a centrifugal clutch.

1 THE BELT MOVES FREELY
During normal use, the toothed plate is not in contact with the clutch and so the plate, and therefore the belt shaft, are free to rotate slowly.

2 THE CLUTCH ENGAGES
A sudden movement makes the toothed plate rotate quickly within the clutch. Centrifugal force makes it slide outward to engage the inner teeth of the clutch.

3 THE BELT LOCKS
Once the clutch has engaged, it rotates to move a pawl, which in turn engages the ratchet. The pawl is fixed to the car body, while the ratchet is attached to the belt shaft. The pawl prevents the ratchet from turning, so locking the belt. When the belt slackens, springs return the parts to their initial positions and free the belt.

BELT

BELT SHAFT

RATCHET

PAWL
ENGAGES AND
LOCKS RATCHET

CLUTCH
MOVES PAWL

BELT SHAFT

TOOTHED PLATE

GYROSCOPE

A spinning gyroscope can balance on a pivot, defying gravity by remaining horizontal while resting just on the tip of its axle. Instead of falling off the pivot, the gyroscope circles around it. The explanation for this amazing feat lies in the effects of precession.

Like all other objects, the rotating wheel of the gyroscope is subjected to gravity. However, as long as the gyroscope spins, precession overcomes gravity by transforming it into a force that causes the gyroscope to circle instead of falling.

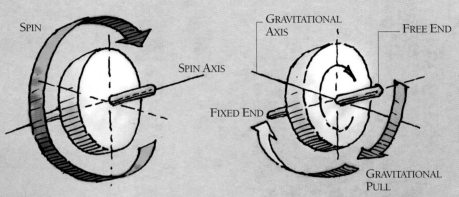

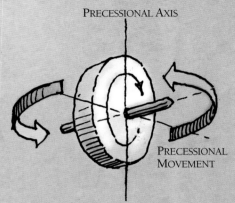

1 THE GYROSCOPE STARTS SPINNING

The gyroscope is set spinning so that its axle is horizontal and the wheel is vertical. The whole gyroscope rotates around the spin axis, which runs along the axle.

2 GRAVITY BEGINS TO ACT

The gyroscope is now placed so that one end of the axle is free to move. Gravity tries to pull this end downward, rotating the gyroscope around a second axis: the gravitational axis.

3 PRECESSION OVERCOMES GRAVITY

At this point, precession occurs. Instead of obeying the pull of gravity, precession makes the gyroscope move in a horizontal circle—in effect rotating it about a third axis, a precessional axis.

CHANGING DIRECTION

If either the wheel or the axle turns in the opposite direction, then the gyroscope precesses in the opposite direction.

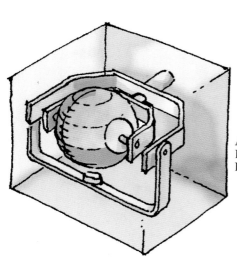

ARTIFICIAL HORIZON

Gyroscopes are very important in navigation. A spinning gyroscope possesses gyroscopic inertia, which makes it resist any change in its direction. The axle of the gyroscope remains pointing in the initial direction to which it is set. In the artificial horizon—an instrument that indicates the angle at which an aircraft banks—a gyroscope controls an indicator. Gimbals allow the gyroscope axle to remain horizontal. As the aircraft banks, the indicator also remains horizontal and shows the angle of the aircraft.

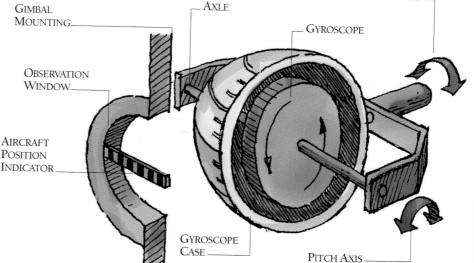

GIMBAL MOUNTING

OBSERVATION WINDOW

AIRCRAFT POSITION INDICATOR

AXLE

GYROSCOPE

ROLL AXIS

GYROSCOPE CASE

PITCH AXIS

GYROCOMPASS

A gyrocompass makes use of the gyroscope to indicate direction. The axis of the gyroscope rotor is set in a north-south direction and the rotor is set spinning. The gyroscope is connected to an indicator so that as the ship or aircraft carrying the compass turns, the gyroscope keeps the indicator pointing north.

However, just as in the toy gyroscope, friction in the gyrocompass can cause it to drift out of true, and this may have to be corrected. In some gyrocompasses, this is done automatically by using the Earth's gravity. The gyroscope is connected to a weight, such as a tube of mercury, that acts as a pendulum. If the gyrocompass begins to point away from north, the pendulum tilts the axis of the rotor. Precession then occurs to bring the axis back to true north.

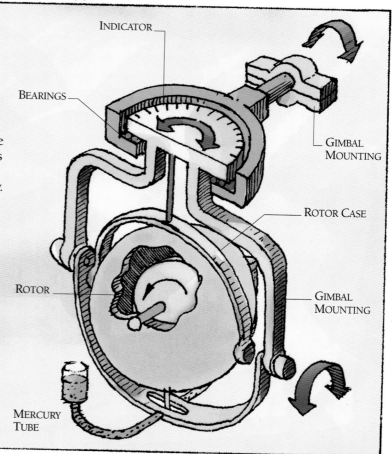

INDICATOR

BEARINGS

GIMBAL MOUNTING

ROTOR CASE

ROTOR

GIMBAL MOUNTING

MERCURY TUBE

THE NON-MAGNETIC COMPASS

A magnetic compass points to the north magnetic pole, which is away from true north, so correction is needed. Because gyrocompasses do not use magnetism, they always point to true north.

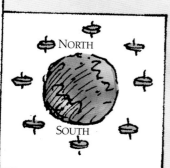

NORTH

SOUTH

SPRINGS

ON A MAMMOTH HARVEST

A great many mammoths, in spite of their generally placid temperament, are ill-suited to inside work. Their preference for the outdoors combined with their tremendous strength makes them marvelous helpers in the field. I well recall seeing mammoths assisting eagerly during a particularly heavy coconut harvest. Instead of climbing each tree and simply dropping the coconuts, which could damage the shells, the farmer used his mammoth to bring the coconuts within reach of a ladder for effortless picking.

SPRINGS THAT REGAIN THEIR SHAPE

Springs have two basic forms—either a coil or a bending bar—and they have three main uses in machines. The first is simply to return something to its previous position. A door-return spring, for example, contracts after being stretched, while the valve springs of a car engine expand after being compressed (see p. 49).

SPRINGS THAT MEASURE FORCE

The second use of springs depends on the amount by which springs change shape when they are subjected to a force. This is exactly proportional to the strength of the force exerted on the spring—the more you pull a spring, the more it stretches. Many weighing machines use springs in this way.

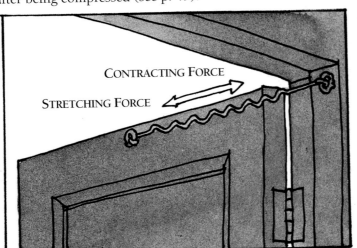

CONTRACTING FORCE

STRETCHING FORCE

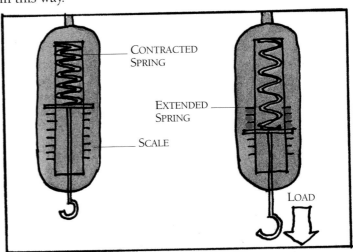

CONTRACTED SPRING

EXTENDED SPRING

SCALE

LOAD

But as I mused on this harmonious partnership between man and mammoth, disaster struck. The unexpected appearance of a mouse so deranged the mammoth that it released the rope. The tree then obeyed its natural desire to return to its original configuration, thereby dispensing the coconuts—and the farmer—far and wide.

SPRINGS THAT STORE ENERGY

The third main use of springs is to store energy. When you stretch or compress a spring, you give it energy to make it move. This energy can be released immediately, as in a door spring, but if not, the energy remains stored. When the spring is released, it gives up the energy. Spring-driven clocks work by releasing the energy stored in springs.

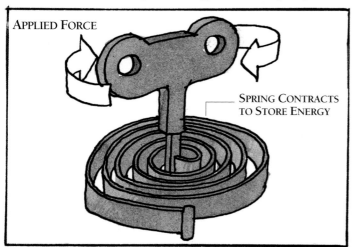

APPLIED FORCE

SPRING CONTRACTS TO STORE ENERGY

ELASTICITY

The special property of springs, their elasticity, is conferred on them by the way their molecules interact. Two main kinds of force operate on the molecules in a material—an attracting force that pulls molecules together, and a repelling force that pushes them apart. Normally these balance so the molecules keep a certain distance apart.

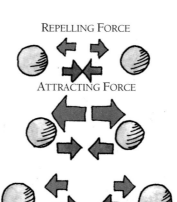

REPELLING FORCE

ATTRACTING FORCE

SPRING AT REST
The attracting and repelling forces are balanced.

SQUEEZED SPRING
Squeezing builds up the repelling force. When released, the force pushes the molecules apart again.

STRETCHED SPRING
Stretching builds up the attracting force. When released, this pulls the molecules back together.

THE STAPLER

A stapler is an everyday device that conceals an ingenious arrangement of springs. It uses both a coil spring and a leaf spring, which feed the staples along the magazine and return the stapler to its original position once it has been used. Pushing down the stapler causes the blade to descend into the magazine, forcing the front staple through the papers. The anvil bends the ends of the staple to clip the papers together. The return spring then raises the magazine and blade, allowing the magazine spring to advance the next staple into position.

BASE PLATE
A projection on the base plate flattens the return spring when the stapler is used. The spring raises the magazine away from the anvil after use.

CAR SUSPENSION

The suspension of a car allows it to drive smoothly over a bumpy road. The wheels may jolt up and down, but springs between the wheel axles and the body of the car flex and take up the force of the jolts. This ensures that the force of the bumping is not transferred to the car. Springs alone produce a bouncing motion, so the suspension also contains dampers, commonly known as shock absorbers. These slow the movement of the springs to prevent the car and its occupants bouncing up and down.

SHOCK ABSORBER
A shock absorber is fixed between the wheel axle and car body. Its piston moves up or down as the suspension spring flexes. As it does so, the oil is squeezed through channels in the piston, slowing the piston's movement.

COIL SPRING
Smaller vehicles have a coil spring and shock absorber attached to each wheel. The axle of the wheel is attached to hinged struts so that it can move up and down. The spring and shock absorber are fixed between the car body and the struts, or "wishbones."

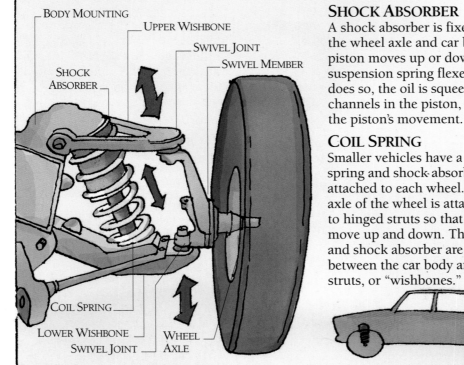

BODY MOUNTING
UPPER WISHBONE
SWIVEL JOINT
SWIVEL MEMBER
SHOCK ABSORBER
COIL SPRING
LOWER WISHBONE
SWIVEL JOINT
WHEEL AXLE

CAR BODY MOUNTING
OIL
CHANNEL
PISTON
VALVE
OIL RESERVOIR
CYLINDER
WHEEL AXLE MOUNTING

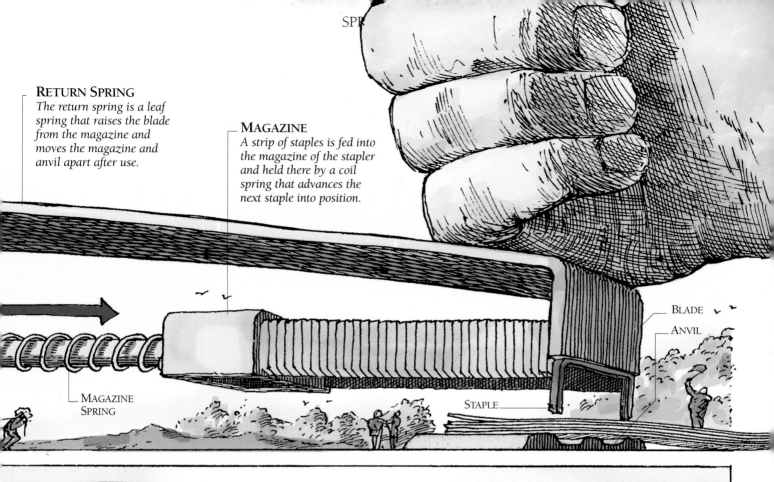

RETURN SPRING

The return spring is a leaf spring that raises the blade from the magazine and moves the magazine and anvil apart after use.

MAGAZINE

A strip of staples is fed into the magazine of the stapler and held there by a coil spring that advances the next staple into position.

BLADE

ANVIL

MAGAZINE
SPRING

STAPLE

LEAF SPRING

Larger vehicles have heavy-duty leaf springs and shock absorbers to cushion the ride. The leaf spring is a stack of steel strips; it is normally slightly curved so that the spring straightens when the vehicle is loaded. The axle is attached at or near the center of the leaf spring, and the ends of the spring are fixed to the body. The shock absorber is fixed between the axle and body.

TORSION BAR

A torsion bar is a steel rod that acts like a spring to take up a twisting force. If the bar is forced to twist in one direction, it resists the movement and then twists back when the force is removed. Many cars contain an anti-roll bar fixed between the front axles. This rotates as the wheels go up and down. If the car begins to roll over on a tight corner, the anti-roll bar prevents the roll from increasing.

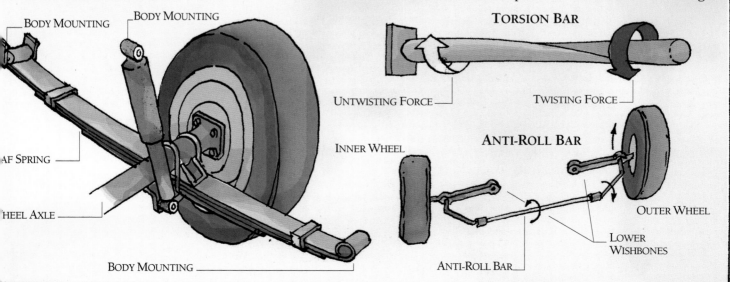

BODY MOUNTING

BODY MOUNTING

LEAF SPRING

WHEEL AXLE

BODY MOUNTING

TORSION BAR

UNTWISTING FORCE

TWISTING FORCE

INNER WHEEL

ANTI-ROLL BAR

OUTER WHEEL

ANTI-ROLL BAR

LOWER
WISHBONES

FRICTION

ON MAMMOTHS AND BATHING

*L*ike children, mammoths in a domestic situation must be bathed with some regularity. Also like children, they tend to see bathing as both an annoying interruption and a needless indignity. Frequent bathing is virtually impossible, but when it must be done the most difficult part of the process is just getting the beast near the tub.

GETTING A GRIP

Friction is a force that appears whenever one surface rubs against another, or when an object moves through water, air, or any other liquid or gas. It always opposes motion. Friction happens because two surfaces in close contact grip each other. The harder they press together, the stronger the grip. The same molecular forces are at work as in springs. Forces between the molecules in the surfaces pull the surfaces together. The closer the molecules get, the stronger the force of friction.

The bathing team have to contend with the mammoth's superior weight, which gives it the better grip on the ground. Only by reducing friction with the soap and marbles—a lubricant and bearings—can they move it.

You can never get the same amount of useful work from a mechanical device as you put into it: friction will always rob you of some of the energy that is transmitted through the machine. Instead of useful motion, this lost energy appears as heat and sound. Excessive heat and strange noises coming from a machine are sure signs that it is not performing well.

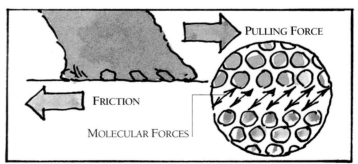

PULLING FORCE

FRICTION

MOLECULAR FORCES

Designers and engineers strive to overcome friction and make machines as efficient as possible. But paradoxically, many machines depend on friction. If it were suddenly to be banished, cars would slide out of control with wheels spinning helplessly. Brakes, which depend on friction, would be of no use, and neither would the clutch. Grinding machines would not make even a scratch, while parachutes would plummet from the sky.

The bathing scene I remember most vividly was not unlike the weighing of a large mammoth in its communal atmosphere. A large sneaker-clad crowd gathered on one side of a bath filled with soap suds. A dirty mammoth sat defiantly on the other. It should be noted that a mammoth's weight is its greatest defense and that just by standing or sitting still, it is able to resist all but the most determined efforts to move it.

Once ropes had been attached to the animal, they were pulled tight. Meanwhile another team used a technique that I had not previously encountered in my researches.

First, they employed second-class levers to raise the beast slightly. Just when I had concluded that they intended to lever it all the way to the tub, some of their number poured a mixture of liquid soap and marbles between the protesting creature and the floor.

The result was astonishing: the animal's resistance was suddenly reduced and, despite its struggles, it was hauled inexorably toward the water. Working simultaneously from both ends, it took little more than half an hour to get the mammoth close enough to the foam-filled tub for a good scrub behind the ears.

CAR TIRE

Car tires use friction to provide traction and steering: they grip the road so that the force of the engine and the force you exert on the steering wheel are converted into forces that act on the tires and propel and turn the car. Tires must grip the road surface in all weather conditions. If a film of water becomes sandwiched between the tire and the road, then friction—and with it traction and steering—is lost. The raised tread on the surface of a tire is designed to maintain friction on a wet road by dispersing the water.

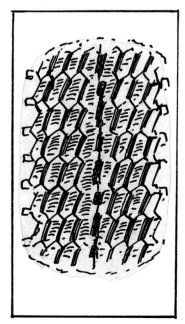

PARACHUTE

As a parachute opens, it develops a large force of friction with the air because it is moving rapidly. Friction is initially greater than gravity so the parachutist slows down. As the speed of the parachute lessens, friction decreases until it equals the force of gravity. At this point, there is no overall force acting on the parachutist, so he or she continues to descend without speeding up or slowing down. This constant rate of fall is slow enough for a safe landing.

FRICTION WITH AIR

GRAVITY

THE CLUTCH

In a car, the clutch makes use of friction to transmit the rotation of the engine crankshaft to the gearbox, and then to the wheels. It can take up the rotation slowly so that the car moves smoothly away.

In a car with a manual gearbox, the clutch is disengaged when the clutch pedal is pressed down.

The pedal operates the thrust pad, which presses on levers at the center of the rotating clutch cover. This raises the pressure plate away from the clutch plate, disconnecting the flywheel, which is turned by the crankshaft, from the transmission shaft. When the clutch pedal is lifted, the springs force the pressure plate and clutch plate against the flywheel. Friction linings on the clutch plate allow the plate to slide before it becomes fully engaged, which prevents jerking.

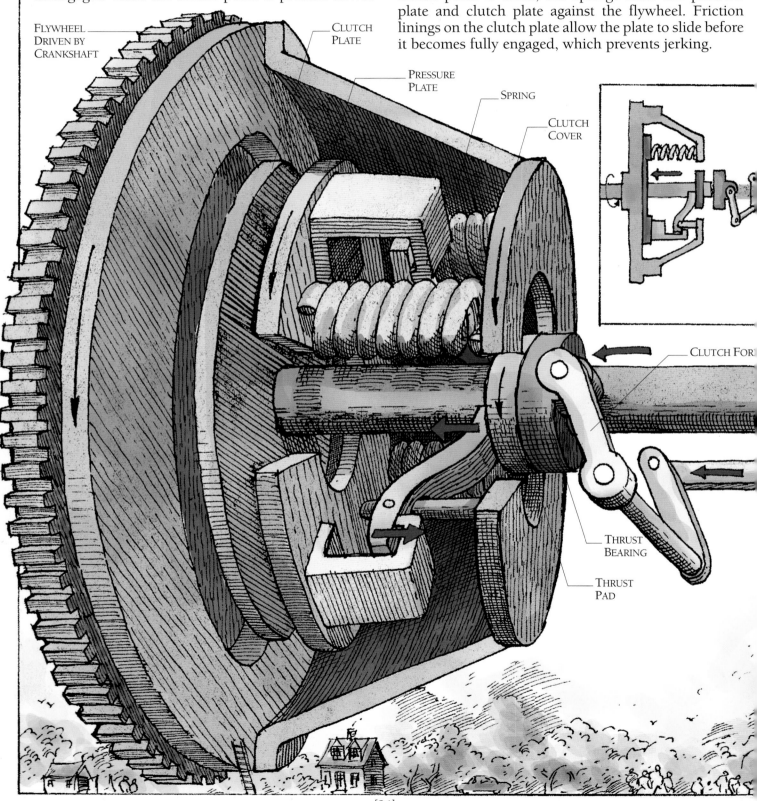

FLYWHEEL DRIVEN BY CRANKSHAFT

CLUTCH PLATE

PRESSURE PLATE

SPRING

CLUTCH COVER

CLUTCH FOR

THRUST BEARING

THRUST PAD

SYNCHROMESH

The synchromesh is a mechanism in a car's gearbox (see pp. 40-41) that enables the driver to change gear easily. It prevents gear wheels inside the gearbox from engaging at different speeds and crunching together. Before any forward gear is selected, gear wheels driven by the engine freewheel on the transmission shaft. For a gear to be engaged, the wheel and shaft need to be brought to the same speed and locked together. The synchromesh uses friction to do this smoothly and quietly.

Pushed by the selector fork, the collar slides along the transmission shaft, rotating with it. The collar fits over a cone on the gear wheel, making the wheel speed up or slow down until both are moving at the same speed. The outer toothed ring on the collar then engages the dog teeth on the cone, locking the collar to the gear wheel.

SYNCHROMESH DISENGAGED

When the synchromesh is disengaged, the collar and gear wheel are not connected, and the gear wheel freewheels on the transmission shaft.

SELECTOR FORK

GEAR WHEEL   DOG TEETH

CONE   TOOTHED RING

COLLAR

GEAR WHEEL

TRANSMISSION SHAFT

SYNCHROMESH ENGAGED

The collar makes contact with the cone, and friction between them brings them to the same speed. The teeth mesh together. The gear wheel is now locked to the transmission shaft and so can transmit power to it from the engine, turning the wheels.

ENGINE

TRANSMISSION SHAFT

GEARBOX

DIFFERENTIAL

CLUTCH

CLUTCH ENGAGED

Releasing the pedal allows the clutch springs to force the clutch plate and flywheel together, so the flywheel drives the transmission shaft.

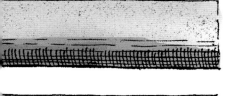

TRANSMISSION SHAFT TO GEARBOX

CLUTCH DISENGAGED

Pressing the pedal pushes in the thrust pad, which in turn pulls back the pressure plate. The flywheel and transmission shaft are now disconnected, so the engine cannot turn the wheels.

CAR BRAKES

To bring a fast-moving car and its passengers to a halt in a few seconds, car brakes must create a greater force than the engine does. Yet this force is produced by friction between surfaces with a total area only about the size of your hands.

Brakes are powerful because the brake pad or shoe and the brake disk or drum are pushed together with great force. In a car with unassisted brakes, the force of the driver's foot is amplified by the hydraulics in the braking system (see p. 128). In a car with power brakes, this hydraulic system is boosted by another system that comes into operation when the brake pedal is pressed, enabling the driver to achieve quicker braking (see p. 127).

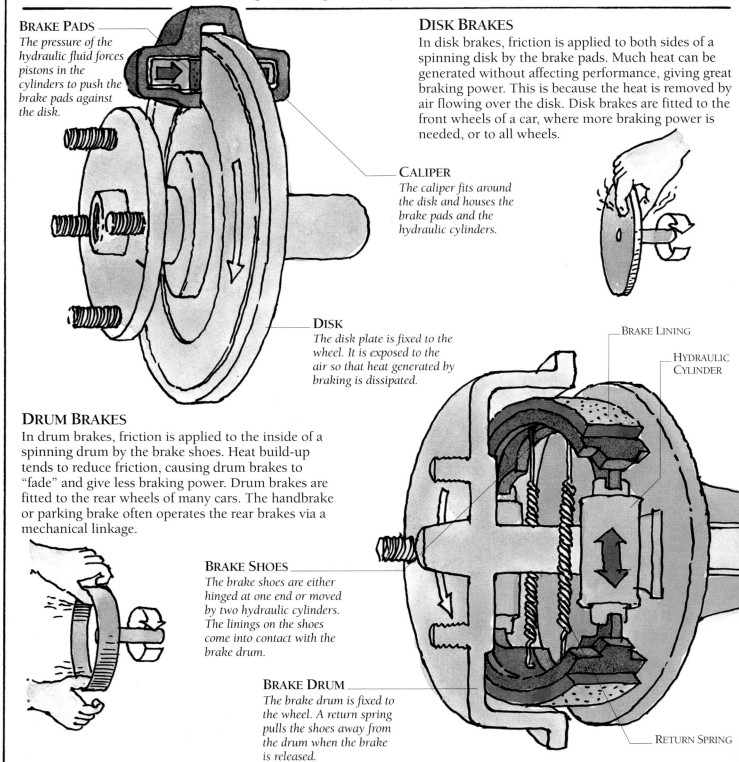

BRAKE PADS

The pressure of the hydraulic fluid forces pistons in the cylinders to push the brake pads against the disk.

DISK BRAKES

In disk brakes, friction is applied to both sides of a spinning disk by the brake pads. Much heat can be generated without affecting performance, giving great braking power. This is because the heat is removed by air flowing over the disk. Disk brakes are fitted to the front wheels of a car, where more braking power is needed, or to all wheels.

CALIPER

The caliper fits around the disk and houses the brake pads and the hydraulic cylinders.

DISK

The disk plate is fixed to the wheel. It is exposed to the air so that heat generated by braking is dissipated.

BRAKE LINING

HYDRAULIC CYLINDER

DRUM BRAKES

In drum brakes, friction is applied to the inside of a spinning drum by the brake shoes. Heat build-up tends to reduce friction, causing drum brakes to "fade" and give less braking power. Drum brakes are fitted to the rear wheels of many cars. The handbrake or parking brake often operates the rear brakes via a mechanical linkage.

BRAKE SHOES

The brake shoes are either hinged at one end or moved by two hydraulic cylinders. The linings on the shoes come into contact with the brake drum.

BRAKE DRUM

The brake drum is fixed to the wheel. A return spring pulls the shoes away from the drum when the brake is released.

RETURN SPRING

OIL RIG

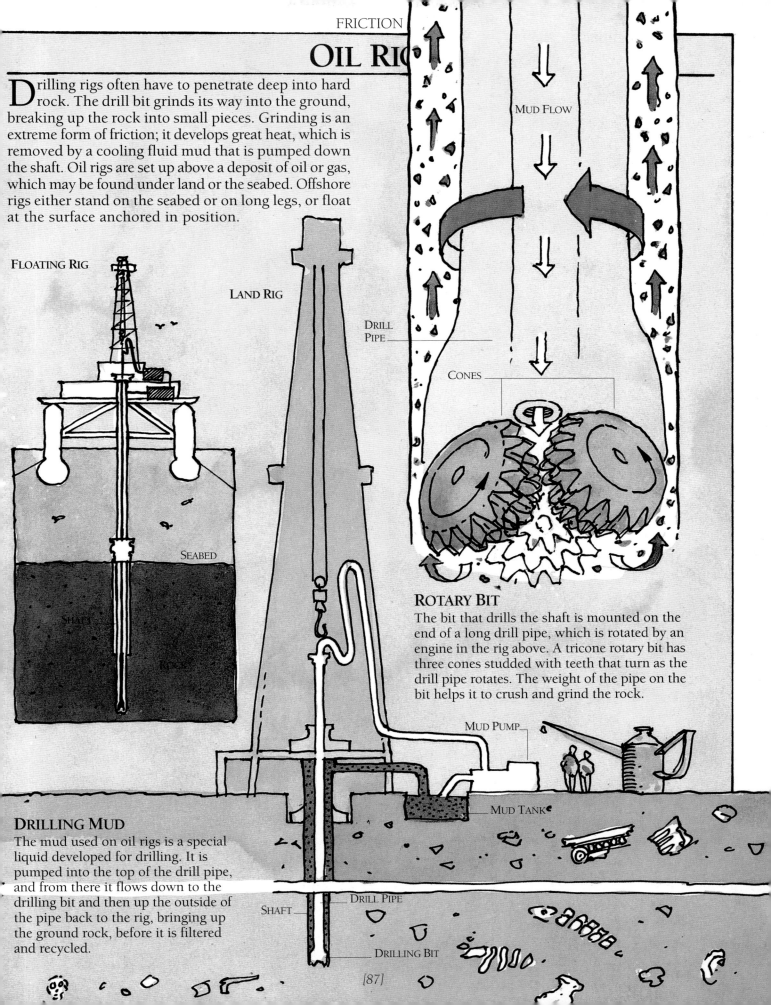

Drilling rigs often have to penetrate deep into hard rock. The drill bit grinds its way into the ground, breaking up the rock into small pieces. Grinding is an extreme form of friction; it develops great heat, which is removed by a cooling fluid mud that is pumped down the shaft. Oil rigs are set up above a deposit of oil or gas, which may be found under land or the seabed. Offshore rigs either stand on the seabed or on long legs, or float at the surface anchored in position.

FLOATING RIG

LAND RIG

SEABED

SHAFT

ROCK

MUD FLOW

DRILL PIPE

CONES

ROTARY BIT

The bit that drills the shaft is mounted on the end of a long drill pipe, which is rotated by an engine in the rig above. A tricone rotary bit has three cones studded with teeth that turn as the drill pipe rotates. The weight of the pipe on the bit helps it to crush and grind the rock.

MUD PUMP

MUD TANK

DRILLING MUD

The mud used on oil rigs is a special liquid developed for drilling. It is pumped into the top of the drill pipe, and from there it flows down to the drilling bit and then up the outside of the pipe back to the rig, bringing up the ground rock, before it is filtered and recycled.

SHAFT

DRILL PIPE

DRILLING BIT

FREEDOM FROM FRICTION

Machines that move themselves or that create movement are limited by friction. In the moving parts of an engine, for example, friction lowers performance and may produce overheating. Reducing friction reduces energy needs and so improves efficiency. This reduction is achieved by minimizing the frictional contact through bearings, streamlining and lubrication.

BALL BEARING

The balls in a ball bearing roll, allowing the inner race and outer race to move freely over each other, rather than scraping. Roller bearings contain cylindrical rollers instead of balls but work in the same way.

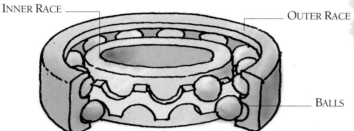

INNER RACE

OUTER RACE

BALLS

CAR LUBRICATION

A car has several sections with moving parts and good lubrication is essential. In the suspension, steering, gearbox and differential, filling with oil or grease is sufficient. The engine, however, needs a special lubrication system to get oil to its components as they work.

Oil is contained in the sump, which is a chamber at the base of the engine. A pump (see p. 124) forces oil up from the sump through the oil filter, which removes dirt particles, and then to all the bearings and other moving parts of the engine, such as the pistons. The parts contain narrow channels that lead the oil to the moving surfaces. The oil then returns to the sump to be recirculated.

OIL PUMP

OIL FILTER

SUMP

PERPETUAL MOTION

Even with the very best bearings, lubricants and streamlining, a little friction still remains. Without a continual supply of fuel or electricity, friction gradually consumes a machine's kinetic energy (its energy of movement) and the machine slows down and stops. The mythical perpetual motion machine—one that, once started, will work forever with no energy input—must remain a myth . . . at least, on Earth.

In space, matters are different. No air exists to cause friction and slow a spacecraft. Once launched into space, a spacecraft is freed from friction. It can continue to move in perpetuity without ever firing its engine again. Thus, in the space probes voyaging outward toward the stars, we have achieved perpetual motion, a pure movement governed only by the celestial mechanics of gravity.

VOLUNTEER
MOLECULES
ENTER·THE·FIRST
WHOOPEE·CUSHION

HARNESSING THE ELEMENTS

INTRODUCTION

IT WAS THE ANCIENT GREEKS who first had the idea that everything is made up of **elements**. They conjured up just four of them—earth, fire, air, and water. As it turned out, the idea was right but the elements wrong. Modern chemical elements are less evocative but more numerous; they make up *more than one hundred basic substances*. Some are commonplace, like oxygen, iron, and carbon; others are rare and precious, such as mercury, uranium, and gold. The Ancient Greeks were also among the first to suggest that all things consist of particles called **atoms**. Elements are substances that contain only one kind of atom. All other substances are compounds of two or more elements in which the atoms group themselves together to form **molecules**.

MORE ABOUT MOLECULES

As you read this, molecules of **oxygen** and **nitrogen** traveling at *supersonic speed* are bombarding you from all directions. You are unaware of this because the molecules (which, along with those of other gases, make up the air) are on the small side. You could get about **400 million million million** of them into an empty matchbox. In fact, it would be truer to say that you could get all those millions of molecules *out* of the matchbox, because the molecules of gases will fill any space open to them. Like five-year-olds, they *dash about in all directions*, crashing into any obstacle they meet. In liquids, the molecules are less energetic, rather like drunken dancers prone to colliding with the walls of the dance hall. The molecules in solids are the least energetic; they huddle together like a flock of sheep shuffling around in a field. In a solid, the molecular bonds are strong, holding the molecules firmly together so that the solid is hard and rigid. The **bonds** between liquid molecules pull them together to give the liquid a set volume, but the bonds are sufficiently weak to allow the liquid to flow. The bonds between gas molecules are weaker still, and they enable the molecules to move apart so the gas expands and fills any space.

STRENGTH IN NUMBERS

Because molecules in liquids and in gases are always on the move, they have **power**. Each one of them may not have much, but together they become a force to be reckoned with. A liner floats because billions of moving water molecules support the hull. Molecules continually bombard any surface they encounter. Each collision produces a little force as the molecule hits the surface and bounces back. Over the whole surface, a large force builds up—*this is known as the pressure of the liquid or gas*. If you squeeze more molecules into the same space, you get **more pressure** as more molecules strike the surface. The pressure produced by this restless movement of molecules is put to work in many ways. Some machines work by producing pressure while others are powered by it.

SPEEDING THINGS UP

If you heat a gas, you are *adding energy to the molecules*, which have no option but to speed up. That is why the pressure of a gas *increases with temperature*—and increasing pressure will make a gas **expand** if at all possible. The expansion of a heated gas is put to use in many machines, from the internal combustion engine in a car to a rocket hurtling toward space. Heating solids and liquids also adds energy to their molecules, *increasing the speed of their vibration and raising their temperature*. Above a certain point, the vibration of molecules is enough to **set them free**: the solid can become a liquid, a liquid can become a gas. The reverse happens if enough heat is lost.

BREAKING THE BONDS

The atoms of elements are made up of even smaller particles— **electrons**, which form the outer shells of each atom, and *protons and neutrons*, which make up its core, or **nucleus**. We tap the energy of electrons—in the form of electrical heat—in everyday devices from hairdryers to heaters. However, breaking the **bonds** that hold together the nucleus of an atom is a more serious business altogether. As we shall see in the last section of "Harnessing the Elements," these bonds are the strongest of all forces. *Breaking them unleashes the most powerful and potentially dangerous source of energy known.*

FLOATING

ON TRANSPORTING A MAMMOTH

*O*nce, *when waiting to board a ferry, I observed further downstream a rival operator attempting to shunt a particularly large mammoth onto a sizeable raft. No sooner had the craft and its protesting cargo been launched than both quickly sank.*

Taken aback by this turn of events, I relinquished my position in line to inquire whether I might not be of assistance. My offer was quickly accepted by the soggy pair. After interviewing those involved and making some hasty calculations, I deduced that the spirit of the water, clearly afraid of the raft's imposing cargo, had simply moved out of the way as the raft was loaded. This left nothing below the raft, and so it sank.

Clearly, a little subterfuge was necessary to keep the cargo afloat. I therefore suggested that the mammoth should be hidden from the spirit of the water by a special device of my own invention.

RAFTS AND BOATS

Although characteristically wayward, the inventor's explanation of the mammoth's adventures contains an element of truth. Water does move out of the way of an immersed object. But rather than leaving nothing below it, the water around an object pushes back and tries to support it. If the water succeeds, the object floats.

Take the case of the raft before the mammoth is on board. Its weight pulls it down into the water. But the water pushes back, supporting the raft with a force called upthrust. The amount of upthrust depends on how much water the raft displaces, or pushes aside, as it enters the water. Upthrust increases as more and more of the raft settles in the water. At some point, the upthrust becomes equal to the weight of the raft and the raft floats.

Now let's load the mammoth. The extra weight makes the raft settle deeper. Although the upthrust increases, it cannot become great enough to equal the weight of the raft and the mammoth because not enough water gets displaced. The raft and its load sink to the bottom.

The boat is a different matter. Because it is hollow, it can settle deeper in the water and displace enough water to provide the necessary upthrust to support the weight of the boat and the mammoth.

Things can also float in a gas and, like the inflated mammoth, a balloon floats in air for the same reason that a boat floats on water. In this case, the upthrust is equal to the weight of air that is displaced. If the weight of the balloon, the air that it contains and the occupants is less than the upthrust, the balloon will rise. If it is greater, the balloon will sink.

THE EFFECT OF DENSITY

Why should a heavy wooden raft float while a pin sinks? And if a steel pin sinks, why does a steel boat float? The answer is density. This factor, rather than weight, determines whether things float or sink.

The density of an object is equal to its mass divided by its volume. Every substance, including water, has its own particular density at a given temperature (density varies as a substance gets hotter or colder). Any solid less dense than water floats, while one that is more dense sinks. However, a hollow object such as a boat floats if its *overall* density—its total mass divided by its total volume—is less than the density of water.

My plans were put into effect. A wooden wall was built around the top of the raft and to everyone's amazement, except of course my own, both raft and cargo floated safely across.

In deference to the beast's obvious displeasure at even the risk of a second dunking, I had suggested that it be clothed in a rubber diving suit. I confess that I am still unable to fully explain what happened shortly after landing. The mammoth was tied up near the dock, wearing the suit and getting some sun. The suit began to expand and to my astonishment the enormous beast rose into the air. Quite why this happened is completely baffling. Perhaps it had something to do with the spirit of the air? We still have so much to learn.

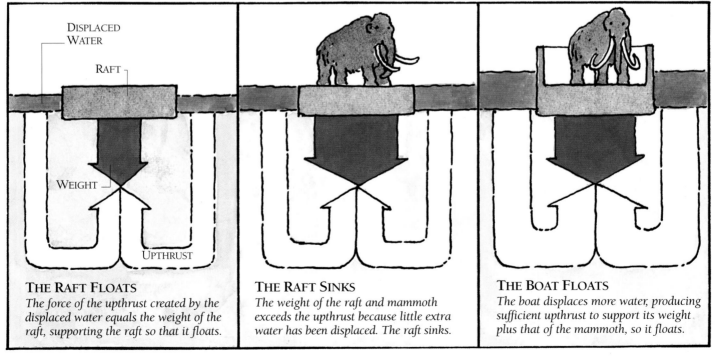

DISPLACED WATER

RAFT

WEIGHT

UPTHRUST

THE RAFT FLOATS
The force of the upthrust created by the displaced water equals the weight of the raft, supporting the raft so that it floats.

THE RAFT SINKS
The weight of the raft and mammoth exceeds the upthrust because little extra water has been displaced. The raft sinks.

THE BOAT FLOATS
The boat displaces more water, producing sufficient upthrust to support its weight plus that of the mammoth, so it floats.

THE SUBMERSIBLE

Submersibles are designed for use at great depths. They need to be able to sink, to rise, and also to float underwater. They do this by altering their weight with a system of ballast tanks that can hold either air or water. If a craft's ballast tanks are flooded with water, the craft's weight increases. If the water is then expelled by compressed air, the weight decreases. By adjusting the amount of water in the tanks, the craft's weight and buoyancy can be precisely regulated.

Submersibles are designed to perform delicate tasks deep underwater, and are therefore designed to withstand high pressure and to be highly maneuverable. They do not need to move at speed and therefore, unlike submarines, they are not streamlined.

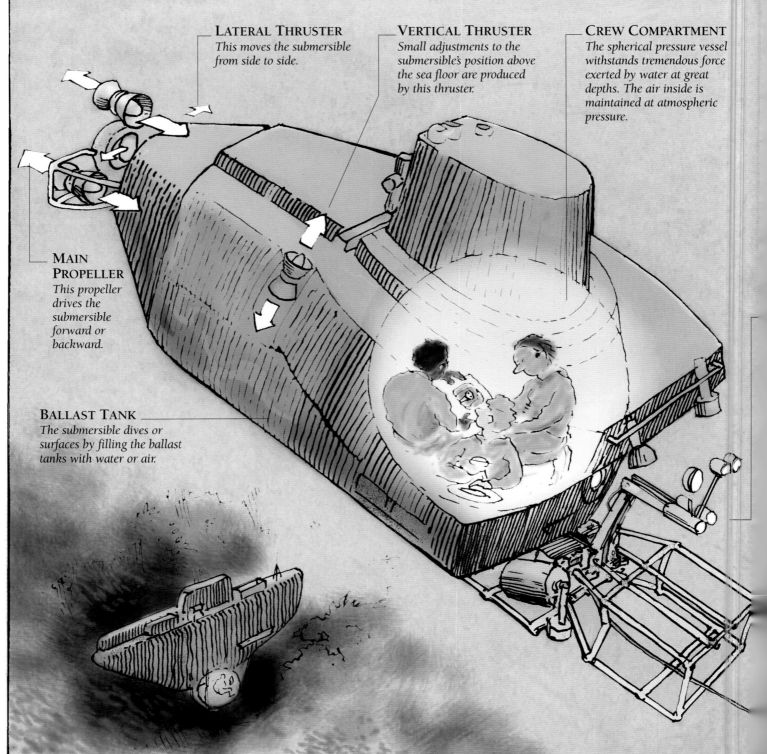

LATERAL THRUSTER
This moves the submersible from side to side.

VERTICAL THRUSTER
Small adjustments to the submersible's position above the sea floor are produced by this thruster.

CREW COMPARTMENT
The spherical pressure vessel withstands tremendous force exerted by water at great depths. The air inside is maintained at atmospheric pressure.

MAIN PROPELLER
This propeller drives the submersible forward or backward.

BALLAST TANK
The submersible dives or surfaces by filling the ballast tanks with water or air.

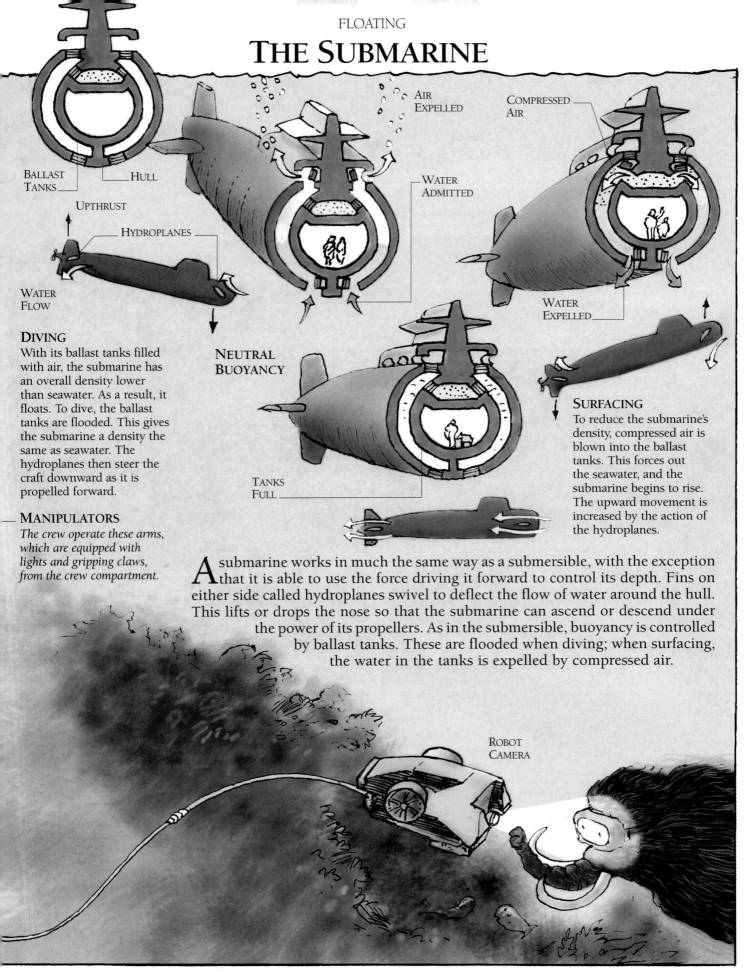

THE SUBMARINE

BALLAST TANKS

HULL

UPTHRUST

HYDROPLANES

WATER FLOW

AIR EXPELLED

WATER ADMITTED

COMPRESSED AIR

WATER EXPELLED

NEUTRAL BUOYANCY

TANKS FULL

DIVING

With its ballast tanks filled with air, the submarine has an overall density lower than seawater. As a result, it floats. To dive, the ballast tanks are flooded. This gives the submarine a density the same as seawater. The hydroplanes then steer the craft downward as it is propelled forward.

MANIPULATORS

The crew operate these arms, which are equipped with lights and gripping claws, from the crew compartment.

SURFACING

To reduce the submarine's density, compressed air is blown into the ballast tanks. This forces out the seawater, and the submarine begins to rise. The upward movement is increased by the action of the hydroplanes.

A submarine works in much the same way as a submersible, with the exception that it is able to use the force driving it forward to control its depth. Fins on either side called hydroplanes swivel to deflect the flow of water around the hull. This lifts or drops the nose so that the submarine can ascend or descend under the power of its propellers. As in the submersible, buoyancy is controlled by ballast tanks. These are flooded when diving; when surfacing, the water in the tanks is expelled by compressed air.

ROBOT CAMERA

PASSENGER BOAT

All powered craft that travel in or on water move by imparting movement to the water or air around them, and they steer by altering the direction in which the water or air flows. In a large ship, power is provided by the propellers, and the direction is governed by a rudder. But large ships also need to be able to control their movement sideways when docking, and their roll during heavy seas. They do this with bow thrusters and stabilizers, two devices that act in the same way as the main propellers and the rudder.

Below the water's surface, the hull is as smooth as possible to reduce the ship's water resistance and increase efficiency. The bow thrusters are recessed, and therefore do not disturb the water flow. The stabilizers are retractable, folding away inside hatches when not in use. At the bow, the hull may project forward beneath the water in a huge bulb. This bulb reduces the bow wave that the ship makes as it slices through the water. The water resistance of the ship is lessened, and this raises the speed or saves fuel.

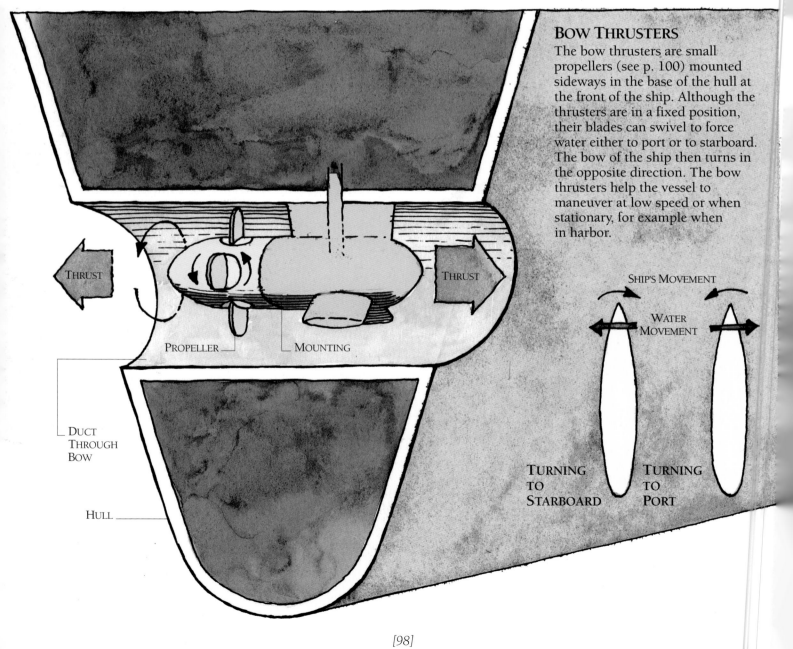

BOW THRUSTERS

The bow thrusters are small propellers (see p. 100) mounted sideways in the base of the hull at the front of the ship. Although the thrusters are in a fixed position, their blades can swivel to force water either to port or to starboard. The bow of the ship then turns in the opposite direction. The bow thrusters help the vessel to maneuver at low speed or when stationary, for example when in harbor.

THRUST

THRUST

PROPELLER

MOUNTING

DUCT THROUGH BOW

HULL

SHIP'S MOVEMENT

WATER MOVEMENT

TURNING TO STARBOARD

TURNING TO PORT

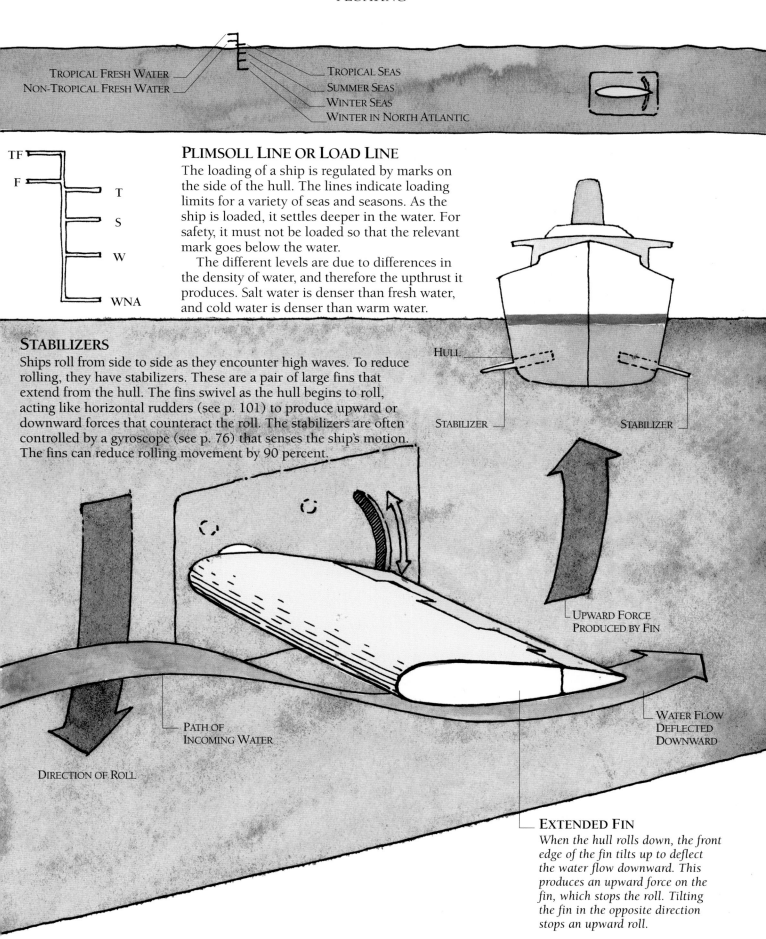

TROPICAL FRESH WATER
NON-TROPICAL FRESH WATER

TROPICAL SEAS
SUMMER SEAS
WINTER SEAS
WINTER IN NORTH ATLANTIC

TF
F
T
S
W
WNA

PLIMSOLL LINE OR LOAD LINE

The loading of a ship is regulated by marks on
the side of the hull. The lines indicate loading
limits for a variety of seas and seasons. As the
ship is loaded, it settles deeper in the water. For
safety, it must not be loaded so that the relevant
mark goes below the water.

   The different levels are due to differences in
the density of water, and therefore the upthrust it
produces. Salt water is denser than fresh water,
and cold water is denser than warm water.

HULL

STABILIZER   STABILIZER

STABILIZERS

Ships roll from side to side as they encounter high waves. To reduce
rolling, they have stabilizers. These are a pair of large fins that
extend from the hull. The fins swivel as the hull begins to roll,
acting like horizontal rudders (see p. 101) to produce upward or
downward forces that counteract the roll. The stabilizers are often
controlled by a gyroscope (see p. 76) that senses the ship's motion.
The fins can reduce rolling movement by 90 percent.

UPWARD FORCE
PRODUCED BY FIN

WATER FLOW
DEFLECTED
DOWNWARD

PATH OF
INCOMING WATER

DIRECTION OF ROLL

EXTENDED FIN

*When the hull rolls down, the front
edge of the fin tilts up to deflect
the water flow downward. This
produces an upward force on the
fin, which stops the roll. Tilting
the fin in the opposite direction
stops an upward roll.*

PASSENGER BOAT

Most craft that travel on water need a source of power to propel them forward and also a means of steering. These requirements are met by propellers and rudders, two devices that work by the same pair of principles.

The first principle is action and reaction. As the blades of a propeller spin, they strike the water and make it move toward the rear of the vessel. The force with which the blades move the water is called the action. The water pushes back on the blades as it begins to move, producing an equal force called the reaction, which drives the propeller forward.

The second principle is called suction. The surface of each propeller blade is curved so that the blade has the shape of an airfoil (see p. 107). Water flows around the blade as it rotates, moving faster over the front surface. The faster motion lowers the water pressure at the front surface, and the blade is sucked forward.

Overall, a combination of reaction and suction drives the spinning propeller through the water.

A rudder affects the water flowing around it in the same way. Reaction and suction produce a turning force that changes the boat's direction.

Propellers drive most surface vessels as well as submarines and submersibles. They also work in air, and power airships and many aircraft. Virtually all forms of water transport and most forms of air transport steer with rudders.

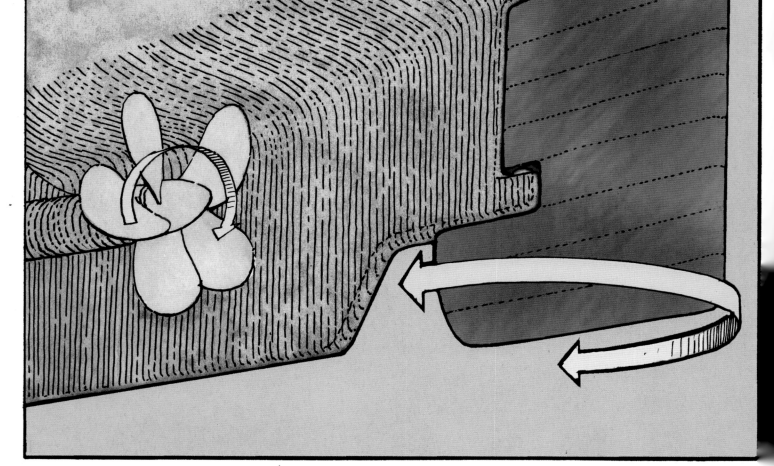

PROPELLER

The blades of a ship's propeller are broad and curved like scimitars to slash strongly through the water. A ship's propeller turns much more slowly than a plane's, but its bigger, broader blades can move lots of water backward, producing a powerful reaction, which pushes the ship forward. Although speedboats have tiny propellers, they spin much faster, so they can still throw enough water back to shoot the boat forward through the sea.

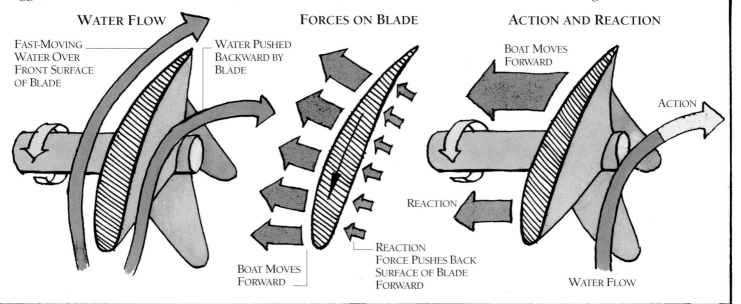

WATER FLOW

FAST-MOVING WATER OVER FRONT SURFACE OF BLADE

WATER PUSHED BACKWARD BY BLADE

FORCES ON BLADE

BOAT MOVES FORWARD

REACTION FORCE PUSHES BACK SURFACE OF BLADE FORWARD

ACTION AND REACTION

BOAT MOVES FORWARD

ACTION

REACTION

WATER FLOW

RUDDER

The rudder acts on the water flowing past the vessel and the backward flow generated by the propeller. The rudder blade swivels to deflect this flow. As the water changes direction, it pushes back with a reaction force and the blade moves in the opposite direction. Suction produced by water flowing around the blade assists reaction. These forces move the stern of the boat and the whole vessel turns around its center so that the bow points in a new direction.

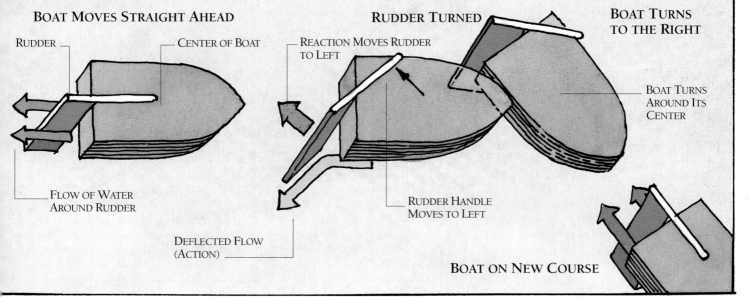

BOAT MOVES STRAIGHT AHEAD

RUDDER

CENTER OF BOAT

FLOW OF WATER AROUND RUDDER

DEFLECTED FLOW (ACTION)

RUDDER TURNED

REACTION MOVES RUDDER TO LEFT

RUDDER HANDLE MOVES TO LEFT

BOAT TURNS TO THE RIGHT

BOAT TURNS AROUND ITS CENTER

BOAT ON NEW COURSE

THE WINDSURFER

Modern sailing craft from the windsurfer to the racing yacht can use the power of the wind to propel them in any direction, no matter which quarter the wind may blow from.

This versatility is achieved with a triangular sail that can be shifted around the boat's mast to engage the wind at various angles. The sail is able to propel the boat at any angle to the wind, except head-on. However, sailing boats are able to make progress into the wind, although in an indirect way. They do this by "tacking," or following a zig-zagging course that keeps the sail at an angle to the wind, and so enables it to provide power.

The windsurfer is the simplest craft with a movable sail. It is basically a raft with a sail on a tilting mast and a small keel beneath. The person aboard the windsurfer grips a curved bar to move the sail in any direction to take advantage of the wind. The sail not only drives the windsurfer forward but also steers it.

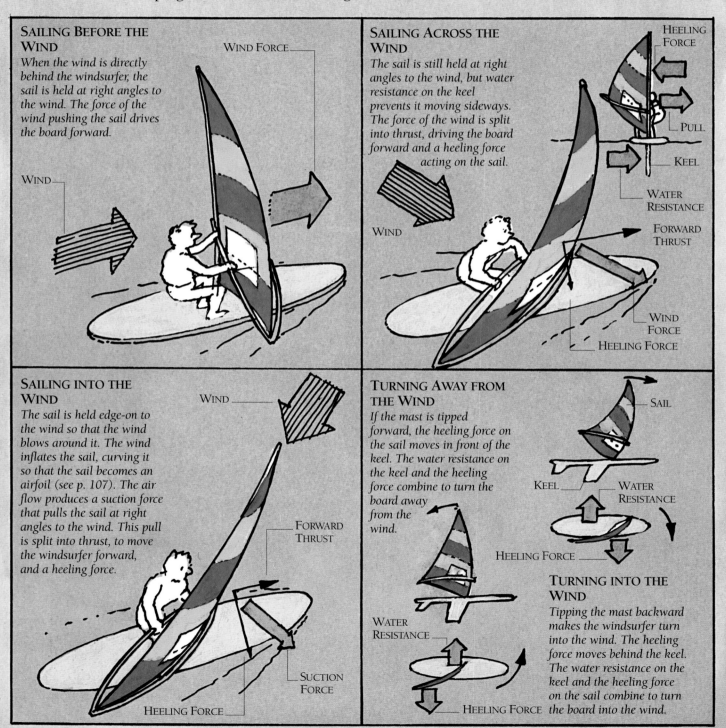

SAILING BEFORE THE WIND

When the wind is directly behind the windsurfer, the sail is held at right angles to the wind. The force of the wind pushing the sail drives the board forward.

WIND FORCE

WIND

SAILING ACROSS THE WIND

The sail is still held at right angles to the wind, but water resistance on the keel prevents it moving sideways. The force of the wind is split into thrust, driving the board forward and a heeling force acting on the sail.

HEELING FORCE

PULL

KEEL

WATER RESISTANCE

FORWARD THRUST

WIND

WIND FORCE

HEELING FORCE

SAILING INTO THE WIND

The sail is held edge-on to the wind so that the wind blows around it. The wind inflates the sail, curving it so that the sail becomes an airfoil (see p. 107). The air flow produces a suction force that pulls the sail at right angles to the wind. This pull is split into thrust, to move the windsurfer forward, and a heeling force.

WIND

FORWARD THRUST

SUCTION FORCE

HEELING FORCE

TURNING AWAY FROM THE WIND

If the mast is tipped forward, the heeling force on the sail moves in front of the keel. The water resistance on the keel and the heeling force combine to turn the board away from the wind.

SAIL

KEEL

WATER RESISTANCE

HEELING FORCE

WATER RESISTANCE

HEELING FORCE

TURNING INTO THE WIND

Tipping the mast backward makes the windsurfer turn into the wind. The heeling force moves behind the keel. The water resistance on the keel and the heeling force on the sail combine to turn the board into the wind.

THE YACHT

A yacht usually has two triangular sails—the mainsail and the jib. The sails propel the yacht before, across or into the wind in the same way as the windsurfer. When sailing into the wind, the two sails combine to act as one large airfoil with a slot in the center. The slot channels air over both sails, producing a powerful suction force. This force splits into two separate forces—thrust that propels the yacht forward and a heeling force that tilts it over. The weight of the tilting hull and keel counteracts the heeling force, while water resistance stops the yacht moving sideways.

A yacht is steered with a rudder (see p. 101), which deflects the flow of water that passes the hull to turn the yacht in the required direction. As the yacht turns, the crew let out or pull in the sails so that they take up the best angle to the wind. A balloon-like spinnaker sail may be used when the yacht is sailing before the wind.

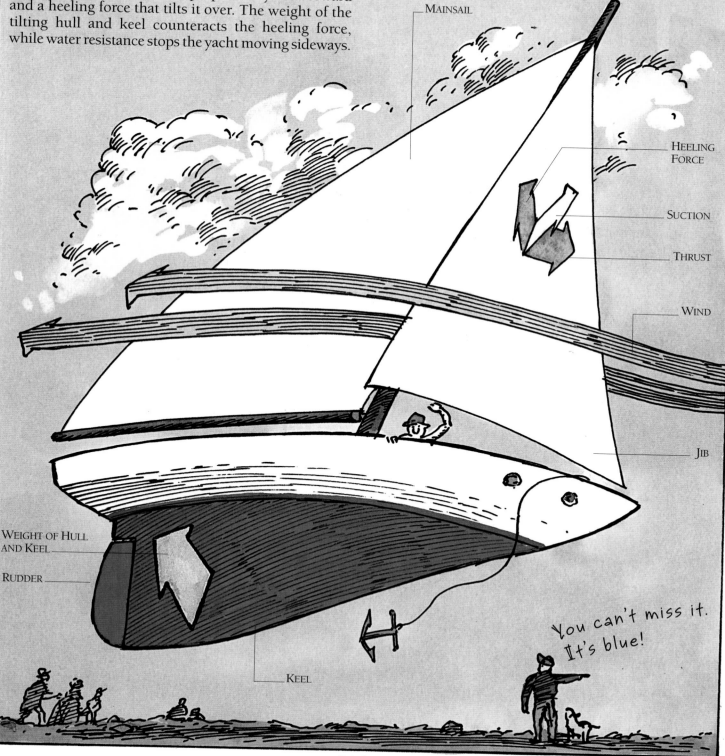

MAINSAIL

HEELING FORCE

SUCTION

THRUST

WIND

JIB

WEIGHT OF HULL AND KEEL

RUDDER

KEEL

You can't miss it. It's blue!

THE AIRSHIP

An airship has a vast envelope that creates a powerful upthrust to lift the substantial weight of the cabin, engine, fans, and passengers. The bulk of the envelope contains helium, a light gas that reduces the weight of the airship so that it is equal to the upthrust, thereby producing neutral buoyancy. Inside the envelope are compartments of air called ballonets. Pumping air out of or into the ballonets decreases or increases the airship's weight and it ascends or descends. The airship also has propellers called ducted fans that drive it through the air and which swivel to maneuver the airship at take-off or landing. Tail fins and a rudder can tilt or turn the whole craft as it floats through the sky. In this way, the airship travels from place to place like an airborne combination of submarine and submersible.

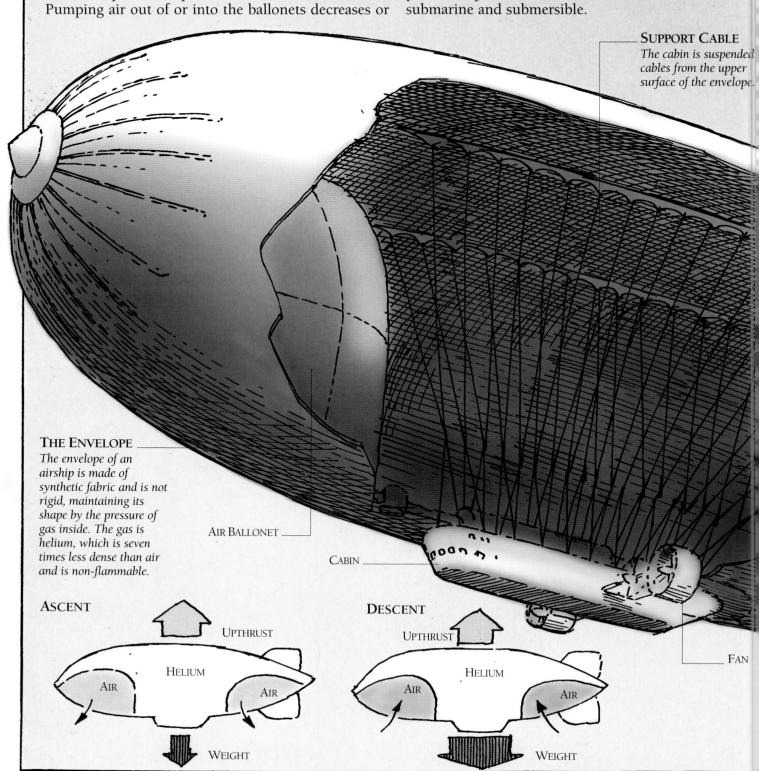

SUPPORT CABLE
The cabin is suspended cables from the upper surface of the envelope.

THE ENVELOPE
The envelope of an airship is made of synthetic fabric and is not rigid, maintaining its shape by the pressure of gas inside. The gas is helium, which is seven times less dense than air and is non-flammable.

AIR BALLONET

CABIN

FAN

ASCENT

UPTHRUST

HELIUM

AIR

AIR

WEIGHT

DESCENT

UPTHRUST

HELIUM

AIR

AIR

WEIGHT

THE HOT-AIR BALLO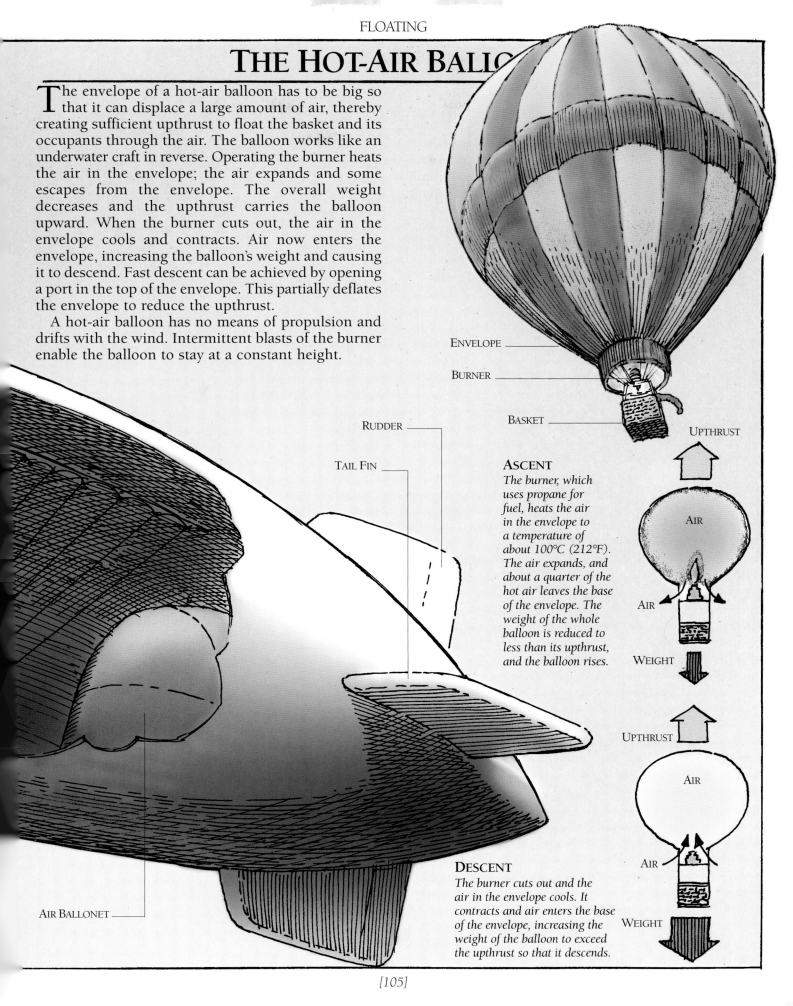

The envelope of a hot-air balloon has to be big so that it can displace a large amount of air, thereby creating sufficient upthrust to float the basket and its occupants through the air. The balloon works like an underwater craft in reverse. Operating the burner heats the air in the envelope; the air expands and some escapes from the envelope. The overall weight decreases and the upthrust carries the balloon upward. When the burner cuts out, the air in the envelope cools and contracts. Air now enters the envelope, increasing the balloon's weight and causing it to descend. Fast descent can be achieved by opening a port in the top of the envelope. This partially deflates the envelope to reduce the upthrust.

A hot-air balloon has no means of propulsion and drifts with the wind. Intermittent blasts of the burner enable the balloon to stay at a constant height.

ENVELOPE

BURNER

BASKET

RUDDER

TAIL FIN

AIR BALLONET

ASCENT
The burner, which uses propane for fuel, heats the air in the envelope to a temperature of about 100°C (212°F). The air expands, and about a quarter of the hot air leaves the base of the envelope. The weight of the whole balloon is reduced to less than its upthrust, and the balloon rises.

UPTHRUST

AIR

AIR

WEIGHT

UPTHRUST

AIR

AIR

WEIGHT

DESCENT
The burner cuts out and the air in the envelope cools. It contracts and air enters the base of the envelope, increasing the weight of the balloon to exceed the upthrust so that it descends.

[105]

FLYING

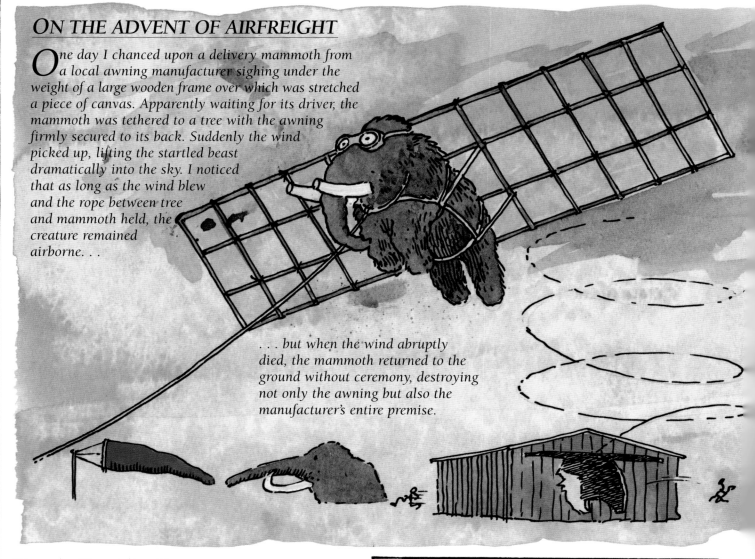

ON THE ADVENT OF AIRFREIGHT

*O*ne day I chanced upon a delivery mammoth from a local awning manufacturer sighing under the weight of a large wooden frame over which was stretched a piece of canvas. Apparently waiting for its driver, the mammoth was tethered to a tree with the awning firmly secured to its back. Suddenly the wind picked up, lifting the startled beast dramatically into the sky. I noticed that as long as the wind blew and the rope between tree and mammoth held, the creature remained airborne. . .

. . . but when the wind abruptly died, the mammoth returned to the ground without ceremony, destroying not only the awning but also the manufacturer's entire premise.

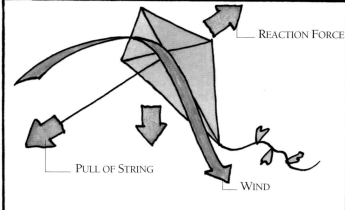

HEAVIER-THAN-AIR FLIGHT

In the struggle to overcome its not inconsiderable weight and launch itself into the air, the mammoth becomes in turn a kite, a glider, and finally a powered aircraft. These are three quite different ways by which an object that is heavier than air can be made to fly.

Like balloons and airships, heavier-than-air machines achieve flight by generating a force that overcomes their weight and which supports them in the air. But because they cannot float in air, they work in different ways to balloons and airships.

Kites employ the power of the wind to keep them aloft, while all winged aircraft, including gliders and helicopters, make use of the airfoil and its power of lift. Airplanes need to be pushed through the air in order to stay aloft—a propeller or a jet engine provides the necessary thrust.

The two principles that govern heavier-than-air flight are the same as those that propel powered vessels—action and reaction, and suction (see pp. 100-101). When applied to flight, suction is known as lift.

REACTION FORCE

PULL OF STRING

WIND

KITE

The kite flies only in a wind, and it is held by its string so that it deflects the wind downward. The wind provides the force for flight. It exerts a reaction that equals the pull of the string and the weight of the kite to support the kite in the air.

*D*uring my own experiments with awning delivery, I discovered that by securing a slightly curved awning to a volunteer mammoth's back, the danger and considerable expense of crash landings could be greatly reduced. Should the wind speed drop or the rope break, the mammoth would usually glide back to Earth in a gentle spiral. I planned one further improvement in which friction-reducing foot-gear would enable the mammoth to leave the ground simply by blowing backward with its trunk.

*H*owever, despite repeated attempts, the mammoth never got far enough off the ground to make this novel form of delivery a practical procedure. Even with the specially designed foot-gear in place, landings remained somewhat unpredictable.

I recall one most unfortunate incident in which a mammoth had to be completely bandaged after an unusually clumsy four-point landing. This resulted in the rather interesting streamlined form depicted here. It is not one that I feel could ever leave the ground.

AIRFOIL

The cross-section of a wing has a shape called an airfoil. As the wing moves through the air, the air divides to pass around the wing. The airfoil is curved so that air passing above the wing moves faster than air passing beneath. Fast-moving air has a lower pressure than slow-moving air. The pressure of the air is therefore greater beneath the wing than above it. This difference in air pressure forces the wing upward. The force is called lift.

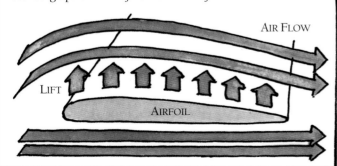

AIR FLOW

LIFT

AIRFOIL

GLIDER

A glider is the simplest kind of winged aircraft. It is first pulled along the ground until it is moving fast enough for the lift generated by the wings to exceed its weight. The glider then rises into the air and flies. After release, the glider continues to move forward as it drops slowly, pulled by a thrust force due to gravity. Friction with the air produces a force called drag that acts to hold the glider back. These two pairs of opposing forces—lift and weight, thrust and drag—act on all aircraft.

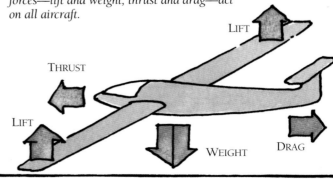

LIFT

THRUST

LIFT

WEIGHT

DRAG

THE AIRPLANE

Adding an engine to a flying machine gives it the power to dispense with winds and air currents that govern the flight of unpowered craft such as balloons and gliders. In order to steer an airplane, a system of flaps is used. These act just like the rudder of a boat (see p. 101). They deflect the air flow and turn or tilt the airplane so that it rotates around its center of gravity, which in all airplanes lies between the wings.

Airplanes usually have one pair of wings to provide lift, and the wings and tail have flaps that turn or tilt the aircraft in flight. Power is provided by a propeller (see p. 100) mounted on the nose, or by several propellers on the wings, or by jet engines (see p. 162) mounted on the wings or tail, or inside the fuselage.

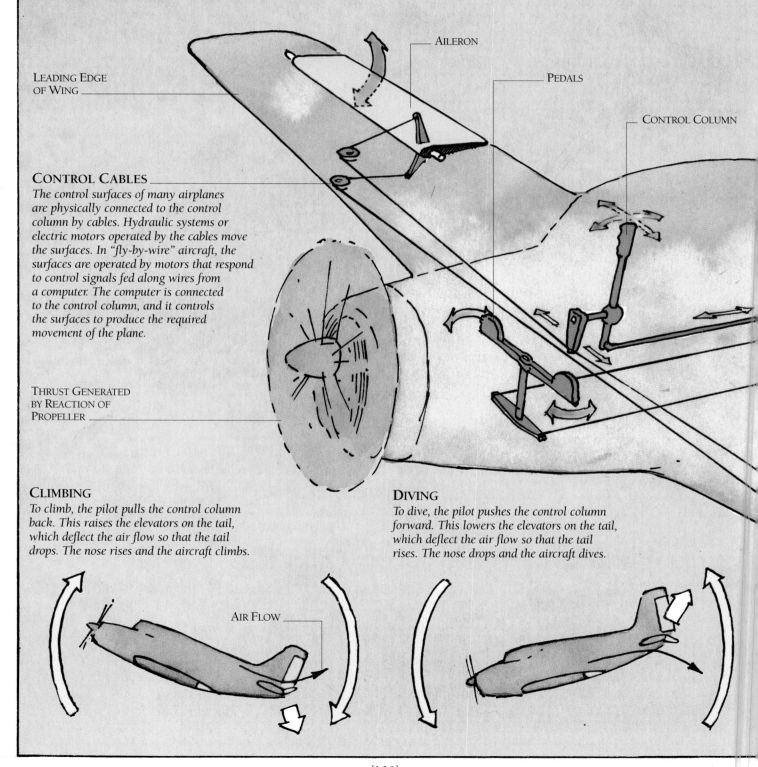

AILERON

LEADING EDGE
OF WING

PEDALS

CONTROL COLUMN

CONTROL CABLES

The control surfaces of many airplanes are physically connected to the control column by cables. Hydraulic systems or electric motors operated by the cables move the surfaces. In "fly-by-wire" aircraft, the surfaces are operated by motors that respond to control signals fed along wires from a computer. The computer is connected to the control column, and it controls the surfaces to produce the required movement of the plane.

THRUST GENERATED
BY REACTION OF
PROPELLER

CLIMBING

To climb, the pilot pulls the control column back. This raises the elevators on the tail, which deflect the air flow so that the tail drops. The nose rises and the aircraft climbs.

DIVING

To dive, the pilot pushes the control column forward. This lowers the elevators on the tail, which deflect the air flow so that the tail rises. The nose drops and the aircraft dives.

AIR FLOW

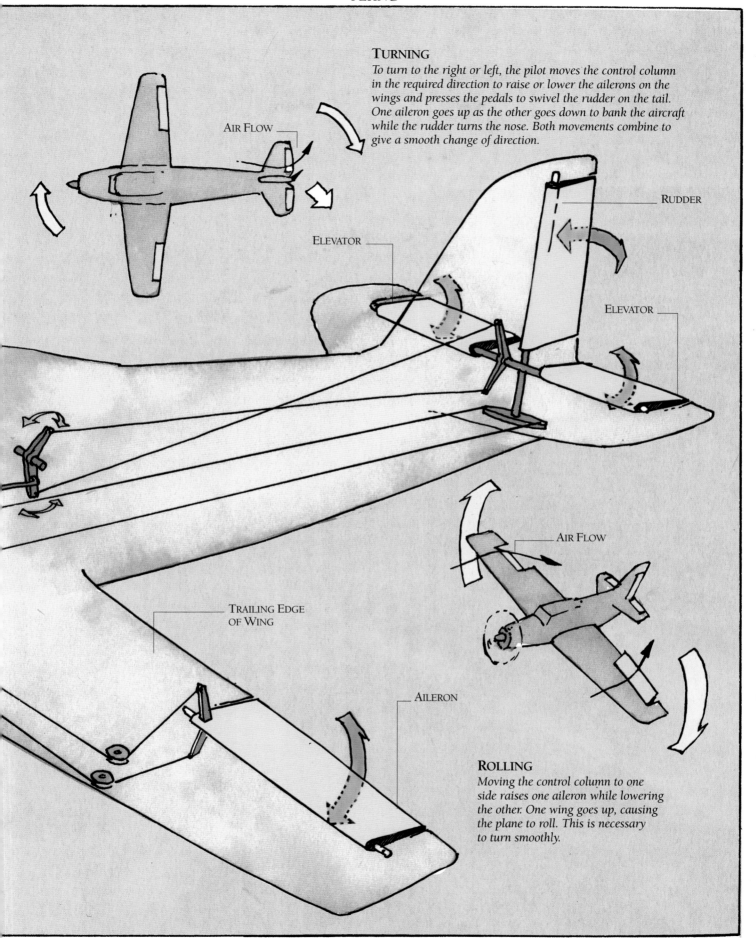

AIR FLOW

TURNING

To turn to the right or left, the pilot moves the control column in the required direction to raise or lower the ailerons on the wings and presses the pedals to swivel the rudder on the tail. One aileron goes up as the other goes down to bank the aircraft while the rudder turns the nose. Both movements combine to give a smooth change of direction.

RUDDER

ELEVATOR

ELEVATOR

AIR FLOW

TRAILING EDGE OF WING

AILERON

ROLLING

Moving the control column to one side raises one aileron while lowering the other. One wing goes up, causing the plane to roll. This is necessary to turn smoothly.

FLYING MACHINES

Many different flying machines now fill our skies. They range from solo sports and airbatic planes to wide-bodied and supersonic jet airliners that carry hundreds of passengers. Some, such as pedal-powered planes, lumber along just above the ground, while others, such as reconnaissance aircraft, streak at three times the speed of sound at a height three times that of Mount Everest.

There are also unpowered gliders, which are carried aloft by a powered airplane and then released, their slow descent occasionally buoyed up by rising warm air currents. Development in other directions has led to helicopters and vertical take-off aircraft, which are capable of rising vertically and hovering in the air. There are also kites of all shapes and sizes, some large enough to carry a person.

Machines also fly through water. Hydrofoils flying through the waves employ exactly the same principles that keep winged airplanes aloft.

GLIDER
Being unpowered, a glider cannot travel fast and so has long, straight wings that produce high lift at very low speed.

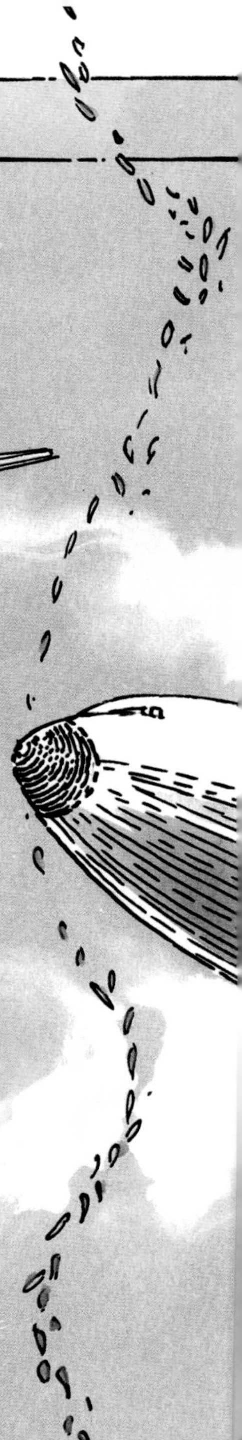

LIGHT AIRCRAFT
Short, straight wings produce good lift and low drag at medium speed. Propellers or jet engines provide the power that produces the lift.

HANG GLIDER
The A-shaped wing inflates in flight to produce an airfoil with low lift and drag, giving low-speed flight with a light load.

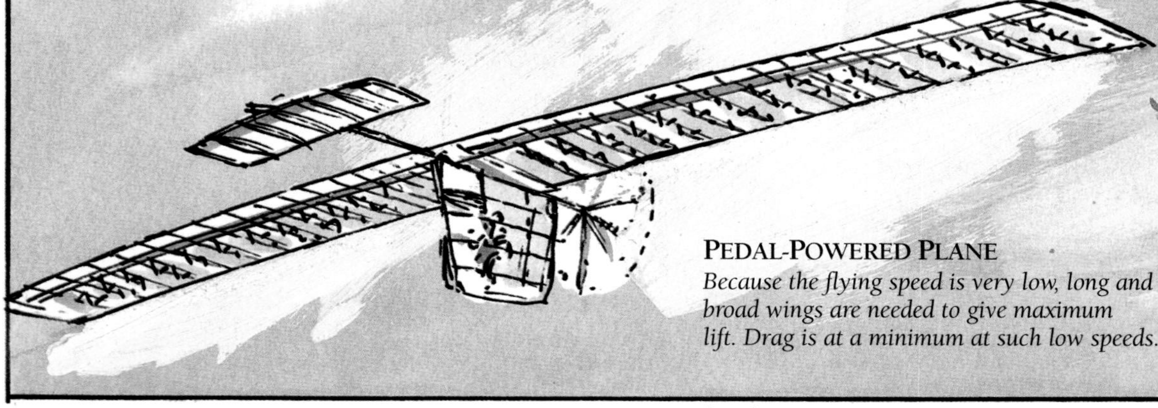

PEDAL-POWERED PLANE
Because the flying speed is very low, long and broad wings are needed to give maximum lift. Drag is at a minimum at such low speeds.

FORWARD-SWEPT WINGS
This experimental design gives high lift and low drag to produce good maneuverability at high speed. Two small forward wings, called canards, aid control.

SWING-WING AIRCRAFT
The wings are straight at take-off and landing to increase lift so that take-off and landing speeds are low. In flight, the wings swing back to reduce drag and enable high-speed flight.

SUPERSONIC AIRLINER
Aircraft that fly faster than the speed of sound often have dart-shaped delta wings. This is because a shock wave forms in the air around the aircraft, and the wings stay inside the shock wave so that control of the aircraft is retained at supersonic speed. Take-off and landing speeds are very high as lift is low.

AIRLINER
Swept-back wings are needed to minimize drag at high speed. However, lift is also reduced, requiring high take-off and landing speeds.

FLAPPING WINGS
This is a highly efficient wing design that you should look out for, particularly in places where bird feeding is encouraged.

What's the big deal?

AIRLINER WING

On a small airplane, the wings need little more than simple hinged ailerons to control flight. An airliner wing, however, experiences enormous and varying forces both in the air and on the ground. To cope with these, it uses an array of complex flaps that change the wing's shape.

During take-off and landing, the wing shape needs to be very different to that needed for cruising. By adjusting the area of the flaps presented to the air, and their angle to it, a pilot is able to vary the amount of lift and drag generated by the wing to suit different phases of the flight.

There are four basic kinds of flaps. Leading-edge flaps line the front edge of the wing, while trailing-edge flaps take up part of the rear edge. These flaps extend to increase the area of the wing, producing more lift and also drag. Spoilers are flaps on top of the wing that rise to reduce lift and increase drag. Ailerons are flaps at the rear edge that are raised or lowered to roll the aircraft in a turn.

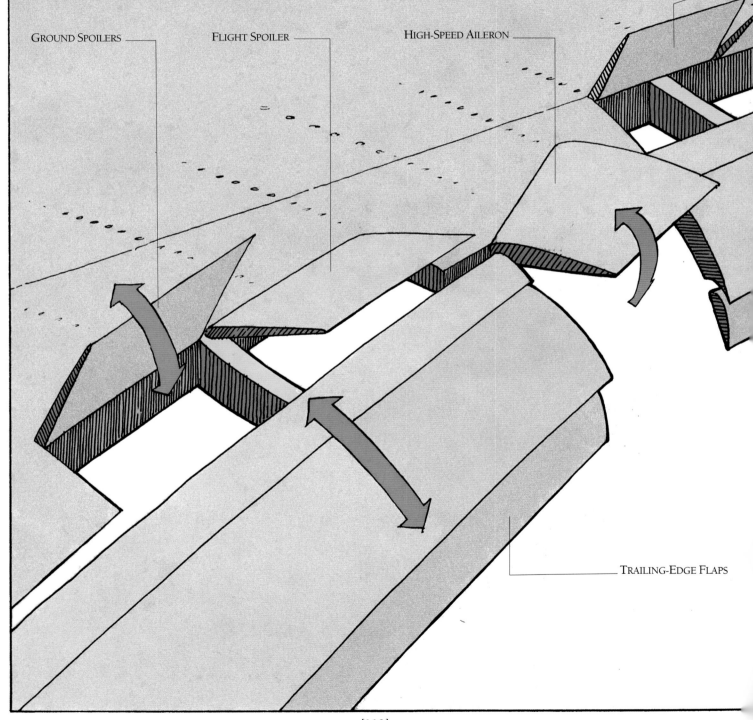

GROUND SPOILERS

FLIGHT SPOILER

HIGH-SPEED AILERON

TRAILING-EDGE FLAPS

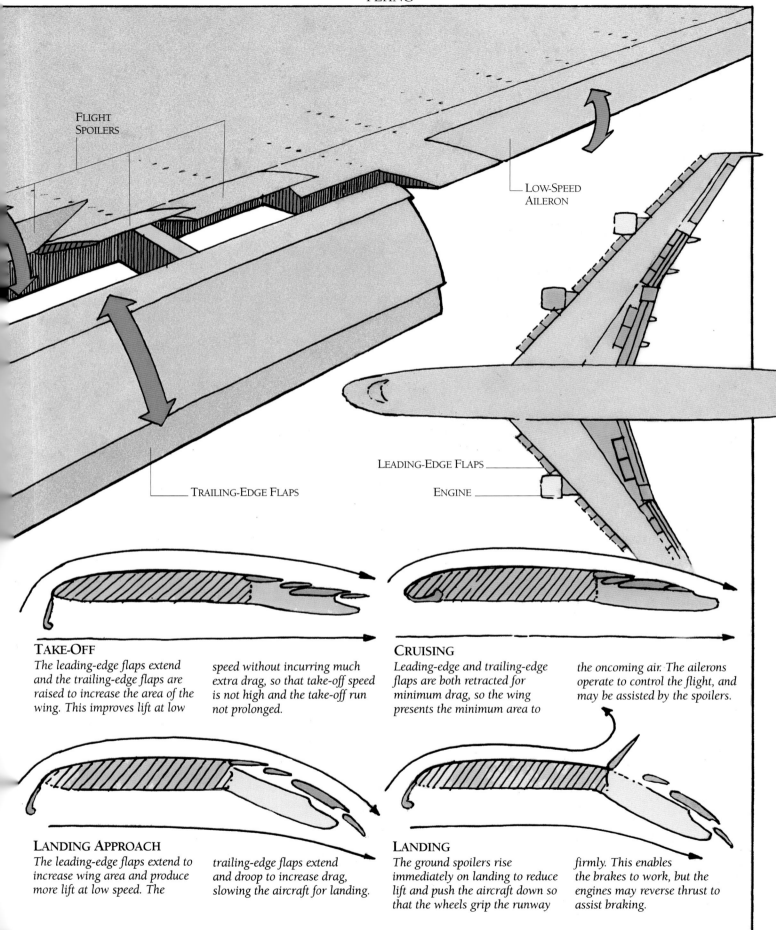

FLIGHT
SPOILERS

LOW-SPEED
AILERON

TRAILING-EDGE FLAPS

LEADING-EDGE FLAPS

ENGINE

TAKE-OFF

The leading-edge flaps extend and the trailing-edge flaps are raised to increase the area of the wing. This improves lift at low speed without incurring much extra drag, so that take-off speed is not high and the take-off run not prolonged.

CRUISING

Leading-edge and trailing-edge flaps are both retracted for minimum drag, so the wing presents the minimum area to the oncoming air. The ailerons operate to control the flight, and may be assisted by the spoilers.

LANDING APPROACH

The leading-edge flaps extend to increase wing area and produce more lift at low speed. The trailing-edge flaps extend and droop to increase drag, slowing the aircraft for landing.

LANDING

The ground spoilers rise immediately on landing to reduce lift and push the aircraft down so that the wheels grip the runway firmly. This enables the brakes to work, but the engines may reverse thrust to assist braking.

THE HELICOPTER

ROTOR BLADES
Most helicopter rotors have from three to six blades. Each is connected to a flapping hinge and a pitch control rod.

With its whirling rotors, a helicopter looks very different from an airplane. Yet, like an airplane, it too uses airfoils for flight (see p. 107). The blades of the helicopter's main rotor have an airfoil shape like the wings of a plane. But whereas a plane has to rush through the air for the wings to develop sufficient lift for flight, the helicopter moves only the rotor blades. As they circle, the blades produce lift to support the helicopter in the air and also to move it in the required direction. The angle at which the blades are set determines how the helicopter flies—hovering, vertical, forward, backward, or sideways.

FLAPPING HINGES
Each rotor blade has a flapping hinge that allows it to flap up and down as it rotates. If the blades did not flap, they would develop uneven lift caused by the helicopter's motion through the air and roll the helicopter over.

ROTOR SHAFT
The rotor shaft drives the rotor blades and the upper swashplate.

PITCH CONTROL RODS
These rods are moved up or down by the upper swashplate as it rotates. They raise or lower the front edge of the rotor blades to change the pitch of the blades.

ROTATING SCISSORS
This link turns the upper swashplate.

UPPER SWASHPLATE
The upper swashplate rotates on bearings above the lower swashplate. It is raised, lowered or tilted by the lower swashplate.

LOWER SWASHPLATE
The lower swashplate does not rotate. It is raised, lowered or tilted by links with the control columns.

HOW THE ROTOR WORKS
As the blades of the main rotor spin around, their angle or pitch can be varied to produce different amounts of lift for different modes of flight. The pitch is controlled by the swashplate, which is connected to two control columns. The swashplate moves up or down or it tilts in response to movements of the columns. It then moves control rods that alter the pitch of the blades.

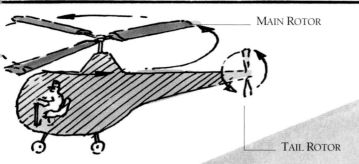

MAIN ROTOR

TAIL ROTOR

VERTICAL FLIGHT

To ascend, the collective pitch control column raises the swashplate and increases the pitch of all the blades by an equal amount. The rotor lift increases to exceed the helicopter's weight so that the

helicopter rises. To descend, the swashplate is lowered. The pitch of all the blades decreases and reduces rotor lift so that the helicopter's weight now exceeds lift and causes it to descend.

HOVERING FLIGHT

The cyclic pitch control column holds the swashplate level, so that each rotor blade has the same pitch and the helicopter does not move forward or backward. The collective pitch

control column raises the swashplate so that the pitch of the blades is sufficiently steep for the rotor to produce just enough lift to equal the weight of the helicopter.

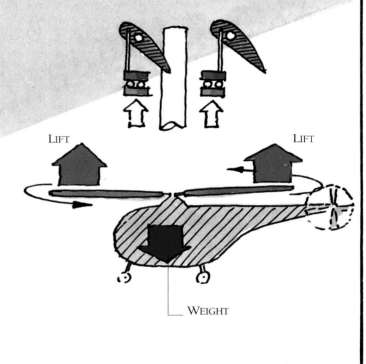

LIFT

LIFT

WEIGHT

ROTOR BLADE

ROTOR BLADE

SWASHPLATE

ROTOR SHAFT

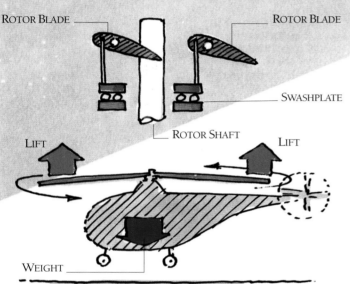

LIFT

LIFT

WEIGHT

FORWARD FLIGHT

The cyclic pitch control column tilts the swashplate forward. The pitch of each blade increases as it moves behind the rotor shaft then decreases as it moves in front. Lift increases over the back of the rotor, tilting the whole rotor forward. The total rotor lift splits into a raising force that supports the helicopter's weight, and thrust that moves it forward.

TOTAL ROTOR LIFT   RAISING FORCE

THRUST

LIFT

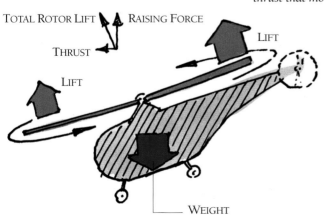

LIFT

LIFT

WEIGHT

LIFT

RAISING FORCE   TOTAL ROTOR LIFT

THRUST

BACKWARD FLIGHT

The cyclic pitch control column tilts the swashplate backward. The pitch of each blade increases as it moves in front of the rotor shaft then decreases as it moves behind. Lift increases over the front of the rotor, producing a backward thrust.

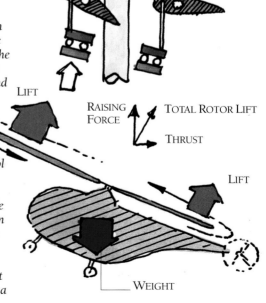

LIFT

WEIGHT

SINGLE-ROTOR HELICOPTER

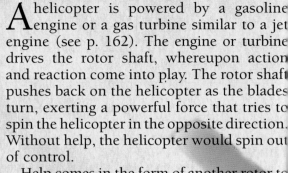

A helicopter is powered by a gasoline engine or a gas turbine similar to a jet engine (see p. 162). The engine or turbine drives the rotor shaft, whereupon action and reaction come into play. The rotor shaft pushes back on the helicopter as the blades turn, exerting a powerful force that tries to spin the helicopter in the opposite direction. Without help, the helicopter would spin out of control.

Help comes in the form of another rotor to counteract the reaction of the main rotor. A so-called single-rotor helicopter also has a tail rotor, which produces thrust like a propeller. The tail rotor not only stops the helicopter spinning, but it also steers the machine in flight. Although the pedals that a helicopter uses to steer are called rudder pedals, the machine does not in fact have a rudder: the pedals control the thrust of the tail rotor.

BACKWARD SPIN

If the blades of a helicopter were held still, the reaction of the rotor would make the helicopter spin around in the opposite direction to the blades' normal rotation.

THRUST OF TAIL ROTOR

DIRECTION OF MAIN ROTOR

REACTION OF MAIN ROTOR

STEERING A SINGLE-ROTOR HELICOPTER

Nomally, the thrust of the tail rotor equals the reaction of the main rotor. The thrust and reaction cancel each out, and no force acts to spin the helicopter.
Operating the rudder pedals to increase the thrust makes the extra thrust turn the helicopter in the same direction as the rotor blades. Decreasing the thrust of the tail rotor allows the reaction of the main rotor to turn the helicopter in the opposite direction.

TWIN-ROTOR HELICOPTER

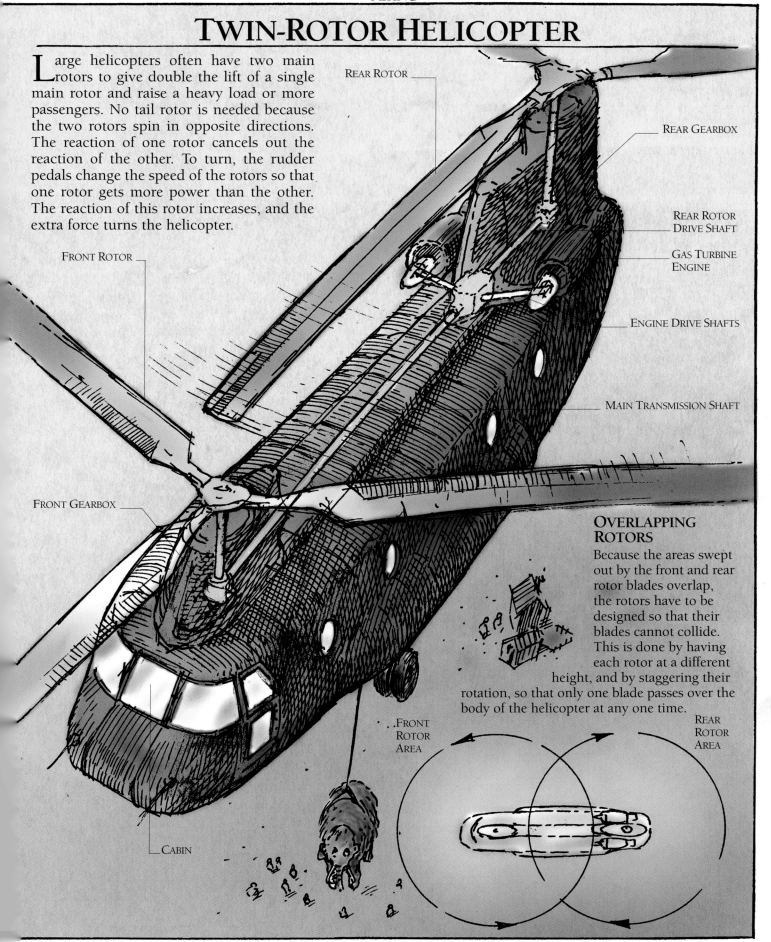

Large helicopters often have two main rotors to give double the lift of a single main rotor and raise a heavy load or more passengers. No tail rotor is needed because the two rotors spin in opposite directions. The reaction of one rotor cancels out the reaction of the other. To turn, the rudder pedals change the speed of the rotors so that one rotor gets more power than the other. The reaction of this rotor increases, and the extra force turns the helicopter.

REAR ROTOR

REAR GEARBOX

REAR ROTOR DRIVE SHAFT

GAS TURBINE ENGINE

ENGINE DRIVE SHAFTS

MAIN TRANSMISSION SHAFT

FRONT ROTOR

FRONT GEARBOX

OVERLAPPING ROTORS

Because the areas swept out by the front and rear rotor blades overlap, the rotors have to be designed so that their blades cannot collide. This is done by having each rotor at a different height, and by staggering their rotation, so that only one blade passes over the body of the helicopter at any one time.

CABIN

FRONT ROTOR AREA

REAR ROTOR AREA

QUADCOPTER

FOUR-ROTOR DRONE

A quadcopter is a helicopter with four rotors. This configuration is both stable and maneuverable in the air. Steering the drone is achieved by changing the relative speed of the rotors. For example, slowing down the front rotors tilts the craft forward so it moves straight ahead.

Small, remote-controlled quadcopters are a type of unmanned aerial vehicle (UAV), also known as drones. Popular with hobbyists, these light, maneuverable craft are often mounted with a camera and used to take photographs or video from the air.

Drones with onboard cameras are useful in police surveillance and scientific research, in search and rescue after natural disasters, and in warfare. In the future, much more autonomous UAVs—those that need little or no human control—may be used to deliver products bought online.

ANTENNA

The antenna receives commands from the handset, and sends images from the camera back to the handset, via radio waves.

GIMBAL

The camera is mounted on a gimbal. This device uses an accelerometer (see p. 241) to keep the camera pointing in the right direction regardless of the orientation of the craft.

DIGITAL CAMERA

HANDSET

The quadcopter is controlled by two joysticks on a small handset. The left joystick increases the speed of all the rotors, making the craft rise or go faster; the right one steers. Live pictures from the camera are displayed on an LCD screen.

LARGER DRONES

Not all UAVs are helicopters, and not all are small—many are the size of a small manned aircraft. They are sometimes used in situations where it would be too dangerous to send a human pilot, such as exploring the mouth of a volcano or flying into enemy territory in a warzone.

THE HYDROFOIL

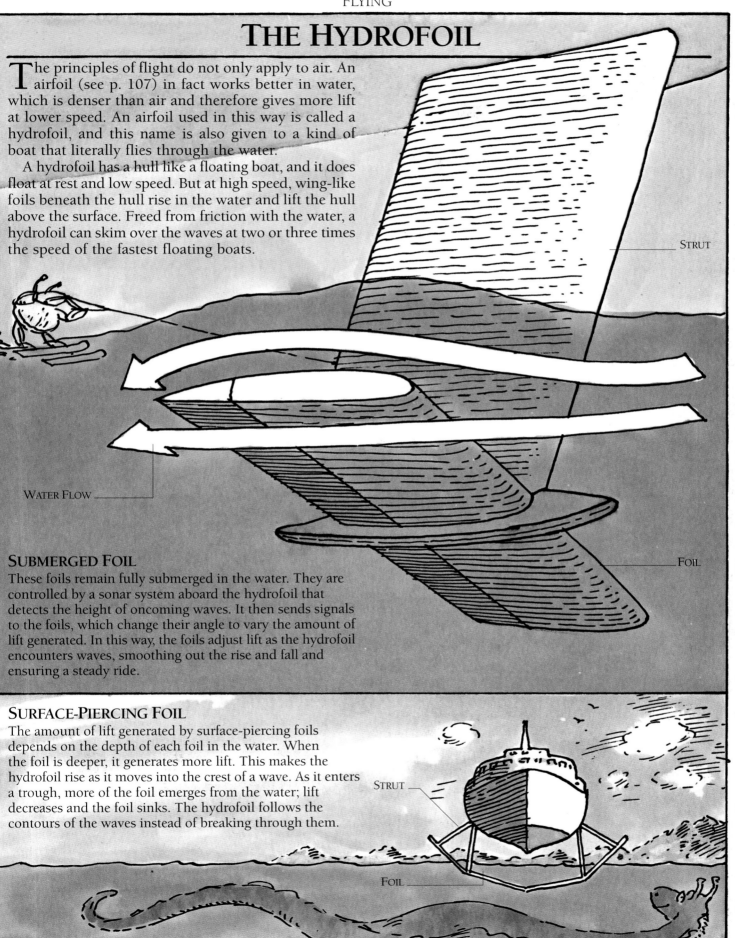

The principles of flight do not only apply to air. An airfoil (see p. 107) in fact works better in water, which is denser than air and therefore gives more lift at lower speed. An airfoil used in this way is called a hydrofoil, and this name is also given to a kind of boat that literally flies through the water.

A hydrofoil has a hull like a floating boat, and it does float at rest and low speed. But at high speed, wing-like foils beneath the hull rise in the water and lift the hull above the surface. Freed from friction with the water, a hydrofoil can skim over the waves at two or three times the speed of the fastest floating boats.

STRUT

WATER FLOW

FOIL

SUBMERGED FOIL

These foils remain fully submerged in the water. They are controlled by a sonar system aboard the hydrofoil that detects the height of oncoming waves. It then sends signals to the foils, which change their angle to vary the amount of lift generated. In this way, the foils adjust lift as the hydrofoil encounters waves, smoothing out the rise and fall and ensuring a steady ride.

SURFACE-PIERCING FOIL

The amount of lift generated by surface-piercing foils depends on the depth of each foil in the water. When the foil is deeper, it generates more lift. This makes the hydrofoil rise as it moves into the crest of a wave. As it enters a trough, more of the foil emerges from the water; lift decreases and the foil sinks. The hydrofoil follows the contours of the waves instead of breaking through them.

STRUT

FOIL

PRESSURE POWER

ON FIGHTING FIRES

Through careful study, I have been able to devise a way to improve both the capacity and range of mammoths in fighting fires. First the mammoth is encouraged to drink as much water as it can hold and still get to the scene of the outbreak. Meanwhile a heavy post is set into the ground a short but safe distance from the fire. The creature is then squeezed against the post in a series of rapid strokes by a large firefighter-operated piston.

PUMPS FOR PRESSURE

The events recorded for all time in the parchment above concern the conversion of the mammoth into a primitive but highly effective pump. Pumps are often required to raise the pressure of a fluid (a liquid or a gas), though they may alternatively reduce the pressure. The change in pressure is then put to work, usually to exert a force and make something move or to cause the fluid to flow.

A pump pushes on the molecules of the fluid that enters the pump, squashing them closer together. Liquids cannot be compressed, because the molecules are already very close together—but they pass on the force, exerting pressure outward in all directions. Exerting pressure on a gas does compress it, because the molecules are much farther apart. The compressed gas exerts a greater pressure outward, in all directions, so the effect is the same. In both cases, the pump increases pressure on the fluid, and the fluid escapes from the pump, if the pressure is lower outside—or passes on the increased pressure in all directions.

SUCTION POWER

A pump may also reduce the pressure of a gas. One way is to increase the volume of the gas so that its molecules become more widely spaced. The mammoth experiences this as the piston is removed, and its empty stomach regains its normal bulk. The pressure of the air inside now becomes less than the pressure of the air outside, and air flows into the mammoth—sucking any nearby object in with it.

PRESSURE AND WEIGHT

Any liquid or gas has a certain pressure by virtue of its weight. When the weight of a liquid or gas presses against a surface within the liquid or gas or against the walls of a container, it creates a pressure on the surface or the walls. Water flows from a tap under pressure because of the weight of the water in the pipe and tank above. Air has a strong pressure because of the great weight of the air in the atmosphere. Suction makes use of this "natural" pressure of the air.

*T*ests show that my apparatus not only completely empties the mammoth, but also dramatically increases the force with which the water is discharged. The only problem with my design occurs if the piston is released too quickly when the mammoth is empty. Naturally, once the pressure is off, the mammoth expands to its original shape and size, resulting in a deep and powerful inhalation. Anyone or anything standing too close to the animal's trunk during this expansion is likely to be sucked bodily into the animal's interior.

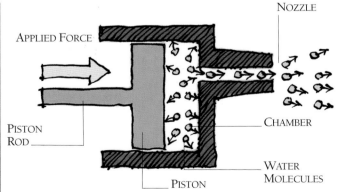

PUMPING OUT

When the piston is pushed in a simple pump, the force creates a high pressure in the water, which the water passes on, exerting pressure outward in all directions. The molecules move to any point where the pressure is lower and they are less crowded. This point is the nozzle of the pump, and the water emerges from it in a jet.

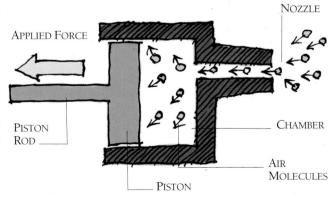

SUCKING IN

As the piston is pulled back, the air pressure in the now empty pump is reduced because the air molecules move apart. The air molecules outside the pump are closer together because the air there is at higher pressure, and so they surge into the pump chamber.

RECIPROCATING PUMPS

PISTON PUMP

In the piston pump, a piston moves up and down inside a cylinder, sucking in water or air at one end and then compressing it to expel it at the other end. A hand-operated water pistol contains the mechanism shown here. A bicycle pump is another simple kind of piston pump.

Pumps increase (or decrease) the pressure of a liquid or gas in two main ways. The piston pump is a reciprocating pump, in which a part such as a piston or diaphragm moves repeatedly to and fro. Rotary pumps compress with a rotating mechanism.

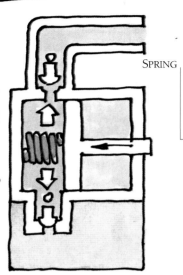

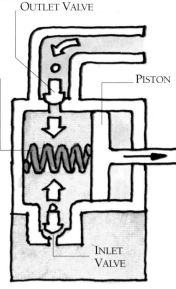

OUTLET VALVE

SPRING

PISTON

INLET VALVE

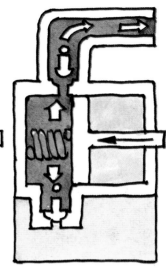

PISTON IN
The piston moves in, increasing the pressure of air in the empty pump. The inlet valve closes, but the outlet valve opens as air escapes.

PISTON OUT
The piston moves back, lowering the air pressure. The outlet valve closes, while the water beneath the pump, which has a higher pressure, flows up into the pump.

PISTON IN
The piston moves in again, increasing the pressure of the water in the pump. The inlet valve closes, but the outlet valve opens to let the water out of the pump.

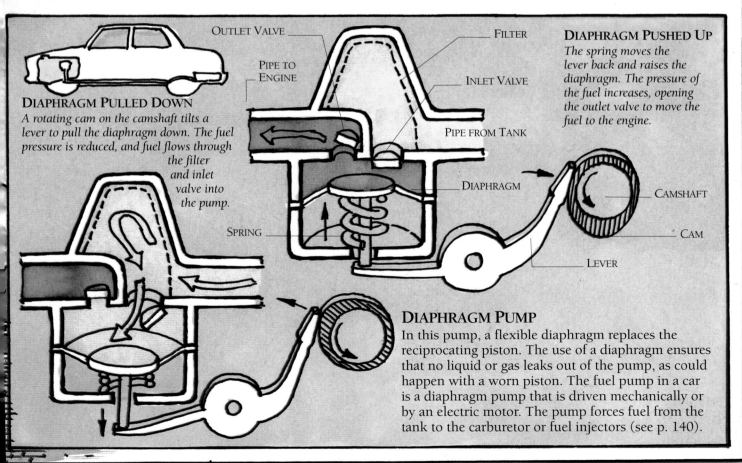

OUTLET VALVE

FILTER

PIPE TO ENGINE

INLET VALVE

PIPE FROM TANK

DIAPHRAGM PUSHED UP
The spring moves the lever back and raises the diaphragm. The pressure of the fuel increases, opening the outlet valve to move the fuel to the engine.

DIAPHRAGM PULLED DOWN
A rotating cam on the camshaft tilts a lever to pull the diaphragm down. The fuel pressure is reduced, and fuel flows through the filter and inlet valve into the pump.

SPRING

DIAPHRAGM

CAMSHAFT

CAM

LEVER

DIAPHRAGM PUMP

In this pump, a flexible diaphragm replaces the reciprocating piston. The use of a diaphragm ensures that no liquid or gas leaks out of the pump, as could happen with a worn piston. The fuel pump in a car is a diaphragm pump that is driven mechanically or by an electric motor. The pump forces fuel from the tank to the carburetor or fuel injectors (see p. 140).

ROTARY PUMPS

GEAR PUMP

The oil that lubricates the engine of a car must be forced at high pressure around channels in the engine (see p. 88). A sturdy and durable gear pump is often used to do the job.

The rotating camshaft of the engine (see pp. 50-51) normally powers the oil pump, driving a shaft that turns a pair of intermeshing gear wheels inside a close-fitting chamber. The oil enters the pump, where it is trapped in the wheels. The wheels carry the oil around to the outlet, where the teeth come together as they intermesh. This squeezes the oil and raises its pressure as it flows to the outlet. The speed of pumping is directly linked to the speed of the engine.

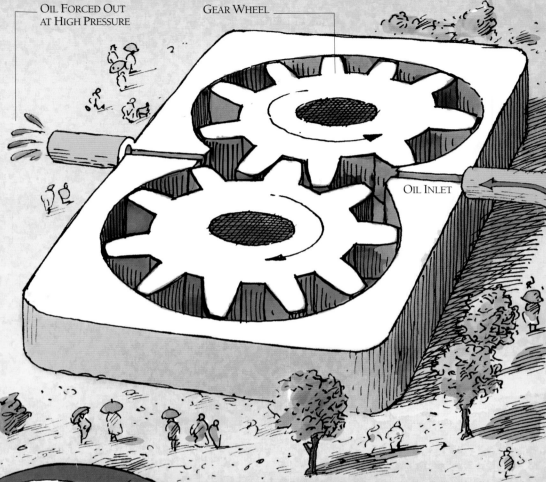

OIL FORCED OUT
AT HIGH PRESSURE

GEAR WHEEL

OIL INLET

OUTLET

VANE

COMPARTMENT

ROTOR

INLET

ROTARY VANE PUMP

This pump contains a chamber with a rotor mounted slightly off-center. The rotor has slots fitted with sliding vanes. As the rotor turns, the vanes are thrown outward against the chamber wall, creating compartments of changing size.

Where the liquid or gas enters the pump, the compartments expand to suck it in. As the fluid is carried around the pump, the compartments get smaller. The fluid is squeezed, and leaves the pump at high pressure. Rotary vane pumps are often used to deliver fuel at gas stations.

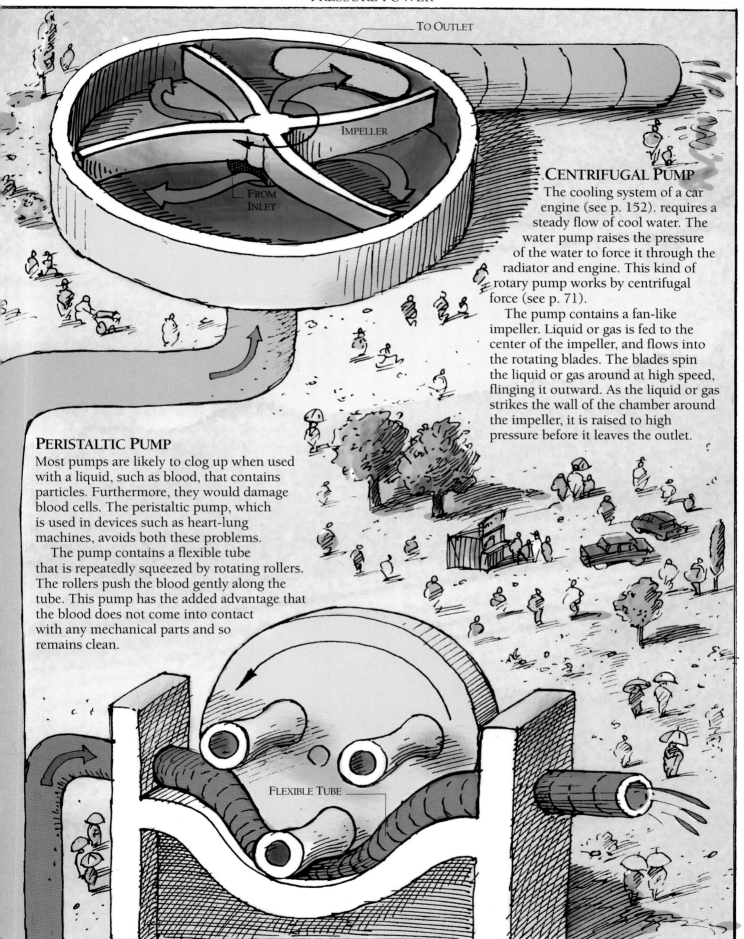

TO OUTLET

IMPELLER

FROM INLET

CENTRIFUGAL PUMP

The cooling system of a car engine (see p. 152). requires a steady flow of cool water. The water pump raises the pressure of the water to force it through the radiator and engine. This kind of rotary pump works by centrifugal force (see p. 71).

The pump contains a fan-like impeller. Liquid or gas is fed to the center of the impeller, and flows into the rotating blades. The blades spin the liquid or gas around at high speed, flinging it outward. As the liquid or gas strikes the wall of the chamber around the impeller, it is raised to high pressure before it leaves the outlet.

PERISTALTIC PUMP

Most pumps are likely to clog up when used with a liquid, such as blood, that contains particles. Furthermore, they would damage blood cells. The peristaltic pump, which is used in devices such as heart-lung machines, avoids both these problems.

The pump contains a flexible tube that is repeatedly squeezed by rotating rollers. The rollers push the blood gently along the tube. This pump has the added advantage that the blood does not come into contact with any mechanical parts and so remains clean.

FLEXIBLE TUBE

PNEUMATIC MACHINES

SUPPORTING A WEIGHT

When air is trapped and squashed inside a container, it's under pressure. This means it pushes upward with force and can support a weight.

DOUBLING THE AREA

If the area of the container is doubled in size, the trapped air can support twice as much weight, even though the pressure is exactly the same.

DOUBLING THE PRESSURE

If the pressure is doubled, the air can also support twice as much weight, even if the container stays the same size.

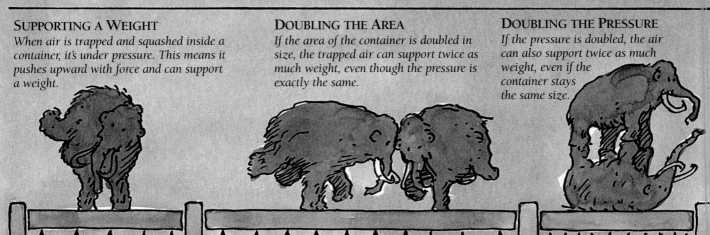

A ir possesses considerable power when placed under pressure, and when compressed it can be used to drive machines. Pneumatic or air-driven machines all make use of the force exerted by air molecules striking a surface. The compressed air exerts a greater pressure than the air on the other side of the surface, which is at atmospheric pressure. The difference in pressure drives the machine.

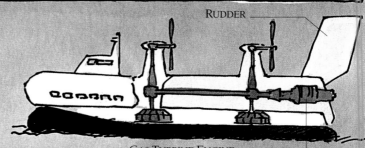

RUDDER

GAS TURBINE ENGINE

HOVERCRAFT

A hovercraft exploits the power of compressed air to lift itself above the surface of the water or ground. Buoyed up by a cushion of air, it can then float and travel rapidly because there is little friction with the water or ground. The hovercraft uses propellers for horizontal movement and rudders for steering. These may operate in the air, as in an aircraft, or underwater like those in a ship. Gas turbines or piston engines drive both the lift fans that compress the air and pump it into the flexible skirt and also the propellers.

INFLATED SKIRT

Compressed air flows beneath the hovercraft. The skirt holds it in to form a high-pressure cushion.

PROPELLER

LIFT FANS

These suck air into the hovercraft, generating enough force to lift the craft above the surface.

UNINFLATED SKIRT

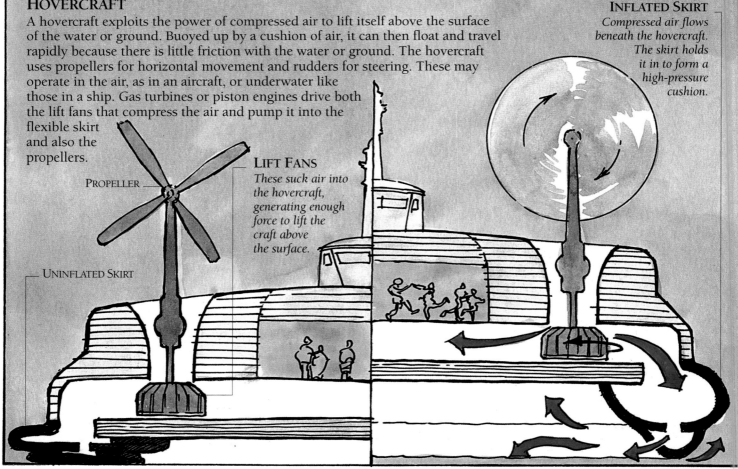

PNEUMATIC DRILL

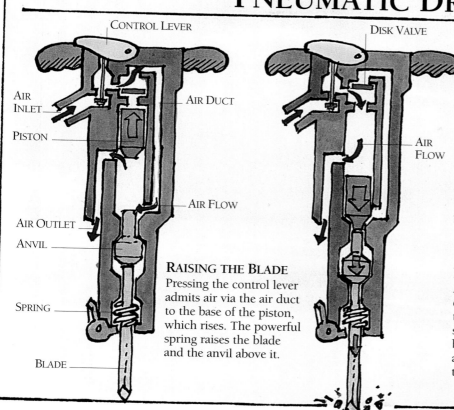

CONTROL LEVER

AIR INLET

AIR DUCT

PISTON

AIR FLOW

AIR OUTLET

ANVIL

SPRING

BLADE

DISK VALVE

AIR FLOW

The force that lifts a hovercraft above the sea is put to use on the road in the reverse direction. The ear-blasting roar that often accompanies road repairs is produced by the pneumatic drill, air hammer or jackhammer. This device is fed with compressed air from a pump as a source of power. The high-pressure air is used to produce a cycle of operations that delivers powerful repeated blows to the tool or blade, which hammers down into the road surface.

RAISING THE BLADE
Pressing the control lever admits air via the air duct to the base of the piston, which rises. The powerful spring raises the blade and the anvil above it.

HAMMERING THE BLADE
Air forced up above the rising piston lifts the disk valve. This diverts the incoming air to the top of the piston, pushing it down. The piston strikes the anvil, which in turn hammers the blade. The falling piston forces air back up the air duct, causing the disk valve to fall and the cycle to begin again.

POWER BRAKES

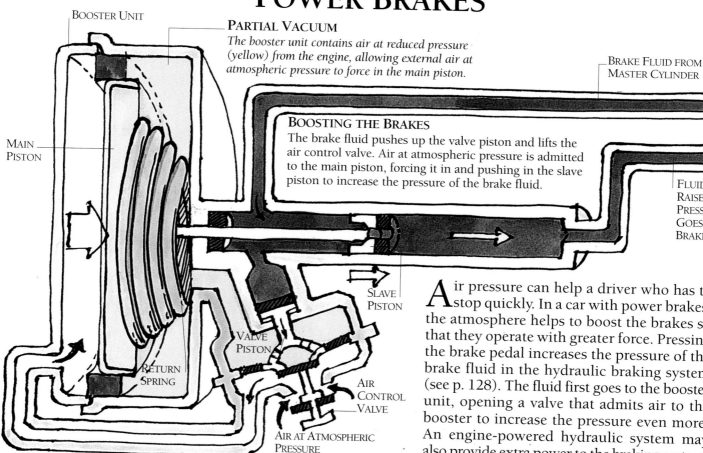

BOOSTER UNIT

PARTIAL VACUUM
The booster unit contains air at reduced pressure (yellow) from the engine, allowing external air at atmospheric pressure to force in the main piston.

BRAKE FLUID FROM MASTER CYLINDER

BOOSTING THE BRAKES
The brake fluid pushes up the valve piston and lifts the air control valve. Air at atmospheric pressure is admitted to the main piston, forcing it in and pushing in the slave piston to increase the pressure of the brake fluid.

MAIN PISTON

FLUID AT RAISED PRESSURE GOES TO BRAKES

SLAVE PISTON

VALVE PISTON

RETURN SPRING

AIR CONTROL VALVE

AIR AT ATMOSPHERIC PRESSURE

Air pressure can help a driver who has to stop quickly. In a car with power brakes, the atmosphere helps to boost the brakes so that they operate with greater force. Pressing the brake pedal increases the pressure of the brake fluid in the hydraulic braking system (see p. 128). The fluid first goes to the booster unit, opening a valve that admits air to the booster to increase the pressure even more. An engine-powered hydraulic system may also provide extra power to the braking system.

HYDRAULIC MACHINES

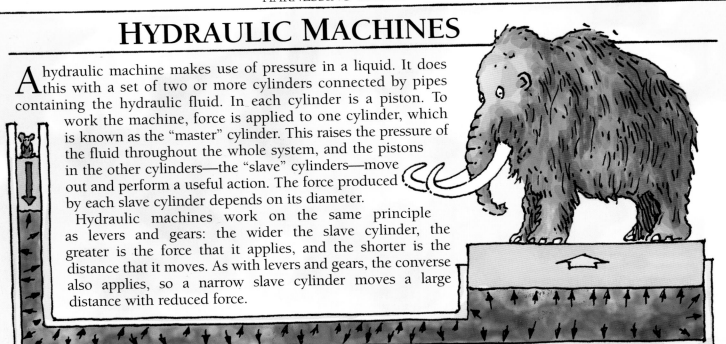

A hydraulic machine makes use of pressure in a liquid. It does this with a set of two or more cylinders connected by pipes containing the hydraulic fluid. In each cylinder is a piston. To work the machine, force is applied to one cylinder, which is known as the "master" cylinder. This raises the pressure of the fluid throughout the whole system, and the pistons in the other cylinders—the "slave" cylinders—move out and perform a useful action. The force produced by each slave cylinder depends on its diameter.

Hydraulic machines work on the same principle as levers and gears: the wider the slave cylinder, the greater is the force that it applies, and the shorter is the distance that it moves. As with levers and gears, the converse also applies, so a narrow slave cylinder moves a large distance with reduced force.

HYDRAULIC BRAKES

Except for the hand-brake, which is operated by a cable, cars use hydraulic braking systems. The brake pedal moves the piston in the master cylinder, raising the pressure of the brake fluid evenly throughout the system. The brake fluid, its pressure boosted by the power-brakes booster unit (see p. 127), then makes pistons in the wheel cylinders move out with great force. These pistons apply the brake pads or shoes to slow the car (see p. 86).

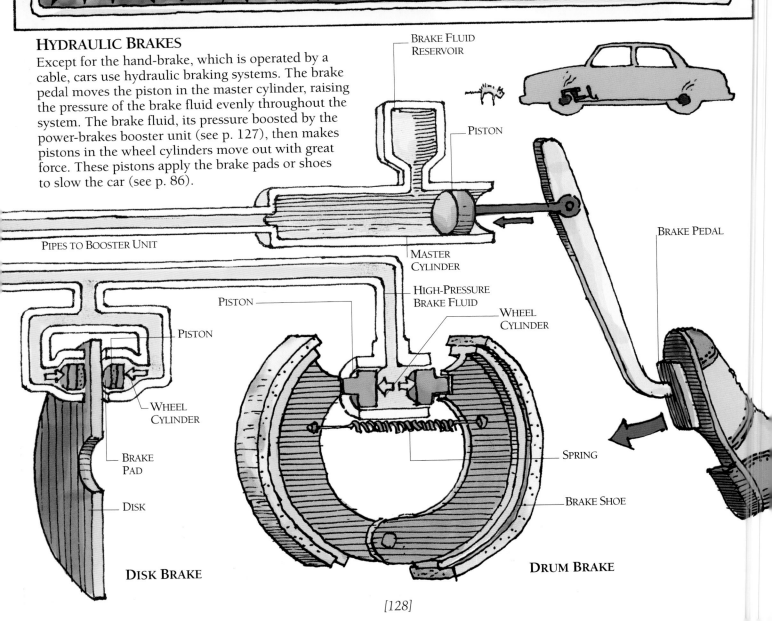

BRAKE FLUID RESERVOIR

PISTON

PISTON

PISTON

PIPES TO BOOSTER UNIT

MASTER CYLINDER

HIGH-PRESSURE BRAKE FLUID

WHEEL CYLINDER

WHEEL CYLINDER

BRAKE PAD

DISK

SPRING

BRAKE SHOE

BRAKE PEDAL

DISK BRAKE

DRUM BRAKE

HYDRAULIC RAM

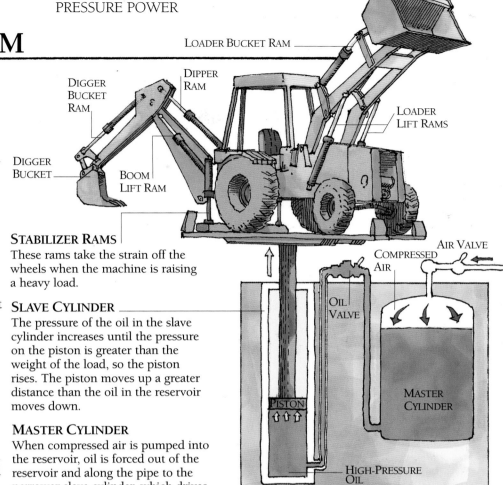

Machines such as the excavator (see p. 23) and firefighter's ladder (see p. 29) work with hydraulic rams. Each ram consists of a piston in a cylinder connected by pipes to a central reservoir of hydraulic fluid. The controls open valves that admit high-pressure fluid to either side of the piston, which then moves in or out with great force and precision.

HYDRAULIC LIFT

A hydraulic lift easily raises the weight of a car. It has only one piston. Air is pumped by a compressor into an oil reservoir, where it increases the pressure of the oil. The oil reservoir acts as the master cylinder. The high-pressure oil then flows to the base of a cylinder, where it forces up a piston, which supports the car's weight. Closing the oil valve keeps the piston extended. To lower the car, the oil and air valves are opened. The compressed air escapes, reducing the oil pressure and allowing the piston to descend.

LOADER BUCKET RAM

DIGGER BUCKET RAM

DIPPER RAM

DIGGER BUCKET

BOOM LIFT RAM

LOADER LIFT RAMS

STABILIZER RAMS

These rams take the strain off the wheels when the machine is raising a heavy load.

SLAVE CYLINDER

The pressure of the oil in the slave cylinder increases until the pressure on the piston is greater than the weight of the load, so the piston rises. The piston moves up a greater distance than the oil in the reservoir moves down.

MASTER CYLINDER

When compressed air is pumped into the reservoir, oil is forced out of the reservoir and along the pipe to the narrower slave cylinder, which drives the piston.

AIR VALVE

COMPRESSED AIR

OIL VALVE

PISTON

MASTER CYLINDER

HIGH-PRESSURE OIL

POWER STEERING

Hydraulics can help with steering a car as well as braking. Power steering reduces the effort of turning the car by using a hydraulic system to boost the force that you apply to the steering wheel. Power-steering systems may use electric motors instead of hydraulics.

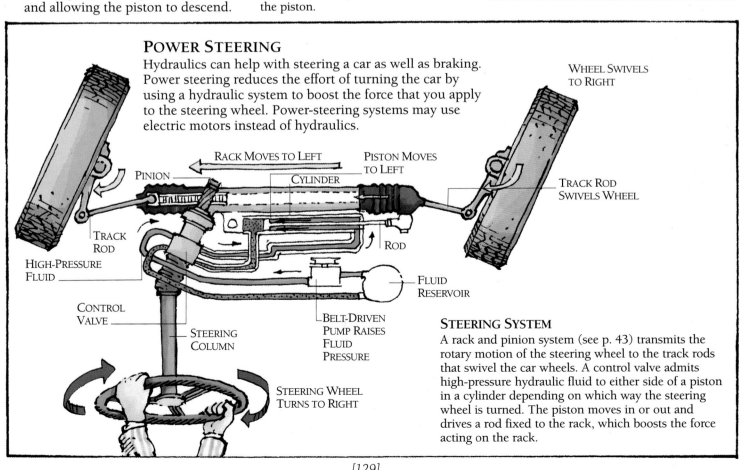

WHEEL SWIVELS TO RIGHT

RACK MOVES TO LEFT

PISTON MOVES TO LEFT

PINION

CYLINDER

TRACK ROD SWIVELS WHEEL

TRACK ROD

ROD

HIGH-PRESSURE FLUID

CONTROL VALVE

STEERING COLUMN

BELT-DRIVEN PUMP RAISES FLUID PRESSURE

FLUID RESERVOIR

STEERING WHEEL TURNS TO RIGHT

STEERING SYSTEM

A rack and pinion system (see p. 43) transmits the rotary motion of the steering wheel to the track rods that swivel the car wheels. A control valve admits high-pressure hydraulic fluid to either side of a piston in a cylinder depending on which way the steering wheel is turned. The piston moves in or out and drives a rod fixed to the rack, which boosts the force acting on the rack.

SUCTION MACHINES

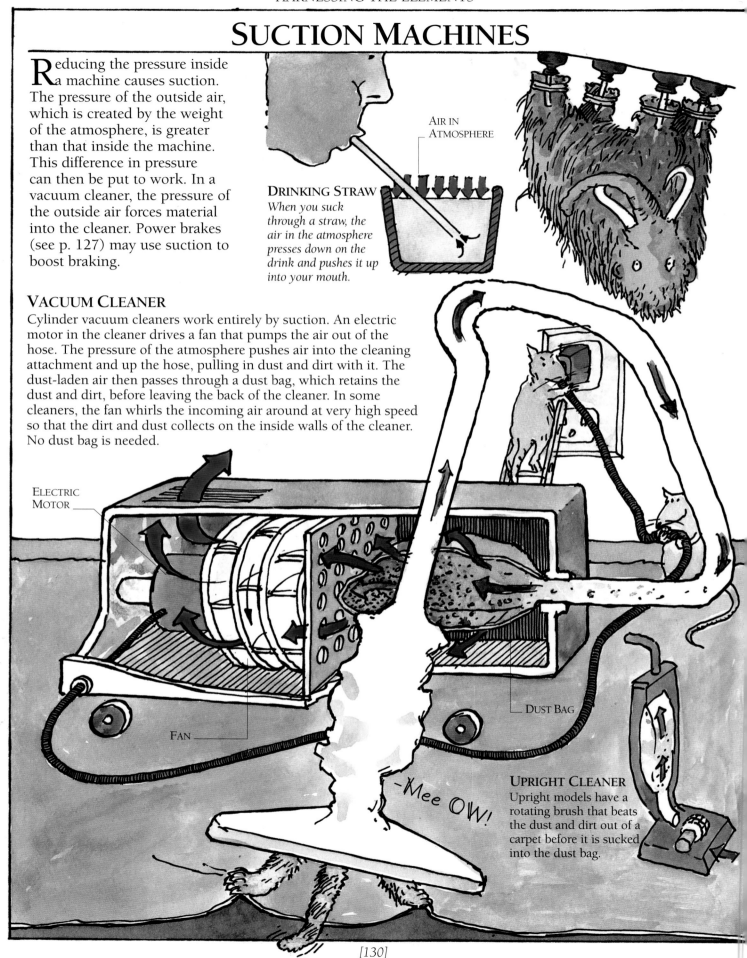

Reducing the pressure inside a machine causes suction. The pressure of the outside air, which is created by the weight of the atmosphere, is greater than that inside the machine. This difference in pressure can then be put to work. In a vacuum cleaner, the pressure of the outside air forces material into the cleaner. Power brakes (see p. 127) may use suction to boost braking.

AIR IN ATMOSPHERE

DRINKING STRAW

When you suck through a straw, the air in the atmosphere presses down on the drink and pushes it up into your mouth.

VACUUM CLEANER

Cylinder vacuum cleaners work entirely by suction. An electric motor in the cleaner drives a fan that pumps the air out of the hose. The pressure of the atmosphere pushes air into the cleaning attachment and up the hose, pulling in dust and dirt with it. The dust-laden air then passes through a dust bag, which retains the dust and dirt, before leaving the back of the cleaner. In some cleaners, the fan whirls the incoming air around at very high speed so that the dirt and dust collects on the inside walls of the cleaner. No dust bag is needed.

ELECTRIC MOTOR

FAN

DUST BAG

-Mee OW!

UPRIGHT CLEANER

Upright models have a rotating brush that beats the dust and dirt out of a carpet before it is sucked into the dust bag.

THE AQUALUNG

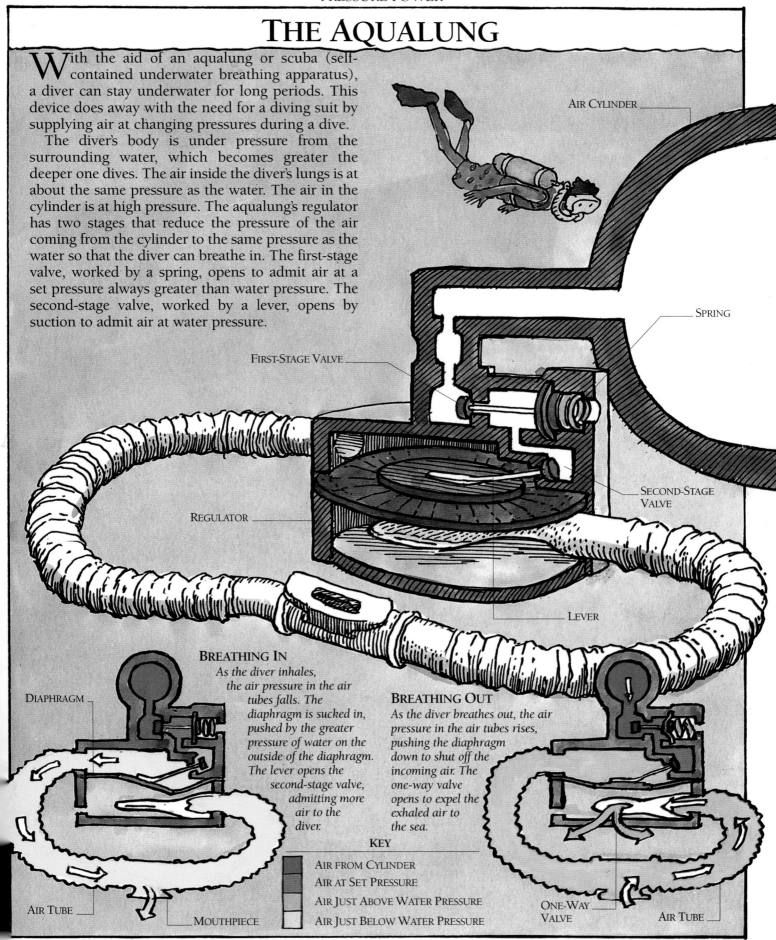

With the aid of an aqualung or scuba (self-contained underwater breathing apparatus), a diver can stay underwater for long periods. This device does away with the need for a diving suit by supplying air at changing pressures during a dive.

The diver's body is under pressure from the surrounding water, which becomes greater the deeper one dives. The air inside the diver's lungs is at about the same pressure as the water. The air in the cylinder is at high pressure. The aqualung's regulator has two stages that reduce the pressure of the air coming from the cylinder to the same pressure as the water so that the diver can breathe in. The first-stage valve, worked by a spring, opens to admit air at a set pressure always greater than water pressure. The second-stage valve, worked by a lever, opens by suction to admit air at water pressure.

AIR CYLINDER

SPRING

FIRST-STAGE VALVE

SECOND-STAGE VALVE

REGULATOR

LEVER

BREATHING IN
As the diver inhales, the air pressure in the air tubes falls. The diaphragm is sucked in, pushed by the greater pressure of water on the outside of the diaphragm. The lever opens the second-stage valve, admitting more air to the diver.

BREATHING OUT
As the diver breathes out, the air pressure in the air tubes rises, pushing the diaphragm down to shut off the incoming air. The one-way valve opens to expel the exhaled air to the sea.

DIAPHRAGM

AIR TUBE

MOUTHPIECE

ONE-WAY VALVE

AIR TUBE

KEY

	AIR FROM CYLINDER
	AIR AT SET PRESSURE
	AIR JUST ABOVE WATER PRESSURE
	AIR JUST BELOW WATER PRESSURE

THE TOILET TANK

Many toilet tanks work with a siphon, which accomplishes the apparently impossible feat of making water (or any other liquid) flow uphill. Provided the open end of the siphon tube is below the level of the surface, the water will flow up the tube, around the bend, and then down to the open end. Operating the toilet cistern starts the siphon flowing. Once the water begins to double back down the siphon tube, air pressure makes the rest of the water follow it.

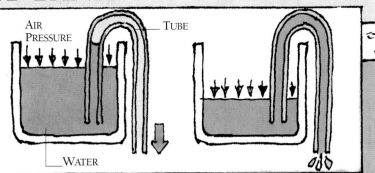

AIR PRESSURE — TUBE

WATER

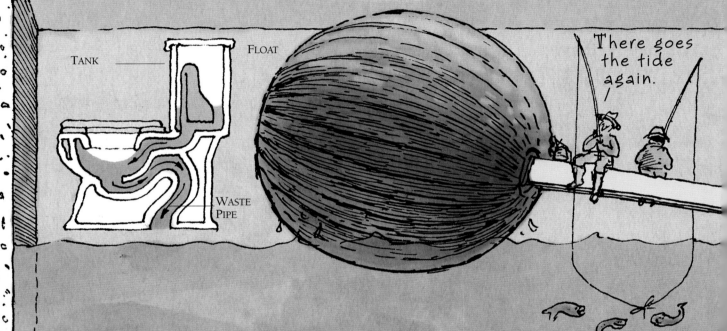

TANK — FLOAT

WASTE PIPE

There goes the tide again.

1 THE TANK FLUSHES

After the handle is pressed down, water is lifted up the siphon tube by the disk. The water reaches the bend in the siphon pipe and then travels around it. As it falls, the water in the tank follows it.

2 THE VALVE OPENS

When the water level in the tank falls below the bottom of the bell, air enters the bell and the siphon is broken. By this time, the float has fallen far enough to open the valve, and water under pressure enters to refill the tank and the float begins to rise again.

3 THE VALVE CLOSES

The rising float gradually shuts the valve, cutting off the water supply. Although the tank is full, the water cannot leave through the siphon tube until the handle is pressed down, forming the siphon once again. The float and valve work together to form a self-regulating mechanism.

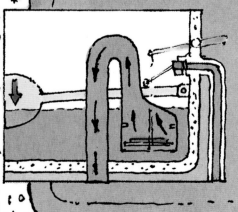

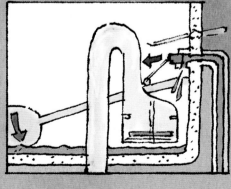

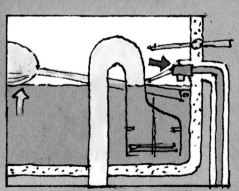

TANK COVER

SIPHON PIPE

HANDLE

VALVE

DISK

BELL

WATER PIPE

PRESSURE GAUGES

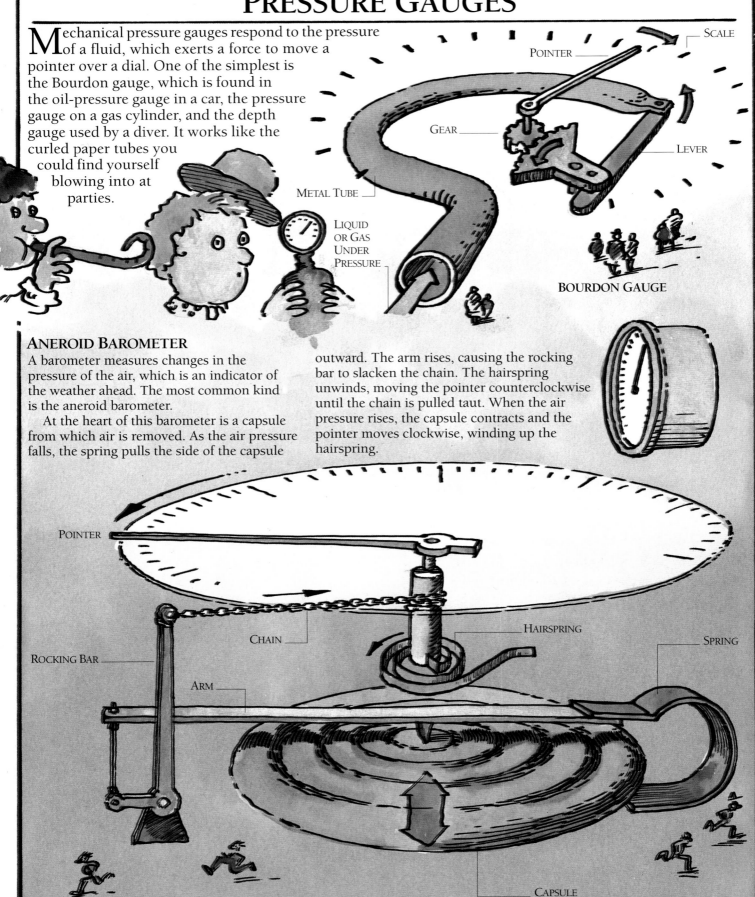

Mechanical pressure gauges respond to the pressure of a fluid, which exerts a force to move a pointer over a dial. One of the simplest is the Bourdon gauge, which is found in the oil-pressure gauge in a car, the pressure gauge on a gas cylinder, and the depth gauge used by a diver. It works like the curled paper tubes you could find yourself blowing into at parties.

SCALE

POINTER

GEAR

LEVER

METAL TUBE

LIQUID OR GAS UNDER PRESSURE

BOURDON GAUGE

ANEROID BAROMETER

A barometer measures changes in the pressure of the air, which is an indicator of the weather ahead. The most common kind is the aneroid barometer.

At the heart of this barometer is a capsule from which air is removed. As the air pressure falls, the spring pulls the side of the capsule outward. The arm rises, causing the rocking bar to slacken the chain. The hairspring unwinds, moving the pointer counterclockwise until the chain is pulled taut. When the air pressure rises, the capsule contracts and the pointer moves clockwise, winding up the hairspring.

POINTER

ROCKING BAR

ARM

CHAIN

HAIRSPRING

SPRING

CAPSULE

THE WATER METER

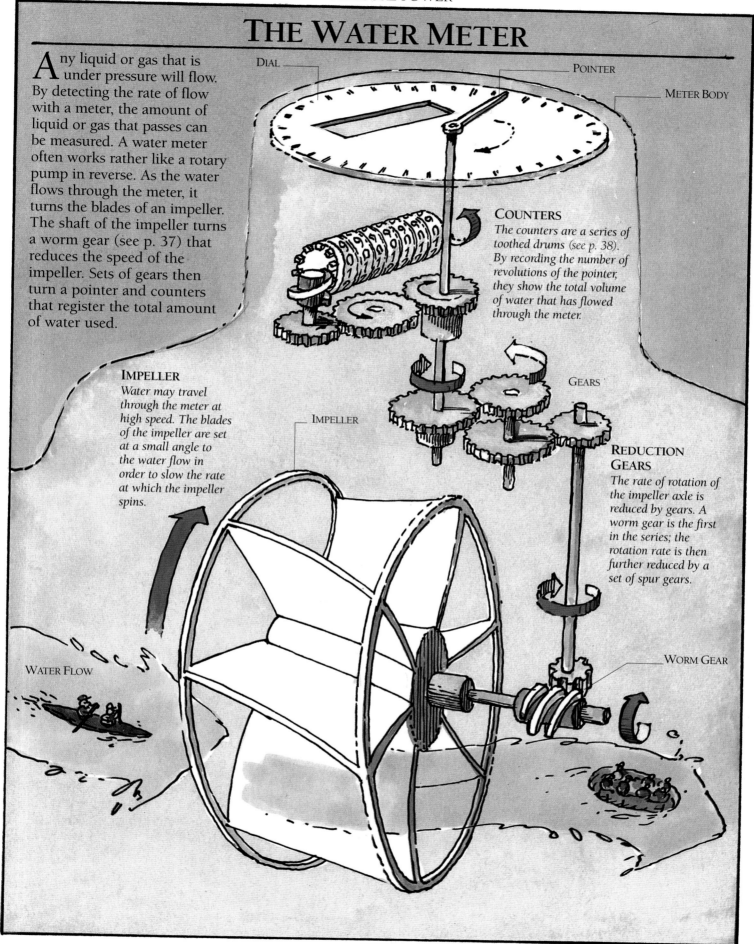

Any liquid or gas that is under pressure will flow. By detecting the rate of flow with a meter, the amount of liquid or gas that passes can be measured. A water meter often works rather like a rotary pump in reverse. As the water flows through the meter, it turns the blades of an impeller. The shaft of the impeller turns a worm gear (see p. 37) that reduces the speed of the impeller. Sets of gears then turn a pointer and counters that register the total amount of water used.

DIAL

POINTER

METER BODY

COUNTERS
The counters are a series of toothed drums (see p. 38). By recording the number of revolutions of the pointer, they show the total volume of water that has flowed through the meter.

GEARS

IMPELLER
Water may travel through the meter at high speed. The blades of the impeller are set at a small angle to the water flow in order to slow the rate at which the impeller spins.

IMPELLER

REDUCTION GEARS
The rate of rotation of the impeller axle is reduced by gears. A worm gear is the first in the series; the rotation rate is then further reduced by a set of spur gears.

WATER FLOW

WORM GEAR

JETS AND SPRAYS

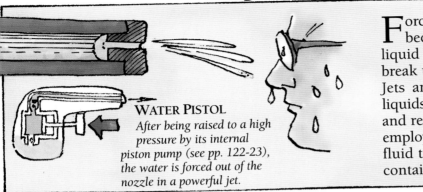

Forcing a liquid through a nozzle requires pressure because the narrow hole restricts the flow. The liquid emerges in a high-pressure jet, which may break up into a spray of droplets as it meets the air. Jets and sprays have many uses, from delivering liquids in a useful form to providing power by action and reaction. Gases, rather than liquids, are usually employed to produce power. A pump may deliver the fluid to the nozzle, as in a dishwasher, or it may be contained under pressure, as in a spray can.

WATER PISTOL

After being raised to a high pressure by its internal piston pump (see pp. 122-23), the water is forced out of the nozzle in a powerful jet.

DISHWASHER

A dishwasher uses hot water under pressure both to power its spray arms, and also to do the cleaning itself. To be effective, the water has to be sprayed in powerful jets from all directions so that it reaches all the dishes and utensils. These are then rinsed by jets of clean water before drying.

THE DISHWASHER CYCLE

1 WATER TREATMENT

Cold water enters through a water softener, which treats the water so that the dishes dry without marks.

2 HEATING

The water fills the base of the dishwasher, where it is heated. Detergent is added.

3 WASHING

The hot water is pumped by the wash pump to the rotating spray arms. It sprays the dishes and returns to the base of the dishwasher, where it is filtered and then recycled.

4 RINSING AND DRYING

After washing, the dirty water is pumped out of the dishwasher and down the drain. Then the dishes are rinsed and dried.

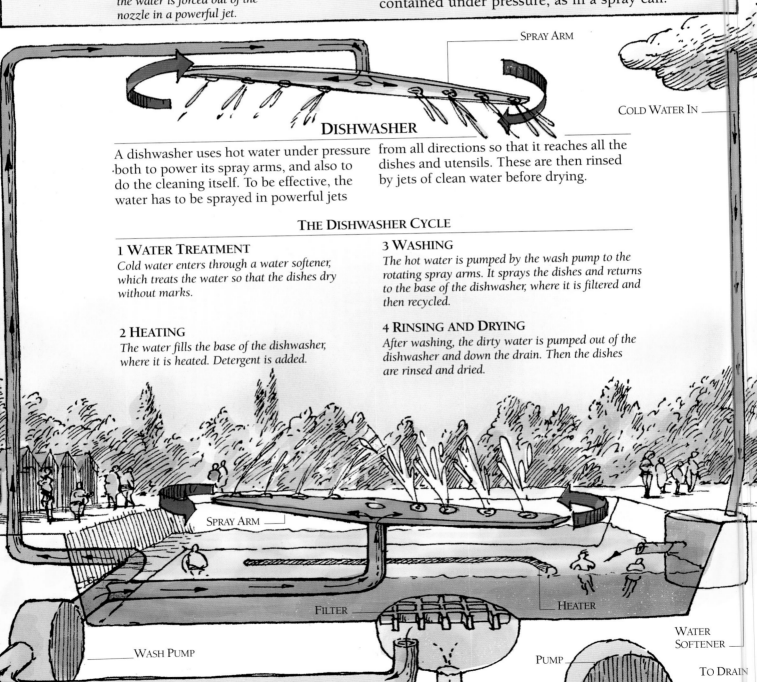

SPRAY ARM

COLD WATER IN

SPRAY ARM

FILTER

HEATER

WATER SOFTENER

WASH PUMP

PUMP

TO DRAIN

JET PACK

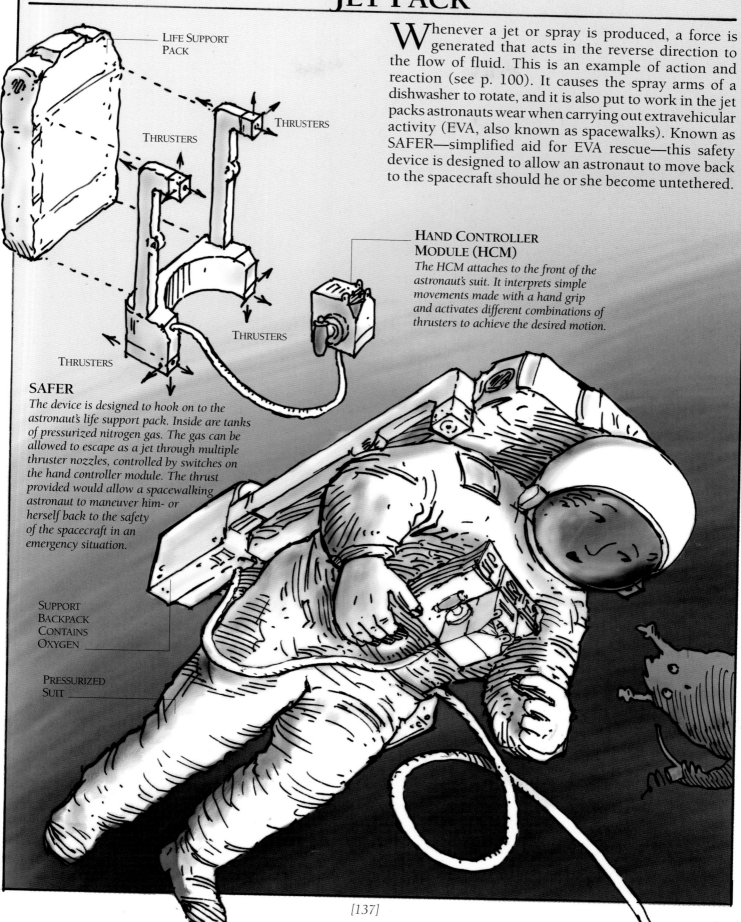

LIFE SUPPORT PACK

THRUSTERS

THRUSTERS

THRUSTERS

THRUSTERS

Whenever a jet or spray is produced, a force is generated that acts in the reverse direction to the flow of fluid. This is an example of action and reaction (see p. 100). It causes the spray arms of a dishwasher to rotate, and it is also put to work in the jet packs astronauts wear when carrying out extravehicular activity (EVA, also known as spacewalks). Known as SAFER—simplified aid for EVA rescue—this safety device is designed to allow an astronaut to move back to the spacecraft should he or she become untethered.

HAND CONTROLLER MODULE (HCM)
The HCM attaches to the front of the astronaut's suit. It interprets simple movements made with a hand grip and activates different combinations of thrusters to achieve the desired motion.

SAFER
The device is designed to hook on to the astronaut's life support pack. Inside are tanks of pressurized nitrogen gas. The gas can be allowed to escape as a jet through multiple thruster nozzles, controlled by switches on the hand controller module. The thrust provided would allow a spacewalking astronaut to maneuver him- or herself back to the safety of the spacecraft in an emergency situation.

SUPPORT BACKPACK CONTAINS OXYGEN

PRESSURIZED SUIT

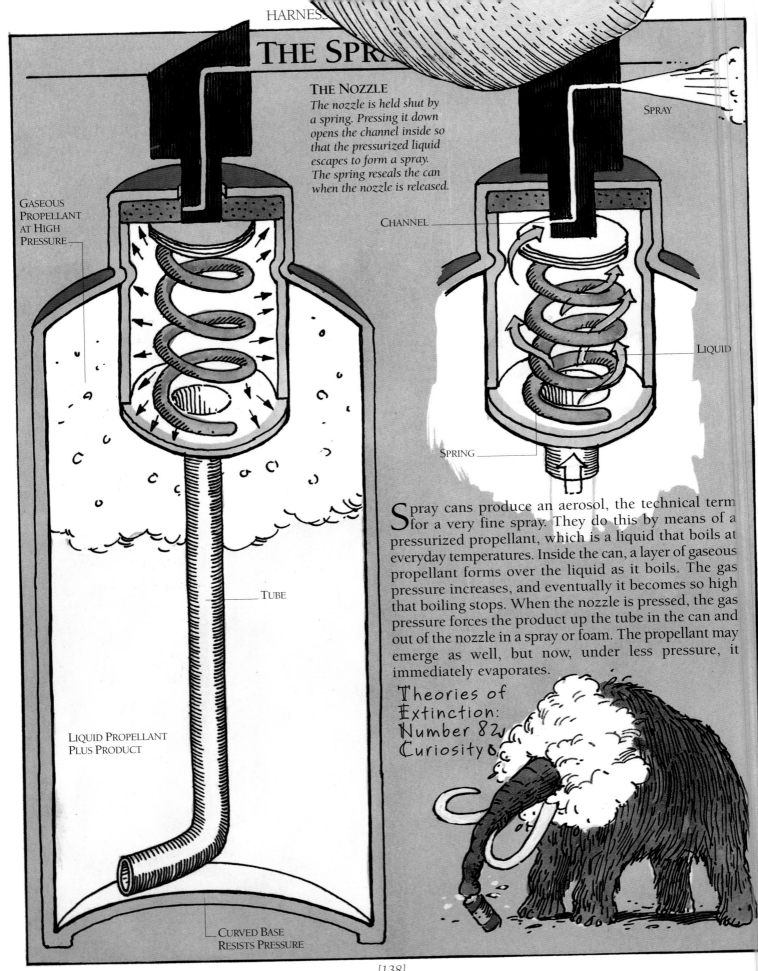

THE NOZZLE

The nozzle is held shut by a spring. Pressing it down opens the channel inside so that the pressurized liquid escapes to form a spray. The spring reseals the can when the nozzle is released.

GASEOUS PROPELLANT AT HIGH PRESSURE

SPRAY

CHANNEL

LIQUID

SPRING

TUBE

LIQUID PROPELLANT PLUS PRODUCT

CURVED BASE RESISTS PRESSURE

Spray cans produce an aerosol, the technical term for a very fine spray. They do this by means of a pressurized propellant, which is a liquid that boils at everyday temperatures. Inside the can, a layer of gaseous propellant forms over the liquid as it boils. The gas pressure increases, and eventually it becomes so high that boiling stops. When the nozzle is pressed, the gas pressure forces the product up the tube in the can and out of the nozzle in a spray or foam. The propellant may emerge as well, but now, under less pressure, it immediately evaporates.

Theories of Extinction: Number 82 Curiosity

THE FIRE EXTINGUISHER

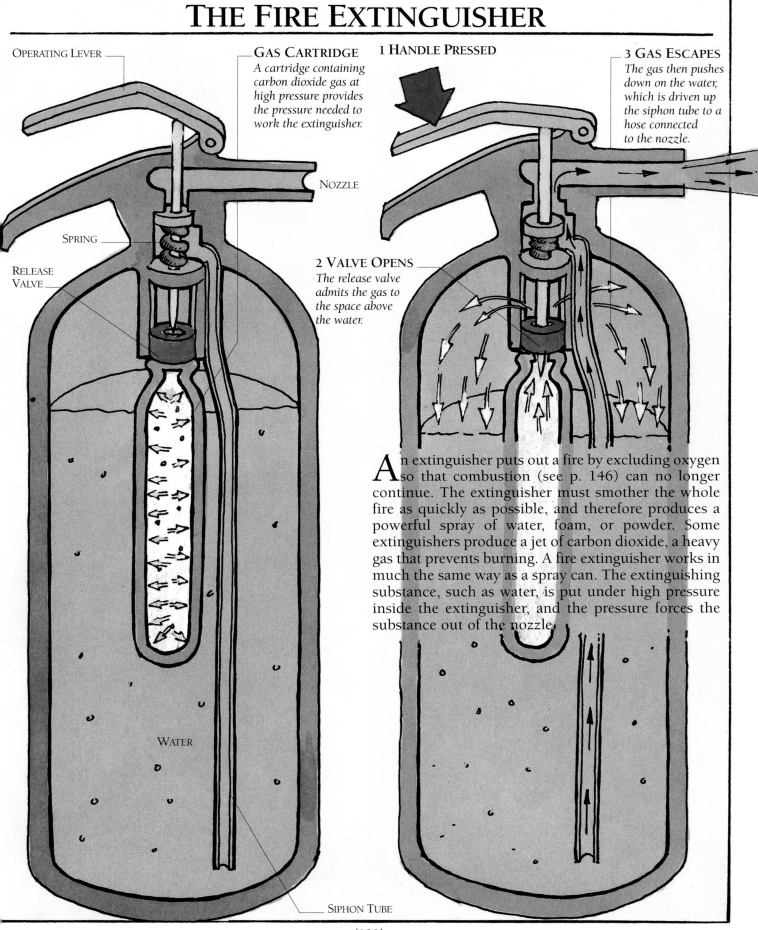

OPERATING LEVER

GAS CARTRIDGE
A cartridge containing carbon dioxide gas at high pressure provides the pressure needed to work the extinguisher.

1 HANDLE PRESSED

3 GAS ESCAPES
The gas then pushes down on the water, which is driven up the siphon tube to a hose connected to the nozzle.

NOZZLE

SPRING

RELEASE VALVE

2 VALVE OPENS
The release valve admits the gas to the space above the water.

An extinguisher puts out a fire by excluding oxygen so that combustion (see p. 146) can no longer continue. The extinguisher must smother the whole fire as quickly as possible, and therefore produces a powerful spray of water, foam, or powder. Some extinguishers produce a jet of carbon dioxide, a heavy gas that prevents burning. A fire extinguisher works in much the same way as a spray can. The extinguishing substance, such as water, is put under high pressure inside the extinguisher, and the pressure forces the substance out of the nozzle.

WATER

SIPHON TUBE

CARBURETOR AND FUEL INJECTION

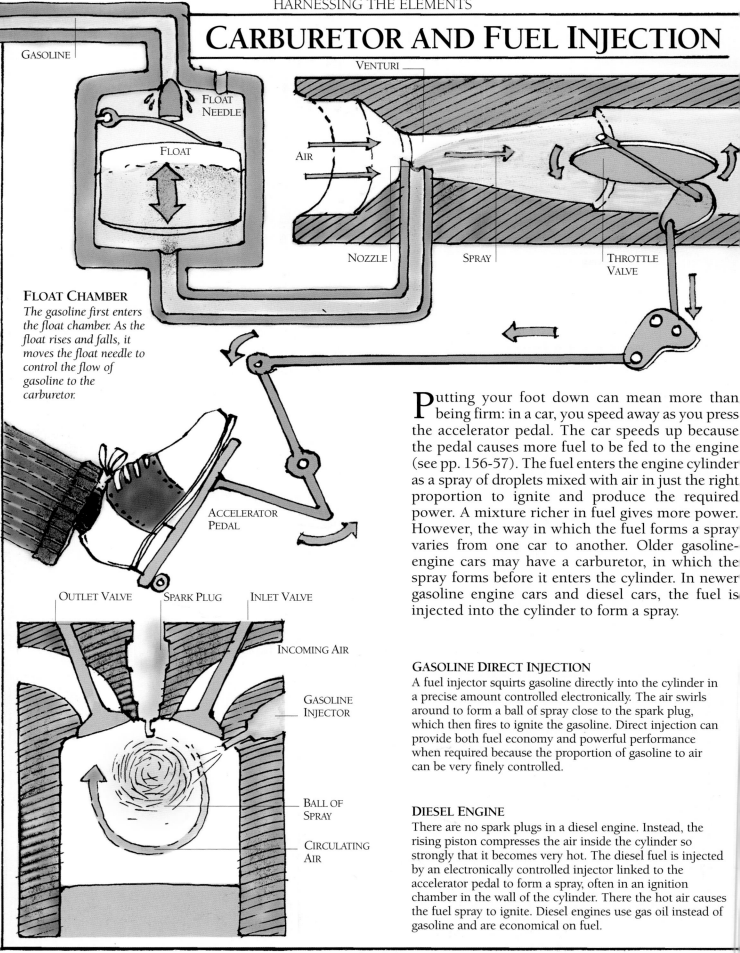

GASOLINE

FLOAT NEEDLE

FLOAT

VENTURI

AIR

NOZZLE   SPRAY   THROTTLE VALVE

FLOAT CHAMBER

The gasoline first enters the float chamber. As the float rises and falls, it moves the float needle to control the flow of gasoline to the carburetor.

ACCELERATOR PEDAL

OUTLET VALVE   SPARK PLUG   INLET VALVE

INCOMING AIR

GASOLINE INJECTOR

BALL OF SPRAY

CIRCULATING AIR

Putting your foot down can mean more than being firm: in a car, you speed away as you press the accelerator pedal. The car speeds up because the pedal causes more fuel to be fed to the engine (see pp. 156-57). The fuel enters the engine cylinder as a spray of droplets mixed with air in just the right proportion to ignite and produce the required power. A mixture richer in fuel gives more power. However, the way in which the fuel forms a spray varies from one car to another. Older gasoline-engine cars may have a carburetor, in which the spray forms before it enters the cylinder. In newer gasoline engine cars and diesel cars, the fuel is injected into the cylinder to form a spray.

GASOLINE DIRECT INJECTION

A fuel injector squirts gasoline directly into the cylinder in a precise amount controlled electronically. The air swirls around to form a ball of spray close to the spark plug, which then fires to ignite the gasoline. Direct injection can provide both fuel economy and powerful performance when required because the proportion of gasoline to air can be very finely controlled.

DIESEL ENGINE

There are no spark plugs in a diesel engine. Instead, the rising piston compresses the air inside the cylinder so strongly that it becomes very hot. The diesel fuel is injected by an electronically controlled injector linked to the accelerator pedal to form a spray, often in an ignition chamber in the wall of the cylinder. There the hot air causes the fuel spray to ignite. Diesel engines use gas oil instead of gasoline and are economical on fuel.

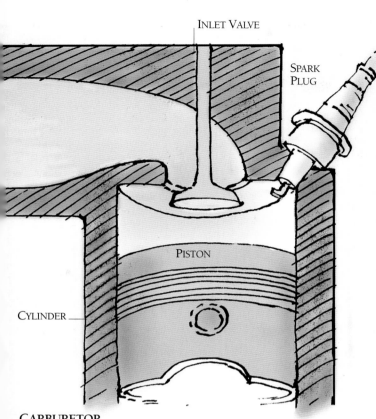

CARBURETOR

As the piston in the cylinder moves down, the inlet valve opens and air is sucked in through the carburetor. This contains a passage with a narrow section called a venturi. Gasoline is fed from a float chamber through a nozzle to the venturi. The air speeds up as it flows through the narrow venturi, and its pressure falls. The low-pressure air sucks gasoline out of the nozzle to form a spray, which goes to the cylinder. In the passage is a throttle valve linked to the accelerator pedal. The valve opens as the pedal is pressed, speeding the flow of air through the carburetor and sucking in more gasoline.

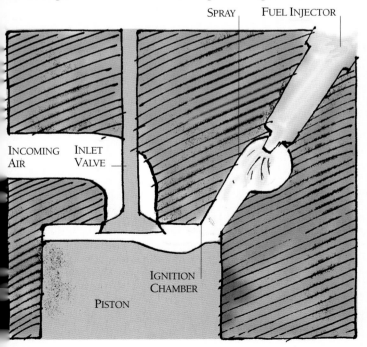

PENS

Many pens work by capillary action, which occurs in a narrow tube or channel. Liquid flows up a narrow tube because the pressure inside is lowered as the molecules at the liquid's surface are attracted to the molecules of the tube. External air pressure then forces the liquid up the tube.

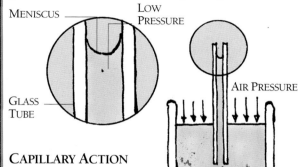

CAPILLARY ACTION

Molecules of water are attracted toward the glass molecules, forming a curve called a meniscus and causing the pressure to drop.

BALLPOINT PEN

At the tip of a ballpoint pen is a tiny metal ball in a socket. Ink flows from the ink tube through a narrow channel to the ball, which rotates to transfer the ink to the paper. The ink dries immediately.

FELT-TIP PEN

The tip of a felt-tip pen contains one or more narrow channels through which ink flows by capillary action as soon as the tip touches the paper.

DIP PEN

A dip pen's nib is split into two halves and has a gap that fills with ink as the pen is dipped in the ink. Capillary action, together with gravity, conducts ink from the gap down the narrow split in the nib to the paper.

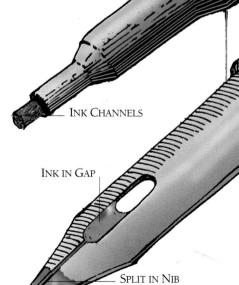

EXPLOITING HEAT

fig. 1

fig. 2

ON THE USES OF MAMMOTH HEAT

There are two things that mammoths enjoy above all else (with the possible exception of swamp grass). They are working at some useful task and sleeping.

During my travels, I have come across a number of situations in which the two have been successfully combined to the benefit of both man and beast.

In figure 1, heat absorbed during a long sleep in the sun or created by chewing swamp grass is used to warm water stored in the animal's trunk. When the trunk is secured vertically, the warmest water rises to the top, making it readily available.

In figure 2, the animal is shown performing its bed-warming function. Heat absorbed or created during the day is transferred from the mammoth to the bed in anticipation of its human occupant. To rouse the beast, either a mouse is slipped under the covers, or the bed's would-be occupant makes squeaking noises. In either case the terrified beast is quickly displaced.

THE NATURE OF HEAT

The mammoth receives heat from the sun in the form of invisible heat rays and makes heat inside its vast bulk by the consumption of swamp grass and other elephantine foods. The heat travels through its body and warms its skin. In the trunk, the heated water rises of its own accord.

Heat is a form of energy that results in the motion of molecules. Molecules are constantly on the move in everything, and the faster they move, the hotter is their possessor. So when anything receives heat energy, its

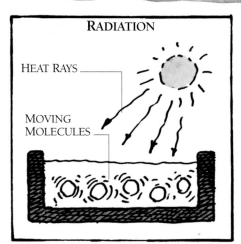

RADIATION

HEAT RAYS

MOVING MOLECULES

molecules speed up; removing heat energy slows them down. Heat travels in three ways—by radiation, conduction, and convection.

RADIATION

Hot things radiate heat rays, or infra-red rays. The rays travel through air or space and strike cooler objects, which warm up. This form of heat transfer is called thermal radiation. The heat rays make the molecules in the surface of the object move about faster. Heat then spreads through the object by conduction or convection.

fig. 3

fig. 4

In figure 3, a hot, sleepy mammoth is employed as a clothes press. To operate the mammoth, one worker tickles the beast behind the ear with a feather. As the mammoth rolls over onto its back in anticipation of having its stomach scratched, a second worker places the garments to be pressed onto the warm spot. When the tickling stops, the mammoth resumes its original position. (I have observed that if the tickling stops before the switching of garments has been completed, the result can be disastrous.)

Figure 4 shows a further development on the principle of the clothes press. In this case, the weight and heat of one or more mammoths is employed to make and cook "Big Mamms." These wafer-thin burgers have become particularly popular with the young and are available with a variety of toppings.

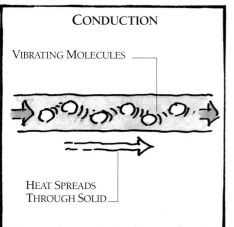

CONDUCTION

VIBRATING MOLECULES

HEAT SPREADS
THROUGH SOLID

CONDUCTION

The molecules in solids vibrate to and fro. When part of the solid is heated, the molecules there vibrate faster. They strike other molecules and make them vibrate faster to spread the heat.

CONVECTION

In liquids and gases the molecules move about. When heated, they also move further apart. A heated liquid or gas expands and rises, while a cooled liquid or gas contracts and sinks. This movement, which is known as convection, spreads the heat.

CONVECTION

HOT LIQUID
EXPANDS
AND RISES

COOL LIQUID
CONTRACTS
AND SINKS

HEAT WAVES

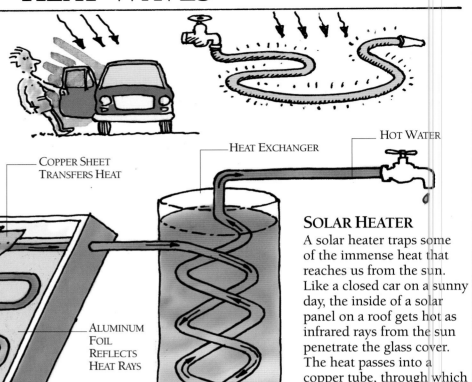

The sun bombards us with a whole range of energy-carrying rays, particularly light rays and infrared rays. These rays, and also microwaves, have similar characteristics: they pass straight through some substances, they are reflected by others and they are absorbed by the remainder. Objects that absorb rays become hot, and this is made use of in a variety of devices including the solar heater and the microwave oven.

COPPER SHEET TRANSFERS HEAT

HEAT EXCHANGER

HOT WATER

SUN'S RAYS

ALUMINUM FOIL REFLECTS HEAT RAYS

BLACK MATERIAL ABSORBS HEAT RAYS

GLASS COVER

PUMP

COPPER TUBE

SOLAR HEATER

A solar heater traps some of the immense heat that reaches us from the sun. Like a closed car on a sunny day, the inside of a solar panel on a roof gets hot as infrared rays from the sun penetrate the glass cover. The heat passes into a copper tube, through which cool water flows. The water takes up the heat and then flows directly to a hot-water tank or (as shown) to a heat exchanger.

COLD WATER SUPPLY

MICROWAVE OVEN

A magnetron produces a beam of microwaves, which have high heating power. The beam strikes a spinning fan, which reflects the waves onto the food from all directions. They pass through the container and enter the food, heating it throughout and cooking the food evenly and quickly.

MICROWAVE HEATING

The microwaves affect the molecules in the food that have separated electric charges (1). Each wave of energy causes the molecules to align (2) and then reverse alignment (3).

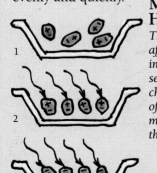

The rapid and repeated twisting increases the temperature.

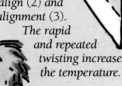

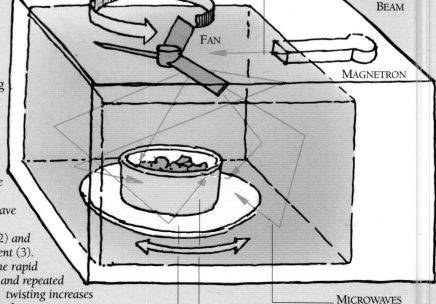

MICROWAVE BEAM

FAN

MAGNETRON

MICROWAVES

TURNTABLE

FOOD

THE VACUUM FLASK

A vacuum flask can keep drinks piping hot—or icy cold—for hours on end. It does this by preventing as much movement of heat as possible, either out of or into the flask.

Inside the flask is a double-walled container of glass or steel. The walls are silvered on the inside to reflect heat rays (which behave like light rays) so that rays cannot leave or enter the flask. Between the container walls is a vacuum, which prevents heat conduction through the walls. The container support and stopper are made of an insulating material, such as cork, that reduces conduction.

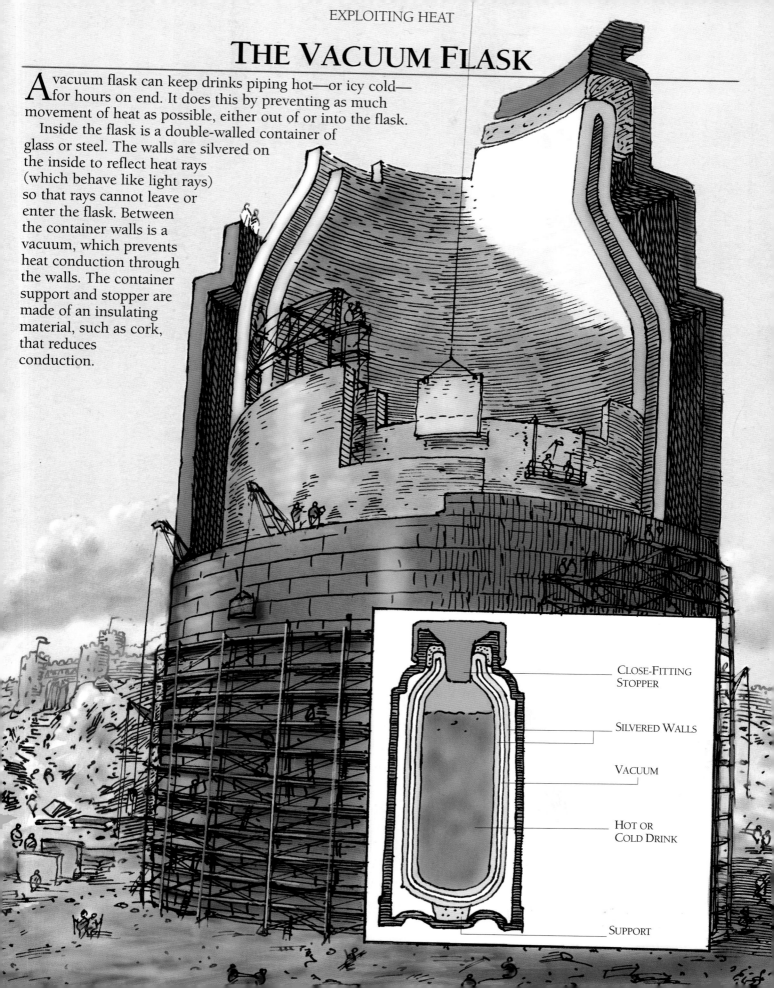

CLOSE-FITTING STOPPER

SILVERED WALLS

VACUUM

HOT OR COLD DRINK

SUPPORT

COMBUSTION MACHINES

FIRE AND WATER

Combustion, or burning, is a chemical reaction in which a fuel combines with oxygen, releasing heat. When the fuel is hydrogen, for example, molecules of hydrogen and oxygen collide and break apart, reforming as fast-moving water molecules and releasing great heat in the process. Most fuels are hydrocarbons (compounds made of carbon and hydrogen). When burned they produce carbon dioxide as well as water (as steam).

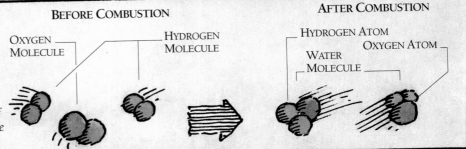

BEFORE COMBUSTION

OXYGEN MOLECULE

HYDROGEN MOLECULE

AFTER COMBUSTION

HYDROGEN ATOM

WATER MOLECULE

OXYGEN ATOM

The heat released by burning fuels is put to use in many machines. In some cases, it is the rapidly expanding gases produced by the combustion that do the work. A bullet (right) and the pistons inside a motor car engine both work in that way. In other cases, it is the heat itself that is useful. In a welding torch (right), the heat melts metals, while in a gas boiler, the heat warms up water to send to radiators and hot water faucets.

GAS BOILER

There are many different designs of gas boiler. Some heat water and send it to an insulated storage tank. Tankless boilers, like this one, heat water only when it is needed. When you turn on the hot tap, the control circuit inside the boiler opens a valve to allow gas into the burners. Cold water drawn through the pipes passes through a heat exchanger—a chamber containing the hot gases produced by combustion. The hot gases heat the water so that when it reaches the tap it is piping hot.

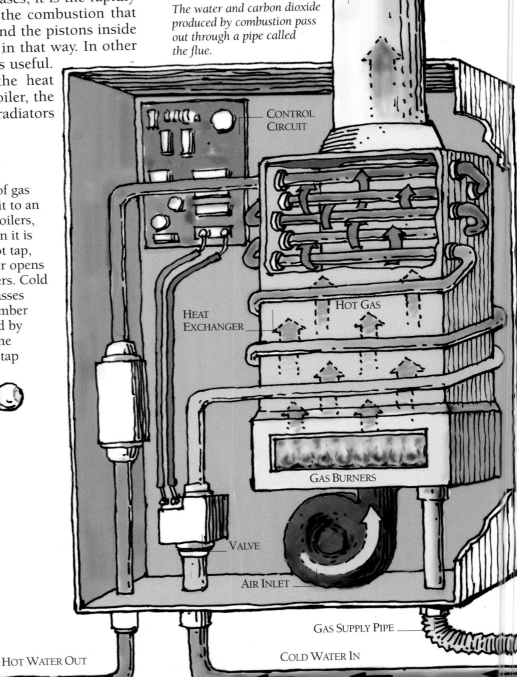

FLUE
The water and carbon dioxide produced by combustion pass out through a pipe called the flue.

CONTROL CIRCUIT

HOT GAS

HEAT EXCHANGER

GAS BURNERS

VALVE

AIR INLET

GAS SUPPLY PIPE

HOT WATER OUT

COLD WATER IN

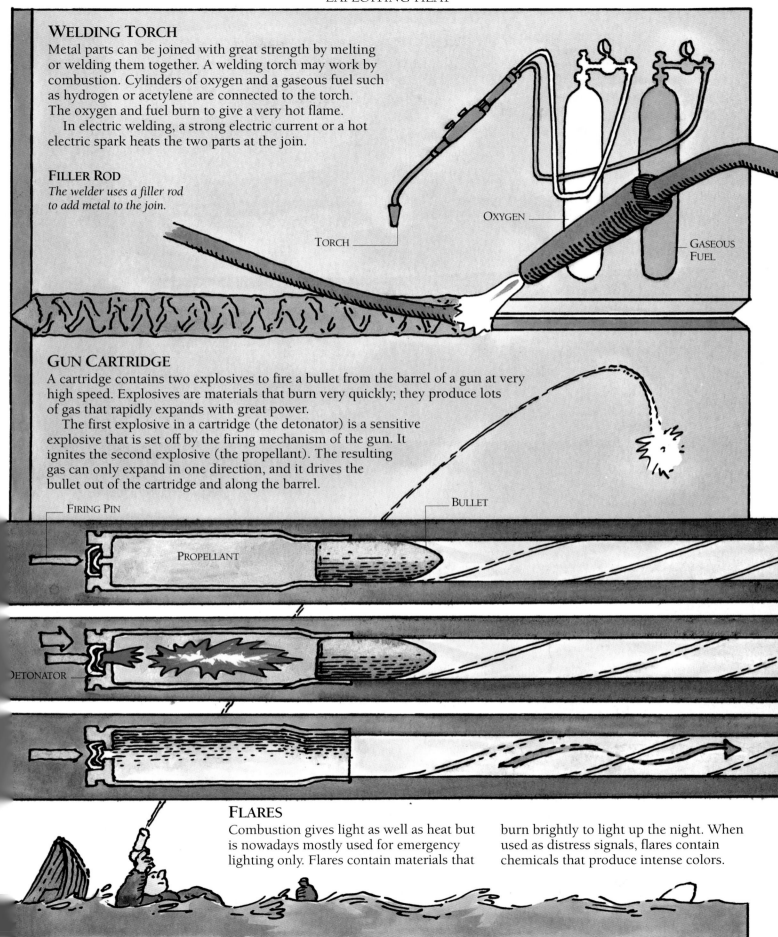

WELDING TORCH

Metal parts can be joined with great strength by melting or welding them together. A welding torch may work by combustion. Cylinders of oxygen and a gaseous fuel such as hydrogen or acetylene are connected to the torch. The oxygen and fuel burn to give a very hot flame.

In electric welding, a strong electric current or a hot electric spark heats the two parts at the join.

FILLER ROD

The welder uses a filler rod to add metal to the join.

OXYGEN

TORCH

GASEOUS FUEL

GUN CARTRIDGE

A cartridge contains two explosives to fire a bullet from the barrel of a gun at very high speed. Explosives are materials that burn very quickly; they produce lots of gas that rapidly expands with great power.

The first explosive in a cartridge (the detonator) is a sensitive explosive that is set off by the firing mechanism of the gun. It ignites the second explosive (the propellant). The resulting gas can only expand in one direction, and it drives the bullet out of the cartridge and along the barrel.

FIRING PIN

BULLET

PROPELLANT

DETONATOR

FLARES

Combustion gives light as well as heat but is nowadays mostly used for emergency lighting only. Flares contain materials that burn brightly to light up the night. When used as distress signals, flares contain chemicals that produce intense colors.

BLAST FURNACE AND STEEL CONVERTER

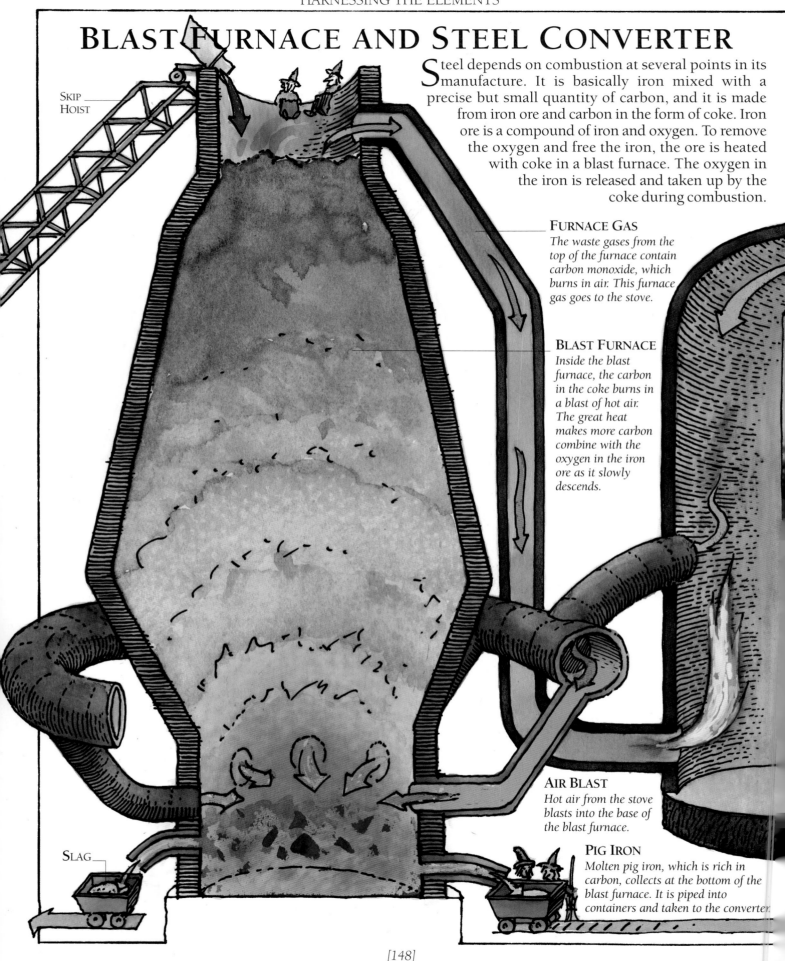

Steel depends on combustion at several points in its manufacture. It is basically iron mixed with a precise but small quantity of carbon, and it is made from iron ore and carbon in the form of coke. Iron ore is a compound of iron and oxygen. To remove the oxygen and free the iron, the ore is heated with coke in a blast furnace. The oxygen in the iron is released and taken up by the coke during combustion.

SKIP HOIST

FURNACE GAS
The waste gases from the top of the furnace contain carbon monoxide, which burns in air. This furnace gas goes to the stove.

BLAST FURNACE
Inside the blast furnace, the carbon in the coke burns in a blast of hot air. The great heat makes more carbon combine with the oxygen in the iron ore as it slowly descends.

AIR BLAST
Hot air from the stove blasts into the base of the blast furnace.

PIG IRON
Molten pig iron, which is rich in carbon, collects at the bottom of the blast furnace. It is piped into containers and taken to the converter.

SLAG

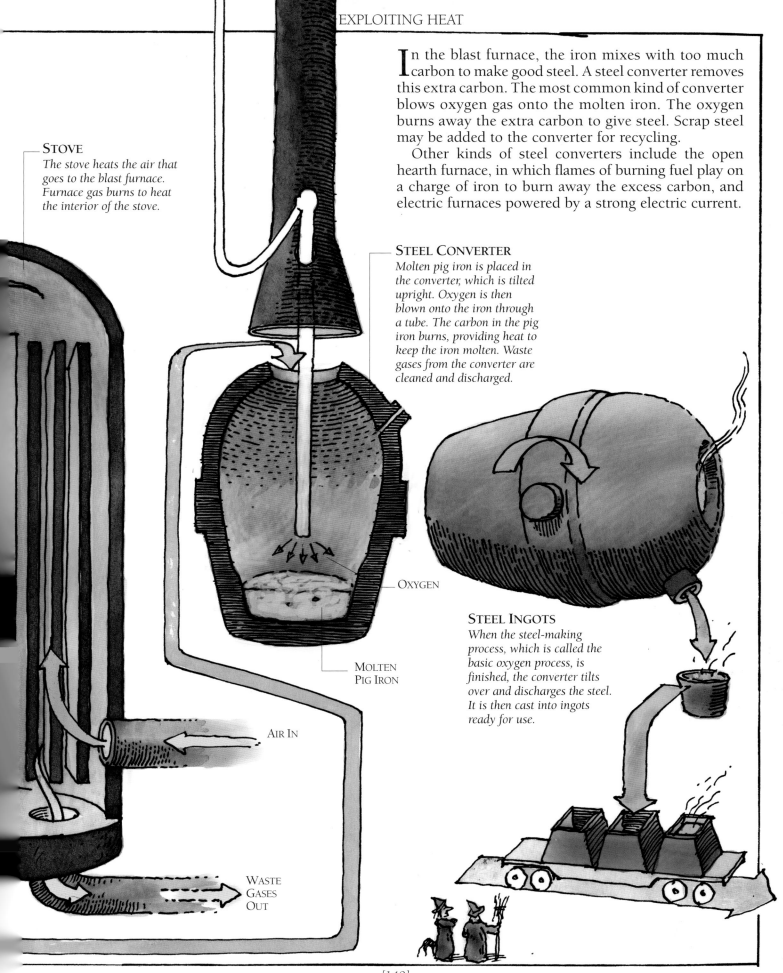

In the blast furnace, the iron mixes with too much carbon to make good steel. A steel converter removes this extra carbon. The most common kind of converter blows oxygen gas onto the molten iron. The oxygen burns away the extra carbon to give steel. Scrap steel may be added to the converter for recycling.

Other kinds of steel converters include the open hearth furnace, in which flames of burning fuel play on a charge of iron to burn away the excess carbon, and electric furnaces powered by a strong electric current.

STOVE
The stove heats the air that goes to the blast furnace. Furnace gas burns to heat the interior of the stove.

STEEL CONVERTER
Molten pig iron is placed in the converter, which is tilted upright. Oxygen is then blown onto the iron through a tube. The carbon in the pig iron burns, providing heat to keep the iron molten. Waste gases from the converter are cleaned and discharged.

OXYGEN

MOLTEN
PIG IRON

STEEL INGOTS
When the steel-making process, which is called the basic oxygen process, is finished, the converter tilts over and discharges the steel. It is then cast into ingots ready for use.

AIR IN

WASTE
GASES
OUT

ELECTRIC HEAT

No form of heating is as convenient as electric heating. It's available at the click of a switch and is totally clean to use, although its generation may very often produce polluting waste through combustion and nuclear fission (see p. 168).

Like all other sources of heat, electricity hastens the motion of molecules, giving them extra energy, which raises their temperature. When an electric current flows along a wire, billions of tiny particles called electrons move among the metal atoms in the wire. The electrons are smaller than the atoms, and jostle the atoms as they pass. The vibration of the metal atoms increases, and the wire gets hotter.

Many machines contain electric heating elements that work in this way. Heat may radiate from the element, as in an electric fire, or the element may be enclosed in an electrically insulating container that heats water, for example, by conduction and convection.

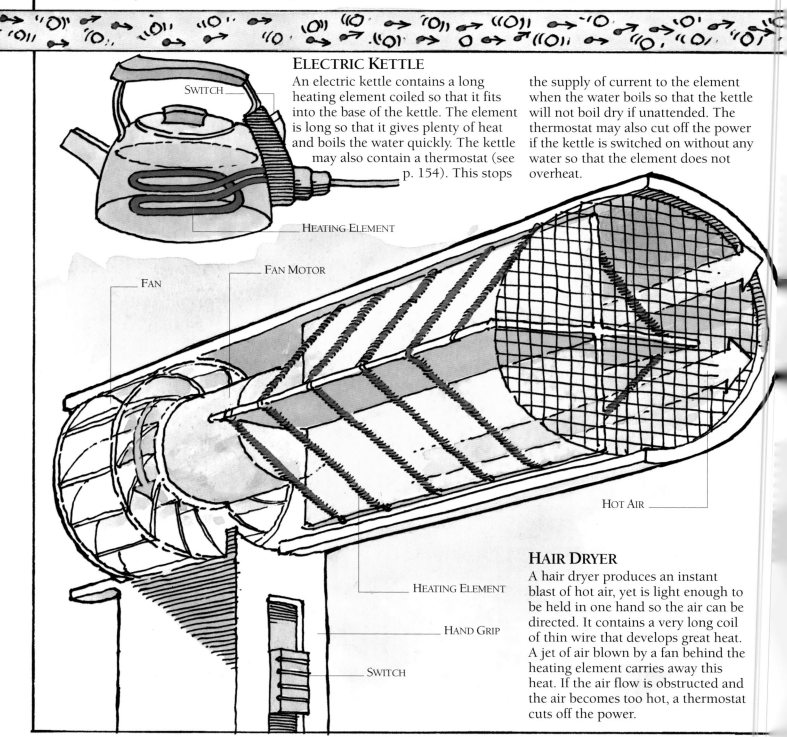

ELECTRIC KETTLE

SWITCH

HEATING ELEMENT

An electric kettle contains a long heating element coiled so that it fits into the base of the kettle. The element is long so that it gives plenty of heat and boils the water quickly. The kettle may also contain a thermostat (see p. 154). This stops the supply of current to the element when the water boils so that the kettle will not boil dry if unattended. The thermostat may also cut off the power if the kettle is switched on without any water so that the element does not overheat.

FAN

FAN MOTOR

HOT AIR

HEATING ELEMENT

HAND GRIP

SWITCH

HAIR DRYER

A hair dryer produces an instant blast of hot air, yet is light enough to be held in one hand so the air can be directed. It contains a very long coil of thin wire that develops great heat. A jet of air blown by a fan behind the heating element carries away this heat. If the air flow is obstructed and the air becomes too hot, a thermostat cuts off the power.

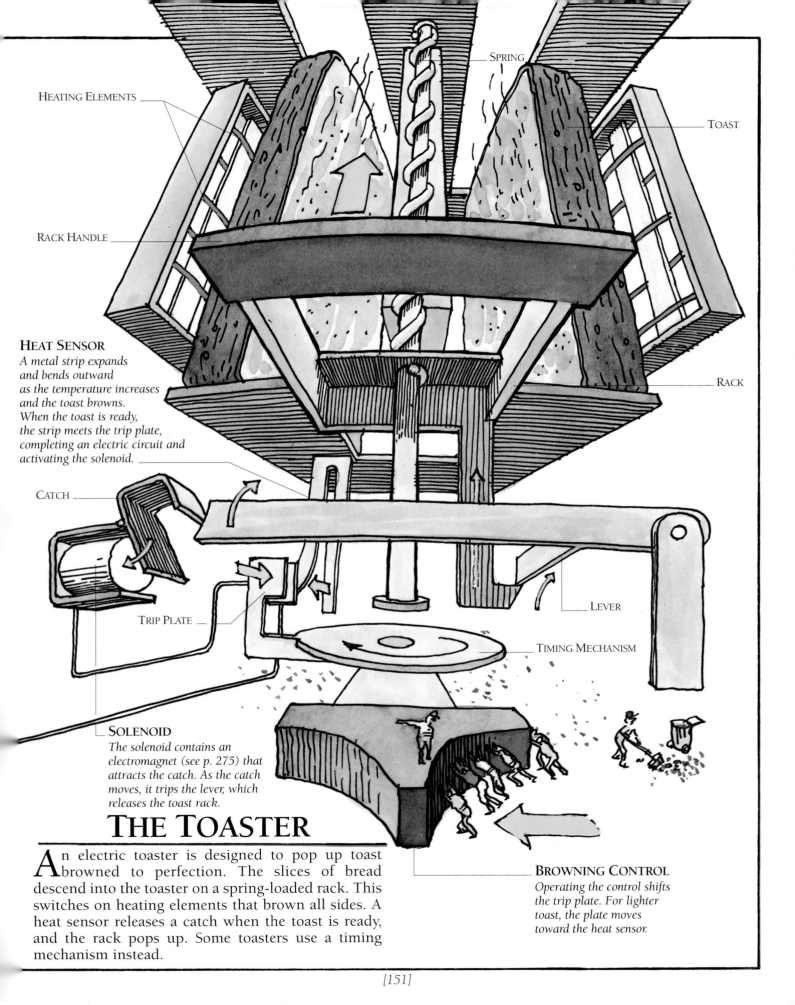

SPRING

HEATING ELEMENTS

TOAST

RACK HANDLE

RACK

HEAT SENSOR
*A metal strip expands
and bends outward
as the temperature increases
and the toast browns.
When the toast is ready,
the strip meets the trip plate,
completing an electric circuit and
activating the solenoid.*

CATCH

TRIP PLATE

LEVER

TIMING MECHANISM

SOLENOID
*The solenoid contains an
electromagnet (see p. 275) that
attracts the catch. As the catch
moves, it trips the lever, which
releases the toast rack.*

THE TOASTER

An electric toaster is designed to pop up toast
browned to perfection. The slices of bread
descend into the toaster on a spring-loaded rack. This
switches on heating elements that brown all sides. A
heat sensor releases a catch when the toast is ready,
and the rack pops up. Some toasters use a timing
mechanism instead.

BROWNING CONTROL
*Operating the control shifts
the trip plate. For lighter
toast, the plate moves
toward the heat sensor.*

REFRIGERATOR

The refrigerator is a machine that makes heat move. It takes heat out of the inside, which in losing its heat becomes cold. The refrigerator moves this heat to the outside, where the heat flows into the air and is lost. Refrigerators work by evaporation. When a liquid turns to vapor, it loses heat and gets colder. This is because the molecules of vapor need energy to move and leave the liquid. This energy comes from the liquid; the molecules left behind have less energy and so the liquid becomes colder.

COMPRESSOR

An electric refrigerator contains a compressor to move a refrigerant (a volatile liquid) around a pipe. The compressor pumps the liquid from the evaporator into the condenser. It then returns through the expansion valve.

EVAPORATOR

The refrigerant leaves the expansion valve at low pressure, causing it to evaporate inside the pipe and get cold. The evaporator is inside the refrigerator and heat flows into the evaporator, making the refrigerator cold.

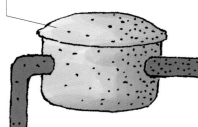

EXPANSION VALVE

CAR COOLING SYSTEM

Most cars have water-cooled engines. A pump (see p. 125) drives the water around channels inside the engine. The hot water then passes through the thermostat to the radiator, where it loses its heat to the air before returning to the pump. In some cars, the hot water also flows through the car's heater.

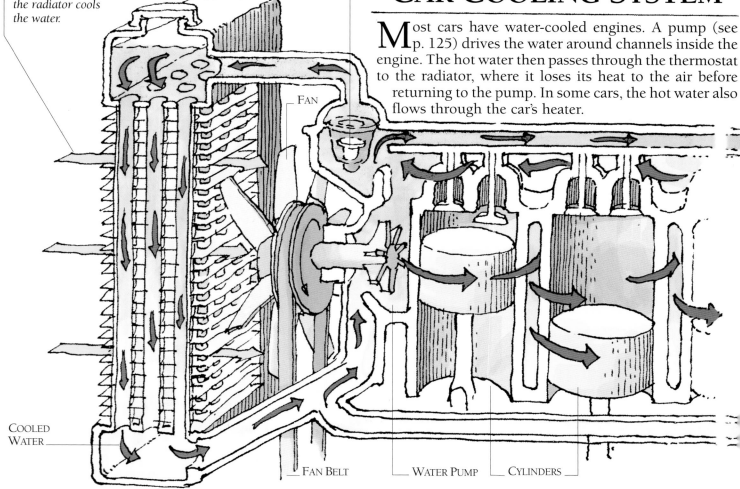

RADIATOR
Air blowing through the radiator cools the water.

THERMOSTAT
(SEE P. 154)

FAN

COOLED WATER

FAN BELT   WATER PUMP   CYLINDERS

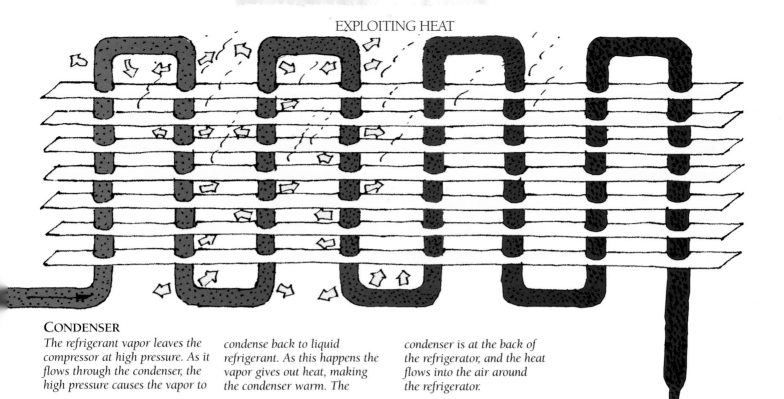

CONDENSER

The refrigerant vapor leaves the compressor at high pressure. As it flows through the condenser, the high pressure causes the vapor to condense back to liquid refrigerant. As this happens the vapor gives out heat, making the condenser warm. The condenser is at the back of the refrigerator, and the heat flows into the air around the refrigerator.

HEATER

The car heater may be part of the cooling system. It contains a heat exchanger, in which the hot water from the engine heats air driven by a fan in the passenger compartment. The warm air then returns to various parts of the passenger compartment.

AIR CONDITIONER

This machine works in the same basic way as a refrigerator. A compressor circulates a refrigerant from an evaporator through a condenser and expansion valve and back to the evaporator. The evaporator is placed over a fan that extracts hot and humid air from the room. It takes heat from the air, making its moisture condense into water droplets. The cool dry air then returns to the room. A fan removes the heat from the condenser outside the room.

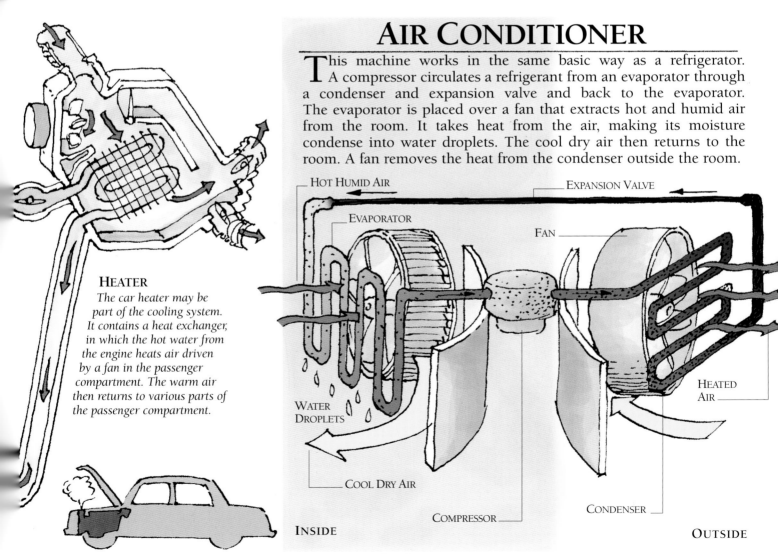

HOT HUMID AIR

EXPANSION VALVE

EVAPORATOR

FAN

WATER DROPLETS

COOL DRY AIR

COMPRESSOR

HEATED AIR

CONDENSER

INSIDE

OUTSIDE

THERMOSTATS

Thermostats are devices that regulate heaters and cooling machines, repeatedly turning them on and off so that they maintain the required temperature. They work by expansion and contraction. As something heats up, its molecules move further apart. The object expands in size. When the object cools, the force pulling the molecules together reasserts itself; the molecules close ranks and the object contracts.

EXPANSION   CONTRACTION

BIMETAL THERMOSTAT

This common thermostat contains a strip of two different metals, often brass and iron. The metals expand and contract by different amounts. The bending produced by heating or cooling the thermostat can be used to activate a heater switch.

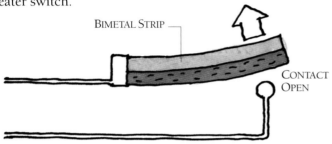

BIMETAL STRIP

CONTACT OPEN

SWITCH OPEN

The strip bends as it gets hotter, opening the contact. The current stops flowing and the heater switches itself off.

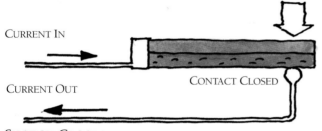

CURRENT IN

CURRENT OUT   CONTACT CLOSED

SWITCH CLOSED

The strip bends back as it cools and makes contact. The current passes and the heater switches itself back on.

ROD THERMOSTAT

Gas ovens and heaters often contain rod thermostats. The control is connected to a steel rod housed in a brass tube. The tube expands or contracts more than the rod, which closes and opens a valve in the flow of gas.

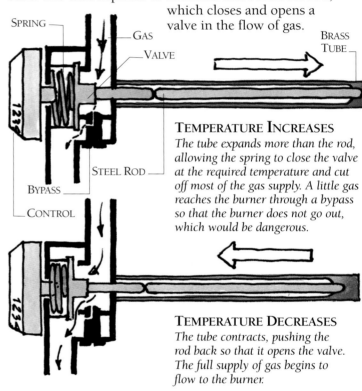

SPRING   GAS

VALVE

BRASS TUBE

STEEL ROD

BYPASS

CONTROL

TEMPERATURE INCREASES

The tube expands more than the rod, allowing the spring to close the valve at the required temperature and cut off most of the gas supply. A little gas reaches the burner through a bypass so that the burner does not go out, which would be dangerous.

TEMPERATURE DECREASES

The tube contracts, pushing the rod back so that it opens the valve. The full supply of gas begins to flow to the burner.

CAR THERMOSTAT

The thermostat in a car cooling system (see p. 152) controls the flow of cooling water to the radiator. Most car thermostats contain wax, which melts when the water gets hot. The wax expands, opening a valve in the water flow. A spring closes the valve when the water cools and the wax solidifies.

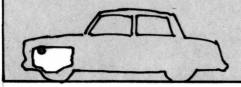

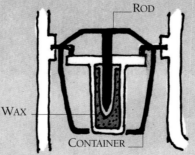

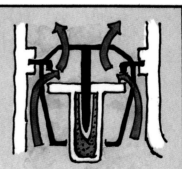

ROD

WAX

CONTAINER

VALVE CLOSED

When the engine is cool, the rod is seated in the wax inside the brass container.

VALVE OPEN

The wax melts and expands, pushing against the rod and forcing the container down.

THERM

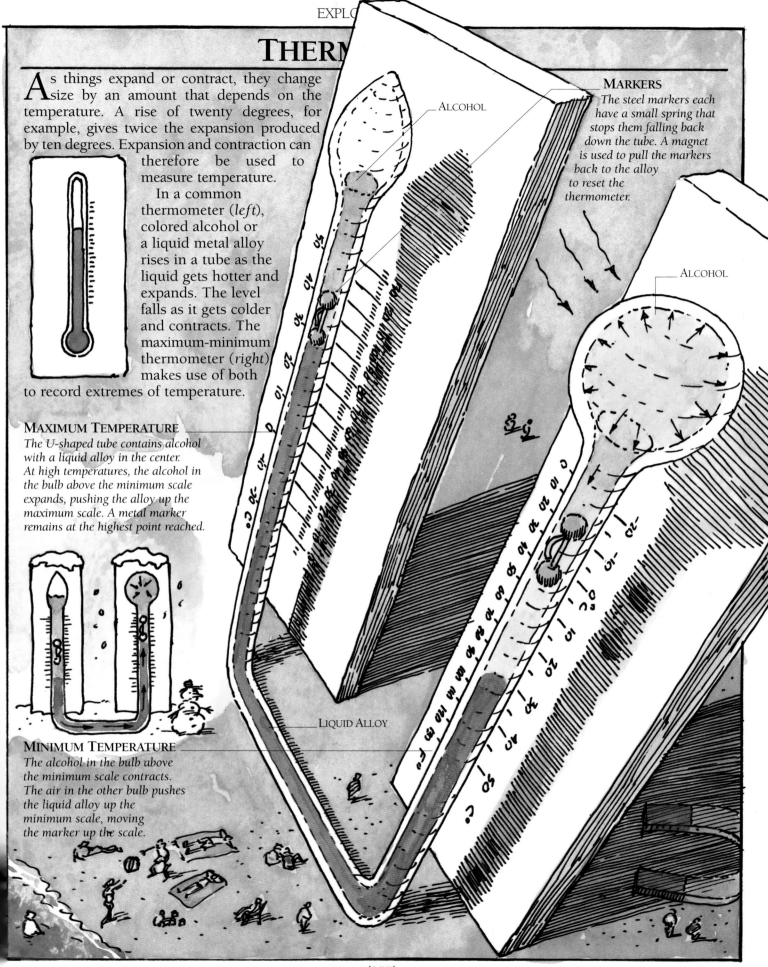

As things expand or contract, they change size by an amount that depends on the temperature. A rise of twenty degrees, for example, gives twice the expansion produced by ten degrees. Expansion and contraction can therefore be used to measure temperature.

In a common thermometer (*left*), colored alcohol or a liquid metal alloy rises in a tube as the liquid gets hotter and expands. The level falls as it gets colder and contracts. The maximum-minimum thermometer (*right*) makes use of both to record extremes of temperature.

ALCOHOL

MARKERS
The steel markers each have a small spring that stops them falling back down the tube. A magnet is used to pull the markers back to the alloy to reset the thermometer.

ALCOHOL

MAXIMUM TEMPERATURE
The U-shaped tube contains alcohol with a liquid alloy in the center. At high temperatures, the alcohol in the bulb above the minimum scale expands, pushing the alloy up the maximum scale. A metal marker remains at the highest point reached.

LIQUID ALLOY

MINIMUM TEMPERATURE
The alcohol in the bulb above the minimum scale contracts. The air in the other bulb pushes the liquid alloy up the minimum scale, moving the marker up the scale.

GASOLINE ENGINE

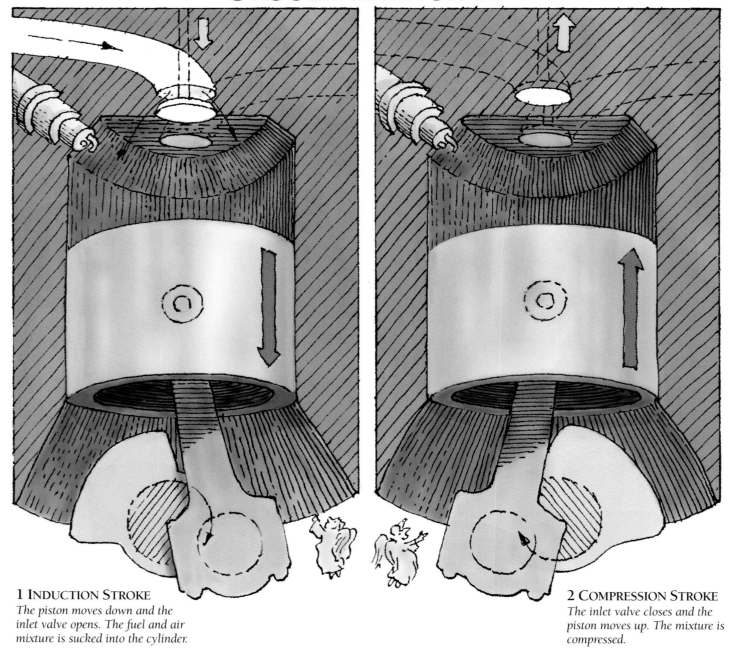

1 INDUCTION STROKE
The piston moves down and the inlet valve opens. The fuel and air mixture is sucked into the cylinder.

2 COMPRESSION STROKE
The inlet valve closes and the piston moves up. The mixture is compressed.

In the gasoline engine, we put heat to use by converting it into motive power. A gasoline engine is often called an internal combustion engine, but this means only that the fuel burns inside the engine. The jet engine and rocket engine are also internal combustion engines.

A gasoline engine burns a mixture of gasoline and air in a cylinder containing a piston. The heat produced causes the air to expand and force down the piston, which turns a crankshaft linked to the wheels.

Most cars have a four-stroke engine. A stroke is one movement of the piston, either up or down. In a four-stroke engine, the engine repeats a cycle of actions (shown above) in which the piston moves four times.

Many light vehicles, such as motorcycles, have two-stroke engines. This kind of engine is simpler in construction than a four-stroke engine, but not as powerful. A two-stroke engine has no valves. Instead there are three ports in the side of the cylinder that the piston opens and closes as it moves up and down. A diesel engine is similar to the gasoline engine, but has no spark plugs (see pp. 140-41).

The exhaust gases that leave the engine contain harmful polluting gases, and may first pass through a catalytic converter. This converts the harmful substances to harmless products. The cleaned-up gases finally go to the silencer before leaving the exhaust.

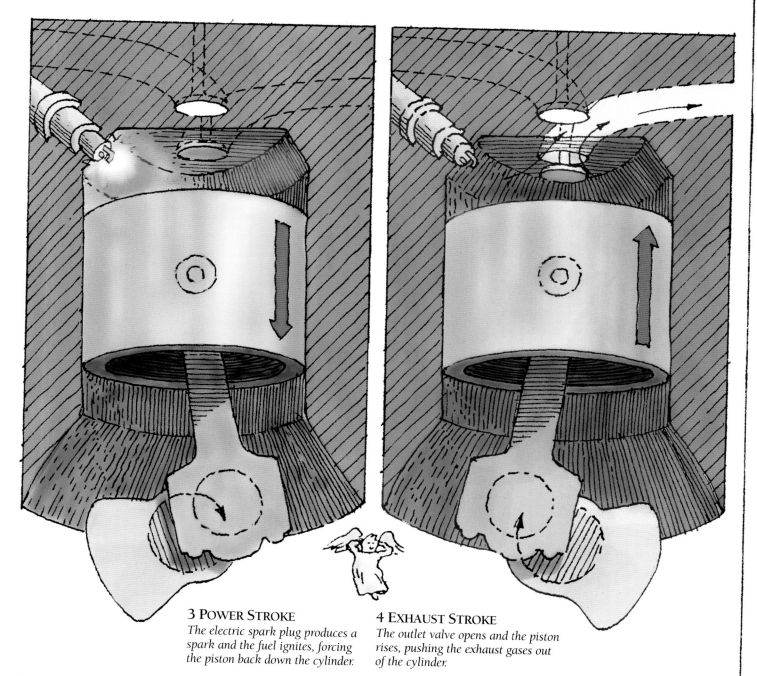

3 POWER STROKE
The electric spark plug produces a spark and the fuel ignites, forcing the piston back down the cylinder.

4 EXHAUST STROKE
The outlet valve opens and the piston rises, pushing the exhaust gases out of the cylinder.

CATALYTIC CONVERTER
The harmful gases include carbon monoxide, nitrogen oxides, and hydrocarbon fuel. In the converter, surfaces coated with catalyst metals change the gases into carbon dioxide, nitrogen, and water vapor. The metals are platinum, palladium, and rhodium.

SILENCER
The exhaust gases leave the engine at high pressure, and would produce intolerable noise if allowed to escape directly. The silencer contains a series of plates with holes, which reduce the pressure of the gases so that they leave the exhaust pipe quietly.

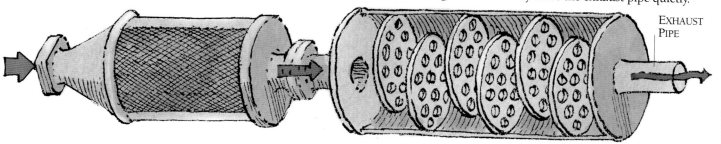

EXHAUST PIPE

HYBRID CARS

A hybrid car has both a gasoline or diesel engine and an electric motor. A conventional motor car is powered by an internal combustion engine (see pp. 156-57). Most conventional cars burn fuel even when they are idling—for example, when they are stopped at traffic lights. And when they brake, all their kinetic energy (the energy of their motion) is lost as heat in the brake pads (see p. 86). An electric car is powered by a battery instead of an engine, and is more efficient: it uses no power when stopped at traffic lights, and

it can retain some of its kinetic energy by a process known as regenerative braking, which uses that energy to charge the battery. Although the battery needs to be charged every day, electric cars can travel up to around 90 miles (150 km) before needing a recharge. Hybrid cars provide the best of both worlds. There are two main types. In a parallel hybrid, the engine can take over when the batteries are low. In a series hybrid, the engine never drives the wheels, but acts only as an onboard electric generator (see pp. 284-85).

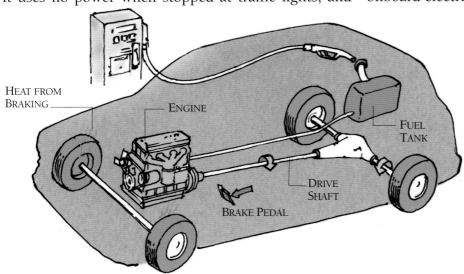

HEAT FROM BRAKING

ENGINE

FUEL TANK

DRIVE SHAFT

BRAKE PEDAL

FILLING UP
Gasoline and diesel produce carbon dioxide when they burn, which contributes to global warming. A hybrid car produces less carbon dioxide and less air pollution.

CONVENTIONAL CAR
In most cars, a gasoline or diesel engine powers the drive shaft that turns the wheels. Energy is provided by filling up at a fuel station. These cars have a long range before they need refueling, but they can be very inefficient, wasting energy when braking to slow down and when idling. Some cars are now fitted with a stop-start engine, which automatically switches off when the car is stationary.

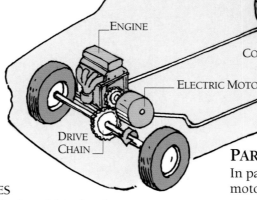

FUEL TANK

BATTERY

ENGINE

COMPUTER

ELECTRIC MOTOR

DRIVE CHAIN

PLUG-IN POINT

ENGINE OR MOTOR
In a parallel hybrid, both the engine and the electric motor are connected to the drive chain and can turn the wheels. Most hybrid cars have front-wheel drive—the drive chain turns the front wheels, not the back— while rear-wheel drive is more common for conventional cars.

PARALLEL HYBRID
In parallel hybrids, the engine and the electric motor can both turn the wheels. An onboard computer monitors the battery's charge level, and decides when the engine should take over. As with other electric vehicles, most hybrids can also be plugged in overnight, to charge their battery.

CONVENTIONAL BRAKES
When the driver presses the brake pedal to slow the car or bring it to a halt, friction in the brake pads and brake linings converts the car's kinetic energy to heat.

CAR STOPS

ENERGY IS LOST AS HEAT

DRIVER BRAKES

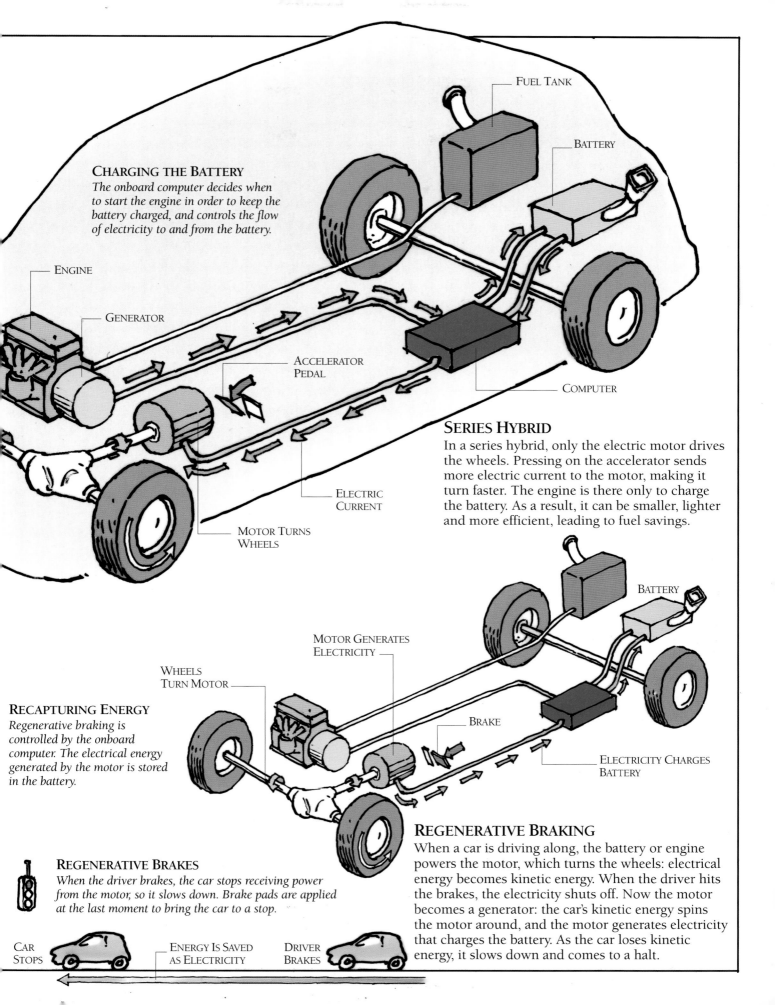

CHARGING THE BATTERY
The onboard computer decides when to start the engine in order to keep the battery charged, and controls the flow of electricity to and from the battery.

FUEL TANK

BATTERY

ENGINE

GENERATOR

ACCELERATOR PEDAL

COMPUTER

ELECTRIC CURRENT

MOTOR TURNS WHEELS

SERIES HYBRID
In a series hybrid, only the electric motor drives the wheels. Pressing on the accelerator sends more electric current to the motor, making it turn faster. The engine is there only to charge the battery. As a result, it can be smaller, lighter and more efficient, leading to fuel savings.

BATTERY

MOTOR GENERATES ELECTRICITY

WHEELS TURN MOTOR

BRAKE

RECAPTURING ENERGY
Regenerative braking is controlled by the onboard computer. The electrical energy generated by the motor is stored in the battery.

ELECTRICITY CHARGES BATTERY

REGENERATIVE BRAKING
When a car is driving along, the battery or engine powers the motor, which turns the wheels: electrical energy becomes kinetic energy. When the driver hits the brakes, the electricity shuts off. Now the motor becomes a generator: the car's kinetic energy spins the motor around, and the motor generates electricity that charges the battery. As the car loses kinetic energy, it slows down and comes to a halt.

REGENERATIVE BRAKES
When the driver brakes, the car stops receiving power from the motor, so it slows down. Brake pads are applied at the last moment to bring the car to a stop.

CAR STOPS

ENERGY IS SAVED AS ELECTRICITY

DRIVER BRAKES

STEAM POWER

The first engine to make use of heat to drive a machine was the steam engine. It employed steam raised in a boiler to drive a piston up and down a cylinder. This engine was vital in the development of the Industrial Revolution, but is now obsolete.

However, the age of steam is by no means over, because steam power provides us with the bulk of our electricity. Thermal power stations, which burn fuels such as coal (shown here) and oil, contain steam turbines to drive the electricity generators—as do nuclear power stations (see pp. 172-73). All power stations are designed to pass as much energy as possible from the fuel to the turbines.

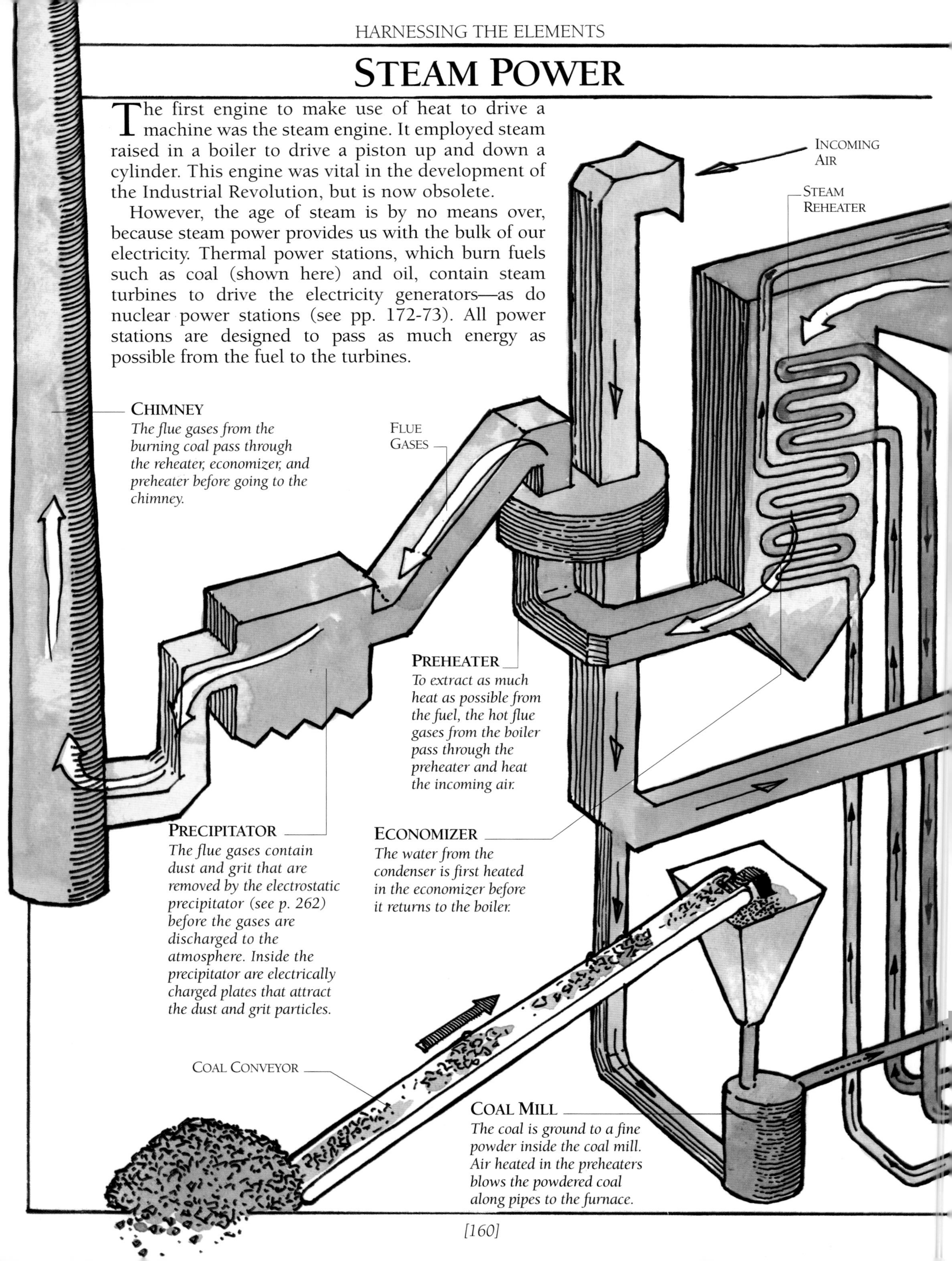

INCOMING AIR

STEAM REHEATER

CHIMNEY
The flue gases from the burning coal pass through the reheater, economizer, and preheater before going to the chimney.

FLUE GASES

PREHEATER
To extract as much heat as possible from the fuel, the hot flue gases from the boiler pass through the preheater and heat the incoming air.

PRECIPITATOR
The flue gases contain dust and grit that are removed by the electrostatic precipitator (see p. 262) before the gases are discharged to the atmosphere. Inside the precipitator are electrically charged plates that attract the dust and grit particles.

ECONOMIZER
The water from the condenser is first heated in the economizer before it returns to the boiler.

COAL CONVEYOR

COAL MILL
The coal is ground to a fine powder inside the coal mill. Air heated in the preheaters blows the powdered coal along pipes to the furnace.

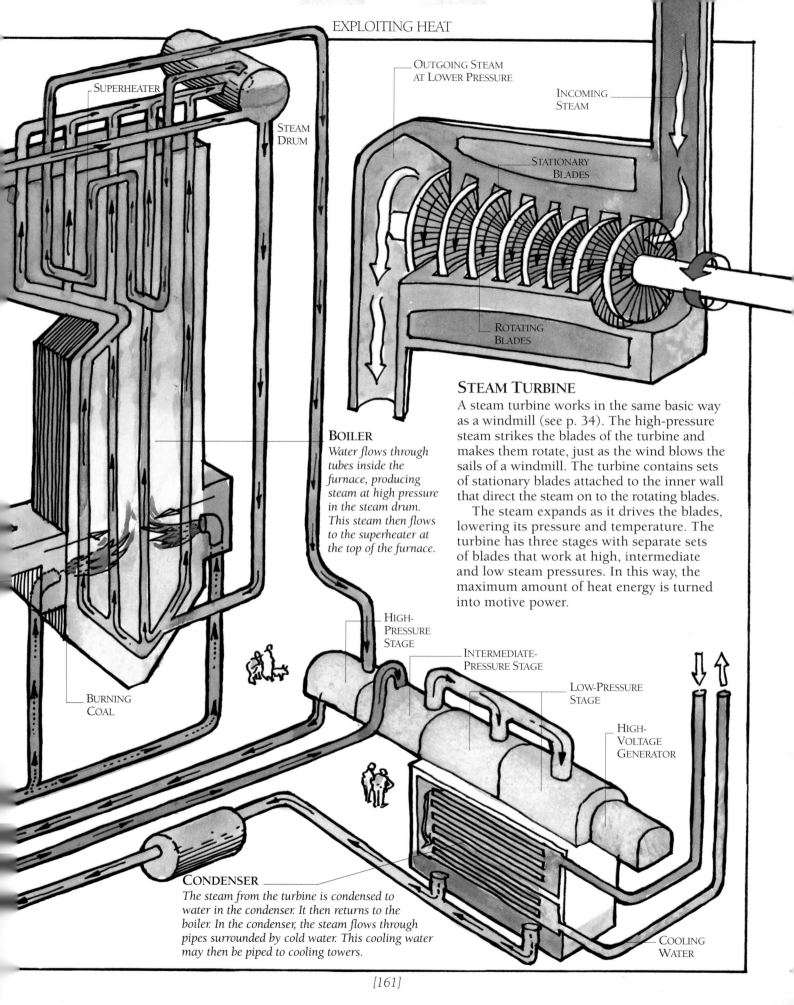

SUPERHEATER

STEAM DRUM

OUTGOING STEAM AT LOWER PRESSURE

INCOMING STEAM

STATIONARY BLADES

ROTATING BLADES

STEAM TURBINE

A steam turbine works in the same basic way as a windmill (see p. 34). The high-pressure steam strikes the blades of the turbine and makes them rotate, just as the wind blows the sails of a windmill. The turbine contains sets of stationary blades attached to the inner wall that direct the steam on to the rotating blades.

The steam expands as it drives the blades, lowering its pressure and temperature. The turbine has three stages with separate sets of blades that work at high, intermediate and low steam pressures. In this way, the maximum amount of heat energy is turned into motive power.

BOILER
Water flows through tubes inside the furnace, producing steam at high pressure in the steam drum. This steam then flows to the superheater at the top of the furnace.

BURNING COAL

HIGH-PRESSURE STAGE

INTERMEDIATE-PRESSURE STAGE

LOW-PRESSURE STAGE

HIGH-VOLTAGE GENERATOR

CONDENSER
The steam from the turbine is condensed to water in the condenser. It then returns to the boiler. In the condenser, the steam flows through pipes surrounded by cold water. This cooling water may then be piped to cooling towers.

COOLING WATER

THE JET ENGINE

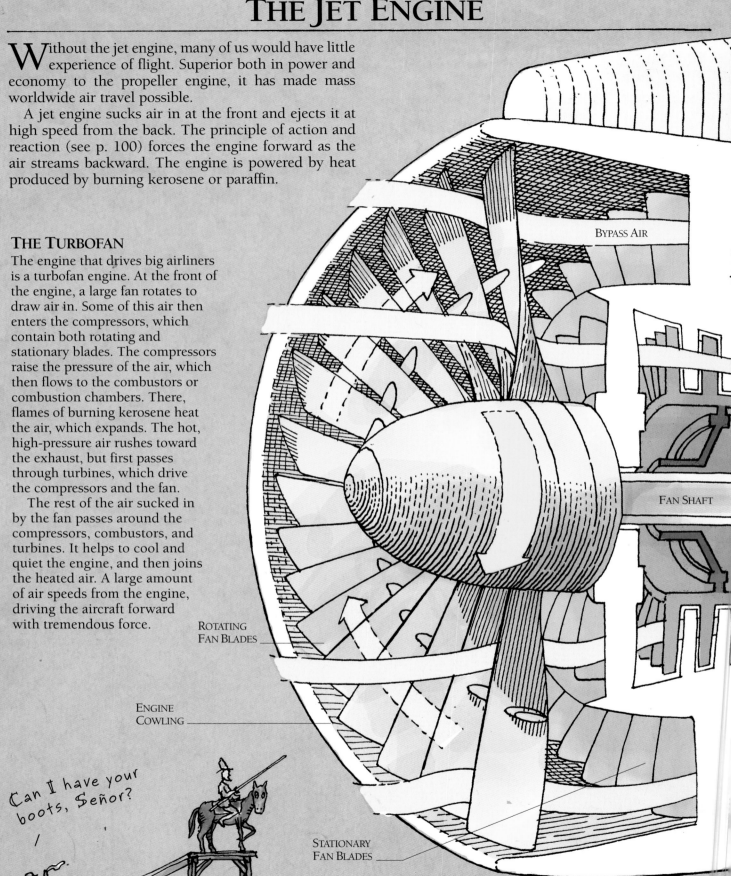

ithout the jet engine, many of us would have little experience of flight. Superior both in power and economy to the propeller engine, it has made mass worldwide air travel possible.

A jet engine sucks air in at the front and ejects it at high speed from the back. The principle of action and reaction (see p. 100) forces the engine forward as the air streams backward. The engine is powered by heat produced by burning kerosene or paraffin.

THE TURBOFAN

The engine that drives big airliners is a turbofan engine. At the front of the engine, a large fan rotates to draw air in. Some of this air then enters the compressors, which contain both rotating and stationary blades. The compressors raise the pressure of the air, which then flows to the combustors or combustion chambers. There, flames of burning kerosene heat the air, which expands. The hot, high-pressure air rushes toward the exhaust, but first passes through turbines, which drive the compressors and the fan.

The rest of the air sucked in by the fan passes around the compressors, combustors, and turbines. It helps to cool and quiet the engine, and then joins the heated air. A large amount of air speeds from the engine, driving the aircraft forward with tremendous force.

BYPASS AIR

FAN SHAFT

ROTATING
FAN BLADES

ENGINE
COWLING

STATIONARY
FAN BLADES

Can I have your boots, Señor?

COMPRESSOR SHAFTS

HEATED AIR

EXHAUST

COMBUSTOR

COMPRESSOR TURBINES

COMPRESSORS

FAN TURBINE

BYPASS DUCT

OUTGOING BYPASS AIR

ROCKET ENGINES

The rocket is the simplest and most powerful kind of heat engine. It burns fuel in a combustion chamber with an open end. The hot gases produced expand greatly and rush from the open end or exhaust at high speed. The rocket moves forward by action and reaction (see p. 100) as the gases exert a powerful force on the chamber walls.

Rockets can work in space because, unlike other heat engines, their fuel does not require air for combustion. It burns without the need for an external oxygen supply.

PAPER CONE

COLORED STARS

EXPLOSIVE CHARGE

CLAY

ROLLED PAPER TUBE

PROPELLANT

FIREWORK ROCKET

Firework rockets are the simplest form of heat engine. They are packed with a propellant, a powder that burns fiercely. The smoke and hot gases stream from the base and drive the rocket upward, while the long stick keeps the rocket's flight straight. The propellant is slowly consumed by combustion, and finally the burning powder ignites an explosive charge that expels the glowing stars.

FUSE

STICK

SOLID-FUEL ROCKET

Many spacecraft are launched by solid-fuel boosters, which are rocket engines that, like firework rockets, contain a solid propellant. A circular or star-shaped channel runs down the center of the propellant. The propellant burns at the surface of this channel, so the channel is the combustion chamber. A solid-fuel booster develops more power if the channel is star-shaped. This is because the channel's area is larger, and a greater volume of hot gases is produced. Solid-fuel rockets can produce great power, but once ignited they cannot be shut down; they fly until all the propellant has burned.

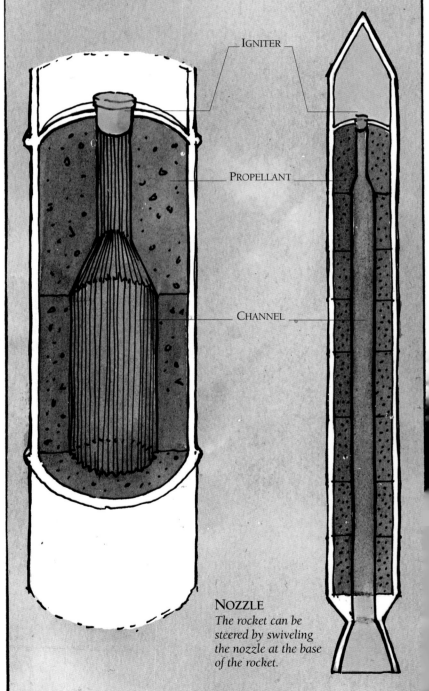

IGNITER

PROPELLANT

CHANNEL

NOZZLE

The rocket can be steered by swiveling the nozzle at the base of the rocket.

LIQUID-FUEL ROCKET

Spacecraft that require repeated firings of their engines, often for maneuvering in space, have liquid-fuel rocket engines. Unlike solid propellants, liquid propellants are fed to the combustion chamber and are burned for as long as necessary. The propellants consist of two liquids, usually called the fuel and the oxidizer. Liquid hydrogen and liquid oxygen are often used. Liquid fuels are usually more energy-rich than solid ones, so liquid-fueled rockets can produce more thrust from the same mass of fuel.

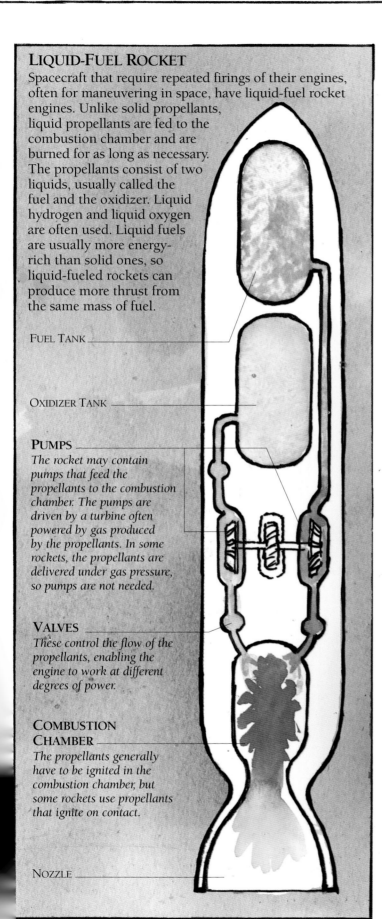

FUEL TANK

OXIDIZER TANK

PUMPS
The rocket may contain pumps that feed the propellants to the combustion chamber. The pumps are driven by a turbine often powered by gas produced by the propellants. In some rockets, the propellants are delivered under gas pressure, so pumps are not needed.

VALVES
These control the flow of the propellants, enabling the engine to work at different degrees of power.

COMBUSTION CHAMBER
The propellants generally have to be ignited in the combustion chamber, but some rockets use propellants that ignite on contact.

NOZZLE

SOLID-FUEL BOOSTERS
Two rocket boosters provide most of the thrust Ariane 5 needs to accelerate off the launch pad. Once the boosters are spent, they are dropped into the ocean to reduce weight.

ARIANE 5

The European Space Agency's Ariane 5 launcher uses both liquid- and solid-fuel rockets to lift satellites and other payloads (cargo) into orbit around Earth. The main engine is a liquid-fuel rocket that uses liquid hydrogen as a fuel and liquid oxygen as the oxidizer. The solid-fuel booster rockets are jettisoned about two minutes after launch.

PAYLOAD
Ariane 5 typically carries two or three satellites inside the top part of the main body. Once the rocket has left Earth's atmosphere, the payload is released and the main body casing is jettisoned into space.

SOLID FUEL BOOSTER

MAIN ENGINE

COMBUSTION CHAMBER
Liquid hydrogen and liquid oxygen are stored in very cold conditions and under very high pressure, to prevent them from turning into gases. They mix and burn inside the main engine's combustion chamber.

NUCLEAR POWER

ON THE GIFT THAT KEPT ON GIVING

During my travels, I once became snowbound in a town that had completely exhausted its fuel supply. On one bitterly cold morning, I awoke to learn that an enormous concrete mammoth had somehow appeared outside the gate. An excited crowd quickly surrounded it, and my professional opinion was sought.

Attached to the mammoth's long flexible trunk I found a note which informed me that this gigantic machine was a gift from a friend. If treated properly, the note continued, the mammoth would give all the heat, in the form of steam, that the town would ever need. In return, all the machine required was plenty of water and an occasional pellet from a bag provided. Scribbled at the bottom of the note was a reminder to bury in heavy containers all the waste material that discharged periodically from the rear of the contraption. The note was not signed.

NUCLEAR REACTIONS

The mechanical mammoth is able to supply such colossal amounts of energy from so little fuel because it runs on nuclear power. Inside is a nuclear reactor that produces heat—but that heat is not generated by burning fuel.

Burning, or combustion, is a chemical reaction. The atoms present in the fuel and the oxygen in the air merely rearrange themselves as burning progresses. The new arrangement of atoms, which yields ash, smoke, and waste gases, has less energy than the original fuel and oxygen. The leftover energy appears as heat.

Inside a nuclear reactor, energy is released not by chemical reactions, but by nuclear reactions. A nuclear reaction involves the nuclei of atoms. Every atom has a nucleus, which is made up of particles called protons and neutrons held together by strong forces. In a nuclear reaction, the protons and neutrons rearrange. In the reactions that take place inside nuclear reactors, large nuclei break apart to form smaller ones. Because these particles are held together by such strong forces, nuclear reactions release more energy than chemical reactions.

We followed the instructions faithfully. A large amount of water was pumped into the concrete creature after which a few pellets were tossed in. It seemed no time at all before, to loud cheers from the assembled populace, clouds of steam began puffing from the mammoth's trunk. A piping system was promptly attached to the trunk to every building in the town. Thereafter, even on the coldest days, everyone, myself included, was warm and cozy. When the waste issued forth, we took it in turns to seal and bury them as the note had instructed.

As the winter wore on, however, the disposal teams grew less and less inclined to turn out to bury the waste, which, after all, seemed harmless enough. Fortunately, I was able to devise a most ingenious way to solve the problem of unsightly waste. A large hole was cut in the wall through which the front end of the mammoth was pushed. Since the rear end of the mammoth stood outside the wall, the waste products could be ignored.

There were those in the town who remained suspicious of the concrete mammoth. They wondered not only how it worked but also where it had come from; could it really be as beneficial as it seemed? But by announcing that I would open up the machine and lead conducted tours of the mechanism, I was able to allay these fears.

However, spring arrived, the snow cleared, and I was on my way again before the promise could be kept. As I left, I noticed that the trees near the waste had yet to burst into leaf.

CONTROLLING NUCLEAR POWER

The people are right to be wary of the nuclear mammoth. A nuclear reaction can, if uncontrolled, produce an enormous explosion, as the immense release of energy takes place almost instantaneously. This is what happens in nuclear weapons. In a nuclear reactor, however, the reactions are controlled and proceed slowly. But there is another danger associated with nuclear reactions: radiation.

When protons and neutrons in the nucleus rearrange, they give out rays that can be harmful, causing diseases in living things. Because of this, nuclear reactors are encased in thick concrete, which absorbs the radiation. Nuclear waste, left over after a reaction has happened, also produces radiation. It remains radioactive for hundreds or thousands of years. It, too, has to be kept in thick concrete and far away from people—often at the bottom of the ocean.

While the reactions inside a nuclear reactor involve large nuclei breaking apart, there is another kind of nuclear reaction, in which small nuclei join together. This second kind is taking place in the sun, and the heat and light it produces supports all life on Earth.

NUCLEAR FISSION

Nuclear power gets its name because the process of power production takes place inside the nucleus. Each atom of fuel contains a central particle called the nucleus, which is itself made up of even smaller particles called protons and neutrons.

The kind of nuclear reaction that happens inside a nuclear reactor is called nuclear fission. The fuel is uranium or plutonium, two very heavy elements that have many protons and neutrons in their nuclei. Fission starts when a fast-moving neutron strikes a nucleus. The nucleus cannot take in the extra neutron, and the whole nucleus breaks apart into two smaller nuclei. Several neutrons are also released and these go on to break more nuclei, which produce more neutrons, and so on. Because the first neutron sets off a chain of fissions, the nuclear reaction is called a chain reaction. Without control, it can multiply rapidly and produce enormous heat in a fraction of a second.

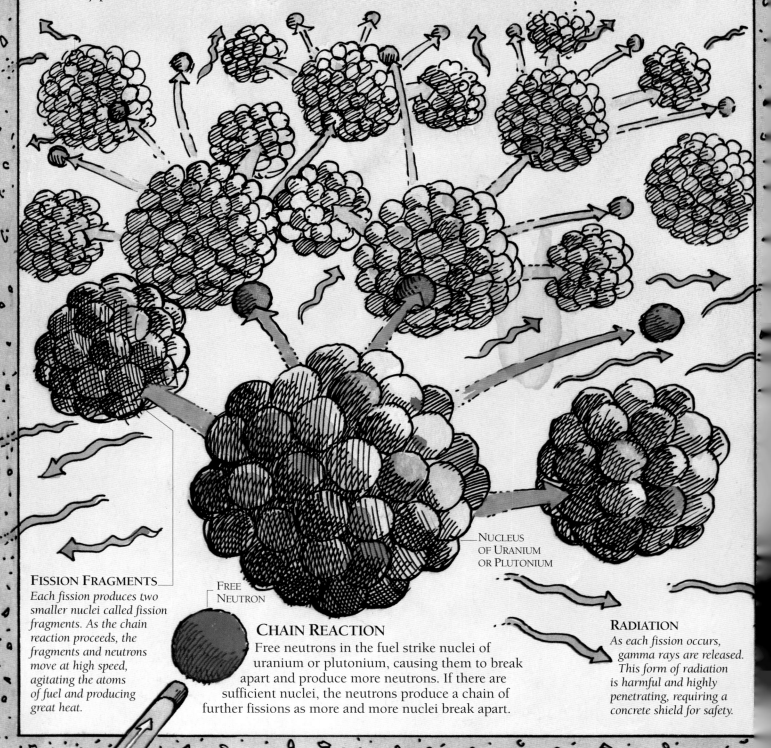

FISSION FRAGMENTS
Each fission produces two smaller nuclei called fission fragments. As the chain reaction proceeds, the fragments and neutrons move at high speed, agitating the atoms of fuel and producing great heat.

FREE
NEUTRON

NUCLEUS
OF URANIUM
OR PLUTONIUM

CHAIN REACTION
Free neutrons in the fuel strike nuclei of uranium or plutonium, causing them to break apart and produce more neutrons. If there are sufficient nuclei, the neutrons produce a chain of further fissions as more and more nuclei break apart.

RADIATION
As each fission occurs, gamma rays are released. This form of radiation is harmful and highly penetrating, requiring a concrete shield for safety.

Nuclear Fusion

Nuclear power can be produced by a process called fusion as well as by fission. In this kind of reaction, the nuclei of the fuel come together and do not break apart. Unlike fission, nuclear fusion occurs only with small atoms with nuclei that contain very few protons and neutrons. The gaseous fuel consists of two different forms of hydrogen, which is the lightest of the elements. To produce nuclear fusion, pairs of nuclei meet so that their protons and neutrons fuse together and become a single nucleus. A spare neutron is left over. The fused nuclei and neutrons move off at high speed, producing great heat. Radiation is not emitted, but the neutrons are harmful.

To get the nuclei to meet and fuse, the atoms must be banged together with tremendous force. This can only be done by heating the fuel to temperatures of millions of degrees. Nuclear fusion powers the sun, and it also occurs in thermonuclear weapons.

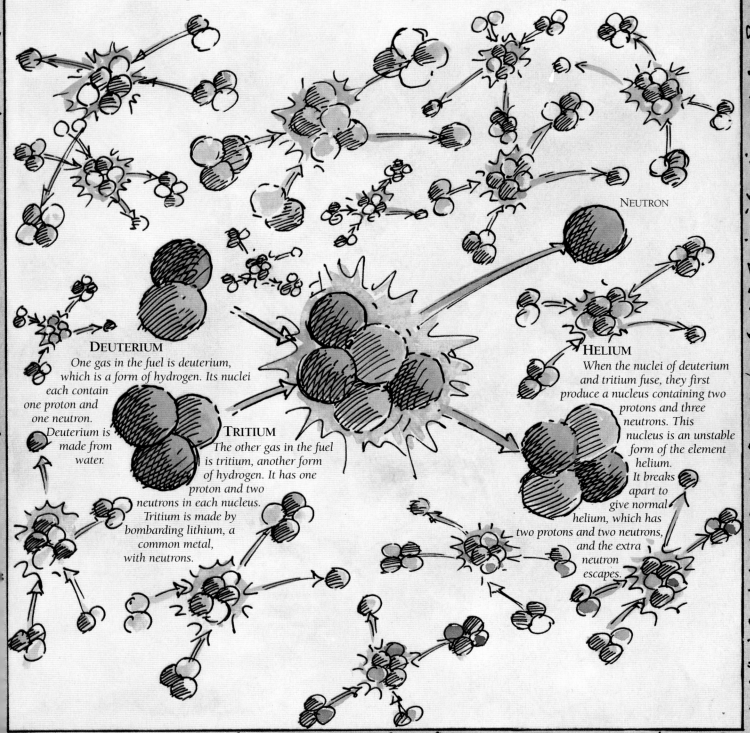

NEUTRON

DEUTERIUM
One gas in the fuel is deuterium, which is a form of hydrogen. Its nuclei each contain one proton and one neutron. Deuterium is made from water.

TRITIUM
The other gas in the fuel is tritium, another form of hydrogen. It has one proton and two neutrons in each nucleus. Tritium is made by bombarding lithium, a common metal, with neutrons.

HELIUM
When the nuclei of deuterium and tritium fuse, they first produce a nucleus containing two protons and three neutrons. This nucleus is an unstable form of the element helium. It breaks apart to give normal helium, which has two protons and two neutrons, and the extra neutron escapes.

NUCLEAR WEAPONS

ATOM BOMB

An atom bomb is also known as a fission bomb because it works by nuclear fission. Inside the bomb is a hollow sphere of uranium or plutonium. The sphere is too big to initiate a chain reaction because neutrons that occur naturally escape from the surface of the sphere without causing fission.

To detonate the bomb, a source of neutrons is shot by the detonator into the center of the sphere. Explosives then crush the sphere around the neutron source. The neutrons cannot now escape. A chain reaction occurs and fission flashes through the uranium or plutonium in a fraction of a second. The bomb explodes with a power equal to thousands of tons (kilotons) of TNT. Intense radiation is also produced.

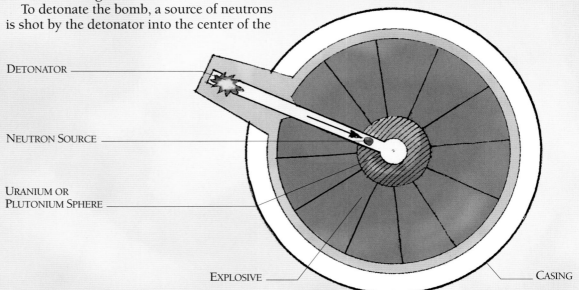

DETONATOR

NEUTRON SOURCE

URANIUM OR
PLUTONIUM SPHERE

EXPLOSIVE

CASING

HYDROGEN BOMB

The hydrogen bomb or H-bomb is a thermonuclear weapon. It works partly by nuclear fusion. Two forms of hydrogen—deuterium and tritium—are compressed at very high temperature to produce instant fusion. These conditions of ultra-high temperature and pressure can only be created by a fission bomb, which is used to trigger fusion in a thermonuclear weapon. Explosives crush all the nuclear materials around a neutron source to detonate the bomb.

Some thermonuclear weapons also contain a jacket of uranium, which produces a blast equal to millions of tons (megatons) of TNT. The neutron bomb, on the other hand, is a fusion weapon of relatively low power that produces penetrating neutrons. The neutrons released by the bomb would kill people, while most buildings would survive the weak blast.

NUCLEAR TESTING

The fallout or debris produced by the explosion of a nuclear weapon is so radioactive that the weapons must be tested in chambers dug deep underground in remote areas. In this way, the atmosphere is not contaminated by the fallout. No nuclear tests have taken place for many years.

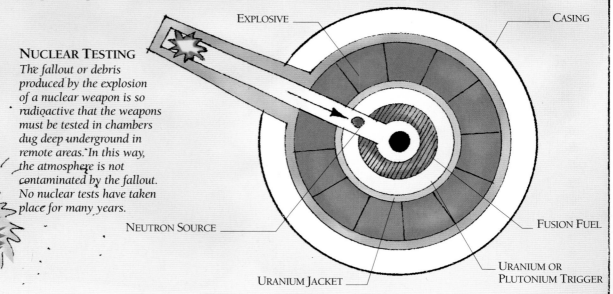

EXPLOSIVE

CASING

NEUTRON SOURCE

FUSION FUEL

URANIUM JACKET

URANIUM OR
PLUTONIUM TRIGGER

FALLOUT

A future nuclear war would not only reduce cities and towns to ruins. Fallout from the nuclear explosions would spread through the atmosphere, bombarding the land with lethal amounts of radiation. The only means of escape would be to live in deep underground shelters away from the fallout. This imprisonment would have to last until the radiation decreased to an acceptable level, which could take many years. Even then, climatic changes, shortage of food and the threat of disease would make life above ground a grim business.

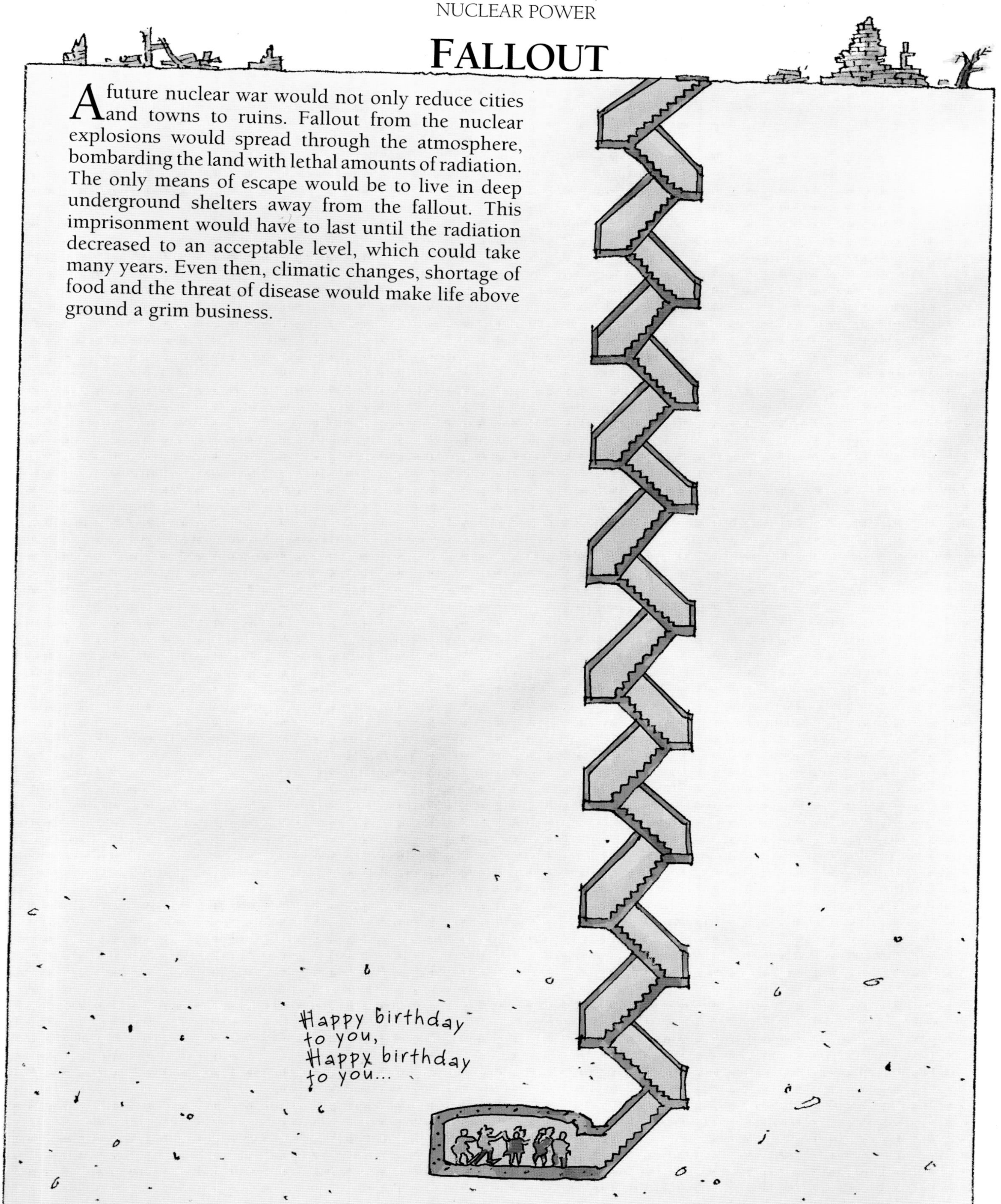

Happy birthday
to you,
Happy birthday
to you...

NUCLEAR REACTOR

The heart of a nuclear power station is its nuclear reactor. Here, immense heat is generated by the fission of uranium fuel. The heat is transferred from the reactor to a steam generator, where it boils water to steam. The rest of the nuclear power station works in the same way as one powered by coal (see pp. 160-61).

In all nuclear reactors, a liquid or gas flows through the core of the reactor and heats up. Its purpose is to take away the heat generated by fission in the reactor core, so it is called a coolant. The main kind of nuclear reactor used in nuclear power stations, the pressurized water reactor (PWR), uses water as the coolant.

FUEL RODS

The fuel consists of pellets of uranium dioxide loaded into long metal tubes. Clusters of these fuel rods are then inserted into the reactor core.

CONTROL RODS

Among the fuel rods are control rods, which contain a substance that absorbs neutrons. Moving the rods in or out of the core controls the flow of neutrons so that fission progresses steadily and provides a constant supply of heat. The reactor is shut down by fully inserting the control rods.

REACTOR CORE

A steel pressure vessel surrounds the core of the pressurized water reactor, which contains the fuel rods and control rods. Neutrons, which occur naturally, start a chain reaction in the fuel and fast neutrons are produced by fission. The coolant (pressurized water) flowing through the core slows the neutrons down. The slow neutrons cause further fission and keep the chain reaction going. Heat produced by fission is passed to the coolant.

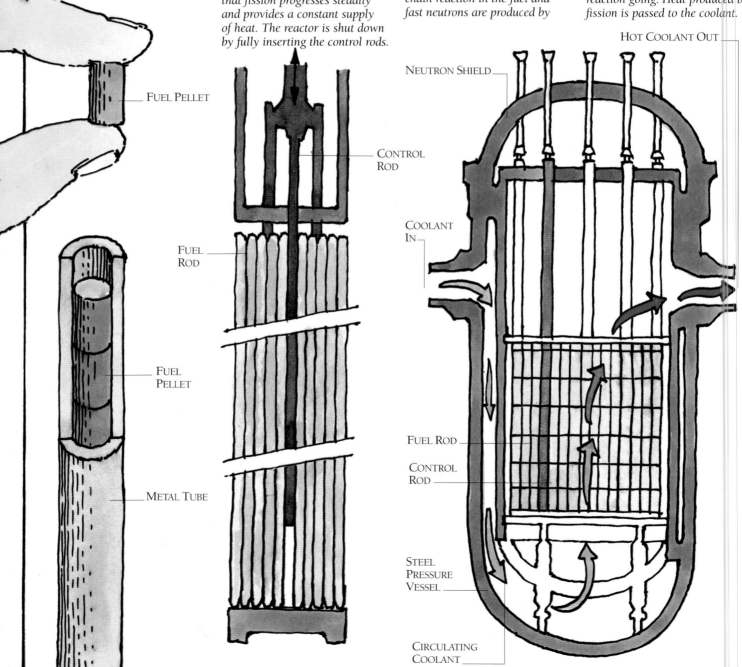

FUEL PELLET

FUEL ROD

FUEL PELLET

METAL TUBE

CONTROL ROD

FUEL ROD

NEUTRON SHIELD

HOT COOLANT OUT

COOLANT IN

FUEL ROD

CONTROL ROD

STEEL PRESSURE VESSEL

CIRCULATING COOLANT

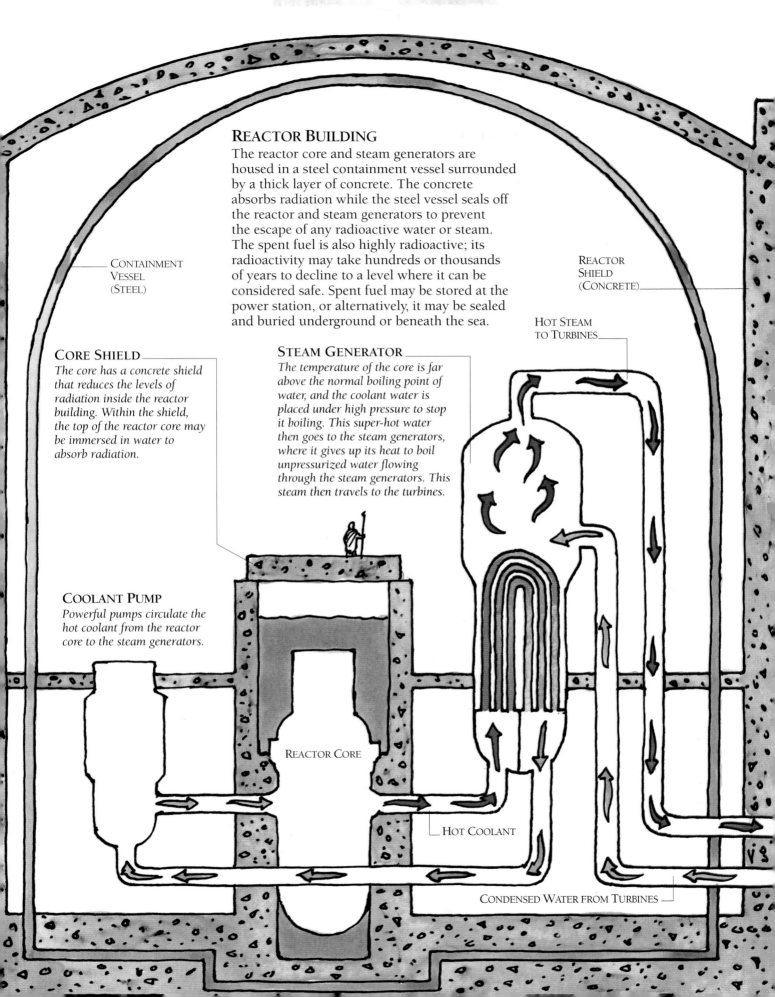

REACTOR BUILDING

The reactor core and steam generators are housed in a steel containment vessel surrounded by a thick layer of concrete. The concrete absorbs radiation while the steel vessel seals off the reactor and steam generators to prevent the escape of any radioactive water or steam. The spent fuel is also highly radioactive; its radioactivity may take hundreds or thousands of years to decline to a level where it can be considered safe. Spent fuel may be stored at the power station, or alternatively, it may be sealed and buried underground or beneath the sea.

CONTAINMENT VESSEL (STEEL)

REACTOR SHIELD (CONCRETE)

HOT STEAM TO TURBINES

CORE SHIELD

The core has a concrete shield that reduces the levels of radiation inside the reactor building. Within the shield, the top of the reactor core may be immersed in water to absorb radiation.

STEAM GENERATOR

The temperature of the core is far above the normal boiling point of water, and the coolant water is placed under high pressure to stop it boiling. This super-hot water then goes to the steam generators, where it gives up its heat to boil unpressurized water flowing through the steam generators. This steam then travels to the turbines.

COOLANT PUMP

Powerful pumps circulate the hot coolant from the reactor core to the steam generators.

REACTOR CORE

HOT COOLANT

CONDENSED WATER FROM TURBINES

FUSION POWER

Nuclear fusion could provide us with almost unlimited power. The fuels for fusion come from materials that are common. Deuterium is made from water and tritium is produced from lithium, which is a metal that occurs widely in minerals. All that is needed is a machine to make them fuse under controlled conditions.

In practice, these conditions are extremely difficult to achieve. The two gases must be heated to a temperature of hundreds of millions of degrees, and kept together for a few seconds. No ordinary container can hold them, and several different systems based on magnetic fields or lasers are being tried.

However, progress is being made; fusion has been achieved on a limited scale, but the amount of energy produced is much less than the energy fed into the fusion machine to create the conditions. Scientists hope that fusion power will advance to become reality early in the next century. If so, we shall possess a source of energy that not only has tremendous power but uses fuels that are abundant. Although a fusion reactor would not be likely to explode and release radioactivity, it would produce radioactive waste in the form of discarded reactor components.

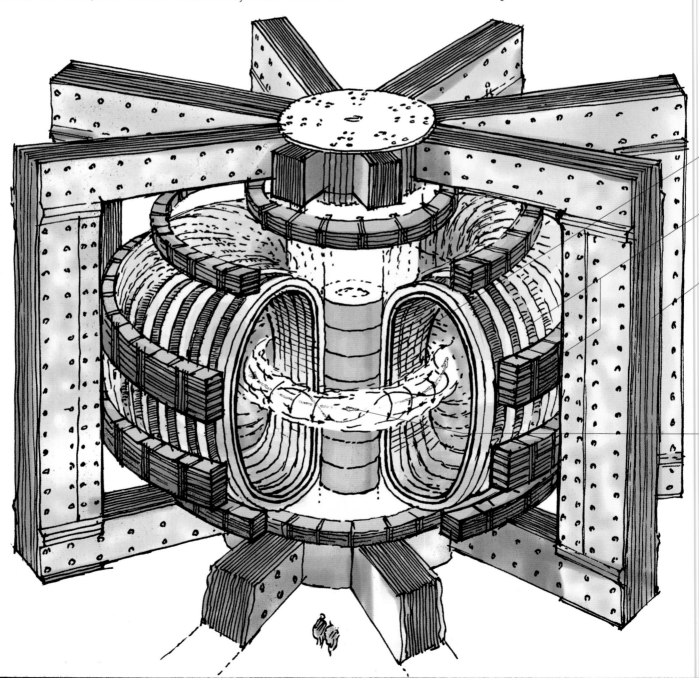

THE TOKAMAK

Most fusion research uses a machine called a tokamak, which was originally developed in Russia. At its heart is a torus—a doughnut-shape tube that contains the gases to be fused. A huge electrical transformer and coils of wire surround the tube. The transformer produces an electric current in the gases, which heats them up to produce an electrically charged mixture, or plasma. At the same time, strong magnetic fields produced by the current and the coils act on the hot gases.

The magnetic fields confine the gases to the center of the torus so that they do not touch the walls. They can then become very hot indeed and begin to fuse. Extra heating can be achieved by bombarding the gases with powerful radio waves, and by injecting beams of particles into the torus.

TORUS
The torus contains a vacuum into which the fuel gases are injected.

MAGNETIC FIELD COILS
These coils are wound around the torus and are supplied with a powerful electric current. A magnetic field is created in the torus.

TRANSFORMER
Electric current supplied to the transformer coils at the center of the machine is stepped up by the transformer coils to create a powerful current in the plasma. This current heats the plasma and produces a second magnetic field around the plasma. The two magnetic fields combine to give a field that confines the plasma to the center of the torus.

PLASMA
The gases fed into the torus are heated to such high temperatures that they become a plasma, a form of super-hot gas that is affected by magnetism. The magnetic field squeezes the plasma into a narrow ring at the center of the torus. The high temperature and pressure cause fusion to occur.

FUSION REACTOR

This is how a fusion reactor of the future could work. Deuterium and tritium are fed into the torus, where they fuse together. Fusion produces non-radioactive helium, which leaves the torus, and high-energy neutrons. Around the torus is a blanket of lithium metal. The neutrons enter the blanket and convert some of the lithium into tritium, which is extracted and goes to the torus. The neutrons also heat up the blanket. This heat is removed by a heat exchanger and goes to a boiler to raise steam for electricity generation. The reactor shield absorbs the low-energy neutrons leaving the blanket.

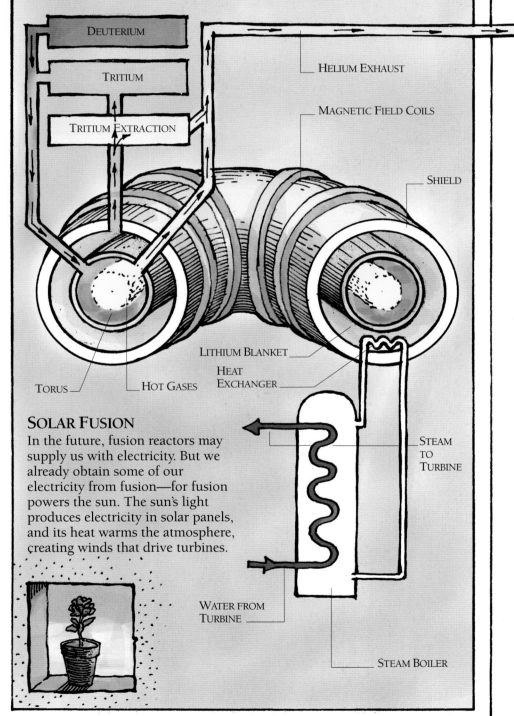

DEUTERIUM

TRITIUM

TRITIUM EXTRACTION

HELIUM EXHAUST

MAGNETIC FIELD COILS

SHIELD

TORUS

HOT GASES

LITHIUM BLANKET

HEAT EXCHANGER

STEAM TO TURBINE

WATER FROM TURBINE

STEAM BOILER

SOLAR FUSION

In the future, fusion reactors may supply us with electricity. But we already obtain some of our electricity from fusion—for fusion powers the sun. The sun's light produces electricity in solar panels, and its heat warms the atmosphere, creating winds that drive turbines.

THE·FIRST
SON·ET·LUMIÈRE
—ATLANTIS

-Very realistic, isn't it?

PART 3
WORKING WITH WAVES

INTRODUCTION

AT EVERY MOMENT OF OUR LIVES, we are bombarded with waves of **energy**. Painful though this may sound, it is actually nothing to get alarmed about, because most of this energy passes by us, or in some cases, right through us, *without having any harmful effect*. However, not all of these waves escape our notice. Through our **senses**, we can detect a small but important part of this ceaseless barrage. We can feel heat energy through our skin, we can see light energy with our eyes, and we can detect sound energy with our ears. But with the help of the machines we can do far more than this: we can communicate over unimaginable distances, bring hidden worlds—both microscopic and astronomic—into view, and reconstruct sights and sounds that would otherwise be *locked away in the past*.

ENERGY ON THE MOVE

When a sewing machine or a gasoline engine is used, it is easy to see where the energy comes from and where it goes to. *Machines that work with waves are different.* You cannot hold waves of energy in order to examine them, and to make things trickier, energy waves behave according to a separate set of **principles** from those that govern physical matter. The important feature of energy waves is that when they are conducted through matter, *it is only the energy itself that moves*. When a stone is dropped into a pond, for example, the ripples spread out from the point where the stone hits the water. But these miniature waves are not made up of water traveling outward. Instead, the water at the surface of the pond just rises and falls, and *only the **energy** moves outward*. The waves used by machines work in just the same way. Every passing wave consists of a regular rise and fall of energy. The distance between successive energy rises is the **wavelength**, and the rate at which they pass is the wave's **frequency**. Both are very important in our perception of waves.

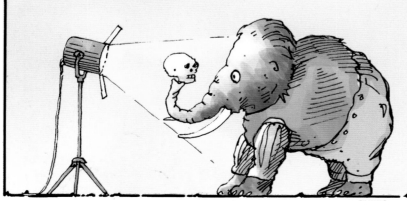

WAVES THROUGH MATTER

The machines in the following pages use *two different types of* **waves**. Of the two, **sound waves** are easier to understand because they consist of vibrations in matter. An individual sound wave is a *chain of vibrating molecules*. When a loudspeaker vibrates, the molecules in the air around it also vibrate. Like the water in the pond, the molecules do not move with the sound, they just *pass on the vibration*. Sound is our perception of this vibration. If something vibrates faster than about 20 times a second, we can hear it—this is the deepest note that human ears can detect. As the vibration speeds up, the **pitch** gets higher. At 20,000 vibrations a second, the pitch becomes too high for us to hear, but not too high for machines such as the **ultrasound scanner,** which uses *high-pitched sound* in the same way as a flying bat to create an image built up of echoes.

WAVES THROUGH SPACE

The second category of waves includes **light** and **radio waves**—members of a family known as *electromagnetic waves*. These mobile forms of energy are often called **rays** instead of waves. The only way these waves differ is in their frequency. Rather than vibrating molecules, electromagnetic waves—light, heat rays, and radio waves—consist of *vibrating electric and magnetic fields*. Because these fields can exist in empty space, electromagnetic waves can travel through nothingness itself. Each wave has a particular **frequency.** In light, we see different frequencies as different **colors** just as higher and lower sound frequencies give treble and bass notes. All electromagnetic waves travel at the *speed of light,* while sound waves crawl along at a millionth of that speed.

COMMUNICATING WITH WAVES

In traveling to us and through us, waves and rays may not just bring energy but may also *communicate meaning*. Waves that are constant, as in the beam of a torch, cannot convey any information. But if that beam is interrupted, or if its brightness can be made to change, then it can carry a message. This is how all wave-borne communications work. By converting these waves to radio waves and electrical waves that can *travel great distances*, sounds and images can flash around the world. The machines on the following pages show something of the vast range of **wave communications**—from a telephone conversation with a next-door neighbor to the feeble signals from a space probe hurtling toward the solar system's distant edge.

LIGHT AND IMAGES

ON SEEING THINGS

My life as an inventor has not been without its setbacks. Perhaps the most distressing was the failure of my athletic trophy business. Having perfected the folding rubber javelin and the stunning crystal discus, I entrusted their production to an apprentice. His initial enthusiasm however soon gave way to strange delusions of giant mammoths.

LIGHT RAYS

All sources of light produce rays that stream out in all directions. When these rays strike objects, they usually bounce off them. If light rays enter our eyes, we either see the source of the light or the object that reflected the rays toward us. The angle of the rays gives the object its apparent size.

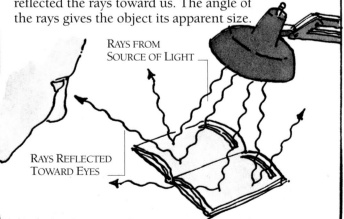

RAYS FROM
SOURCE OF LIGHT

RAYS REFLECTED
TOWARD EYES

EYESIGHT

The lens of the eye bends the light rays that come from an object. It forms an image of the object on the light-sensitive retina of the eye, and this image is then changed to nerve impulses that travel to the brain. The image is in fact upside down on the retina, but the brain interprets it as upright.

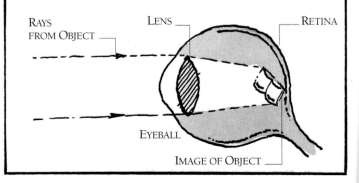

RAYS
FROM OBJECT

LENS

RETINA

EYEBALL

IMAGE OF OBJECT

ssuming that he was simply overworked, I reduced his hours and improved ventilation in the workshop. But his condition deteriorated and one day he confronted me in my laboratory, claiming that miniature mammoths had invaded the premises. He insisted that a procession of these creatures was making its way across the wall, accompanied by a trail of smoke. Within the hour, word reached us that the workshop and all its contents had mysteriously burned to the ground. I realized that the frightened youth must have knocked over a candle as he fled, and although very disappointed at the loss, I decided to humor him and attribute the disaster to the spirits.

FORMING IMAGES

As light rays enter and leave transparent materials such as glass, they bend or refract. Seen through a lens, a nearby object appears to be much bigger because the rays enter the eye in a wider angle than they would without it. This is why the mammoth's eye is magnified by the discus.

Lenses can also throw images onto a surface. Cones of rays from every point on the object are bent by the lens to meet at the surface. The cones cross, inverting the mammoths, while the sun's rays meet to form a hot spot on the wall.

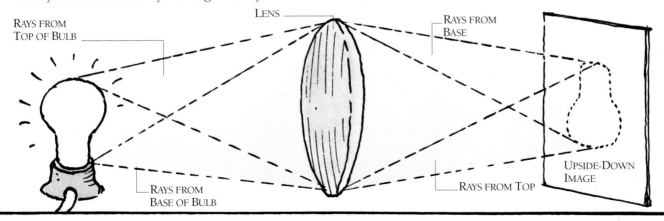

RAYS FROM TOP OF BULB

LENS

RAYS FROM BASE

RAYS FROM BASE OF BULB

RAYS FROM TOP

UPSIDE-DOWN IMAGE

LET THERE BE LIGHT

In both incandescence and luminescence, the light is produced by electrons. In the filament of an incandescent light bulb, the electrons are free of their atoms, and vibrate when hot, producing light. In a fluorescent lamp or an LED, the light is produced by electrons that are bound to their atoms. The electrons gain extra energy—typically from electricity or heat—causing them to move farther from the nucleus at the center of the atom. Just as gravity pulls a stone thrown into the air back down to the ground, electric forces in the atom pull electrons back down to their original positions. But while the stone produces sound as it lands with a bump, electrons release light.

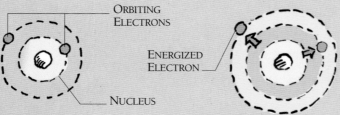

STABLE ATOM
Inside an atom, electrons move in a number of concentric orbits around the nucleus.

ELECTRONS MOVE OUT
Heat or electricity provides enough energy to make the electrons "jump" to higher orbits.

ELECTRONS FALL BACK
When the electrons fall back, their extra energy is emitted as a ray of light.

CANDLE FLAME

Millions of tiny soot particles in the hot flame produce the yellow incandescent glow of a candle. When the candle is lit, wax melts, rises up the wick, vaporizes, and burns in the air. The combustion (see p. 146) of the wax produces both the heat and the soot particles.

SOOT PARTICLES

FLAME

WICK

WAX

FLUORESCENT TUBE

A fluorescent strip light is a glass tube containing mercury vapor. Heated electrodes at each end of the tube release electrons that pass through the vapor and excite electrons in the mercury atoms, causing them to emit invisible ultraviolet light. The ultraviolet rays strike a phosphor coating on the inside of the tube, energizing electrons in the phosphor and making them glow with visible light.

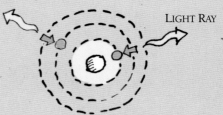

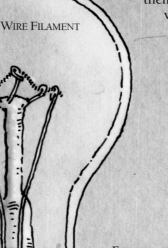

WIRE FILAMENT

GLASS TUBE

PHOSPHOR COATING

MERCURY ATOM

ELECTRON

ELECTRODE HEATED BY ELECTRIC CURRENT

INCANDESCENT BULB

Inside an incandescent bulb, electric current passes through a thin metal filament and makes the filament very hot, so that it glows. These bulbs are very inefficient, because most of the energy is lost as heat.

LIGHTING

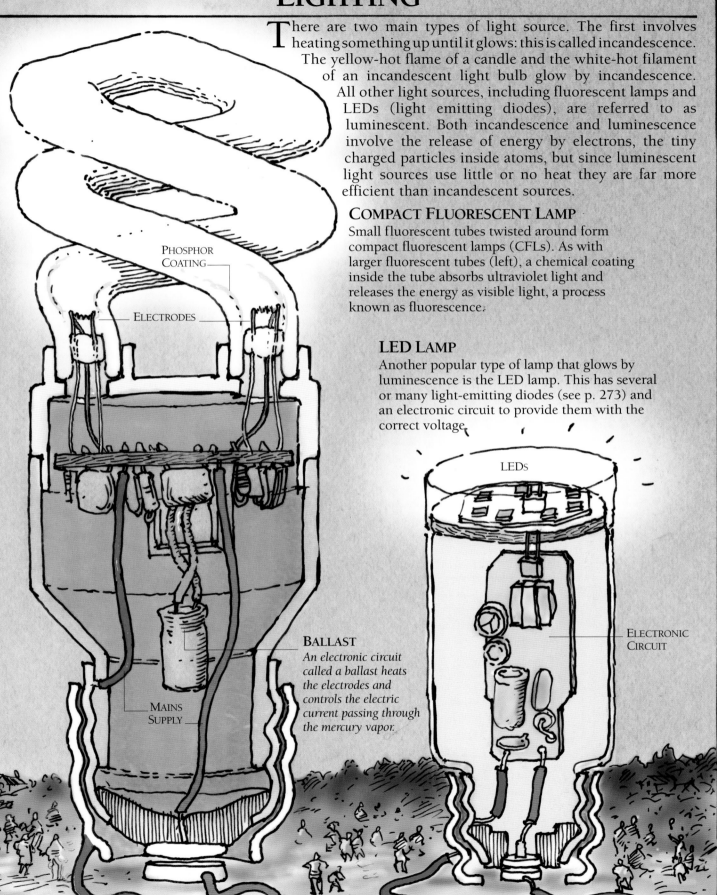

There are two main types of light source. The first involves heating something up until it glows: this is called incandescence. The yellow-hot flame of a candle and the white-hot filament of an incandescent light bulb glow by incandescence. All other light sources, including fluorescent lamps and LEDs (light emitting diodes), are referred to as luminescent. Both incandescence and luminescence involve the release of energy by electrons, the tiny charged particles inside atoms, but since luminescent light sources use little or no heat they are far more efficient than incandescent sources.

COMPACT FLUORESCENT LAMP

Small fluorescent tubes twisted around form compact fluorescent lamps (CFLs). As with larger fluorescent tubes (left), a chemical coating inside the tube absorbs ultraviolet light and releases the energy as visible light, a process known as fluorescence.

LED LAMP

Another popular type of lamp that glows by luminescence is the LED lamp. This has several or many light-emitting diodes (see p. 273) and an electronic circuit to provide them with the correct voltage.

PHOSPHOR COATING

ELECTRODES

LEDs

BALLAST
An electronic circuit called a ballast heats the electrodes and controls the electric current passing through the mercury vapor.

ELECTRONIC CIRCUIT

MAINS SUPPLY

ADDING COLORS

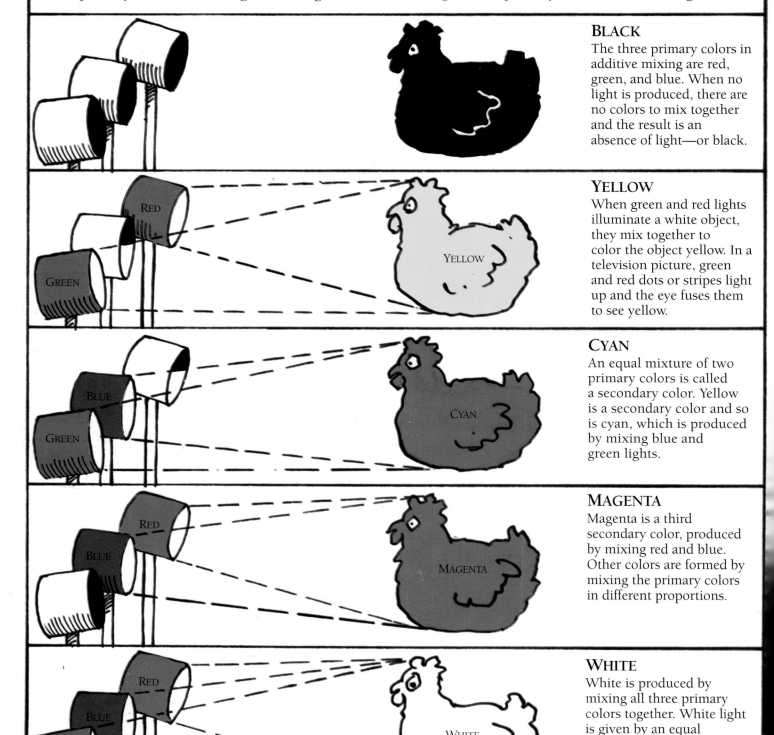

Many of the color images we see are not quite what they seem. Instead of being composed of all the colors that we perceive, they are actually made of three primary colors mixed together. Images that are sources of light, such as pictures on an LCD screen (see p. 246), combine colors by "additive" mixing. Stage lights produce a range of colors by additive mixing of three primary colors at various brightnesses.

BLACK

The three primary colors in additive mixing are red, green, and blue. When no light is produced, there are no colors to mix together and the result is an absence of light—or black.

YELLOW

When green and red lights illuminate a white object, they mix together to color the object yellow. In a television picture, green and red dots or stripes light up and the eye fuses them to see yellow.

CYAN

An equal mixture of two primary colors is called a secondary color. Yellow is a secondary color and so is cyan, which is produced by mixing blue and green lights.

MAGENTA

Magenta is a third secondary color, produced by mixing red and blue. Other colors are formed by mixing the primary colors in different proportions.

WHITE

White is produced by mixing all three primary colors together. White light is given by an equal mixture of red, green, and blue lights.

SUBTRACTING COLORS

Images produced by mixing printing inks (see pp. 216-17) and paints form colors by "subtractive" mixing. This gives different colors to additive mixing because the pictures themselves are not sources of light. The pictures reflect some of the primary colors in the white light that illuminates them, and absorb or subtract the other primary colors. We see the reflected primary colors added together.

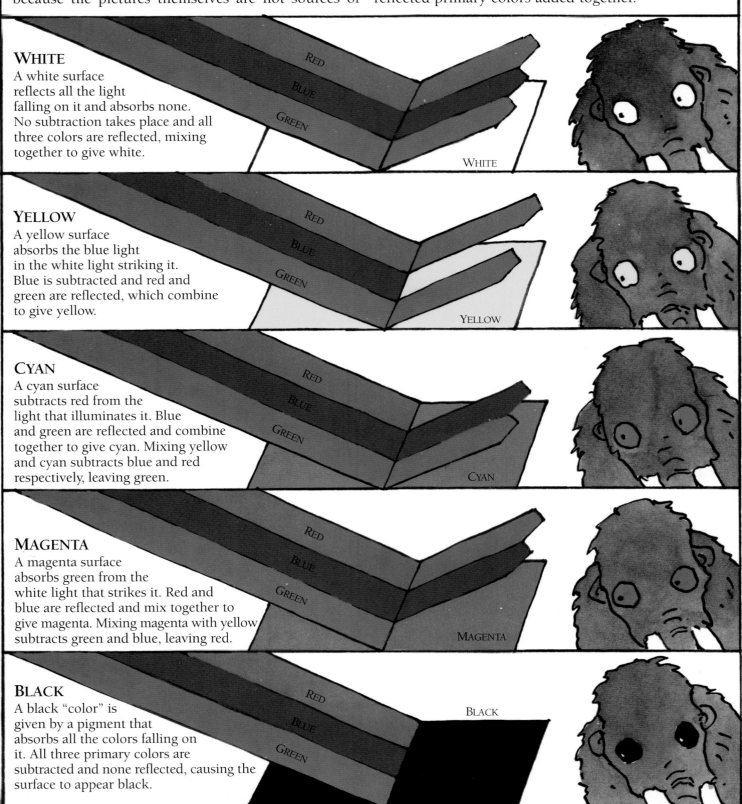

WHITE

A white surface reflects all the light falling on it and absorbs none. No subtraction takes place and all three colors are reflected, mixing together to give white.

YELLOW

A yellow surface absorbs the blue light in the white light striking it. Blue is subtracted and red and green are reflected, which combine to give yellow.

CYAN

A cyan surface subtracts red from the light that illuminates it. Blue and green are reflected and combine together to give cyan. Mixing yellow and cyan subtracts blue and red respectively, leaving green.

MAGENTA

A magenta surface absorbs green from the white light that strikes it. Red and blue are reflected and mix together to give magenta. Mixing magenta with yellow subtracts green and blue, leaving red.

BLACK

A black "color" is given by a pigment that absorbs all the colors falling on it. All three primary colors are subtracted and none reflected, causing the surface to appear black.

MIRRORS

Aflat mirror reflects the light rays that strike it so that the rays leave the surface of the mirror at exactly the same angle that they meet it. The light rays enter the eye as if they had come directly from an object behind the mirror, and we therefore see an image of the object in the mirror. This image is a "virtual" image: it cannot be projected on a screen. It is also reversed. Images formed by two mirrors, as in the periscope, are not reversed because the second mirror corrects the image.

PERISCOPE

The periscope makes it possible to see around corners. It has one mirror to capture light rays from an object and sends them to another mirror, which directs the rays into the eye.

IMAGE

CONVEX MIRROR

OBJECT

DRIVING MIRROR

A driving mirror is a convex mirror, which curves toward the viewer. It reflects light rays from an image so that they diverge. The eye sees an image that is reduced in size, giving the mirror a wide field of view.

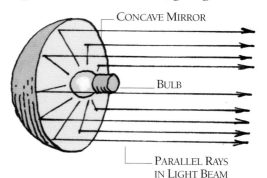

CONCAVE MIRROR

BULB

PARALLEL RAYS IN LIGHT BEAM

HEADLAMP MIRROR

In headlights and torches, a concave mirror is placed behind the bulb. The light rays are reflected by the curved surface so that they are parallel and form a narrow and bright beam of light.

ENDOSCOPE

FIBER OPTICS

Fiber optic devices depend on internal reflection, which allows light to pass along a narrow filament of very pure glass. The light-conducting fibers used by instruments such as the endoscope have a glass coating that reflects light rays along the fiber core. An image formed by a lens on one end of a cable of fibers appears at the other end, no matter how much the cable twists. Each fiber carries part of the image. Optical fibers also carry light signals over long distances in telecommunications (see pp. 236-37).

LIGHT PATH

IMAGE LENS

LIGHT

By using an endoscope, a doctor can easily see what is going on inside a body without cutting it open. A narrow tube containing fiber optic cables or guides is inserted into a channel in the body, such as the throat. Light guides transmit light along the fibers to light up the interior. The image guide sends a picture of the interior back along the tube, where it is viewed in an eyepiece. The tube also contains air and water pipes as well as a channel for small surgical instruments. Wires control the bending of the tube.

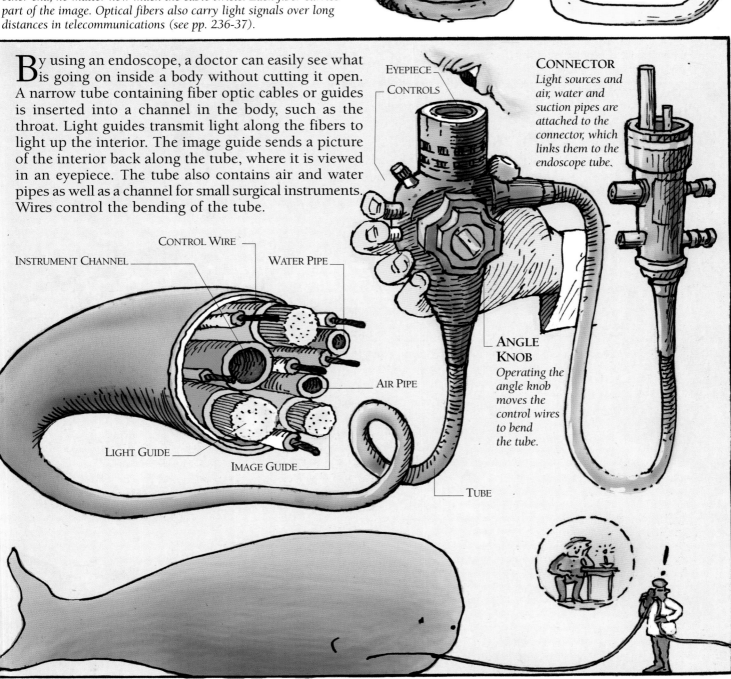

EYEPIECE

CONTROLS

CONNECTOR
Light sources and air, water and suction pipes are attached to the connector, which links them to the endoscope tube.

INSTRUMENT CHANNEL

CONTROL WIRE

WATER PIPE

AIR PIPE

LIGHT GUIDE

IMAGE GUIDE

ANGLE KNOB
Operating the angle knob moves the control wires to bend the tube.

TUBE

LENSES

Lenses are of great importance in devices that use light. Optical instruments such as cameras, projectors, microscopes, and telescopes all produce images with lenses, while many of us see the world through lenses that correct poor sight. Lenses work by refraction, which is the bending of light rays that occurs as rays leave one transparent material and enter another. In the case of lenses, the two materials involved are glass and air. Lenses in glasses and contact lenses are used to supplement the lens in the eye (see p. 180) when it cannot otherwise bend the rays by the angle required to form a sharp image.

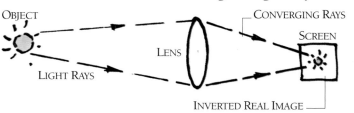

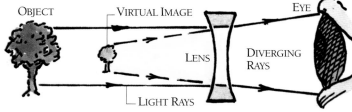

CONVEX LENS

A convex lens is thicker at the center than the edges. Light rays from an object pass through it and converge to form a "real" image—one that can be seen on a screen.

CONCAVE LENS

A concave lens is thicker at the edges than the center. It makes light rays diverge. The eye receives these rays and sees a smaller "virtual" image (see p. 186) of the object.

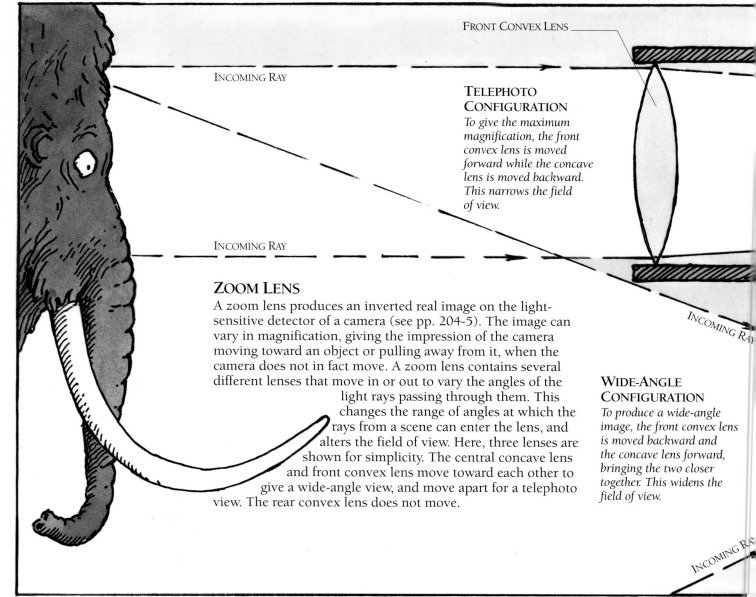

TELEPHOTO CONFIGURATION

To give the maximum magnification, the front convex lens is moved forward while the concave lens is moved backward. This narrows the field of view.

ZOOM LENS

A zoom lens produces an inverted real image on the light-sensitive detector of a camera (see pp. 204-5). The image can vary in magnification, giving the impression of the camera moving toward an object or pulling away from it, when the camera does not in fact move. A zoom lens contains several different lenses that move in or out to vary the angles of the light rays passing through them. This changes the range of angles at which the rays from a scene can enter the lens, and alters the field of view. Here, three lenses are shown for simplicity. The central concave lens and front convex lens move toward each other to give a wide-angle view, and move apart for a telephoto view. The rear convex lens does not move.

WIDE-ANGLE CONFIGURATION

To produce a wide-angle image, the front convex lens is moved backward and the concave lens forward, bringing the two closer together. This widens the field of view.

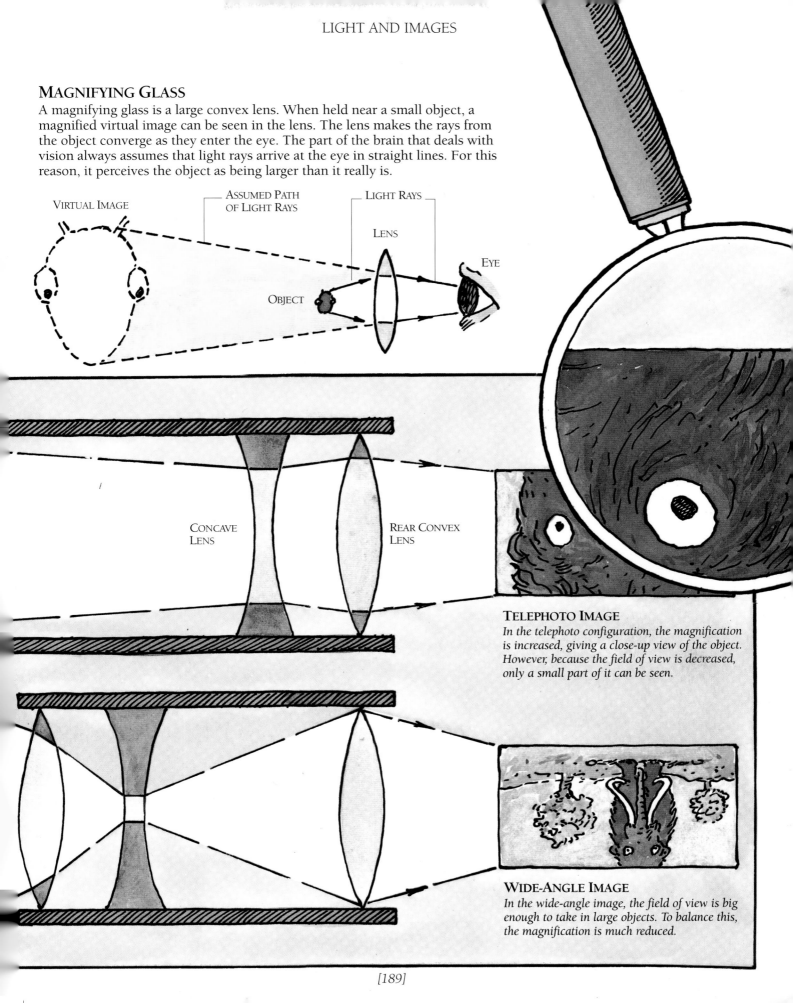

MAGNIFYING GLASS

A magnifying glass is a large convex lens. When held near a small object, a magnified virtual image can be seen in the lens. The lens makes the rays from the object converge as they enter the eye. The part of the brain that deals with vision always assumes that light rays arrive at the eye in straight lines. For this reason, it perceives the object as being larger than it really is.

VIRTUAL IMAGE

ASSUMED PATH OF LIGHT RAYS

LIGHT RAYS

LENS

EYE

OBJECT

CONCAVE LENS

REAR CONVEX LENS

TELEPHOTO IMAGE

In the telephoto configuration, the magnification is increased, giving a close-up view of the object. However, because the field of view is decreased, only a small part of it can be seen.

WIDE-ANGLE IMAGE

In the wide-angle image, the field of view is big enough to take in large objects. To balance this, the magnification is much reduced.

TELESCOPES

A telescope gives a close-up view of a distant object, which, in the case of an astronomical telescope viewing a far-off planet or galaxy, is very distant indeed. Most telescopes work in the same basic way, which is to produce a real image of the object inside the telescope tube. The eyepiece lens then views this image in the same way as a magnifying glass (see p. 189). The viewer looks at a very close real image, which therefore appears large. The degree of magnification depends mainly on the power of the eyepiece lens.

REFRACTING TELESCOPE

In a refracting telescope, an objective lens forms the real image that is viewed by the eyepiece lens. The image is upside down but this is not important in astronomy. A terrestrial telescope gives an upright view. It contains an extra convex lens that forms an upright real image and the eyepiece lens views this image.

REFLECTING TELESCOPE

In a reflecting telescope, a large concave primary mirror forms the real image that is then viewed by an eyepiece lens. Usually, a secondary mirror reflects the rays from the primary mirror so that the real image forms beneath the mirror or to the side. This is more convenient for viewing.

Reflecting telescopes are important in astronomy because the primary mirror can be very wide. This enables it to collect a lot of light, making faint objects visible. Collecting light from an object is often more important than magnifying it because distant stars do not appear bigger even when magnified.

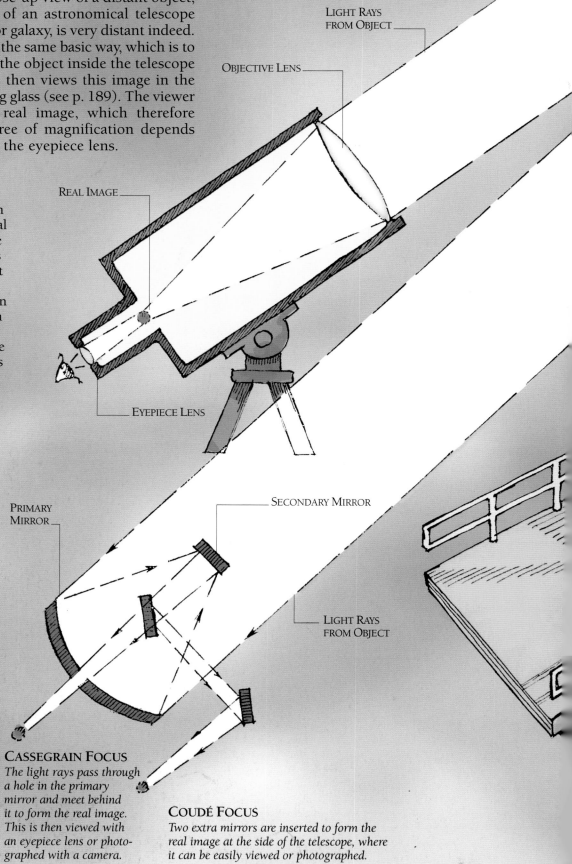

LIGHT RAYS FROM OBJECT

OBJECTIVE LENS

REAL IMAGE

EYEPIECE LENS

PRIMARY MIRROR

SECONDARY MIRROR

LIGHT RAYS FROM OBJECT

CASSEGRAIN FOCUS
The light rays pass through a hole in the primary mirror and meet behind it to form the real image. This is then viewed with an eyepiece lens or photographed with a camera.

COUDÉ FOCUS
Two extra mirrors are inserted to form the real image at the side of the telescope, where it can be easily viewed or photographed.

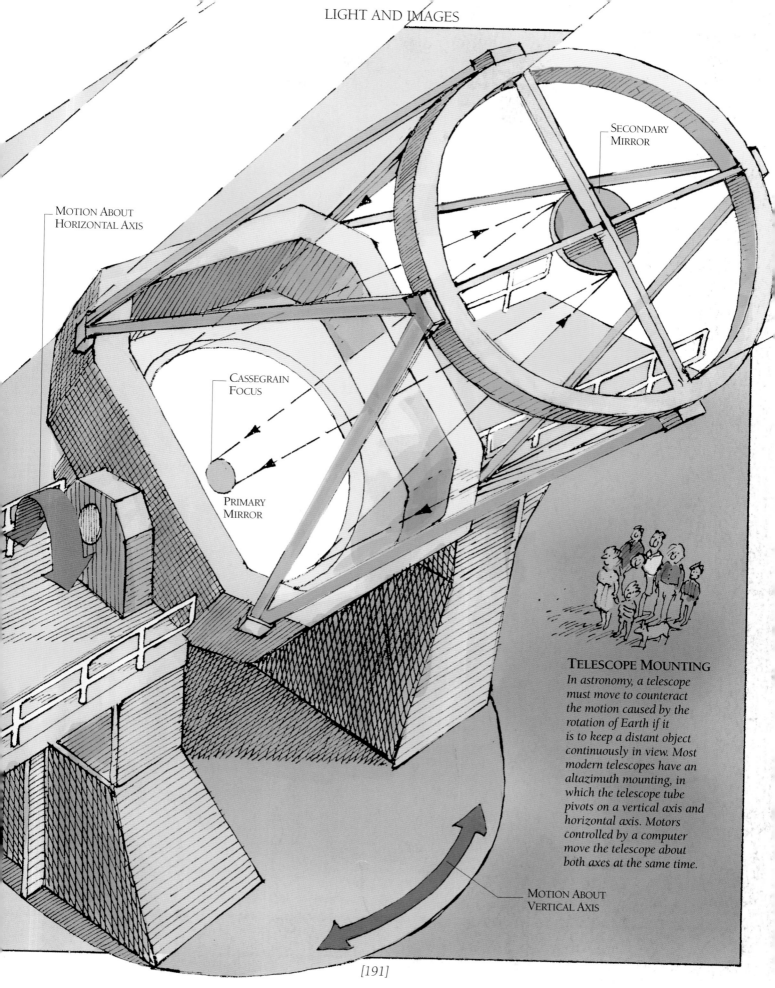

MOTION ABOUT
HORIZONTAL AXIS

SECONDARY
MIRROR

CASSEGRAIN
FOCUS

PRIMARY
MIRROR

TELESCOPE MOUNTING

*In astronomy, a telescope
must move to counteract
the motion caused by the
rotation of Earth if it
is to keep a distant object
continuously in view. Most
modern telescopes have an
altazimuth mounting, in
which the telescope tube
pivots on a vertical axis and
horizontal axis. Motors
controlled by a computer
move the telescope about
both axes at the same time.*

MOTION ABOUT
VERTICAL AXIS

BINOCULARS

A pair of binoculars is basically two small refracting telescopes that together produce a stereoscopic or three-dimensional view. Each eye sees a separate close-up view, but the brain combines them to perceive an image that has depth.

Binoculars are different from telescopes in one respect. They contain a pair of prisms between the objective and eyepiece lenses. The faces of the prisms reflect the light rays internally so that an upright non-reversed image is seen. The prisms also lengthen the light path between the lenses, which narrows the field of view and increases magnification in a short tube. In addition, the two objective lenses may be farther apart than the eyes, which enhances stereoscopic vision.

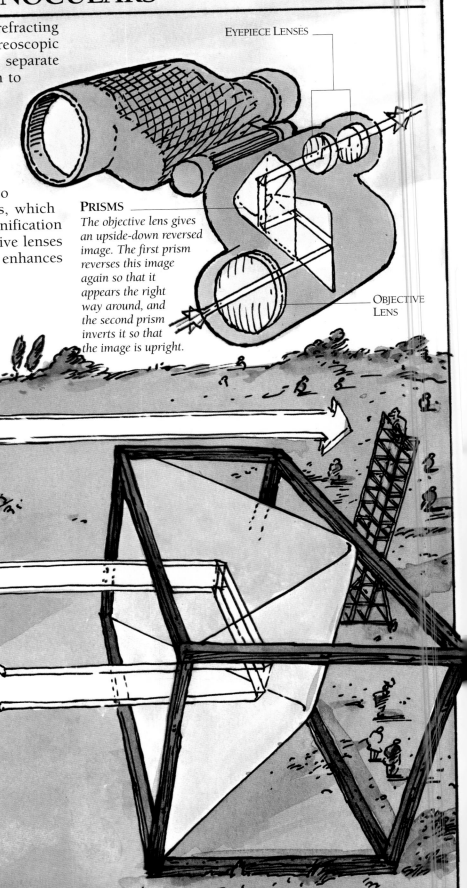

EYEPIECE LENSES

PRISMS
The objective lens gives an upside-down reversed image. The first prism reverses this image again so that it appears the right way around, and the second prism inverts it so that the image is upright.

OBJECTIVE LENS

MICROSCOPES

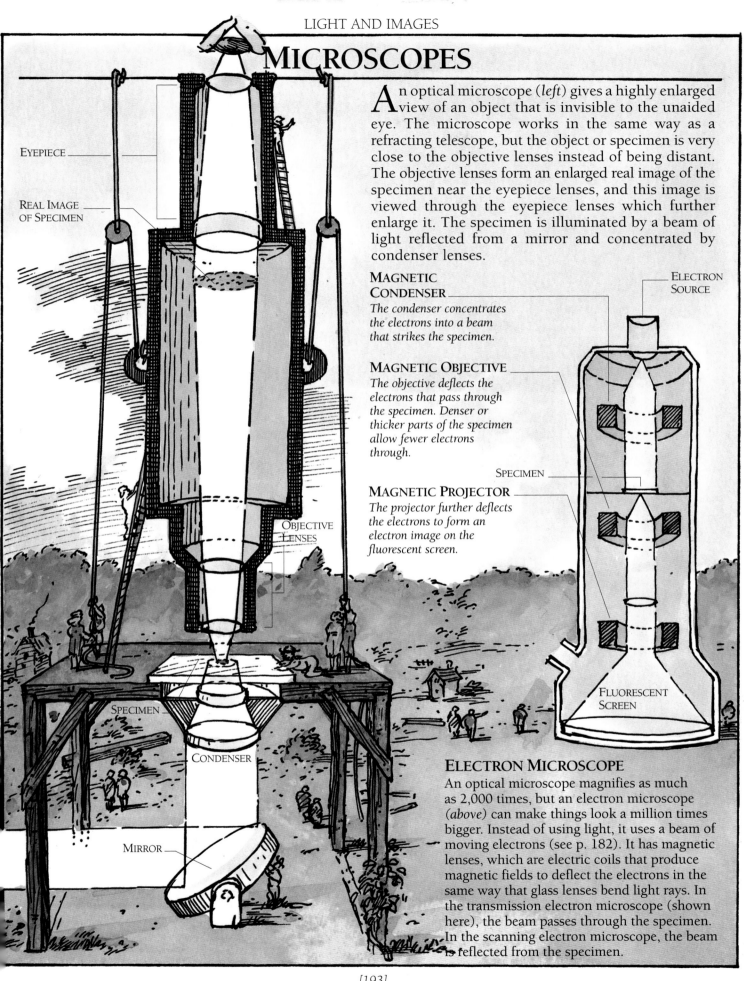

An optical microscope (*left*) gives a highly enlarged view of an object that is invisible to the unaided eye. The microscope works in the same way as a refracting telescope, but the object or specimen is very close to the objective lenses instead of being distant. The objective lenses form an enlarged real image of the specimen near the eyepiece lenses, and this image is viewed through the eyepiece lenses which further enlarge it. The specimen is illuminated by a beam of light reflected from a mirror and concentrated by condenser lenses.

EYEPIECE

REAL IMAGE OF SPECIMEN

OBJECTIVE LENSES

SPECIMEN

CONDENSER

MIRROR

MAGNETIC CONDENSER
The condenser concentrates the electrons into a beam that strikes the specimen.

MAGNETIC OBJECTIVE
The objective deflects the electrons that pass through the specimen. Denser or thicker parts of the specimen allow fewer electrons through.

MAGNETIC PROJECTOR
The projector further deflects the electrons to form an electron image on the fluorescent screen.

ELECTRON SOURCE

SPECIMEN

FLUORESCENT SCREEN

ELECTRON MICROSCOPE
An optical microscope magnifies as much as 2,000 times, but an electron microscope (*above*) can make things look a million times bigger. Instead of using light, it uses a beam of moving electrons (see p. 182). It has magnetic lenses, which are electric coils that produce magnetic fields to deflect the electrons in the same way that glass lenses bend light rays. In the transmission electron microscope (shown here), the beam passes through the specimen. In the scanning electron microscope, the beam is reflected from the specimen.

POLARIZED LIGHT

Light rays are electromagnetic waves: their energy consists of vibrating electric and magnetic fields (see p. 243). In normal light rays, these fields vibrate in planes at random angles. In polarized light, all the rays vibrate in the same plane. The direction of this plane is the plane in which the electric field vibrates. Polarizing filters are found in, among other things, anti-glare sunglasses and liquid crystal displays.

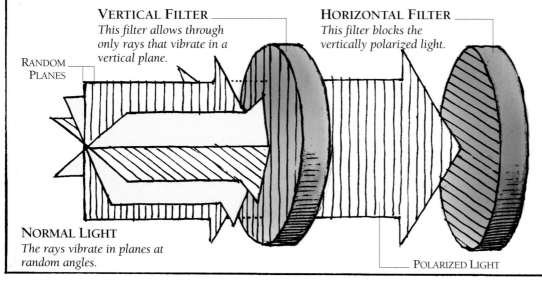

VERTICAL FILTER
This filter allows through only rays that vibrate in a vertical plane.

HORIZONTAL FILTER
This filter blocks the vertically polarized light.

RANDOM PLANES

NORMAL LIGHT
The rays vibrate in planes at random angles.

POLARIZED LIGHT

POLARIZING FILTERS

A polarizing filter blocks all rays except those vibrating in a certain plane. If polarized light strikes a filter whose plane is at right angles to the plane of the rays, then no light passes.

Polarizing sunglasses work in this way. Light reflected from shiny surfaces is partly polarized, and the sunglasses are polarizing filters. They block the polarized light and reduce glare.

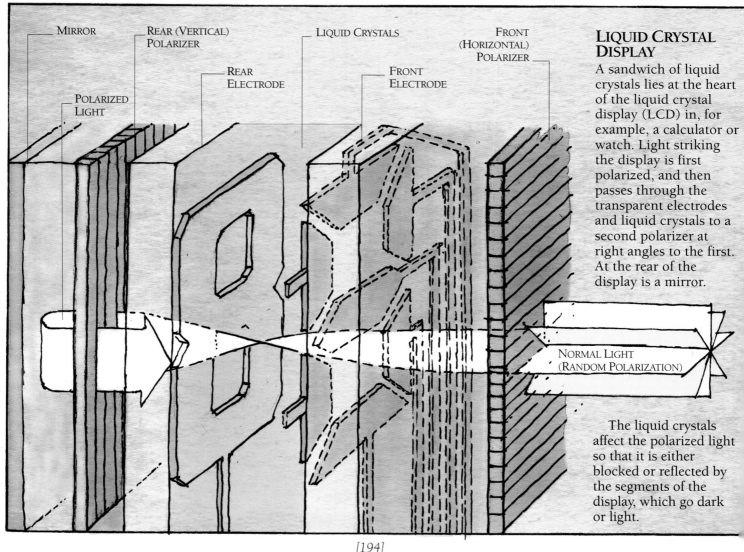

MIRROR

REAR (VERTICAL) POLARIZER

LIQUID CRYSTALS

FRONT (HORIZONTAL) POLARIZER

REAR ELECTRODE

FRONT ELECTRODE

POLARIZED LIGHT

NORMAL LIGHT (RANDOM POLARIZATION)

LIQUID CRYSTAL DISPLAY

A sandwich of liquid crystals lies at the heart of the liquid crystal display (LCD) in, for example, a calculator or watch. Light striking the display is first polarized, and then passes through the transparent electrodes and liquid crystals to a second polarizer at right angles to the first. At the rear of the display is a mirror.

The liquid crystals affect the polarized light so that it is either blocked or reflected by the segments of the display, which go dark or light.

LIQUID CRYSTALS

Liquid crystals are liquid materials with molecules arranged in patterns similar to those of crystals. The molecules are normally twisted, and when polarized light passes through liquid crystals, its plane of vibration twists through a right angle.

A weak electric current changes the pattern of molecules in liquid crystals. It causes the molecules to line up so that polarized light is no longer affected. The liquid crystals are sandwiched between two transparent electrodes, which pass light rays and deliver the electric current.

By arranging liquid crystals in segments, numbers and letters can be produced in a liquid crystal display (see p. 361). An LCD in a television (see pp. 246-47) works in a similar way, but has a backlight behind the display.

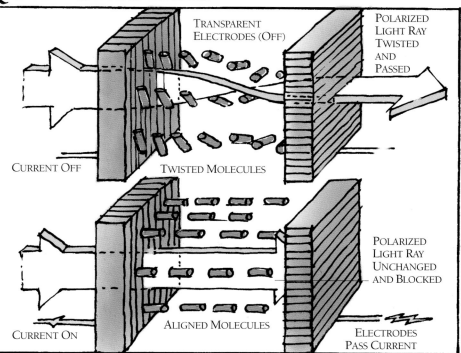

TRANSPARENT ELECTRODES (OFF)

POLARIZED LIGHT RAY TWISTED AND PASSED

CURRENT OFF

TWISTED MOLECULES

POLARIZED LIGHT RAY UNCHANGED AND BLOCKED

CURRENT ON

ALIGNED MOLECULES

ELECTRODES PASS CURRENT

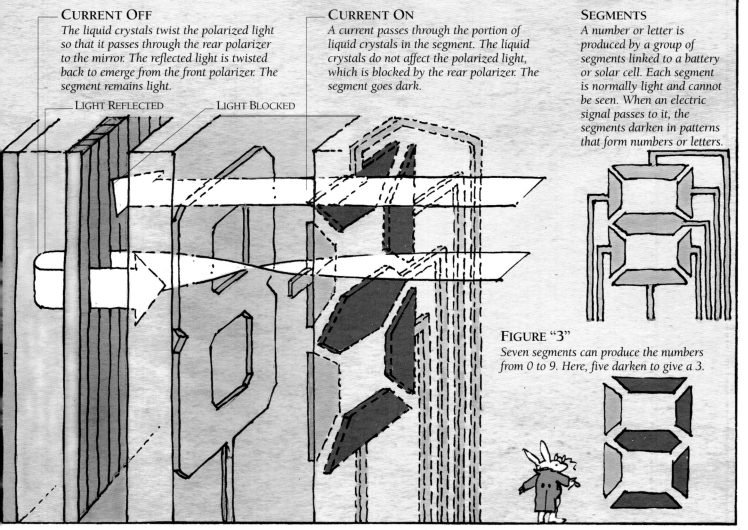

CURRENT OFF
The liquid crystals twist the polarized light so that it passes through the rear polarizer to the mirror. The reflected light is twisted back to emerge from the front polarizer. The segment remains light.

LIGHT REFLECTED   LIGHT BLOCKED

CURRENT ON
A current passes through the portion of liquid crystals in the segment. The liquid crystals do not affect the polarized light, which is blocked by the rear polarizer. The segment goes dark.

SEGMENTS
A number or letter is produced by a group of segments linked to a battery or solar cell. Each segment is normally light and cannot be seen. When an electric signal passes to it, the segments darken in patterns that form numbers or letters.

FIGURE "3"
Seven segments can produce the numbers from 0 to 9. Here, five darken to give a 3.

LASER

A laser produces a narrow beam of very bright light, either firing brief pulses of light or forming a continuous beam. Laser stands for light amplification by stimulated emission of radiation. Unlike ordinary light, laser light is "coherent," meaning that all the rays have exactly the same wavelength and are all in phase, vibrating together to produce a beam of great intensity.

A laser beam may either be of visible light, or of invisible infrared rays. Visible light lasers are used in digital recording and fiber-optic communications as well as in surveying and distance measurement, and give results of very high quality and accuracy. The intense heat of a powerful infrared laser beam is sufficient to cut metal.

1 EXCITING THE ATOMS

In a laser, energy is first stored in a lasing medium, which may be a solid, liquid, or gas. The energy excites atoms in the medium, raising them to a high-energy state. One excited atom then spontaneously releases a light ray. In a gas laser, shown here, electrons in an electric current excite the gas atoms.

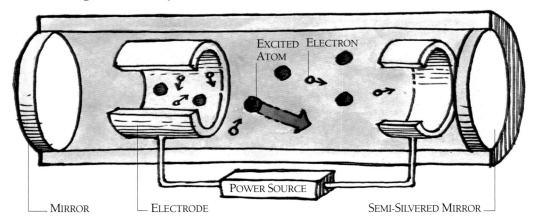

EXCITED ATOM   ELECTRON

MIRROR   ELECTRODE   POWER SOURCE   SEMI-SILVERED MIRROR

2 LIGHT BUILDS UP

The ray of light from the excited atom strikes another excited atom, causing it also to emit a light ray. These rays then strike more excited atoms, and the process of light production grows. The mirrors at the ends of the tube reflect the light rays so that more and more excited atoms release light.

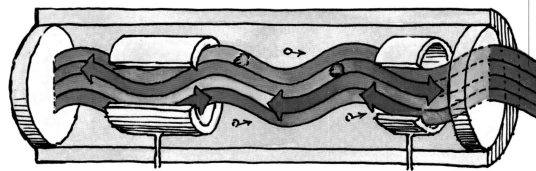

LASER BEAM

3 THE LASER FIRES

As each excited atom emits a light ray, the new ray vibrates in step with the ray that strikes the atom. All the rays are in step, and the beam becomes bright enough to pass through the semi-silvered mirror and leave the laser. The energy is released as laser light.

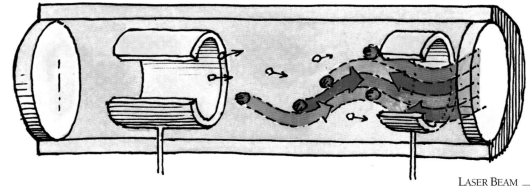

GAS LASER

A gas laser produces a continuous beam of laser light as the gas atoms absorb energy from the electrons moving through the gas and then release this energy as light.

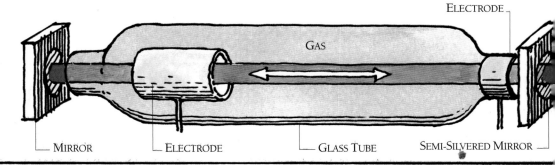

ELECTRODE

GAS

MIRROR   ELECTRODE   GLASS TUBE   SEMI-SILVERED MIRROR

HOLOGRAPHY

One very important application of lasers is holography, the production of images that are three-dimensional and that appear to have depth just like a real object. Holography requires light of a single exact wavelength, which can only be produced by a laser.

In holography, the light beam from a laser is split into two beams. One beam, the object beam, lights up the object. The second beam, the reference beam, goes to a photographic plate or film placed near the object. When developed, the plate or film becomes a hologram, in which a three-dimensional image of the object can be seen (see pp. 198-99).

MAKING A HOLOGRAM

The photographic plate or film receives laser light from the object and from the reference beam. The arrangement here produces a reflection hologram, which gives an image in ordinary light. For a transmission hologram, which is viewed with a laser, the two beams strike the same side of the plate or film.

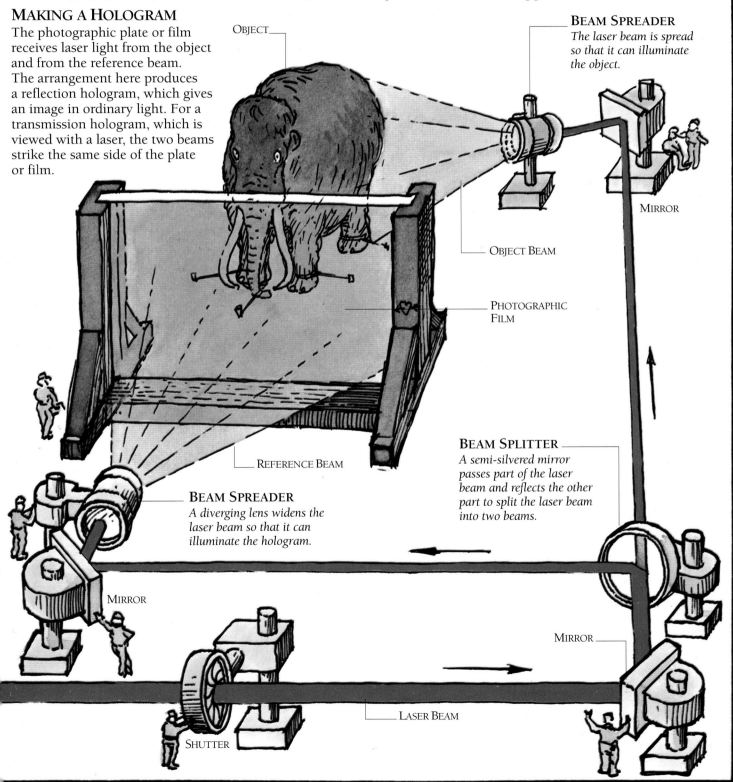

OBJECT

BEAM SPREADER
The laser beam is spread so that it can illuminate the object.

MIRROR

OBJECT BEAM

PHOTOGRAPHIC FILM

REFERENCE BEAM

BEAM SPREADER
A diverging lens widens the laser beam so that it can illuminate the hologram.

BEAM SPLITTER
A semi-silvered mirror passes part of the laser beam and reflects the other part to split the laser beam into two beams.

MIRROR

MIRROR

SHUTTER

LASER BEAM

HOLOGRAM

A reflection hologram is made with a photographic plate or film and laser light (see p. 197). In the plate or film, light first reflected by the object meets light coming directly from the laser. Each pair of rays—one from every point on the surface of the object and one in the reference beam—interferes. The two rays give light if the interference is "constructive" or they cancel each other out to give dark if the interference is "destructive." Over the whole hologram, an interference pattern forms as all the pairs of rays meet. This pattern depends on the energy levels of the rays coming from the object, which vary with the brightness of its surface.

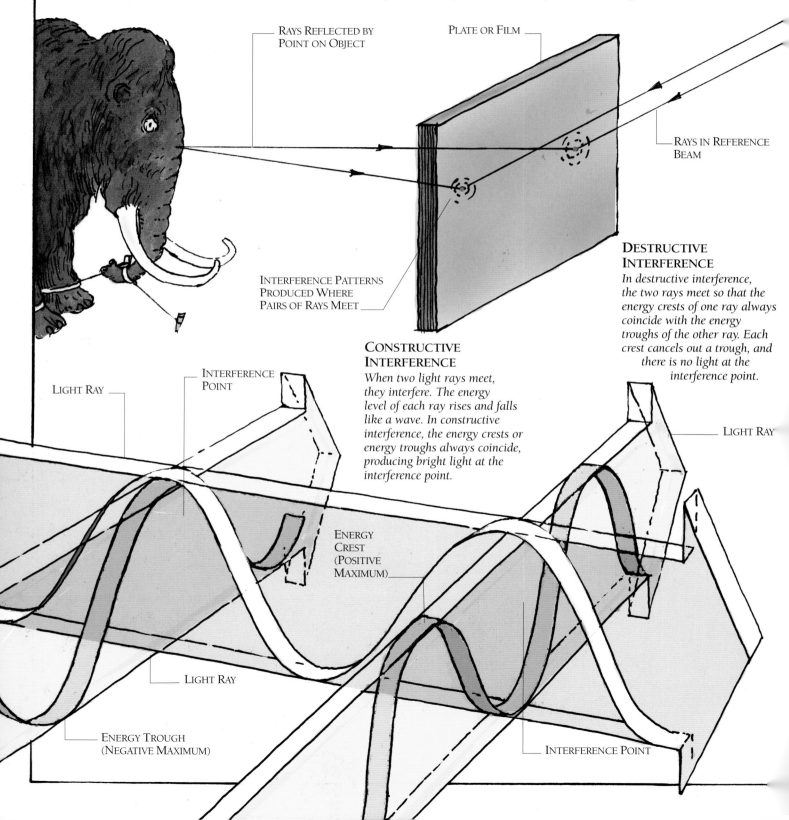

RAYS REFLECTED BY POINT ON OBJECT

PLATE OR FILM

RAYS IN REFERENCE BEAM

INTERFERENCE PATTERNS PRODUCED WHERE PAIRS OF RAYS MEET

DESTRUCTIVE INTERFERENCE

In destructive interference, the two rays meet so that the energy crests of one ray always coincide with the energy troughs of the other ray. Each crest cancels out a trough, and there is no light at the interference point.

CONSTRUCTIVE INTERFERENCE

When two light rays meet, they interfere. The energy level of each ray rises and falls like a wave. In constructive interference, the energy crests or energy troughs always coincide, producing bright light at the interference point.

LIGHT RAY

INTERFERENCE POINT

LIGHT RAY

ENERGY CREST (POSITIVE MAXIMUM)

LIGHT RAY

ENERGY TROUGH (NEGATIVE MAXIMUM)

INTERFERENCE POINT

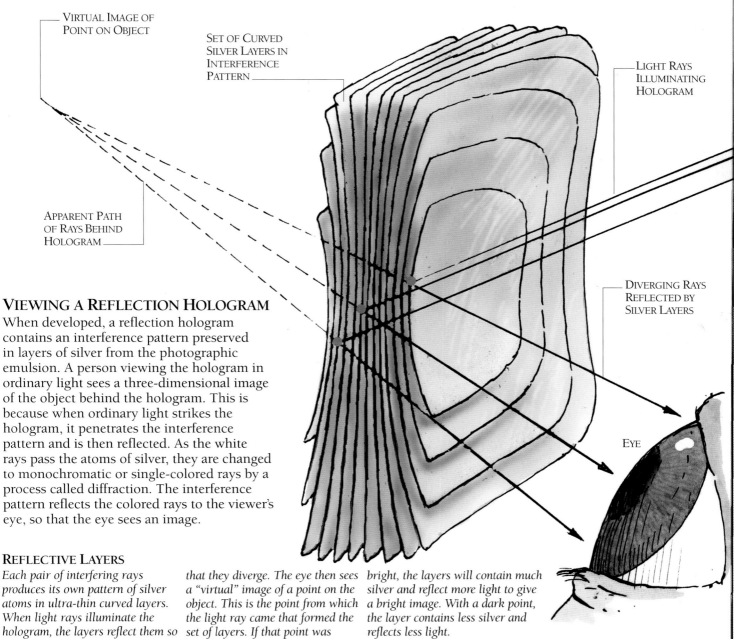

VIRTUAL IMAGE OF
POINT ON OBJECT

SET OF CURVED
SILVER LAYERS IN
INTERFERENCE
PATTERN

LIGHT RAYS
ILLUMINATING
HOLOGRAM

APPARENT PATH
OF RAYS BEHIND
HOLOGRAM

DIVERGING RAYS
REFLECTED BY
SILVER LAYERS

EYE

VIEWING A REFLECTION HOLOGRAM

When developed, a reflection hologram contains an interference pattern preserved in layers of silver from the photographic emulsion. A person viewing the hologram in ordinary light sees a three-dimensional image of the object behind the hologram. This is because when ordinary light strikes the hologram, it penetrates the interference pattern and is then reflected. As the white rays pass the atoms of silver, they are changed to monochromatic or single-colored rays by a process called diffraction. The interference pattern reflects the colored rays to the viewer's eye, so that the eye sees an image.

REFLECTIVE LAYERS

Each pair of interfering rays produces its own pattern of silver atoms in ultra-thin curved layers. When light rays illuminate the hologram, the layers reflect them so *that they diverge. The eye then sees a "virtual" image of a point on the object. This is the point from which the light ray came that formed the set of layers. If that point was* *bright, the layers will contain much silver and reflect more light to give a bright image. With a dark point, the layer contains less silver and reflects less light.*

SEEING IN DEPTH

In a hologram, each eye sees many points formed by different sets of layers in the interference pattern. This gives an image of the object. The two eyes look at different parts of the hologram and so see separate images of the object. The brain combines them to give a three-dimensional image.

The image in each eye is produced by different parts of the hologram formed by rays that left the original object at different angles. Each side of the hologram is formed by rays coming from that side of the object. Moving your head therefore brings another side of the object into view and your view of the image changes.

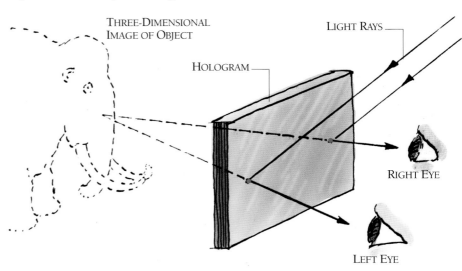

THREE-DIMENSIONAL
IMAGE OF OBJECT

HOLOGRAM

LIGHT RAYS

RIGHT EYE

LEFT EYE

BLU-RAY PLAYER

Blu-ray disks store huge amounts of digital information, usually high-definition video or games for use in video game consoles. On the shiny underside of the disk is a spiral track that carries the bits—binary 1s and 0s (see opposite)—coded into a sequence of tiny indentations called pits. Tens or hundreds of billions of bits are read every second by a violet-blue-colored laser beam that reflects off the spiral track. The disc spins at up to 10,000 revolutions per minute, depending on the kind of information being read and whether the laser is reading from the center or the outer edge of the disc.

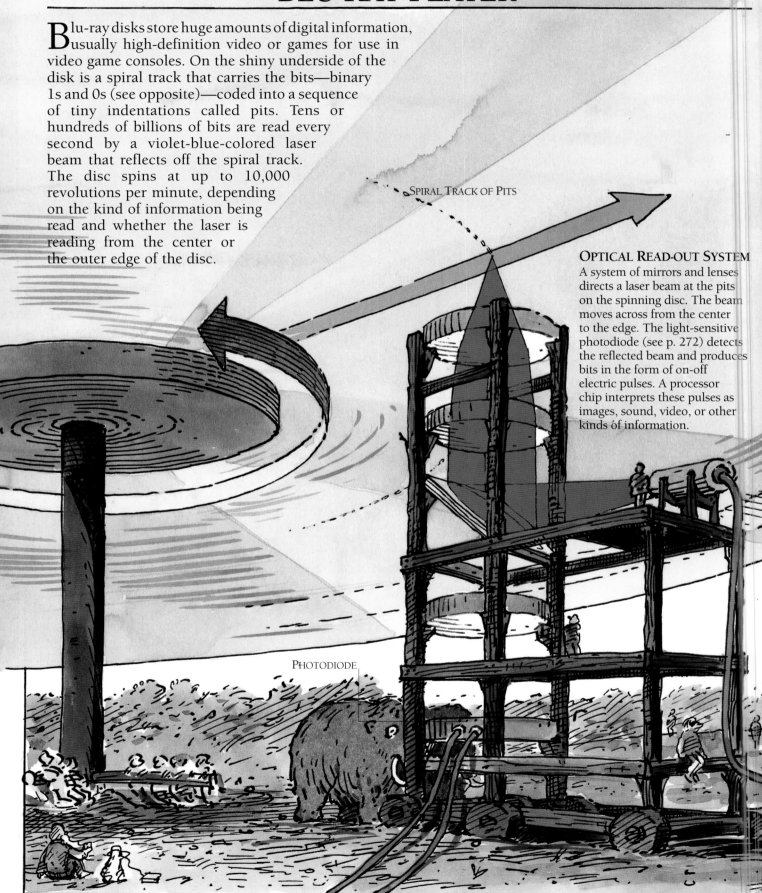

SPIRAL TRACK OF PITS

OPTICAL READ-OUT SYSTEM

A system of mirrors and lenses directs a laser beam at the pits on the spinning disc. The beam moves across from the center to the edge. The light-sensitive photodiode (see p. 272) detects the reflected beam and produces bits in the form of on-off electric pulses. A processor chip interprets these pulses as images, sound, video, or other kinds of information.

PHOTODIODE

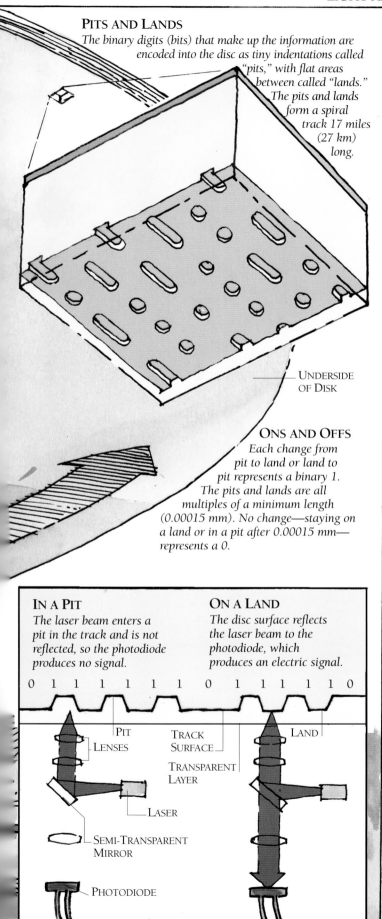

PITS AND LANDS

The binary digits (bits) that make up the information are encoded into the disc as tiny indentations called "pits," with flat areas between called "lands." The pits and lands form a spiral track 17 miles (27 km) long.

UNDERSIDE OF DISK

ONS AND OFFS

Each change from pit to land or land to pit represents a binary 1. The pits and lands are all multiples of a minimum length (0.00015 mm). No change—staying on a land or in a pit after 0.00015 mm— represents a 0.

IN A PIT
The laser beam enters a pit in the track and is not reflected, so the photodiode produces no signal.

ON A LAND
The disc surface reflects the laser beam to the photodiode, which produces an electric signal.

0 1 1 1 1 1 0 1 1 1 1 0

PIT

LENSES

TRACK SURFACE

LAND

TRANSPARENT LAYER

LASER

SEMI-TRANSPARENT MIRROR

PHOTODIODE

OTHER OPTICAL DISCS

A Blu-ray disc is an "optical disc," because it is read using light from a laser beam. Two other common types of optical disc are the compact disc (CD) and the digital versatile disc (DVD). Both have the same arrangement of pits and lands as a Blu-ray, but cannot hold anywhere near as much information, because the pits and lands are of a different size.

CDS AND DVDS

While it is common for people to download music from the Internet, CDs are still a popular way to buy and play music. Some gaming consoles use CDs, and some computer software is distributed on CD-ROM (read-only memory). The DVD format is older than Blu-ray, but remains a popular way to buy films. Many computers are fitted with CD or DVD drives, which can read these optical discs, and most can also write digital information onto "recordable" optical discs (CD-R and DVD-R). A Blu-ray player can play CDs and DVDs, but CD players and DVD players cannot play Blu-ray discs.

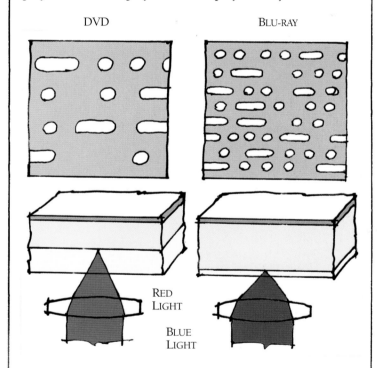

DVD

BLU-RAY

RED LIGHT

BLUE LIGHT

DVD AND BLU-RAY

The blue laser of a Blu-ray player can read much finer detail than the red laser of a DVD player. This is because, with a shorter wavelength, blue light can be focused to a much smaller dot on the disc's surface. As a result, the pits and lands can be made much smaller, and the track much narrower than on a DVD. That is why a Blu-ray disc holds much more information than a DVD. One problem with the blue laser used in Blu-ray players is that it is more prone to being blurred by any imperfections in the protective plastic layer. For that reason, that layer is much thinner so the light does not have to pass through so much plastic to reach the pits and lands, though the layer also has to be tough.

PHOTOGRAPHY

ON MAMMOTH PICTURES

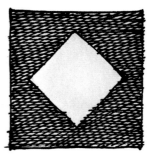

*W*hile *playing golf one day, I noticed that the grass in the specified caddy
waiting areas was considerably lower and less green than the grass in the
sunlight. I played on, but my mind was no longer on the game. If the image of
a mammoth could be made on the grass accidentally, I reasoned, then
perhaps images of other things could be made intentionally?*

*Returning to my workshop, I begged the assistance of the family
next door for my first experiment. I asked them to sleep in a line on the
grass outside. They were reluctant. I offered to pay
them and they were soon snoring away.*

PRESERVED IN SILVER

Film photography uses silver, rather than grass, to preserve
images. Light-sensitive compounds of silver on the plastic
film break down when exposed to light. The result is tiny
specks of silver wherever light has fallen—the image
preserved on the film. The film has to be developed, to make
more silver form where the film has been exposed.
This makes a "negative," because light areas of a scene are
represented by dark silver areas on the film. The whole
process has to be repeated, this time with photographic
paper instead of film, to form a positive image.

EXPOSURE
*Where the light from the bright parts of an image reaches
the film, the silver compound begins to break down,
forming atoms of silver.*

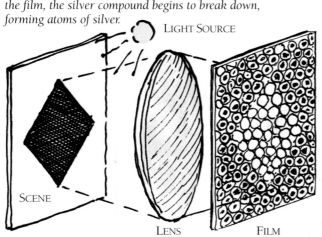

LIGHT SOURCE

SCENE

LENS

FILM

DEVELOPMENT
*A chemical called a developer causes
visible grains of silver to form wherever
the dark silver atoms are present.*

NEGATIVE
*The negative image is then
projected onto photographic
paper, the process repeated
to produce a positive image.*

fig 1

fig 2

fig 3

I had them return for the next five days and lie in exactly the same spot. By the end of the week I had a perfect image of my neighbors. The procedure soon caught on, and eventually even school groups could be seen lying motionless on the workshop's lawns.

However, several drawbacks arose that I had not foreseen. The images required continuous trimming once the subjects left the picture. They were also difficult to display as well as being astronomically expensive to frame. Had I been able to shrink people before they were recorded, I am convinced that my discovery would have had a bright future.

DIGITAL PHOTOGRAPHY

Most photography today is digital. An electronic sensor instead of film captures the image. The sensor has a grid of thousands or millions of light-sensitive elements, and is connected to the camera's battery. Light falling on an element causes that element to allow electric current to flow—the brighter the light, the greater the current. The electric currents then pass through an analog-digital converter (see p. 322) and an image processor, forming a digital image, which is stored on a removable memory card (see pp. 334-35).

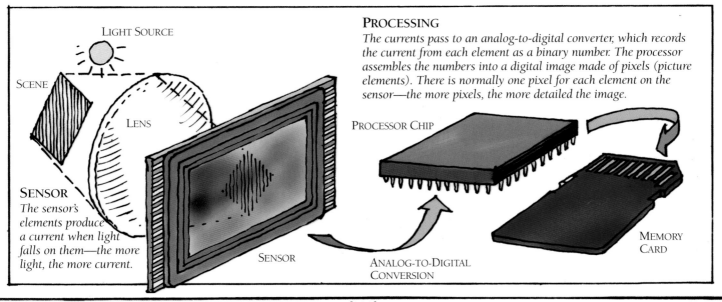

LIGHT SOURCE

SCENE

LENS

SENSOR
The sensor's elements produce a current when light falls on them—the more light, the more current.

SENSOR

ANALOG-TO-DIGITAL CONVERSION

PROCESSING
The currents pass to an analog-to-digital converter, which records the current from each element as a binary number. The processor assembles the numbers into a digital image made of pixels (picture elements). There is normally one pixel for each element on the sensor—the more pixels, the more detailed the image.

PROCESSOR CHIP

MEMORY CARD

DIGITAL SINGLE-LENS REFLEX CAMERA

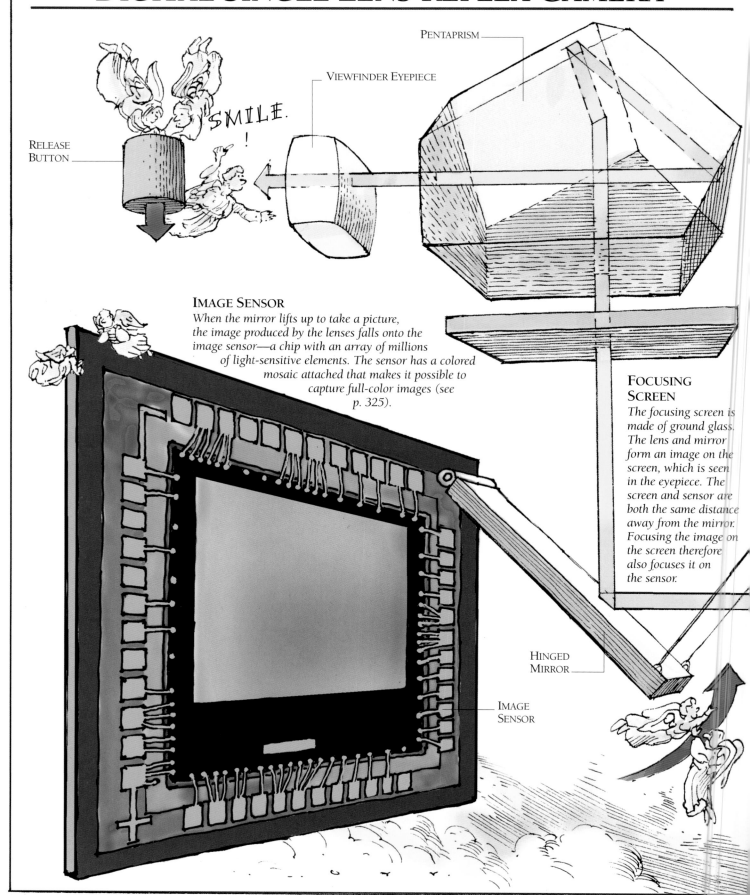

PENTAPRISM

VIEWFINDER EYEPIECE

RELEASE BUTTON

SMILE!

IMAGE SENSOR
When the mirror lifts up to take a picture, the image produced by the lenses falls onto the image sensor—a chip with an array of millions of light-sensitive elements. The sensor has a colored mosaic attached that makes it possible to capture full-color images (see p. 325).

FOCUSING SCREEN
The focusing screen is made of ground glass. The lens and mirror form an image on the screen, which is seen in the eyepiece. The screen and sensor are both the same distance away from the mirror. Focusing the image on the screen therefore also focuses it on the sensor.

HINGED MIRROR

IMAGE SENSOR

Some cameras have two different sets of lenses: one to view the image and one to throw it onto the image sensor. Many photographers prefer to view the actual image that will fall on the sensor before taking a picture. The digital single-lens reflex (DSLR) camera is so named because it uses a single collection of lenses for viewing and for taking the picture. A hinged mirror, angled at 45 degrees in front of the sensor, reflects the light beam from the lens onto a focusing screen above the mirror. The image forms on this screen, and light from it is reflected by the faces of a pentaprism (five-sided prism) into the viewfinder eyepiece. The various reflections turn the viewfinder image upright and the right way around. When the shutter release is pressed, the mirror rises and the light beam strikes the sensor.

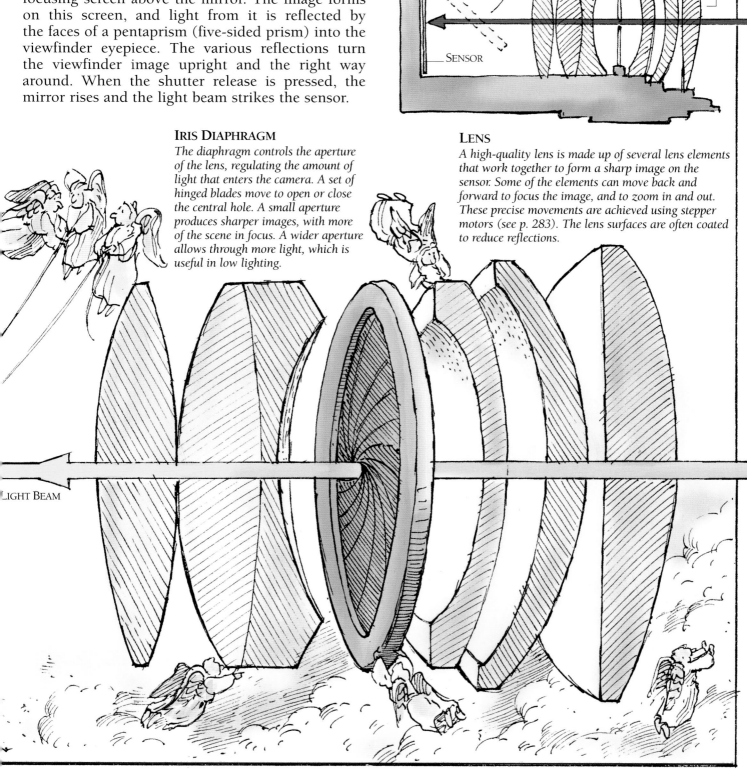

VIEWFINDER EYEPIECE

FOCUSING SCREEN

LENS

PENTAPRISM

DIAPHRAGM

MIRROR

SENSOR

IRIS DIAPHRAGM

The diaphragm controls the aperture of the lens, regulating the amount of light that enters the camera. A set of hinged blades move to open or close the central hole. A small aperture produces sharper images, with more of the scene in focus. A wider aperture allows through more light, which is useful in low lighting.

LENS

A high-quality lens is made up of several lens elements that work together to form a sharp image on the sensor. Some of the elements can move back and forward to focus the image, and to zoom in and out. These precise movements are achieved using stepper motors (see p. 283). The lens surfaces are often coated to reduce reflections.

LIGHT BEAM

DIGITAL VIDEO

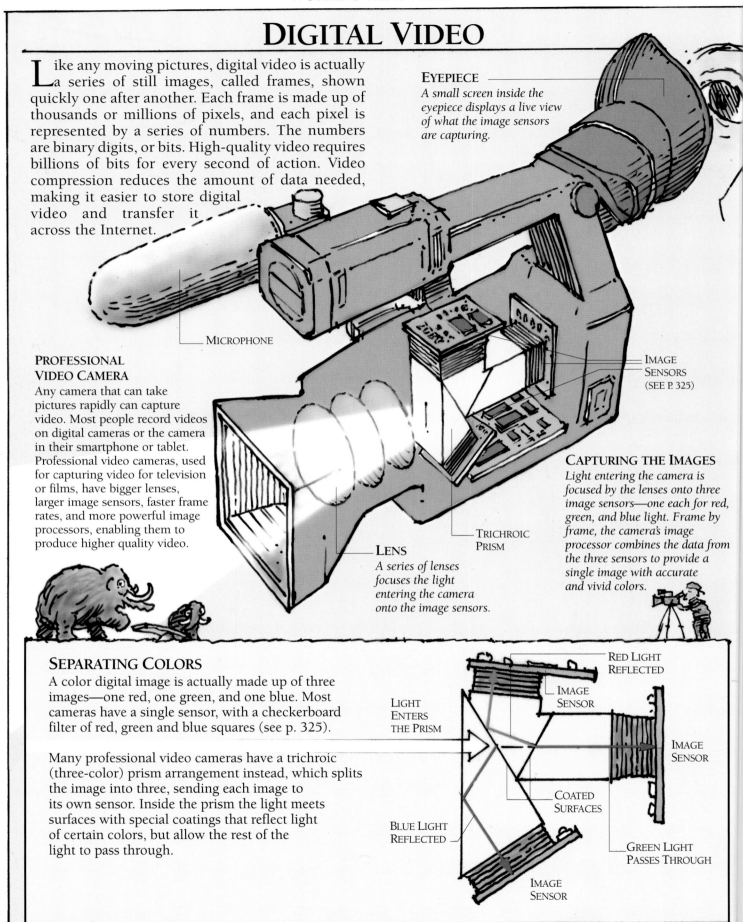

Like any moving pictures, digital video is actually a series of still images, called frames, shown quickly one after another. Each frame is made up of thousands or millions of pixels, and each pixel is represented by a series of numbers. The numbers are binary digits, or bits. High-quality video requires billions of bits for every second of action. Video compression reduces the amount of data needed, making it easier to store digital video and transfer it across the Internet.

EYEPIECE
A small screen inside the eyepiece displays a live view of what the image sensors are capturing.

MICROPHONE

PROFESSIONAL VIDEO CAMERA

Any camera that can take pictures rapidly can capture video. Most people record videos on digital cameras or the camera in their smartphone or tablet. Professional video cameras, used for capturing video for television or films, have bigger lenses, larger image sensors, faster frame rates, and more powerful image processors, enabling them to produce higher quality video.

IMAGE SENSORS (SEE P. 325)

TRICHROIC PRISM

LENS
A series of lenses focuses the light entering the camera onto the image sensors.

CAPTURING THE IMAGES
Light entering the camera is focused by the lenses onto three image sensors—one each for red, green, and blue light. Frame by frame, the camera's image processor combines the data from the three sensors to provide a single image with accurate and vivid colors.

SEPARATING COLORS

A color digital image is actually made up of three images—one red, one green, and one blue. Most cameras have a single sensor, with a checkerboard filter of red, green and blue squares (see p. 325).

Many professional video cameras have a trichroic (three-color) prism arrangement instead, which splits the image into three, sending each image to its own sensor. Inside the prism the light meets surfaces with special coatings that reflect light of certain colors, but allow the rest of the light to pass through.

LIGHT ENTERS THE PRISM

RED LIGHT REFLECTED

IMAGE SENSOR

IMAGE SENSOR

COATED SURFACES

BLUE LIGHT REFLECTED

GREEN LIGHT PASSES THROUGH

IMAGE SENSOR

PICTURE QUALITY

Pixels are the tiny elements that together form the picture you see on the screen. The more pixels each frame has, the more detail will be present in that frame, and the clearer the video will be. The dimensions of a video image, in terms of the number of pixels along the horizontal and vertical edges, is called its resolution. Most modern televisions can display video at a resolution of 1920 x 1080. The higher the resolution, the more bits are needed to represent each frame.

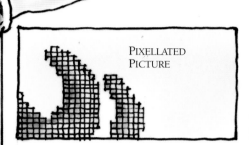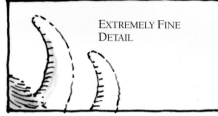

PIXELLATED PICTURE

PIXELS ONLY VISIBLE CLOSE UP

EXTREMELY FINE DETAIL

LOW RESOLUTION
On low resolution video, such as videos streamed across a slow connection to the Internet, the pixels may be clearly visible.

HIGH DEFINITION (HD)
A standard HD television picture is 1920 x 1080. Some TVs can display ultra-high definition (UHD), up to 3840 x 2160.

4K RESOLUTION
Digital video displayed in cinemas is typically 4096 x 2160, called 4K. The images are extremely clear and lifelike.

VIDEO COMPRESSION

High-quality digital video requires billions of bits every second, quickly filling up a hard disk or memory card (see pp. 334-35). The camera's image processor "compresses" the video, so that it takes up much less space. It uses a code to represent areas of each frame that are very similar, and areas that change little from frame to frame. The code requires far fewer bits than the raw image. A processor in a television or computer can then use the same code to reconstruct the frames for display.

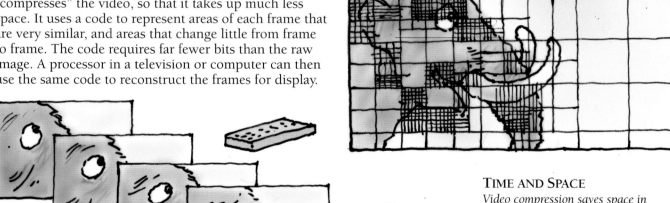

ONLY THE MAMMOTH'S EYE CHANGES FROM FRAME TO FRAME

TIME AND SPACE

Video compression saves space in digital storage media, such as memory cards. Large areas of this frame are almost identical and can be represented as blocks of a single color.

VIDEO PROJECTOR

Digital video captured by a video camera and stored on a hard disk or memory card can be projected onto a large screen for viewing. There are two main types of projector. LCD (liquid crystal display) projectors work in the same way as an LCD screen (see p. 246), except that the light shining through the LCD is focused onto a screen. A DLP (digital light processing) projector uses millions of tiny mirrors to turn on and off the individual pixels that make up each frame of video.

PROJECTOR CASE

BEAM DISPLAYING RED FRAME SHINES ONTO A SCREEN

LENS

DLP PROJECTOR

Light from a bright lamp passes through a rotating color filter and onto a chip called a digital micromirror device. Here, millions of tiny moving mirrors reflect light toward or away from an ordinary mirror. This bounces the light through a lens, which focuses the light on a screen.

MIRROR

CIRCUIT BOARD

COLOR WHEEL

DIGITAL MICROMIRROR DEVICE (DMD)

COLOR WHEEL
The projector displays red, green, and blue versions of each frame in quick succession, thanks to a rapidly rotating color wheel. The brain combines them into a full-color frame.

BRIGHT LIGHT SOURCE

MAKING THE IMAGE
Just like any digital image, each frame is made up of millions of pixels. The DMD controls how much light reaches the screen for each pixel.

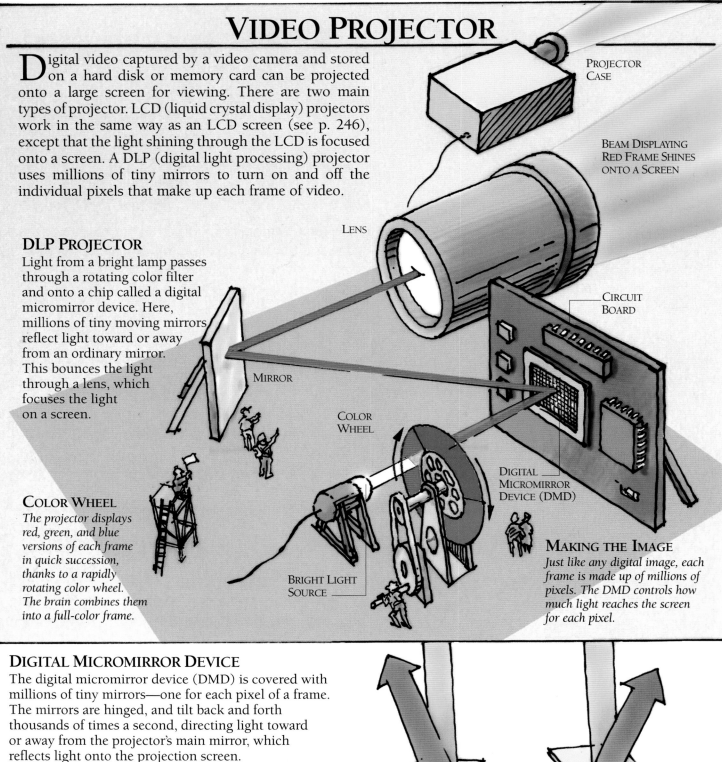

DIGITAL MICROMIRROR DEVICE

The digital micromirror device (DMD) is covered with millions of tiny mirrors—one for each pixel of a frame. The mirrors are hinged, and tilt back and forth thousands of times a second, directing light toward or away from the projector's main mirror, which reflects light onto the projection screen. The more times the mirror tilts to the "on" position, the brighter the pixel it produces.

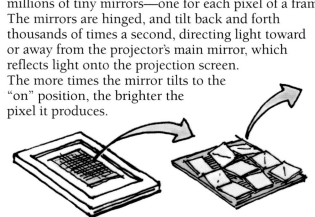

MIRROR IS "ON"
Micromirror reflects light onto the projector's main mirror.

MIRROR IS "OFF"
Micromirror reflects light away from the projector's main mirror.

3D MOVIES

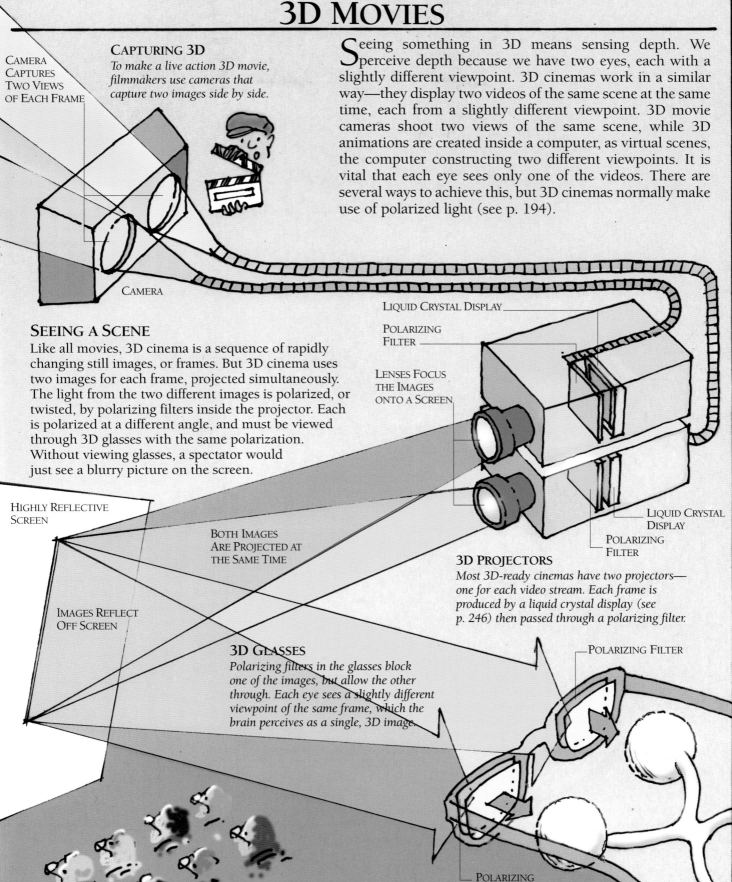

CAPTURING 3D
To make a live action 3D movie, filmmakers use cameras that capture two images side by side.

CAMERA CAPTURES TWO VIEWS OF EACH FRAME

CAMERA

Seeing something in 3D means sensing depth. We perceive depth because we have two eyes, each with a slightly different viewpoint. 3D cinemas work in a similar way—they display two videos of the same scene at the same time, each from a slightly different viewpoint. 3D movie cameras shoot two views of the same scene, while 3D animations are created inside a computer, as virtual scenes, the computer constructing two different viewpoints. It is vital that each eye sees only one of the videos. There are several ways to achieve this, but 3D cinemas normally make use of polarized light (see p. 194).

SEEING A SCENE
Like all movies, 3D cinema is a sequence of rapidly changing still images, or frames. But 3D cinema uses two images for each frame, projected simultaneously. The light from the two different images is polarized, or twisted, by polarizing filters inside the projector. Each is polarized at a different angle, and must be viewed through 3D glasses with the same polarization. Without viewing glasses, a spectator would just see a blurry picture on the screen.

LIQUID CRYSTAL DISPLAY

POLARIZING FILTER

LENSES FOCUS THE IMAGES ONTO A SCREEN

LIQUID CRYSTAL DISPLAY

POLARIZING FILTER

HIGHLY REFLECTIVE SCREEN

BOTH IMAGES ARE PROJECTED AT THE SAME TIME

IMAGES REFLECT OFF SCREEN

3D PROJECTORS
Most 3D-ready cinemas have two projectors—one for each video stream. Each frame is produced by a liquid crystal display (see p. 246) then passed through a polarizing filter.

POLARIZING FILTER

3D GLASSES
Polarizing filters in the glasses block one of the images, but allow the other through. Each eye sees a slightly different viewpoint of the same frame, which the brain perceives as a single, 3D image.

POLARIZING FILTER

PRINTING

MODERN METHODS OF PRINTING

The mammoth mint works by a printing process known as letterpress, the oldest of the three main methods now in use. The other two are gravure and lithography. Here we show flat printing plates for simplicity. Printing presses often have curved plates that rotate to print multiple copies on sheets or strips of paper, but the principles involved are the same.

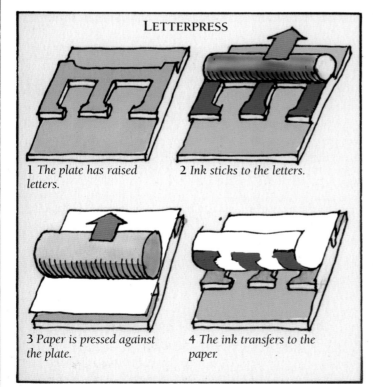

LETTERPRESS

1 The plate has raised letters.

2 Ink sticks to the letters.

3 Paper is pressed against the plate.

4 The ink transfers to the paper.

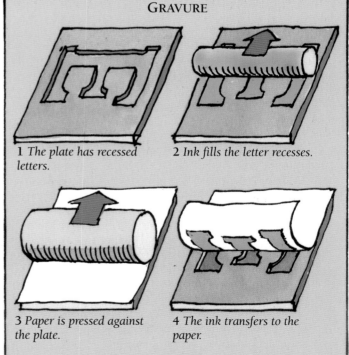

GRAVURE

1 The plate has recessed letters.

2 Ink fills the letter recesses.

3 Paper is pressed against the plate.

4 The ink transfers to the paper.

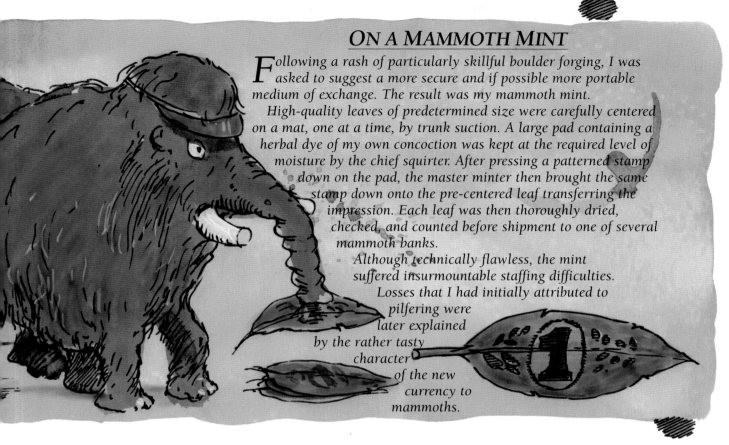

ON A MAMMOTH MINT

Following a rash of particularly skillful boulder forging, I was asked to suggest a more secure and if possible more portable medium of exchange. The result was my mammoth mint.

High-quality leaves of predetermined size were carefully centered on a mat, one at a time, by trunk suction. A large pad containing a herbal dye of my own concoction was kept at the required level of moisture by the chief squirter. After pressing a patterned stamp down on the pad, the master minter then brought the same stamp down onto the pre-centered leaf transferring the impression. Each leaf was then thoroughly dried, checked, and counted before shipment to one of several mammoth banks.

Although technically flawless, the mint suffered insurmountable staffing difficulties. Losses that I had initially attributed to pilfering were later explained by the rather tasty character of the new currency to mammoths.

The processes here show printing in a single color. In full-color printing, a number of inks are applied one after the other by different rollers. Three colored inks, together with black, can produce a complete range of hues by the process of color subtraction.

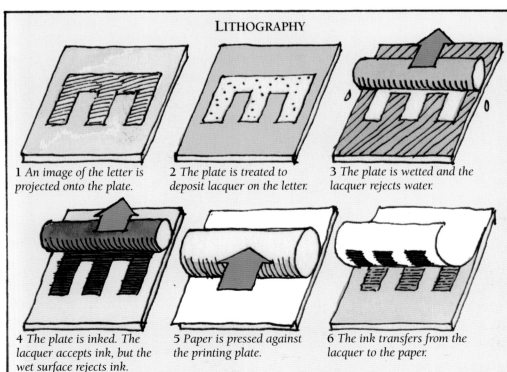

LITHOGRAPHY

1 *An image of the letter is projected onto the plate.*

2 *The plate is treated to deposit lacquer on the letter.*

3 *The plate is wetted and the lacquer rejects water.*

4 *The plate is inked. The lacquer accepts ink, but the wet surface rejects ink.*

5 *Paper is pressed against the printing plate.*

6 *The ink transfers from the lacquer to the paper.*

PRINTING ON STONE

Lithography first used stone printing plates, hence its name which means "writing on stone." An artist can draw on the stone with a greasy substance that attracts ink, and the ink is transferred to paper in a press. Modern litho printing uses light-sensitive plates on which text and images can be deposited by photography. In offset litho printing, the ink is first transferred to a cylinder that then prints the paper.

PAPERMAKING

Printing is of little use without paper. A sheet of paper is a flattened mesh of interlocking plant fibers, mainly of wood and cotton. Making paper involves reducing a plant to its fibers, and then aligning them and coating the fibers with materials such as glues, pigments, and mineral fillers.

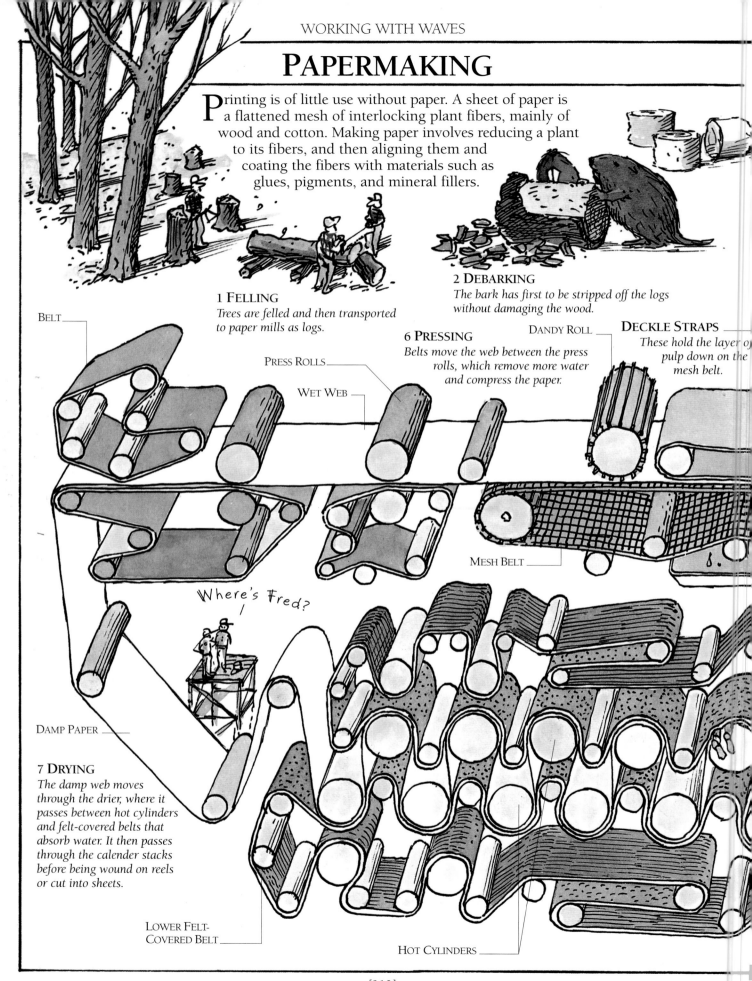

1 FELLING
Trees are felled and then transported to paper mills as logs.

2 DEBARKING
The bark has first to be stripped off the logs without damaging the wood.

BELT

6 PRESSING
Belts move the web between the press rolls, which remove more water and compress the paper.

PRESS ROLLS

WET WEB

DANDY ROLL

DECKLE STRAPS
These hold the layer of pulp down on the mesh belt.

MESH BELT

Where's Fred?

DAMP PAPER

7 DRYING
The damp web moves through the drier, where it passes between hot cylinders and felt-covered belts that absorb water. It then passes through the calender stacks before being wound on reels or cut into sheets.

LOWER FELT-COVERED BELT

HOT CYLINDERS

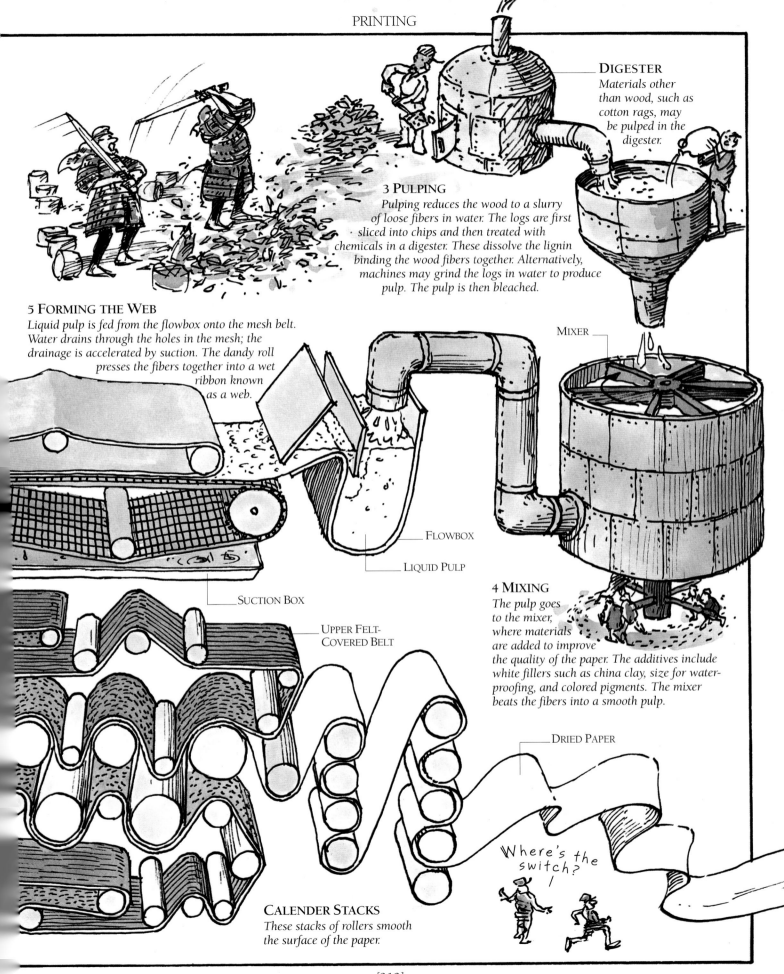

DIGESTER
Materials other than wood, such as cotton rags, may be pulped in the digester.

3 PULPING
Pulping reduces the wood to a slurry of loose fibers in water. The logs are first sliced into chips and then treated with chemicals in a digester. These dissolve the lignin binding the wood fibers together. Alternatively, machines may grind the logs in water to produce pulp. The pulp is then bleached.

5 FORMING THE WEB
Liquid pulp is fed from the flowbox onto the mesh belt. Water drains through the holes in the mesh; the drainage is accelerated by suction. The dandy roll presses the fibers together into a wet ribbon known as a web.

MIXER

FLOWBOX

LIQUID PULP

SUCTION BOX

4 MIXING
The pulp goes to the mixer, where materials are added to improve the quality of the paper. The additives include white fillers such as china clay, size for waterproofing, and colored pigments. The mixer beats the fibers into a smooth pulp.

UPPER FELT-COVERED BELT

DRIED PAPER

Where's the switch?

CALENDER STACKS
These stacks of rollers smooth the surface of the paper.

PRINTING PLATE

When a book like *The Way Things Work Now* is printed, all the color pictures in it are produced using just four different colored inks. The inks are in the three secondary colors—yellow, magenta, and cyan (see p. 185)—plus black, which is also used for the book's text. Each ink is printed by a separate printing plate. Computer software separates the images into these component colors, and a separate printing plate is produced to print each ink.

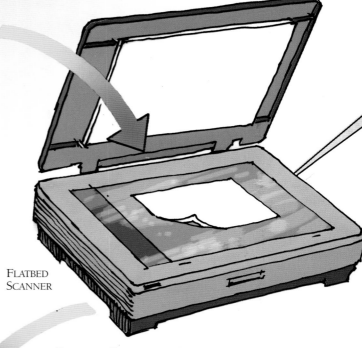

FLATBED
SCANNER

PREPARING IMAGES

The images in this book have been drawn by hand and fed into a computer in digital form—as binary 1s and 0s—using a scanner. Some books use photographs, which are produced in digital cameras, or images produced by illustration software. These are already in digital form, so can be manipulated by the computer, using design software that lays out the images on a book's pages.

PAGE DESIGN

Desktop publishing software allows the designer to see exactly how the text and images will look on the printed page.

theories of
Extinction
Number 37:
Garden hose
experiments

IMAGE SCANNING

An image scanner (see pp. 326-27) uses a light source and an image sensor to capture a picture in digital form. It breaks the image down into millions of red, green, and blue pixels (see p. 203), each recorded as a binary number. The digital image the scanner sends to a computer is a detailed and faithful digital representation of the original drawing.

DESKTOP PUBLISHING

A designer uses desktop publishing software to form the page layouts of the book. The images are placed on the page and text is entered in typefaces of different sizes and styles. Once the book has been designed, the same desktop publishing software is used to prepare the pages for printing by making CMYK color separations for each page (above right).

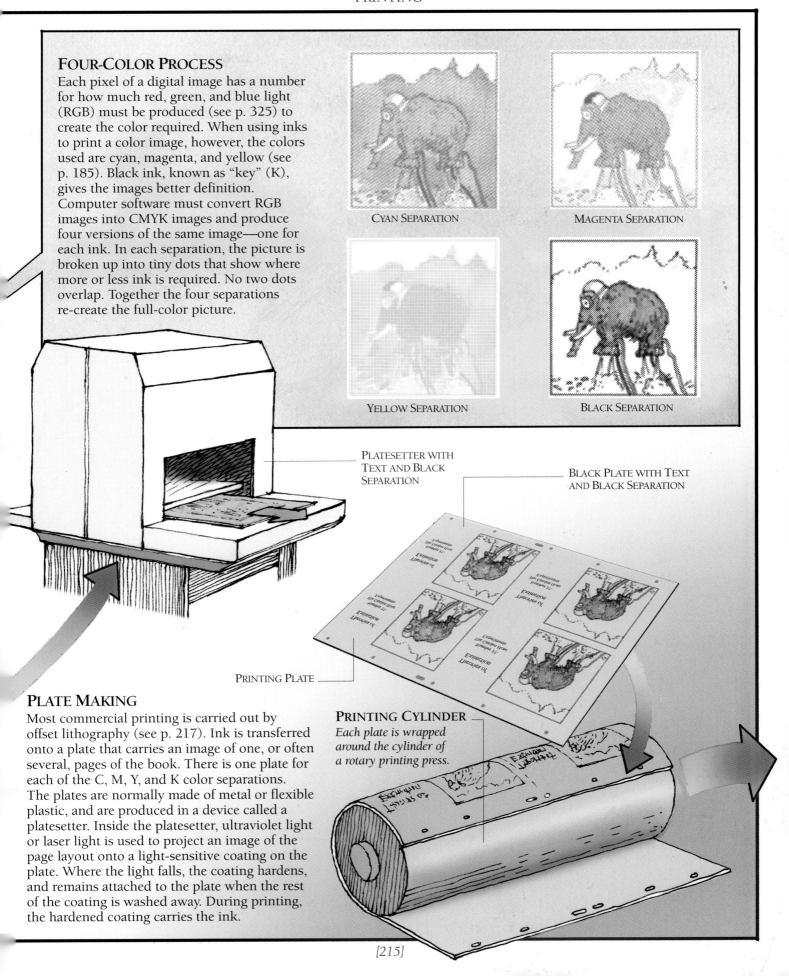

FOUR-COLOR PROCESS

Each pixel of a digital image has a number for how much red, green, and blue light (RGB) must be produced (see p. 325) to create the color required. When using inks to print a color image, however, the colors used are cyan, magenta, and yellow (see p. 185). Black ink, known as "key" (K), gives the images better definition. Computer software must convert RGB images into CMYK images and produce four versions of the same image—one for each ink. In each separation, the picture is broken up into tiny dots that show where more or less ink is required. No two dots overlap. Together the four separations re-create the full-color picture.

CYAN SEPARATION

MAGENTA SEPARATION

YELLOW SEPARATION

BLACK SEPARATION

PLATESETTER WITH TEXT AND BLACK SEPARATION

BLACK PLATE WITH TEXT AND BLACK SEPARATION

PRINTING PLATE

PLATE MAKING

Most commercial printing is carried out by offset lithography (see p. 217). Ink is transferred onto a plate that carries an image of one, or often several, pages of the book. There is one plate for each of the C, M, Y, and K color separations. The plates are normally made of metal or flexible plastic, and are produced in a device called a platesetter. Inside the platesetter, ultraviolet light or laser light is used to project an image of the page layout onto a light-sensitive coating on the plate. Where the light falls, the coating hardens, and remains attached to the plate when the rest of the coating is washed away. During printing, the hardened coating carries the ink.

PRINTING CYLINDER

Each plate is wrapped around the cylinder of a rotary printing press.

PRINTING PRESS

The printing press, as its name implies, prints by pressing paper against an inked plate. Large printing presses are rotary machines in which the printing plate is fitted around a cylinder. As the cylinder rotates, cut sheets or a web (continuous strip) of paper pass rapidly through the press and are printed while on the move. Presses that print in color have four or more printing cylinders so that the color separations are printed immediately one after the other. Quick-drying inks prevent smudging.

SHEET-FED OFFSET PRESS

This book, like many books and magazines, has been printed by offset lithography, a process that combines speed with quality printing. Sheet-fed presses are mainly used for printing books because print quality is very high. Sheets of paper are fed into the press and pass through four printing units that print in yellow, magenta, cyan, and black. The three colors form color pictures, while the black plate adds contrast to the pictures and prints black text. The sheets are printed first on one side, and are then fed back into the machine for printing on the reverse side.

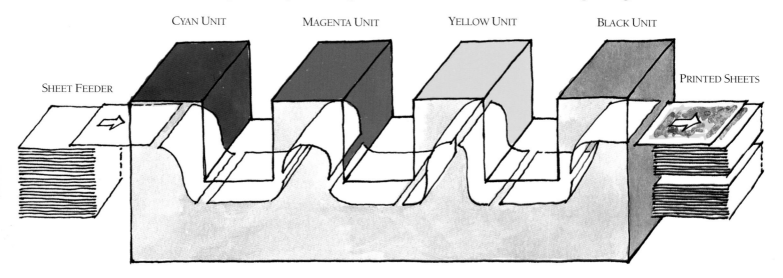

CYAN UNIT MAGENTA UNIT YELLOW UNIT BLACK UNIT

SHEET FEEDER PRINTED SHEETS

WEB OFFSET PRESS

Web offset presses achieve very high speed as well as good quality, and are often used to print magazines and newspapers. Large reels feed the web into the press, which is then printed with four or more colors. Each printing unit usually contains two sets of printing cylinders so that both sides of the paper are printed at the same time. After leaving the press, the web continues on to folding and cutting machines (see p. 218).

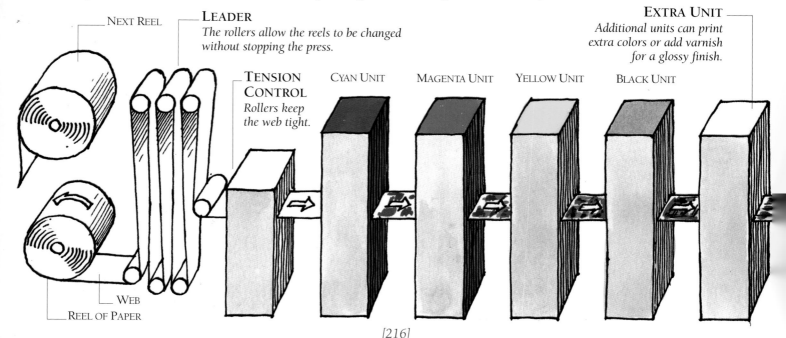

NEXT REEL

LEADER
The rollers allow the reels to be changed without stopping the press.

EXTRA UNIT
Additional units can print extra colors or add varnish for a glossy finish.

TENSION CONTROL
Rollers keep the web tight.

CYAN UNIT MAGENTA UNIT YELLOW UNIT BLACK UNIT

WEB

REEL OF PAPER

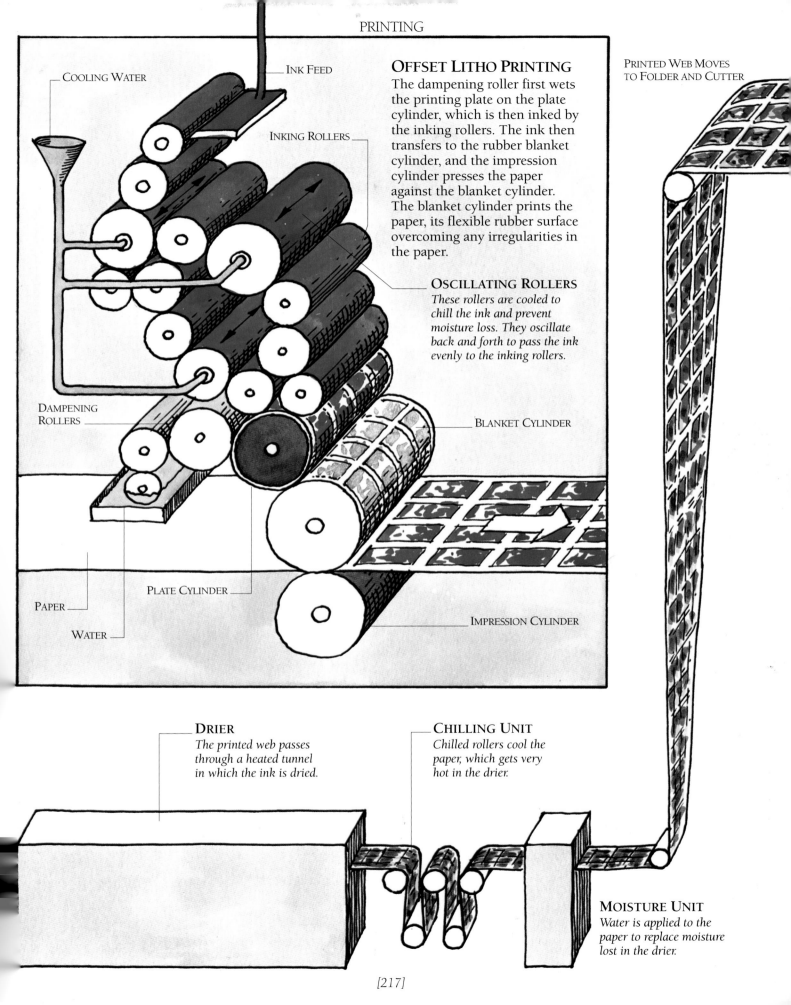

COOLING WATER

INK FEED

INKING ROLLERS

OFFSET LITHO PRINTING

The dampening roller first wets the printing plate on the plate cylinder, which is then inked by the inking rollers. The ink then transfers to the rubber blanket cylinder, and the impression cylinder presses the paper against the blanket cylinder. The blanket cylinder prints the paper, its flexible rubber surface overcoming any irregularities in the paper.

OSCILLATING ROLLERS

These rollers are cooled to chill the ink and prevent moisture loss. They oscillate back and forth to pass the ink evenly to the inking rollers.

PRINTED WEB MOVES TO FOLDER AND CUTTER

DAMPENING ROLLERS

BLANKET CYLINDER

PAPER

WATER

PLATE CYLINDER

IMPRESSION CYLINDER

DRIER

The printed web passes through a heated tunnel in which the ink is dried.

CHILLING UNIT

Chilled rollers cool the paper, which gets very hot in the drier.

MOISTURE UNIT

Water is applied to the paper to replace moisture lost in the drier.

BOOKBINDING

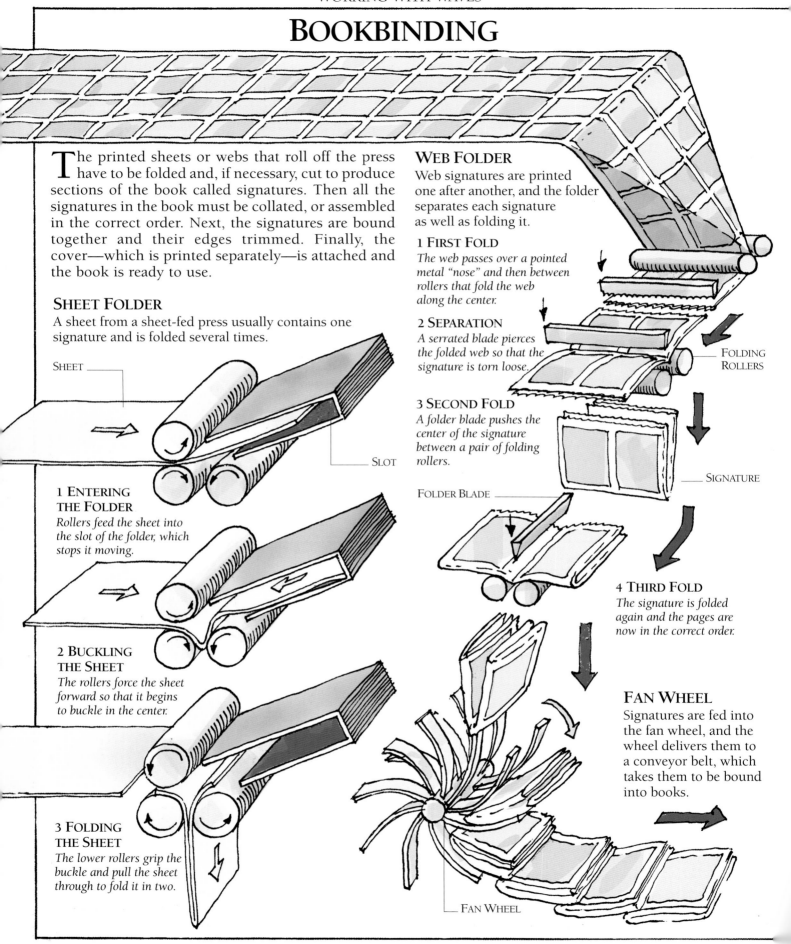

The printed sheets or webs that roll off the press have to be folded and, if necessary, cut to produce sections of the book called signatures. Then all the signatures in the book must be collated, or assembled in the correct order. Next, the signatures are bound together and their edges trimmed. Finally, the cover—which is printed separately—is attached and the book is ready to use.

SHEET FOLDER

A sheet from a sheet-fed press usually contains one signature and is folded several times.

SHEET

SLOT

1 ENTERING THE FOLDER

Rollers feed the sheet into the slot of the folder, which stops it moving.

2 BUCKLING THE SHEET

The rollers force the sheet forward so that it begins to buckle in the center.

3 FOLDING THE SHEET

The lower rollers grip the buckle and pull the sheet through to fold it in two.

WEB FOLDER

Web signatures are printed one after another, and the folder separates each signature as well as folding it.

1 FIRST FOLD

The web passes over a pointed metal "nose" and then between rollers that fold the web along the center.

2 SEPARATION

A serrated blade pierces the folded web so that the signature is torn loose.

3 SECOND FOLD

A folder blade pushes the center of the signature between a pair of folding rollers.

FOLDING ROLLERS

SIGNATURE

FOLDER BLADE

4 THIRD FOLD

The signature is folded again and the pages are now in the correct order.

FAN WHEEL

Signatures are fed into the fan wheel, and the wheel delivers them to a conveyor belt, which takes them to be bound into books.

FAN WHEEL

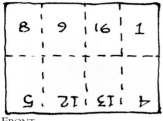

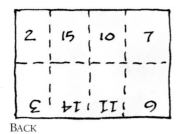

FRONT   BACK

SIGNATURES

The pages in the signature are printed on the sheet or web in a particular order. When folded the right way the pages in each signature will be in the correct sequence. Signatures may contain various numbers of pages: most books have signatures of 16, 24, or 32 pages.

FIRST FOLD

SECOND FOLD

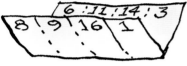

THIRD FOLD

16-PAGE SIGNATURE

The sheet or web is four pages wide and the signature two pages deep. It is folded in the center three times.

HAND BINDING

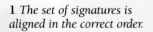

1 *The set of signatures is aligned in the correct order.*

2 *The backs of the signatures are sewn together.*

3 *Glue is applied to hold the signatures together. The pages are then trimmed.*

4 *A lining is glued to the spine (back) of the book.*

5 *The case (cover) is glued to the lining.*

SIGNATURES

CASE

LINING

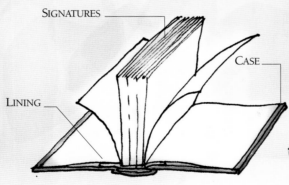

THE FINISHED BOOK

Machine binding follows much the same sequence of operations as hand binding, although sometimes glue is used without sewing.

ELECTRONIC PAPER

Unlike the displays used in most tablets and smartphones, which work by emitting their own light, electronic paper has no light source of its own. Instead, it works by reflecting light much like real paper does. This means it uses far less battery power than LCDs and OLED screens and is much easier to read in bright sunlight. Most electronic paper displays use electronic ink, which is made of millions of tiny microcapsules containing black and white pigments. Letters and images are formed by causing the black pigments to move to the top of certain microcapsules, while the white "paper" background is formed by microcapsules with the white pigment at the top. An alternative technology called electrowetting can display color images. Electronic paper has many uses, from ebook readers and advertising posters to price labels and even some road signs.

MICROCAPSULES

Each microcapsule is about the same diameter as a human hair. It is filled with a transparent fluid in which electrically charged black and white particles are suspended. A single, densely packed layer of microcapsules makes up the display.

WHITE PARTICLES
REFLECT LIGHT

BLACK PARTICLES
ABSORB LIGHT

TINY TRANSISTORS

Beneath the layer of microcapsules is an array of transistors that control whether a particular point on the screen is black or white. Each transistor is connected to an electrode and acts like a switch that makes the electrode either positively or negatively charged. This attracts or repels the black and white particles.

TRANSPARENT
SURFACE

TRANSISTOR

ELECTRODE

MICROCAPSULE

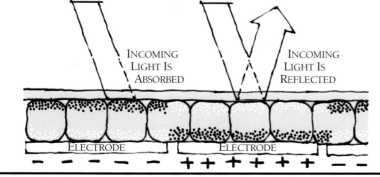

INCOMING
LIGHT IS
ABSORBED

INCOMING
LIGHT IS
REFLECTED

ELECTRODE   ELECTRODE

− − −   + + + + + + +   − −

MICROPARTICLES

The black particles inside the microcapsules are negatively charged and the white ones are positively charged. A negative electric charge on an electrode beneath the microcapsules causes the black particles to migrate toward the top of the display, and the white ones to drop down to the bottom. The particles then remain in these positions—power only needs to be applied to change the display.

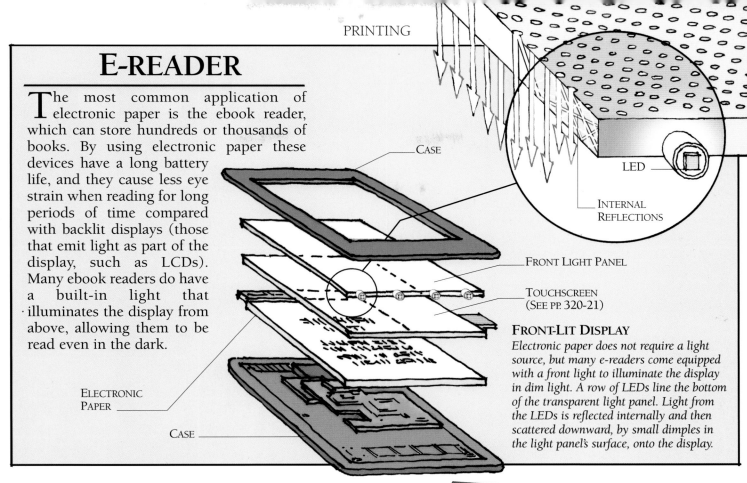

E-READER

The most common application of electronic paper is the ebook reader, which can store hundreds or thousands of books. By using electronic paper these devices have a long battery life, and they cause less eye strain when reading for long periods of time compared with backlit displays (those that emit light as part of the display, such as LCDs). Many ebook readers do have a built-in light that illuminates the display from above, allowing them to be read even in the dark.

CASE

LED

INTERNAL REFLECTIONS

FRONT LIGHT PANEL

TOUCHSCREEN
(SEE PP. 320-21)

ELECTRONIC PAPER

CASE

FRONT-LIT DISPLAY

Electronic paper does not require a light source, but many e-readers come equipped with a front light to illuminate the display in dim light. A row of LEDs line the bottom of the transparent light panel. Light from the LEDs is reflected internally and then scattered downward, by small dimples in the light panel's surface, onto the display.

ELECTROWETTING DISPLAY

The pigments of electronic ink take time to move positions, and the whole image must be cleared before the next image is displayed. By contrast, an electrowetting display can change very rapidly from one image to the next, allowing it to display video. Built onto a reflective white plastic sheet are millions of tiny compartments. Inside each one is a small amount of black liquid. The liquid moves back and forth like a curtain over the reflective white surface, absorbing light or allowing it to be reflected.

COLOR FILTER

A color filter on top of the compartments works in the same way as a mosaic filter in a digital camera (see p. 325). The color of each pixel of the image is created by a group of three subpixels—one red, one blue, and one green. Some electrowetting displays use red, green, and blue colored oils instead.

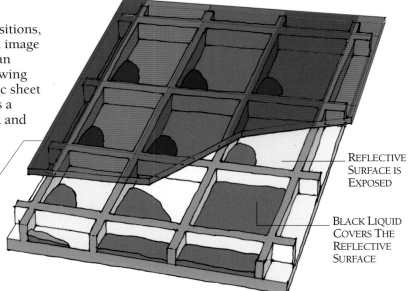

REFLECTIVE SURFACE IS EXPOSED

BLACK LIQUID COVERS THE REFLECTIVE SURFACE

RED SUBPIXEL IS BRIGHT

GREEN SUBPIXEL IS DIM

BLUE SUBPIXEL IS OFF

LOTS OF LIGHT IS REFLECTED

SOME LIGHT IS REFLECTED

NO LIGHT IS REFLECTED

ELECTROWETTING

To make the black liquid uncover or cover the reflective surface at the bottom of each compartment, an electric voltage is applied to an electrode beneath the reflective layer. The voltage causes the liquid to "bead" as water does on a waxed surface. When the voltage turns off, the liquid "wets" the surface, spreading out flat and covering the reflective surface.

SOUND AND MUSIC

ON PLAYING THE MAMMOTH

While I do not profess to understand the "modern" music, I have long been involved in the development of the mammoth as an instrument. In my earliest experiments, a trio of courageous musicians produced the most remarkable assortment of sounds from a single properly tuned and securely tethered beast. The tusks, when struck by wooden mallets, gave a rich melodic chime. The great belly, played with leather-covered mallets, offered a sonorous thud. The tail, secured by a flexible tree trunk, produced a soothing twang when plucked. By moving the tree trunk to either stretch or relax the tail, the plucker could achieve many different notes. But perhaps the most extraordinary sound was that produced voluntarily by the animal itself. As the mammoth slipped into the spirit of the music, it issued periodic trumpet blasts from its great trunk. The trio became a quartet in which man and nature achieved an unforgettable harmony.

MAKING SOUND

All sound producers emit sound by making something vibrate. As a vibrating object moves to and fro, it sets up sound waves in the air. The waves consist of alternate regions of high and low pressure, which are known as compressions and rarefactions. As the object's surface moves forward into the air, it produces a compression. The surface then moves back, producing a rarefaction. Together each compression and rarefaction makes up a sound wave, and the waves move out in all directions at high speed. The stronger the vibrations, the greater the pressure difference between each compression and rarefaction and the louder the sound.

The vibrations that set up sounds can be produced in a number of different ways. The simplest is hitting an object: the energy from the blow vibrates the object and these vibrations are transmitted to the air. Plucking a taut string (or tail) makes it vibrate, while releasing air under pressure into a hollow tube (such as a trunk) can also set up vibrations in the air.

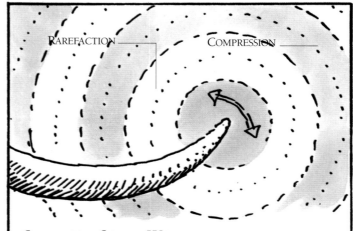

SETTING UP SOUND WAVES
Hitting an object like a tusk makes it vibrate, and this vibration is then transmitted to the air around the object. The vibration needed to create an audible sound wave has to have a rate of more than 20 compressions and 20 rarefactions per second.

More recent experiments have focused on the mammoth as an ensemble instrument. Perhaps the best known of these undertakings was my arrangement for four mammoths, tethered in order of size. Although the instruments often grew restless during rehearsals, the twelve musicians, comprising four tusk-tappers, four stomach-thumpers, and four tail-twangers, became highly proficient at playing them. The performance was a feast not only for the ears but also for the eyes.

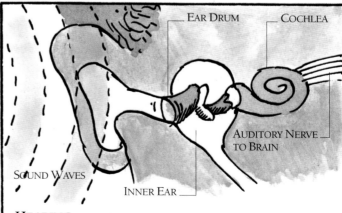

The popularity of massed mammoth music reached its peak with the creation of the Mammoth Tabernacle Choir. While I personally never saw or heard it, I am assured that the effect, especially at close range, was nothing short of stunning.

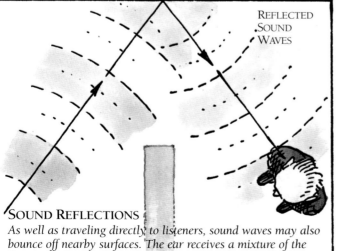

REFLECTED SOUND WAVES

SOUND REFLECTIONS

As well as traveling directly to listeners, sound waves may also bounce off nearby surfaces. The ear receives a mixture of the direct sound and echoes. If the reflecting surfaces are fairly distant, the reflected sound will take much longer to reach the ear and separate echoes will be heard.

EAR DRUM   COCHLEA

AUDITORY NERVE TO BRAIN

SOUND WAVES

INNER EAR

HEARING

As sound waves enter the ear, the pressure differences between successive compressions and rarefactions set the ear drum vibrating. These vibrations pass to the cochlea in the inner ear, where they are converted into electric signals. The signals travel along the auditory nerve to the brain, and the sound is heard.

WOODWIND INSTRUMENTS

Woodwind instruments are not necessarily made of wood, many of them, like the saxophone, being metal, but they do require wind to make a sound. They consist basically of a tube, usually with a series of holes. Air is blown into the top of the tube, either across a hole or past a flexible reed. This makes the air inside the tube vibrate and give out a note. The pitch of the note depends on the length of the tube, a shorter tube giving a higher note, and also on which holes are covered. Blowing harder makes the sound louder.

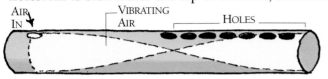

ALL HOLES COVERED
Covering all seven holes in a simple pipe makes the air in the whole tube vibrate, giving the note middle C.

FIRST THREE HOLES COVERED
This shortens the vibrating air column to two-thirds of the tube, giving the higher note G.

FIRST FIVE HOLES COVERED
This extends the vibrating air column to four-fifths of the total length of the tube, giving an E.

KEYS AND CURVES
To produce deep notes, woodwind instruments have to be quite long. The tube is therefore curved so that the player can hold the instrument, as in this alto saxophone. Keys allow the fingers to open and close holes all along the instrument.

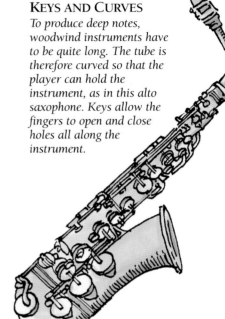

EDGE-BLOWN WOODWINDS
In the flute and recorder, the player blows air over an edge in the mouthpiece. This sets the air column inside the instrument vibrating.

SINGLE-REED WOODWINDS
In the clarinet and saxophone, the mouthpiece contains a single reed that vibrates to set the air column inside the instrument vibrating.

DOUBLE-REED WOODWINDS
The oboe, cor anglais, and bassoon have a mouthpiece made of a double reed that vibrates to set the air column inside the instrument vibrating.

FINGERHOLES
In a short and simple woodwind instrument, such as the recorder, the fingers can cover all the holes directly.

PADS
Several woodwinds have holes that are larger than the fingers, requiring the fingers to press pads to cover the holes.

KEYS
Holes that are out of reach of the fingers are covered by pressing sprung keys attached to pads.

BRASS INSTRUMENTS

Brass instruments are in fact mostly made of brass, and consist of a long pipe that is usually coiled and has no holes. The player blows into a mouthpiece at one end of the pipe, the vibration of the lips setting the air column vibrating throughout the tube. The force of the lips varies to make the vibrating column divide into two halves, three thirds, and so on. This gives an ascending series of notes called harmonics. Opening extra lengths of tubing then gives other notes that are not in this harmonic series.

LOW PRESSURE
With low lip pressure, the air column vibrates in two halves and each half gives the note middle C. The length of the tube is therefore twice as long as a woodwind instrument sounding the same note.

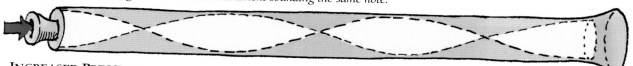

INCREASED PRESSURE
Raising the lip pressure makes the air column vibrate in three thirds. Each vibrating section is two-thirds the length of the previous section, raising the pitch of the note to G.

INCREASED LENGTH
To play an E, which is not in the harmonic series, the player keeps the air vibrating in three thirds and increases the total length of the tube. Each vibrating section becomes four-fifths the length for middle C.

THE TROMBONE
The trombone has a section of tubing called a slide that can be moved in and out. The player pushes out the slide to lengthen the vibrating air column and produce notes that are not in the harmonic series.

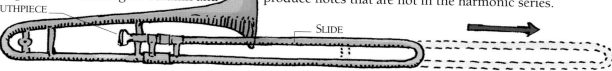

MOUTHPIECE

SLIDE

THE TRUMPET
The trumpet has three pistons that are pushed down to open extra sections of tubing and play notes that are not in the harmonic series. Up to six different notes are obtained by using different combinations of the three pistons.

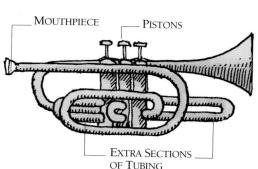

MOUTHPIECE   PISTONS

EXTRA SECTIONS OF TUBING

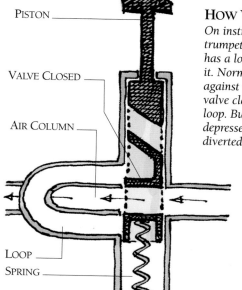

PISTON

VALVE CLOSED

AIR COLUMN

LOOP

SPRING

HOW VALVES WORK
On instruments such as the trumpet and tuba, each valve has a loop of tubing attached to it. Normally, the spring pushes against the piston, keeping the valve closed and shutting off the loop. But when the piston is depressed, the air column is diverted through the loop.

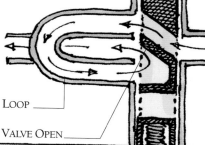

LOOP

VALVE OPEN

STRING AND PERCUSSION INSTRUMENTS

String instruments form a large group of musical instruments that includes the violin family and guitar, and also harps, zithers, and the piano. All these instruments make a sound by causing a taut string to vibrate. The string may be bowed, as with the violin family, plucked as in guitars, harps, and zithers, or struck by a hammer as in the piano (see pp. 26-27). The pitch of the note produced depends on three factors—the length, weight, and tension of the string. A shorter, lighter, or tighter string gives a higher note.

In many string instruments, the strings themselves do not make much sound. Their vibration is passed to the body of the instrument, which resonates to increase the level of sound that is heard.

STRING — FINGERBOARD —

TUNING PEG

Percussion instruments are struck, usually with sticks or mallets, to make a sound. Often the whole instrument vibrates and makes a crack or crash, as in castanets and cymbals. Their sound does not vary in pitch and can only be made louder or softer. Drums contain stretched skins, which may vibrate to give a pitched note. As with strings, tightening the skin makes the note higher in pitch and smaller drums give higher notes.

Tuned percussion instruments, such as the xylophone, have sets of bars that each give a definite note. The pitch of the note depends on the size of the bar, a smaller bar giving a higher pitch.

THE KETTLE-DRUM

Kettledrums or timpani make sounds with a definite pitch, which can be varied. Pressing a pedal or turning screws pulls the hoop down to tighten the skin and raise the pitch, or releases the hoop to slacken the skin and lower the pitch.

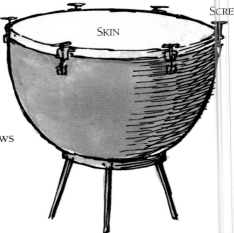

SCRE

SKIN

THE VIOLIN

The violin and its relatives are the most expressive of string instruments. The violin has four strings of different weights. These are wound around tuning pegs to produce the correct amount of tension, and they sound four "open" notes when they are plucked or bowed. The performer stops the strings to obtain other notes, pressing one or more strings against the fingerboard to shorten the section that vibrates, thus raising the pitch of the string.

The front and back of the violin are connected by a short sound post, which transmits vibrations to the back. The whole body vibrates and the sound emerges through the f-shaped sound holes on the front of the instrument.

SKIN

HOOP

TENSIONING SCREW

SHELL

BAR

RESONATORS

Air inside tubes called resonators under the bars vibrates to make the notes louder.

RESONATOR

THE XYLOPHONE

The xylophone and similar instruments such as the vibraphone and marimba have sets of bars arranged like a piano keyboard. Each bar gives out a particular note when struck with a mallet, the longer bars sounding deeper notes.

MICROPH...

A microphone is a kind of electric ear in that it too converts sound waves into an electric signal. The voltage of the microphone signal depends on the pressure of the sound wave—or in other words, on the volume of sound. The frequency at which its voltage varies depends on the other important characteristic of the sound wave, the frequency or pitch.

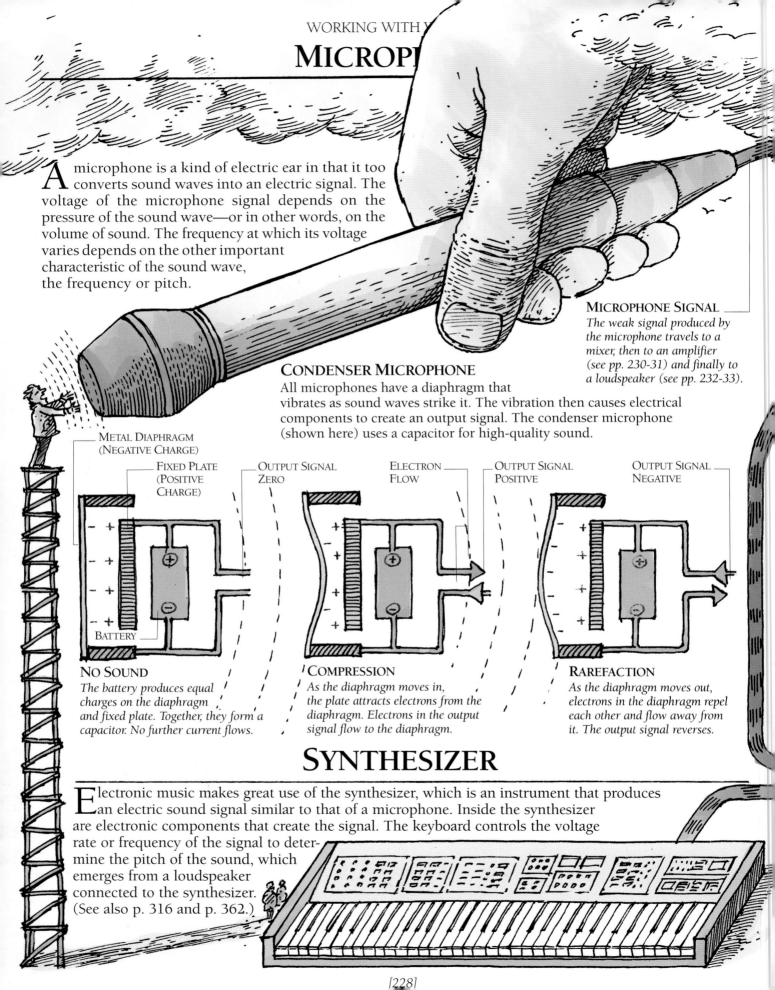

MICROPHONE SIGNAL
The weak signal produced by the microphone travels to a mixer, then to an amplifier (see pp. 230-31) and finally to a loudspeaker (see pp. 232-33).

CONDENSER MICROPHONE
All microphones have a diaphragm that vibrates as sound waves strike it. The vibration then causes electrical components to create an output signal. The condenser microphone (shown here) uses a capacitor for high-quality sound.

METAL DIAPHRAGM (NEGATIVE CHARGE)

FIXED PLATE (POSITIVE CHARGE)

OUTPUT SIGNAL ZERO

ELECTRON FLOW

OUTPUT SIGNAL POSITIVE

OUTPUT SIGNAL NEGATIVE

BATTERY

NO SOUND
The battery produces equal charges on the diaphragm and fixed plate. Together, they form a capacitor. No further current flows.

COMPRESSION
As the diaphragm moves in, the plate attracts electrons from the diaphragm. Electrons in the output signal flow to the diaphragm.

RAREFACTION
As the diaphragm moves out, electrons in the diaphragm repel each other and flow away from it. The output signal reverses.

SYNTHESIZER

Electronic music makes great use of the synthesizer, which is an instrument that produces an electric sound signal similar to that of a microphone. Inside the synthesizer are electronic components that create the signal. The keyboard controls the voltage rate or frequency of the signal to determine the pitch of the sound, which emerges from a loudspeaker connected to the synthesizer. (See also p. 316 and p. 362.)

ELECTRIC GUITAR

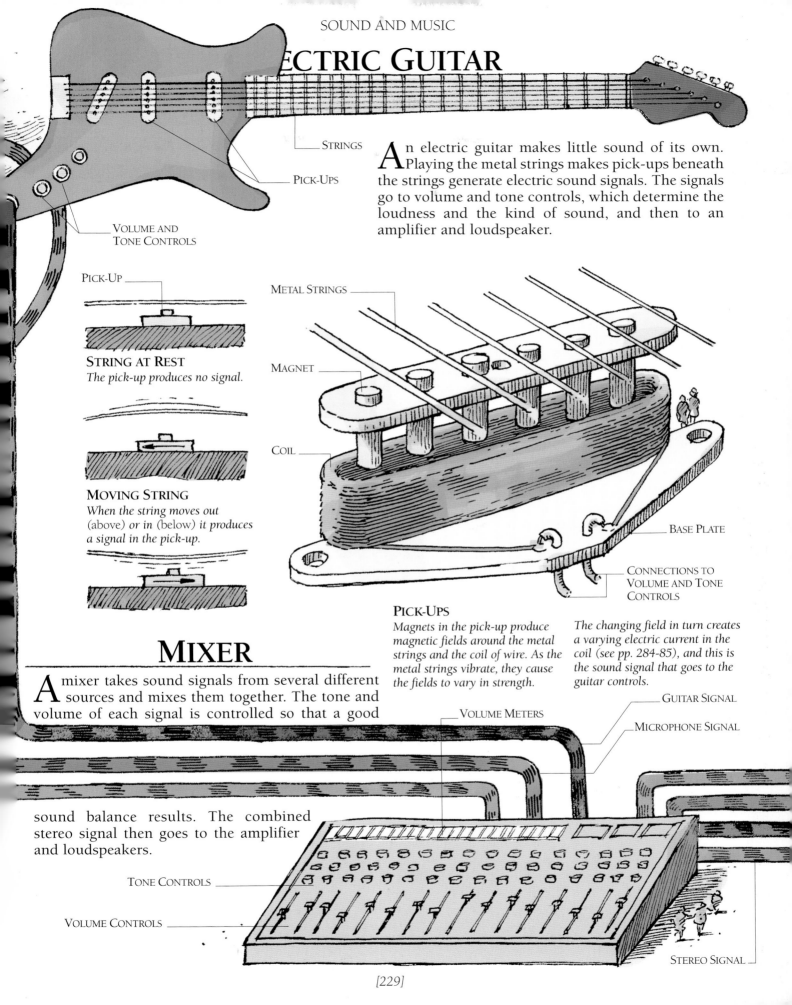

STRINGS

PICK-UPS

VOLUME AND
TONE CONTROLS

An electric guitar makes little sound of its own. Playing the metal strings makes pick-ups beneath the strings generate electric sound signals. The signals go to volume and tone controls, which determine the loudness and the kind of sound, and then to an amplifier and loudspeaker.

PICK-UP

STRING AT REST
The pick-up produces no signal.

MOVING STRING
When the string moves out (above) or in (below) it produces a signal in the pick-up.

METAL STRINGS

MAGNET

COIL

BASE PLATE

CONNECTIONS TO
VOLUME AND TONE
CONTROLS

PICK-UPS
Magnets in the pick-up produce magnetic fields around the metal strings and the coil of wire. As the metal strings vibrate, they cause the fields to vary in strength.

The changing field in turn creates a varying electric current in the coil (see pp. 284-85), and this is the sound signal that goes to the guitar controls.

MIXER

A mixer takes sound signals from several different sources and mixes them together. The tone and volume of each signal is controlled so that a good sound balance results. The combined stereo signal then goes to the amplifier and loudspeakers.

GUITAR SIGNAL

MICROPHONE SIGNAL

VOLUME METERS

TONE CONTROLS

VOLUME CONTROLS

STEREO SIGNAL

AMPLIFIER

An amplifier increases the voltage of a weak signal from a microphone, mixer, electric instrument, radio tuner or CD player, giving it enough power to drive a loudspeaker or earphone. It works by using the weak signal to regulate the flow of a much stronger current, which normally comes from a battery or the mains supply. The key components that regulate the flow of the strong current are usually transistors. These two pages show the principles of amplification with a basic single-transistor amplifier.

RAREFACTION IN SOUND WAVE

A transistor is a small sandwich of two types of semiconductor, so called because their conductivity changes as the transistor works. The two *n*-type (negative) pieces have some free electrons, while the *p*-type (positive) piece has "holes" into which the electrons can fit. The three pieces are known as the emitter, base, and collector. When the microphone diaphragm moves out, electrons from the weak sound signal fill holes in the *p*-type semiconductor. This blocks the electrons from the power supply.

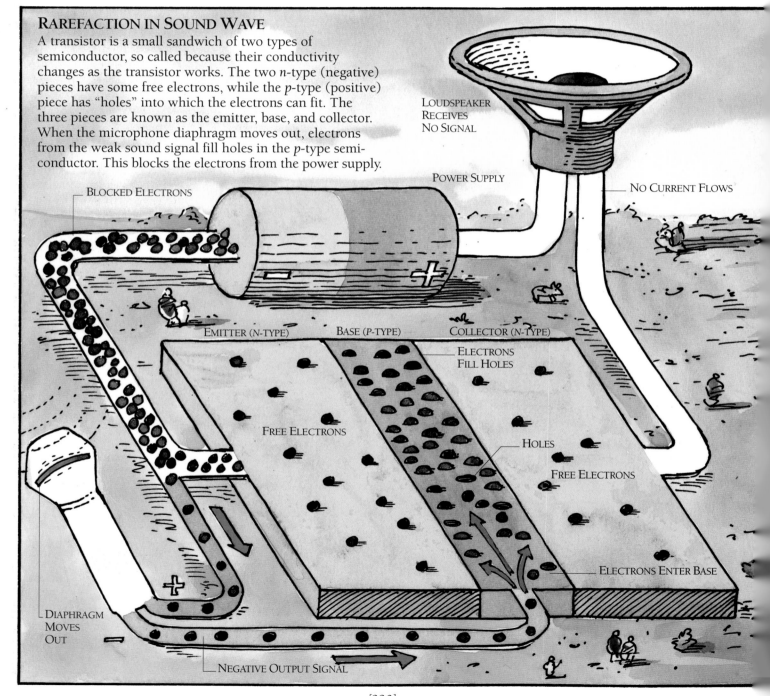

LOUDSPEAKER RECEIVES NO SIGNAL

POWER SUPPLY

NO CURRENT FLOWS

BLOCKED ELECTRONS

EMITTER (N-TYPE)

BASE (P-TYPE)

COLLECTOR (N-TYPE)

ELECTRONS FILL HOLES

FREE ELECTRONS

HOLES

FREE ELECTRONS

ELECTRONS ENTER BASE

DIAPHRAGM MOVES OUT

NEGATIVE OUTPUT SIGNAL

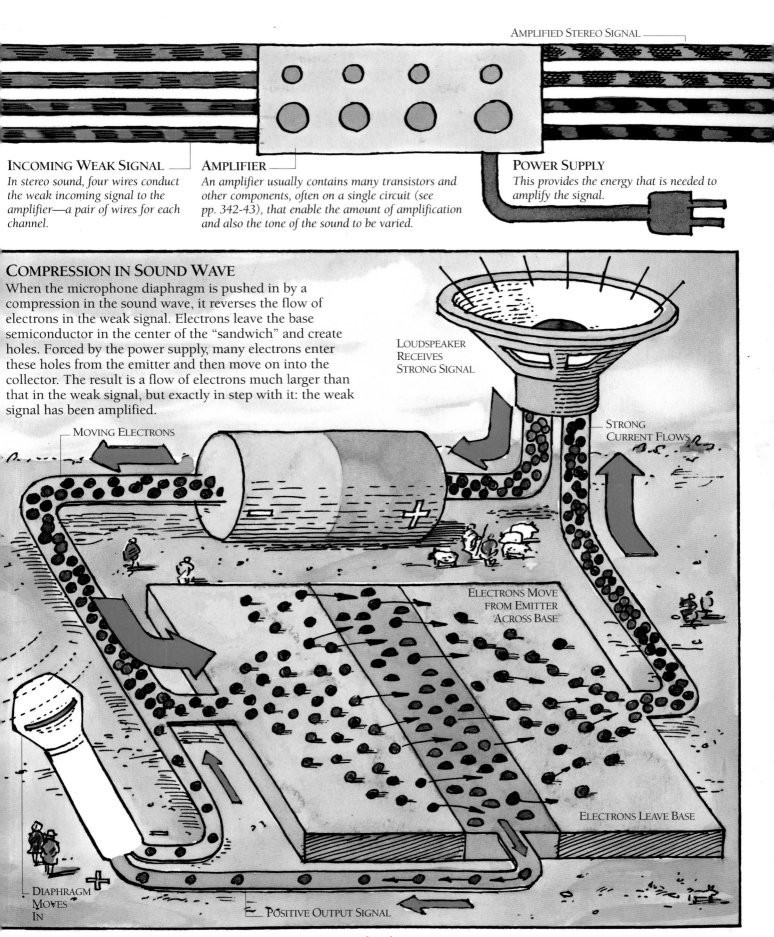

AMPLIFIED STEREO SIGNAL

INCOMING WEAK SIGNAL
In stereo sound, four wires conduct the weak incoming signal to the amplifier—a pair of wires for each channel.

AMPLIFIER
An amplifier usually contains many transistors and other components, often on a single circuit (see pp. 342-43), that enable the amount of amplification and also the tone of the sound to be varied.

POWER SUPPLY
This provides the energy that is needed to amplify the signal.

COMPRESSION IN SOUND WAVE

When the microphone diaphragm is pushed in by a compression in the sound wave, it reverses the flow of electrons in the weak signal. Electrons leave the base semiconductor in the center of the "sandwich" and create holes. Forced by the power supply, many electrons enter these holes from the emitter and then move on into the collector. The result is a flow of electrons much larger than that in the weak signal, but exactly in step with it: the weak signal has been amplified.

LOUDSPEAKER RECEIVES STRONG SIGNAL

MOVING ELECTRONS

STRONG CURRENT FLOWS

ELECTRONS MOVE FROM EMITTER ACROSS BASE

ELECTRONS LEAVE BASE

DIAPHRAGM MOVES IN

POSITIVE OUTPUT SIGNAL

LOUDSPEAKER

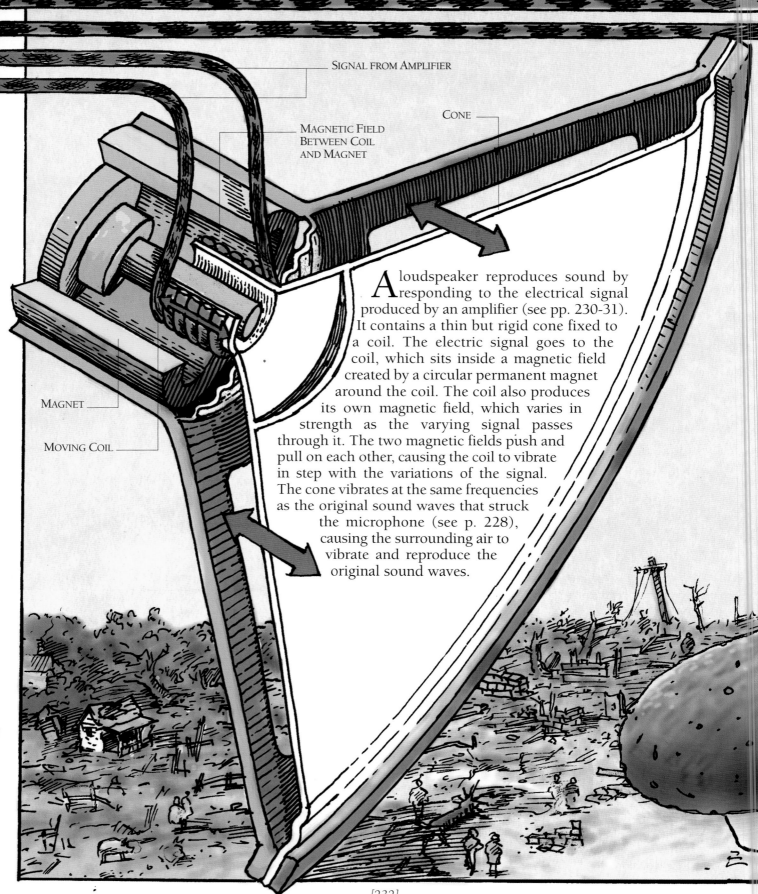

SIGNAL FROM AMPLIFIER

CONE

MAGNETIC FIELD
BETWEEN COIL
AND MAGNET

MAGNET

MOVING COIL

A loudspeaker reproduces sound by responding to the electrical signal produced by an amplifier (see pp. 230-31). It contains a thin but rigid cone fixed to a coil. The electric signal goes to the coil, which sits inside a magnetic field created by a circular permanent magnet around the coil. The coil also produces its own magnetic field, which varies in strength as the varying signal passes through it. The two magnetic fields push and pull on each other, causing the coil to vibrate in step with the variations of the signal. The cone vibrates at the same frequencies as the original sound waves that struck the microphone (see p. 228), causing the surrounding air to vibrate and reproduce the original sound waves.

EARPHONE

An earphone is basically a miniature loudspeaker, and works in the same way. Just as two loudspeakers are normally used, a pair of earphones are usually worn, and these can reproduce stereophonic sound. Two pairs of wires carry a pair of sound signals originating from two or more microphones or other sound sources (see pp. 228-31). Although the sounds go directly to each ear, the stereophonic effect causes the voices or instruments to spread out and have locations in space between the two earphones or loudspeakers.

INSIDE AN EARPHONE
The signal goes to a coil fixed to a diaphragm and suspended around a magnet. The coil and diaphragm vibrate to reproduce the sound.

GRILL

SOFT COVER

MAGNET

COIL

DIAPHRAGM

PLUG
The wires from the amplifier end in a socket. The earphone plug fits in the socket and contacts in the plug transfer the electric signal to the wires leading to each earphone.

THE RECORD PLAYER

A record player takes disks that revolve at 33 or 45 revolutions per minute, each side containing one spiral groove. The recording system, now obsolescent, is analog. The number and depth of the contours in the groove wall correspond to the varying frequency and loudness of the sound waves being recorded.

The record rests on a rotating turntable, and the pick-up arm in the player has a cartridge with a stylus that rests in the groove and vibrates as the record revolves. The vibrations of the stylus make the cartridge produce a stereo electric signal. This signal then goes to an amplifier and pair of loudspeakers to reproduce the recorded sound.

SPINDLE

TURNTABLE

BELT DRIVE
Many turntables are driven by a belt that runs around a drive spindle turned by the motor. This system prevents motor vibration reaching the record.

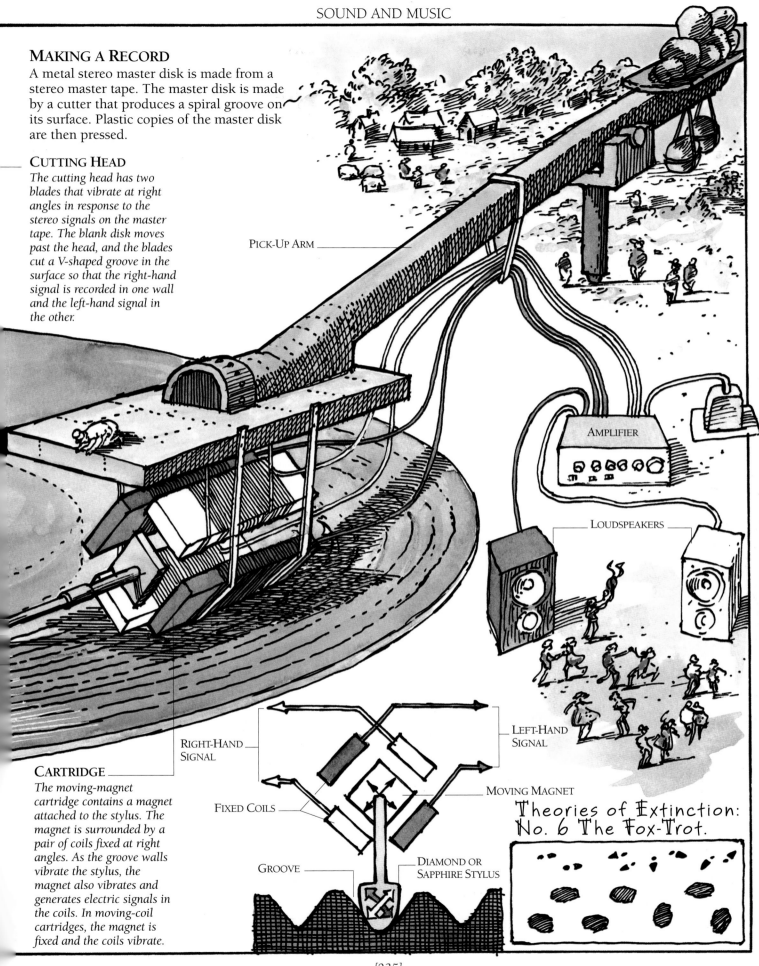

MAKING A RECORD

A metal stereo master disk is made from a stereo master tape. The master disk is made by a cutter that produces a spiral groove on its surface. Plastic copies of the master disk are then pressed.

CUTTING HEAD

The cutting head has two blades that vibrate at right angles in response to the stereo signals on the master tape. The blank disk moves past the head, and the blades cut a V-shaped groove in the surface so that the right-hand signal is recorded in one wall and the left-hand signal in the other.

PICK-UP ARM

AMPLIFIER

LOUDSPEAKERS

RIGHT-HAND SIGNAL

LEFT-HAND SIGNAL

FIXED COILS

MOVING MAGNET

CARTRIDGE

The moving-magnet cartridge contains a magnet attached to the stylus. The magnet is surrounded by a pair of coils fixed at right angles. As the groove walls vibrate the stylus, the magnet also vibrates and generates electric signals in the coils. In moving-coil cartridges, the magnet is fixed and the coils vibrate.

GROOVE

DIAMOND OR SAPPHIRE STYLUS

Theories of Extinction: No. 6 The Fox-Trot.

TELECOMMUNICATIONS

ON THE CONVEYING OF MESSAGES

While on a mammoth watch in the mountainous southern area, I was asked for some advice in the matter of communication between remote villages. It appeared that the age-old system of conveying messages— which relied on catapulting couriers from one place to another—was critically threatened by a shortage of both volunteers and also paper. After inspecting the catapults and calculating certain distances and elevations, I devised a completely new system. Instead of relying on dwindling manpower, I suggested that the messages could be carried through the air in the form of stones.

INSTANT SOUNDS AND IMAGES

Telecommunications are communications at a distance beyond the range of unaided hearing or eyesight. In order to send messages without delay over long distances, a fast-moving signal carrier is required. The method of telecommunication recorded above uses catapulted rocks as the signal carriers. The rocks are hurled aloft in a sequence that encodes a message, and when they land, the sequence is decoded and the message read.

Modern telecommunications use electricity, light, and radio as very swift signal carriers. They carry signals representing sounds, images, and computer data, which may be either analog signals that vary continuously in level, or digital signals made up of on-off pulses. The carrier—an electric current, light beam or radio wave—is often "modulated" by combining it with the analog or digital signal so that the carrier is made to vary in the same way as the signal. The modulated current, beam, or wave is then sent to a receiver. A detector in the receiver extracts the signal from the carrier and reproduces the sound, image, or data.

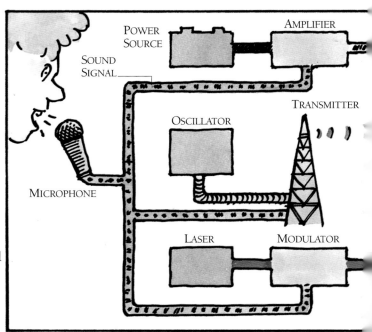

POWER SOURCE

AMPLIFIER

SOUND SIGNAL

TRANSMITTER

OSCILLATOR

MICROPHONE

LASER

MODULATOR

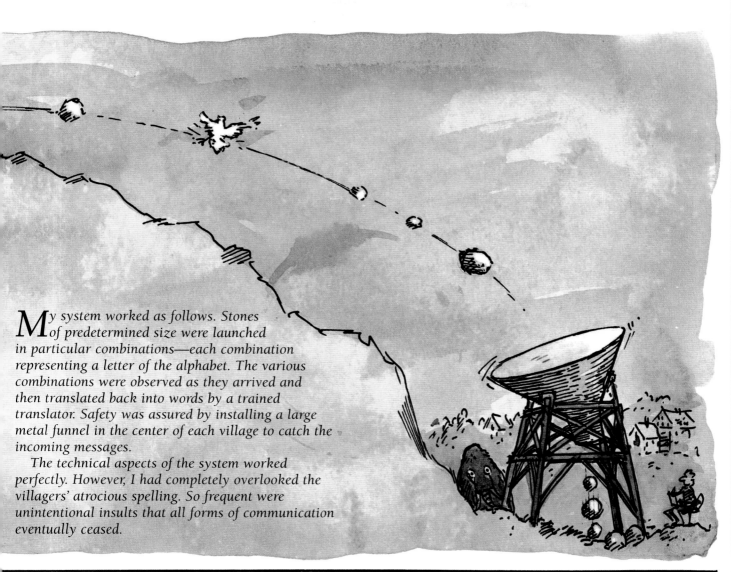

*M*y system worked as follows. Stones of predetermined size were launched in particular combinations—each combination representing a letter of the alphabet. The various combinations were observed as they arrived and then translated back into words by a trained translator. Safety was assured by installing a large metal funnel in the center of each village to catch the incoming messages.

The technical aspects of the system worked perfectly. However, I had completely overlooked the villagers' atrocious spelling. So frequent were unintentional insults that all forms of communication eventually ceased.

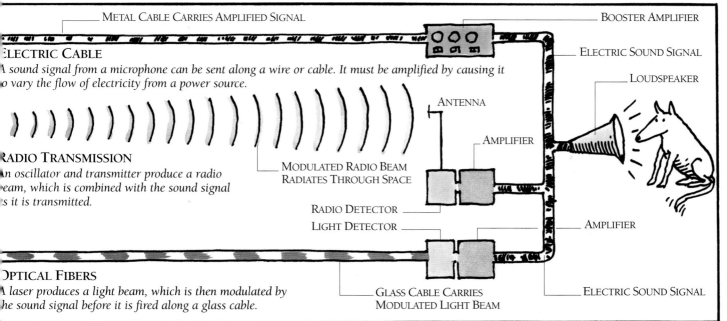

METAL CABLE CARRIES AMPLIFIED SIGNAL

BOOSTER AMPLIFIER

ELECTRIC CABLE

A sound signal from a microphone can be sent along a wire or cable. It must be amplified by causing it to vary the flow of electricity from a power source.

ELECTRIC SOUND SIGNAL

LOUDSPEAKER

ANTENNA

RADIO TRANSMISSION

An oscillator and transmitter produce a radio beam, which is combined with the sound signal as it is transmitted.

AMPLIFIER

MODULATED RADIO BEAM
RADIATES THROUGH SPACE

RADIO DETECTOR

LIGHT DETECTOR

AMPLIFIER

OPTICAL FIBERS

A laser produces a light beam, which is then modulated by the sound signal before it is fired along a glass cable.

GLASS CABLE CARRIES
MODULATED LIGHT BEAM

ELECTRIC SOUND SIGNAL

TELEPHONE NETWORK

The global telephone network enables us to speak to people anywhere in the world. Using metal cables, radio links and fiber-optic cables, a call from a fixed telephone goes through a series of local and main exchanges that route it to another telephone. A mobile phone connects by radio to a nearby base station, which provides coverage over a hexagonal area known as a cell. Each cell has a base station and varies in size depending on the number of callers in the cell. As a mobile phone moves from one cell to another, it automatically connects to the base station in the next cell so that the call can continue. Each base station routes the call to a mobile exchange, which connects to the main exchange in the network. A telephone's mouthpiece and earpiece work in the same way as a microphone (see p. 228) and earphone (see p. 233). Mobile networks also support text messaging and picture messaging, and allow users to connect to the Internet.

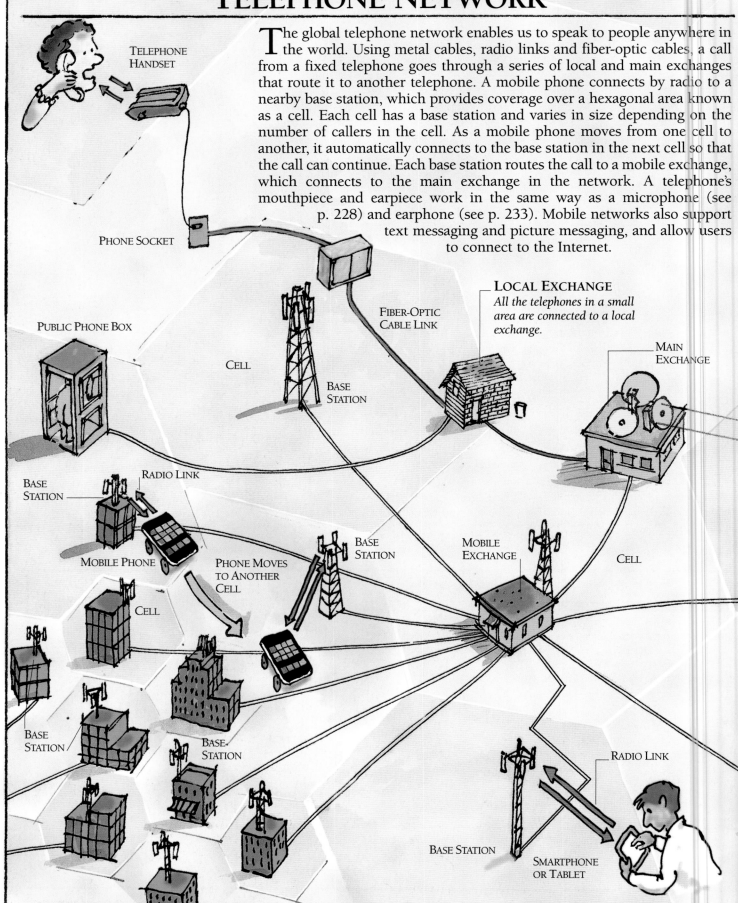

TELEPHONE HANDSET

PHONE SOCKET

PUBLIC PHONE BOX

FIBER-OPTIC CABLE LINK

LOCAL EXCHANGE
All the telephones in a small area are connected to a local exchange.

CELL

BASE STATION

MAIN EXCHANGE

BASE STATION

RADIO LINK

MOBILE PHONE

PHONE MOVES TO ANOTHER CELL

CELL

BASE STATION

MOBILE EXCHANGE

CELL

BASE STATION

BASE STATION

BASE STATION

RADIO LINK

BASE STATION

SMARTPHONE OR TABLET

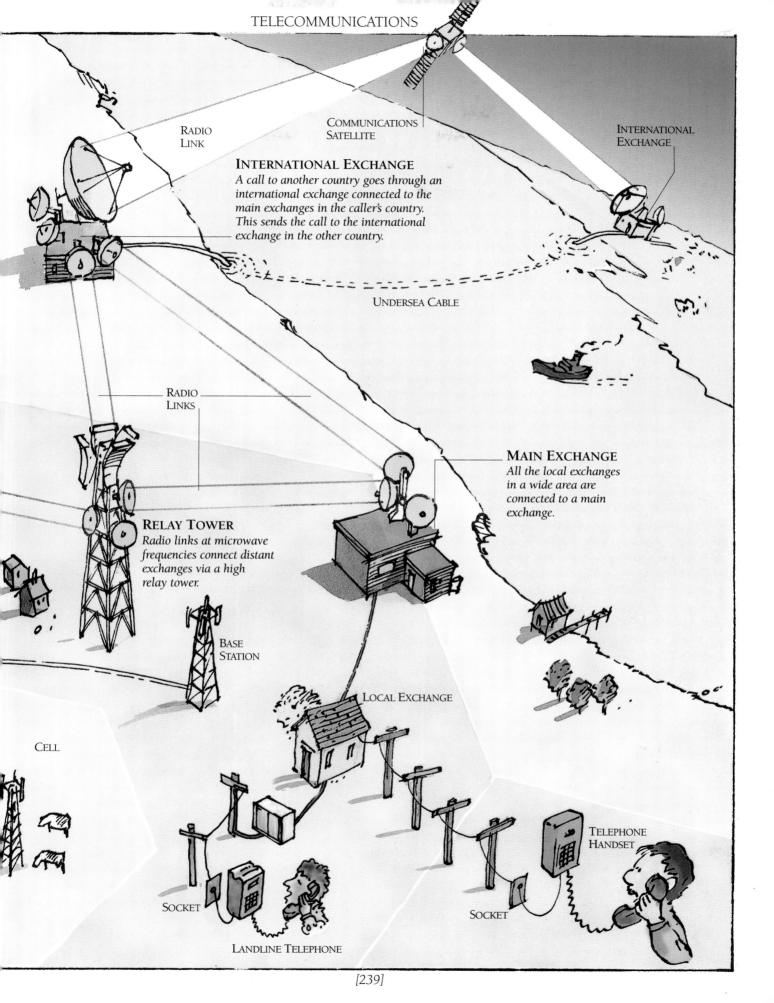

COMMUNICATIONS
SATELLITE

RADIO
LINK

INTERNATIONAL
EXCHANGE

INTERNATIONAL EXCHANGE

*A call to another country goes through an
international exchange connected to the
main exchanges in the caller's country.
This sends the call to the international
exchange in the other country.*

UNDERSEA CABLE

RADIO
LINKS

MAIN EXCHANGE

*All the local exchanges
in a wide area are
connected to a main
exchange.*

RELAY TOWER

*Radio links at microwave
frequencies connect distant
exchanges via a high
relay tower.*

BASE
STATION

CELL

LOCAL EXCHANGE

TELEPHONE
HANDSET

SOCKET

SOCKET

LANDLINE TELEPHONE

SMARTPHONE

A smartphone is really a handheld computer that can run a wide range of different software applications (apps), including web browsers, as well as communicating via the telephone network. An antenna allows it to send and receive radio waves encoded with digital sound, using the same techniques as digital radio broadcasting.

A microphone picks up the caller's speech, and can record sounds. A small loudspeaker produces the sound of the other person's voice, and can also play music. The speaker also alerts the user to incoming calls and messages, while a vibrating motor can achieve the same thing by making the phone buzz. The main form of input is a touchscreen, although most smartphones are also equipped with speech recognition, and can respond to spoken commands. The phone can detect movement, including a change in its orientation, thanks to a miniature accelerometer (see opposite page).

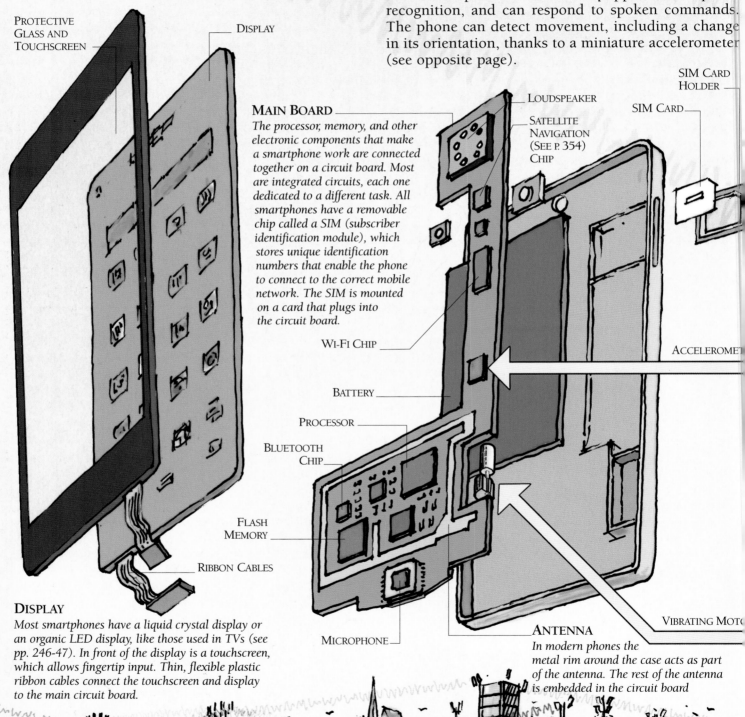

PROTECTIVE GLASS AND TOUCHSCREEN

DISPLAY

MAIN BOARD

The processor, memory, and other electronic components that make a smartphone work are connected together on a circuit board. Most are integrated circuits, each one dedicated to a different task. All smartphones have a removable chip called a SIM (subscriber identification module), which stores unique identification numbers that enable the phone to connect to the correct mobile network. The SIM is mounted on a card that plugs into the circuit board.

LOUDSPEAKER

SATELLITE NAVIGATION (SEE P. 354) CHIP

SIM CARD HOLDER

SIM CARD

WI-FI CHIP

ACCELEROMET

BATTERY

PROCESSOR

BLUETOOTH CHIP

FLASH MEMORY

RIBBON CABLES

DISPLAY

Most smartphones have a liquid crystal display or an organic LED display, like those used in TVs (see pp. 246-47). In front of the display is a touchscreen, which allows fingertip input. Thin, flexible plastic ribbon cables connect the touchscreen and display to the main circuit board.

MICROPHONE

VIBRATING MOTO

ANTENNA

In modern phones the metal rim around the case acts as part of the antenna. The rest of the antenna is embedded in the circuit board

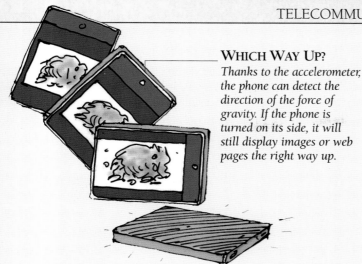

WHICH WAY UP?

Thanks to the accelerometer, the phone can detect the direction of the force of gravity. If the phone is turned on its side, it will still display images or web pages the right way up.

ACCELEROMETER

A smartphone accelerometer works on the same principle as the accelerometer found in an autopilot (see p. 293), but it is much smaller. It can detect changes in the speed of the phone, such as sudden movements—and crucially it can detect changes in the phone's orientation. The accelerometer is particularly useful when displaying images or playing games, both of which need the display to switch between portrait (upright) and landscape (on its side) orientations. The accelerometer in a smartphone is a tiny chip made by sculpting silicon, using similar techniques to those used in manufacturing microprocessors (see pp. 342-43).

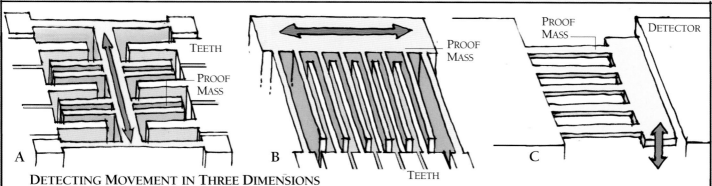

DETECTING MOVEMENT IN THREE DIMENSIONS

There are three sections to the accelerometer, each detecting accelerations in one axis: backward-forward (A), left-right (B) and up-down (C). The first two are composed of a large number of very thin silicon "teeth" set close to a moving weight called a proof mass. The other section works in a similar way, but the proof mass moves up and down next to a silicon detector.

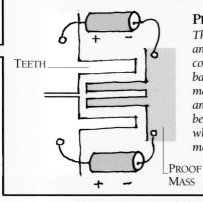

PHONE NOT MOVING

The accelerometer's teeth and the proof mass are both connected to the phone's battery. This means the proof mass is electrically charged, and there is an electric field between adjacent teeth, but when the proof mass is not moving, no current can flow.

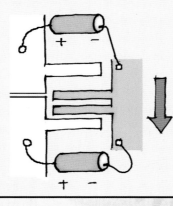

PHONE MOVING

When the proof mass moves, its electric charge disrupts the electric field around the teeth. This causes electric charges to move around the circuit. In other words, it creates an electric current. The phone's processor compares currents in each of the three axes to work out how much the phone is moving and in which direction.

SILENT MODE

A smartphone can be set to silent, so that it doesn't ring out loud. When the phone is in silent mode a user can still be alerted to calls and messages, thanks to a vibrating motor. This is a small electric motor with an off-center mass attached to the spindle. The whole motor vibrates, in the same way that a spin dryer shakes when all the wet clothes inside it have bunched up on one side. The same technology is used in games controllers (see p. 328) to make the controller shake in your hands when a certain action has been completed (sometimes called "haptic" or force feedback).

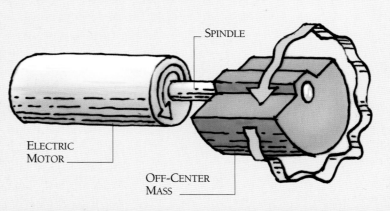

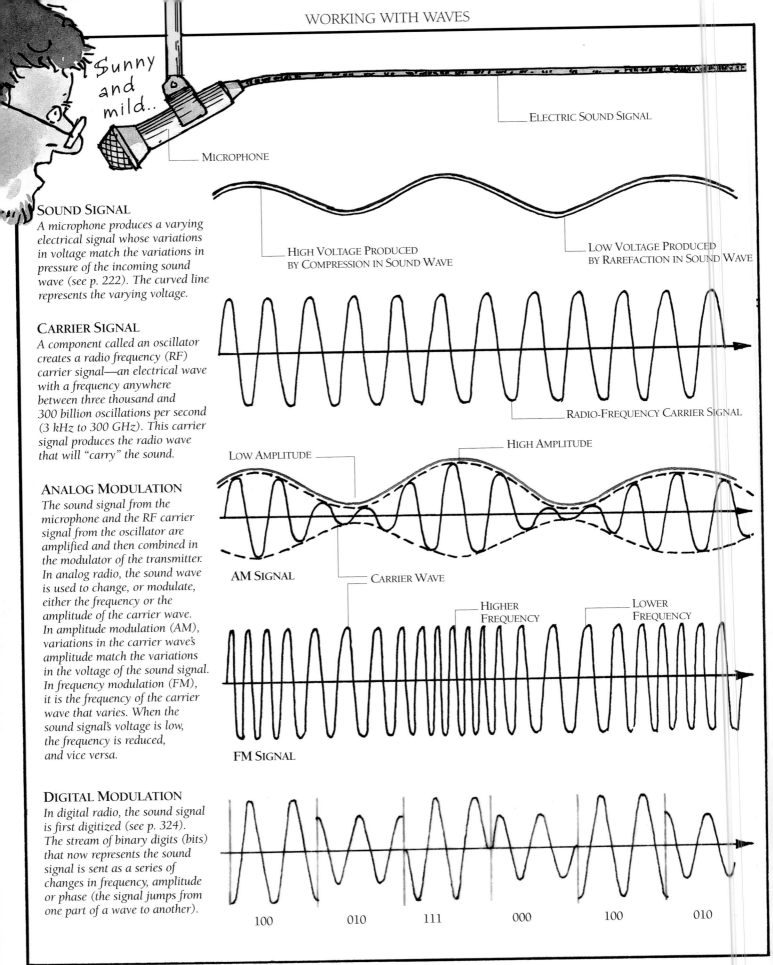

Sunny and mild..

ELECTRIC SOUND SIGNAL

MICROPHONE

SOUND SIGNAL

A microphone produces a varying electrical signal whose variations in voltage match the variations in pressure of the incoming sound wave (see p. 222). The curved line represents the varying voltage.

HIGH VOLTAGE PRODUCED BY COMPRESSION IN SOUND WAVE

LOW VOLTAGE PRODUCED BY RAREFACTION IN SOUND WAVE

CARRIER SIGNAL

A component called an oscillator creates a radio frequency (RF) carrier signal—an electrical wave with a frequency anywhere between three thousand and 300 billion oscillations per second (3 kHz to 300 GHz). This carrier signal produces the radio wave that will "carry" the sound.

RADIO-FREQUENCY CARRIER SIGNAL

HIGH AMPLITUDE

LOW AMPLITUDE

ANALOG MODULATION

The sound signal from the microphone and the RF carrier signal from the oscillator are amplified and then combined in the modulator of the transmitter. In analog radio, the sound wave is used to change, or modulate, either the frequency or the amplitude of the carrier wave. In amplitude modulation (AM), variations in the carrier wave's amplitude match the variations in the voltage of the sound signal. In frequency modulation (FM), it is the frequency of the carrier wave that varies. When the sound signal's voltage is low, the frequency is reduced, and vice versa.

AM SIGNAL

CARRIER WAVE

HIGHER FREQUENCY

LOWER FREQUENCY

FM SIGNAL

DIGITAL MODULATION

In digital radio, the sound signal is first digitized (see p. 324). The stream of binary digits (bits) that now represents the sound signal is sent as a series of changes in frequency, amplitude or phase (the signal jumps from one part of a wave to another).

100   010   111   000   100   010

RADIO TRANSMITTER

Radio waves are produced by feeding a rapidly varying electrical signal to the antenna of a transmitter. The signal makes the electrons in the antenna move rapidly up and down, creating ripples of electrical and magnetic energy that radiate outward. Like all waves, radio waves have a particular frequency and wavelength. Frequency, measured in hertz (Hz), is the number of waves produced each second. Wavelength is the length of each complete wave in meters. A radio wave with a high frequency has a short wavelength, and one with a low frequency has a long wavelength. The strength of a wave—equivalent to the distance from the peak to the trough on a graph of the wave—is called the amplitude. In order to broadcast sound, radio transmitters produce "modulated" waves: the original sound signal is superimposed on a radio wave so that the radio wave "carries" the sound by continuously changing the wave's frequency and amplitude.

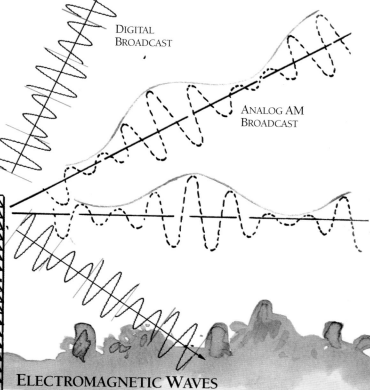

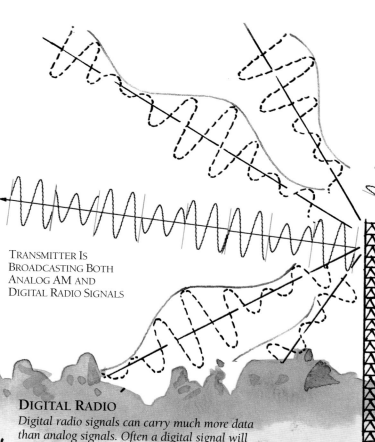

DIGITAL BROADCAST

ANALOG AM BROADCAST

TRANSMITTER IS BROADCASTING BOTH ANALOG AM AND DIGITAL RADIO SIGNALS

DIGITAL RADIO

Digital radio signals can carry much more data than analog signals. Often a digital signal will provide information such as the name of the song currently playing and the name of the DJ, as well as the name of the radio station.

AMPLIFICATION AND TRANSMISSION

A radio transmitter creates a modulated signal and sends it through a powerful amplifier and then on to the mast or antenna of the transmitter. Radio carrier waves, which are modulated in exactly the same way as the modulated signal, radiate from the transmitter. A radio mast broadcasts several carrier waves at different frequencies, each carrying a different sound signal. Every radio station or channel broadcasting from the transmitter has a different frequency.

ELECTROMAGNETIC WAVES

Radio waves are part of a large family of rays and waves known as electromagnetic waves. They consist of electric and magnetic fields that vibrate at right angles to each other. Both vibrate at the same frequency.

Light rays are also electromagnetic, and so too are radar, microwaves, infrared rays, ultraviolet rays, and X-rays. All electromagnetic waves move at the speed of light, which is 186,000 miles per second (300,000 kilometers per second). They travel through air and space.

VARYING ELECTRIC FIELD

VARYING MAGNETIC FIELD

RADIO RECEIVER

A radio receiver is essentially a transmitter in reverse. Radio waves strike the antenna connected to the receiver. They affect the metal atoms, producing weak electric carrier signals in the antenna. The receiver then selects the carrier signal of the required station or channel. It extracts the sound signal from the carrier signal, and this signal goes to an amplifier and loudspeaker to reproduce the sound.

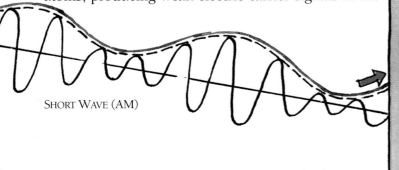

SHORT WAVE (AM)

MEDIUM WAVE (AM)

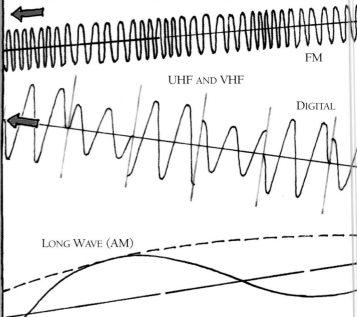

FM

UHF AND VHF

DIGITAL

LONG WAVE (AM)

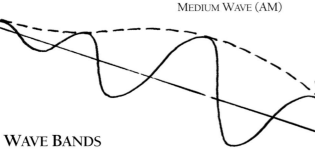

WAVE BANDS

The carrier frequencies radio stations use to broadcast their programs are grouped into bands. The bands with lower frequency carrier signals, with longer wavelengths, are called long wave, medium wave, and short wave. These bands are used to broadcast AM radio. Bands with higher frequency signals are called very high frequency (VHF) and ultra-high frequency (UHF), and are used for FM and digital radio. An antenna receives hundreds of different radio broadcasts at the same time.

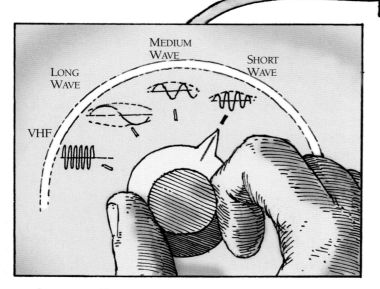

ANALOG RADIO

Each analog radio station uses a different carrier frequency. The radio receiver is tuned first to the correct band, and then to the correct frequency within it. Circuits inside the receiver remove the carrier wave to leave the original sound signal, which is amplified and sent to a loudspeaker (see pp. 232-33).

DIGITAL RADIO

Many digital stations share the same carrier frequency. Like data on a computer network (see p. 349), the digital sound is delivered in packets, labeled to identify which station they are from. A processor inside the radio identifies the relevant packets and reconstructs the sound by putting them in the correct order.

RADIO SIGNALS

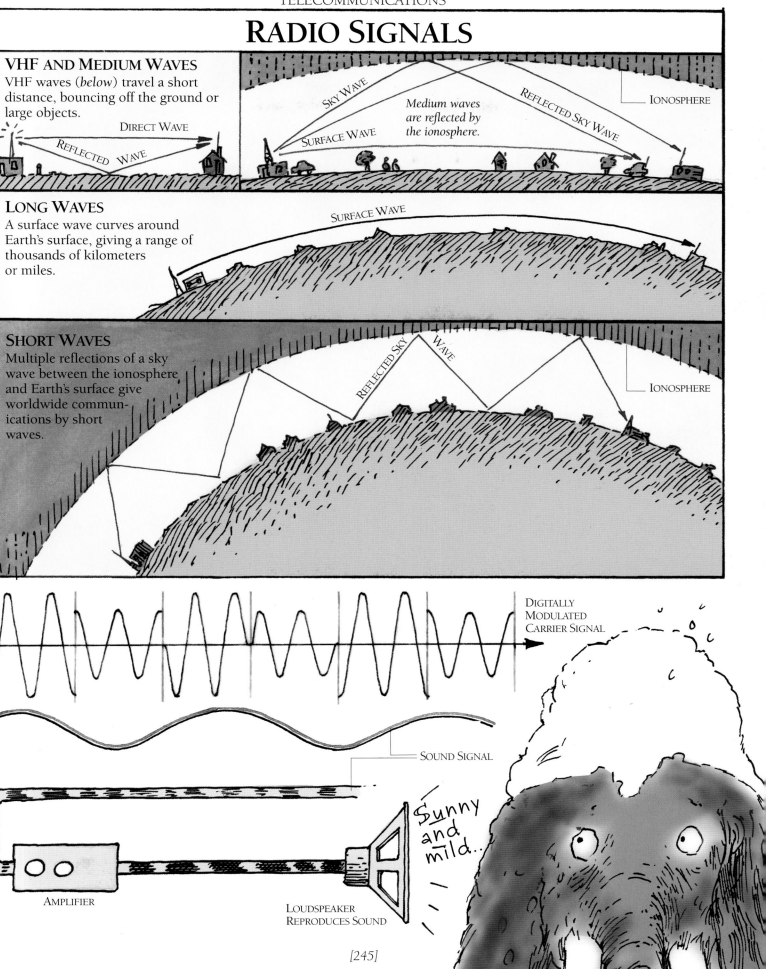

VHF AND MEDIUM WAVES

VHF waves (*below*) travel a short distance, bouncing off the ground or large objects.

DIRECT WAVE

REFLECTED WAVE

SKY WAVE

SURFACE WAVE

Medium waves are reflected by the ionosphere.

REFLECTED SKY WAVE

IONOSPHERE

LONG WAVES

A surface wave curves around Earth's surface, giving a range of thousands of kilometers or miles.

SURFACE WAVE

SHORT WAVES

Multiple reflections of a sky wave between the ionosphere and Earth's surface give worldwide communications by short waves.

REFLECTED SKY WAVE

IONOSPHERE

DIGITALLY MODULATED CARRIER SIGNAL

SOUND SIGNAL

AMPLIFIER

LOUDSPEAKER REPRODUCES SOUND

Sunny and mild...

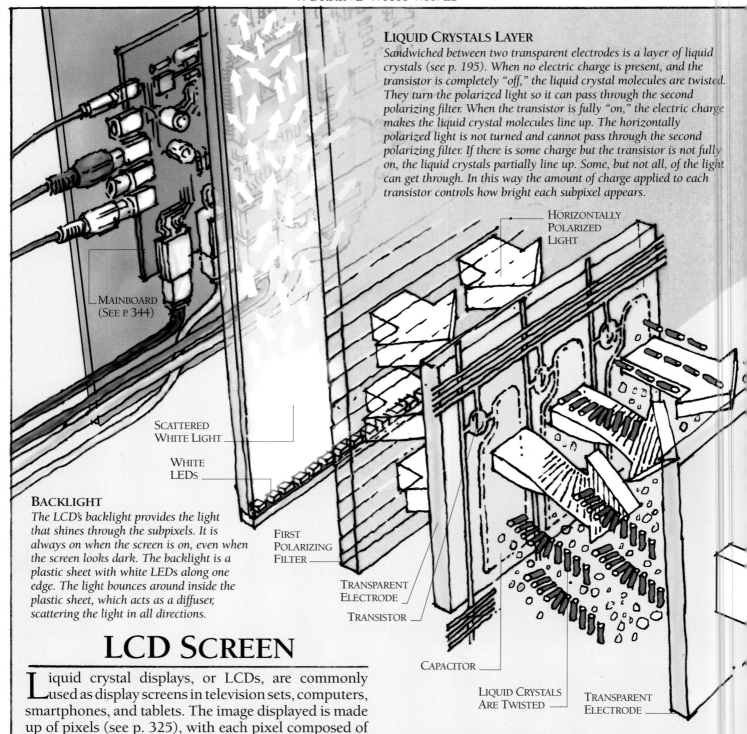

LIQUID CRYSTALS LAYER

Sandwiched between two transparent electrodes is a layer of liquid crystals (see p. 195). When no electric charge is present, and the transistor is completely "off," the liquid crystal molecules are twisted. They turn the polarized light so it can pass through the second polarizing filter. When the transistor is fully "on," the electric charge makes the liquid crystal molecules line up. The horizontally polarized light is not turned and cannot pass through the second polarizing filter. If there is some charge but the transistor is not fully on, the liquid crystals partially line up. Some, but not all, of the light can get through. In this way the amount of charge applied to each transistor controls how bright each subpixel appears.

HORIZONTALLY POLARIZED LIGHT

MAINBOARD (SEE P. 344)

SCATTERED WHITE LIGHT

WHITE LEDS

FIRST POLARIZING FILTER

TRANSPARENT ELECTRODE

TRANSISTOR

CAPACITOR

LIQUID CRYSTALS ARE TWISTED

TRANSPARENT ELECTRODE

BACKLIGHT

The LCD's backlight provides the light that shines through the subpixels. It is always on when the screen is on, even when the screen looks dark. The backlight is a plastic sheet with white LEDs along one edge. The light bounces around inside the plastic sheet, which acts as a diffuser, scattering the light in all directions.

LCD SCREEN

Liquid crystal displays, or LCDs, are commonly used as display screens in television sets, computers, smartphones, and tablets. The image displayed is made up of pixels (see p. 325), with each pixel composed of three subpixels—one red, one blue, and one green. The subpixels are controlled by transistors, which receive signals from a processor on the screen's mainboard. A sequence of polarizing filters and liquid crystals blocks or allows light through depending on how much charge is sent to each transistor. The subpixels are addressed one by one in rapid sequence. In high-definition TV, for example, there are 2 million pixels per frame, and 25 frames per second. This means 6 million subpixels are addressed one after the other in the 1/25th of a second duration of a frame.

THREE SUBPIXELS

Light from the backlight passes through a polarizing filter (see p. 194), which only allows horizonally polarized light through. Each subpixel has its own transistor, mounted on a transparent electrode. The signal sent to the transistor determines how much light is able to pass through a second polarizing filter and therefore reach the screen (see above). The subpixels are addressed one at a time. Each has a tiny capacitor (a device that can store electric charge), so the subpixel "remembers" the signal from the transistor until it is addressed again when the next frame is displayed.

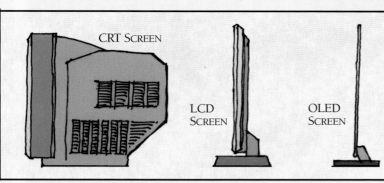

SHRINKING MONITORS

LCD screens are much thinner than older, bulkier CRT (cathode ray tube) screens. A new technology called OLED (organic light-emitting diode) allows for displays that are even thinner. An OLED display screen works in a very similar way to an LCD screen: each subpixel is addressed by a transistor controlled by the monitor's processor. But OLED subpixels produce their own light, rather than relying on a backlight. This allows for richer colors and an ultra-slim screen.

CRT Screen

LCD Screen

OLED Screen

TRANSPARENT ELECTRODE

The second transparent electrode does not carry any electric circuits. Instead it is scored with microscopic marks that make the liquid crystals, when no charge is present, twist around in exactly the right way to turn the light through the second polarizing filter.

COLOR PIXELS

All the pixels in a digital image are produced by combining different amounts of red, green and blue light (see p. 184 and p. 325). The LED backlight in an LCD screen is a white light source: to produce the colors of each subpixel tiny color filters are used, which allow through only red, green or blue light. Varying the amount of white light that reaches each subpixel controls how light or dark that subpixel appears. When seen together on the screen, three subpixels combine to create one pixel.

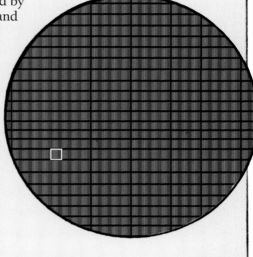

COLOR FILTERS

BLUE LIGHT CANNOT PASS THROUGH SECOND POLARIZER

SECOND POLARIZING FILTER

NO BLUE LIGHT REACHES THE SCREEN

SOME GREEN LIGHT REACHES THE SCREEN

LOTS OF RED LIGHT REACHES THE SCREEN

TOGETHER THE COLORS APPEAR ORANGE

ORANGE PIXEL

A grid of tiny color filters just behind the second polarizing filter allows through only red, green, or blue light. Here, a red subpixel at 100 percent brightness, a green subpixel at 50 percent, and a blue subpixel at 0 percent combine to give an orange pixel.

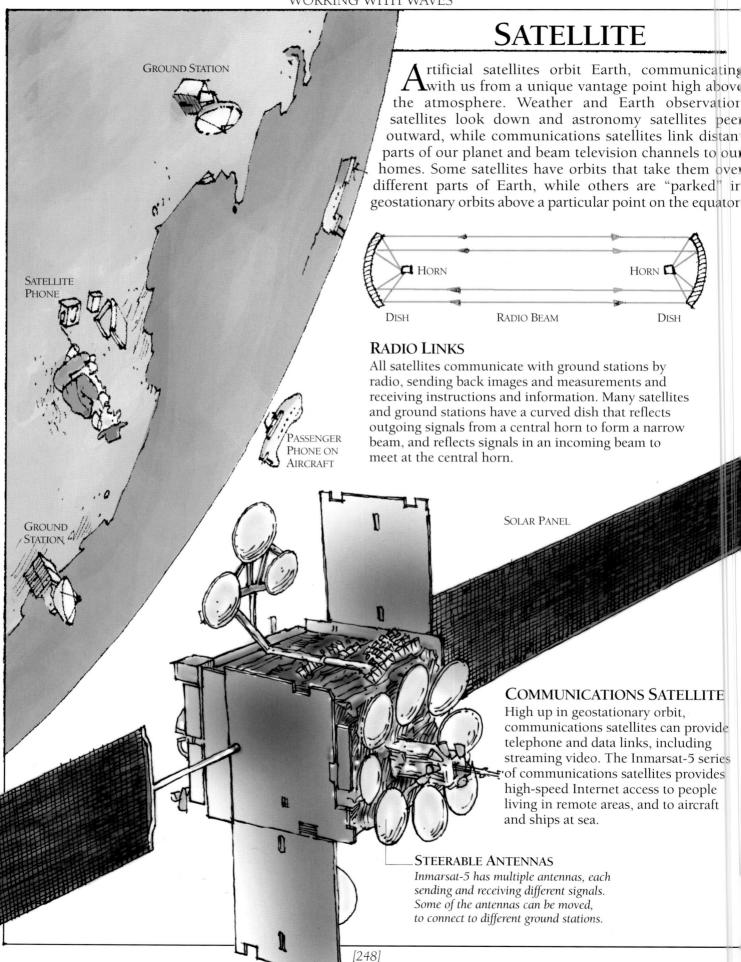

SATELLITE

Artificial satellites orbit Earth, communicating with us from a unique vantage point high above the atmosphere. Weather and Earth observation satellites look down and astronomy satellites peer outward, while communications satellites link distant parts of our planet and beam television channels to our homes. Some satellites have orbits that take them over different parts of Earth, while others are "parked" in geostationary orbits above a particular point on the equator.

GROUND STATION

SATELLITE PHONE

PASSENGER PHONE ON AIRCRAFT

GROUND STATION

HORN

HORN

DISH

RADIO BEAM

DISH

RADIO LINKS

All satellites communicate with ground stations by radio, sending back images and measurements and receiving instructions and information. Many satellites and ground stations have a curved dish that reflects outgoing signals from a central horn to form a narrow beam, and reflects signals in an incoming beam to meet at the central horn.

SOLAR PANEL

COMMUNICATIONS SATELLITE

High up in geostationary orbit, communications satellites can provide telephone and data links, including streaming video. The Inmarsat-5 series of communications satellites provides high-speed Internet access to people living in remote areas, and to aircraft and ships at sea.

STEERABLE ANTENNAS

Inmarsat-5 has multiple antennas, each sending and receiving different signals. Some of the antennas can be moved, to connect to different ground stations.

POLAR ORBIT

Landsat-8 orbits at a height of 705 km (438 miles) and passes over both poles 14 times every day. This polar orbit allows Landsat-8 to survey the whole of the planet.

EARTH OBSERVATION SATELLITE

Earth observation satellites gather enormous amounts of information about our planet, from a perfect vantage point in space. Landsat-8 has two main instruments on board: the operational land imager is sensitive to visible light and infrared, and captures high-resolution images of the ground and oceans, while the thermal infrared sensor can measure the temperature of the ground, sea or atmosphere, to help scientists studying land use or climate change.

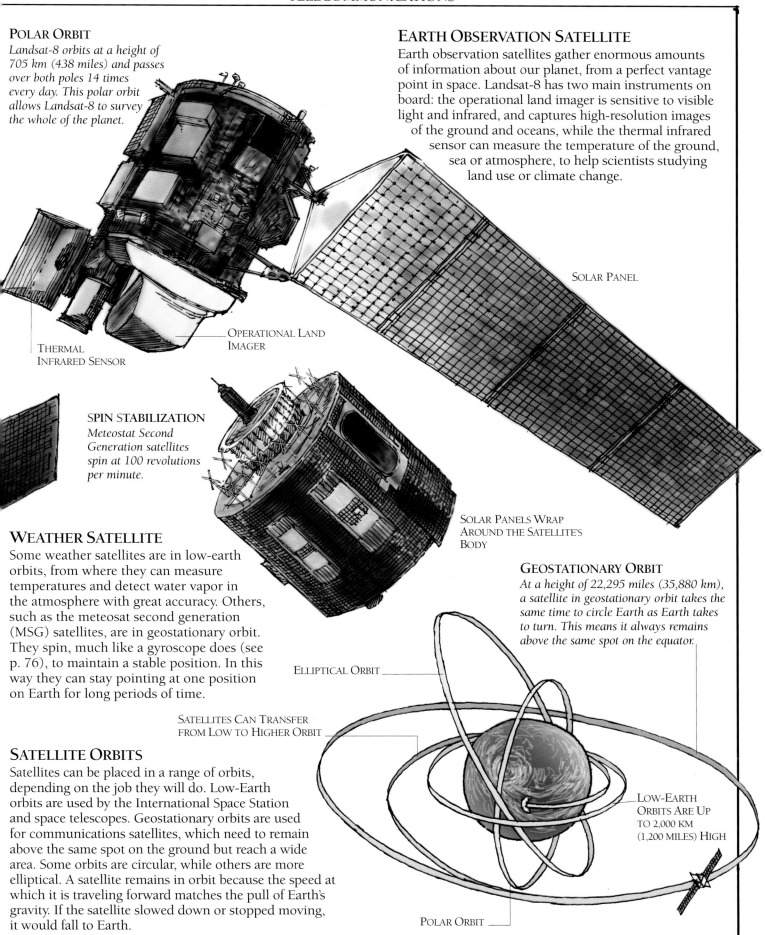

SOLAR PANEL

THERMAL INFRARED SENSOR

OPERATIONAL LAND IMAGER

SPIN STABILIZATION

Meteostat Second Generation satellites spin at 100 revolutions per minute.

SOLAR PANELS WRAP AROUND THE SATELLITE'S BODY

WEATHER SATELLITE

Some weather satellites are in low-earth orbits, from where they can measure temperatures and detect water vapor in the atmosphere with great accuracy. Others, such as the meteosat second generation (MSG) satellites, are in geostationary orbit. They spin, much like a gyroscope does (see p. 76), to maintain a stable position. In this way they can stay pointing at one position on Earth for long periods of time.

GEOSTATIONARY ORBIT

At a height of 22,295 miles (35,880 km), a satellite in geostationary orbit takes the same time to circle Earth as Earth takes to turn. This means it always remains above the same spot on the equator.

ELLIPTICAL ORBIT

SATELLITES CAN TRANSFER FROM LOW TO HIGHER ORBIT

SATELLITE ORBITS

Satellites can be placed in a range of orbits, depending on the job they will do. Low-Earth orbits are used by the International Space Station and space telescopes. Geostationary orbits are used for communications satellites, which need to remain above the same spot on the ground but reach a wide area. Some orbits are circular, while others are more elliptical. A satellite remains in orbit because the speed at which it is traveling forward matches the pull of Earth's gravity. If the satellite slowed down or stopped moving, it would fall to Earth.

LOW-EARTH ORBITS ARE UP TO 2,000 KM (1,200 MILES) HIGH

POLAR ORBIT

RADIO TELESCOPE

Many objects in the universe send out radio waves, and a radio telescope can be used to detect them. A large, curved metal dish collects the radio waves and reflects them to a focus point above the center of the dish, rather as the curved mirror of a reflecting telescope gathers light waves from space (see p. 190). At this point, an antenna intercepts the radio waves and turns them into a weak electric signal. The signal then goes to a computer. Radio telescopes detect very weak waves, and can also communicate with spacecraft.

By detecting radio waves coming from galaxies and other objects in space, radio telescopes have discovered the existence of many previously unknown bodies. It is possible to make visible images of radio sources by scanning the telescope or a group of telescopes across the source. This yields a sequence of signals from different parts of the source, which the computer can process to form an image. Differences in frequency of the signals give information about the composition and motion of the radio source.

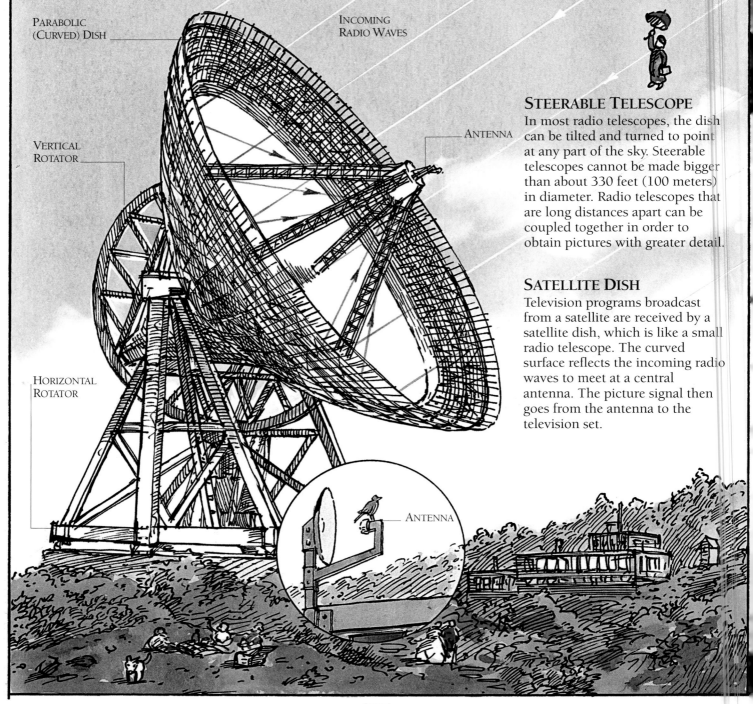

PARABOLIC (CURVED) DISH

INCOMING RADIO WAVES

VERTICAL ROTATOR

ANTENNA

HORIZONTAL ROTATOR

ANTENNA

STEERABLE TELESCOPE
In most radio telescopes, the dish can be tilted and turned to point at any part of the sky. Steerable telescopes cannot be made bigger than about 330 feet (100 meters) in diameter. Radio telescopes that are long distances apart can be coupled together in order to obtain pictures with greater detail.

SATELLITE DISH
Television programs broadcast from a satellite are received by a satellite dish, which is like a small radio telescope. The curved surface reflects the incoming radio waves to meet at a central antenna. The picture signal then goes from the antenna to the television set.

SPACE TELESCOPE

Observing space from the ground, telescopes peer through Earth's turbulent atmosphere, which limits the clarity of the images they produce. The atmosphere blocks certain types of electromagnetic waves coming from space. To produce the clearest possible views, astronomers launch telescopes into orbit above Earth's atmosphere. Many space telescopes are in use, but the most successful and best known is the Hubble Space Telescope, launched in 1990. It has detected faint and distant objects and produced more detailed pictures of known objects, greatly expanding our knowledge of the universe.

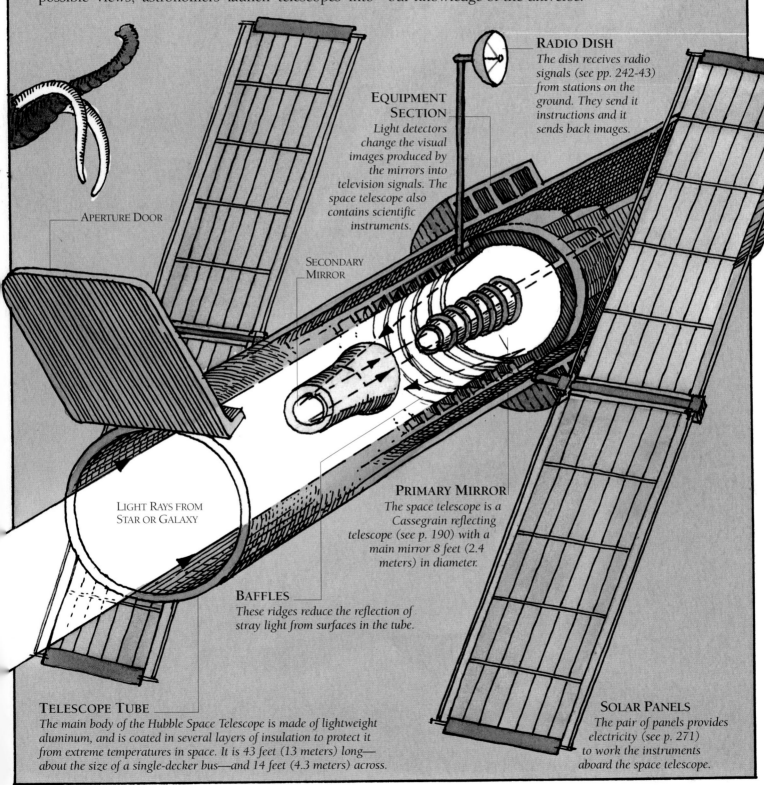

RADIO DISH
The dish receives radio signals (see pp. 242-43) from stations on the ground. They send it instructions and it sends back images.

EQUIPMENT SECTION
Light detectors change the visual images produced by the mirrors into television signals. The space telescope also contains scientific instruments.

APERTURE DOOR

SECONDARY MIRROR

LIGHT RAYS FROM STAR OR GALAXY

PRIMARY MIRROR
The space telescope is a Cassegrain reflecting telescope (see p. 190) with a main mirror 8 feet (2.4 meters) in diameter.

BAFFLES
These ridges reduce the reflection of stray light from surfaces in the tube.

TELESCOPE TUBE
The main body of the Hubble Space Telescope is made of lightweight aluminum, and is coated in several layers of insulation to protect it from extreme temperatures in space. It is 43 feet (13 meters) long—about the size of a single-decker bus—and 14 feet (4.3 meters) across.

SOLAR PANELS
The pair of panels provides electricity (see p. 271) to work the instruments aboard the space telescope.

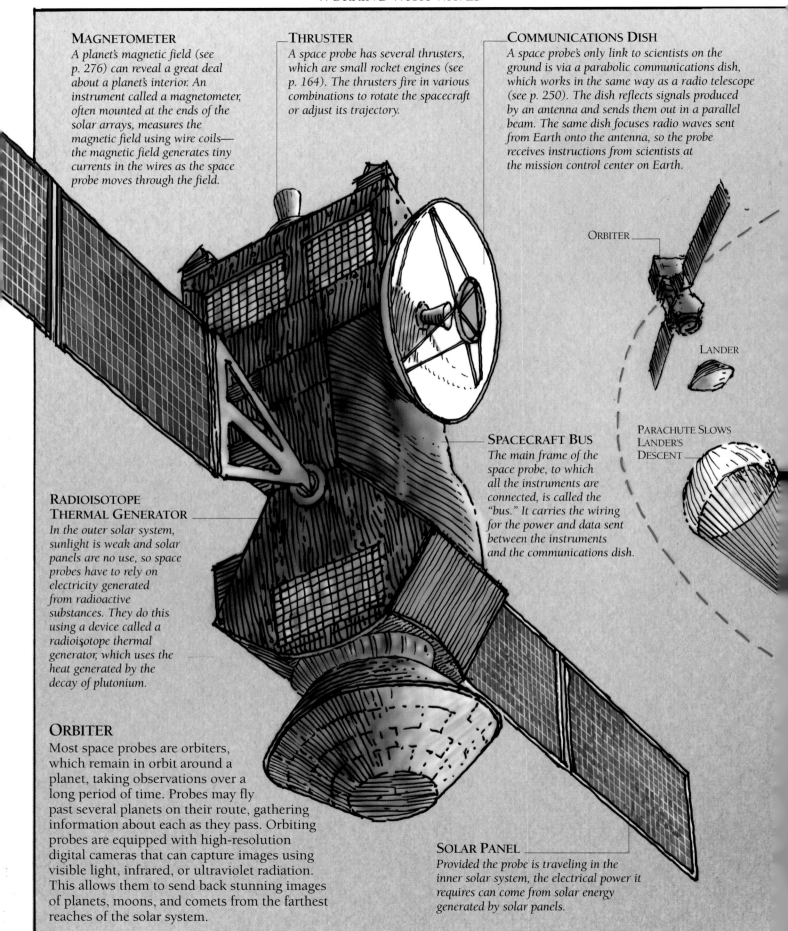

MAGNETOMETER

A planet's magnetic field (see p. 276) can reveal a great deal about a planet's interior. An instrument called a magnetometer, often mounted at the ends of the solar arrays, measures the magnetic field using wire coils— the magnetic field generates tiny currents in the wires as the space probe moves through the field.

THRUSTER

A space probe has several thrusters, which are small rocket engines (see p. 164). The thrusters fire in various combinations to rotate the spacecraft or adjust its trajectory.

COMMUNICATIONS DISH

A space probe's only link to scientists on the ground is via a parabolic communications dish, which works in the same way as a radio telescope (see p. 250). The dish reflects signals produced by an antenna and sends them out in a parallel beam. The same dish focuses radio waves sent from Earth onto the antenna, so the probe receives instructions from scientists at the mission control center on Earth.

ORBITER

LANDER

PARACHUTE SLOWS LANDER'S DESCENT

SPACECRAFT BUS

The main frame of the space probe, to which all the instruments are connected, is called the "bus." It carries the wiring for the power and data sent between the instruments and the communications dish.

RADIOISOTOPE THERMAL GENERATOR

In the outer solar system, sunlight is weak and solar panels are no use, so space probes have to rely on electricity generated from radioactive substances. They do this using a device called a radioisotope thermal generator, which uses the heat generated by the decay of plutonium.

ORBITER

Most space probes are orbiters, which remain in orbit around a planet, taking observations over a long period of time. Probes may fly past several planets on their route, gathering information about each as they pass. Orbiting probes are equipped with high-resolution digital cameras that can capture images using visible light, infrared, or ultraviolet radiation. This allows them to send back stunning images of planets, moons, and comets from the farthest reaches of the solar system.

SOLAR PANEL

Provided the probe is traveling in the inner solar system, the electrical power it requires can come from solar energy generated by solar panels.

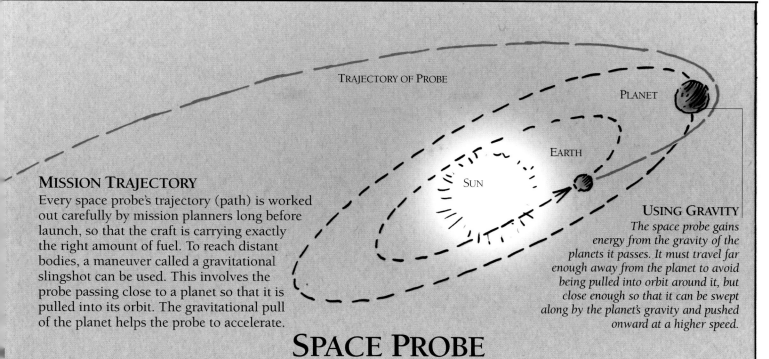

MISSION TRAJECTORY

Every space probe's trajectory (path) is worked out carefully by mission planners long before launch, so that the craft is carrying exactly the right amount of fuel. To reach distant bodies, a maneuver called a gravitational slingshot can be used. This involves the probe passing close to a planet so that it is pulled into its orbit. The gravitational pull of the planet helps the probe to accelerate.

TRAJECTORY OF PROBE

PLANET

EARTH

SUN

USING GRAVITY

The space probe gains energy from the gravity of the planets it passes. It must travel far enough away from the planet to avoid being pulled into orbit around it, but close enough so that it can be swept along by the planet's gravity and pushed onward at a higher speed.

SPACE PROBE

The ultimate limits of communications are reached with unmanned space probes, which have sent us detailed pictures and information from every planet, and several comets, moons, and dwarf planets, in the solar system. A space probe may orbit a planet or moon, or carry a lander, which reaches its surface to send back geological and atmospheric data, and close-up pictures of distant worlds and their surfaces. Probes have visited the farthest reaches of the solar system by using mission trajectories that depend on the gravitational pull of planets along the way to increase the craft's speed without using any fuel.

Communication to and from space probes is by radio waves. These waves travel nearly 186,000 miles (300,000 kilometers) every second—but the distances between planets are so great, it still takes several hours for signals to pass between probes in the outer solar system and ground stations on Earth. As a result, space probes must be able to carry out tasks by themselves. These involve measuring magnetic fields and capturing high-resolution digital images. All the onboard instruments and communications equipment need electrical power, which may come from solar panels or generators powered by radioactive substances.

LANDER

Space probes that reach the surface of a planet or other celestial body are called landers. They may be released from an orbiting probe, which relays messages to and from the lander, while also capturing information about the planet from its bird's-eye view. Roving landers can move across the surface of the planet, examining rock samples and taking detailed photographs.

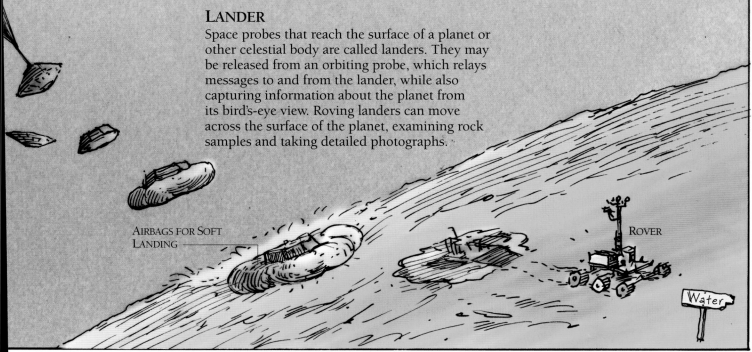

AIRBAGS FOR SOFT LANDING

ROVER

Water

THE
DISCOVERY
OF·MAGNETIC
NORTH

ELECTRICITY & AUTOMATION

INTRODUCTION

THE POWER BEHIND ELECTRICITY comes from particles that are among the smallest things known to science. These are **electrons**, and they are normally found in **atoms**. Each one bears a *minute negative electric charge*. When an electric current flows through a wire, these tiny particles surge through the metal in unimaginable numbers. In a current of 1 ampere, sufficient to light a flashlight bulb, for example, *6 million million million electrons* pass any point in just **one second**. Each electron moves relatively slowly, but the energy transfers from electron to electron *at the speed of light*. Today, many machines are driven by electric motors and governed by electrical control devices, while others use electricity to carry information. This branch of technology assumes greater and greater importance as machines go **digital**, a subject that is explored in depth in Part 5.

EXPLOITING ELECTRONS

The machines in this part of the book either produce **electricity** or use it in various ways. Many use the ability of moving electrons to create a **magnetic field** around them. *Magnetic fields attract and repel each other with great force.* Machines that use electric motors move by harnessing the push and pull of magnetic fields created around wires that carry electricity. Electric generators, which produce our main supply of electricity, also make use of magnetic fields. And magnets themselves possess a magnetic field because of the *motion of the electrons within their atoms*. So all machines that exploit magnetism in one way or another are ultimately using electrons. Electrons also produce **electric fields**, which have the same ability to attract and repel as magnetic fields do.

The principles that govern the flow of electricity are *exactly the same in all electrical machines*. The electrons always need **energy** to make them move. They always travel in a set direction (from **negative** to **positive**) at a set speed. Furthermore, they will always produce *particular effects* while they are on the move. **Magnetism** is one. So too are **heat** and **light**, as we have already seen in Part 2. Electrons have other ways of producing light as well as rays that are invisible and even sounds that cannot be heard, but all are highly useful.

ELECTRICITY AND MOVEMENT

As a source of **power**, electricity has no rival. It is *clean, silent, can be turned on and off instantly,* and can be fed easily to where it is needed. Electric machines that produce movement are extraordinarily diverse. At first sight, there is little similarity between, for example, a quartz wristwatch and an electric locomotive. However, both use the **motive force** produced by the magnetic effects of an electric current—although the current used by a train is *hundreds of thousands of times greater* than that which flows in a watch.

MACHINES THAT CONTROL THEMSELVES

Amounts of electric charge and the flow of electric current can vary—so can **voltage**, which is *a measure of how much energy each electron has.* As a result, electric charge, current or voltage can be used as **signals**, either to convey information or automatically control how a machine works. This is put to use in electronic devices—anything from sensors like metal detectors and automatic doors to digital devices such as computers and smartphones. In **digital electronics**, the current and voltage represent numbers, using the binary number system, which has just two digits: 0 and 1. For example, an electronic circuit can store "no charge" (0) or "charge" (1), or a circuit could have no current flowing (0) versus a current flowing (1), or could be at low voltage (0) or higher voltage (1). Sequences of just these two digits can make any number—so, the number we know as 28 is 11100, for example, while 29 is 11101. In digital devices, these **binary numbers** represent text characters, images, or sounds, as well as sets of instructions (programs) that control the device. Sophisticated digital electronic circuits that manipulate the charges, currents, and voltages representing binary numbers are the basis of many automatic devices, including a smartphone that will connect to the Internet whenever a signal is available, or a robot that can sense the world around it and act accordingly.

ELECTRICITY

ON MAMMOTH ATTRACTION

*O*ne day, I happened upon a mammoth whose hair had been lovingly combed. The hairdresser, in fact, was just about to return her creation to its owner. No sooner had the perfectly coiffed animal stepped into the street, however, than a combination of litter, loose laundry, and stray cats flew into the air and secured themselves to the startled beast's freshly combed coat. It is common knowledge that a well-groomed individual is more attractive, but never before had I seen this so forcefully illustrated.

STATIC ELECTRICITY

All things are made up of atoms, and within atoms are even smaller particles called electrons. Electrons each have an electric charge, and this charge, which is considered to be negative, is the fundamental cause of electricity.

Static electricity is so-called because it involves electrons that are moved from one place to another rather than ones that flow in a current. In an object with no static electric charge, all the atoms have their normal number of electrons. If some of the electrons are then transferred to another object by, for example, vigorous rubbing or brushing, the other object becomes negatively charged while the object that loses electrons becomes positively charged. An electric field is set up around each object.

Unlike charges always attract each other and like charges always repel each other. This is the reason why the mammoth finds itself festooned with rubbish after its brushing, and why a comb rubbed with a cloth will attract pieces of paper. Rubbing or brushing creates a charge and therefore an electric field. The field affects objects nearby, producing an unlike charge in them, and the unlike charges are drawn together.

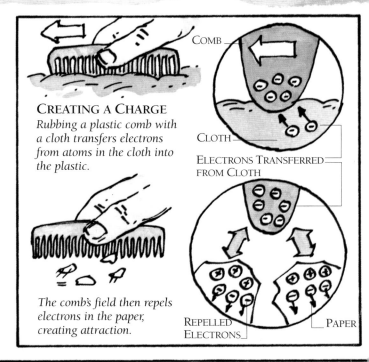

CREATING A CHARGE
Rubbing a plastic comb with a cloth transfers electrons from atoms in the cloth into the plastic.

The comb's field then repels electrons in the paper, creating attraction.

COMB

CLOTH

ELECTRONS TRANSFERRED FROM CLOTH

REPELLED ELECTRONS

PAPER

ON MAMMOTH LEMONS

At harvest time, I once watched with great admiration as lemons were gathered with mammoth assistance. Large specimens were harpooned, the mammoths being equipped with copper lances, and their riders with zinc ones—a lightweight improvement of my own devising. During my visit, the riders did complain of suffering powerful shudderings, which they somehow attributed to their new equipment, but I was able to assure them that of course there could be no connection.

As each team boldly rode into action, the air was almost electric.

CURRENT ELECTRICITY

Current electricity is produced by electrons on the move. Unlike static electricity, current electricity can exist only in a conductor—that is, a material such as a metal that allows electrons to pass freely through it.

In order to make electrons move, a source of energy is needed. This energy can be in the form of light, heat, or pressure, or it can be the energy produced by a chemical reaction. Chemical energy is the source of power in a battery-powered circuit. The mammoth and its rider suffer a surge of electric current because they inadvertently form this type of circuit. Lemons contain acid, which reacts with the zinc and copper in the lances. Atoms in the acid take electrons from the copper atoms and transfer them to the zinc atoms. The electrons then flow through the materials connected to the two metal lances. The zinc lance, which releases the negatively charged electrons, is the negative terminal of the lemon battery. The copper lance, which receives the electrons, is the positive terminal. Whereas an ordinary lemon would not produce sufficient electrons to give a big current, the giant lemon yields enough to produce a violent shock.

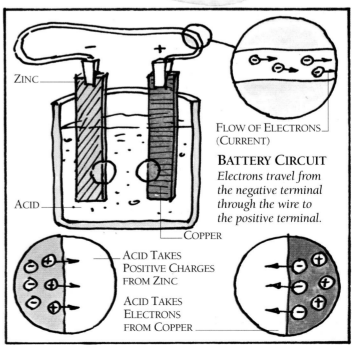

ZINC

ACID

COPPER

FLOW OF ELECTRONS (CURRENT)

BATTERY CIRCUIT
Electrons travel from the negative terminal through the wire to the positive terminal.

ACID TAKES POSITIVE CHARGES FROM ZINC

ACID TAKES ELECTRONS FROM COPPER

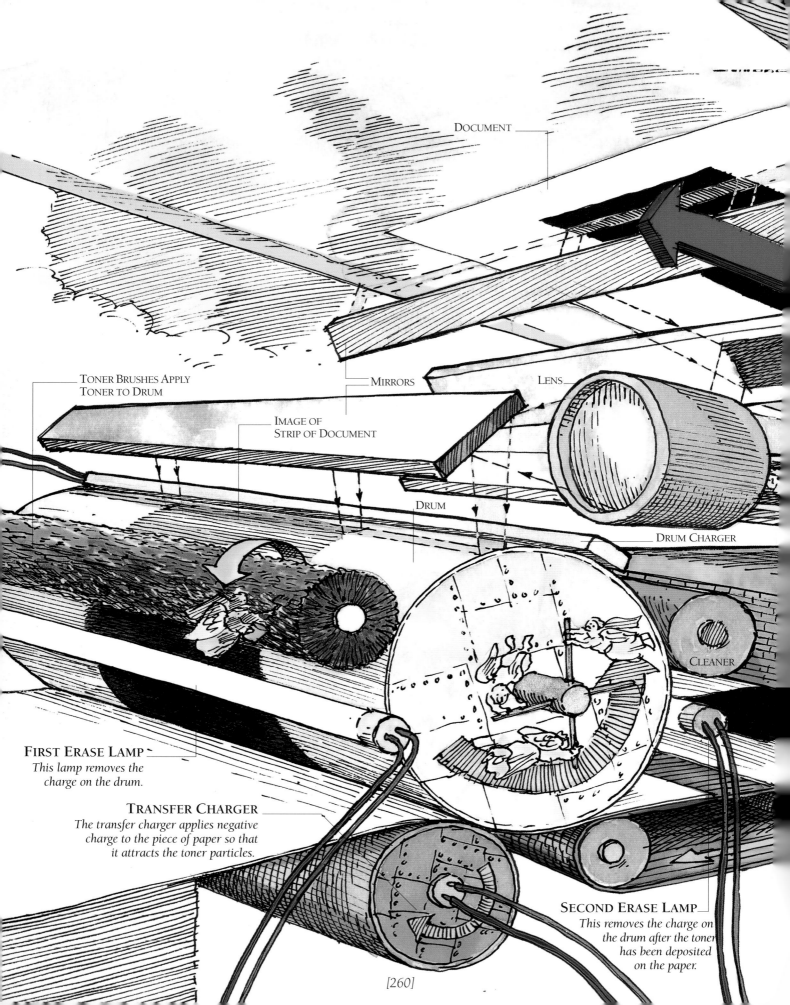

DOCUMENT

MIRRORS

LENS

TONER BRUSHES APPLY
TONER TO DRUM

IMAGE OF
STRIP OF DOCUMENT

DRUM

DRUM CHARGER

CLEANER

FIRST ERASE LAMP
*This lamp removes the
charge on the drum.*

TRANSFER CHARGER
*The transfer charger applies negative
charge to the piece of paper so that
it attracts the toner particles.*

SECOND ERASE LAMP
*This removes the charge on
the drum after the toner
has been deposited
on the paper.*

THE PHOTOCOPIER

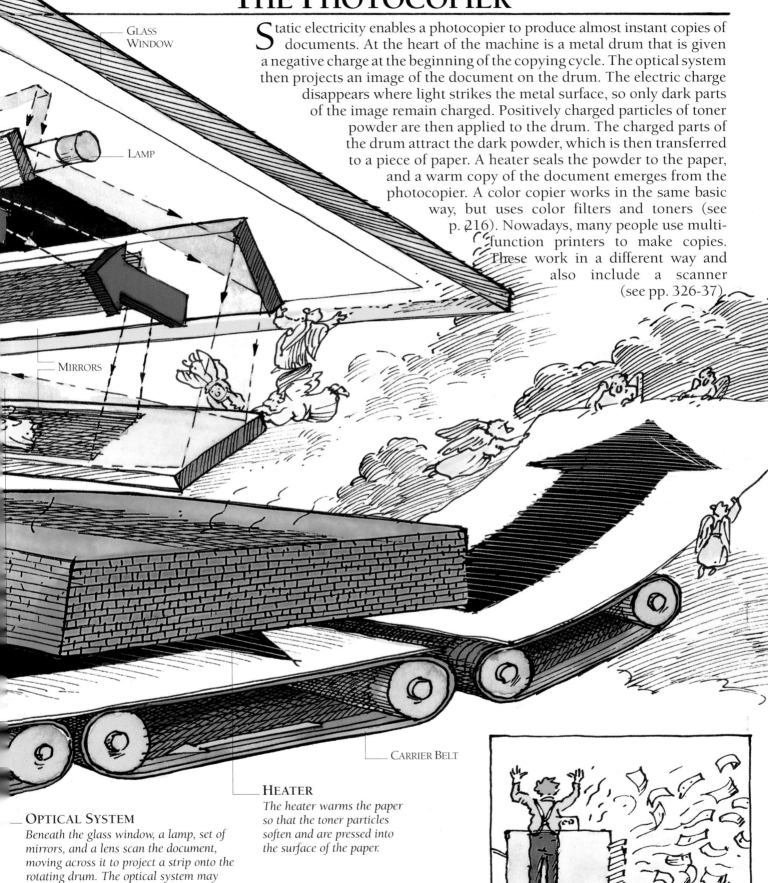

Static electricity enables a photocopier to produce almost instant copies of documents. At the heart of the machine is a metal drum that is given a negative charge at the beginning of the copying cycle. The optical system then projects an image of the document on the drum. The electric charge disappears where light strikes the metal surface, so only dark parts of the image remain charged. Positively charged particles of toner powder are then applied to the drum. The charged parts of the drum attract the dark powder, which is then transferred to a piece of paper. A heater seals the powder to the paper, and a warm copy of the document emerges from the photocopier. A color copier works in the same basic way, but uses color filters and toners (see p. 216). Nowadays, many people use multi-function printers to make copies. These work in a different way and also include a scanner (see pp. 326-37).

GLASS WINDOW

LAMP

MIRRORS

CARRIER BELT

HEATER
The heater warms the paper so that the toner particles soften and are pressed into the surface of the paper.

OPTICAL SYSTEM
Beneath the glass window, a lamp, set of mirrors, and a lens scan the document, moving across it to project a strip onto the rotating drum. The optical system may enlarge or reduce the size of the image on the drum.

AIR CLEANER

The most effective kind of air cleaner uses an electrostatic precipitator to remove very fine particles, such as dust and pollen, from the air in a room. The precipitator works by giving a positive charge to particles in the air and then trapping them with a negatively charged grid. The cleaner may also contain filters to remove dust and odors, and finally an ionizer to add negative ions to the clean air.

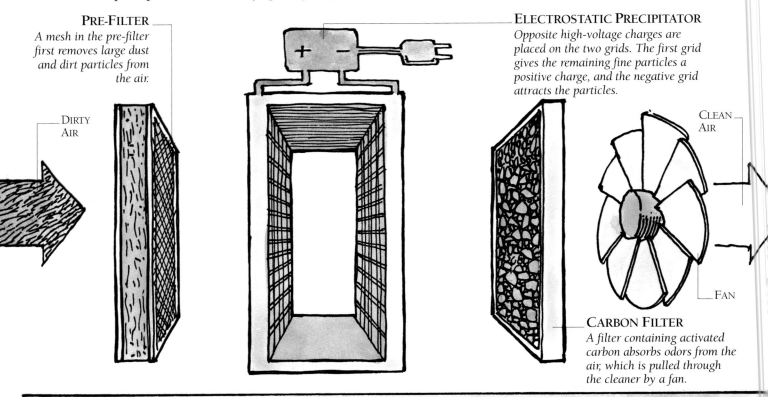

PRE-FILTER
A mesh in the pre-filter first removes large dust and dirt particles from the air.

DIRTY AIR

ELECTROSTATIC PRECIPITATOR
Opposite high-voltage charges are placed on the two grids. The first grid gives the remaining fine particles a positive charge, and the negative grid attracts the particles.

CLEAN AIR

FAN

CARBON FILTER
A filter containing activated carbon absorbs odors from the air, which is pulled through the cleaner by a fan.

LIGHTNING CONDUCTOR

CHARGE BUILD-UP
A thunderstorm creates regions of strong negative electric charge at the base of clouds. These charges cause strong positive charges to form in the ground.

NEGATIVE CHARGE IN CLOUD BASE

POSITIVE CHARGE IN GROUND

LIGHTNING DISCHARGE
The very strong electric fields produce ions and free electrons in the air. The air can then conduct electricity and a flash of lightning surges through it.

IONIZER

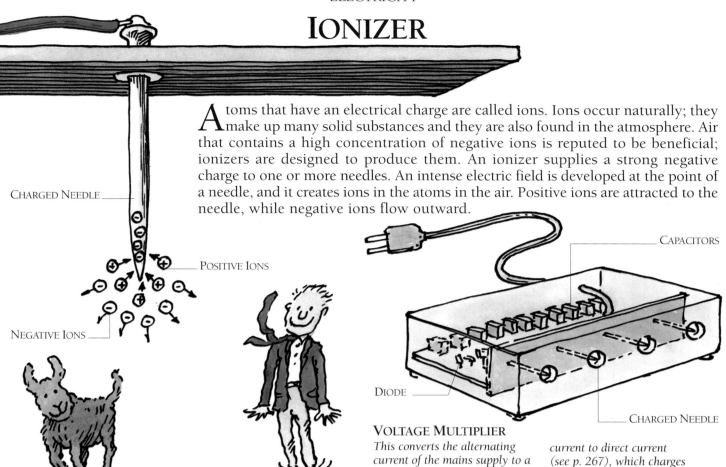

Atoms that have an electrical charge are called ions. Ions occur naturally; they make up many solid substances and they are also found in the atmosphere. Air that contains a high concentration of negative ions is reputed to be beneficial; ionizers are designed to produce them. An ionizer supplies a strong negative charge to one or more needles. An intense electric field is developed at the point of a needle, and it creates ions in the atoms in the air. Positive ions are attracted to the needle, while negative ions flow outward.

CHARGED NEEDLE

POSITIVE IONS

NEGATIVE IONS

CAPACITORS

DIODE

CHARGED NEEDLE

VOLTAGE MULTIPLIER

This converts the alternating current of the mains supply to a high-voltage direct current that charges the ionizer needles. The diodes change the alternating *current to direct current (see p. 267), which charges the capacitors. The capacitors store increasing amounts of charge to raise the voltage.*

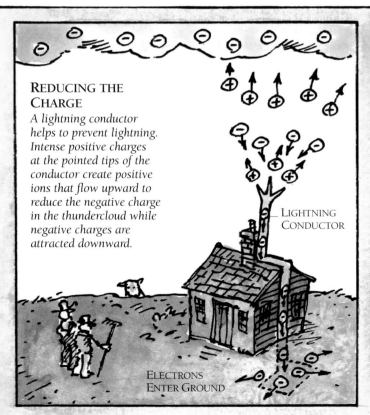

REDUCING THE CHARGE

A lightning conductor helps to prevent lightning. Intense positive charges at the pointed tips of the conductor create positive ions that flow upward to reduce the negative charge in the thundercloud while negative charges are attracted downward.

LIGHTNING CONDUCTOR

ELECTRONS ENTER GROUND

CONDUCTING THE CHARGE TO EARTH

If lightning does strike, it tends to follow the ion path and hits the lightning conductor. The powerful current flows down the cable and enters the ground without causing any damage.

SELF-WINDING WATCH

PIEZOELECTRICITY

Exerting pressure on certain crystals and ceramics can cause them to produce an electric charge. This effect is called piezoelectricity, from the Greek word *piezein* meaning to press, and it is put to use in several electrical devices. In many substances, the atoms are in the form of ions (see p. 263), which are held together very tightly by their electric charges. Quartz, for example, has positive silicon ions and negative oxygen ions. Pressing the quartz displaces the ions so that negative ions move toward one side of the crystal and positive ions toward the other. The opposite faces develop negative and positive charges, which can be very powerful. The reverse happens too: applying an electric signal to a crystal makes it vibrate at a precise natural frequency, as in a quartz oscillator.

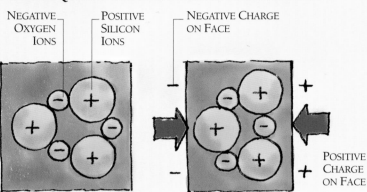

NORMAL QUARTZ CRYSTAL CRYSTAL UNDER PRESSURE

NEGATIVE OXYGEN IONS

POSITIVE SILICON IONS

NEGATIVE CHARGE ON FACE

POSITIVE CHARGE ON FACE

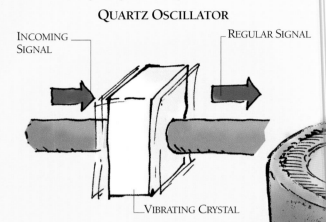

QUARTZ OSCILLATOR

INCOMING SIGNAL

REGULAR SIGNAL

VIBRATING CRYSTAL

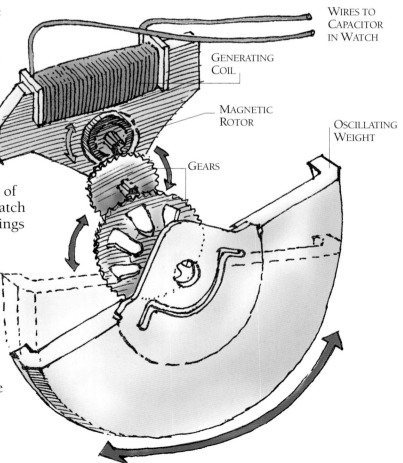

A quartz watch (see opposite page) consumes very little power, but its battery will eventually run out and have to be replaced. The self-winding, or kinetic, watch is a quartz watch that uses the principles of piezoelectricity to keep good time, but does not require a battery. It generates its own electricity simply by using the movement of the wearer's wrist. Inside the watch is an oscillating weight that swings to and fro as the watch moves. The oscillating motion is transferred through a set of gears to a tiny magnetic rotor that rotates at speeds of up to 100,000 revolutions per minute and induces bursts of electric current in a generating coil. The current then goes to the capacitor of the watch to be stored for use by the watch's quartz oscillator and motor.

WIRES TO CAPACITOR IN WATCH

GENERATING COIL

MAGNETIC ROTOR

OSCILLATING WEIGHT

GEARS

QUARTZ CLOCK

Piezoelectricity provides a simple method of accurate time-keeping. Many clocks and watches contain a quartz crystal oscillator that controls the hands or display. Power from a small battery makes the crystal vibrate and it gives out pulses of current at a very precise rate or frequency. A microchip reduces this rate to one pulse per second, and this signal controls the motor that turns the hands or activates the display.

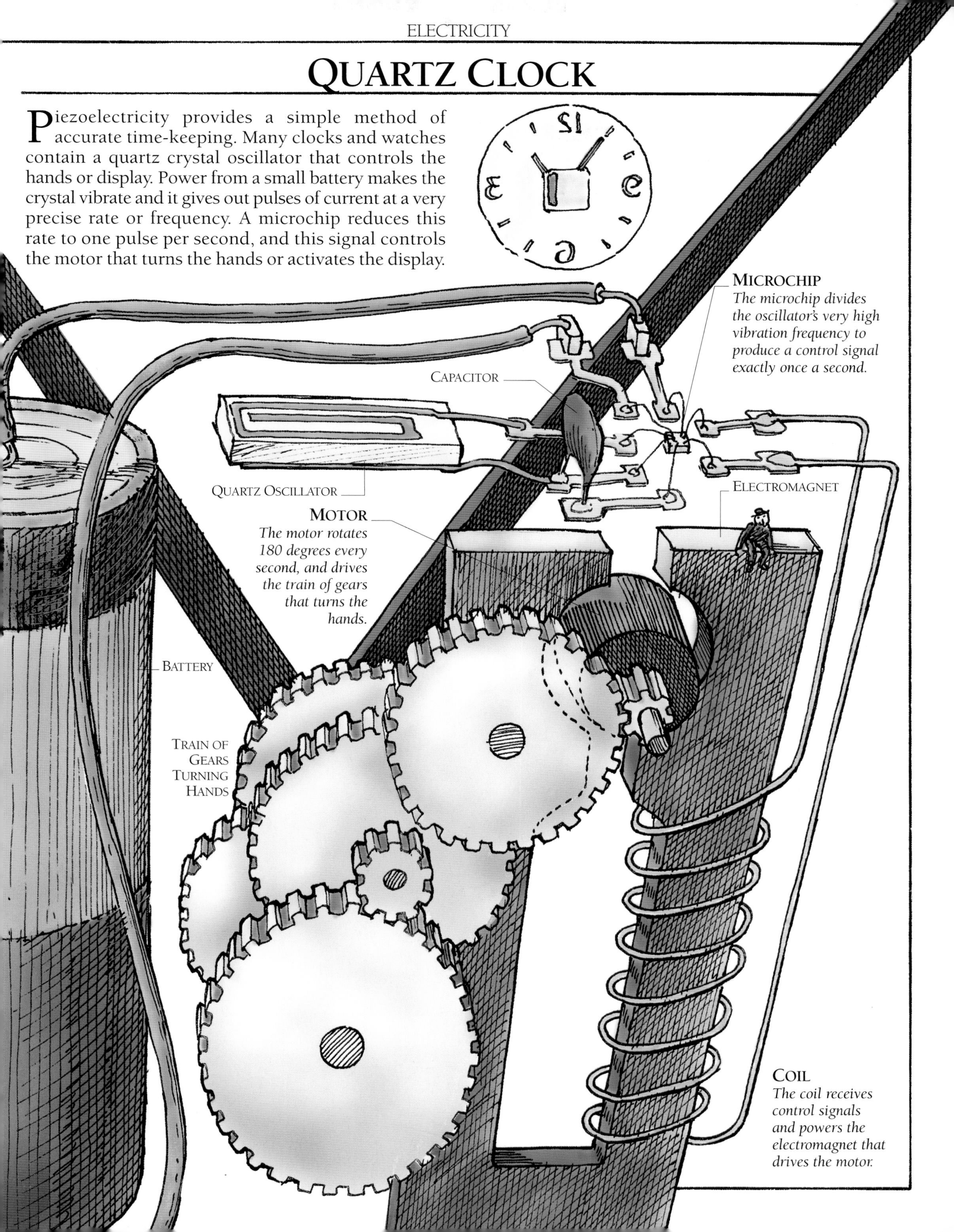

MICROCHIP
The microchip divides the oscillator's very high vibration frequency to produce a control signal exactly once a second.

CAPACITOR

QUARTZ OSCILLATOR

ELECTROMAGNET

MOTOR
The motor rotates 180 degrees every second, and drives the train of gears that turns the hands.

BATTERY

TRAIN OF GEARS TURNING HANDS

COIL
The coil receives control signals and powers the electromagnet that drives the motor.

THE CURRENT CART

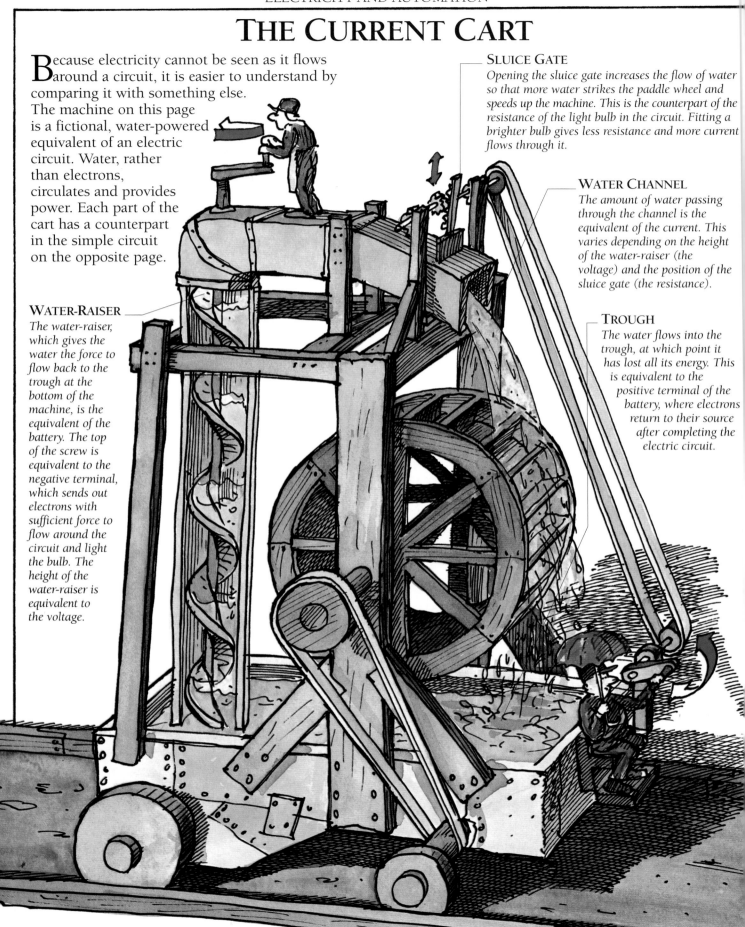

Because electricity cannot be seen as it flows around a circuit, it is easier to understand by comparing it with something else. The machine on this page is a fictional, water-powered equivalent of an electric circuit. Water, rather than electrons, circulates and provides power. Each part of the cart has a counterpart in the simple circuit on the opposite page.

SLUICE GATE

Opening the sluice gate increases the flow of water so that more water strikes the paddle wheel and speeds up the machine. This is the counterpart of the resistance of the light bulb in the circuit. Fitting a brighter bulb gives less resistance and more current flows through it.

WATER CHANNEL

The amount of water passing through the channel is the equivalent of the current. This varies depending on the height of the water-raiser (the voltage) and the position of the sluice gate (the resistance).

WATER-RAISER

The water-raiser, which gives the water the force to flow back to the trough at the bottom of the machine, is the equivalent of the battery. The top of the screw is equivalent to the negative terminal, which sends out electrons with sufficient force to flow around the circuit and light the bulb. The height of the water-raiser is equivalent to the voltage.

TROUGH

The water flows into the trough, at which point it has lost all its energy. This is equivalent to the positive terminal of the battery, where electrons return to their source after completing the electric circuit.

ELECTRIC CIRCUIT

All devices and machines powered by current electricity contain an electric circuit. A source of electricity, usually a battery or generator, drives electrons through a wire to the part of the machine that provides power or releases energy. The electrons then return along a wire to the source and complete the circuit. The source produces a certain number of volts, which is a measure of the electrical force that sends the electrons around the circuit. The current, which is the amount of electricity that flows, is measured in amps or amperes. The working part of the circuit has a resistance measured in ohms.

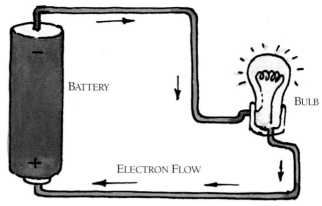

BATTERY

BULB

ELECTRON FLOW

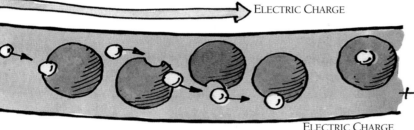

ONE-WAY FLOW

LOOSE ELECTRONS MOVE FROM ONE ATOM TO NEXT

METAL ATOM

ELECTRON FROM SOURCE

DIRECT CURRENT (DC)

The electric current produced by a battery and solar cell is direct current. The electrons flow in one direction from the negative terminal of the source to the positive terminal. Although individual electrons move very slowly, the electric charge travels very much faster. This is because the arriving electrons collide with loose electrons in the metal atoms, making them leave one atom and collide with the next. Like shunting railway trucks, the shift in electrons progresses very rapidly along the wire, making the electric charge move very quickly.

ELECTRIC CHARGE

ELECTRIC CHARGE

TWO-WAY FLOW

ELECTRIC CHARGE

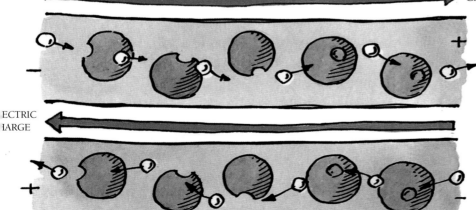

ALTERNATING CURRENT (AC)

The main supply is usually not direct current but alternating current. Here, the electrons move to and fro 50 times a second, because the terminals of the supply repeatedly change from positive to negative and vice versa. This makes no difference to a light bulb, which lights up when the current flows in either direction.

BATTERIES

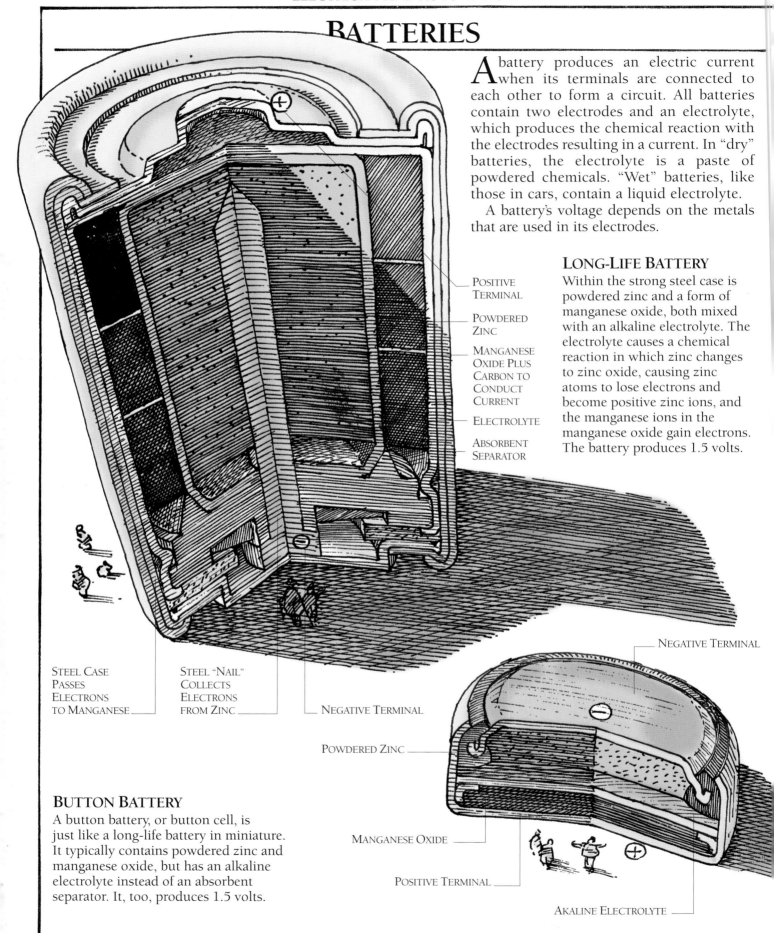

A battery produces an electric current when its terminals are connected to each other to form a circuit. All batteries contain two electrodes and an electrolyte, which produces the chemical reaction with the electrodes resulting in a current. In "dry" batteries, the electrolyte is a paste of powdered chemicals. "Wet" batteries, like those in cars, contain a liquid electrolyte.

A battery's voltage depends on the metals that are used in its electrodes.

LONG-LIFE BATTERY
Within the strong steel case is powdered zinc and a form of manganese oxide, both mixed with an alkaline electrolyte. The electrolyte causes a chemical reaction in which zinc changes to zinc oxide, causing zinc atoms to lose electrons and become positive zinc ions, and the manganese ions in the manganese oxide gain electrons. The battery produces 1.5 volts.

POSITIVE TERMINAL

POWDERED ZINC

MANGANESE OXIDE PLUS CARBON TO CONDUCT CURRENT

ELECTROLYTE

ABSORBENT SEPARATOR

STEEL CASE PASSES ELECTRONS TO MANGANESE

STEEL "NAIL" COLLECTS ELECTRONS FROM ZINC

NEGATIVE TERMINAL

NEGATIVE TERMINAL

POWDERED ZINC

MANGANESE OXIDE

POSITIVE TERMINAL

AKALINE ELECTROLYTE

BUTTON BATTERY
A button battery, or button cell, is just like a long-life battery in miniature. It typically contains powdered zinc and manganese oxide, but has an alkaline electrolyte instead of an absorbent separator. It, too, produces 1.5 volts.

CAR BATTERY

The battery in a car is designed to produce the strong current needed to turn the starter motor (see p. 73). It does this by using a number of cells linked together. When running, the engine turns a generator that feeds current back into the battery to recharge it.

A car battery contains plates of lead oxide and lead metal, immersed in a sulfuric acid electrolyte. As the battery produces current, both kinds of plate change to lead sulfate. Feeding a current into the battery reverses the chemical reaction.

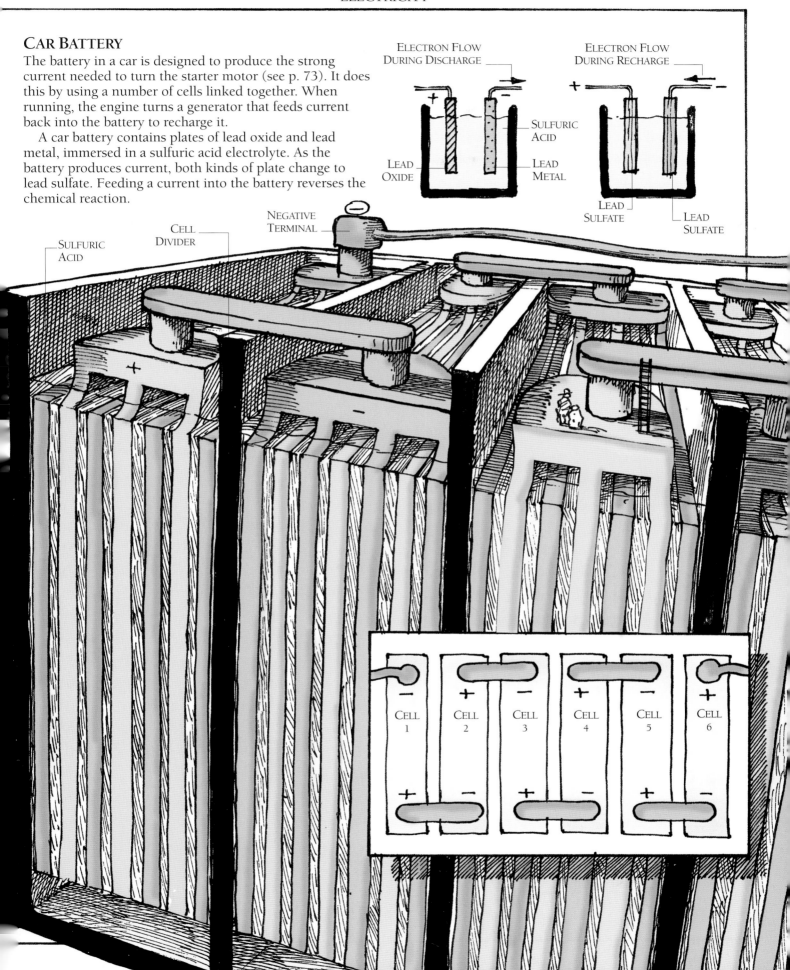

ELECTRON FLOW DURING DISCHARGE

SULFURIC ACID

LEAD OXIDE

LEAD METAL

ELECTRON FLOW DURING RECHARGE

LEAD SULFATE

LEAD SULFATE

SULFURIC ACID

CELL DIVIDER

NEGATIVE TERMINAL

CELL 1

CELL 2

CELL 3

CELL 4

CELL 5

CELL 6

CAR TEMPERATURE GAUGE

Electrical temperature gauges and thermometers depend on the changing resistance of a heat-sensitive element. The resistance varies with temperature, so that the amount of current flowing depends on how hot the element gets.

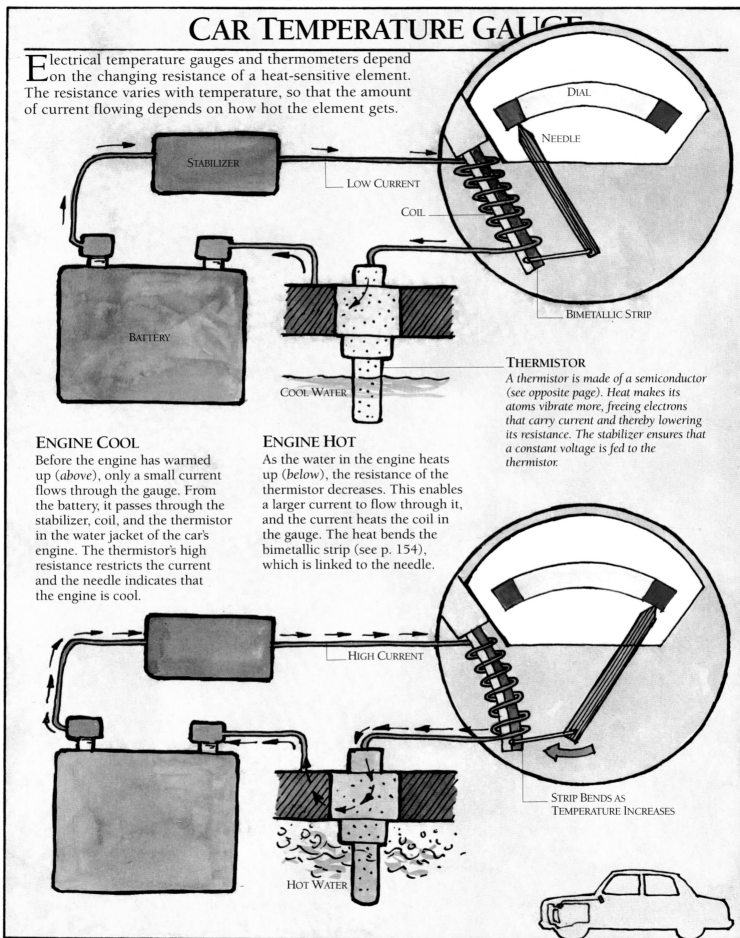

DIAL

NEEDLE

STABILIZER

LOW CURRENT

COIL

BATTERY

BIMETALLIC STRIP

COOL WATER

THERMISTOR

A thermistor is made of a semiconductor (see opposite page). Heat makes its atoms vibrate more, freeing electrons that carry current and thereby lowering its resistance. The stabilizer ensures that a constant voltage is fed to the thermistor.

ENGINE COOL

Before the engine has warmed up (*above*), only a small current flows through the gauge. From the battery, it passes through the stabilizer, coil, and the thermistor in the water jacket of the car's engine. The thermistor's high resistance restricts the current and the needle indicates that the engine is cool.

ENGINE HOT

As the water in the engine heats up (*below*), the resistance of the thermistor decreases. This enables a larger current to flow through it, and the current heats the coil in the gauge. The heat bends the bimetallic strip (see p. 154), which is linked to the needle.

HIGH CURRENT

STRIP BENDS AS
TEMPERATURE INCREASES

HOT WATER

SOLAR CELL

A solar cell generates electricity when light falls on it. Large panels of cells power satellites, while strips of a few cells provide the much smaller current needed to power calculators. Like many electronic devices, solar cells depend on semiconductors. These are materials in which the flow of electrons can be controlled—in this case, to generate a low current. Each cell contains two layers of different types of silicon. The silicon atoms are arranged in a lattice in which other atoms containing extra or fewer atoms are inserted.

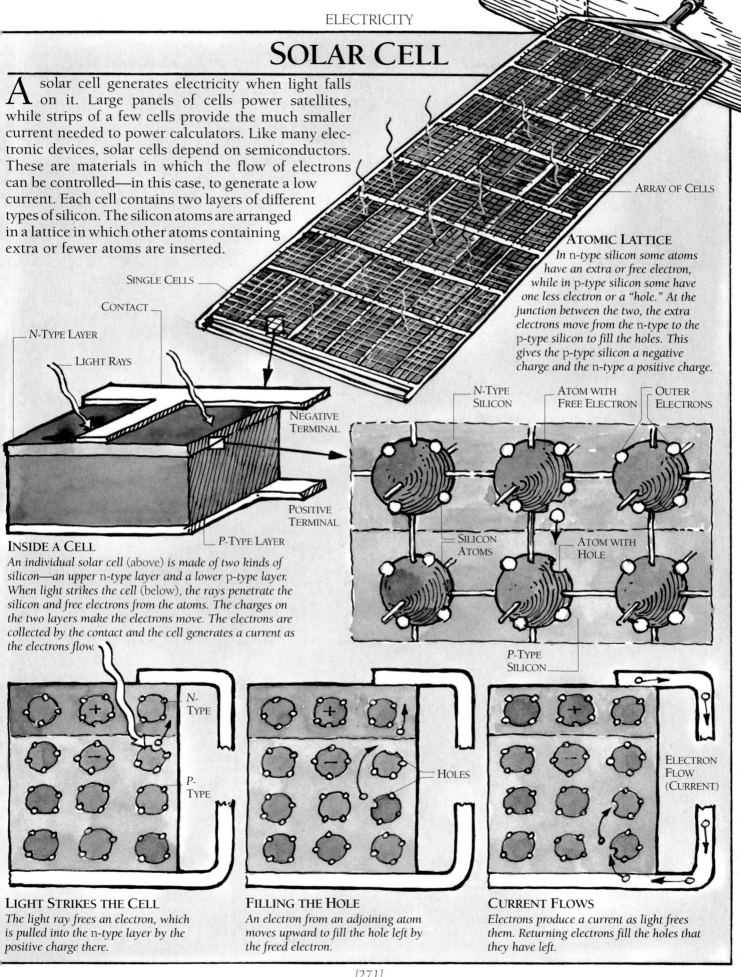

ARRAY OF CELLS

SINGLE CELLS

CONTACT

N-TYPE LAYER

LIGHT RAYS

NEGATIVE TERMINAL

POSITIVE TERMINAL

P-TYPE LAYER

ATOMIC LATTICE

In n-type silicon some atoms have an extra or free electron, while in p-type silicon some have one less electron or a "hole." At the junction between the two, the extra electrons move from the n-type to the p-type silicon to fill the holes. This gives the p-type silicon a negative charge and the n-type a positive charge.

N-TYPE SILICON

ATOM WITH FREE ELECTRON

OUTER ELECTRONS

SILICON ATOMS

ATOM WITH HOLE

P-TYPE SILICON

INSIDE A CELL

An individual solar cell (above) is made of two kinds of silicon—an upper n-type layer and a lower p-type layer. When light strikes the cell (below), the rays penetrate the silicon and free electrons from the atoms. The charges on the two layers make the electrons move. The electrons are collected by the contact and the cell generates a current as the electrons flow.

N-TYPE

P-TYPE

HOLES

ELECTRON FLOW (CURRENT)

LIGHT STRIKES THE CELL

The light ray frees an electron, which is pulled into the n-type layer by the positive charge there.

FILLING THE HOLE

An electron from an adjoining atom moves upward to fill the hole left by the freed electron.

CURRENT FLOWS

Electrons produce a current as light frees them. Returning electrons fill the holes that they have left.

REMOTE CONTROL UNIT

DIODE

A diode allows current to flow in one direction but not in the other. It consists of a *p-n* semiconductor junction (see p. 271). When a positive terminal is connected to the *p*-type layer (*far right*), the positive charge of the terminal attracts electrons and a full current flows. On reversing the connections (*right*), the negative charge of the *p*-type layer opposes electron flow. A low current flows as a few electrons freed by atomic vibrations cross the juction.

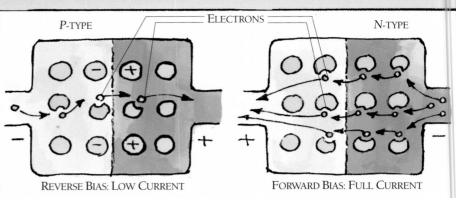

P-TYPE   ELECTRONS   N-TYPE

REVERSE BIAS: LOW CURRENT   FORWARD BIAS: FULL CURRENT

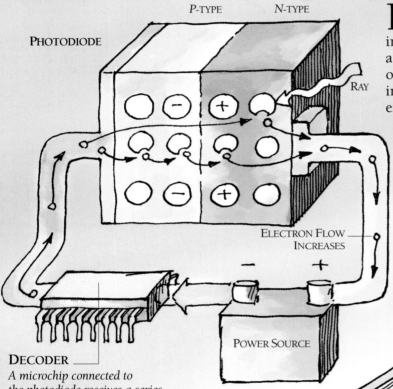

P-TYPE   N-TYPE

PHOTODIODE

RAY

ELECTRON FLOW INCREASES

POWER SOURCE

DECODER

A microchip connected to the photodiode receives a series of electrical pulses in binary code as the beam flashes on and off. A barcode reader (see p. 337), and a Blu-ray player (see pp. 200-201) work in a similar way.

PHOTODIODE

POWER LEADS

P ressing a button on the remote control unit for a television or Blu-ray player transmits a beam of invisible infrared rays to the set. The beam contains a digital code signal similar to that given when a key of a computer keyboard is pressed. The receiver unit in the TV detects the signal and decodes it, for example to change channel or volume. Both the transmitter and receiver work with diodes, but in each case the diodes function in opposite ways.

RECEIVER UNIT

The receiver unit contains a photodiode, which is a diode sensitive to light or infrared rays. It is connected in reverse bias so that normally only a low current flows through it. When rays strike the diode, they free some electrons, increasing the current to produce a signal, which goes to the decoder.

INFRARED BEAM

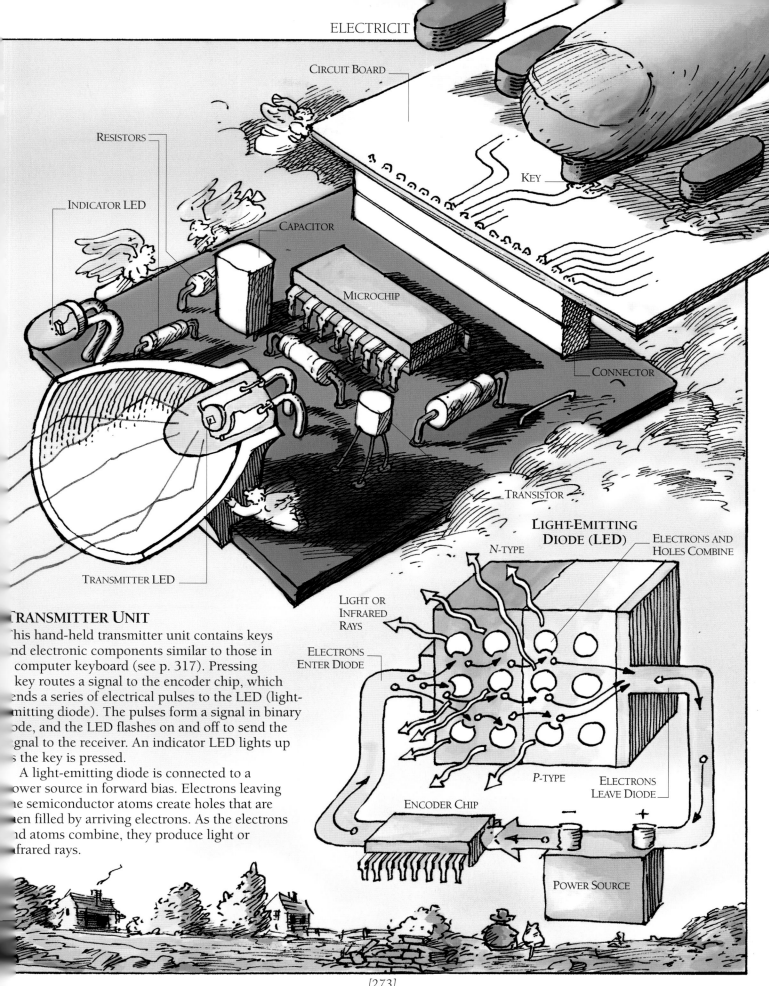

CIRCUIT BOARD

RESISTORS

INDICATOR LED

CAPACITOR

KEY

MICROCHIP

CONNECTOR

TRANSMITTER LED

TRANSISTOR

LIGHT-EMITTING DIODE (LED)

N-TYPE

ELECTRONS AND HOLES COMBINE

LIGHT OR INFRARED RAYS

ELECTRONS ENTER DIODE

P-TYPE

ELECTRONS LEAVE DIODE

ENCODER CHIP

_ +

POWER SOURCE

TRANSMITTER UNIT

This hand-held transmitter unit contains keys
nd electronic components similar to those in
computer keyboard (see p. 317). Pressing
key routes a signal to the encoder chip, which
ends a series of electrical pulses to the LED (light-
mitting diode). The pulses form a signal in binary
ode, and the LED flashes on and off to send the
gnal to the receiver. An indicator LED lights up
s the key is pressed.

A light-emitting diode is connected to a
ower source in forward bias. Electrons leaving
e semiconductor atoms create holes that are
en filled by arriving electrons. As the electrons
nd atoms combine, they produce light or
frared rays.

MAGNETISM

ON SHOEING A MAMMOTH

*W*orking mammoths wear out their shoes with great rapidity, so it was with extreme interest that I watched a blacksmith fitting new improved shoes to a volunteer beast. The test had mixed results. Shoe wear was reduced to zero, but only because a strange and powerful attraction between opposite shoes prevented all movement on the part of the wearer.

WHERE NORTH MEETS SOUTH

A magnet is a seemingly ordinary piece of metal or ceramic that is surrounded by an invisible field of force that affects any magnetic material within it. All magnets have two poles. When magnets are brought together, a north pole always attracts a south pole, while pairs of like poles repel each other. Bar magnets are the simplest permanent magnets. Horseshoe magnets, which have such an unfortunate effect when used as mammoth footwear, are bar magnets bent so that their poles are brought close together.

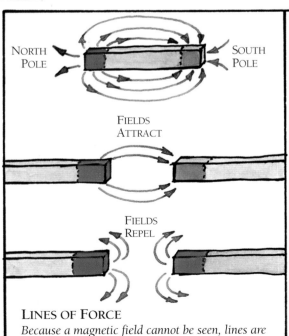

NORTH POLE

SOUTH POLE

FIELDS ATTRACT

FIELDS REPEL

LINES OF FORCE
Because a magnetic field cannot be seen, lines are used to show the direction of the field.

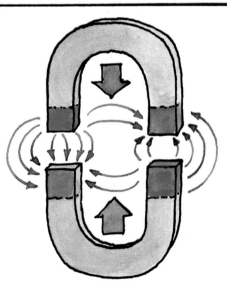

MAGNETIC ATTRACTION
The lines of force extend from the north pole of one magnet to the south pole of the other, pulling the magnets together.

ON A MAMMOTH CLOTHES DRYER

The problem of how to dry out weatherproof clothing worn by working mammoths in damp climates has long taxed my ingenuity. On one occasion, I designed a hollow dryer modeled on the form of a standing mammoth, which was intended to prevent shrinkage of the garments. I accordingly had a blacksmith put my plans into effect, and in no time he was happily coiling some sturdy wire around an iron bar supported on wooden legs.

What happened next was both startling and inexplicable. A sudden thunderstorm swept overhead and a bolt of lightning hit one end of the coil, and at that very instant all the blacksmith's tools flew through the air and attached themselves to the work in progress. The project was promptly abandoned.

ELECTRICAL MAGNETS

When an electric current flows through a wire, a magnetic field is produced around it. The field produced by a single wire is not very strong, so to increase it, the wire is wound into a coil. This concentrates the magnetic field, especially if an iron bar is placed in the center of the field. Electromagnets can be very powerful—as the blacksmith finds out.

A sudden burst of current momentarily transforms his clothes dryer into a powerful electromagnet, which attracts all nearby iron objects to its poles.

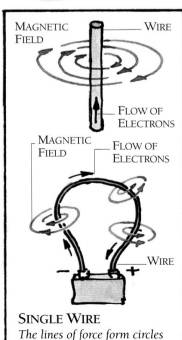

MAGNETIC FIELD — **WIRE**

FLOW OF ELECTRONS

MAGNETIC FIELD — **FLOW OF ELECTRONS**

WIRE

SINGLE WIRE
The lines of force form circles around the wire.

COIL OF WIRE
The lines of force of all the loops in a coil combine to produce a field that is similar to the field around a bar magnet. The poles of the electromagnet are at either end of the coil.

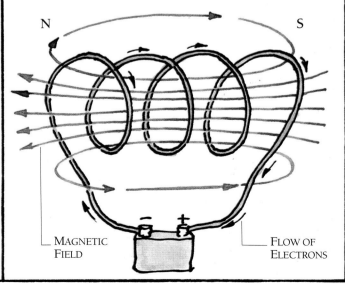

N   S

MAGNETIC FIELD

FLOW OF ELECTRONS

MAGNETS AT WORK

MAGNETIC COMPASS

Earth has its own magnetic field. A compass needle will align itself so that it points toward the north and south magnetic poles, along lines of force that run in the direction of the field. The magnetic poles are situated away from the geographical poles.

MAGNETIC INDUCTION

A magnet is able to pick up a piece of steel or iron because its magnetic field flows into the metal. This turns the metal into a temporary magnet, and the two magnets then attract each other.

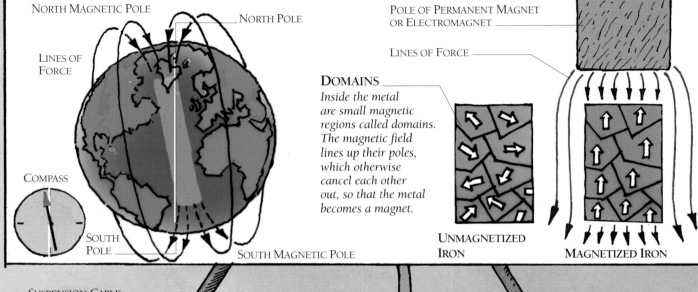

NORTH MAGNETIC POLE

NORTH POLE

LINES OF FORCE

COMPASS

SOUTH POLE

SOUTH MAGNETIC POLE

POLE OF PERMANENT MAGNET OR ELECTROMAGNET

LINES OF FORCE

DOMAINS

Inside the metal are small magnetic regions called domains. The magnetic field lines up their poles, which otherwise cancel each other out, so that the metal becomes a magnet.

UNMAGNETIZED IRON

MAGNETIZED IRON

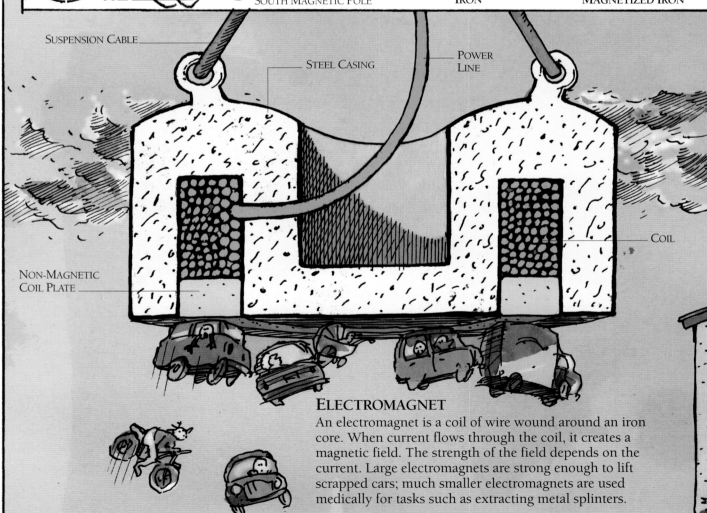

SUSPENSION CABLE

STEEL CASING

POWER LINE

COIL

NON-MAGNETIC COIL PLATE

ELECTROMAGNET

An electromagnet is a coil of wire wound around an iron core. When current flows through the coil, it creates a magnetic field. The strength of the field depends on the current. Large electromagnets are strong enough to lift scrapped cars; much smaller electromagnets are used medically for tasks such as extracting metal splinters.

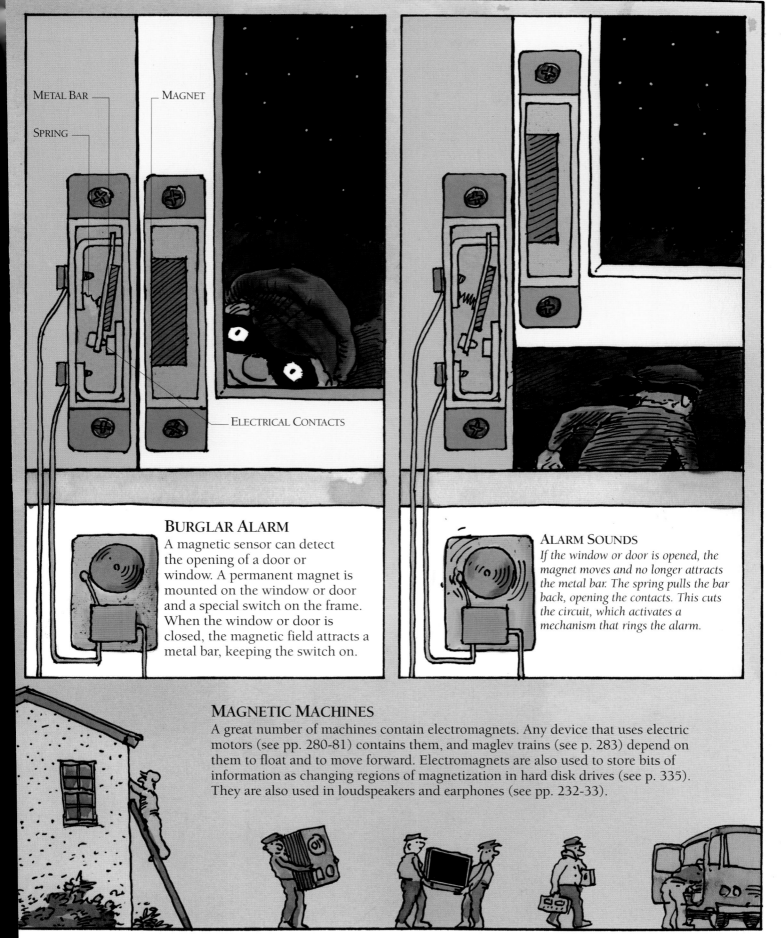

METAL BAR

MAGNET

SPRING

ELECTRICAL CONTACTS

BURGLAR ALARM

A magnetic sensor can detect the opening of a door or window. A permanent magnet is mounted on the window or door and a special switch on the frame. When the window or door is closed, the magnetic field attracts a metal bar, keeping the switch on.

ALARM SOUNDS

If the window or door is opened, the magnet moves and no longer attracts the metal bar. The spring pulls the bar back, opening the contacts. This cuts the circuit, which activates a mechanism that rings the alarm.

MAGNETIC MACHINES

A great number of machines contain electromagnets. Any device that uses electric motors (see pp. 280-81) contains them, and maglev trains (see p. 283) depend on them to float and to move forward. Electromagnets are also used to store bits of information as changing regions of magnetization in hard disk drives (see p. 335). They are also used in loudspeakers and earphones (see pp. 232-33).

THE ELECTRIC BELL

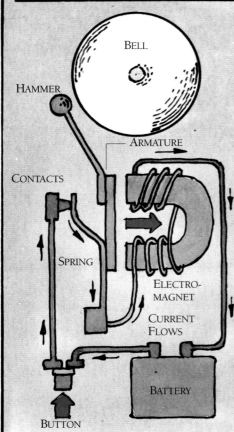

O ne of the many everyday uses of electromagnetism is the electric bell. The button at the door is an electric switch that sends current from a power source such as a battery to the striking mechanism. This makes a hammer move to and fro several times a second, sounding a metal bell. An electromagnet and a spring alternately pull the hammer.

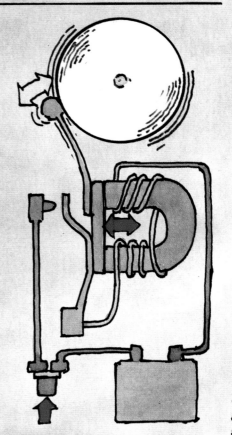

BELL

HAMMER

ARMATURE

CONTACTS

SPRING

ELECTRO-MAGNET

CURRENT FLOWS

BATTERY

BUTTON

PRESSING THE BUTTON

When the button is pressed, the contacts are first closed. Current flows through the contacts and the spring to the electromagnet, which produces a magnetic field. This field attracts the iron armature, which moves toward the electromagnet against the spring and makes the hammer strike the bell.

THE BELL SOUNDS

As the hammer strikes the bell, the movement of the armature opens the contacts. The current stops flowing to the electromagnet, which loses its magnetism. The spring pulls the armature back, and the hammer moves away from the bell. The contacts then close again, and the cycle repeats itself for as long as the button is pressed.

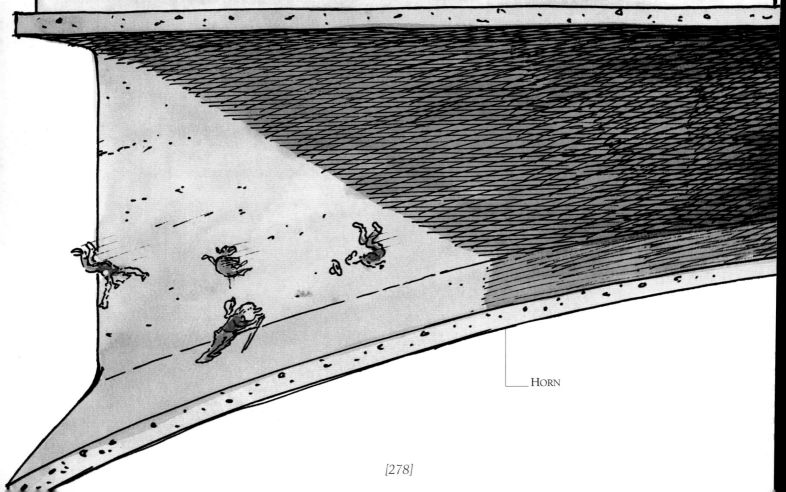

HORN

THE ELECTRIC HORN

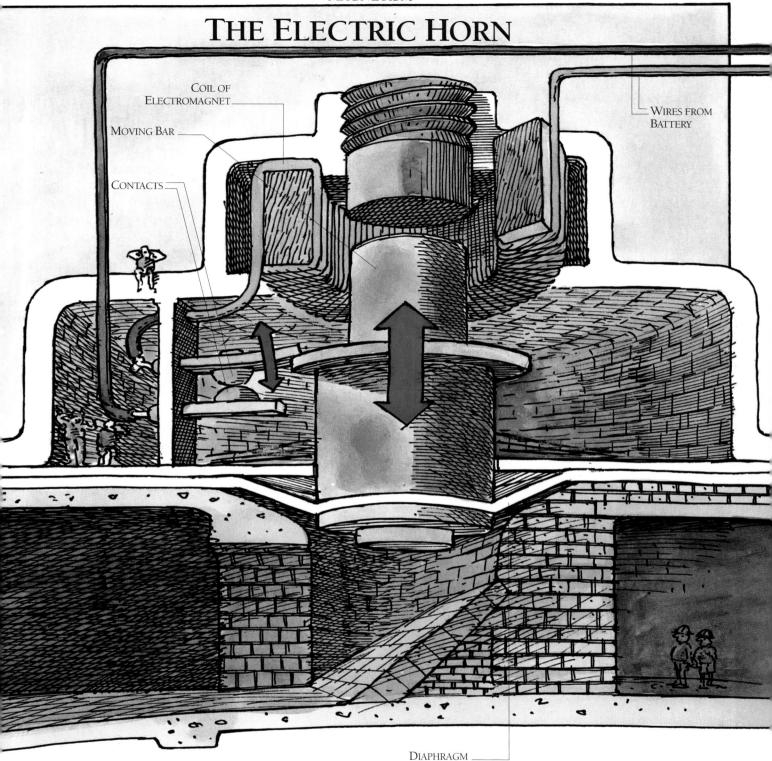

COIL OF
ELECTROMAGNET

MOVING BAR

CONTACTS

WIRES FROM
BATTERY

DIAPHRAGM

The horn of a motor vehicle is another example of the use of magnetism to produce sound by a simple vibration. The mechanism of a horn is rather similar to that of an electric bell, with a set of contacts repeatedly closing and opening to interrupt the flow of current to an electromagnet. Here, an iron bar moves up and down inside the coil of the electromagnet as the magnetic field switches on and off. The bar is attached to a diaphragm, which vibrates rapidly and gives out a loud sound.

The horn, as here, may have an actual bell-shaped horn attached to the diaphragm. This resonates to give a penetrating note and projects the sound forward.

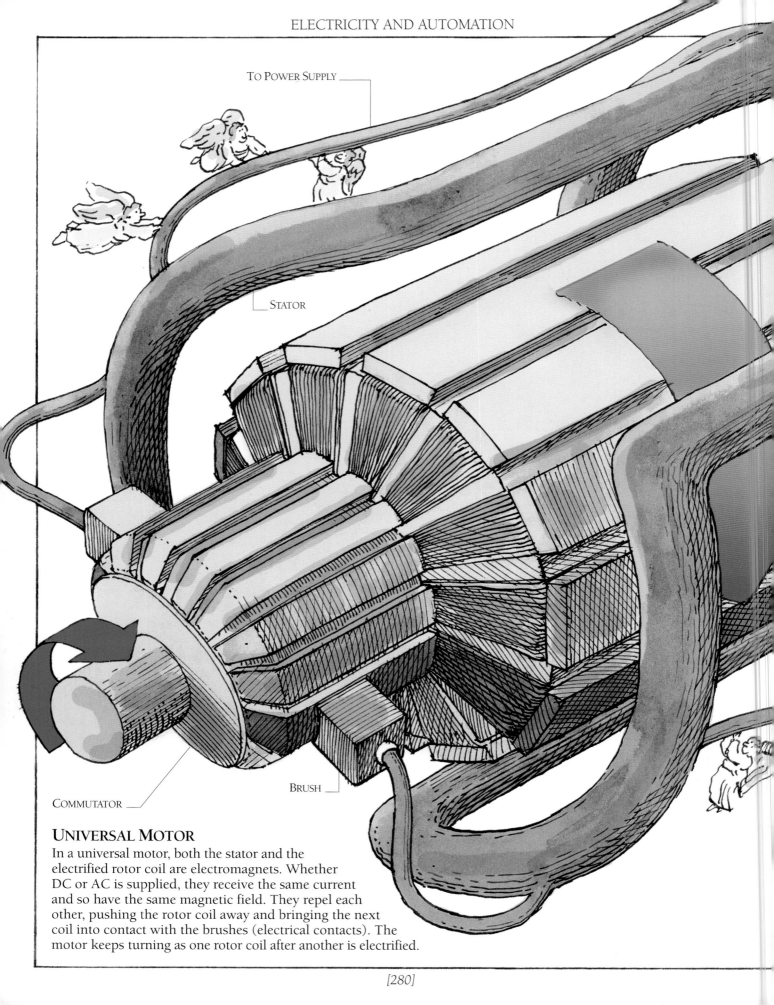

TO POWER SUPPLY

STATOR

COMMUTATOR

BRUSH

UNIVERSAL MOTOR

In a universal motor, both the stator and the
electrified rotor coil are electromagnets. Whether
DC or AC is supplied, they receive the same current
and so have the same magnetic field. They repel each
other, pushing the rotor coil away and bringing the next
coil into contact with the brushes (electrical contacts). The
motor keeps turning as one rotor coil after another is electrified.

ELECTRIC MOTOR

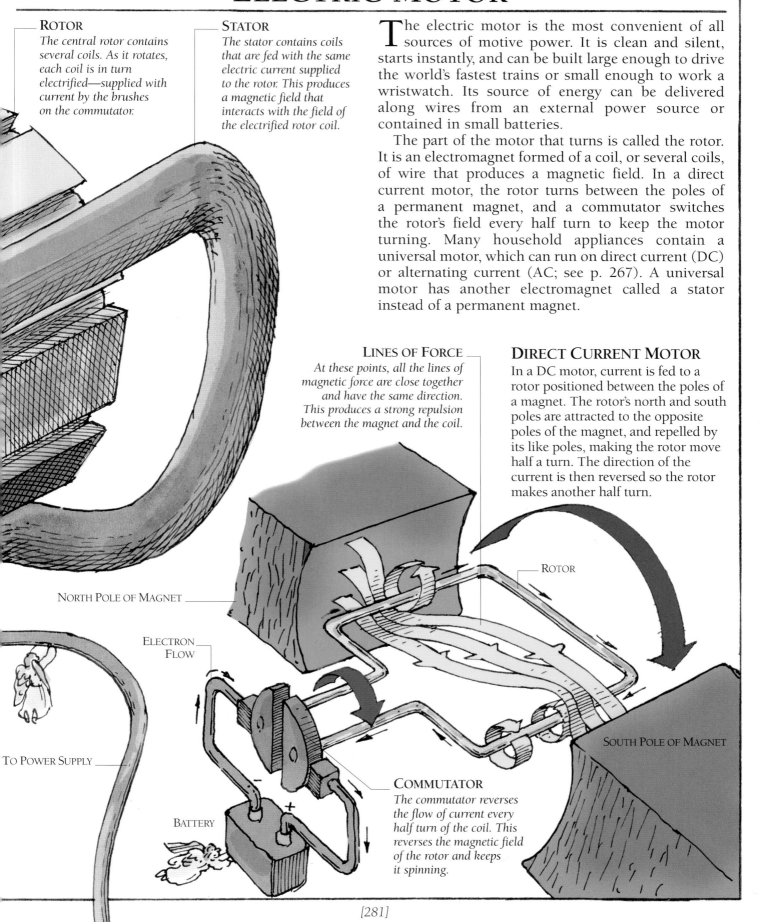

ROTOR
The central rotor contains several coils. As it rotates, each coil is in turn electrified—supplied with current by the brushes on the commutator.

STATOR
The stator contains coils that are fed with the same electric current supplied to the rotor. This produces a magnetic field that interacts with the field of the electrified rotor coil.

The electric motor is the most convenient of all sources of motive power. It is clean and silent, starts instantly, and can be built large enough to drive the world's fastest trains or small enough to work a wristwatch. Its source of energy can be delivered along wires from an external power source or contained in small batteries.

The part of the motor that turns is called the rotor. It is an electromagnet formed of a coil, or several coils, of wire that produces a magnetic field. In a direct current motor, the rotor turns between the poles of a permanent magnet, and a commutator switches the rotor's field every half turn to keep the motor turning. Many household appliances contain a universal motor, which can run on direct current (DC) or alternating current (AC; see p. 267). A universal motor has another electromagnet called a stator instead of a permanent magnet.

LINES OF FORCE
At these points, all the lines of magnetic force are close together and have the same direction. This produces a strong repulsion between the magnet and the coil.

DIRECT CURRENT MOTOR
In a DC motor, current is fed to a rotor positioned between the poles of a magnet. The rotor's north and south poles are attracted to the opposite poles of the magnet, and repelled by its like poles, making the rotor move half a turn. The direction of the current is then reversed so the rotor makes another half turn.

ROTOR

NORTH POLE OF MAGNET

ELECTRON FLOW

TO POWER SUPPLY

SOUTH POLE OF MAGNET

BATTERY

COMMUTATOR
The commutator reverses the flow of current every half turn of the coil. This reverses the magnetic field of the rotor and keeps it spinning.

3D PRINTER

A 3D printer produces 3D objects from computer-generated virtual models created by computer-aided design (CAD) software or by scanning real objects with a laser beam. The printer's computer gives each point on the virtual model's surface a set of three numbers—one number for each axis (left-right, forward-backward and up-down). It can then use these coordinates to send precise instructions to very accurate motors called stepper motors in control of a printing head. The head deposits plastic layer by layer, constructing a solid replica of the virtual model.

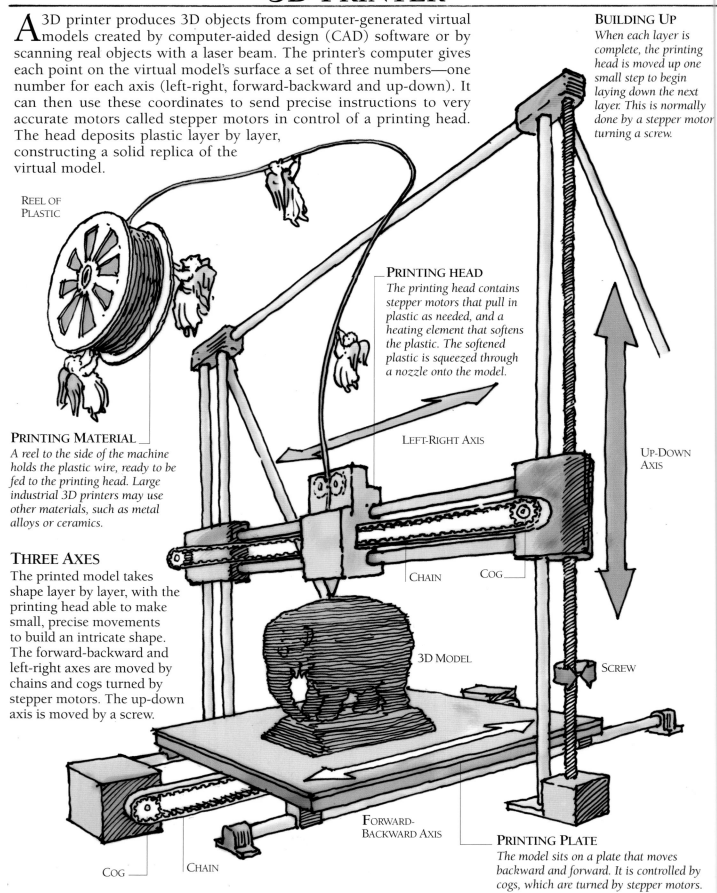

BUILDING UP
When each layer is complete, the printing head is moved up one small step to begin laying down the next layer. This is normally done by a stepper motor turning a screw.

REEL OF PLASTIC

PRINTING HEAD
The printing head contains stepper motors that pull in plastic as needed, and a heating element that softens the plastic. The softened plastic is squeezed through a nozzle onto the model.

LEFT-RIGHT AXIS

UP-DOWN AXIS

PRINTING MATERIAL
A reel to the side of the machine holds the plastic wire, ready to be fed to the printing head. Large industrial 3D printers may use other materials, such as metal alloys or ceramics.

CHAIN

COG

THREE AXES
The printed model takes shape layer by layer, with the printing head able to make small, precise movements to build an intricate shape. The forward-backward and left-right axes are moved by chains and cogs turned by stepper motors. The up-down axis is moved by a screw.

3D MODEL

SCREW

COG

CHAIN

FORWARD-BACKWARD AXIS

PRINTING PLATE
The model sits on a plate that moves backward and forward. It is controlled by cogs, which are turned by stepper motors.

STEPPER MOTOR

A crucial component of a 3D printer is the stepper motor—an electric motor that moves in tiny steps. A stepper motor's rotor—the part that turns—is a permanent magnet. It has two sets of teeth, one at the magnet's north pole and one at the south pole. The two sets of teeth are offset, so that only one set will line up with teeth on the motor's stators—the parts that stay still. The stators are electromagnets whose poles can be reversed, pulling the rotor around one tiny step. Stepper motors are found in many other precision devices, including computer printers and scanners.

STATORS

This stepper motor has eight static stators arranged around the rotor. The stators have teeth that align with one set of teeth on the rotor. When the stator is a north pole, it attracts the teeth on the rotor's south pole and repels the teeth on the rotor's north pole. Switching the stator to a south pole repels the rotor's south pole teeth and attracts its north pole teeth, causing the motor to move around one tiny step.

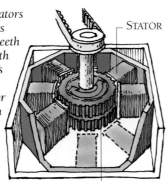

STATOR

ROTOR

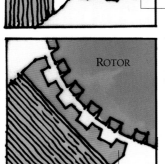

SOUTH POLE

NORTH POLE

OFFSET TEETH

The teeth on the rotor's south pole (blue) are offset by exactly one half step relative to the teeth of the rotor's north pole (red).

BEFORE A STEP

The teeth of the rotor's south pole align with the teeth of the stator, which are currently a north pole (red).

ROTOR

STATOR TEETH: NORTH POLE

MAKING A STEP

The stator's poles reverse, so the stator teeth now present a south pole (blue). The rotor moves one step, so that the teeth of its north pole align with the stator teeth.

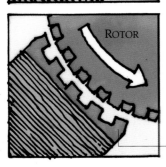

ROTOR

STATOR TEETH: SOUTH POLE

MAGLEV TRAIN

A maglev has no wheels, instead using magnetic fields to levitate itself above a track. Thus freed from friction with the rails, the train can float along the track. The train shown here uses the attractive system of levitation, in which electromagnets attached to the train run below the suspension rail and rise toward it to lift the train.

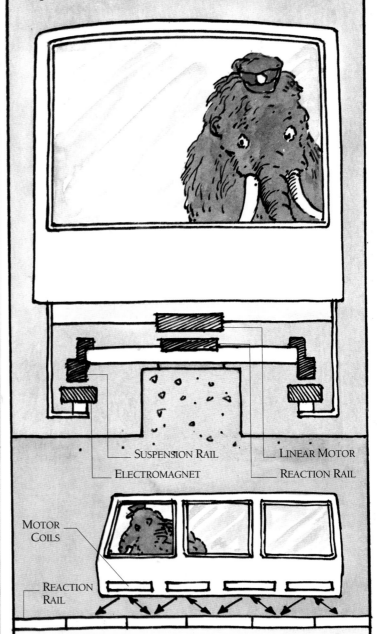

SUSPENSION RAIL

ELECTROMAGNET

LINEAR MOTOR

REACTION RAIL

MOTOR COILS

REACTION RAIL

LINEAR INDUCTION MOTOR

A form of electric motor called an induction motor drives the maglev train. Coils on the train generate a magnetic field in which the poles shift along the train. The field induces electric currents in the reaction rail, which in turn generates its own magnetic field. The two fields interact so that the shifting field pulls the floating train along the track.

ELECTRIC GENERATOR

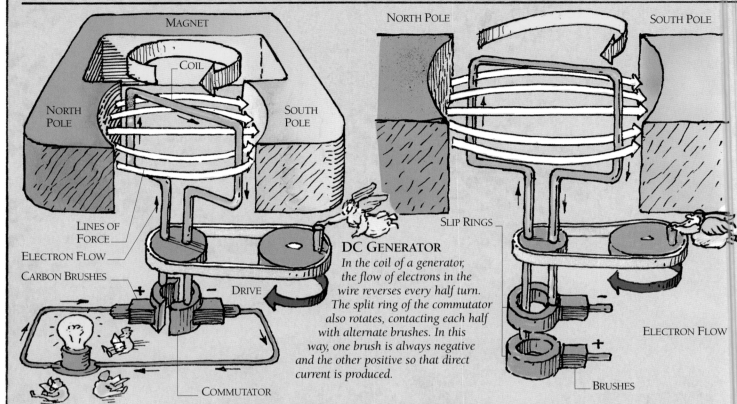

MAGNET

COIL

NORTH POLE

SOUTH POLE

NORTH POLE

SOUTH POLE

LINES OF FORCE

ELECTRON FLOW

CARBON BRUSHES

DRIVE

SLIP RINGS

ELECTRON FLOW

COMMUTATOR

BRUSHES

DC GENERATOR

In the coil of a generator, the flow of electrons in the wire reverses every half turn. The split ring of the commutator also rotates, contacting each half with alternate brushes. In this way, one brush is always negative and the other positive so that direct current is produced.

An electric generator works by electromagnetic induction—it uses magnetism to make electricity. The power source spins a coil between the poles of a magnet or electromagnet. As it cuts through the lines of force, an electric current flows through the coil.

AC GENERATOR – FIRST HALF TURN

An alternating current (AC) generator contains two slip rings connected to the end of the coil. As the current reverses in the coil, an alternating current emerges from the brushes. When part of the coil cuts the lines of force near the magnet's north pole, the electrons move up the wire, producing a positive charge at the lower slip ring.

POWER SUPPLY

The large generators in power stations are powered by steam turbines, water turbines, or gas turbines, which work like the turbines in jet engines (see p. 162). The electricity reaches our homes through a network of power lines carrying current at a very high voltage, which reduces energy losses in transmission. Transformers then step down the voltage to different levels for use in industry and in the home.

POWER LINE

At high voltage, the current is capable of sparking considerable distances through air. For safety, the lines are suspended from high pylons by long insulators.

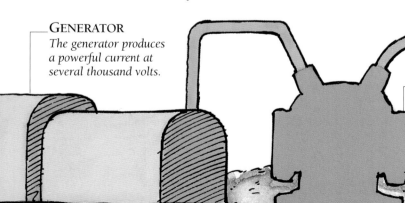

GENERATOR

The generator produces a powerful current at several thousand volts.

TRANSMISSION TRANSFORMER

This steps up the voltage to several hundred thousand volts to reduce energy losses.

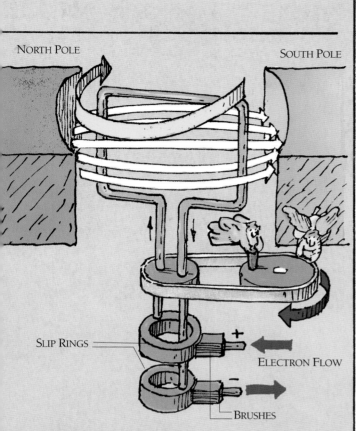

SLIP RINGS

ELECTRON FLOW

BRUSHES

AC GENERATOR – SECOND HALF TURN

The same part of the coil has now turned to cut the lines of force near the magnet's south pole. Electrons now flow down the wire to produce a negative charge at the lower slip ring, reversing the current flow. The frequency of the current reversal produced by an AC generator depends on the speed at which the coil rotates.

TRANSFORMER

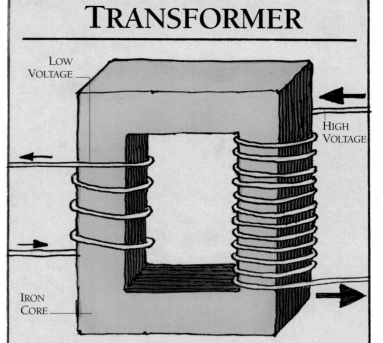

LOW VOLTAGE

HIGH VOLTAGE

IRON CORE

A transformer changes the voltage of an alternating current. The input current goes to a primary coil wound around an iron core. The output current emerges from a secondary coil also wound around the core. The alternating input current produces a magnetic field that continually switches on and off. The core transfers this field to the secondary coil, where it induces an output current. The degree of change in voltage depends on the ratio of turns in the coils; the transformer shown here steps up or steps down the voltage three times.

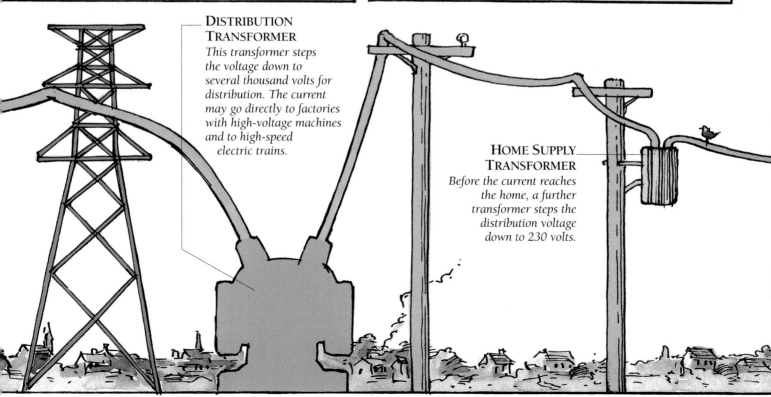

DISTRIBUTION TRANSFORMER

This transformer steps the voltage down to several thousand volts for distribution. The current may go directly to factories with high-voltage machines and to high-speed electric trains.

HOME SUPPLY TRANSFORMER

Before the current reaches the home, a further transformer steps the distribution voltage down to 230 volts.

THE TWO-WAY SWITCH

Once a supply of electricity has entered the home, it is metered and then distributed to power points and light switches. The two-way switch is a common part of a domestic electric circuit. In it, a pair of switches is connected so that pressing either turns a light on or off. Each switch has two sets of contacts linked by a pair of wires. Moving the switch up or down closes one set of contacts and opens the other set. To turn the light on, the sets of contacts at the ends of either of the two wires must close.

Many appliances have a third wire connected to their metal casing, which links through the wiring circuit to the ground. If the appliance is faulty and a live wire touches the case, the strong current is immediately conducted to the ground.

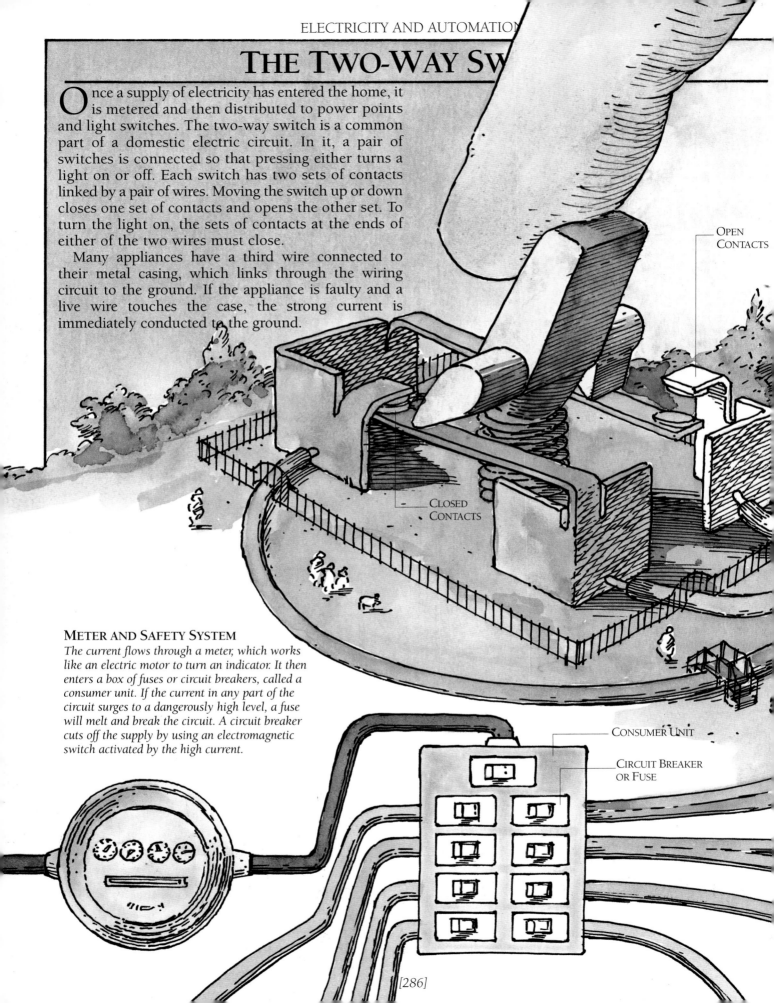

OPEN
CONTACTS

CLOSED
CONTACTS

METER AND SAFETY SYSTEM
The current flows through a meter, which works like an electric motor to turn an indicator. It then enters a box of fuses or circuit breakers, called a consumer unit. If the current in any part of the circuit surges to a dangerously high level, a fuse will melt and break the circuit. A circuit breaker cuts off the supply by using an electromagnetic switch activated by the high current.

CONSUMER UNIT

CIRCUIT BREAKER
OR FUSE

OPEN CONTACTS

CLOSED CONTACTS

POWER
SOCKETS

EARTH
SOCKET

EARTH WIRE

CAR IGNITION SYSTEM

Electromagnetism enables a car to start and also keeps it running by producing the sparks that ignite the fuel. At a twist of the ignition key, the starter motor draws direct current from the battery to start the engine. Producing the powerful magnetic field needed in the starter motor requires a hefty current, one that is too strong to pass through the ignition switch. So a solenoid, activated by a low current

passing through the ignition switch, passes a high current to the starter motor.

In electromechanical ignition systems, like the one shown here, the contact breaker in the distributor opens and interrupts the supply of low-voltage current to the induction coil. The magnetic field around the primary winding collapses, inducing a high voltage in the secondary winding. The distributor then passes the current to the spark plugs. In electronic ignition, the contact breaker is replaced by an electronic switch.

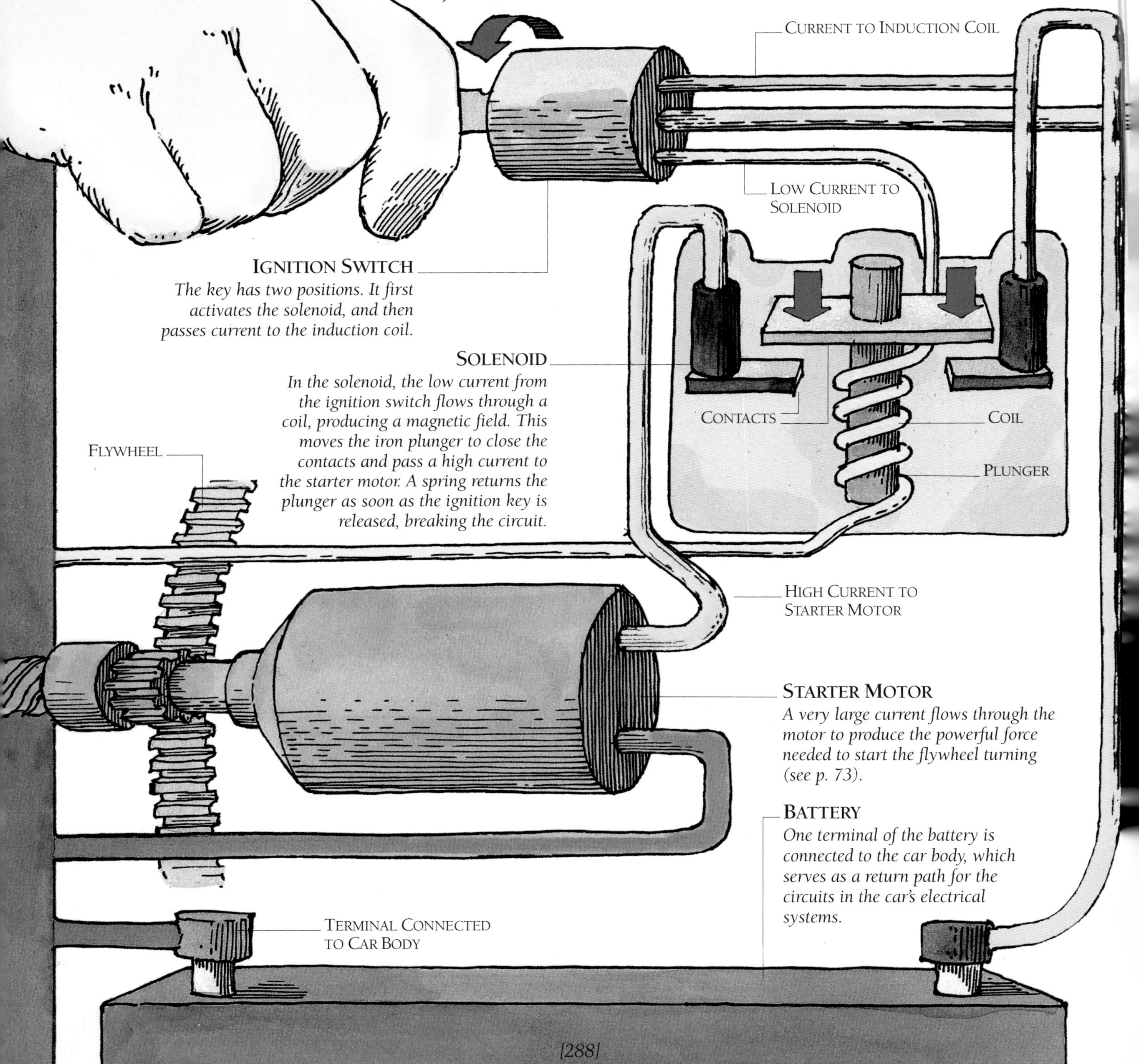

CURRENT TO INDUCTION COIL

LOW CURRENT TO SOLENOID

IGNITION SWITCH

The key has two positions. It first activates the solenoid, and then passes current to the induction coil.

SOLENOID

In the solenoid, the low current from the ignition switch flows through a coil, producing a magnetic field. This moves the iron plunger to close the contacts and pass a high current to the starter motor. A spring returns the plunger as soon as the ignition key is released, breaking the circuit.

CONTACTS

COIL

PLUNGER

FLYWHEEL

HIGH CURRENT TO STARTER MOTOR

STARTER MOTOR

A very large current flows through the motor to produce the powerful force needed to start the flywheel turning (see p. 73).

BATTERY

One terminal of the battery is connected to the car body, which serves as a return path for the circuits in the car's electrical systems.

TERMINAL CONNECTED TO CAR BODY

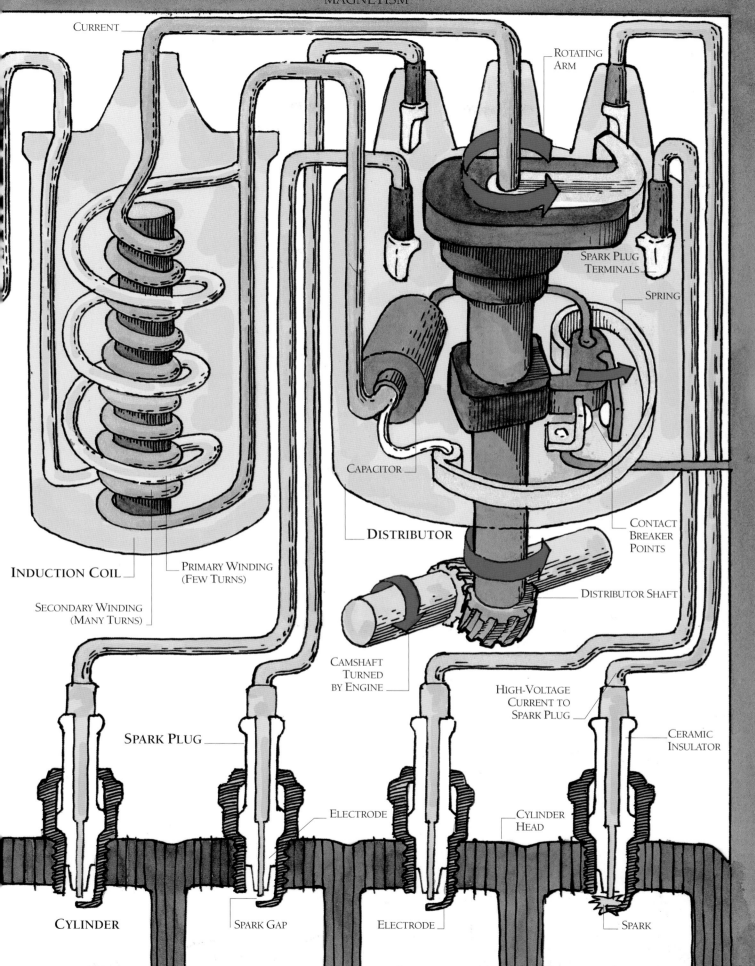

CURRENT

ROTATING
ARM

SPARK PLUG
TERMINALS

SPRING

CAPACITOR

DISTRIBUTOR

CONTACT
BREAKER
POINTS

INDUCTION COIL

PRIMARY WINDING
(FEW TURNS)

DISTRIBUTOR SHAFT

SECONDARY WINDING
(MANY TURNS)

CAMSHAFT
TURNED
BY ENGINE

HIGH-VOLTAGE
CURRENT TO
SPARK PLUG

SPARK PLUG

CERAMIC
INSULATOR

ELECTRODE

CYLINDER
HEAD

CYLINDER

SPARK GAP

ELECTRODE

SPARK

SENSORS AND DETECTORS

ON MAMMOTH SENSITIVITY

*E*motionally and physically, mammoths are highly sensitive creatures. Their physical sensitivity can be exploited in numerous ways, assuming always that their emotional sensitivity can be controlled. A selection of such applications is here depicted. In figure 1, the trunk of a sleeping mammoth is used as a pressure-operated alarm to frighten away burglars.

*I*n figure 2, the trunk of a sleeping mammoth is secured to the ceiling to act as a smoke detector. Plants obscure the creature's bulk and also provide it with occasional snacks.

fig 1

fig 2

*I*n figures 3, 4, and 5, a highly trained mammoth is used as a metal detector. Once a piece of luggage has been tested, there is no question about the location of bulky items. Chances are that at least some of them are metal.

fig 3

fig 4

fig 5

In figures 6 and 7, the mammoth's trunk is employed as a highly sensitive mobile breath analyzer.

fig 6

fig 7

Figure 8 illustrates my automated ski lift. By continually consuming water, the mammoth's weight increases until it exceeds that of the loaded car, which automatically ascends.

Figure 9 shows the specially designed squeezer. This forces the water out of the mammoth so the car automatically descends.

fig 8

fig 9

DISCOVERY AND MEASUREMENT

Sensors and detectors are devices that are used to detect the presence of something and often to measure it. Alarm systems sense the direct evidence of unwanted visitations, such as the tell-tale tread of a burglar or the airborne particles of smoke from a fire. Other sensors and detectors employ penetrating rays or magnetic fields to locate and reveal objects that cannot be seen. Measuring instruments, from seismographs to radar speed traps, are sensors and detectors that react to something specific and then register its quantity.

Sensors and detectors are also very important as essential components of automatic machines. Many machines, for example the autopilot in an aircraft, use feedback. This means that their sensors measure the machine's performance and then feed the results back to control the power output. This in turn affects the performance, which is measured by the sensors . . . and so on in an endless loop. By sensing their own performance, automatic machines keep within set limits. The mammoth-powered weight-sensing ski lift is a simple automatic machine.

SEISMOGRAPH

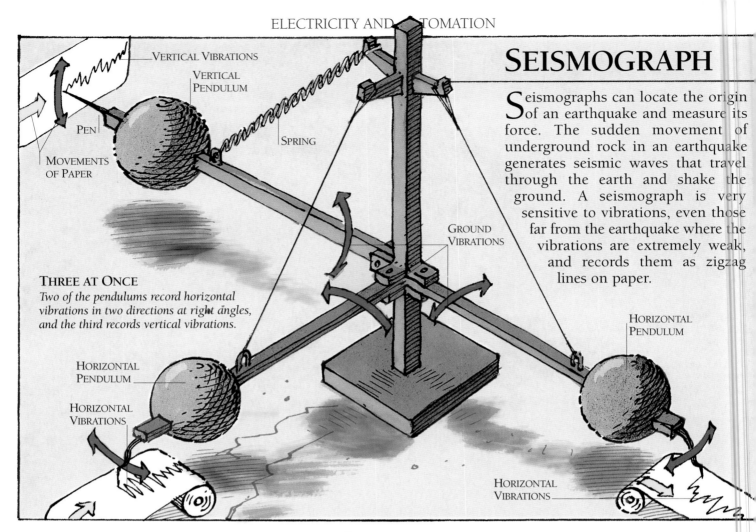

Seismographs can locate the origin of an earthquake and measure its force. The sudden movement of underground rock in an earthquake generates seismic waves that travel through the earth and shake the ground. A seismograph is very sensitive to vibrations, even those far from the earthquake where the vibrations are extremely weak, and records them as zigzag lines on paper.

VERTICAL VIBRATIONS

VERTICAL PENDULUM

PEN

SPRING

MOVEMENTS OF PAPER

GROUND VIBRATIONS

THREE AT ONCE
Two of the pendulums record horizontal vibrations in two directions at right angles, and the third records vertical vibrations.

HORIZONTAL PENDULUM

HORIZONTAL PENDULUM

HORIZONTAL VIBRATIONS

HORIZONTAL VIBRATIONS

AIRBAG

In front of and possibly to each side of the occupants of a car is a concealed bag and gas generator containing an igniter and solid propellant. If the car crashes, a crash sensor triggers the igniter, which fires the propellant. A large volume of nitrogen gas (not air) is generated and inflates the bag in about 30 milliseconds. The bag emerges, and then deflates gently as the head of the occupant sinks into it.

AIRBAG WARNING LIGHT

CRASH SENSOR

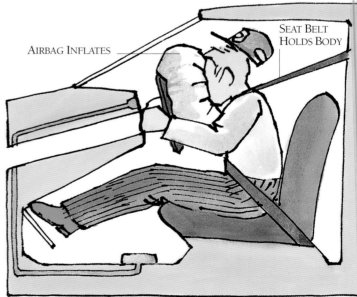

AIRBAG INFLATES

SEAT BELT HOLDS BODY

AUTOPILOT

By comparing the arrival times of the seismic waves at several seismographs in different places, the location of the earthquake can be pinpointed. The strength of the vibrations enables the intensity of the earthquake to be estimated. Seismographs can also detect vibrations from underground nuclear tests. The simple seismograph shown here operates mechanically; more advanced seismographs have vibration detectors that work electromagnetically.

BASIC SEISMOGRAPH
The seismograph is basically a pendulum mounted horizontally or vertically. It has a heavy mass with a high inertia (see p. 70). As the ground shakes, the rest of the detector vibrates around the mass and a pen fixed to the pendulum marks the vibrations on a moving roll of paper.

The guidance system of an aircraft operates the controls to correct drifting and keep it on course. It has two main parts. The autopilot keeps the aircraft flying at a set height and direction, using gyroscopes (see p. 76) to detect changes in height or direction. The other part of the guidance system continually checks the position to keep the aircraft to its route, altering height and direction when required. In it, accelerometers mounted on a level platform stabilized by gyroscopes measure the forces acting on the plane. Inertia causes a spring-mounted armature to remain still as coils beneath it move, inducing an electric signal in the coils that measures the force.

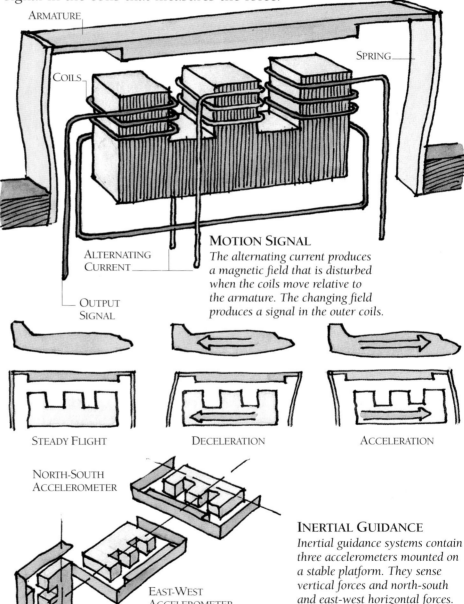

ARMATURE

SPRING

COILS

ALTERNATING CURRENT

OUTPUT SIGNAL

MOTION SIGNAL
The alternating current produces a magnetic field that is disturbed when the coils move relative to the armature. The changing field produces a signal in the outer coils.

STEADY FLIGHT   DECELERATION   ACCELERATION

CRASH SENSOR
The sensor that detects the sudden deceleration of the car in a crash is a microchip containing a tiny square linked by thin strips to a frame.

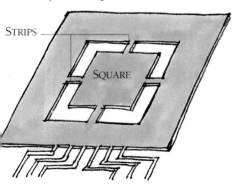

STRIPS

SQUARE

Because of the square's inertia, the movements of the car stretch or compress the strips, changing their electrical resistance in the same way as a strain gauge (see p. 323). In a crash, the sensor puts out a strong signal and this triggers the air bag.

NORTH-SOUTH ACCELEROMETER

EAST-WEST ACCELEROMETER

VERTICAL ACCELEROMETER

INERTIAL GUIDANCE
Inertial guidance systems contain three accelerometers mounted on a stable platform. They sense vertical forces and north-south and east-west horizontal forces. In this way, the accelerometers can detect all the movements of the aircraft. Their signals go to a computer that calculates the aircraft's current altitude and latitude and longitude to keep it on course.

BREATH TESTER

Several sensors are designed to detect the presence of specific substances. A breath tester detects and measures the concentration of alcohol in the breath, which is an accurate indication of the amount of alcohol in the blood. Breath testers use either a fuel cell (shown here) or infrared rays, which are absorbed by alcohol vapor. Testing drivers with a breath tester enables police to check alcohol levels in a matter of seconds.

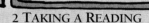

LIGHT A   TIMER   LIGHT B

PRESSURE SENSOR

2 TAKING A READING
The driver blows into a tube until first light A and then light B come on. The lights are linked to a pressure sensor and timer to provide the correct breath sample. The READ button is then pressed, which raises the diaphragm to admit the sample to the fuel cell. Alcohol in the air causes the fuel cell to produce a current.

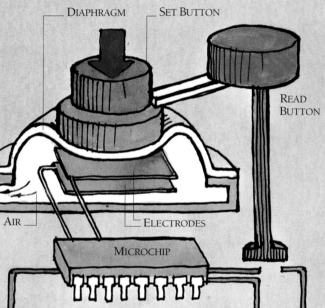

DIAPHRAGM   SET BUTTON

READ BUTTON

AIR

ELECTRODES

MICROCHIP

1 PREPARING THE TESTER
The SET button is pressed first to lower the diaphragm and empty the fuel cell of air. The fuel cell contains two platinum electrodes connected to a microchip.

BATTERY

BREATH SAMPLE

DISPLAY READS ZERO

3 ALCOHOL LEVEL
The microchip measures the voltage of the cell and converts it into a signal that goes to the display. This shows the alcohol level.

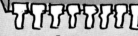

SMOKE DETECTOR

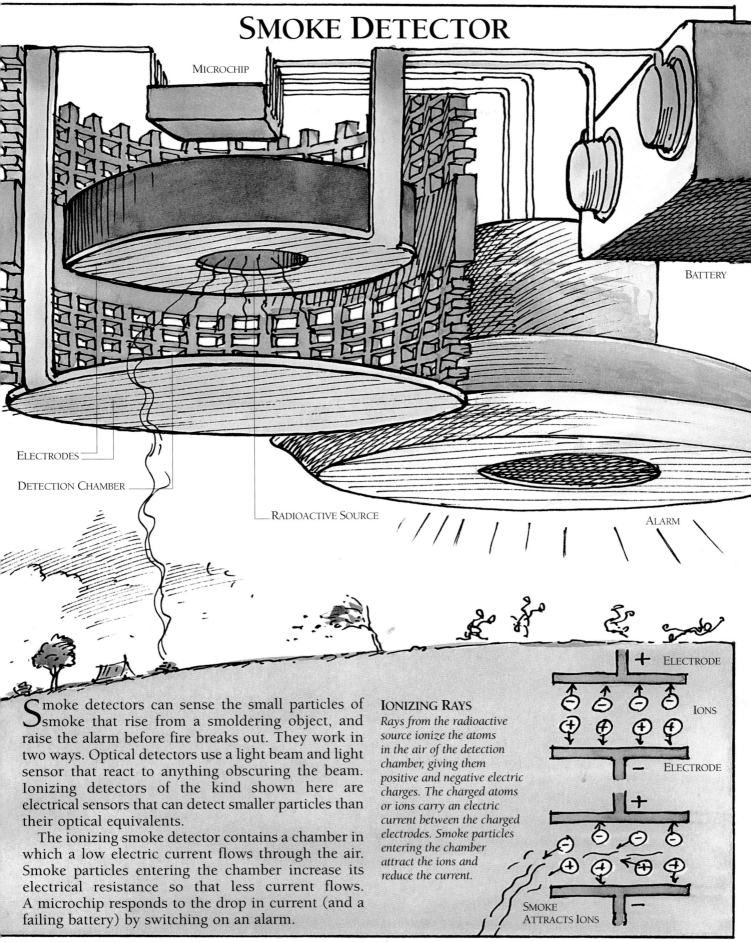

MICROCHIP

BATTERY

ELECTRODES

DETECTION CHAMBER

RADIOACTIVE SOURCE

ALARM

Smoke detectors can sense the small particles of smoke that rise from a smoldering object, and raise the alarm before fire breaks out. They work in two ways. Optical detectors use a light beam and light sensor that react to anything obscuring the beam. Ionizing detectors of the kind shown here are electrical sensors that can detect smaller particles than their optical equivalents.

The ionizing smoke detector contains a chamber in which a low electric current flows through the air. Smoke particles entering the chamber increase its electrical resistance so that less current flows. A microchip responds to the drop in current (and a failing battery) by switching on an alarm.

IONIZING RAYS

Rays from the radioactive source ionize the atoms in the air of the detection chamber, giving them positive and negative electric charges. The charged atoms or ions carry an electric current between the charged electrodes. Smoke particles entering the chamber attract the ions and reduce the current.

ELECTRODE

IONS

ELECTRODE

SMOKE ATTRACTS IONS

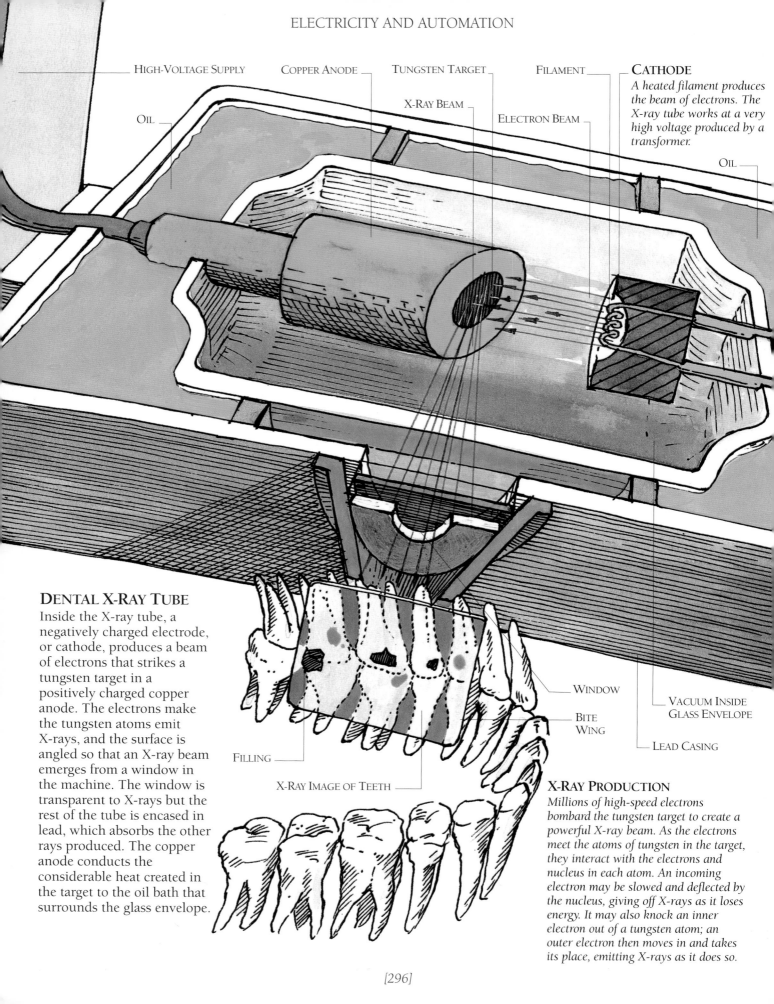

HIGH-VOLTAGE SUPPLY

OIL

COPPER ANODE

X-RAY BEAM

TUNGSTEN TARGET

FILAMENT

ELECTRON BEAM

CATHODE
A heated filament produces the beam of electrons. The X-ray tube works at a very high voltage produced by a transformer.

OIL

WINDOW

BITE WING

VACUUM INSIDE GLASS ENVELOPE

LEAD CASING

FILLING

X-RAY IMAGE OF TEETH

DENTAL X-RAY TUBE

Inside the X-ray tube, a negatively charged electrode, or cathode, produces a beam of electrons that strikes a tungsten target in a positively charged copper anode. The electrons make the tungsten atoms emit X-rays, and the surface is angled so that an X-ray beam emerges from a window in the machine. The window is transparent to X-rays but the rest of the tube is encased in lead, which absorbs the other rays produced. The copper anode conducts the considerable heat created in the target to the oil bath that surrounds the glass envelope.

X-RAY PRODUCTION

Millions of high-speed electrons bombard the tungsten target to create a powerful X-ray beam. As the electrons meet the atoms of tungsten in the target, they interact with the electrons and nucleus in each atom. An incoming electron may be slowed and deflected by the nucleus, giving off X-rays as it loses energy. It may also knock an inner electron out of a tungsten atom; an outer electron then moves in and takes its place, emitting X-rays as it does so.

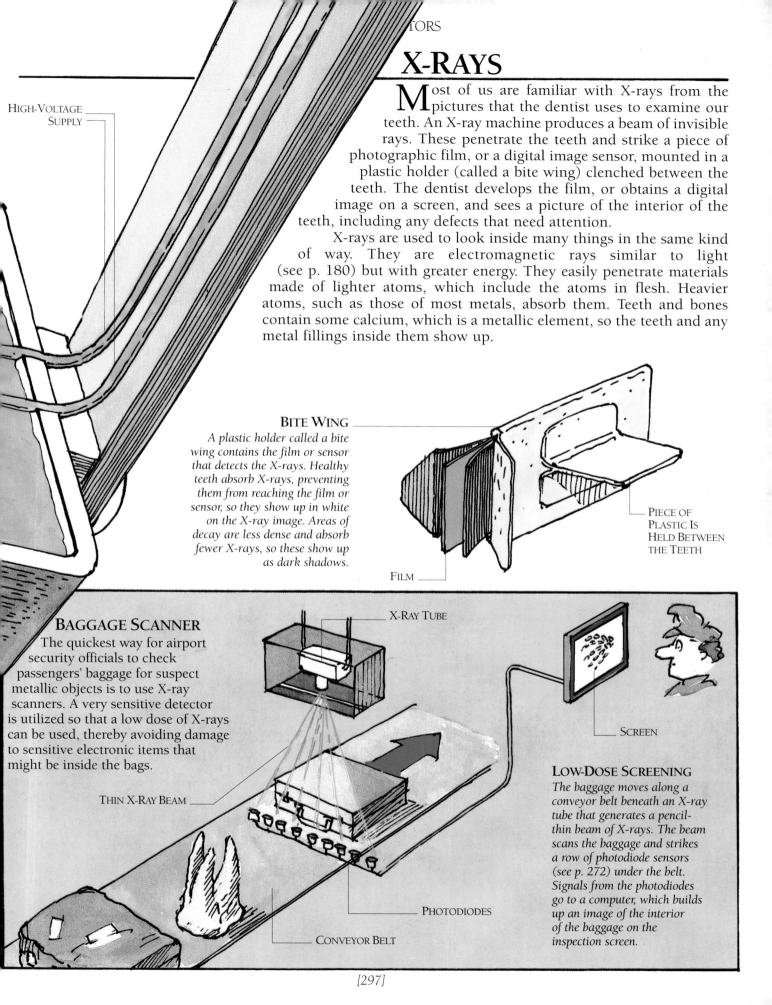

X-RAYS

Most of us are familiar with X-rays from the pictures that the dentist uses to examine our teeth. An X-ray machine produces a beam of invisible rays. These penetrate the teeth and strike a piece of photographic film, or a digital image sensor, mounted in a plastic holder (called a bite wing) clenched between the teeth. The dentist develops the film, or obtains a digital image on a screen, and sees a picture of the interior of the teeth, including any defects that need attention.

X-rays are used to look inside many things in the same kind of way. They are electromagnetic rays similar to light (see p. 180) but with greater energy. They easily penetrate materials made of lighter atoms, which include the atoms in flesh. Heavier atoms, such as those of most metals, absorb them. Teeth and bones contain some calcium, which is a metallic element, so the teeth and any metal fillings inside them show up.

HIGH-VOLTAGE SUPPLY

BITE WING

A plastic holder called a bite wing contains the film or sensor that detects the X-rays. Healthy teeth absorb X-rays, preventing them from reaching the film or sensor, so they show up in white on the X-ray image. Areas of decay are less dense and absorb fewer X-rays, so these show up as dark shadows.

PIECE OF PLASTIC IS HELD BETWEEN THE TEETH

FILM

BAGGAGE SCANNER

The quickest way for airport security officials to check passengers' baggage for suspect metallic objects is to use X-ray scanners. A very sensitive detector is utilized so that a low dose of X-rays can be used, thereby avoiding damage to sensitive electronic items that might be inside the bags.

X-RAY TUBE

SCREEN

THIN X-RAY BEAM

LOW-DOSE SCREENING

The baggage moves along a conveyor belt beneath an X-ray tube that generates a pencil-thin beam of X-rays. The beam scans the baggage and strikes a row of photodiode sensors (see p. 272) under the belt. Signals from the photodiodes go to a computer, which builds up an image of the interior of the baggage on the inspection screen.

PHOTODIODES

CONVEYOR BELT

SONAR

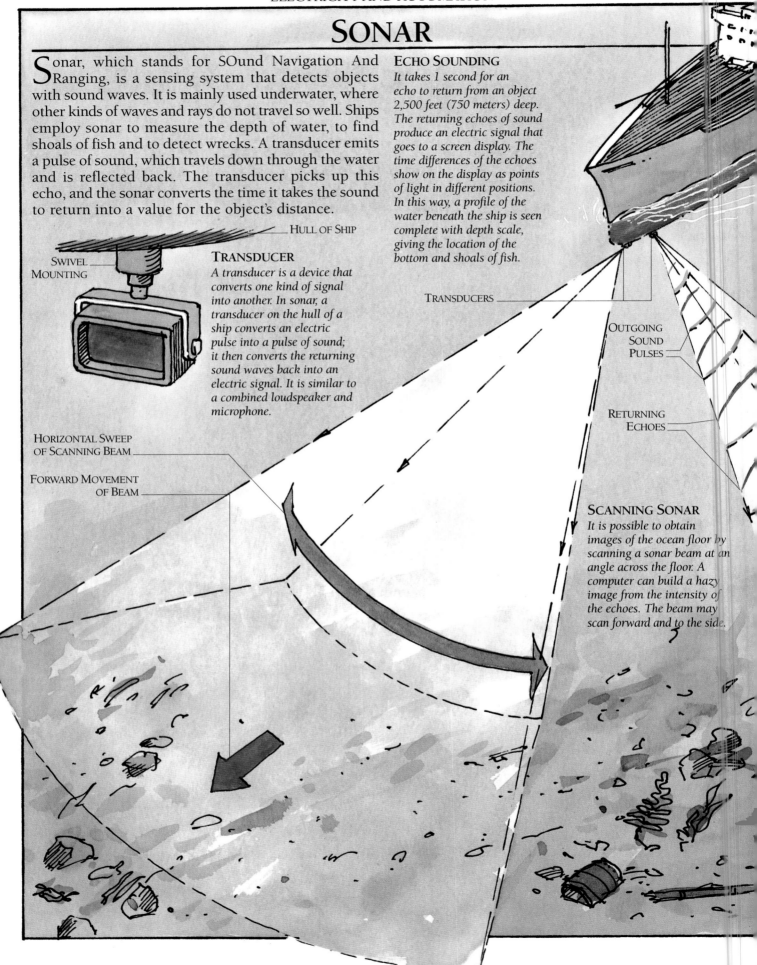

Sonar, which stands for SOund Navigation And Ranging, is a sensing system that detects objects with sound waves. It is mainly used underwater, where other kinds of waves and rays do not travel so well. Ships employ sonar to measure the depth of water, to find shoals of fish and to detect wrecks. A transducer emits a pulse of sound, which travels down through the water and is reflected back. The transducer picks up this echo, and the sonar converts the time it takes the sound to return into a value for the object's distance.

HULL OF SHIP

SWIVEL MOUNTING

TRANSDUCER

A transducer is a device that converts one kind of signal into another. In sonar, a transducer on the hull of a ship converts an electric pulse into a pulse of sound; it then converts the returning sound waves back into an electric signal. It is similar to a combined loudspeaker and microphone.

ECHO SOUNDING

It takes 1 second for an echo to return from an object 2,500 feet (750 meters) deep. The returning echoes of sound produce an electric signal that goes to a screen display. The time differences of the echoes show on the display as points of light in different positions. In this way, a profile of the water beneath the ship is seen complete with depth scale, giving the location of the bottom and shoals of fish.

TRANSDUCERS

OUTGOING SOUND PULSES

RETURNING ECHOES

SCANNING SONAR

It is possible to obtain images of the ocean floor by scanning a sonar beam at an angle across the floor. A computer can build a hazy image from the intensity of the echoes. The beam may scan forward and to the side.

HORIZONTAL SWEEP OF SCANNING BEAM

FORWARD MOVEMENT OF BEAM

ULTRASOUND SCANNER

The principles of sonar are put to important use in the ultrasound scanner. This machine can produce an image of an unborn child inside its mother. Pulses of sound from a probe scan across the interior of the body. A computer uses the returning echoes to build up a cross-section image of the mother and baby.

The scanner produces pulses of ultrasound, which is sound with a frequency range that lies above the limit of human hearing. Ultrasound is used not to spare the ears of doctor, mother, and baby, but because it has a shorter wavelength and so enables the computer to produce more detail in the image.

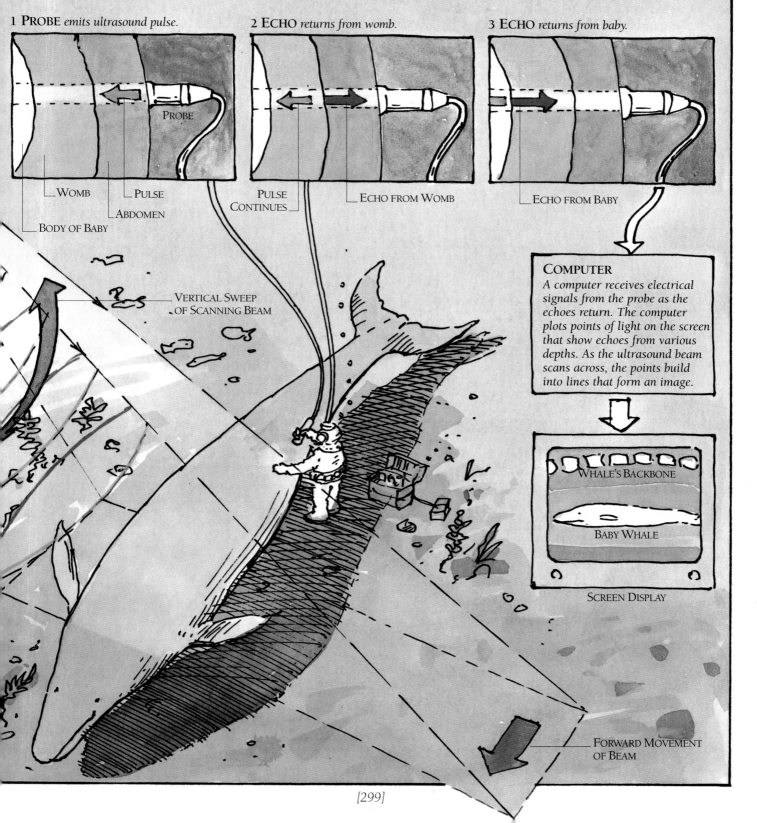

1 PROBE *emits ultrasound pulse.*

WOMB
ABDOMEN
PULSE
PROBE
BODY OF BABY

2 ECHO *returns from womb.*

PULSE CONTINUES
ECHO FROM WOMB

3 ECHO *returns from baby.*

ECHO FROM BABY

VERTICAL SWEEP OF SCANNING BEAM

COMPUTER
A computer receives electrical signals from the probe as the echoes return. The computer plots points of light on the screen that show echoes from various depths. As the ultrasound beam scans across, the points build into lines that form an image.

WHALE'S BACKBONE
BABY WHALE
SCREEN DISPLAY

FORWARD MOVEMENT OF BEAM

RADAR

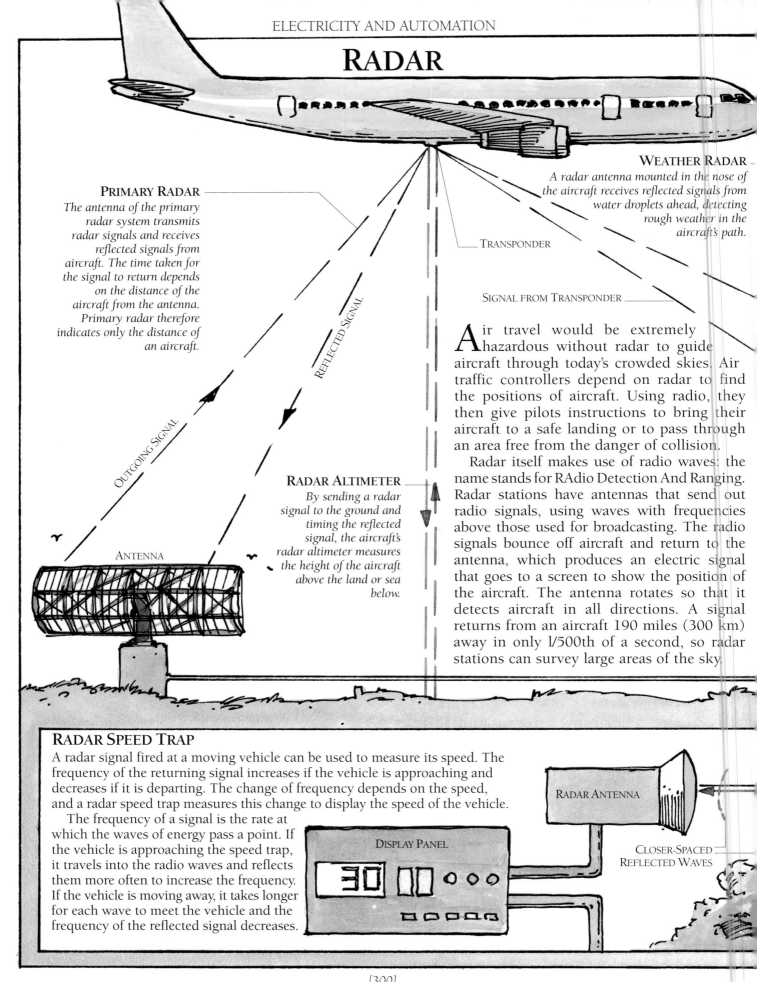

WEATHER RADAR
A radar antenna mounted in the nose of the aircraft receives reflected signals from water droplets ahead, detecting rough weather in the aircraft's path.

PRIMARY RADAR
The antenna of the primary radar system transmits radar signals and receives reflected signals from aircraft. The time taken for the signal to return depends on the distance of the aircraft from the antenna. Primary radar therefore indicates only the distance of an aircraft.

TRANSPONDER

SIGNAL FROM TRANSPONDER

REFLECTED SIGNAL

OUTGOING SIGNAL

RADAR ALTIMETER
By sending a radar signal to the ground and timing the reflected signal, the aircraft's radar altimeter measures the height of the aircraft above the land or sea below.

ANTENNA

Air travel would be extremely hazardous without radar to guide aircraft through today's crowded skies. Air traffic controllers depend on radar to find the positions of aircraft. Using radio, they then give pilots instructions to bring their aircraft to a safe landing or to pass through an area free from the danger of collision.

Radar itself makes use of radio waves: the name stands for RAdio Detection And Ranging. Radar stations have antennas that send out radio signals, using waves with frequencies above those used for broadcasting. The radio signals bounce off aircraft and return to the antenna, which produces an electric signal that goes to a screen to show the position of the aircraft. The antenna rotates so that it detects aircraft in all directions. A signal returns from an aircraft 190 miles (300 km) away in only 1/500th of a second, so radar stations can survey large areas of the sky.

RADAR SPEED TRAP

A radar signal fired at a moving vehicle can be used to measure its speed. The frequency of the returning signal increases if the vehicle is approaching and decreases if it is departing. The change of frequency depends on the speed, and a radar speed trap measures this change to display the speed of the vehicle.

The frequency of a signal is the rate at which the waves of energy pass a point. If the vehicle is approaching the speed trap, it travels into the radio waves and reflects them more often to increase the frequency. If the vehicle is moving away, it takes longer for each wave to meet the vehicle and the frequency of the reflected signal decreases.

RADAR ANTENNA

DISPLAY PANEL

30

CLOSER-SPACED REFLECTED WAVES

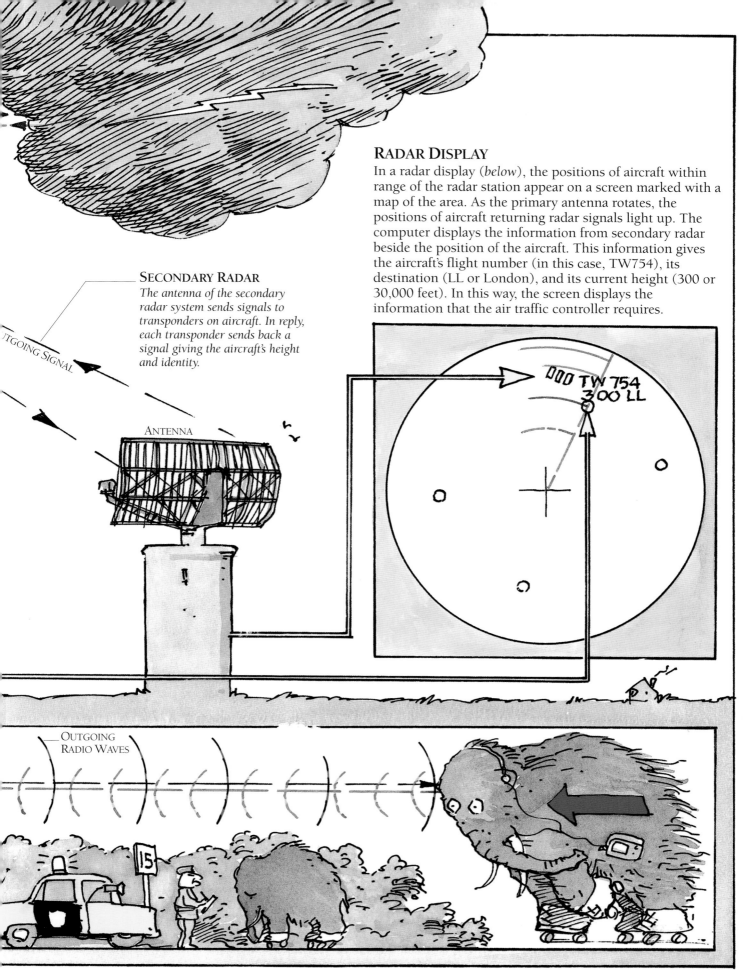

SECONDARY RADAR

The antenna of the secondary radar system sends signals to transponders on aircraft. In reply, each transponder sends back a signal giving the aircraft's height and identity.

JTGOING SIGNAL

ANTENNA

RADAR DISPLAY

In a radar display (*below*), the positions of aircraft within range of the radar station appear on a screen marked with a map of the area. As the primary antenna rotates, the positions of aircraft returning radar signals light up. The computer displays the information from secondary radar beside the position of the aircraft. This information gives the aircraft's flight number (in this case, TW754), its destination (LL or London), and its current height (300 or 30,000 feet). In this way, the screen displays the information that the air traffic controller requires.

TW 754
300 LL

OUTGOING
RADIO WAVES

METAL DETECTOR

The technology that enables us to discover buried treasure also invisibly frisks people at airports and controls traffic lights. All these machines are basically metal detectors, and they work by electromagnetic induction (see pp. 284-85).

When a piece of metal passes through a magnetic field or the field passes through the metal, the field produces electric eddy currents that circulate in the metal. The eddy currents in turn produce their own magnetic field, and metal detectors work by detecting this field.

PULSE OF CURRENT

MAGNETIC FIELD OF COIL

COIL

CAN LID.

SINGLE-COIL DETECTOR

A current fed to the coil produces a magnetic field around it. Eddy currents induced in the metal can lid generate a magnetic field that in turn induces an opposite current in the now inactive coil.

OPPOSITE CURRENT

MAGNETIC FIELD OF LID

EDDY CURRENTS

DETECTOR COILS

The transmit and receive coils overlap so that each induces a current in the other. Normally the two currents cancel out, but the magnetic field of a metal object distorts this balance and a low current appears in the receive coil.

TRANSMIT COIL

RECEIVE COIL

DETECTOR HEAD

In the metal detector head, one coil usually transmits a magnetic field and another coil picks up the magnetic field produced by a metal object below. The receive coil produces an electric signal that indicates a find.

AIRPORT DETECTOR

The gateways of metal detectors in airports contain coils similar in principle to the coils in a metal detector. A receiver detects distortions of the transmitted field caused by metal possessions on the person passing through the gateway. The coils are shielded on the outside so that people passing nearby do not trigger the detector.

LOOP IN ROAD

MAGNETIC FIELD INDUCED IN CAR

FLOW OF ELECTRONS

LOOP IN ROAD

MAGNETIC FIELD OF LOOP

TRAFFIC LIGHTS

Traffic lights may sense the arrival of vehicles. Some work like upside-down metal detectors. A loop of wire in the road surface is connected to the box that controls the lights. A current passes through the loop. As a vehicle moves overhead, it produces a signal in the loop. The signal goes to the control box to register the vehicle's arrival. Other lights use radar detectors to sense a vehicle.

SECURITY SCANNER

A full-body scanner enables security staff at airports and other high-security locations to detect suspicious objects on a person without having to touch that person. The scanner uses high-frequency radio waves—not magnetic fields and eddy currents like an ordinary walk-through scanner. It is called a millimeter wave detector, because it uses radio waves with a wavelength of about a millimeter, whose frequency is much higher than radio waves used for broadcasting (see p. 244). These waves penetrate clothing but are reflected by skin and other tissues, and by any objects concealed under clothing.

SCANNER
The subject to be scanned walks up a ramp to the booth. When inside, the subject must stand very still, to allow a clear picture to be captured.

RADIO WAVES
While the subject stands still, two vertical bars rotate around the booth. These bars are made up of discs that function as both transmitters and receivers. They send out high-frequency radio waves, which reflect off the subject and are picked up again. The waves pass through clothing and bounce off the body or concealed objects.

TRANSMITTERS/RECEIVERS
There are two vertical stacks of transmitters/receivers that move around the subject, to scan the whole body, front and back.

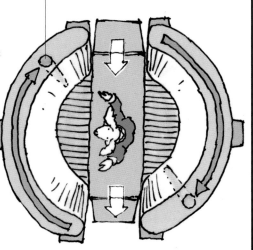

TRANSMISSION
The transmitters on the bars all radiate at the same time, producing a wavefront whereby the outgoing radio waves are all in step with each other.

TRANSMITTED WAVES

REFLECTION
Different things reflect or absorb waves in different waves, so the reflected waves are not in step. This enables a computer to build up a 3D image of the subject.

REFLECTED WAVES

DISPLAY
The pictures produced by the scanner are displayed on a computer monitor, enabling security staff to see any objects concealed beneath the subject's clothing.

BODY SCANNER

Doctors can see into the body using body scanners. These can produce images of internal organs, locating defects and diseases. Some scanners work by passing X-rays or gamma rays through the body. The most useful scanner is an MRI (magnetic resonance imaging) scanner, which works with nuclear magnetic resonance (NMR). Inside, the patient is bombarded by a strong magnetic field and then by pulses of radio waves. These are harmless, unlike X-rays and gamma rays. The nuclei in the body's atoms produce magnetic signals that detectors pick up, and a computer forms an image from these.

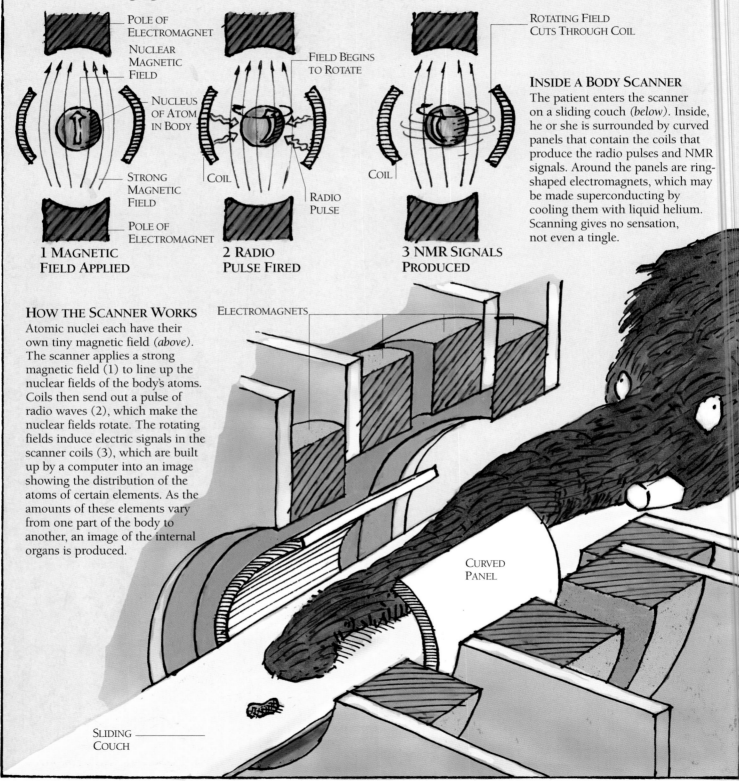

POLE OF ELECTROMAGNET

NUCLEAR MAGNETIC FIELD

NUCLEUS OF ATOM IN BODY

STRONG MAGNETIC FIELD

POLE OF ELECTROMAGNET

1 MAGNETIC FIELD APPLIED

FIELD BEGINS TO ROTATE

COIL

RADIO PULSE

2 RADIO PULSE FIRED

ROTATING FIELD CUTS THROUGH COIL

COIL

3 NMR SIGNALS PRODUCED

INSIDE A BODY SCANNER

The patient enters the scanner on a sliding couch (*below*). Inside, he or she is surrounded by curved panels that contain the coils that produce the radio pulses and NMR signals. Around the panels are ring-shaped electromagnets, which may be made superconducting by cooling them with liquid helium. Scanning gives no sensation, not even a tingle.

HOW THE SCANNER WORKS

Atomic nuclei each have their own tiny magnetic field (*above*). The scanner applies a strong magnetic field (1) to line up the nuclear fields of the body's atoms. Coils then send out a pulse of radio waves (2), which make the nuclear fields rotate. The rotating fields induce electric signals in the scanner coils (3), which are built up by a computer into an image showing the distribution of the atoms of certain elements. As the amounts of these elements vary from one part of the body to another, an image of the internal organs is produced.

ELECTROMAGNETS

CURVED PANEL

SLIDING COUCH

ADVANCED BURGLAR ALARMS

Burglar alarms can detect even the slightest movement made by an intruder. There are two kinds of alarms—active detectors and passive detectors. They usually sit high in the corner of a room, silently checking that all is well.

An active detector sends invisible beams of microwaves or ultrasonic waves throughout the room. Every object in the room reflects the beams back to the detector. A beam reflected from a stationary object, such as furniture, is unchanged in frequency. But a moving object causes a change in frequency. This is the same effect as that used by a radar speed trap (see p. 300). The detector registers the change in frequency and sounds the alarm.

A passive detector works with infrared rays. All objects give off invisible infrared rays (or heat rays) depending on their temperature. Warmer objects give off stronger rays than cold objects. The detector senses any change in the level of infrared rays received from the room. The body heat of an intruder increases the level and activates the alarm.

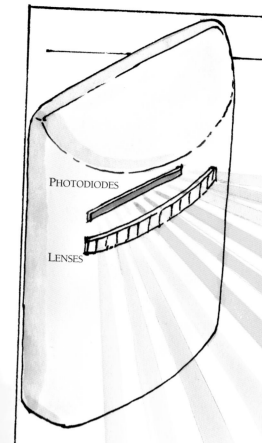

PHOTODIODES

LENSES

PASSIVE INFRARED MOVEMENT DETECTOR

The detector contains a line of lenses that focus infrared rays on a set of photodiodes (see p. 272). Each one collects infrared rays from a different part of the room. The alarm is triggered only when the level of infrared rays received by any photodiode changes over a period of time. The body heat of an intruder moving across the room causes the level on some photodiodes to increase and then decrease.

RAYS FROM COOL
STATIONARY OBJECTS

INFRARED RAYS
FROM WARM
MOVING TAIL

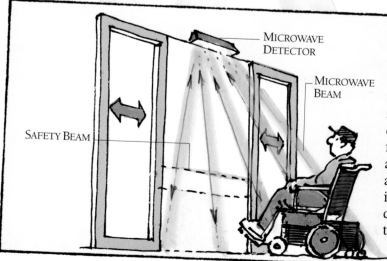

MICROWAVE
DETECTOR

MICROWAVE
BEAM

SAFETY BEAM

AUTOMATIC DOOR

When you approach an automatic door, an invisible and harmless beam of microwaves from a detector above the door strikes you. Because you are moving toward the door, the frequency of the beam increases as it returns to the detector—like the active burglar alarm above. The detector registers the increase and triggers a mechanism to open the door. An invisible safety beam and detector in the door detect your presence in the doorway and prevent the door closing until you have passed through.

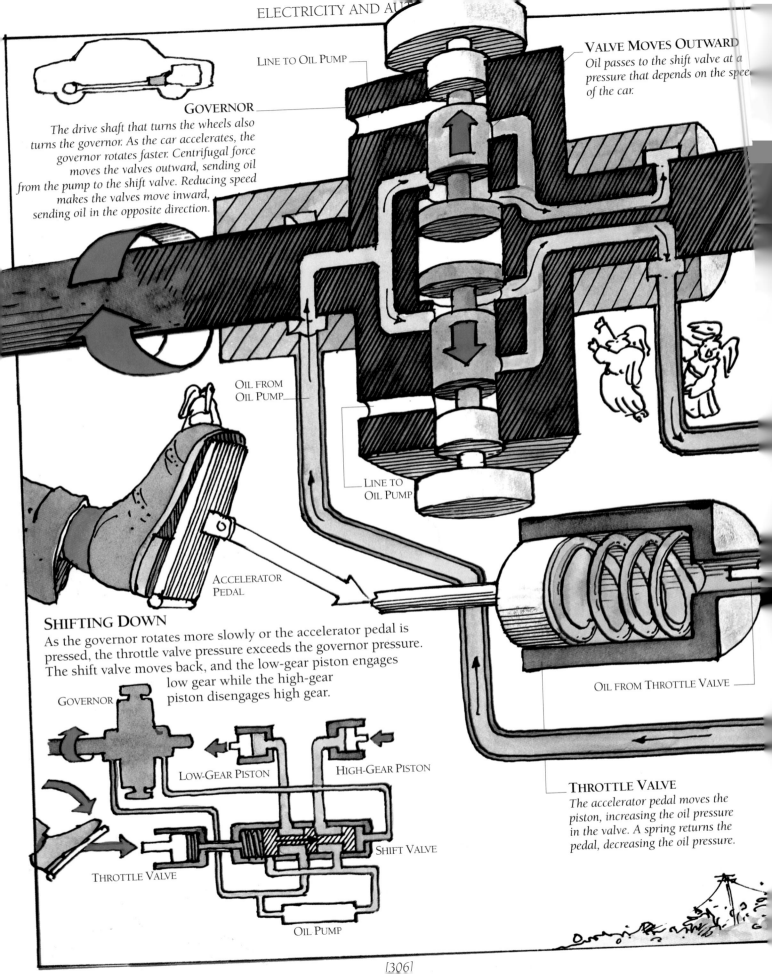

LINE TO OIL PUMP

GOVERNOR

The drive shaft that turns the wheels also turns the governor. As the car accelerates, the governor rotates faster. Centrifugal force moves the valves outward, sending oil from the pump to the shift valve. Reducing speed makes the valves move inward, sending oil in the opposite direction.

VALVE MOVES OUTWARD

Oil passes to the shift valve at a pressure that depends on the speed of the car.

OIL FROM OIL PUMP

LINE TO OIL PUMP

ACCELERATOR PEDAL

SHIFTING DOWN

As the governor rotates more slowly or the accelerator pedal is pressed, the throttle valve pressure exceeds the governor pressure. The shift valve moves back, and the low-gear piston engages low gear while the high-gear piston disengages high gear.

GOVERNOR

LOW-GEAR PISTON   HIGH-GEAR PISTON

THROTTLE VALVE

SHIFT VALVE

OIL PUMP

OIL FROM THROTTLE VALVE

THROTTLE VALVE

The accelerator pedal moves the piston, increasing the oil pressure in the valve. A spring returns the pedal, decreasing the oil pressure.

AUTOMATIC TRANSMISSION

Automatic transmission makes driving easy because there is no gear lever and clutch pedal to operate. The mechanism responds to the speed of the car and automatically changes to a higher or lower gear as the car's speed rises and falls. It can also sense the position of the accelerator pedal.

The control system works by oil pressure. Each gear change is controlled by a shift valve. A governor linked to the wheels and a throttle valve operated by the pedal supply oil at different pressures to the shift valve. The valve moves accordingly and routes oil to the gear change mechanisms in the transmission.

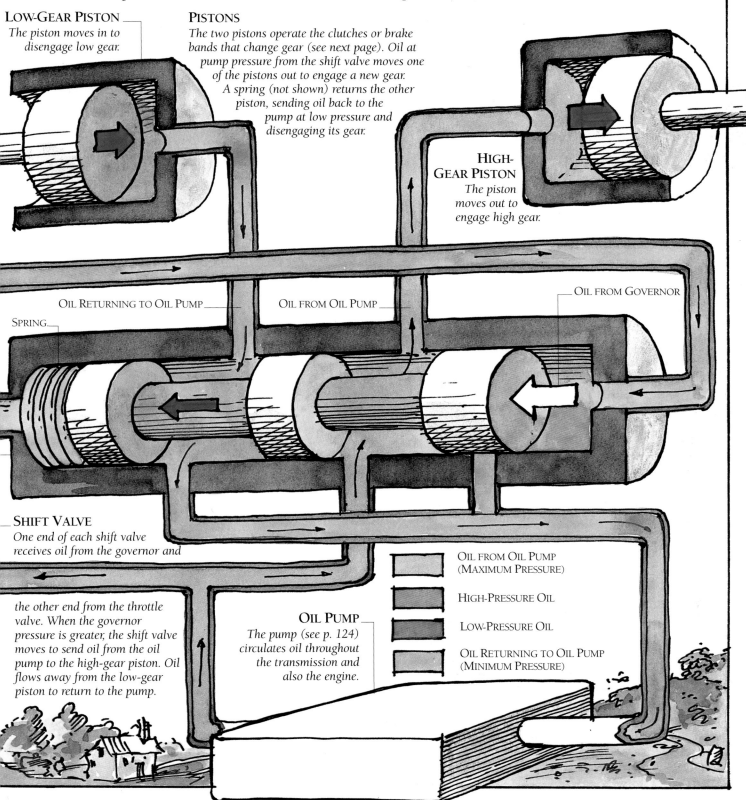

LOW-GEAR PISTON
The piston moves in to disengage low gear.

PISTONS
The two pistons operate the clutches or brake bands that change gear (see next page). Oil at pump pressure from the shift valve moves one of the pistons out to engage a new gear. A spring (not shown) returns the other piston, sending oil back to the pump at low pressure and disengaging its gear.

HIGH-GEAR PISTON
The piston moves out to engage high gear.

OIL RETURNING TO OIL PUMP

OIL FROM OIL PUMP

OIL FROM GOVERNOR

SPRING

SHIFT VALVE
One end of each shift valve receives oil from the governor and the other end from the throttle valve. When the governor pressure is greater, the shift valve moves to send oil from the oil pump to the high-gear piston. Oil flows away from the low-gear piston to return to the pump.

OIL PUMP
The pump (see p. 124) circulates oil throughout the transmission and also the engine.

OIL FROM OIL PUMP (MAXIMUM PRESSURE)

HIGH-PRESSURE OIL

LOW-PRESSURE OIL

OIL RETURNING TO OIL PUMP (MINIMUM PRESSURE)

AUTOMATIC TRANSMISSION

An automatic transmission contains two main parts, the torque converter and automatic gearbox. The torque converter passes power from the engine flywheel to the gearbox. It does this progressively and smoothly so that starting and changing gear are not jerky, acting rather like the clutch in a manual gearbox (see p. 84).

The automatic gearbox contains two sets of epicyclic gears (see p. 39) in which gear wheels rotate at different speeds. Overall, except in top gear, the speed of the flywheel is reduced so that the car wheels turn more slowly but with more force. Reverse gear reverses the direction of the wheels.

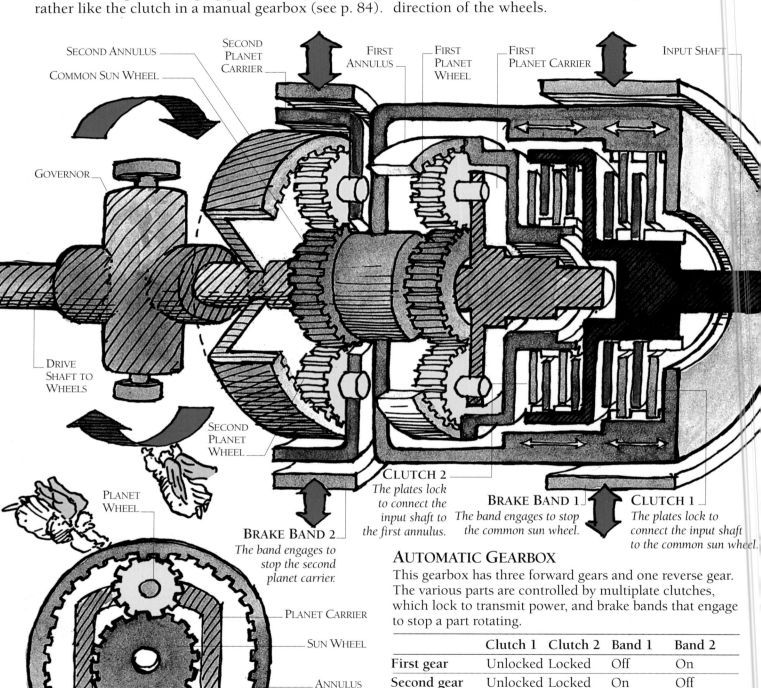

SECOND ANNULUS

COMMON SUN WHEEL

SECOND PLANET CARRIER

FIRST ANNULUS

FIRST PLANET WHEEL

FIRST PLANET CARRIER

INPUT SHAFT

GOVERNOR

DRIVE SHAFT TO WHEELS

SECOND PLANET WHEEL

PLANET WHEEL

BRAKE BAND 2
The band engages to stop the second planet carrier.

CLUTCH 2
The plates lock to connect the input shaft to the first annulus.

BRAKE BAND 1
The band engages to stop the common sun wheel.

CLUTCH 1
The plates lock to connect the input shaft to the common sun wheel.

PLANET CARRIER

SUN WHEEL

ANNULUS

EPICYCLIC GEAR
Each part either rotates or is locked so that other parts rotate around it.

PLANET WHEEL

AUTOMATIC GEARBOX

This gearbox has three forward gears and one reverse gear. The various parts are controlled by multiplate clutches, which lock to transmit power, and brake bands that engage to stop a part rotating.

	Clutch 1	Clutch 2	Band 1	Band 2
First gear	Unlocked	Locked	Off	On
Second gear	Unlocked	Locked	On	Off
Third gear	Locked	Locked	Off	Off
Reverse gear	Locked	Unlocked	Off	On

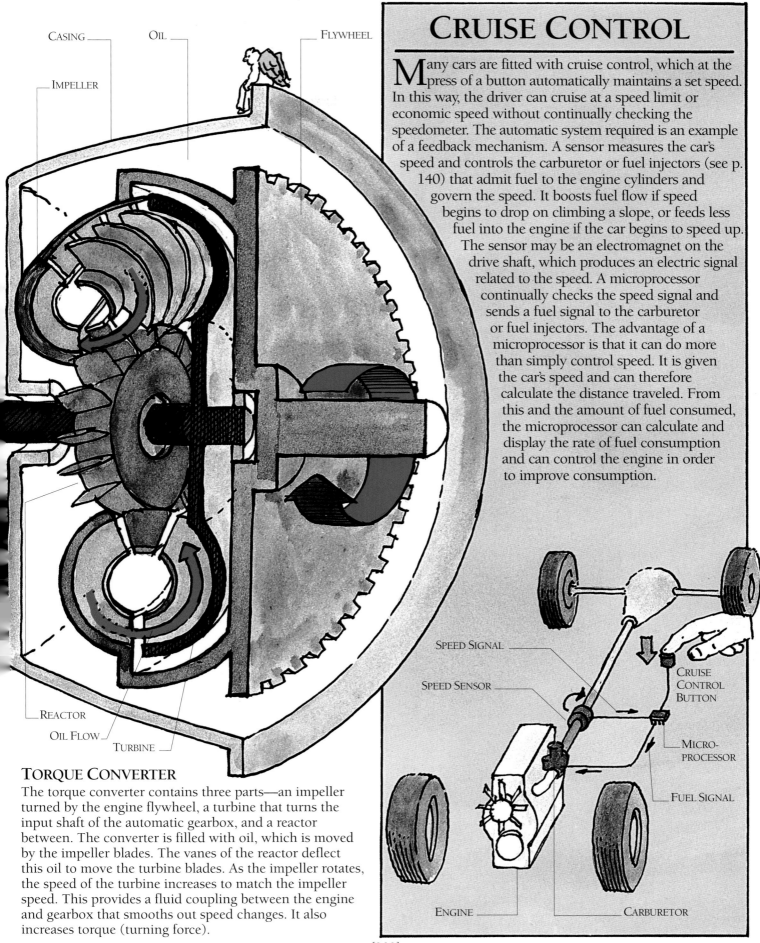

CASING · OIL · FLYWHEEL

IMPELLER

REACTOR

OIL FLOW

TURBINE

CRUISE CONTROL

Many cars are fitted with cruise control, which at the press of a button automatically maintains a set speed. In this way, the driver can cruise at a speed limit or economic speed without continually checking the speedometer. The automatic system required is an example of a feedback mechanism. A sensor measures the car's speed and controls the carburetor or fuel injectors (see p. 140) that admit fuel to the engine cylinders and govern the speed. It boosts fuel flow if speed begins to drop on climbing a slope, or feeds less fuel into the engine if the car begins to speed up. The sensor may be an electromagnet on the drive shaft, which produces an electric signal related to the speed. A microprocessor continually checks the speed signal and sends a fuel signal to the carburetor or fuel injectors. The advantage of a microprocessor is that it can do more than simply control speed. It is given the car's speed and can therefore calculate the distance traveled. From this and the amount of fuel consumed, the microprocessor can calculate and display the rate of fuel consumption and can control the engine in order to improve consumption.

SPEED SIGNAL

SPEED SENSOR

CRUISE CONTROL BUTTON

MICRO-PROCESSOR

FUEL SIGNAL

ENGINE · CARBURETOR

TORQUE CONVERTER

The torque converter contains three parts—an impeller turned by the engine flywheel, a turbine that turns the input shaft of the automatic gearbox, and a reactor between. The converter is filled with oil, which is moved by the impeller blades. The vanes of the reactor deflect this oil to move the turbine blades. As the impeller rotates, the speed of the turbine increases to match the impeller speed. This provides a fluid coupling between the engine and gearbox that smooths out speed changes. It also increases torque (turning force).

PART 5

THE DIGITAL DOMAIN

& THE LAST MAMMOTH

THE LAST MAMMOTH

CHAPTER ONE

Mammoth stood in the stream stuffing clumps of swamp grass into his mouth. As the tender juices trickled down his throat, he contemplated the pros and cons of the solitary life. On the one hand, he didn't have to share the dwindling harvest with any other mammoths—because there were no other mammoths. But, on the other hand, he was terribly lonely. He wondered how he had come to be the last mammoth and where the rest of his proud species had gone. A large oil slick floated by. He marveled at its iridescence before ambling off in search of more food.

The trail of dwindling swamp grass led to an imposing wall and an entrance presided over by a character who introduced himself as Bill. Bill announced that this was his "digital domain" and that it was full of wonderful and amazing things, all of which were intended to improve the quality of life but none of which had been fully tested. While Bill spoke with enthusiasm about the future, Mammoth could only dwell on the past. Lonely thoughts filled his tiny brain, releasing a single tear that inadvertently saturated Bill's tennis shoes. Recognizing the mammoth's distress, Bill suggested they work together. He and his digital staff needed someone (or some thing) to process. And the mammoth was obviously desperate for companionship. So it came to pass that Mammoth, who generally distrusted high walls, warily entered Bill's gates.

He was immediately surrounded by enthusiastic white-coated workers who began recording every aspect of his considerable being. This was not exactly the kind of companionship he'd been hoping for. One group measured him from top to bottom while another tackled him head to tail. A third group was assigned to gauge his considerable weight. Even those things that could not be so easily measured, such as voice and smell, were meticulously noted.

Within hours, everything about the last mammoth had been reduced to numbers, which Bill copied on large white cards. He informed Mammoth that although they were very good numbers indeed, they weren't actually the right kind of numbers for the digital domain. If they were going to be useful in helping find true companionship, these numbers would first have to be changed.

Along one side of an enormous pumpkin patch, eight rows of crates had been laid out. Each row was half as long as the one that preceded it. The first and longest row contained one hundred and twenty-eight crates, the second contained sixty-four, and so on. When Bill held up the card inscribed with the number 237 (the mammoth's height in centimeters), a team of farm hands quickly harvested exactly 237 pumpkins.

Then, moving row by row from longest to shortest, they placed one of these pumpkins in each crate. If they couldn't fill an entire row completely, they simply skipped it. As soon as all the pumpkins had been appropriately crated, Bill drew Mammoth's attention to the pattern of pumpkins along the bottom of all eight rows.

He explained that in the language of the digital domain, the relatively simple number 237 was now "pumpkin, pumpkin, pumpkin, no-pumpkin, pumpkin, pumpkin, no-pumpkin, pumpkin." "That's progress," he added proudly. Mammoth was having a little trouble with this concept but really shook his head when Bill suggested that "pumpkin" and "no-pumpkin" were equally important. To Mammoth this was like saying swamp grass and no swamp grass were equally filling.

Bill supervised as the pumpkins from the first crate of each row were hung on a long clothesline. Special care was taken to keep them in exactly the same order. For each "no-pumpkin," a space was left. However, since this happened to be a Tuesday, these spaces were filled with single pieces of wet laundry. When pumpkin, pumpkin, pumpkin, sock, pumpkin, pumpkin, underpants, pumpkin had been secured to the line, the whole thing began to move slowly out of view. "Come on, Mammoth," shouted Bill. "We've got work to do."

MAKING BITS

The mammoth found the digital domain unfamiliar and confusing. While we are familiar with the computers and other devices the digital domain makes possible, the way these things work is bewildering to many of us. The thing that all digital devices share is that they work with numbers. The mammoth finds its dimensions, image, and sound changed into numbers as it goes digital. Similarly, all digital machines begin a task by converting things like these into numbers. Instead of the decimal form that uses the ten digits 0 to 9, numbers in the digital domain are binary numbers, which use only two digits, 0 and 1, and which are much more convenient for machines. These digits are called bits—short for "binary digits."

The mammoth observes that its height, measured in decimal centimeters as 237, becomes, in the digital domain, a set of eight crates, some containing a pumpkin and others empty. The sequence of full and empty crates is a binary number containing eight digits or bits: 237 is full-full-full-empty-full-full-empty-full. When writing binary numbers, we use the two numerals 1 and 0 to represent bits, 1 meaning full or yes and 0 meaning empty or no, so that the decimal number 237 becomes 11101101.

In the decimal system that we are all familiar with, each place value is ten times the value of the place to its right—a decimal number may be made up of thousands, hundreds, tens, and ones. The decimal number 237 is made up of two 100s, three 10s, and seven 1s. In the binary system, each place value is twice the one to its right—that's why the rows of pumpkin crates can hold 128, 64, 32, 16 pumpkins, and so on. As Mammoth discovered, 237 in binary is 11101101: this tells us that the number is reached by adding one 128, one 64, one 32, one 8, one 4, and one 1.

In a digital machine, bits take a form just as physical as pumpkins. They manifest themselves primarily as electric charges in which the electricity is switched either on or off. Here, 237 becomes on-on-on-off-on-on-off-on. Numbers represented by on-off electrical signals and on-off light signals flash to and fro along the pathways of digital machines in huge quantities at great speed. Digital machines can handle vast amounts of numbers arranged in countless ways, allowing them to carry out a huge variety of complex tasks very quickly. Furthermore, bits are rugged: they do not easily degrade as they rush about the digital domain. Being born survivors, bits enable digital machines to work at superior levels of quality and reliability.

FINGERTIP INPUT

Every digital device, from computers and smartphones to digital cameras and Blu-ray players, needs input in the form of bits (binary digits, 1s and 0s). The input might be a command, to make the device do what we want, or it might be data, such as text for a document or a digitized sound or image (see pp. 324-25). Many devices allow the user to input commands or data by pressing on keys or buttons—on a keypad, computer keyboard, or musical keyboard, for example. Each key on a keypad or keyboard produces a unique group of bits when it is pressed. A specific combination of key presses might represent a code, such as a PIN number (see p. 336) for a cash machine.

CASH MACHINE AND ELECTRONIC LOCK

Getting cash out of a machine is simply a matter of inserting your card, then typing your PIN number and the amount required on the keypad. You also type in a code number on a similar keyboard to open an electronic lock. Like the number keys on the computer keyboard opposite, the keys act as switches to generate a sequence of on-off electric pulses forming the bits in the numbers. From a cash machine, these bits go to the bank's central computer, which checks the PIN number and debits your account before instructing the machine to pay out. In the lock, the bits go to a chip that checks the number. If it is correct, the chip produces an electric signal that frees the bolt so that the door can be opened.

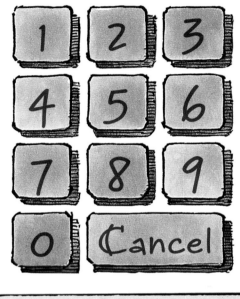

KEYPAD
The CANCEL button enables you to delete any wrong key presses and start again.

ELECTRIC KEYBOARD

Electronic music equipment conforms to a standard called MIDI (Musical Instrument Digital Interface). When you play a note on a MIDI keyboard, it sends out a digital code number, made of three bytes (three groups of eight bits). The first byte is a command, such as "turn this note on." The second is the actual note—middle C is 00111100 (decimal 60), for example. The third byte represents the force with which the key is pressed. The bytes go to a synthesizer in the keyboard, to software in a computer, or to a separate synthesizer, and you hear the note played loudly or softly.

INSTANT MUSICAL SCRIBE
The MIDI bits can go to a computer, which displays the music in written form on the screen as you play.

CONTROLS
You can operate the sound controls with one hand as you play with the other.

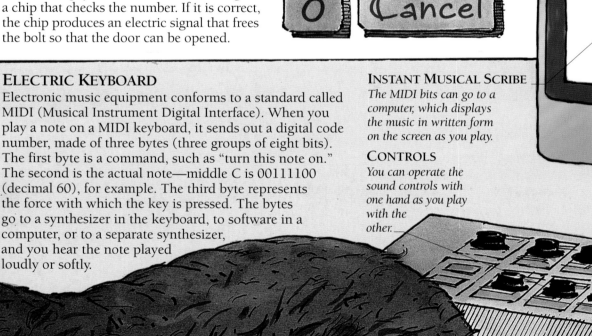

COMPUTER KEYBOARD

Only about half of the hundred or so keys on a computer keyboard produce characters—letters, numbers, and signs. Pressing the other keys makes the computer take action, and more options become available by pressing two or even three keys at once. This versatility is possible because pressing a key causes the keyboard to generate an electric signal forming a code number that identifies the key. The code number is in the form of bits made up of on-off electric pulses. This digital signal passes to the computer's processor, along a USB cable (see p. 369) or via a wireless connection. The processor interprets the code number or combination of numbers either to display a character or to take action.

3 KEYBOARD CHIP
The chip is an integrated circuit that sends out a regular signal through its connecting pins along pairs of lines to all the key contacts. When the signal in one pair changes, the chip generates a code for the key connected to that pair of lines.

4 LETTER b APPEARS ONSCREEN
The key code is sent wirelessly via Bluetooth (or, in some keyboards, along a wire) to the computer's processor. There, the code is converted to a binary number: 01100010 (98), the code number for the lowercase letter b.

RUBBER DOME RETURNS KEY TO ORIGINAL POSITION

RUBBER SHEET UNDER THE KEYS PROTECTS INTERNAL WORKINGS

1 PRESSING KEY B
A metal contact in a rubber dome under key B touches two contacts at the ends of a pair of lines from the keyboard chip.

DOME AND METAL CONTACT

2 SCANNING SIGNAL
As the contacts meet, a scanning signal sent along the lines from the keyboard chip changes strength.

CONTACTS AT ENDS OF PAIR OF LINES FROM KEYBOARD CHIP

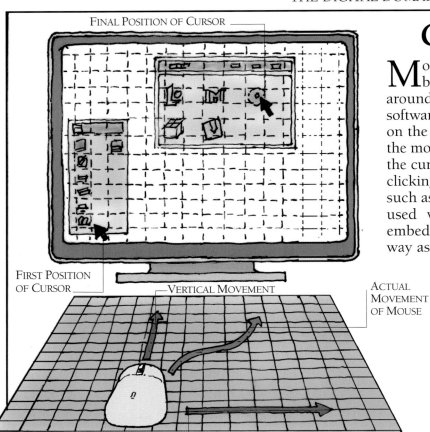

FINAL POSITION OF CURSOR

FIRST POSITION
OF CURSOR

VERTICAL MOVEMENT

ACTUAL
MOVEMENT
OF MOUSE

HORIZONTAL MOVEMENT

COMPUTER MOUSE

Most desktop computers have a mouse, which can be used to access software and files, move files around within folders, or interact directly with software. A small cursor (often a sloping arrow) moves on the computer's screen, mirroring the movement of the mouse across a mouse pad or other surface. When the cursor is located on the desired part of the screen, clicking a button on the mouse carries out a command, such as opening a file. Laptop computers can also be used with a mouse, but most have a trackpad embedded in the keyboard, which works in the same way as a touchscreen (see pp. 320-21).

ICONS AND HOTSPOTS

Icons are small images on a computer's screen that represent programs or operations. These areas are "hot," which means they respond to mouse clicks. They work because every point on the screen has a pair of coordinates: numbers that give its horizontal and vertical position. The computer initially gives the cursor two position numbers, and it appears at that position. Moving the mouse sends signals to the computer that change the cursor's coordinates, and the cursor shifts accordingly.

OPTICAL MOUSE

Most mice are optical—they use light to work out their position. Light from an LED (see p. 273) passes into a plastic light guide, which directs the light onto the surface on which the mouse is resting. A tiny digital camera collects light scattered from the surface and sends images to the computer.

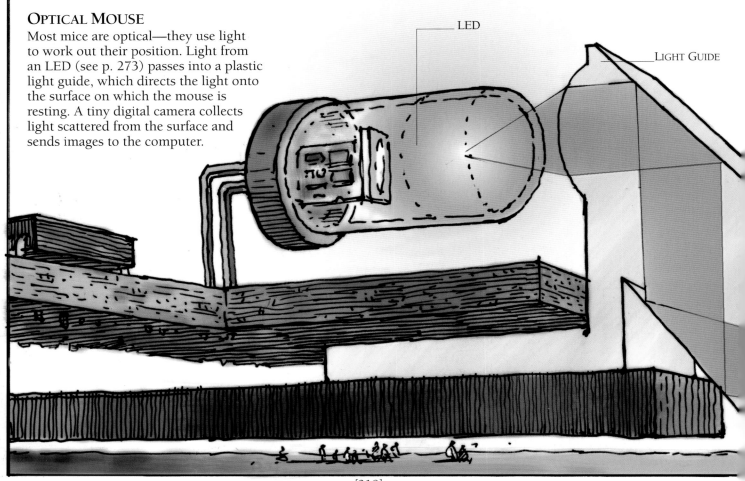

LED

LIGHT GUIDE

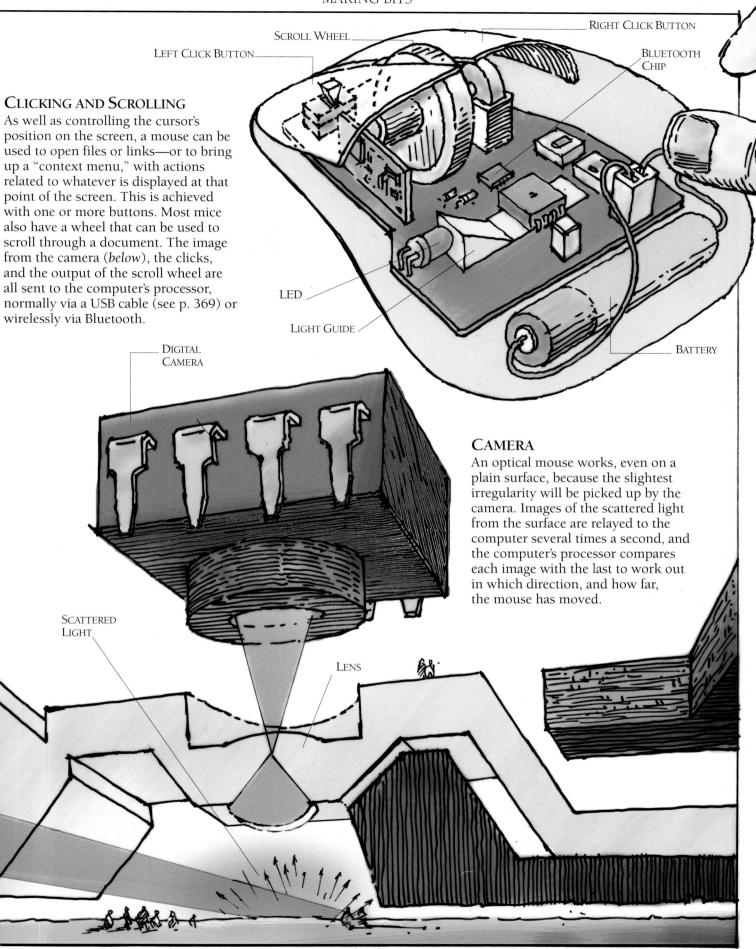

SCROLL WHEEL

RIGHT CLICK BUTTON

LEFT CLICK BUTTON

BLUETOOTH CHIP

CLICKING AND SCROLLING

As well as controlling the cursor's position on the screen, a mouse can be used to open files or links—or to bring up a "context menu," with actions related to whatever is displayed at that point of the screen. This is achieved with one or more buttons. Most mice also have a wheel that can be used to scroll through a document. The image from the camera (*below*), the clicks, and the output of the scroll wheel are all sent to the computer's processor, normally via a USB cable (see p. 369) or wirelessly via Bluetooth.

LED

LIGHT GUIDE

BATTERY

DIGITAL CAMERA

CAMERA

An optical mouse works, even on a plain surface, because the slightest irregularity will be picked up by the camera. Images of the scattered light from the surface are relayed to the computer several times a second, and the computer's processor compares each image with the last to work out in which direction, and how far, the mouse has moved.

SCATTERED LIGHT

LENS

TOUCHSCREEN

With a smartphone or tablet, you can order a pizza, find directions, take a photo, browse the Web, and so much more, all using the touch of a finger. On top of the device's display screen but beneath the outer protective glass is a grid of two sets of fine, transparent wires mounted at right angles to each other. These carry pulses of electric current. Holding a finger close to one part of the grid affects the currents flowing through the wires. This enables a controller chip inside the device to work out the finger's location and feed this information to the device's main processor.

FINGERTIP CONTROL

A touchscreen allows users to interact with what is shown onscreen, by changing the display according to touch input. It can be used to manipulate images or enter text via an onscreen keyboard.

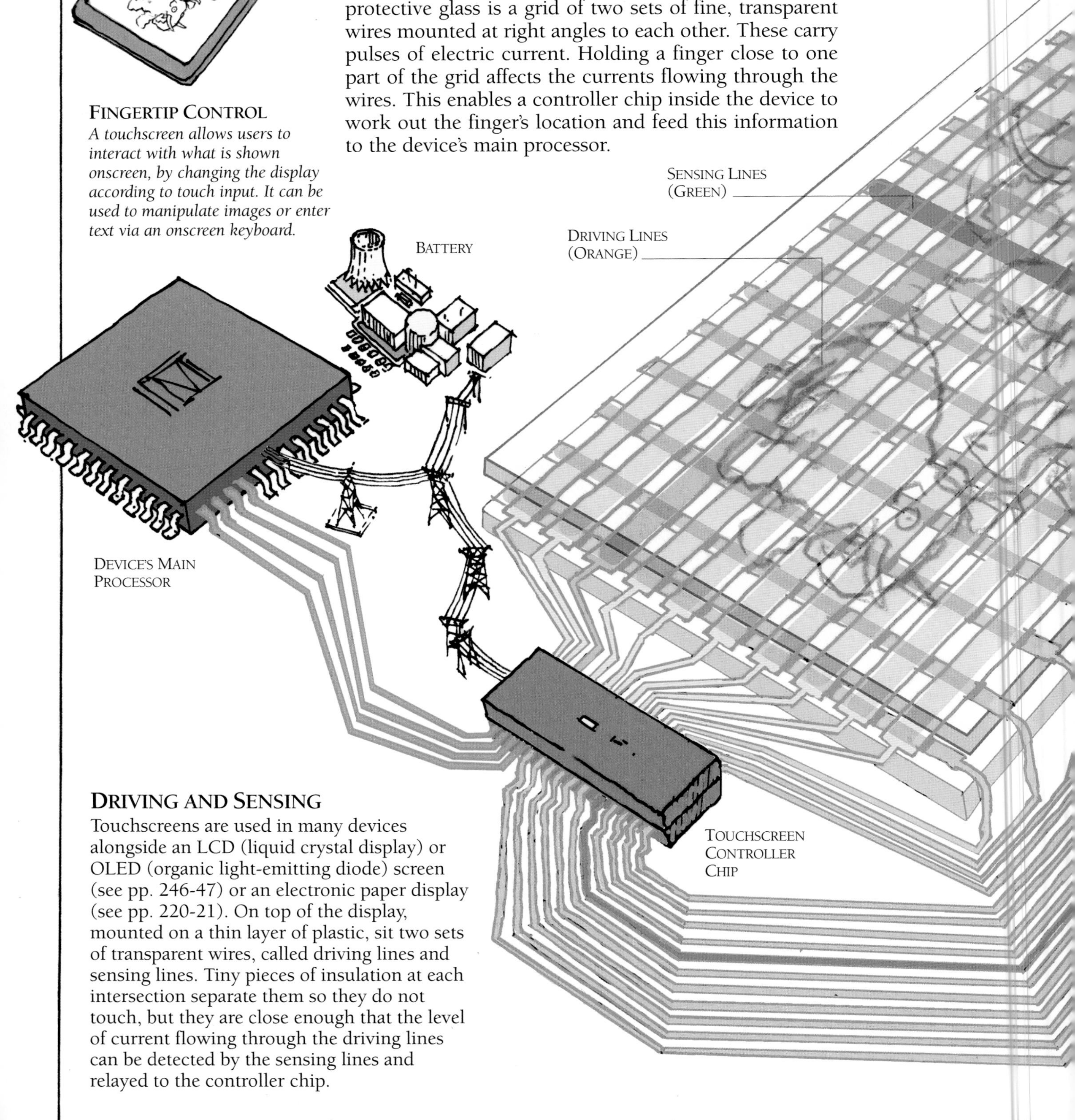

BATTERY

SENSING LINES (GREEN)

DRIVING LINES (ORANGE)

DEVICE'S MAIN PROCESSOR

TOUCHSCREEN CONTROLLER CHIP

DRIVING AND SENSING

Touchscreens are used in many devices alongside an LCD (liquid crystal display) or OLED (organic light-emitting diode) screen (see pp. 246-47) or an electronic paper display (see pp. 220-21). On top of the display, mounted on a thin layer of plastic, sit two sets of transparent wires, called driving lines and sensing lines. Tiny pieces of insulation at each intersection separate them so they do not touch, but they are close enough that the level of current flowing through the driving lines can be detected by the sensing lines and relayed to the controller chip.

SCANNING

The controller chip sends electric currents down each driving line in turn and detects the level of current flowing through the sensing lines—again, one after the other. In a typical smartphone, there are about 10 driving lines and 15 sensing lines, so the controller has to monitor around 150 individual crossing points. The chip monitors every crossing point about 100 times every second.

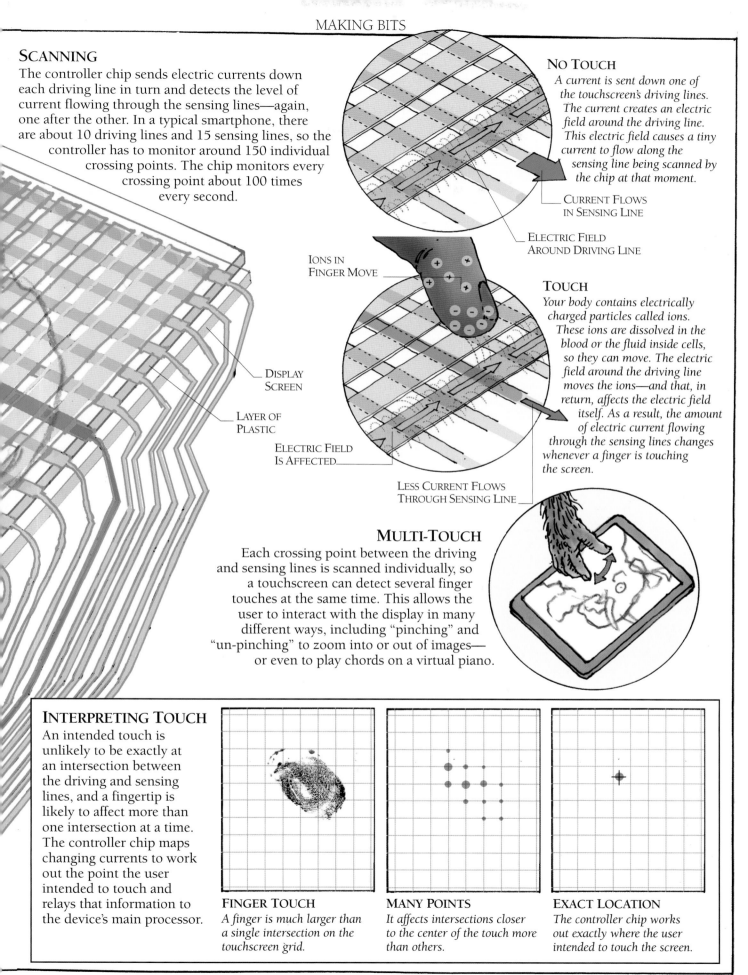

NO TOUCH

A current is sent down one of the touchscreen's driving lines. The current creates an electric field around the driving line. This electric field causes a tiny current to flow along the sensing line being scanned by the chip at that moment.

CURRENT FLOWS
IN SENSING LINE

ELECTRIC FIELD
AROUND DRIVING LINE

IONS IN
FINGER MOVE

DISPLAY
SCREEN

LAYER OF
PLASTIC

ELECTRIC FIELD
IS AFFECTED

TOUCH

Your body contains electrically charged particles called ions. These ions are dissolved in the blood or the fluid inside cells, so they can move. The electric field around the driving line moves the ions—and that, in return, affects the electric field itself. As a result, the amount of electric current flowing through the sensing lines changes whenever a finger is touching the screen.

LESS CURRENT FLOWS
THROUGH SENSING LINE

MULTI-TOUCH

Each crossing point between the driving and sensing lines is scanned individually, so a touchscreen can detect several finger touches at the same time. This allows the user to interact with the display in many different ways, including "pinching" and "un-pinching" to zoom into or out of images— or even to play chords on a virtual piano.

INTERPRETING TOUCH

An intended touch is unlikely to be exactly at an intersection between the driving and sensing lines, and a fingertip is likely to affect more than one intersection at a time. The controller chip maps changing currents to work out the point the user intended to touch and relays that information to the device's main processor.

FINGER TOUCH
A finger is much larger than a single intersection on the touchscreen grid.

MANY POINTS
It affects intersections closer to the center of the touch more than others.

EXACT LOCATION
The controller chip works out exactly where the user intended to touch the screen.

SIGNAL INPUT

There are many digital machines and systems that do not need fingertip input of information. They set about making bits unaided, needing little or no control. Digital thermometers and electronic scales constantly measure temperature and weight. Many digital machines respond to incoming sound waves or light rays, changing them into sequences of binary numbers so that you can capture speech or music digitally or take digital pictures. Once sound and light are in digital form, machines can process the numbers and do amazing things.

One very special device makes this possible: the analog-digital converter. It is the main gateway from our environment—the analog world—to the digital domain. Ours is a world of movement and forces, of heat, light, and sound. All these are analog quantities, meaning that they vary continuously, rising and falling in level or intensity.

These variations are turned into sequences of numbers, or sets of bits, in a digital machine or system. First, a detector or sensor converts the varying levels of heat, weight, sound, or light into an analog or varying electric signal. Then an analog-digital converter chip measures the voltage of this signal at frequent intervals and changes each number of volts into a binary number made up of bits in the form of on-off electric pulses. These bits then progress through the digital domain.

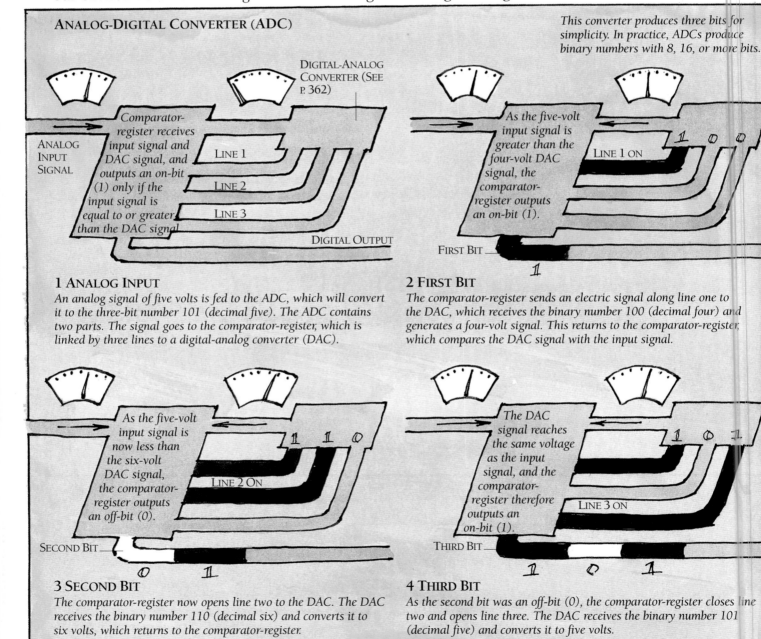

ANALOG-DIGITAL CONVERTER (ADC)

This converter produces three bits for simplicity. In practice, ADCs produce binary numbers with 8, 16, or more bits.

DIGITAL-ANALOG CONVERTER (SEE P. 362)

ANALOG INPUT SIGNAL

Comparator-register receives input signal and DAC signal, and outputs an on-bit (1) only if the input signal is equal to or greater than the DAC signal.

LINE 1
LINE 2
LINE 3

DIGITAL OUTPUT

1 ANALOG INPUT
An analog signal of five volts is fed to the ADC, which will convert it to the three-bit number 101 (decimal five). The ADC contains two parts. The signal goes to the comparator-register, which is linked by three lines to a digital-analog converter (DAC).

As the five-volt input signal is greater than the four-volt DAC signal, the comparator-register outputs an on-bit (1).

LINE 1 ON

FIRST BIT

2 FIRST BIT
The comparator-register sends an electric signal along line one to the DAC, which receives the binary number 100 (decimal four) and generates a four-volt signal. This returns to the comparator-register, which compares the DAC signal with the input signal.

As the five-volt input signal is now less than the six-volt DAC signal, the comparator-register outputs an off-bit (0).

LINE 2 ON

SECOND BIT

3 SECOND BIT
The comparator-register now opens line two to the DAC. The DAC receives the binary number 110 (decimal six) and converts it to six volts, which returns to the comparator-register.

The DAC signal reaches the same voltage as the input signal, and the comparator-register therefore outputs an on-bit (1).

LINE 3 ON

THIRD BIT

4 THIRD BIT
As the second bit was an off-bit (0), the comparator-register closes line two and opens line three. The DAC receives the binary number 101 (decimal five) and converts it to five volts.

DIGITAL THERMOMETER

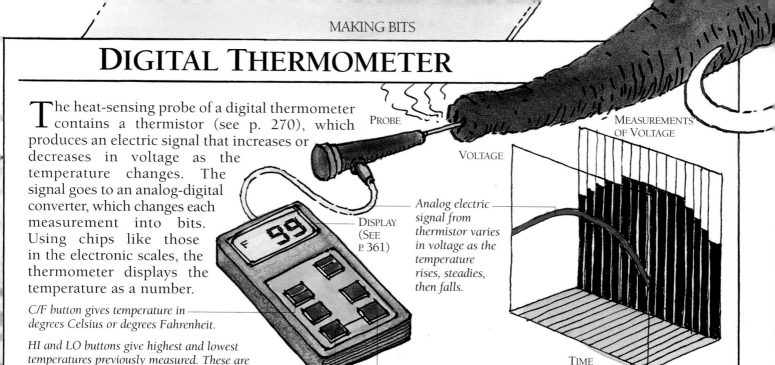

The heat-sensing probe of a digital thermometer contains a thermistor (see p. 270), which produces an electric signal that increases or decreases in voltage as the temperature changes. The signal goes to an analog-digital converter, which changes each measurement into bits. Using chips like those in the electronic scales, the thermometer displays the temperature as a number.

C/F button gives temperature in degrees Celsius or degrees Fahrenheit.

HI and LO buttons give highest and lowest temperatures previously measured. These are stored as bits in the thermometer's memory.

PROBE

VOLTAGE

DISPLAY (SEE P. 361)

Analog electric signal from thermistor varies in voltage as the temperature rises, steadies, then falls.

MEASUREMENTS OF VOLTAGE

TIME

F 99

ELECTRONIC SCALES

DETECTING WEIGHT

The weight of the letter very slightly bends the beam, which stretches or compresses the thin wire in the strain gauge. This changes the electric resistance of the wire so that the voltage of the current flowing through the gauge also changes.

STRAIN GAUGE CONTAINS TWO WIRE LOOPS

SECOND STRAIN GAUGE UNDER BEAM

ANALOG-DIGITAL CONVERTER

PROCESSOR CHIP

DISPLAY CHIP

MEMORY CHIP

BUTTON CONTROLLER CHIP

OFF BUTTON

ON BUTTON

DISPLAY (SEE P. 361)

OUNCES/GRAMS BUTTON

RESET BUTTON

VOLTAGE

WEIGHT OF PAN PLUS PURCHASE

STRAIN GAUGE SIGNAL

WEIGHT OF PAN

MEASUREMENTS OF VOLTAGE

TIME

Like this postal scale, electronic weighing machines used in shops contain a strain gauge that detects the weight of a purchase. The gauge sends out an analog electric signal that varies in voltage with the weight, and an analog-digital converter changes the voltage into a binary number consisting of on-off electric pulses. These bits go to the scale's processor, which calculates the weight, subtracts the weight of the pan (stored in the memory), and may also calculate the price. The result goes to the display.

DIGITIZING SOUND

Digital sound is stored and played back on digital devices such as computers and smartphones, and can be downloaded or streamed over the Internet. Digitizing sound begins with an electrical sound signal—a rapidly varying voltage that is a copy of the sound wave. The voltage is measured, or sampled, thousands of times every second, and groups of bits represent each sample. Using the bits, a digital-analog converter can reconstruct the sound wave and reproduce the original sound.

SOUND TRAVELS
THROUGH AIR
TO MICROPHONE

SOUND WAVES

Sound sources vibrate hundreds or thousands of times every second and cause disturbances in air pressure that radiate outward like ripples on a pond.

VOLTAGE COPIES
PATTERN OF
SOUND WAVE

ANALOG TO DIGITAL

Sound causes a diaphragm in a microphone (see p. 228) to vibrate at the same rate as the variations of pressure in the sound wave. The movement of the diaphragm creates a varying voltage that is a direct copy, or analog, of the varying pressure. This signal passes to an analog-digital converter (see p. 322), which measures the size of the voltage thousands of times a second and represents each sample as a binary number. The numbers are stored and processed in a digital device's memory and processor chips.

SAMPLING

The graph shows a tiny part of the sound signal. The vertical axis shows the levels of voltage, the horizontal axis time in milliseconds (thousandths of a second). Each sample is shown as a dot.

SOUND QUALITY

The more times the voltage is sampled every second, and the more precisely the voltage is measured, the more faithfully the original sound will be represented. Increasing these factors increases the number of bits (binary 1s and 0s) required to represent the sound. Typical rates for high-quality audio are 44,100 samples per second and 16 bits per sample. With so much data, high-quality audio files may take more time to send and receive, and more space to store.

PART OF SIGNAL
EXPANDED
BELOW

ANALOG SIGNAL

A sound signal is a complicated wave whose pattern is unique to the particular sound being made.

VOLTAGE SAMPLE
REPRESENTED AS
BINARY NUMBER
(E.G., 11000001)

VOLTAGE

TIME

STREAM OF BITS (11000001, 10011001, 01110110, 01011100…)

MEMORY CHIP
STORES THE SOUND

REPRODUCTION

Sound is reproduced when a digital-analog converter reconstructs the sound signal from the stream of bits.

COMPRESSION FOR PLAYBACK

To make audio files smaller, less audible parts of the sound can be left out, reducing the number of bits. A common form of compression is MP3.

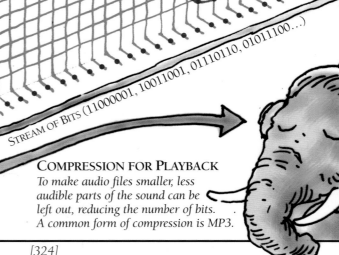

DIGITIZING IMAGES

Images are represented in digital devices as collections of individual squares called picture elements, or pixels. Each pixel is represented by a group of bits in a binary number. The more bits per pixel, and the more pixels, the better the image quality. Inside a digital camera (see pp. 204-5), an image formed by the lens is captured on a sensor—a silicon chip with an array of millions of light-sensitive elements that allow electric current to flow when light falls on them. The more light falls on them, the more current they produce. The current is measured, and its level is represented as a binary number by an analog-digital converter. The numbers from all the elements make up the digital image.

MAMMOTH PHOTOGRAPHED IN A RED HAT

DIGITAL CAMERA
Lenses focus light to form an image on the sensor at the back of the camera.

SILICON CHIP

COLORED FILTER

PHOTODIODE

MICROLENS FOCUSES LIGHT ON PHOTODIODE

LIGHT PASSES THROUGH FILTER TO PHOTODIODE

IMAGE SENSOR

The light-sensitive elements on an image sensor are photodiodes (see p. 272). Electric current is measured from each photodiode in turn, and the measurement is recorded as a binary number. The more bits that are used for each pixel's measurement, the more accurately the current can be recorded and the better the representation of the image will be—and the more photodiodes there are, the more detailed the digital image will be. High-quality images are very large files, but compression can help reduce the size (see p. 207).

PHOTODIODE
The sensor is connected to a circuit in the camera and is constantly supplied with electricity, but a current will flow through and activate a particular photodiode only when light falls on it. The brighter the light, the greater the current will be.

COLOR IMAGES
Photodiodes can detect only brightness, not color. Each one has a color filter—red, green, or blue— which together enable the sensor to capture images in millions of shades of color.

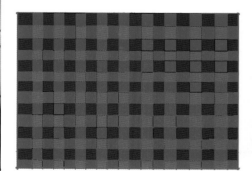

1. RED, GREEN, AND BLUE
The array of red, green, and blue colored filters on the front of the sensor makes each photodiode sensitive to only one of those three primary colors.

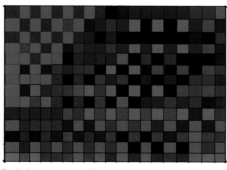

2. MOSAIC OF BRIGHTNESS
Since each photodiode is sensitive only to either red, green, or blue, the image captured by the sensor is a mosaic of pixels of those three colors, at different levels of brightness.

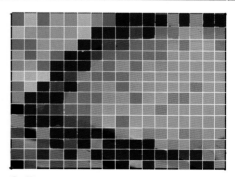

3. DE-MOSAICING
Software inside the camera finds the true colors of the image from the mosaic of red, green, and blue squares by comparing the brightness of each pixel with its neighbors.

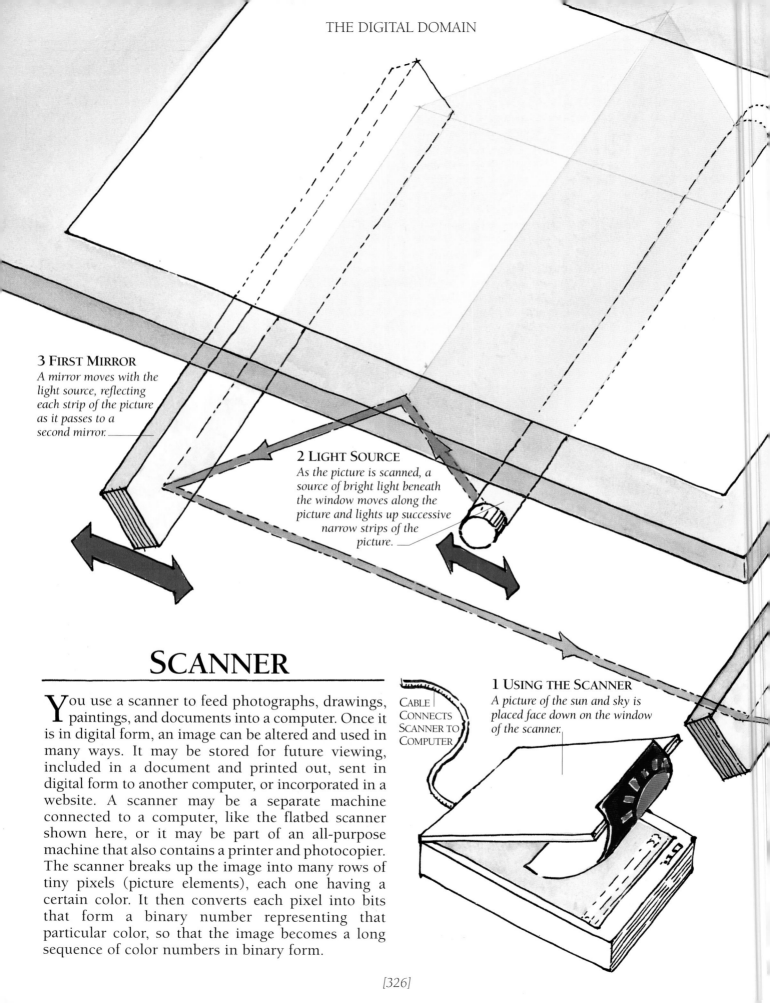

3 FIRST MIRROR

A mirror moves with the light source, reflecting each strip of the picture as it passes to a second mirror.

2 LIGHT SOURCE

As the picture is scanned, a source of bright light beneath the window moves along the picture and lights up successive narrow strips of the picture.

SCANNER

You use a scanner to feed photographs, drawings, paintings, and documents into a computer. Once it is in digital form, an image can be altered and used in many ways. It may be stored for future viewing, included in a document and printed out, sent in digital form to another computer, or incorporated in a website. A scanner may be a separate machine connected to a computer, like the flatbed scanner shown here, or it may be part of an all-purpose machine that also contains a printer and photocopier. The scanner breaks up the image into many rows of tiny pixels (picture elements), each one having a certain color. It then converts each pixel into bits that form a binary number representing that particular color, so that the image becomes a long sequence of color numbers in binary form.

CABLE CONNECTS SCANNER TO COMPUTER

1 USING THE SCANNER

A picture of the sun and sky is placed face down on the window of the scanner.

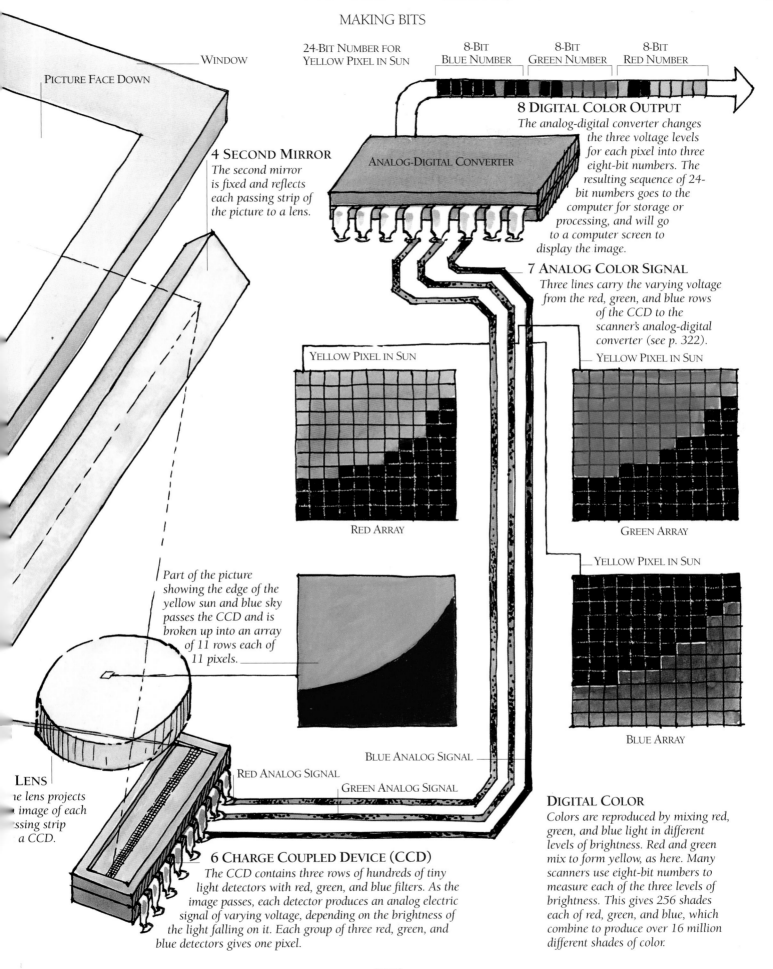

WINDOW

PICTURE FACE DOWN

24-BIT NUMBER FOR
YELLOW PIXEL IN SUN

8-BIT
BLUE NUMBER

8-BIT
GREEN NUMBER

8-BIT
RED NUMBER

8 DIGITAL COLOR OUTPUT

*The analog-digital converter changes
the three voltage levels
for each pixel into three
eight-bit numbers. The
resulting sequence of 24-
bit numbers goes to the
computer for storage or
processing, and will go
to a computer screen to
display the image.*

4 SECOND MIRROR

*The second mirror
is fixed and reflects
each passing strip of
the picture to a lens.*

ANALOG-DIGITAL CONVERTER

7 ANALOG COLOR SIGNAL

*Three lines carry the varying voltage
from the red, green, and blue rows
of the CCD to the
scanner's analog-digital
converter (see p. 322).*

YELLOW PIXEL IN SUN

YELLOW PIXEL IN SUN

RED ARRAY

GREEN ARRAY

YELLOW PIXEL IN SUN

*Part of the picture
showing the edge of the
yellow sun and blue sky
passes the CCD and is
broken up into an array
of 11 rows each of
11 pixels.*

BLUE ARRAY

BLUE ANALOG SIGNAL

GREEN ANALOG SIGNAL

RED ANALOG SIGNAL

LENS

*e lens projects
image of each
ssing strip
a CCD.*

DIGITAL COLOR

*Colors are reproduced by mixing red,
green, and blue light in different
levels of brightness. Red and green
mix to form yellow, as here. Many
scanners use eight-bit numbers to
measure each of the three levels of
brightness. This gives 256 shades
each of red, green, and blue, which
combine to produce over 16 million
different shades of color.*

6 CHARGE COUPLED DEVICE (CCD)

*The CCD contains three rows of hundreds of tiny
light detectors with red, green, and blue filters. As the
image passes, each detector produces an analog electric
signal of varying voltage, depending on the brightness of
the light falling on it. Each group of three red, green, and
blue detectors gives one pixel.*

GAMES CONTROLLER

A video games console is a powerful computer. The controller enables a player to interact with a host of games—from tricky puzzles to fast-paced action—by relaying the player's inputs to the console via USB cables (see p. 369) or wireless connections, normally Bluetooth. The most common type is a hand controller, which has a selection of buttons and at least one joystick. Each button controls a specific action and works as a switch. Pressing the button completes a circuit on the circuit board inside the controller, sending a stream of bits to the console, which matches the data to the software instructions and triggers the appropriate action. Moving the joystick allows the player to control the direction and angle of the action.

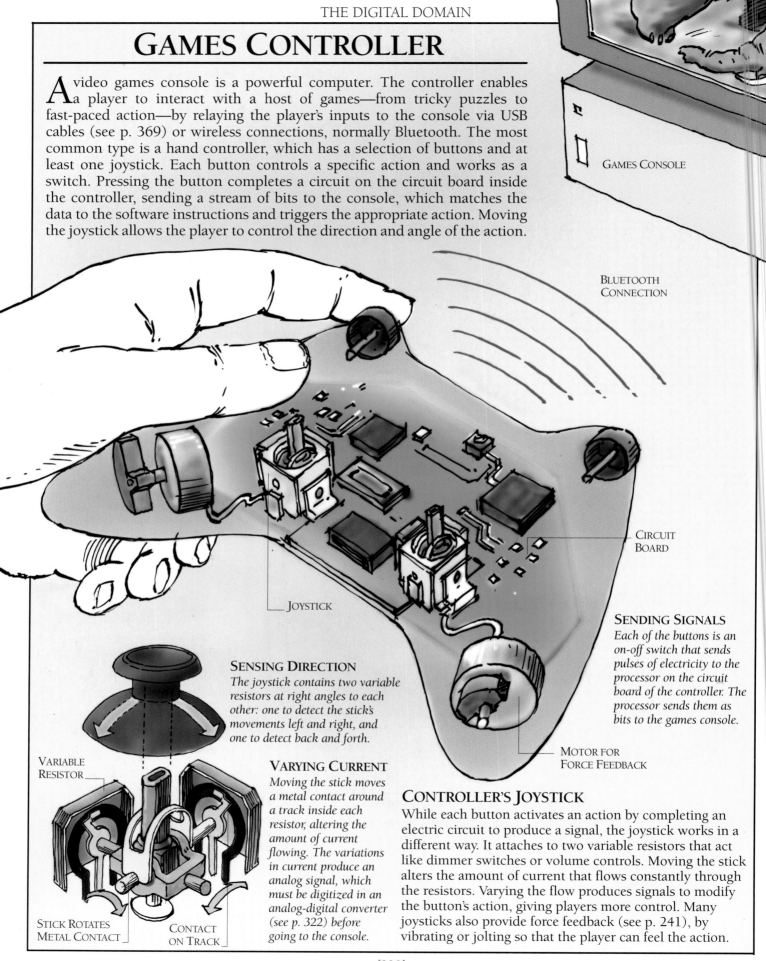

GAMES CONSOLE

BLUETOOTH CONNECTION

CIRCUIT BOARD

JOYSTICK

SENDING SIGNALS
Each of the buttons is an on-off switch that sends pulses of electricity to the processor on the circuit board of the controller. The processor sends them as bits to the games console.

MOTOR FOR FORCE FEEDBACK

VARIABLE RESISTOR

STICK ROTATES METAL CONTACT

CONTACT ON TRACK

SENSING DIRECTION
The joystick contains two variable resistors at right angles to each other: one to detect the stick's movements left and right, and one to detect back and forth.

VARYING CURRENT
Moving the stick moves a metal contact around a track inside each resistor, altering the amount of current flowing. The variations in current produce an analog signal, which must be digitized in an analog-digital converter (see p. 322) before going to the console.

CONTROLLER'S JOYSTICK

While each button activates an action by completing an electric circuit to produce a signal, the joystick works in a different way. It attaches to two variable resistors that act like dimmer switches or volume controls. Moving the stick alters the amount of current that flows constantly through the resistors. Varying the flow produces signals to modify the button's action, giving players more control. Many joysticks also provide force feedback (see p. 241), by vibrating or jolting so that the player can feel the action.

CHAPTER TWO

*T*he other end of the rope was attached
to a rolling stepladder behind which
stood a tall set of shelves. Every shelf
was individually numbered and divided
into eight compartments. A worker
placed each arriving pumpkin into its
own compartment once again, taking
special care to maintain their order.
Where there was a no-pumpkin or piece
of laundry, that compartment was left
empty. Even to the mammoth this seemed
a somewhat overly complicated way of
drying clothes, but this too he assumed
must be "progress."

As Mammoth turned the corner, he was stunned by an overwhelming sight. Rows and rows of shelves filled with pumpkins and no-pumpkins extended as far as the eye could see. For the first time in his life, he actually felt small. A shudder suddenly rippled through his pungent body. He had entered the digital domain and even allowed himself to be processed in the hope of finding companionship. But now, as he gazed at all the pumpkins before him, he felt more insignificant than ever. His quest seemed hopeless.

*E*ven though every shelf had its own number, he wondered how anyone, including Bill, could possibly keep track of all these pumpkins—never mind the no-pumpkins. As Mammoth looked around for reassurance, he noticed that all the shelves were served by another even larger ladder. When Bill called out a particular shelf number, the ladder was rolled against that bank of shelves and then the entire eight-compartment pattern was removed. It was then attached to one of two moving ropes and carried off.

STORING BITS

The mammoth watches as its personal details are stored for future use. The eight-bit sequences of pumpkins are placed in numbered racks so that any sequence can be found and sent elsewhere.

Bits enter and leave storage as on-off electric pulses. But in its memory units, a digital machine or system stores the bits in other forms. The bits may be parked in the memory just for a short time, or the memory may hold the bits for a long time or even permanently.

Digital machines store two classes of bits: programs and data. A program is a set of instructions that direct the machine to carry out a particular task, such as word processing, taking pictures, or playing a game. The instructions consist of bits that form code numbers for actions to be taken. Data consists of bits that make up information required by the program or produced as the program runs, such as words, images, or points scored.

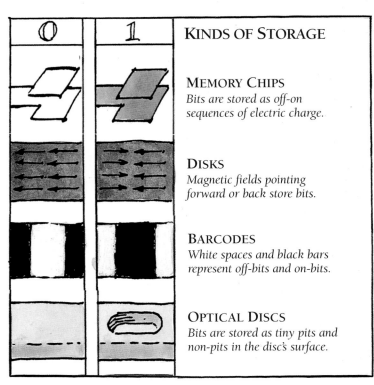

KINDS OF STORAGE

MEMORY CHIPS
Bits are stored as off-on sequences of electric charge.

DISKS
Magnetic fields pointing forward or back store bits.

BARCODES
White spaces and black bars represent off-bits and on-bits.

OPTICAL DISCS
Bits are stored as tiny pits and non-pits in the disc's surface.

BITS AND BYTES

Every memory device has a certain storage capacity that is measured in bytes. A byte is a tiny amount—just eight bits—that stores in binary form any decimal number from 0 to 255; larger numbers require two or more bytes. Memory capacity is measured in units bigger than single bytes. One kilobyte (1 KB) is 1,024 bytes; one megabyte (1 MB) is 1,048,576 bytes; and one gigabyte (1 GB) is 1,073,741,824 bytes. Each byte has its own location in the memory, and this is identified by an address number. A digital machine keeps a record of which byte is stored where, and works through a list of address numbers to retrieve the bits in a set of bytes.

ONE BYTE

Eight bits make up one byte. Letters, numerals, and signs are represented by eight-bit code numbers: the letter "a" is 01100001 (decimal 97). So one byte stores one letter.

ONE KILOBYTE

One kilobyte is just over a thousand bytes. This amount of memory can store the letters in about 150 words, or half a page of a novel.

OPTICAL DISC

Compact discs (CDs), DVDs, and Blu-rays (see pp. 200-201) store data as tiny indentations on spiral tracks. A CD can store about 700 MB, a standard DVD up to 4.7 GB, and a standard Blu-ray disc up to 25 GB.

REMOVABLE STORAGE

A USB flash drive (see p. 334) has a capacity of several gigabytes—enough to store the text from hundreds or thousands of novels.

HARD DISK AND SSD

A computer needs huge amounts of storage, for holding documents, images, music, and video. Most have a hard disk drive or a solid-state drive (SSD), which can hold several terabytes (one terabyte = 1,024 GB).

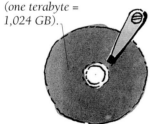

Do you have a copy of 'The Typewriter's Revenge?'

Shhhhhh . . . . . .

SQUEEZING BITS

The amount of data that can be stored in a memory device can be greatly increased by a mathematical process called data compression. For example, rather than store all the original numbers produced by the input unit, the machine may store the first number and then calculate and store only the differences between each successive number. This difference can be very small, or even zero (as in adjacent parts of a digital image of the same color). This compression process greatly reduces the number of bits to be stored—by a factor of up to 200 to 1 in digital video (see p. 207). When the compressed bits are retrieved from the memory, the digital device decompresses them, reversing the mathematical process to reconstitute the original sets of bits.

PINS AND PASSWORDS

Secure digital machines and systems, such as cash machines and e-mail, ask you to type in a PIN (personal identification number) or a password. The machine or system contains the PIN or password stored in its memory as a set of bits. It compares the bits that you type in with the set in its memory. Only if they match does the machine allow you to proceed.

COMPUTER MEMORY

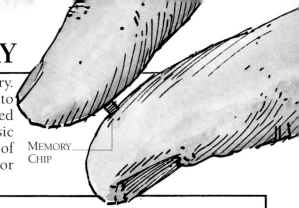

MEMORY CHIP

On a computer's motherboard (see p. 344) are two kinds of memory. Random-access memory (RAM) is used as working memory to store any programs that are running and any information they need to make them work. Read-only memory (ROM) stores the basic programs that make the device work. Both are arrays of millions of transistors (see p. 341) on integrated circuits (chips). Each transistor stores either a 1, if it is switched on, or a 0, if it is switched off.

RANDOM-ACCESS MEMORY (RAM)

The main working memory of a digital machine consists of RAM chips. These hold data and programs, but only for as long as these bits are required; they are constantly replaced by new sets of bits as the machine is used. The bits can be stored at any available groups of memory cells, hence the name "random-access." More RAM may make the machine work faster.

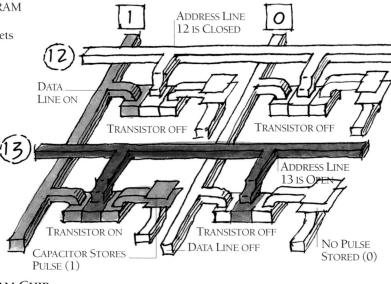

1   ADDRESS LINE 12 IS CLOSED   0

(12)

DATA LINE ON

TRANSISTOR off   TRANSISTOR off

(13)

ADDRESS LINE 13 IS OPEN

TRANSISTOR ON

CAPACITOR STORES PULSE (1)

TRANSISTOR off DATA LINE off

NO PULSE STORED (0)

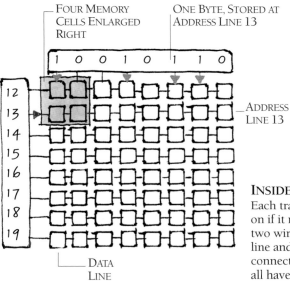

FOUR MEMORY CELLS ENLARGED RIGHT   ONE BYTE, STORED AT ADDRESS LINE 13

1 0 0 1 0 1 1 0

12
13
14
15
16
17
18
19

ADDRESS LINE 13

DATA LINE

INSIDE A RAM CHIP

Each transistor in a RAM chip is turned on if it receives an electric current from two wires simultaneously: an address line and a data line. Each address line connects to a group of transistors, which all have the same address. The address lines are switched on in turn, then a current is fed or not fed along the data lines. When a transistor turns on, it stores a tiny charge in a capacitor. To retrieve the bits, the "on" capacitors discharge, sending an electric pulse back along the data line.

READ-ONLY MEMORY (ROM)

The bits held in a ROM chip are permanent and cannot be changed. A ROM inside a computer or other digital device contains start-up routines that spring into action when the computer is switched on. A ROM chip contains a grid of memory cells consisting of transistors that are linked to address lines and data lines as in a RAM chip. Some of the address line links are cut when the chip is made. To retrieve bits, power goes to all the cells. It passes through only the linked transistors at an address, which are switched on to give the on-pulses in the bits that are stored in the ROM. The cut links switch off the other transistors at that address, and give the off-pulses.

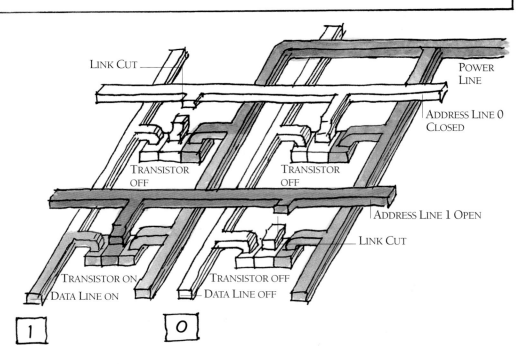

LINK CUT

POWER LINE

ADDRESS LINE 0 CLOSED

TRANSISTOR OFF   TRANSISTOR OFF

ADDRESS LINE 1 OPEN

LINK CUT

TRANSISTOR ON DATA LINE ON   TRANSISTOR OFF DATA LINE OFF

1   0

FLASH STORAGE

Flash memory is used on USB memory sticks, on memory cards used in digital cameras, on smartphones, and in high-capacity storage drives. It is called "solid-state memory" because there are no moving parts and it comes on integrated circuits, or "chips." Flash memory chips are similar to the chips used for RAM (see p. 333). RAM chips are volatile—that means the bits they store are only retained while the chips are supplied with power. Turn off the computer (or other digital device), and the contents of RAM are lost. Flash memory chips are nonvolatile—they retain the bits even when the device is powered down. They are used as backup storage, to store programs and data that are not currently being used.

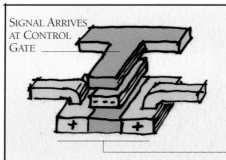

SIGNAL ARRIVES AT CONTROL GATE

FLOATING GATE BECOMES CHARGED, AND REMAINS SO TO STORE ONE BIT

TRANSISTOR SWITCHES ON WHEN THERE IS A SIGNAL AT THE CONTROL GATE

FLOATING GATE TRANSISTOR
Inside a flash memory chip, transistors turning off or on represent binary 0s and 1s, just as they do in a RAM chip. However, unlike in a RAM chip, the bit remains stored even when the computer is turned off, thanks to a "floating gate." When a signal turns on the transistor, the floating gate becomes electrically charged. The charge remains on the floating gate until a new signal changes it.

FLASH CHIPS
Flash chips are small and have no moving parts, so they are portable and durable, and can be used in tablets and smartphones. Most digital cameras have removable, secure digital cards, which have flash chips to store images. Flash chips are also used in storage devices called USB flash drives and solid-state drives that plug into computers. Inside these storage devices, a chip called a microcontroller communicates with the host device's processor, and controls the flow of bits to and from flash chips.

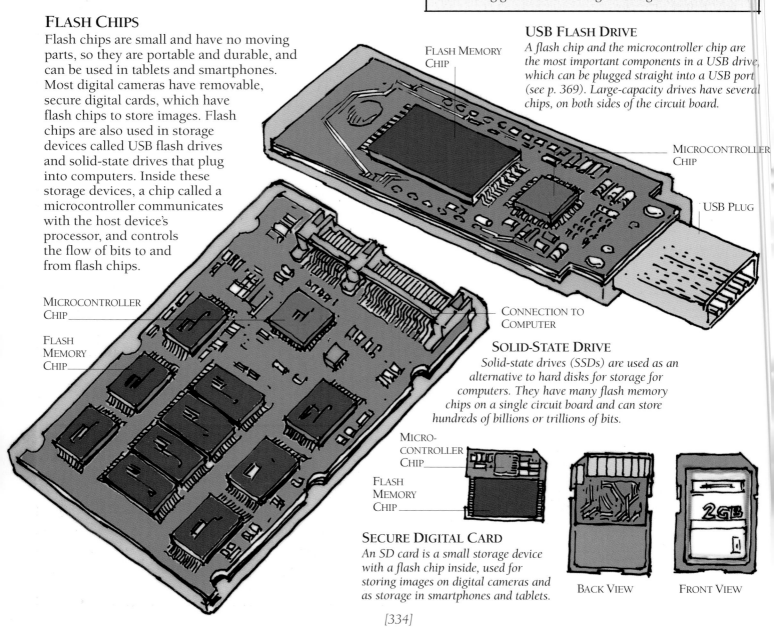

FLASH MEMORY CHIP

USB FLASH DRIVE
A flash chip and the microcontroller chip are the most important components in a USB drive, which can be plugged straight into a USB port (see p. 369). Large-capacity drives have several chips, on both sides of the circuit board.

MICROCONTROLLER CHIP

USB PLUG

MICROCONTROLLER CHIP

FLASH MEMORY CHIP

CONNECTION TO COMPUTER

SOLID-STATE DRIVE
Solid-state drives (SSDs) are used as an alternative to hard disks for storage for computers. They have many flash memory chips on a single circuit board and can store hundreds of billions or trillions of bits.

MICRO-CONTROLLER CHIP

FLASH MEMORY CHIP

SECURE DIGITAL CARD
An SD card is a small storage device with a flash chip inside, used for storing images on digital cameras and as storage in smartphones and tablets.

2GB

BACK VIEW   FRONT VIEW

HARD DISK STORAGE

All digital devices need backup storage, to hold the bits that represent software and the letters and numbers, sounds and images that can be called up into RAM (see p. 333) to be manipulated or output. Most laptops and other computers use hard disk drives, which contain rapidly spinning discs with bits stored magnetically. Hard disk drives are also commonplace in digital video recorders (DVRs) that can record television programs and play them from the drive.

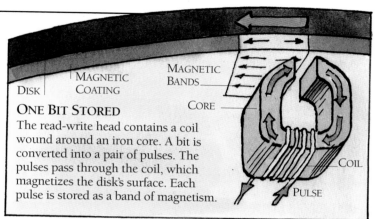

ONE BIT STORED

The read-write head contains a coil wound around an iron core. A bit is converted into a pair of pulses. The pulses pass through the coil, which magnetizes the disk's surface. Each pulse is stored as a band of magnetism.

PLATTERS AND HEADS

A hard disk drive consists of several flat metal or ceramic disks called platters, coated with a thin layer of magnetic material. Tiny coils on the ends of read-write heads—one above and one below each disc—read and write the disc. Read-write heads are on the ends of levers called actuator arms, which swing to any point on the disk's surface.

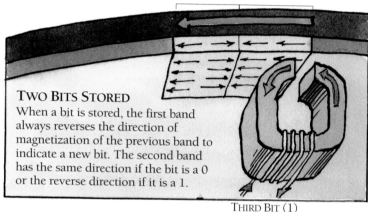

TWO BITS STORED

When a bit is stored, the first band always reverses the direction of magnetization of the previous band to indicate a new bit. The second band has the same direction if the bit is a 0 or the reverse direction if it is a 1.

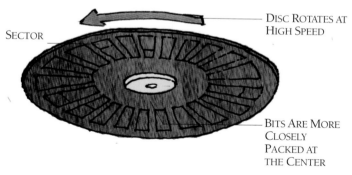

SECTORS AND TRACKS

Bits are encoded onto the disks' surfaces as changes in the direction of magnetization in tiny regions of the magnetic coating (see right). A typical hard disk drive can store gigabytes (GB)—billions of bytes—or terabytes (TB)—trillions of bytes—of data; a byte being a unit of eight bits. The bits are arranged along circular tracks, not a single spiral track as they are on a Blu-ray disk (see pp. 200-201). Each track is divided into sectors, each with a capacity of 4,096 bytes—so every byte that is stored on a disk can be located by its track and sector. Each sector begins with a sequence of bytes called a "header," which contains information about what data is stored where within that sector. The tracks close to the edge of the disk are much longer than those near the center. Other hard disks keep the same number of sectors per track, so the bits are more spread out farther from the center.

THREE BITS STORED

Three bits—101—have now been stored in six bands. The bands create a circular track on the surface of the disk. Some of the bits stored form a directory giving the names and locations of files.

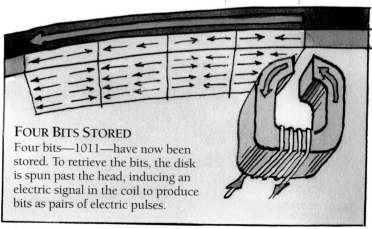

FOUR BITS STORED

Four bits—1011—have now been stored. To retrieve the bits, the disk is spun past the head, inducing an electric signal in the coil to produce bits as pairs of electric pulses.

IDENTIFICATION AND TRACKING

Information that identifies people can help them access restricted areas or make quick and easy payments. For example, many hotels give guests plastic cards with a sequence of bits stored in a magnetic strip. The bits are stored as changing directions of magnetism, as on a hard disk (see p. 335), and act as a passcode, giving the guest access to the correct room. The magnetic strip on a credit or debit card stores the customer's name, account number, and PIN—the personal identification number that a card reader or cash machine uses to check the customer's identity. The same details are stored on a flash memory chip on the card, which can also be read wirelessly, using a technique called radio frequency identification. RFID has many other uses, including tracking goods in warehouses, shops and during delivery.

CHIP AND PIN

On a credit or debit card, the details stored in the magnetic strip are also present in a flash memory chip (see p. 334) in the card. A card reader in a shop or cash machine reads the information through metal contacts on the chip, and the customer has to enter the same PIN that is stored in the memory. Most cards can also be used to make contactless payments using radio frequency identification (see opposite). For this, thin wires running around the edge of the chip form an antenna to intercept radio waves transmitted by a wireless card reader, so that the card only needs to be held close to the reader. Since no PIN is required, contactless payments are used only in transactions involving small amounts of money.

CARD READER

Swiping the magnetic strip through a reader generates tiny electric currents in a coil of wire inside the reader. A computer interprets the currents as bits to reconstruct the information.

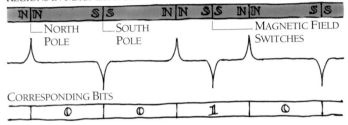

REGIONS IN MAGNETIC COATING

NORTH POLE   SOUTH POLE   MAGNETIC FIELD SWITCHES

CORRESPONDING BITS

0   0   1   0

MAGNETIC STRIP

The north and south poles of tiny magnetic regions switch at regular distances along the card, each time registering a 0— unless they switch in between, in which case a 1 is registered.

METAL CONTACTS

FLASH CHIP

CONNECTING WIRES

RFID ANTENNA

ENCRYPTION

The information held in the flash memory of the chip is coded, or encrypted, so that the person reading the card cannot discover the PIN.

RADIO FREQUENCY IDENTIFICATION (RFID)

RFID is not only used in chip and PIN cards. Tags containing a chip and antenna can be used to track clothing and other products. By reading the information on the chip, warehouses and stores can monitor where the item came from, how much stock they have for that product, and whether they need to order more of it. Tags can even be used to track pets, farm animals, or wildlife. Radio waves from an antenna in an RFID reader produce a tiny current in the wires of the RFID chip, which activates the chip. In response, the activated chip broadcasts a small radio signal of its own, encoded with information. The RFID reader detects this signal and relays the information as bits to a computer to process.

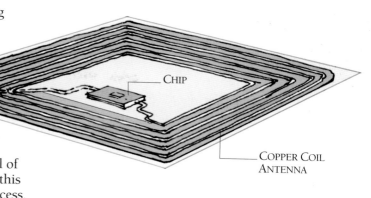

CHIP

COPPER COIL ANTENNA

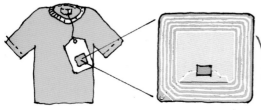

TAGGED ITEM

RFID TAG

RADIO WAVES

RFID READER

STOCK COMPUTER

BARCODE

The pattern of white and black stripes on a barcode provides another way to identify and track products. A barcode reader's laser beams scan across the stripes, and the pattern is read from the amount of reflected light entering a photodiode (see p. 272)—more is reflected off the white stripes than the black. The reader sends the signal created by the photodiode to a computer, which interprets the pattern and checks the code against a database of available products. Barcodes can be used to track everything from mail and medicines to airline passengers and their luggage.

LASER BEAM

TWO-PART BARCODE

780751 302158

GUARD BAR

UNIVERSAL PRODUCT CODE

Barcodes work with decimal numbers, using a system called the Universal Product Code (UPC). A white or black stripe can be one, two, three, or four units wide. Each number from 0 to 9 has a different pattern of four stripes that is seven units wide. Represented by its unique pattern, a 6 cannot be misread as a 9, for example, if the label is scanned upside down or back to front. The extra-long stripes at each end and in the middle, called guard bars, mark where the code starts and stops.

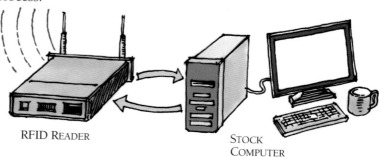

4 STRIPES MAKE UP 7 UNIT WIDTHS, E.G., 1 + 2 + 1 + 3 = 7

| 2 | 2 | 2 | 1 | 1 | 2 | 3 | 1 | 1 | 2 | 1 | 3 | 1 | 1 | 1 |

1

5

8

2221 PATTERN REPRESENTS THE NUMBER 1

1231 PATTERN REPRESENTS THE NUMBER 5

1213 PATTERN REPRESENTS THE NUMBER 8

111 IS STOP / START CODE

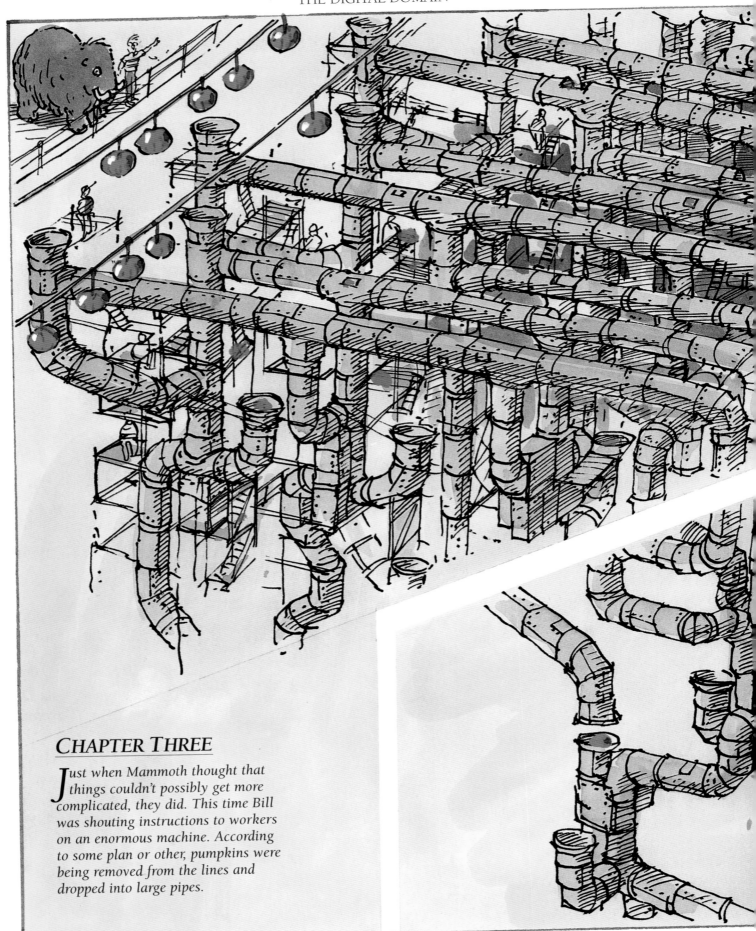

CHAPTER THREE

Just when Mammoth thought that things couldn't possibly get more complicated, they did. This time Bill was shouting instructions to workers on an enormous machine. According to some plan or other, pumpkins were being removed from the lines and dropped into large pipes.

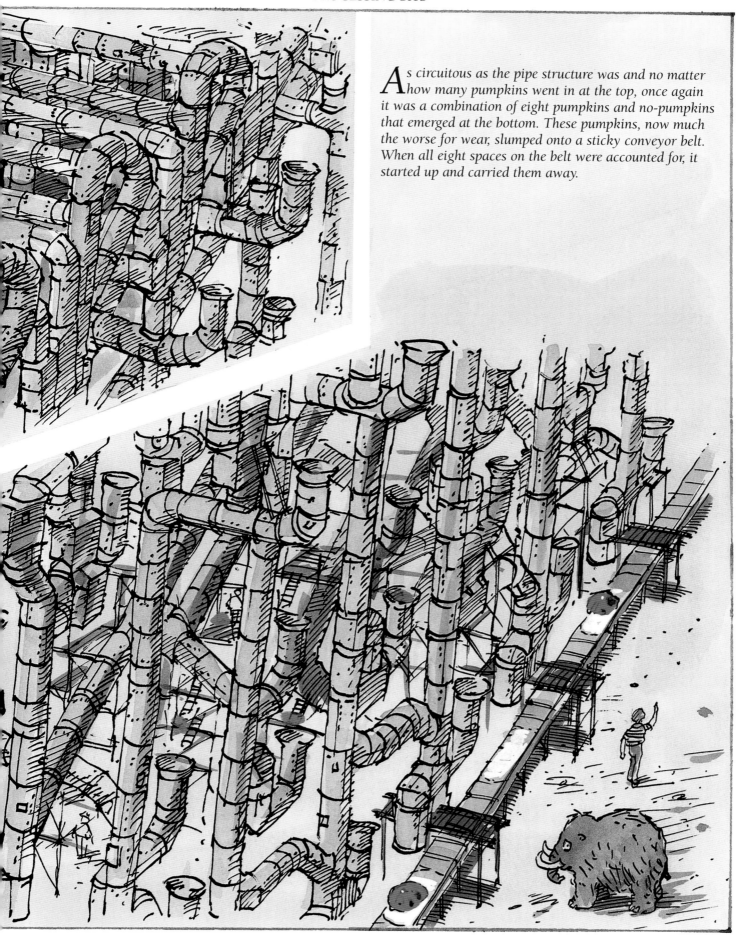

As circuitous as the pipe structure was and no matter how many pumpkins went in at the top, once again it was a combination of eight pumpkins and no-pumpkins that emerged at the bottom. These pumpkins, now much the worse for wear, slumped onto a sticky conveyor belt. When all eight spaces on the belt were accounted for, it started up and carried them away.

Bill explained to Mammoth that as the pumpkins traveled through the huge machine, they operated a series of spring-loaded gates. The opening and closing of these gates actually determined the precise pattern of pumpkins that would eventually emerge onto the conveyor belt. When they reached a couple of prototype gates in the test area, Bill sensed that his oversize companion was finally beginning to appreciate the ingenuity and technical sophistication of these contraptions. But then he realized that, in fact, it was their trunklike geometry that had struck a familiar chord. For the first time in ages, Mammoth was feeling a little less alone.

PROCESSING BITS

The mammoth now looks on as the bits representing its personal details arrive from the storage racks and are processed. The sequences of pumpkins drop into a vast and complex processing machine, where they approach gates that open to pass them or close to block them, so that new sequences of pumpkins emerge and continue on through the digital domain. The gates are worked by other combinations of pumpkins arriving from other racks.

Every digital machine and system contains a processor or CPU (central processing unit), which is a microchip containing hundreds of millions of miniature electronic gates called logic gates. Bits in the form of on-off electric pulses come from the memory and flash to the gates, which pass or block incoming bits so that new sets of bits emerge. These new bits are the result of the task set by the machine's program, and they pass back to the memory or forward to the next part of the machine.

LOGIC GATES

The processor in a digital machine or system is a type of miniature electronic brain housed in a powerful microchip. It receives two groups of bits from the machine's memory: program bits that direct the processor to carry out a task, and data bits that are processed to give a result. Every step consists of simple arithmetic performed electronically at great speed.

Inside the processor chip are billions of tiny transistors (see p. 343). These are connected to make hundreds of millions of logic gates, and the transistors inside them rapidly switch on and off to pass or block bits in order to perform binary arithmetic. The bits consist of on-off electric pulses with a high voltage (on or binary 1) or a zero or low voltage (off or binary 0).

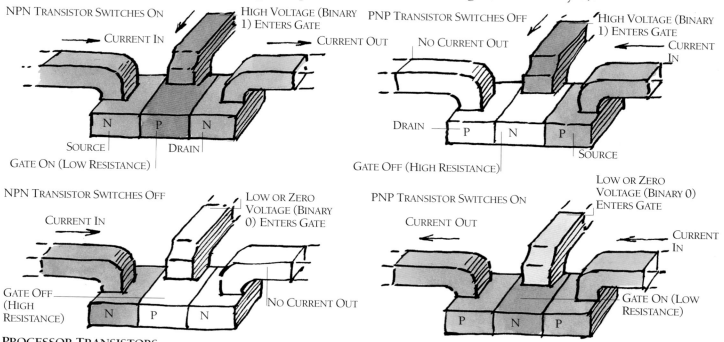

PROCESSOR TRANSISTORS

A transistor is a sandwich of two types of semiconductor, *n*-type and *p*-type, with opposite electrical properties. It contains three pieces: the source, gate, and drain, arranged n-p-n or p-n-p. An electric current is fed to the source and a controlling bit (an on-pulse or off-pulse) goes to the gate. This may cause the electrical resistance of the gate to decrease so that the transistor switches on and passes the current. Alternatively, the resistance of the gate increases and the transistor switches off and blocks the current.

NOT GATE

Arithmetic occurs when a digital machine has to compare two numbers, as in clicking an icon with the mouse (see p. 318). The processor subtracts one number from the other: if the result is zero, the numbers are the same. This kind of arithmetical action enables machines to make decisions. The NOT gate is the simplest of several kinds of logic gates performing arithmetic inside the processor. It changes an on-bit (binary 1) to an off-bit (binary 0) and vice versa, and contains an NPN transistor fed with a low voltage and a PNP transistor fed with a high voltage. This is the real electronic version of the mechanical NOT gate encountered by the mammoth opposite. Other logic gates have more complex groups of transistors using two or more bits, but work in a similar way to pass either a high or low voltage.

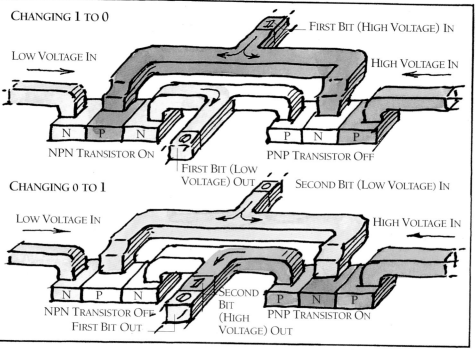

MICROCHIP

A microchip or integrated circuit is a thin sliver of silicon less than 1 cm (0.4 inch) square. A special type of microchip, called a microprocessor, is the central processing unit (see p. 344) of computers and other digital devices. It contains billions of electronic components connected together to form key parts of the microprocessor, such as logic gates (see p. 341) and memory cells (see p. 333).

A chip's components and their connections are all made at the same time, built up in layers of material in complex miniature patterns. The layers of patterns are made with "masks" produced by reducing large patterns photographically. These two pages illustrate the manufacture of a single transistor in a microchip.

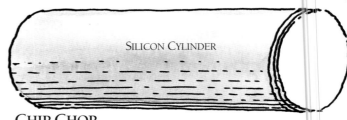

SILICON CYLINDER

CHIP CHOP

A microchip is made mostly of *p*-type silicon (see p. 271). A cylinder of silicon is produced and then sliced into wafers about 0.25 mm (0.01 inch) thick. Each wafer is treated, using broadly the same methods shown below, to make hundreds of microchips. The wafers are then tested and chopped up into individual chips. These are inspected under a microscope before being packaged.

MAKING A TRANSISTOR

1 FIRST MASKING
The silicon base is first coated with silicon dioxide, which does not conduct electricity, and then with a substance called photoresist. Shining ultraviolet light through a patterned mask hardens the photoresist. The unexposed parts remain soft.

2 FIRST ETCHING
A solvent dissolves away the soft, unexposed layer of photoresist, revealing a part of the silicon dioxide. This is then chemically etched to reduce its thickness. The hardened photoresist is then dissolved to leave a ridge of silicon dioxide.

3 SECOND MASKING
Layers of polysilicon, which conducts electricity, and photoresist are applied. Then a second masking exposes and hardens part of the photoresist.

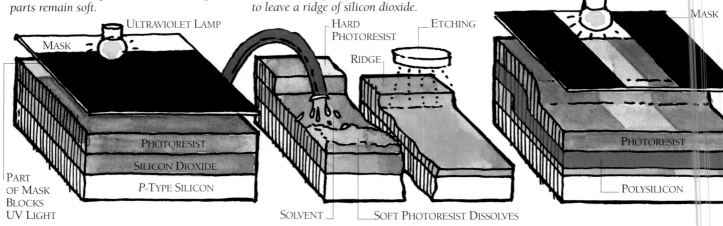

ULTRAVIOLET LAMP
MASK
PHOTORESIST
SILICON DIOXIDE
P-TYPE SILICON
PART OF MASK BLOCKS UV LIGHT
HARD PHOTORESIST
RIDGE
ETCHING
SOLVENT
SOFT PHOTORESIST DISSOLVES
MASK
PHOTORESIST
POLYSILICON

4 SECOND ETCHING
The unexposed photoresist is dissolved, and then an etching treatment removes the polysilicon and silicon dioxide beneath it. This reveals two strips of p-type silicon.

5 DOPING
The hard photoresist is removed. The layers now undergo an operation called doping, which transforms the newly revealed strips of p-type silicon into n-type silicon.

6 THIRD MASKING AND ETCHING
Layers of silicon dioxide and photoresist are added. Masking and etching creates holes through to the doped silicon and central polysilicon strip.

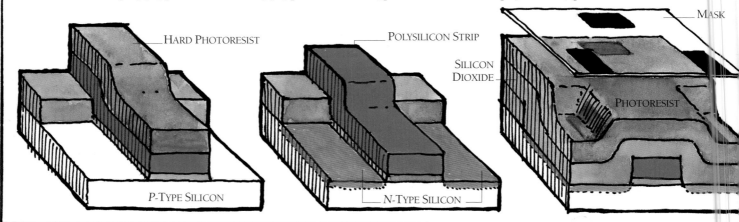

HARD PHOTORESIST
P-TYPE SILICON
POLYSILICON STRIP
N-TYPE SILICON
SILICON DIOXIDE
MASK
PHOTORESIST

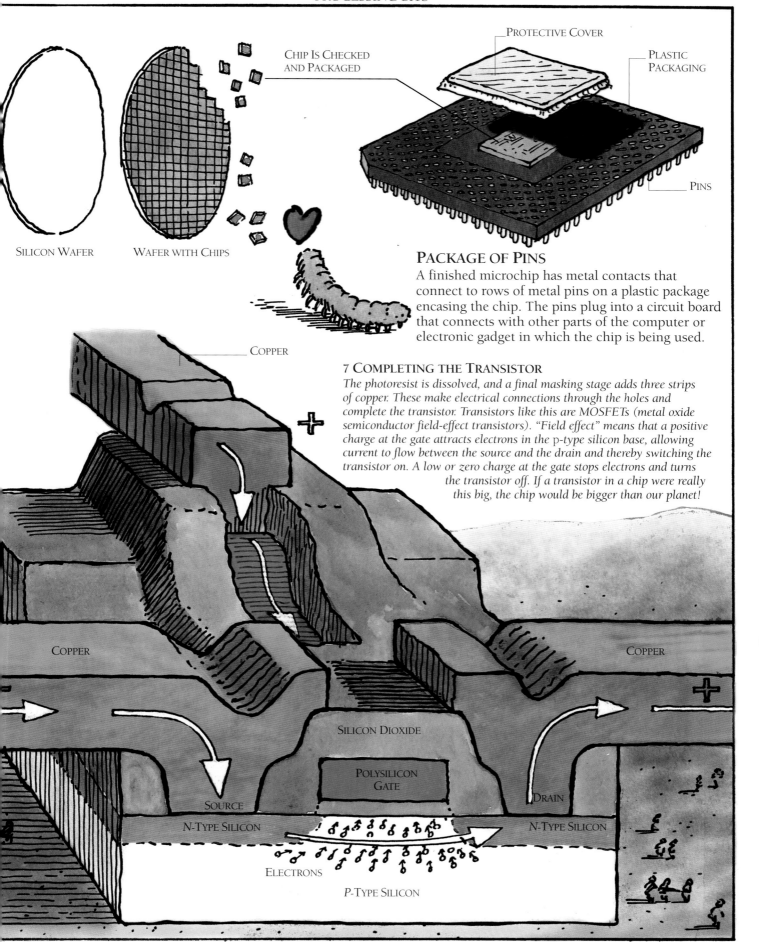

CHIP IS CHECKED
AND PACKAGED

PROTECTIVE COVER

PLASTIC
PACKAGING

PINS

SILICON WAFER

WAFER WITH CHIPS

PACKAGE OF PINS

A finished microchip has metal contacts that connect to rows of metal pins on a plastic package encasing the chip. The pins plug into a circuit board that connects with other parts of the computer or electronic gadget in which the chip is being used.

7 COMPLETING THE TRANSISTOR

The photoresist is dissolved, and a final masking stage adds three strips of copper. These make electrical connections through the holes and complete the transistor. Transistors like this are MOSFETs (metal oxide semiconductor field-effect transistors). "Field effect" means that a positive charge at the gate attracts electrons in the p-type silicon base, allowing current to flow between the source and the drain and thereby switching the transistor on. A low or zero charge at the gate stops electrons and turns the transistor off. If a transistor in a chip were really this big, the chip would be bigger than our planet!

COPPER

COPPER

COPPER

SILICON DIOXIDE

POLYSILICON
GATE

SOURCE

DRAIN

N-TYPE SILICON

N-TYPE SILICON

ELECTRONS

P-TYPE SILICON

MOTHERBOARD

Inside every digital machine, microchips and other electronic components are all connected to a circuit board called a mainboard or motherboard, linked together by electrical pathways called buses. The two most important components are the processor, or CPU, and the random access memory, or RAM. The processor accepts bits, in the form of electrical pulses, from connected input devices such as a keyboard, and carries out millions of calculations every second. The results of the calculations may be stored on a hard disk, sent to connected output devices such as a monitor, or sent to other digital devices over a network.

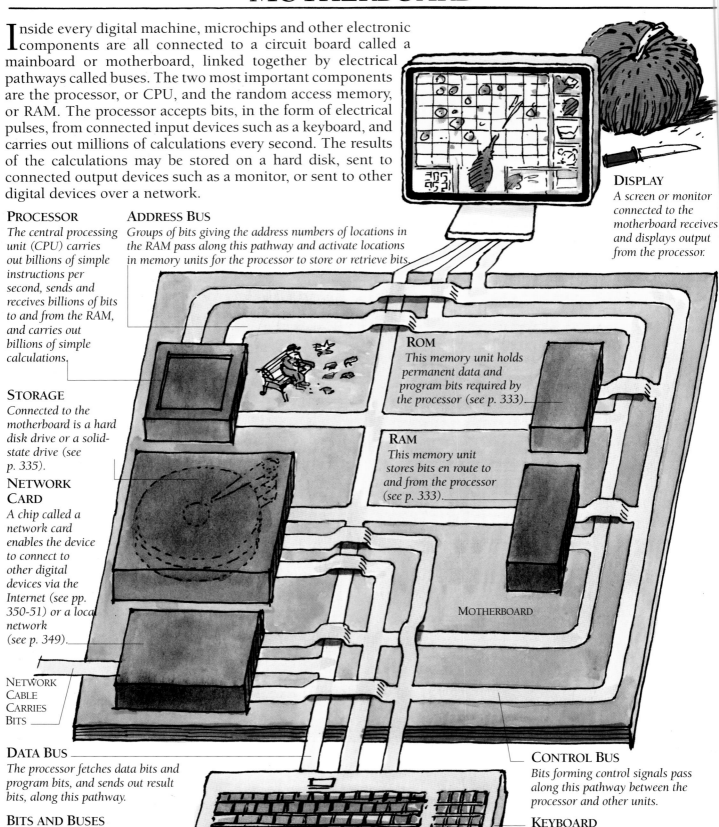

DISPLAY
A screen or monitor connected to the motherboard receives and displays output from the processor.

PROCESSOR
The central processing unit (CPU) carries out billions of simple instructions per second, sends and receives billions of bits to and from the RAM, and carries out billions of simple calculations.

ADDRESS BUS
Groups of bits giving the address numbers of locations in the RAM pass along this pathway and activate locations in memory units for the processor to store or retrieve bits.

ROM
This memory unit holds permanent data and program bits required by the processor (see p. 333).

RAM
This memory unit stores bits en route to and from the processor (see p. 333).

STORAGE
Connected to the motherboard is a hard disk drive or a solid-state drive (see p. 335).

NETWORK CARD
A chip called a network card enables the device to connect to other digital devices via the Internet (see pp. 350-51) or a local network (see p. 349).

MOTHERBOARD

NETWORK CABLE CARRIES BITS

DATA BUS
The processor fetches data bits and program bits, and sends out result bits, along this pathway.

BITS AND BUSES
The buses and processor handle bits in groups of 8, 16, 32, 64, etc.—the faster the device, the bigger the groups it can handle.

CONTROL BUS
Bits forming control signals pass along this pathway between the processor and other units.

KEYBOARD
This is an input unit that produces data bits required by the processor (see p. 317).

SOFTWARE

Every digital device becomes little more than a useless chunk of processed sand and oil without software. This is the general name for the programs that instruct devices how to carry out tasks. They are called "software" to contrast with "hardware," the device itself. Written by programmers using computers, software consists of complex instruction codes in the form of bits. The programs may be distributed in microchips inserted directly into a device's mainframe, downloaded over the Internet, or, in the case of video games, stored on Blu-ray discs. Software may be inbuilt and give a device one task, enabling a digital camera to take pictures, for example. A computer can be given different software for a huge range of tasks, including word processing and desktop publishing, editing photographs and videos, playing games, producing music, browsing the Web, tracking cyclones, or monitoring meteors across the night sky.

Operating System

Every digital device needs an operating system, which is the program that governs the basic way in which the device works and enables you to use it. In a computer, this is a program such as Windows, iOS/OS X, or Android that makes the computer respond to the mouse. The operating system is stored on the hard disk so that it may be upgraded or improved when necessary.

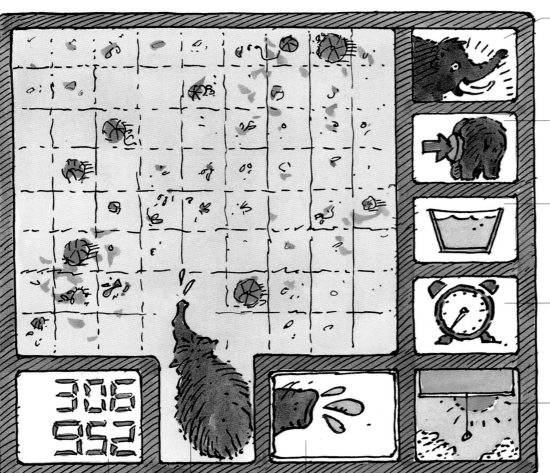

ANGLE BUTTON
Click here to change the angle of the mammoth's trunk. A higher angle could make the mammoth squirt the water farther—but not always.

SQUIRT FORCE BUTTON
More force sends the water farther. But too much force could make the water miss the pumpkin patch altogether!

WATER BUTTON
Clicking here changes the amount of water that the mammoth sucks up and squirts out. Too little water will parch the pumpkins; too much will drown them.

COUNTDOWN BUTTON
This button controls the amount of time for each go. The computer counts down as you play, and stops play when the time reaches zero.

WEATHER BUTTON
Click here to control the amount of sunshine. Too much sun will dry out the patch; too little will not provide enough sunlight for rapid growth.

SCORE PANEL
This shows the biggest pumpkin's weight. The top figure is your score, and the lower figure the highest score.

TRUNK DIRECTION
Click on the mammoth to make the mammoth swivel its trunk.

SQUIRT BUTTON
Click here to make the mammoth squirt. The computer's processor stores all the chosen factors in the memory. Using mathematical formulas in the program, the processor calculates the path of the water and growth of the pumpkin hit. It then works out the display images so that you see the mammoth squirt the water and the pumpkin grow, and it updates the score.

PUMPKIN PATCH
The object of this game is to grow the biggest pumpkin in the time allowed. You get the mammoth to squirt water over the pumpkins. There are many factors to consider. There are the direction and angle of the trunk and the squirt force, so that the water will hit a promising pumpkin. The amount of water and the weather will also affect growth.

CHAPTER FOUR

Mammoth and Bill followed the belt into a large clearing in which eight ovens and eight chefs stood waiting.

"Hi, Bill." "Hi, Bill." "Hi, Bill." "Hi, Bill."

"Hi, Bill." "Hi, Bill." "Hi, Bill." "Hi, Bill."

When a pumpkin came to rest in front of a particular oven, the chef assigned to that oven would scoop it into a waiting pie crust.

Then he or she would light a fire in their oven and prepare to bake the pie. When a no-pumpkin arrived in front of an oven, that particular chef would do absolutely nothing. Since smoke was produced only by those ovens that were lit, a pattern of smoke and no-smoke was created that matched exactly the pumpkin/no-pumpkin pattern.

Bill admitted that in an earlier system they had simply launched the pumpkin patterns to distant locations, but complaints from various communities along the route, not to mention birdwatchers, had necessitated a redesign. What Bill didn't explain, because he enjoyed surprises, was that his workers had been using these smoke signals to gather information about the lifestyles and habitat of mammoths from a distant museum of natural history.

It didn't much matter what Bill was saying or not saying since Mammoth was far too busy snorting in as much warm pumpkin pie air as possible. To his great relief, the digital domain finally smelled of something other than metal, plastic, and wet laundry. A sudden "whistle-thud," "whistle-thud" told Bill that information was already coming back in response to his most recent smoke requests.

"Come on, Mammoth," he shouted. "We're almost there."

*J*ust around the corner from the ovens, a set of eight funnels and eight chutes had been set up to catch apples and no-apples, which were hurtling through the air. While Bill considered the apple rather low-tech and a little behind the times, he was clearly excited by the arrival of any information. To Mammoth's surprise and delight, the eight chutes ended above a tray of sweet-smelling chocolate syrup. After dropping through the funnels, the apples from each arriving sequence rolled down the chutes, shot through the gooey tray, and slid across a narrow strip of paper, leaving a distinct chocolate smear. After a set of eight smears or no-smears had been made, the marked portion of the paper was yanked out of the way in order to record the next set.

SENDING BITS

The digital domain now reveals itself to be immense. Bits are no longer just patterns of pumpkins to be transported short distances. They are transformed into other kinds of bits that can fly swiftly through the air over huge distances to distant processors and memory stores. The bits return in different patterns carrying numbers that represent new kinds of information. These may include images and sounds, like those that the mammoth warily provided when it entered the digital domain.

Many digital systems involve communications in which bits are sent between machines. One computer, for example, can send an e-mail to another and moments later receive a reply. Digital communications have revolutionized telephone, radio, and TV, greatly improving sound and picture quality and offering more ways, often interactive, of using these services. Millions of computers worldwide can now communicate with each other on the Internet. Bits can arrive from anywhere, ready to proceed to the next step in the digital domain and—along with original homegrown bits—finally be put to use.

COMPUTER NETWORKS

Most homes have a type of computer network called a LAN (Local Area Network), which enables computers and other digital devices to connect to one another and to the Internet. Each device can send and receive millions of bits every second, along wired links called Ethernet cables, or wirelessly through the air, via Wi-Fi. Every device can be identified by an address—and at the heart of the network is a device called a router, which ensures that the network traffic reaches the correct destination.

WI-FI
CONNECTION

LAPTOP

MEDIA PLAYER

It is not only computers that can connect to a local network. A media player can play music, photos, and movies stored on other connected devices, such as a desktop computer at the office.

NETWORK ADDRESSES

The router assigns an Internet Protocol, or IP, address to every device on the network, including itself. An IP address is normally made up of between four and eight numbers—for example, 192.168.0.12. When one device needs to send some pieces of information to another, it sends a request to the router labeled with the destination IP address.

TELEPHONE LINE, OPTICAL FIBER OR CABLE CONNECTION

BREAKING IT DOWN

Information on a network travels in chunks, each several thousand bits long, called packets. This enables the network to work more efficiently than if it was sending large files in one go. Every packet contains the IP addresses of both the source and destination devices. The destination device assembles the packets to reproduce the original information.

TABLET

WI-FI
CONNECTION

WI-FI

The most common way for networked devices to communicate with the router in a LAN is by Wi-Fi, which carries streams of bits in a similar way to digital radio (see p. 242).

ROUTER

DESKTOP
COMPUTER

WI-FI
CONNECTION

MEDIA SERVER

The desktop computer's hard disk or SSD (see pp. 334-35) holds movies, music, and images that can be streamed via the router to the media player and other devices connected to the LAN.

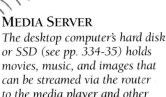

ROUTER

The router controls the traffic on the LAN, but it also acts as a gateway to the Internet, which is a vast network of interconnected networks. The router has a public IP address as well as its local (private) IP address, and can forward traffic to any device on any network in the world. Traffic to other networks on the Internet passes out of the house along telephone lines, cable TV cables, or optical fibers. The router keeps track of any packets it sends out from devices on its own network, so that it knows where to forward any packets it receives from the Internet.

SMARTPHONE

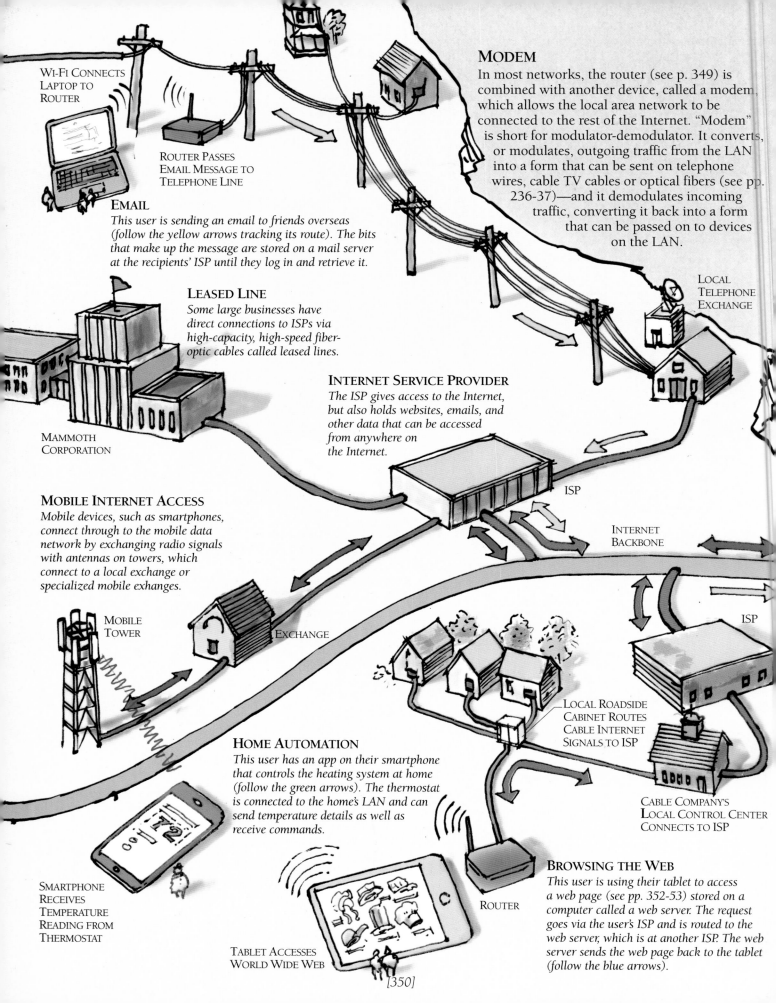

WI-FI CONNECTS LAPTOP TO ROUTER

ROUTER PASSES EMAIL MESSAGE TO TELEPHONE LINE

EMAIL

This user is sending an email to friends overseas (follow the yellow arrows tracking its route). The bits that make up the message are stored on a mail server at the recipients' ISP until they log in and retrieve it.

MODEM

In most networks, the router (see p. 349) is combined with another device, called a modem, which allows the local area network to be connected to the rest of the Internet. "Modem" is short for modulator-demodulator. It converts, or modulates, outgoing traffic from the LAN into a form that can be sent on telephone wires, cable TV cables or optical fibers (see pp. 236-37)—and it demodulates incoming traffic, converting it back into a form that can be passed on to devices on the LAN.

LOCAL TELEPHONE EXCHANGE

LEASED LINE

Some large businesses have direct connections to ISPs via high-capacity, high-speed fiber-optic cables called leased lines.

INTERNET SERVICE PROVIDER

The ISP gives access to the Internet, but also holds websites, emails, and other data that can be accessed from anywhere on the Internet.

MAMMOTH CORPORATION

ISP

MOBILE INTERNET ACCESS

Mobile devices, such as smartphones, connect through to the mobile data network by exchanging radio signals with antennas on towers, which connect to a local exchange or specialized mobile exhanges.

INTERNET BACKBONE

ISP

MOBILE TOWER

EXCHANGE

LOCAL ROADSIDE CABINET ROUTES CABLE INTERNET SIGNALS TO ISP

HOME AUTOMATION

This user has an app on their smartphone that controls the heating system at home (follow the green arrows). The thermostat is connected to the home's LAN and can send temperature details as well as receive commands.

CABLE COMPANY'S LOCAL CONTROL CENTER CONNECTS TO ISP

SMARTPHONE RECEIVES TEMPERATURE READING FROM THERMOSTAT

ROUTER

BROWSING THE WEB

This user is using their tablet to access a web page (see pp. 352-53) stored on a computer called a web server. The request goes via the user's ISP and is routed to the web server, which is at another ISP. The web server sends the web page back to the tablet (follow the blue arrows).

TABLET ACCESSES WORLD WIDE WEB

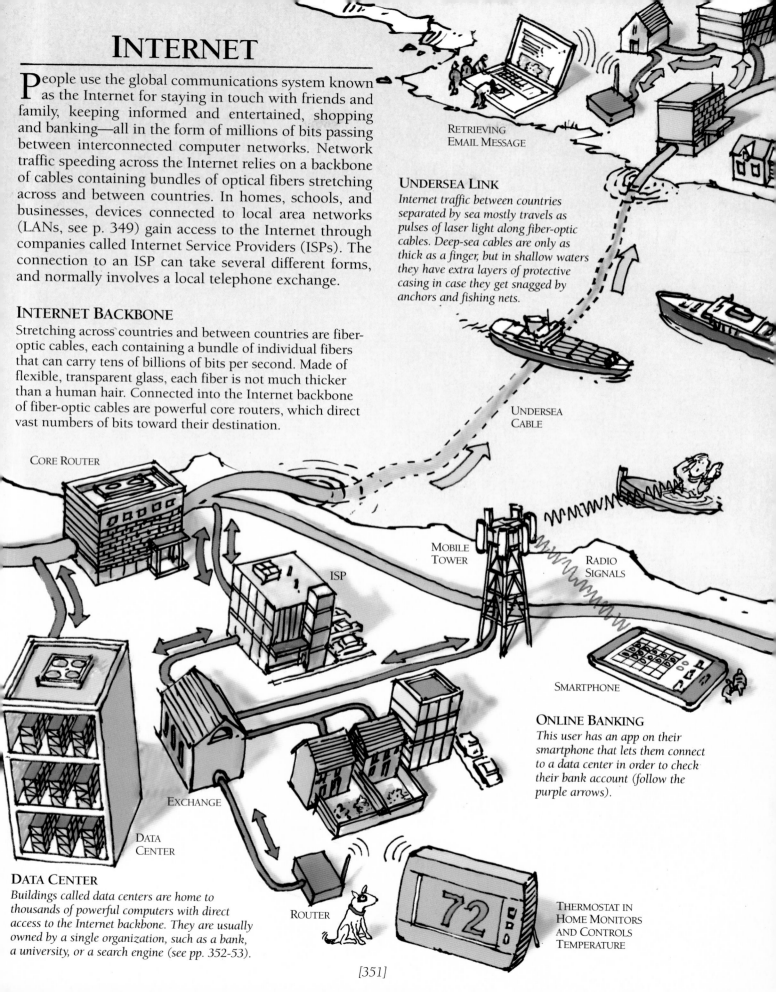

INTERNET

People use the global communications system known as the Internet for staying in touch with friends and family, keeping informed and entertained, shopping and banking—all in the form of millions of bits passing between interconnected computer networks. Network traffic speeding across the Internet relies on a backbone of cables containing bundles of optical fibers stretching across and between countries. In homes, schools, and businesses, devices connected to local area networks (LANs, see p. 349) gain access to the Internet through companies called Internet Service Providers (ISPs). The connection to an ISP can take several different forms, and normally involves a local telephone exchange.

INTERNET BACKBONE

Stretching across countries and between countries are fiber-optic cables, each containing a bundle of individual fibers that can carry tens of billions of bits per second. Made of flexible, transparent glass, each fiber is not much thicker than a human hair. Connected into the Internet backbone of fiber-optic cables are powerful core routers, which direct vast numbers of bits toward their destination.

RETRIEVING EMAIL MESSAGE

UNDERSEA LINK

Internet traffic between countries separated by sea mostly travels as pulses of laser light along fiber-optic cables. Deep-sea cables are only as thick as a finger, but in shallow waters they have extra layers of protective casing in case they get snagged by anchors and fishing nets.

UNDERSEA CABLE

CORE ROUTER

MOBILE TOWER

RADIO SIGNALS

ISP

SMARTPHONE

ONLINE BANKING

This user has an app on their smartphone that lets them connect to a data center in order to check their bank account (follow the purple arrows).

EXCHANGE

DATA CENTER

DATA CENTER

Buildings called data centers are home to thousands of powerful computers with direct access to the Internet backbone. They are usually owned by a single organization, such as a bank, a university, or a search engine (see pp. 352-53).

ROUTER

72

THERMOSTAT IN HOME MONITORS AND CONTROLS TEMPERATURE

WORLD WIDE WEB

The most common way to use the Internet is to run a program called a browser that can access pages of information stored on computers called servers. Each page contains links to other pages, forming a web of interconnected information—the World Wide Web. Billions of people follow these links to surf the Web for information, entertainment, and business. Some pages are written and uploaded to a server, where they remain, ready to be downloaded by a browser onto a user's computer or other Internet-connected device.

Other pages, such as search results and online bank statements, are produced on request, selecting and updating information that is relevant only to the user requesting them. On interactive pages, such as social media pages, users can modify the content. Every page has a unique address that identifies it—as does any other piece of information available on the Web, such as a digital image, sound, or video file. Each of these items is a resource, and its address (such as www.example.com) is called a uniform resource locator, or URL.

WI-FI CONNECTS LAPTOP TO ROUTER

SEARCHING THE WEB

The best way to find information on the Web is to use a search engine. Words typed into a form on the search engine's web page are sent to a data center (see p. 351), where the search engine company holds a vast index of web pages. The search engine finds pages containing the words being searched for, and sends the URLs of those pages back to the browser.

1. SEARCH TERMS
This user types the search term "mammoth fur science" into a form on the search engine web page.

2. SENDING THE REQUEST
The request is sent first to the router (see p. 349) and then across the Internet to a data center owned by the search engine company.

3. SEARCHING THE INDEX
At the data center, a computer scans an index of web pages, looking for "mammoth," "fur," and "science." The more often the words appear in a page, and the closer together they are, the more relevant the page is likely to be.

MAMMOTH LIST OF RESULTS

DATA CENTER

CLICKING ON A LINK

The search engine computer at the data center prepares a web page that contains the results of the search—a list of the web pages it has found that are relevant to the information the user is looking for. It sends the results page via the Internet back to the user's computer. Each result that appears on the list is accompanied by a link to its URL. Clicking on one of the links instructs the brower to download that particular web page.

4. REQUESTING A WEB PAGE
When the user clicks on a page's URL, the computer sends a request, via the router, across the Internet to the server where that web page is stored. Most servers are owned by an Internet Service Provider (ISP).

WEB SERVER,
OWNED BY
WISE OWLS INC.

SCIENTIST SCANS RARE SAMPLE OF
MAMMOTH FUR FOR WEB PAGE

5. SENDING THE WEB PAGE

One of the search engine results that looked promising to the user was a page written by a scientist who studies mammoth fur. The web server sends the page and the images it contains back to the user's computer, via the Internet.

WRITING WEB PAGES

Web pages are written in a computer language called hypertext markup language (HTML), which enables web designers to mark up, or style, how the text will look when it is displayed on a screen. HTML uses "tags" to mark up the text—for example, <p> to make new paragraphs, <img> to insert pictures, and <a> to insert links to other pages and resources such as images and videos. These links are called hyperlinks, and each hides a URL. When a web page is displayed in a browser window, clicking or tapping on a hyperlink causes the browser to download the linked resource. Text containing these hyperlinks is called hypertext.

HYPERLINKS DISPLAYED
IN COLOR AND
UNDERLINED

EACH IMAGE
HAS ITS
OWN URL

6. VIEWING THE WEB PAGE

When the web page and its images have been received, the browser displays them as a page. The page also contains links to other URLs for other pages, images, sounds, and videos on the fascinating topic of mammoth fur.

SATELLITE NAVIGATION

You can find out where you are, anywhere in the world, using satellite navigation. A receiving device, often installed in a ship or a car, picks up digital radio signals from navigation satellites orbiting Earth. Each satellite broadcasts a precise time and location signal. By comparing the signals from several satellites, the receiver can work out its own position. The position is then shown on a map, and can be tracked in real time, as the device moves. Smartphones can fulfill the same function, using antennas and microchips that detect the satellite signals, combined with maps stored in their memory or downloaded over the Internet.

SHOWING THE WAY

Smartphone apps can use satellite signals to display the user's location on a map. Software allows the user to key in their desired destination and receive turn-by-turn directions in order to reach it.

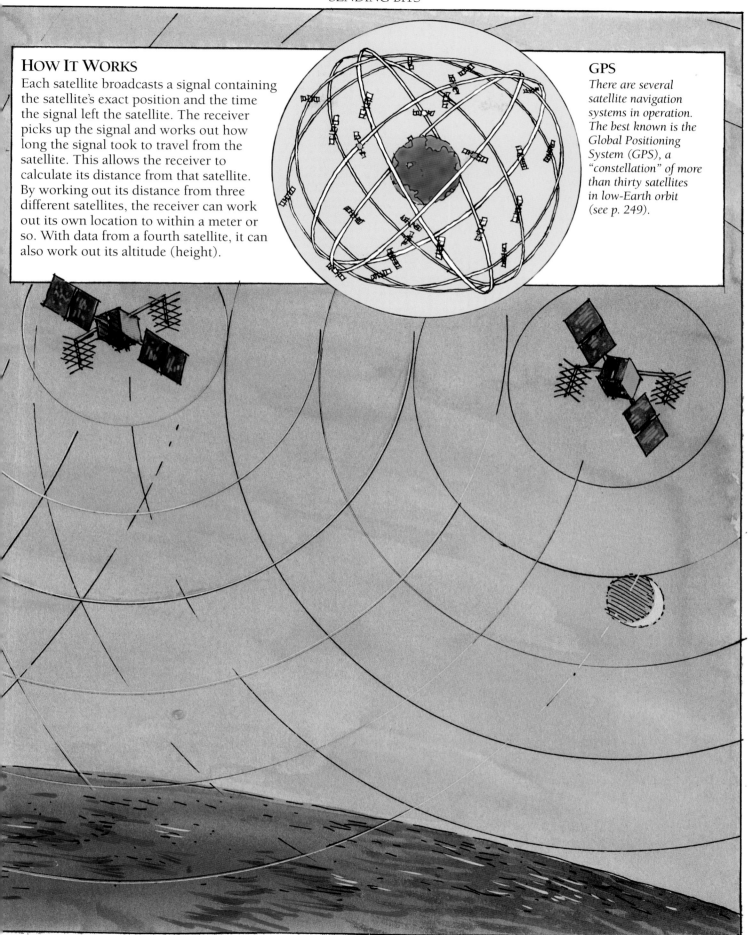

HOW IT WORKS

Each satellite broadcasts a signal containing the satellite's exact position and the time the signal left the satellite. The receiver picks up the signal and works out how long the signal took to travel from the satellite. This allows the receiver to calculate its distance from that satellite. By working out its distance from three different satellites, the receiver can work out its own location to within a meter or so. With data from a fourth satellite, it can also work out its altitude (height).

GPS

There are several satellite navigation systems in operation. The best known is the Global Positioning System (GPS), a "constellation" of more than thirty satellites in low-Earth orbit (see p. 249).

CHAPTER FIVE

"Well, here we go," said Bill, coaxing the reluctant mammoth away from a pile of discarded chocolate-coated apples and into a large building where workers were fastening the last of the smeared strips together. They had created a single, large piece of paper, which they then stretched between two rollers.

Pressed into the floor in the center of the space were four footprints, which to Mammoth's amazement precisely matched his own. No sooner had he placed his feet in them than two small orchestras complete with sheet music were rolled into position next to his ears. Mammoth was already beginning to feel a little claustrophobic, and when a large piece of machinery gently wrapped itself around his head, he let out an extraordinary wail.

At that very moment, the musicians began to play—
or more accurately to re-create—almost identical
trumpeting sounds. Then the paper began to roll past his
eyes, which made the individual smears blur together,
creating not only an amazing landscape but one which
seemed to be in motion. When Mammoth turned his head
to follow a particular sound, the scene shifted in exactly
that direction. Endless clumps of swamp grass swayed
gently in the breeze.

Most important, however, he thought he saw other
mammoths—lots of them. He couldn't believe his tear-filled
eyes. The years of loneliness were over. Solitary wandering
would be a thing of the past. As the sounds grew louder and
more wonderfully cacophonous, his head swung back and
forth to take it all in. Feeling a pleasant dizziness, he stood
still for a moment and noticed that one particularly
beautiful mammoth was approaching him.

USING BITS

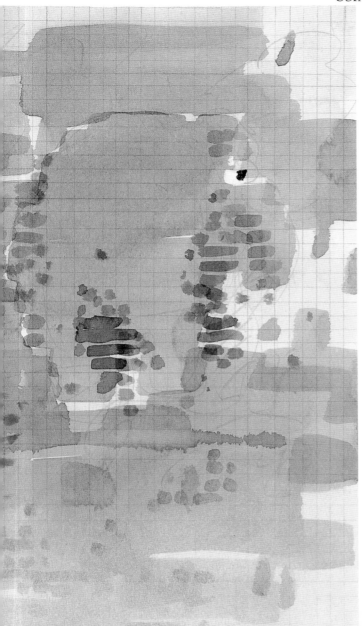

On its journey through the digital domain, the mammoth first saw personal details such as its dimensions, image, and sound changed into numbers. These were stored, then processed to produce new numbers, while yet more numbers arrived from elsewhere. The purpose of this number crunching now becomes clear as the bits representing the numbers are turned back into images and sounds so the mammoth can experience a virtual mammoth world. Aided by imperfect eyesight, and a little credulity, he sees and hears mammoths cavorting all around him.

The new friends are, in fact, near-replicas of himself. The original bits giving the mammoth's details have been processed to produce bits that form images of a variety of mammoths in motion. The sound bits have undergone processing to provide a vocabulary of calls. From the mammoth museum have come bits representing a typical mammoth landscape, and bits that give information on mammoth lifestyles so that the virtual mammoths will move and call realistically.

But for us, the digital domain becomes an actual reality as the bits that have been made by an input unit of a digital machine, communicated to the machine, stored in its memory, and processed by its processor, are changed back into forms that we can understand and use. The bits become words, numbers, images, sounds, or movements in output units such as printers, screens, loudspeakers, simulators, and robots.

NUMBERS AT WORK

Thus do numbers serve us. Digital machines have changed the world and the ways in which we live because almost everything can be represented by a string of numbers. Once something is in numerical form, the numbers can be easily and swiftly changed to represent actions that are difficult or impossible to achieve by mechanical means. Digital machines not only outstrip and outperform their mechanical forebears. They inspire new kinds of things, new things to do, and new ways in which things are to work.

He was helplessly in love. She was wearing a bow in her hair and a name tag. He was at some kind of mammoth software convention. And then he remembered that mammoths didn't attend conventions! They flouted them. But she came closer and raised her trunk to kiss him. This was too good to be true. He decided to stop thinking. He closed his eyes and raised his trunk to return the caress. He tasted . . . chocolate. Chocolate? His eyes suddenly flew open. All he saw were smears.

Not the little smears, but big smears. The kind of smears you get when you drag a drooling trunk across a piece of chocolate-covered paper. He was stunned. Then he was furious. He shook the contraption from his head. The orchestras took cover where they could. By the time Mammoth calmed down, he was devastated. He felt cheated. Humiliated. It had all been some kind of trick. "Not a trick," said Bill somewhat defensively. "Progress."

DIRECT OUTPUT

S equences of bits in the form of on-off electric pulses arrive at the output unit of a digital machine or system. If they are then arranged in a grid or array, bits representing an image or a character, such as a letter, form a pattern that reproduces the image or character. The bits go directly to a printer mechanism to be printed in this pattern. Bits representing characters also go directly to alphanumeric displays.

INCOMING BITS
(SEE P. 352)

INK-JET PRINTER

Also known as a bubble-jet printer, this printer contains a print head that moves back and forth across the sheet of paper, which moves up after each pass. The print head fires tiny jets of ink onto the paper to produce rows of dots that build up into images and characters. Each on-pulse (binary 1) fires the print head to ink a dot; an off-pulse (binary 0) does not fire the head.

PRINT HEAD

The head contains an ink chamber, and vertical rows of very fine nozzles that fire jets of quick-drying ink at the paper.

INK-JET
NOZZLES

CABLE BRINGING BITS
TO PRINT HEAD

PRINT JOBS

The computer processes the document to be printed and sends it, with information about paper size and number of copies, as a binary file called a print job. The print job can be sent along a USB cable (see p. 369) or over a network (see p. 349).

INK-JET NOZZLES

An enlarged view of the nozzles. Each one fires about 10,000 times a second.

INSIDE AN INK-JET

An ink-jet printer works by forming bubbles in the ink, hence its other name of bubble-jet printer.

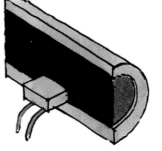

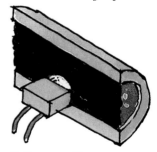

1 INK TUBE
Inside each nozzle of the print head is a tube containing a heating element. Ink is fed to it.

2 BUBBLE FORMS
A pulse of electricity heats up the element, instantly vaporizing some of the ink to form a bubble.

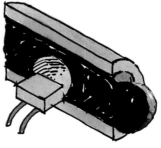

3 BUBBLE EXPANDS
The bubble grows rapidly as the heating continues, and begins to force some ink out of the tube.

4 TUBE FIRES
A jet of ink leaves the tube, and the heating stops. The bubble collapses, sucking in more ink.

COLOR PRINTER

Color ink-jet printers contain four separate print heads that fire jets of yellow, magenta, cyan and black inks at the paper. The colored dots merge to form a full-color picture (see pp. 185 and 216). Three eight-bit color numbers in the digital color signal (see p. 327) give the shade of each color to be printed, and the print head fires a varying number of separate small dots. A light shade results from a few small dots spaced out, and a heavy shade from lots of close-spaced dots. A color laser printer works in the same basic way, except that the paper makes four passes and the drum is fed with toner powder in the four different colors.

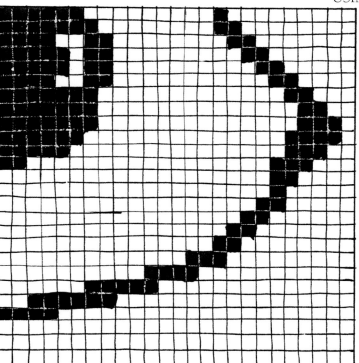

EYE TO EYE
A printed picture or document consists of a grid of rows of tiny dots printed one after another. From normal viewing distance, the dots merge together to form images and characters. This is a print of the eye scanned on page 325.

LASER PRINTER
The printing action of a laser printer is exactly the same as a photocopier (see p.260). The incoming on-off bits cause a laser or LED (see p. 273) to fire rows of on-off flashes of light at the printing drum and build up dots in the image.

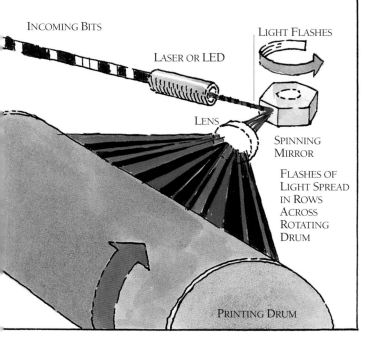

INCOMING BITS

LIGHT FLASHES

LASER OR LED

LENS

SPINNING MIRROR

FLASHES OF LIGHT SPREAD IN ROWS ACROSS ROTATING DRUM

PRINTING DRUM

ALPHANUMERIC DISPLAY
A simple display showing numbers, made up of the ten decimal numerals from 0 to 9, appears on many digital machines. These include the pocket calculator, digital watch, digital thermometer, and digital scales. Some machines, such as radio sets, also display letters of the alphabet. Each character (numeral or letter) is formed of several segments; numerals contain seven segments. On-off bits go directly to the segments in the display, and the on bits cause some of the segments to go dark. The resulting pattern of dark segments forms a number or letter.

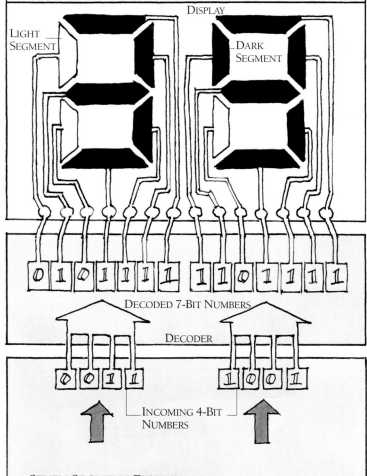

DISPLAY

LIGHT SEGMENT

DARK SEGMENT

DECODED 7-BIT NUMBERS

DECODER

INCOMING 4-BIT NUMBERS

SEVEN-SEGMENT DISPLAY
The segments in an alphanumeric display work with liquid crystals (see pp. 194-95). Natural light is either reflected from the display, or a light source is placed behind it. When an electric current goes to the segment, the liquid crystals inside it block the light so that the segment goes dark. Bits representing the characters to be displayed go to the display decoder. For numerals that have seven segments, these bits may be the four-bit binary equivalents of the decimal numerals to be displayed, so that 0011 arrives to become a 3, and 1001 arrives to become a 9. The decoder changes the four-bit numbers to seven-bit numbers, and each of the seven bits controls one of the segments. An on-bit (binary 1) causes a current to go to the segment and darken it; an off-bit (binary 0) stops the current and lightens the segment.

SIGNAL OUTPUT

DIGITAL-ANALOG CONVERTER (DAC)

Output units that produce sound through loudspeakers and earphones, as well as images on screens, do not work directly with bits. They require an analog electric signal with a varying voltage. The incoming digital sound and image signal, which consists of bits in the form of on-off electric pulses, first passes through a digital-analog converter. This is the reverse of the analog-digital converter that changes sound and light to bits when they enter the digital domain (see p. 322).

THREE-BIT CONVERTER

The converter shown here turns the three-bit digital signal 101 (on-off-on) into an analog signal of five volts. Only three bits are shown for simplicity. In practice, DACs convert digital signals of 8, 16, or more bits.

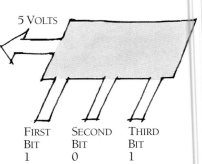

5 VOLTS

FIRST BIT 1 SECOND BIT 0 THIRD BIT 1

CURRENT OF 5 VOLTS EMERGES FROM DAC

INSIDE A DAC

The incoming bits go to separate wires connected to transistor switches. These control an electric current going to resistors that reduce the voltage of the current to a half, a quarter, an eighth, and so on.

4 VOLTS
RESISTOR REDUCES VOLTAGE TO A HALF

0 VOLTS
RESISTOR REDUCES VOLTAGE TO A QUARTER IF TRANSISTOR 2 IS ON

1 VOLT

TRANSISTOR 1 ON

TRANSISTOR 2 OFF

TRANSISTOR 3 ON

RESISTOR REDUCES VOLTAGE TO AN EIGHTH

8-VOLT CURRENT GOES TO ALL TRANSISTORS

1
FIRST BIT

0
SECOND BIT

1
THIRD BIT

DOUBLE, DOUBLE

Each resistor has double the value of the next resistor, which ensures that the value of the final voltage is equal to the binary number fed to the DAC: 101 in binary is 5 in decimal.

DIGITAL SOUND

Inside a digital device, such as a smartphone or tablet, sound is represented digitally, as a sequence of bits—thousands or millions of bits for every second of sound. To reproduce the sound, the bits pass through a DAC, which converts them to an analog signal. The signal passes to an amplifier, which makes the signal powerful enough to drive the speaker (see p. 232). The speaker produces a sound wave that is a copy of the analog signal.

INCOMING DIGITAL SIGNAL

DIGITAL-ANALOG CONVERTER

LOUDSPEAKER CONE

AMPLIFIED SIGNAL

ANALOG SOUND SIGNAL

AMPLIFIER

MAKING SOUND WAVES

The cone of a loudspeaker vibrates in step with the variations in the signal, producing a sound wave that is a copy of the analog signal.

SPEECH RECOGNITION

When you talk into a smartphone, its processor can work out the words you say by identifying the sounds that make up spoken language, which are known as phonemes. The sound of your voice is a mixture of many different frequencies (see p. 242), from low-pitched to high-pitched. Each phoneme has a different mixture of frequencies, so the processor identifies each phoneme by analyzing the sound wave your voice produces.

SMARTPHONE

SOUND WAVES TRAVEL THROUGH THE AIR

ELECTRICAL SIGNAL

SPECTROGRAM

LONGER WAVES ARE LOW FREQUENCY

SHORTER WAVES ARE HIGH FREQUENCY

1 BREAKING IT DOWN

The phone's microphone captures the sound of your voice as an electrical signal, which is a precise copy of the sound wave. The processor breaks down the signal into its various frequencies, producing a pattern called a spectrogram, which has low frequencies at the bottom and high frequencies at the top. Different phonemes produce different patterns on the spectrogram. As each phoneme is spoken, the mixture of frequencies changes, and so does the spectogram.

PHONEMES

The smartphone compares the spectrogram of the incoming sound with examples of each of the prerecorded phonemes stored in the phone's memory. The range of phonemes depends on which language is being used—for example, English has 44.

36

CHANGING PATTERNS

Phonemes are produced by closing or opening your lips or the back of your throat, or by pushing your tongue against your teeth or the roof of your mouth. Each action dramatically changes the mixture of sounds that make up your speech.

FINDING A MATCH

The smartphone's processor identifies which phoneme is being spoken at any moment.

SILENCE IN BETWEEN WORDS

3 PHRASES AND SENTENCES

Recognizing speech is a difficult process—not least because some words sound the same but have very different meanings. Once the phone's processor has identified which phonemes have been spoken, a program called a language model uses the rules of grammar to analyze each sequence of words, to help be more certain which words have actually been spoken. How the processor responds depends on whether the speech is a voice command, such as "Phone Mom," dictation for a text message or email, or a question—in which case the phone will have to connect to the Internet to find an answer.

2 RECONSTRUCTING THE WORDS

The processor connects the phonemes together one after the other, to reconstruct the words that have been spoken. The words can now be represented as sequences of bits inside the phone, just as they would be if they had been typed in on a keyboard (see p. 317).

VIRTUAL REALITY

The one way in which you can enter a digital domain is to put on a virtual reality headset. You find yourself in a world created by the computer. Objects are moving all around you, and you can hear their sounds. As you move your head, the scene and sounds move too, just as if you were actually there and looking around, up, or down. In fact, you are looking at two small screens and listening to earphones. The computer connected to the headset is able to react to your movements because the headset contains a sensor that detects your head movements.

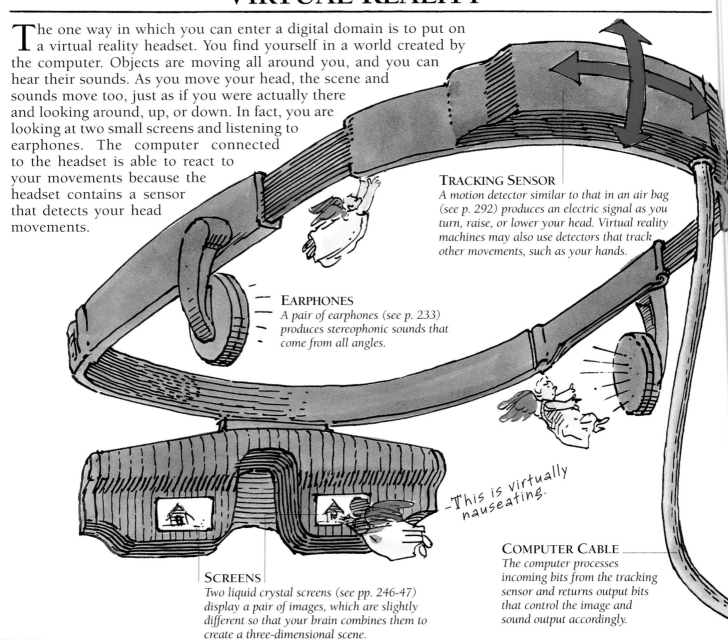

TRACKING SENSOR
A motion detector similar to that in an air bag (see p. 292) produces an electric signal as you turn, raise, or lower your head. Virtual reality machines may also use detectors that track other movements, such as your hands.

EARPHONES
A pair of earphones (see p. 233) produces stereophonic sounds that come from all angles.

—This is virtually nauseating.

COMPUTER CABLE
The computer processes incoming bits from the tracking sensor and returns output bits that control the image and sound output accordingly.

SCREENS
Two liquid crystal screens (see pp. 246-47) display a pair of images, which are slightly different so that your brain combines them to create a three-dimensional scene.

1 LOOKING AHEAD
You see a three-dimensional view of a doghouse as the pair of screens display two images of the doghouse.

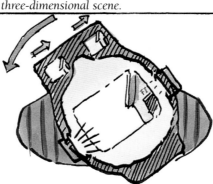

2 LOOKING AROUND
You hear a dog barking in your left ear. As you turn your head toward it, the images shift to the right.

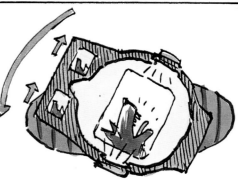

3 LOOKING LEFT
The dog appears, and the barking sound is now in front as sounds come from both earphones.

FLIGHT SIMULATOR

Virtual reality is a valuable way of training aircraft pilots. A flight simulator contains a mock-up of the aircraft flight deck. The pilot sits at the controls and through the windows sees a real airport and moving pictures of scenes that occur during takeoff, flight, and landing. The pictures are generated by a powerful computer connected to the controls. As the pilot handles the controls, the computer processes the operations and sends output bits back to the simulator. These move the picture, vary the instrument displays, sound warnings, and tilt the flight deck exactly as if the aircraft were flying. The computer can switch to night landings or foggy weather, or conditions that require an emergency landing such as an engine failure. It can also record a "flight" and replay it so that the pilot and instructor can go back over the training exercise.

PROJECTORS
High-quality projectors throw adjacent sections of a wide, color, computer-generated picture onto a curved screen that extends around the flight deck. Half of the screen can be seen here with two of the three projectors working.

CURVED MIRROR
The pilot looks through the windows of the flight deck at a wide, curved mirror that extends around the windows. The mirror reflects the back-projected picture on the screen. This optical system makes the image appear to be a long way off. Half of the mirror is shown here.

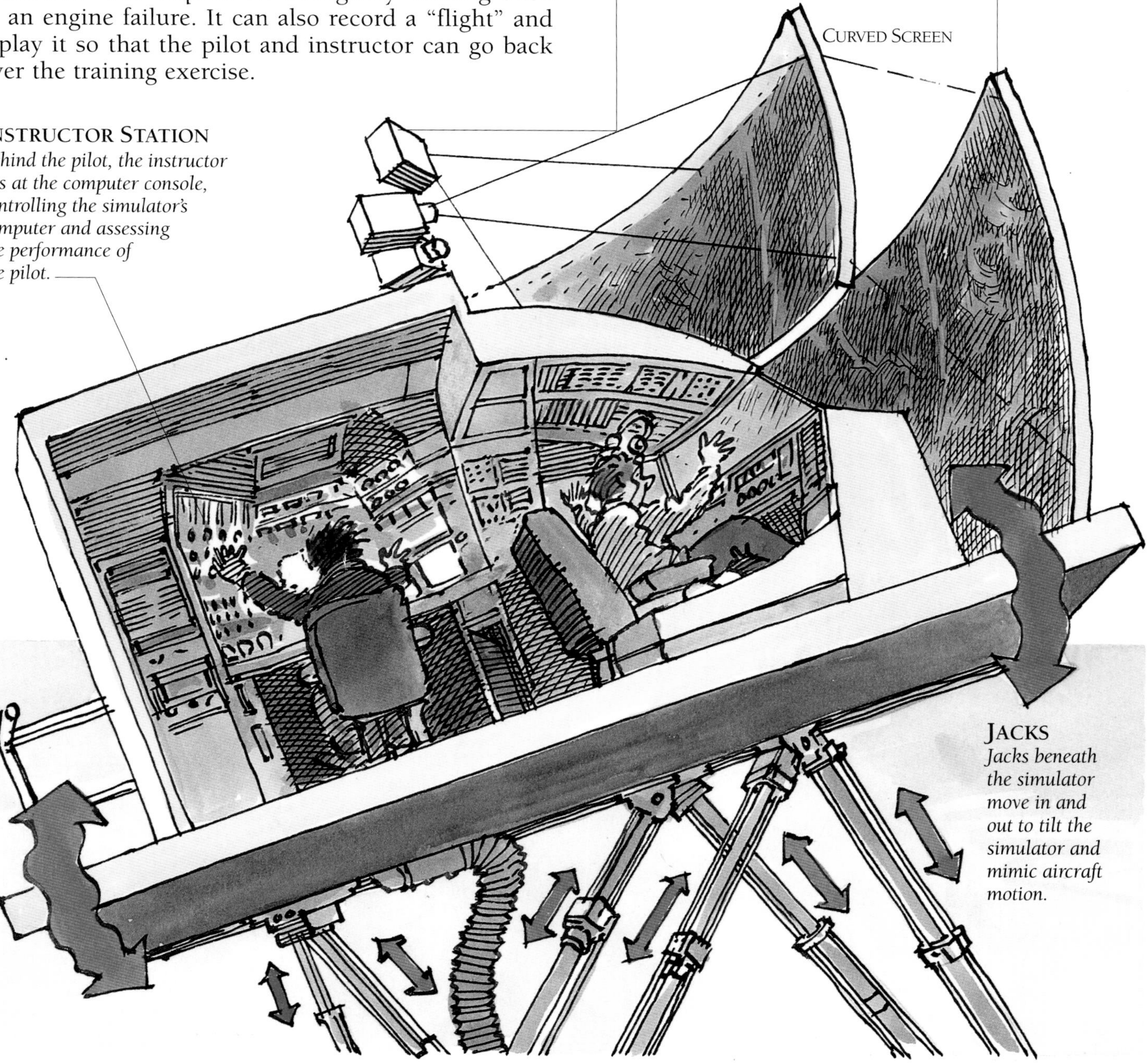

CURVED SCREEN

INSTRUCTOR STATION
Behind the pilot, the instructor sits at the computer console, controlling the simulator's computer and assessing the performance of the pilot.

JACKS
Jacks beneath the simulator move in and out to tilt the simulator and mimic aircraft motion.

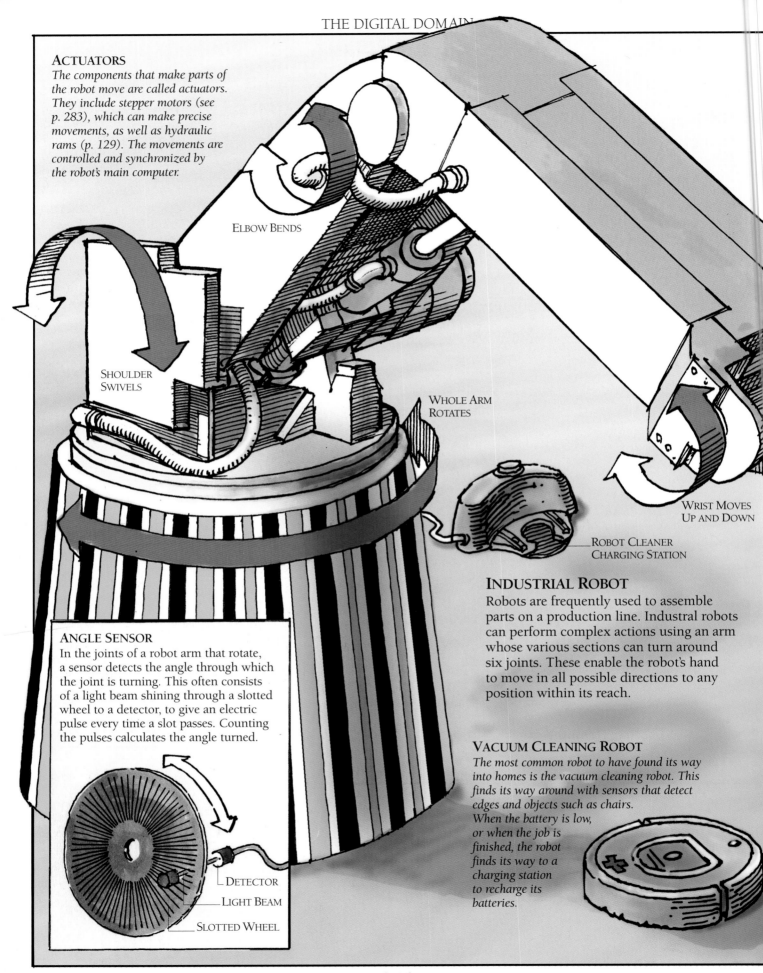

ACTUATORS

The components that make parts of the robot move are called actuators. They include stepper motors (see p. 283), which can make precise movements, as well as hydraulic rams (p. 129). The movements are controlled and synchronized by the robot's main computer.

ELBOW BENDS

SHOULDER SWIVELS

WHOLE ARM ROTATES

WRIST MOVES UP AND DOWN

ROBOT CLEANER CHARGING STATION

ANGLE SENSOR

In the joints of a robot arm that rotate, a sensor detects the angle through which the joint is turning. This often consists of a light beam shining through a slotted wheel to a detector, to give an electric pulse every time a slot passes. Counting the pulses calculates the angle turned.

DETECTOR

LIGHT BEAM

SLOTTED WHEEL

INDUSTRIAL ROBOT

Robots are frequently used to assemble parts on a production line. Industral robots can perform complex actions using an arm whose various sections can turn around six joints. These enable the robot's hand to move in all possible directions to any position within its reach.

VACUUM CLEANING ROBOT

The most common robot to have found its way into homes is the vacuum cleaning robot. This finds its way around with sensors that detect edges and objects such as chairs. When the battery is low, or when the job is finished, the robot finds its way to a charging station to recharge its batteries.

ROBOT

The robot is the ultimate machine, able to carry out a wide range of physical tasks. A sophisticated computer directs the movements of the robot's arms, legs, or other appendages, sending output bits to electric or hydraulic motors that move the joints by precise amounts. The computer can be programmed with a particular set of movements that the robot can repeat exactly over and over again without ever getting tired. Therefore it is an ideal machine for factory work, especially on assembly lines producing complicated machines such as cars. Some robots can handle parts, fitting them in place precisely, while other robots can hold and operate tools such as welding torches and paint sprayers. Robots are used in many other applications, including carrying out scientific surveys in dangerous environments, picking and packing products in warehouses, and helping to care for elderly patients in hospitals or at home. Walking on two legs (bipedalism) is a real challenge for a robot. It is achieved with accelerometers (see p. 241) and pressure sensors constantly feeding back to a robot's computer, which rapidly adjusts joints in its legs to keep its balance. Some robots can recognize certain objects and faces, thanks to onboard video cameras and sophisticated image-recognition software. As computing power increases, artificial intelligence is allowing some robots to become more and more autonomous.

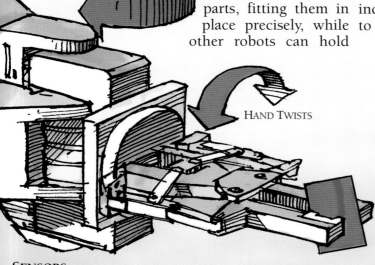

FOREARM ROTATES

HAND TWISTS

SENSORS

Sensors relay information back to the robot's main computer. Pressure sensors enable the computer to work out if it has picked up an object, and to adjust its grasp to make sure that it doesn't break an object it is holding.

ROBOT VISION

Video cameras provide a robot with vision, which gives useful feedback to help it accomplish tasks. An onboard computer runs image-recognition software, which can help identify things to avoid or to aim for. For example, a football-playing robot can identify the ball, the goal, and other players. With two video cameras, set slightly apart like human eyes, a robot acquires a sense of depth to help it accurately work out distances—important when kicking a ball to score a goal or to pass to a teammate.

BIPEDAL HUMANOID ROBOT

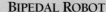

BIPEDAL ROBOT

Bipedal robots can be programmed to play football, interacting autonomously with other robot team members, tackling, and kicking the ball—but rarely breaking the rules of the game.

COMPUTER

A computer—desktop, laptop, tablet, or smartphone—is the ultimate digital device. It can communicate quickly with other digital devices and link to the Internet, using Wi-Fi, Bluetooth, and network cables. A computer's mainboard contains a powerful processor chip as well as large amounts of RAM to run the software applications. Software and data are stored on a hard disk or solid state drive, while additional storage can be connected in the form of flash drives and external hard disks. Computers have many different forms of input and output. Most of these "peripherals" connect via USB cables.

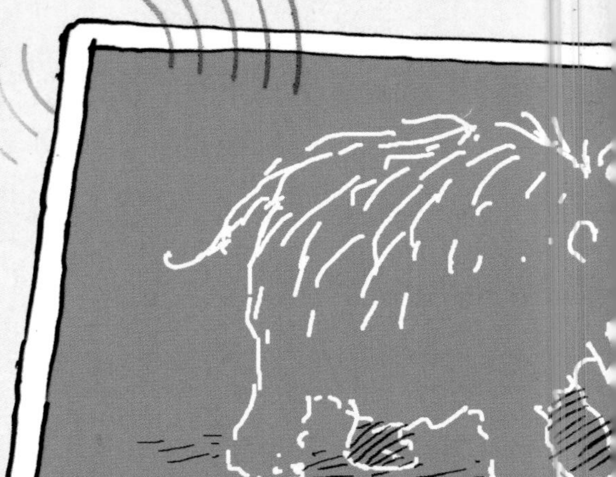

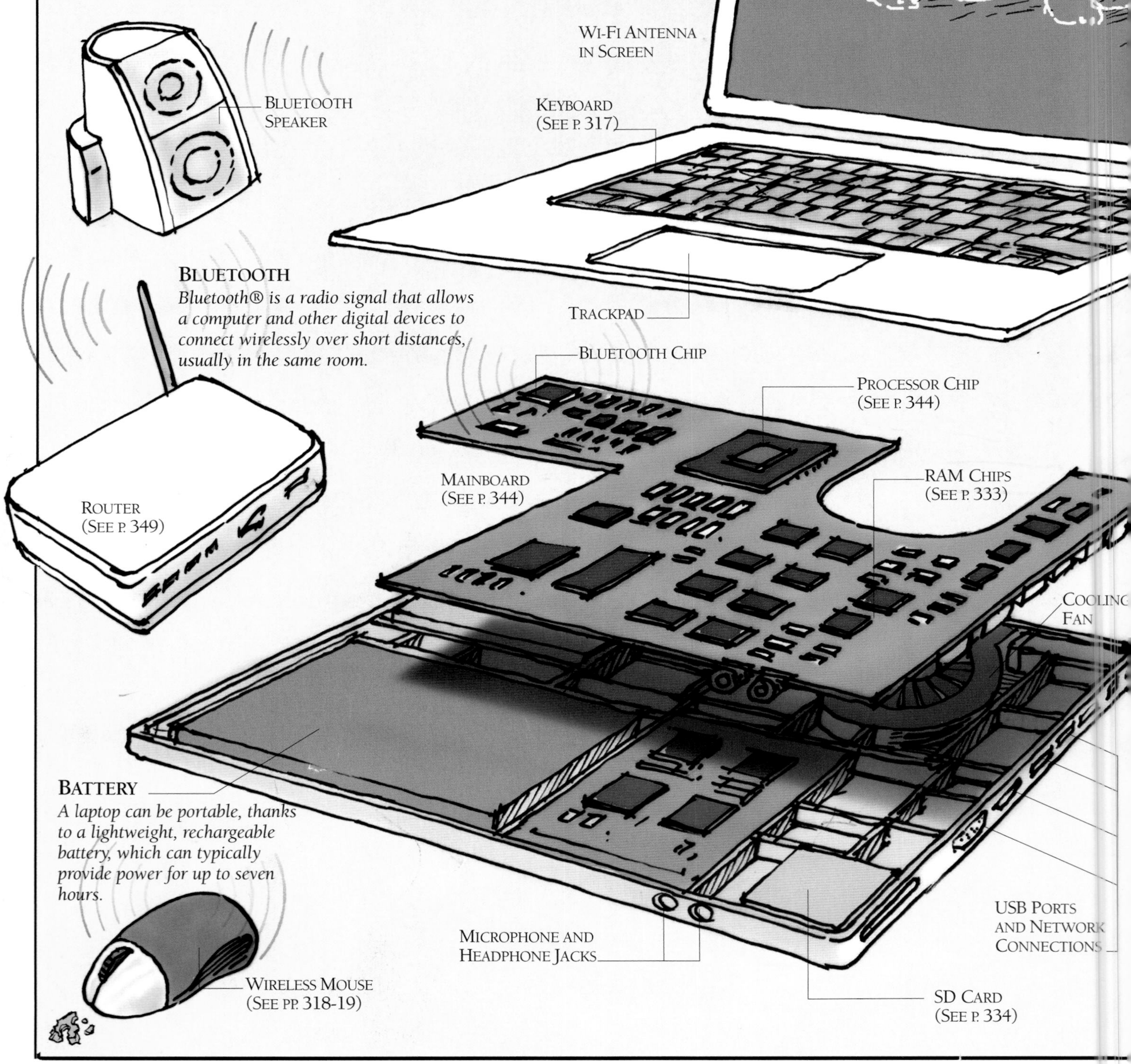

WI-FI ANTENNA
IN SCREEN

BLUETOOTH
SPEAKER

KEYBOARD
(SEE P. 317)

TRACKPAD

BLUETOOTH

Bluetooth® is a radio signal that allows a computer and other digital devices to connect wirelessly over short distances, usually in the same room.

BLUETOOTH CHIP

PROCESSOR CHIP
(SEE P. 344)

MAINBOARD
(SEE P. 344)

RAM CHIPS
(SEE P. 333)

ROUTER
(SEE P. 349)

COOLING
FAN

BATTERY

A laptop can be portable, thanks to a lightweight, rechargeable battery, which can typically provide power for up to seven hours.

MICROPHONE AND
HEADPHONE JACKS

USB PORTS
AND NETWORK
CONNECTIONS

WIRELESS MOUSE
(SEE PP. 318-19)

SD CARD
(SEE P. 334)

GETTING CONNECTED

The most common way to connect peripherals such as external storage devices, printers, and digital cameras is to use a USB cable. A computer acts as a USB hub, which means it can connect several USB devices at the same time. USB stands for "universal serial bus." A serial connection is one in which the binary digits are transferred one-by-one, but nevertheless USB cables can carry billions of binary digits (gigabits, or Gb) every second. There are several standard fittings, which allow different devices to connect together. They are known as "A," "B," or "C" fittings.

MINI USB B

USB A

USB B

USB C

PRINTER

Modern printers can also function as scanners (see pp. 326-27). They typically connect to a computer via USB, or wirelessly across a local network (see p. 349).

USB C

MULTIFUNCTION PRINTER

USB FLASH DRIVE
(SEE P. 334)

DIGITAL CAMERA
(SEE PP. 204-5)

USB A

EXTERNAL HARD DRIVE
(SEE P. 333)

CONNECTING PERIPHERALS

Input and output peripherals can be connected via ports on the edge of the mainboard. This is one way, for example, of transferring photographs from a digital camera to a computer.

USB A TO
USB B CABLE

MIDI KEYBOARD
(SEE P. 316)

SUPERMARKET

Every time you make a purchase at a supermarket checkout, you come into contact with a huge digital system. The supermarket company uses a vast computer network built around the central computer at the head office. This communicates to a ring of depots in different locations. Each depot computer links in turn to a ring of individual stores. Each store contains an in-store computer that is connected to the computer in each checkout. The central computer is also linked to a network of bank computers.

IN-STORE COMPUTER
Digital signals pass to and from the central computer via the in-store computer. Every night, this updates each checkout computer with price changes and new products.

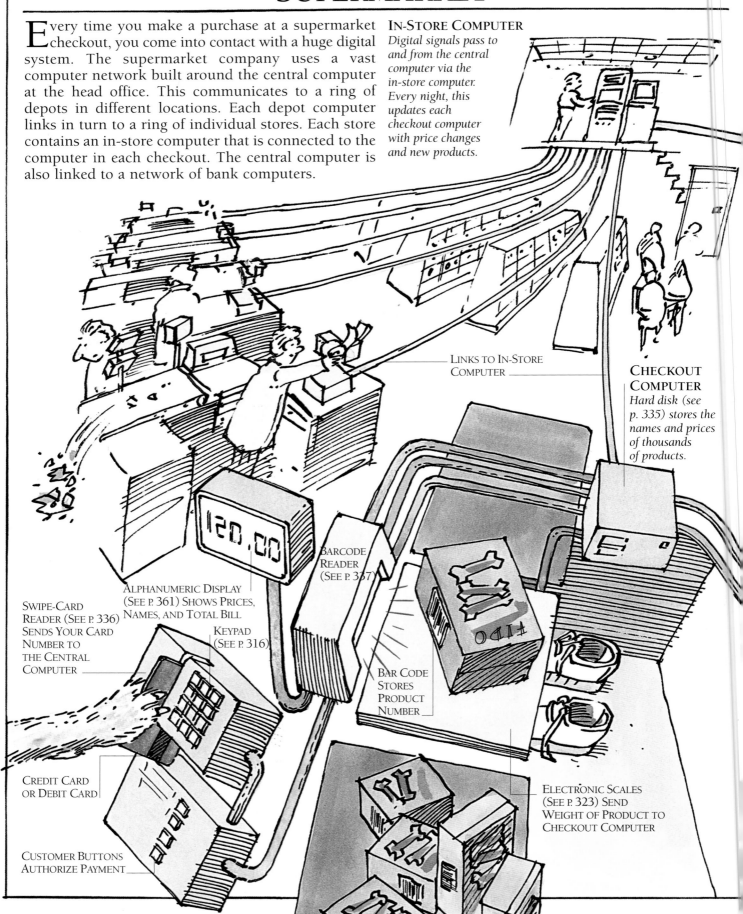

LINKS TO IN-STORE COMPUTER

CHECKOUT COMPUTER
Hard disk (see p. 335) stores the names and prices of thousands of products.

BARCODE READER (SEE P. 357)

ALPHANUMERIC DISPLAY (SEE P. 361) SHOWS PRICES, NAMES, AND TOTAL BILL

SWIPE-CARD READER (SEE P. 336) SENDS YOUR CARD NUMBER TO THE CENTRAL COMPUTER

KEYPAD (SEE P. 316)

BAR CODE STORES PRODUCT NUMBER

CREDIT CARD OR DEBIT CARD

CUSTOMER BUTTONS AUTHORIZE PAYMENT

ELECTRONIC SCALES (SEE P. 323) SEND WEIGHT OF PRODUCT TO CHECKOUT COMPUTER

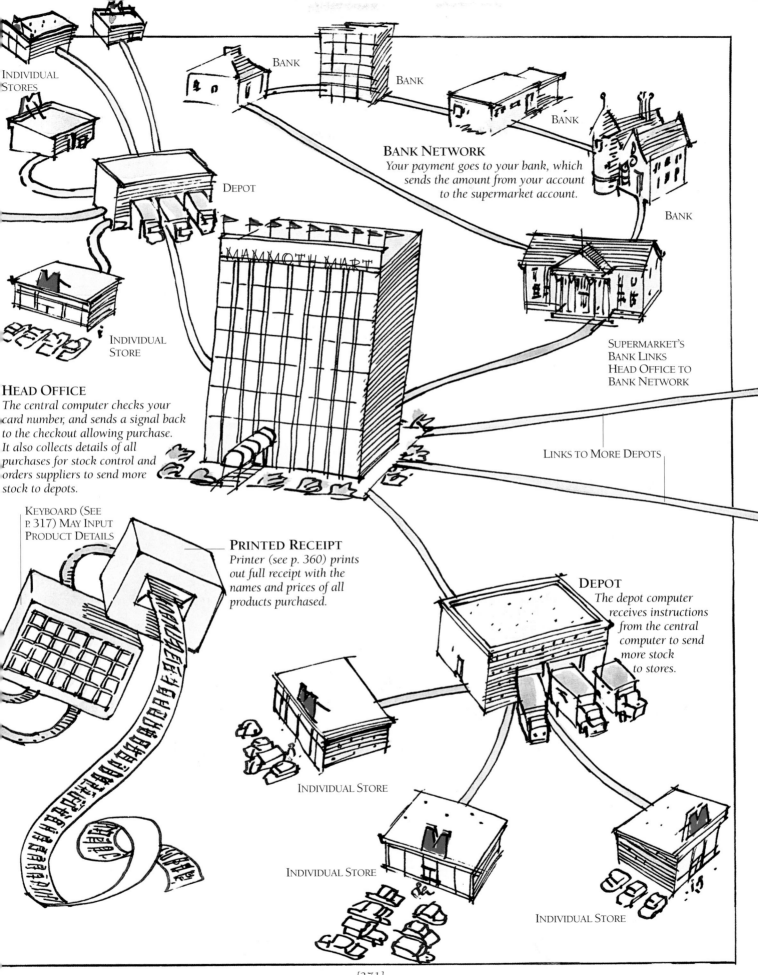

INDIVIDUAL
STORES

BANK

BANK

DEPOT

BANK

BANK NETWORK
*Your payment goes to your bank, which
sends the amount from your account
to the supermarket account.*

BANK

INDIVIDUAL
STORE

HEAD OFFICE
*The central computer checks your
card number, and sends a signal back
to the checkout allowing purchase.
It also collects details of all
purchases for stock control and
orders suppliers to send more
stock to depots.*

SUPERMARKET'S
BANK LINKS
HEAD OFFICE TO
BANK NETWORK

LINKS TO MORE DEPOTS

KEYBOARD (SEE
P. 317) MAY INPUT
PRODUCT DETAILS

PRINTED RECEIPT
*Printer (see p. 360) prints
out full receipt with the
names and prices of all
products purchased.*

DEPOT
*The depot computer
receives instructions
from the central
computer to send
more stock
to stores.*

INDIVIDUAL STORE

INDIVIDUAL STORE

INDIVIDUAL STORE

EPILOGUE

While Mammoth had been impressed by much of the digital domain, there was also plenty about it that left him feeling uncomfortable. In the end, it was just too much, too big, too fast, and too unfamiliar. Mammoths, after all, had never really embraced the concept of progress, and this one wasn't going to start now. In fact, as he left the digital domain, he had no intention of ever returning. Bill, smiling down from the top of the wall, knew differently. While it was true that the mammoth hadn't developed much of an appreciation for digital technology and all that it could complicate, he had developed a real taste for pumpkin pie and apples smeared in chocolate. These were a pleasant and entirely compatible replacement for swamp grass, which would soon be extinct. And Bill was the only supplier for miles and miles.

EUREKA!

THE INVENTION OF MACHINES

THE INCLINED PLANE

People have to eat to live and, necessity being ever the mother of invention, the very first machines to be invented were the tools used by prehistoric people in hunting and gathering their food. Stones crudely chipped to form tools date back more than 3 million years, and stone axes and spearheads litter archaeological sites down to the dawn of civilization. In cutting tools, the inclined plane became the first principle of technology to be put to work. On a larger scale, it may have enabled people to build at least one of the Seven Wonders of the World—the Great Pyramid. This was built in Egypt in 2600 BCE using high earth ramps to raise great stone blocks into position.

THE PLOW

The plow was invented in the Middle East in about 3500 BCE. At first, it was little more than a digging stick drawn by a person or an ox, but this primitive plow enabled people to dig deeper than before. Plants could put down stronger roots in plowed soil, increasing crop yields and enabling farmers to produce a surplus of food. The plow thus freed some people from the necessity of growing their food.

LOCKS

Locks existed in Ancient Egypt, and they made use of pins in the same way as the cylinder lock. The application of the inclined plane to the key, made by Linus Yale in the United States in 1848, is one of those fundamental inventions that long outlive their maker, and the cylinder lock is still often called a Yale lock. The lever lock dates from 1778 and was invented by British engineer Robert Barron. The design resulted from a need to prevent burglars from taking wax impressions inside locks and then making keys from them, and it too proved to be a fundamental advance.

THE ZIPPER

The zipper took quite a time to make its mark. It was invented by American engineer Whitcomb Judson in 1891, not in its present form as a clothes fastener, but as a device to do up boots. It did not take off until 1918, when the US Navy realized that Judson's invention would make an ideal fastener for flying suits. The name zipper, coined in 1926, clinched its success.

THE CAN OPENER

Methods of preserving food in sealed containers were invented in the early 1800s, at first using glass jars and then tin cans. The cans were ideal for transporting food, but opening them could be a problem. At first, a hammer and chisel—a crude use of the inclined plane—had to serve. Claw-like devices and levered blades were then devised to open cans, not without some

danger to the user. The safe and simple can openers that we have today were not invented until the 1930s, more than a century after the appearance of the tin can.

LEVERS

Levers also originated in ancient times in devices such as hoes, oars, and slings. People realized intuitively that levers could aid their muscle power, but it took a genius to explain how levers work. The genius was the Ancient Greek scientist Archimedes (287–212 BCE), who first defined the principle of levers. He illustrated it with the famous adage "Give me a place to stand and I will move the Earth"—meaning that if he had a lever sufficiently long, he could shift the Earth by his own efforts.

The formulation of the principle of levers was a landmark in the development of science and technology. Archimedes' insight explained not only levers, because the same principle lies behind the inclined plane, gears and belts, pulleys, and screws. Furthermore, Archimedes showed that by making observations and experiments, it was possible to deduce the basic principles that explain why things work.

WEIGHING MACHINES

The first device to make precise use of levers was invented long before Archimedes' time. This was the balance or scales used for weighing, which dates back from 3500 BCE. It may seem odd that a precision instrument was required so long ago; however, what had to be weighed was no ordinary material—it was gold. Gold dust was used as currency in the ancient civilizations of the Middle East, and amounts of it had to be weighed very precisely in order to assess their value.

KEYBOARD MACHINES

The piano was invented in Italy in 1709 by Bartolomeo Christofori, who sought a way of varying the volume of a keyboard by using levers to strike the strings with different amounts of force. His success is reflected in the instrument's name: the pianoforte or "soft-loud." The lever system was later improved to increase the response of the piano, resulting in the highly expressive instrument that affected the whole course of music.

THE WHEEL AND AXLE

The development of mechanical power has its origins in the wheel and axle. The first machines to make use of this device may well have been the windlass and the winch. The Greek physician Hippocrates, who was born in 460 BCE, employed a windlass to stretch the limbs of his patients, a treatment uncomfortably like the rack of medieval torture chambers. Winches have been used to draw water from wells for many centuries.

THE WATERWHEEL AND WINDMILL

The waterwheel dates back to Greece in about 100 BCE, and it was developed by the Romans to power water mills grinding corn. The wheel had horizontal blades angled so that a stream of falling water could turn the wheel. Its advantage was that the vertical shaft of the wheel drove the horizontal grindstone directly. The bad news was that it required fast-flowing water and produced little power. The vertical waterwheel, first described by a Roman writer in about 15 BCE, is far more practical and it soon replaced the Greek wheel.

Rather like the first waterwheel, the first windmill was powered by a horizontal wheel bearing vertical sails. It was invented in Iran in about 640 CE. The vertical windmill, also more practical, was invented in Europe in about 1170.

TURBINES

Modern turbines are a product of the Industrial Revolution, when the demand for power soared as factories developed. Engineers investigated blade design,

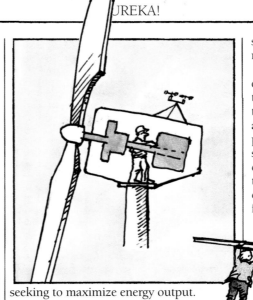

seeking to maximize energy output. The Francis turbine, invented by James Francis in 1850 and now common in power stations, was literally a product of lateral thinking because Francis made the water flow inward instead of outward.

GEARS AND BELTS

Belts are simple devices, seen in the chains of buckets that lifted water in ancient times. The basic forms of gears were known by the first century CE. An extraordinary early application of gears is the Antikythera mechanism, a mechanical calendar made in Greece in about 100 BCE and recovered from a wreck sunk off the Greek island of Antikythera. This machine had 25 bronze gear wheels forming a complex train of gears that could move pointers to indicate the future positions of the sun and moon as well as the times when certain stars would rise or set.

CLOCKS

A rack-and-pinion gear was used in a water clock built by the Greek inventor Ctesibius in about 250 BCE. The water clock was an ancient device in which water dropped at a constant rate into a container, the level of the water indicating the time. Ctesibius improved it by having a float raise a rack that turned a pinion connected to a pointer on a drum. The pointer turned to indicate the time in the

same way as the hour hand of a mechanical clock.

The oldest surviving mechanical clocks date from the late 1300s. Gears transmitted the constant movement of a regulator to the hands or to a bell. A good regulator appeared only with the discovery of the pendulum in 1581 by the great Italian scientist Galileo, who timed a swinging chandelier with his pulse and realized that the time taken for each swing was always constant. Even so, it took nearly a century for the first pendulum clocks to appear.

THE EPICYCLIC GEAR

The sun-and-planet or epicyclic gear is of much more recent origin than other types. It was invented in 1781 by the great British engineer James Watt, who is best known for improving the steam engine. Watt needed a device to turn the reciprocating motion of the piston of his steam engine into rotary motion, but he could not use the crank because someone else had patent protection on it. Watt's alternative was the epicyclic gear, now found in salad spinners, automatic transmissions, and many other devices.

THE DIFFERENTIAL

This first appeared in the "south-pointing carriage" invented in China in the third century CE. The two-wheeled carriage was surmounted by a figure that always pointed south, no matter how the carriage turned as it moved. The figure was set to south, and then a differential driven by the wheels turned the figure in the opposite direction from the carriage so that it still pointed south.

Such a machine must have appeared magical to the people of the time. However, calculations show that the mechanism could not have been sufficiently precise for the figure to point south for long. Within 3 miles (5 km) it could well have been pointing north instead!

CAMS AND CRANKS

Cams and cranks are old devices too— the cam appearing in the drop hammer and the crank in a winding handle. Their application in the sewing machine was developed during the early 1800s, the first successful sewing machine being produced in the United States by Isaac Singer in 1851. The four-stroke internal combustion engine, which similarly depends on the controlling movement of cams and cranks, was first put to use in the motorcar by Karl Benz in 1885. These two machines are still with us in their basic form today, along with their inventors' names.

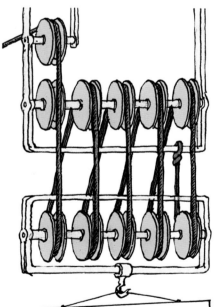

PULLEYS

Simple cranes using single pulley wheels were invented some 3,000 years ago, and compound pulleys with several wheels date back to about the 400s BCE. Archimedes is said to have invented a compound pulley that was able to haul a ship ashore. The shadoof, a counter-weighted lifting machine, is also of ancient origin.

THE ELEVATOR AND ESCALATOR

The elevator is a relatively recent invention, the reason being that buildings had to reach quite a height before they became necessary. Although elevators are intended for public use, the very first elevator had exactly the opposite purpose. It was built in 1743 at the Palace of Versailles for the French king Louis XV. Counterbalanced by weights and operated by hand, the elevator carried the king in total privacy from one floor to another.

The modern safety elevator is the invention of the American engineer Elisha Otis, who dramatically demonstrated its effectiveness in 1854. He ordered the rope of the elevator carrying himself to be cut. The emergency braking system was automatically activated, and the elevator did not fall.

Escalators date from the 1890s. The first models were basically moving belts and had no steps, so could only carry people up or down a gentle incline.

SCREWS

The screw is yet another machine associated with Archimedes, for the earliest known is the water-lifting auger know as Archimedes' screw. However, it may well have been invented before his time. The screw press, which contains the form of screw used in nuts and bolts, was first described by Hero of Alexandria.

Metal screws were used as a superior alternative to nails in 1556, when the German mining engineer Agricola described how to screw leather to wood to make durable bellows. The screwdriver, however, did not follow until 1780.

THE COMBINE HARVESTER

The combine harvester is the most important invention in farming since the plow, and a modern harvester makes use of several augers that work in exactly the same way as Archimedes' screw. The first combine harvester was built in 1835 by combining a horse-drawn reaper and a threshing machine. It took a century to develop the harvester into an effective self-powered machine.

THE MICROMETER

This important device based on the screw was invented in 1772 by James Watt. Watt's micrometer worked in much the same way as the modern micrometer, and was accurate to one-thousandth of an inch (a fiftieth of a millimeter).

ROTATING WHEELS

Ancient peoples could easily move heavy loads by rolling them on logs, and one would expect that the wheel developed in this way. But this is not the case. Unlike a roller, a wheel requires an axle on which to turn and so the potter's wheel was the first true wheel. It was invented in the Middle East in about 3500 BCE. From the potter's wheel, the wheel was soon developed for transport.

THE BICYCLE

The first bicycles were pushed along by the feet and not pedaled. They were novelties rather than a serious means of transport, and were known as hobby-horses. Kirkpatrick Macmillan, a blacksmith, invented the pedal-operated bicycle in Britain in 1839. Raising the feet from the ground to turn the pedals required the rider to make use of precession to balance.

GYROCOMPASS

The inherent stability or gyroscopic inertia of devices such as spinning tops has been known for centuries, but the development of the gyroscope in machines is more recent. Its most important application, the gyrocompass, was invented by American Elmer Sperry and first demonstrated on a US Navy ship in 1911.

SPRINGS

Springs are also of ancient origin, being used in early locks. Metal springs date from the 1500s, when leaf springs were invented to provide a primitive suspension for road carriages. Springs did not become common until two centuries later, when coil springs were invented.

SPRING BALANCE AND HAIRSPRING

The principle behind the spring balance—that the extension of a spring is proportional to the force acting on it—was discovered by the English scientist Robert Hooke in 1678 and is known as Hooke's Law. Hooke also invented the spiral spring known as a hairspring, which is used as a regulator in mechanical watches and which made portable timepieces possible.

FRICTION

People have been making use of friction ever since they first set foot on the ground, and the first friction devices to pound grain into flour date back to the beginnings of civilization.

THE PARACHUTE

This was one of several inventions that were forecast by Leonardo da Vinci, who drew one in 1485. Understandably, neither Leonardo nor anyone else was very keen to try out the idea in practice. However, there was little need for parachutes until the first balloons took to the air three centuries later. The first parachute descent proper took place in 1797, when the French balloonist André Garnerin successfully dropped 2,230 feet (680 meters). Early parachutes were fashioned like huge parasols and similarly named, being proof against a *chute* or fall rather than the sun.

DRILLING MACHINES

Drilling, which is basically pounding or grinding, is a surprisingly old activity. The Chinese drilled oil wells some hundreds of yards or meters deep as early as the third century BCE. They dropped a metal drilling tool into the hole to break up the rock. The first modern oil well, drilled by Edwin Drake in Pennsylvania in 1859, was drilled in the same way.

BEARINGS

Devices to reduce friction are of ancient origin, the first being log rollers placed under an object that was to be moved.

To work effectively, a wheel needs bearings on its axle. These were invented in France and Germany in about 1000 BCE. The bearings were made of wood and then greased to improve speed and lengthen their life. Modern bearings date back to the late 1700s. They made the development of machines during the Industrial Revolution all the more effective.

FLOATING

The first form of transport to progress under its own power was the raft. In prehistoric times, people must have hitched rides on uprooted trees that happened to be floating down rivers. Rafts borne on ocean currents probably carried people across the world's oceans long before recorded history.

The earliest known hollow boats date back to about 8000 BCE. These were canoes dug out of tree trunks, which were paddled through the water.

The principle of flotation, which explains how things float, was one of the many achievements of Archimedes, the great scientist who lived in Sicily (then a Greek colony) in the 200s BCE. He is reputed to have made this discovery in his bath and then ran naked into the street shouting the inventor's classic cry of "Eureka," which means "I have found it."

Although the principle that Archimedes put forward explained that an iron boat could float, nobody really believed this, and all boats and ships were made of wood until just over two centuries ago. The development of the iron ship coincided with the development of a powerful steam engine, which drove paddle wheels in boats.

SUBMARINES

Traveling under the water and into the air can be risky ventures, and required intrepid pioneers. Understandably, perhaps, the inventors of both the first submarine and balloon persuaded other people to try out their craft.

The first proper submarine took to the water in 1776 during the American War of Independence. It was an egg-shaped wooden vessel invented by the American engineer David Bushnell; it went into action (unsuccessfully) against a British warship. The *Turtle*, as it was called, was very much a forerunner of the modern submersible, having ballast tanks and propellers.

BALLOONS

The first balloon to carry passengers was a hot-air balloon invented by the Montgolfier brothers in France in 1783. It made its first flight in November of that year at Paris, and flew 5 miles (8 km). A few days later the first gas-filled balloon took to the Parisian skies, piloted by its inventor, Jacques Charles. It contained hydrogen, which also lifted the first airship into the air in 1852. This machine, which was steam-powered, was invented by the French engineer Henri Giffard.

SAILS AND PROPELLERS

Sails powered boats along the River Nile in Egypt as long ago as 4000 BCE. These were square sails, which could sail only before the wind. The triangular sail, which is able to sail into the wind, first appeared in about 300 CE in boats on the Arabian Sea.

The propeller was invented in 1836 by Francis Pettit Smith in Britain and John Ericsson in the United States. It first powered a seagoing ship, appropriately called the *Archimedes*, in 1839.

FLYING

The first people to fly were Chinese criminals lifted by large kites. The explorer Marco Polo reported the use of such kites for punishment in the 1200s, but kite flying was also used to look out over enemy territory. Then, five centuries later, balloons began to carry people aloft.

THE AIRFOIL

The principle behind the airfoil – that increasing the velocity of a gas or liquid lowers its pressure—was discovered by the Swiss scientist Daniel Bernoulli in 1738, and the basic form of the winged aircraft was developed during the 1800s. Its design was due to the British engineer Sir George Cayley, who flew the first glider in 1849. This machine carried a child. Four years later, Cayley's coachman (against his will) became the first

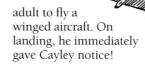

adult to fly a winged aircraft. On landing, he immediately gave Cayley notice!

POWERED FLIGHT

The invention of powered flight is indelibly associated with the Wright brothers, who flew the first powered airplane at Kitty Hawk in North Carolina, USA, in 1903. Unlike all modern aircraft, the wings of the Wrights' flying machine did not have ailerons. This development came in 1908 in aircraft built by the British engineer Henry Farman.

THE HELICOPTER

Like the Wrights' powered airplane, the development of the helicopter was contingent upon the invention of a light but powerful engine—the gasoline engine. The very first helicopter, built by Paul Cornu, whirled unsteadily into the air in France in 1907. The development of a reliable helicopter took about 30 years.

THE HYDROFOIL

The first use of the principle of the airfoil was not in air but in water. In Britain in 1861, Thomas Moy tested wings by fixing them beneath a boat and found that the wings raised the hull above the water. Thus the hydrofoil was born before the airplane. The production of a practical hydrofoil took place in Italy, developed by Enrico Forlanini in the 1910s.

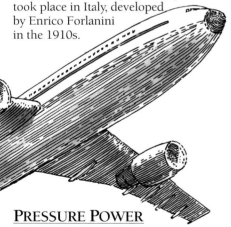

PRESSURE POWER

The achievements of Archimedes inspired generations of inventors and engineers. First was Ctesibius, who lived at Alexandria in Egypt. Ctesibius was renowned for his self-powered devices, notably the first organ. Water was a convenient source of power, and in this instrument, he used the pressure of water to drive air into the pipes; the resulting music was ear-splitting.

PUMPS AND JETS

The water-lifting pump is another invention credited to Ctesibius. However, the slow development of pumps able to produce a continuous jet of water enabled the Great Fire to destroy much of London in 1666. The first proper fire engine did not appear until 1721. The pump was invented by the British engineer Richard Newsham. It was a reciprocating pump with two pistons driven alternately up and down by hand. The fire engine was reputed

to produce a jet of water nearly 160 feet (50 meters) high and to be strong enough to smash a window.

Portable fire extinguishers were developed in the nineteenth century, powered at first by compressed air and then by carbon dioxide.

HYDRAULICS AND PNEUMATICS

An understanding of pressure in both air and water came with the work of the French scientist Blaise Pascal. In the mid-1600s, he discovered the principle that governs the action of pressure on a surface. Pascal's principle explains both

hydraulics and pneumatics. One of its latest consequences is the hovercraft, which was invented in 1955 by the British engineer Christopher Cockerell. This machine began life as a pair of tin cans linked up to a vacuum cleaner, which demonstrated that an air cushion could produce sufficient pressure to support a hovercraft.

SUCTION MACHINES

The vacuum cleaner also began life in Britain, where it was invented by Hubert Booth in 1901. Again, a simple demonstration sufficed to prove its viability: Booth sucked air through a handkerchief to show how it could pick up dirt. However, a practical machine was developed in the United States in 1908 by

William Hoover, and it is his name that has always been associated with the vacuum cleaner. Its distant relative, the aqualung, is also firmly associated with its inventor, the French oceanographer Jacques Cousteau. The aqualung was developed during World War II, and Cousteau subsequently used it to pioneer exploration of the seabed.

IRON AND STEEL MAKING

Iron making dates from 1500 BCE when the Hittites, in what is now Turkey, built furnaces to smelt iron ore with charcoal and so produce the metal itself. The process did not develop further until 1709, when the British iron maker Abraham Darby substituted coke for charcoal and added limestone. His furnace needed a powerful blast of air to burn the coke, but it could make iron in large quantities—a factor that helped to bring about the Industrial Revolution.

The large-scale production of steel from

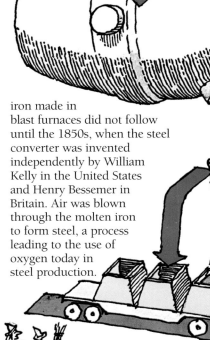

iron made in blast furnaces did not follow until the 1850s, when the steel converter was invented independently by William Kelly in the United States and Henry Bessemer in Britain. Air was blown through the molten iron to form steel, a process leading to the use of oxygen today in steel production.

in 1876. He was able to produce liquid oxygen with it, but such a cold liquid was difficult to keep. James Dewar, a British scientist, developed the vacuum flask in 1892 to store liquid oxygen, but it has since found far wider use in storing hot drinks.

STEAM POWER

The use of heat to provide motive power came in a brilliant invention by the Greek engineer Hero in the first century CE. He built the first steam engine, a little device that spouted jets of steam and whirled around rather like a lawn sprinkler. Hero's engine was of no practical use, and the steam engine vanished until the 1700s, when it was developed in Britain, notably by James Watt. The steam turbine was invented by another Briton, Charles Parsons, in 1884

GASOLINE, DIESEL, AND JET ENGINES

The gasoline engine followed the development of oil drilling in the mid-1800s and also the invention of a four-stroke engine running on gas at about the same time. The first two-stroke engine was invented in 1878, but it was a gasoline-powered four-stroke engine that came to power the horseless carriage. A practical gasoline engine was principally the work of the German engineer Gottlieb Daimler, who developed it in 1883, fitting it first to a boat and then in 1885 to a bicycle. However, it was another German, Karl Benz, who built the first practical motorcar in 1885.

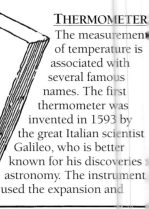

The diesel engine was perfected by Rudolf Diesel in 1897, a year before the invention of the carburetor.

The gasoline engine spurred the invention of the airplane, while the jet engine, being cheaper and faster, has brought us mass worldwide air travel. The jet engine was invented by the British engineer Frank Whittle in 1930.

THE FLUSH TOILET

The water closet, the first of many euphemisms (though more accurate than most) for the flush toilet, dates back to 1589, when it was invented by Sir John Harington, a British nobleman who was a godson of Queen Elizabeth I. The cistern in Harington's invention worked with a valve that released the flow of water. Harington recommended that it be flushed once or preferably twice a day.

Harington's important contribution to the history of technology was centuries ahead of its time, and the water closet did not attain its present form until the late 1800s. The use of a siphon, which does away with valves that can leak, dates from that period.

EXPLOITING HEAT

Harnessing heat was a key technological achievement. The discovery of fire, which happened in China over half a million years ago, provided heat for cooking and warmth. Millennia were to pass before heat was to be turned to much more advanced uses such as smelting metals and providing motive power.

THE REFRIGERATOR AND VACUUM FLASK

Although preserving food by keeping it in an ice-filled pit is an art some 4,000 years old, the first machine capable of reducing temperatures was not built until 1851. James Harrison, an Australian printer, noticed when cleaning type with ether that the type became very cold as the ether evaporated. Using this idea, he built an ether refrigerator. However, it was not very successful, being unable to compete with ice imported all the way from America.

The first practical refrigerator, which used ammonia as the refrigerant, was made by the German scientist Karl von Linde

THERMOMETER

The measurement of temperature is associated with several famous names. The first thermometer was invented in 1593 by the great Italian scientist Galileo, who is better known for his discoveries in astronomy. The instrument used the expansion and contraction of a volume of gas, and was very inaccurate as well as bulky.

The first thermometer to use mercury was invented by German physicist Gabriel Fahrenheit in 1714, and he also devised a temperature scale that bears his name.

GUNPOWDER AND ROCKETS

Heat also became a source of power in gunpowder, the first explosive, which appeared in China about a thousand years ago. Gunpowder had other uses too, and by the 1200s, rockets fueled by gunpowder were being fired in China.

The first person to propose that rockets be used for spaceflight was not an engineer, but a Russian schoolteacher named Konstantin Tsiolkovsky. At the turn of this century, he realized that rockets powered by liquid-fuel engines working in several separate stages would be required to provide the immense power necessary to carry people into space. However, Tsiolkovsky was a visionary and did not build rockets himself.

Liquid-fuel rocket engines were pioneered by the American engineer Robert Goddard, who first launched one in 1926. The first space rocket was built by the Russian engineer Sergei Korolev. It used liquid fuel to launch the first satellite, Sputnik 1, in October 1957, just a century after Tsiolkovsky was born.

NUCLEAR POWER

The basis of nuclear power was discovered in 1905 by the great German-born scientist Albert Einstein. In his Special Theory of Relativity, Einstein explained that a little mass could theoretically be converted into a lot of energy.

Nuclear fission is the practical application of Einstein's theory, and was first achieved in the laboratory of the Italian scientist Enrico Fermi in 1934. Fermi did not realize at the time that fission had in fact occurred, and it was not until 1939 that other nuclear scientists were able to confirm that fission was

possible, and with it the release of enormous amounts of energy. This information was kept secret as World War II loomed, and Fermi and the other scientists went to the United States. There, at the prompting of Einstein, a crash program to build a nuclear reactor went ahead in the fear that Germany might build a fission bomb first. Fermi constructed the first experimental nuclear reactor in 1942.

The first atomic bomb was tested in the United States in July 1945, shortly after the defeat of Germany, and it was Japan that suffered the first, and so far the only, use of nuclear weapons. The hydrogen bomb was first tested by the United States in 1952. The first nuclear reactor to produce electricity was built in Russia in 1954.

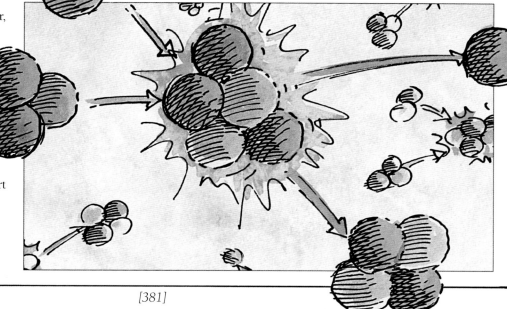

LIGHT AND IMAGES

People must have begun observing how light behaves thousands of years ago. They could see where it came from, and they could see that it was reflected by bright smooth surfaces and cast a shadow when something got in its way. The Greek philosopher Euclid was certainly familiar with the basic principles of optics around 300 BCE, and Alhazen, the famous Arab scholar, wrote an important treatise on the subject in the 900s CE. But no one knew anything about the nature of light until 1666, when Isaac Newton discovered the color spectrum, and 1678, when Dutch mathematician Christiaan Huygens suggested that light is composed of waves. Until then, Newton's assertion that light is made up of particles or "corpuscles" was regarded as more convincing.

ELECTRIC LIGHTS

The American inventor Thomas Edison is usually credited with inventing the electric light. In reality, however, he was beaten to the punch by a British competitor, Joseph Wilson Swan. Swan's filament lamp, not unlike Edison's, had been unveiled nearly a year before Edison's in December 1878. Incandescent lamps are relatively inefficient compared with fluorescent lamps, which give off little heat. Henri Becquerel, the discoverer of radioactivity,

made the first experiments with fluorescence in 1859, but it was not until 1934 that the American physicist Arthur H. Compton developed the first fluorescent lamp for general use in homes and offices.

MIRRORS

"Natural" mirrors made of polished obsidian (a natural glass) were in use in Turkey 7,500 years ago, but the earliest manufactured mirrors were highly polished copper, bronze, and brass. Pliny the Elder mentions glass backed with tin or silver in the first century CE, but silvering did not come into widespread use until the Venetians found a way of doing it in the thirteenth century. A German chemist, Justus von Liebig, invented the modern silvering process in 1835. Modern applications of reflecting surfaces include the periscope and the endoscope. Periscopes were developed for use in submarines in France in 1854. The flexible endoscope using glass fibers with special coatings to reflect images around corners came into use in 1958.

LENSES

The Roman Emperor Nero (37–68 CE) was one of the first people to use a lens (although he may not have realized it) when he watched performances in the arena through a fragment of emerald that just happened to be of the right shape to benefit his poor eyesight. Spherical lenses used as burning glasses were certainly known by the 900s, when Alhazen described how they work. The first lenses to come into general use were convex lenses in spectacles, some-time around 1287 in Italy. The zoom lens, giving a correctly focused image at a range of focal lengths, was developed for use in the movie industry in the 1930s.

TELESCOPES

Lenses had been in use for centuries before Hans Lippershey, a Dutch spectacle maker, happened upon the marvelous invention of the telescope. In 1608, he looked at a nearby church steeple through two lenses placed one in front of the other and found that it was magnified. The working telescopes that followed Lippershey's discovery all suffered from poor image quality caused by the refraction of light through the glass lenses. Isaac Newton solved this problem in 1668 by making a reflecting telescope that worked with mirrors rather than lenses. Binoculars are essentially two telescopes arranged side by side. They first appeared in a Paris opera house in 1823; although it is not known who invented them, they rapidly became popular for use both indoors and outside.

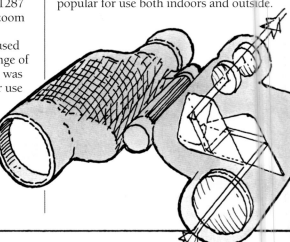

MICROSCOPES

Magnifying glasses have been used as long as convex spectacle lenses have existed, and they were developed into excellent single-lens microscopes by a Dutch merchant, Anton van Leeuwenhoek, in the mid-1600s. By using a tiny bead-like lens, he was able to obtain magnifications of up to 200 times.

The origin of the compound microscope, which has two lenses, is shrouded in some mystery. Another Dutch spectacle maker, Zacharias Janssen, has been credited with inventing the compound microscope in 1590. However, it seems unlikely that this would have preceded the discovery of the telescope, and Janssen's son is thought to have made up the story. Galileo is believed to have experimented with lenses for microscopy, but the biographers of the Dutch-born scientist Cornelius Drebbel insist that he built the first compound microscope in 1619. The first electron microscope was built over three centuries later in Germany in 1928.

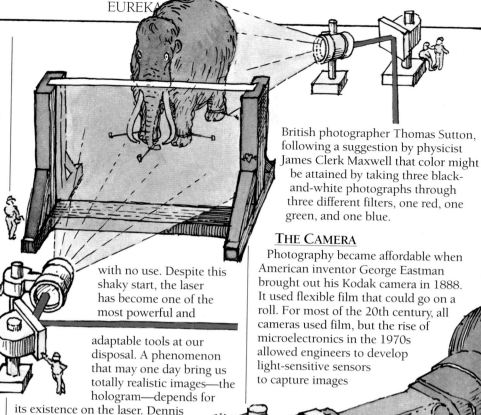

with no use. Despite this shaky start, the laser has become one of the most powerful and adaptable tools at our disposal. A phenomenon that may one day bring us totally realistic images—the hologram—depends for its existence on the laser. Dennis Gabor invented the hologram in 1947, but he could not put his idea into practice until he had a coherent light source, in other words a laser.

British photographer Thomas Sutton, following a suggestion by physicist James Clerk Maxwell that color might be attained by taking three black-and-white photographs through three different filters, one red, one green, and one blue.

THE CAMERA

Photography became affordable when American inventor George Eastman brought out his Kodak camera in 1888. It used flexible film that could go on a roll. For most of the 20th century, all cameras used film, but the rise of microelectronics in the 1970s allowed engineers to develop light-sensitive sensors to capture images electronically, and processor chips to digitize them. Digital cameras have now become the norm.

PHOTOGRAPHY

Photography was invented when Joseph Niepce, a Frenchman, found a way of fixing an image created in a camera obscura ("dark room" or box), a device that had been used for many years previously as a drawing aid for artists. He took his first photograph in 1826. Niepce's young partner, Louis Daguerre, invented a new process in 1837. Eventually it reduced exposure times to under half a minute, making portrait photography hugely popular. But modern photography is based on two breakthroughs made by the British inventor William Fox-Talbot in 1839: the negative-positive method of printmaking, which allows many copies to be made of one exposure, and development of the latent image, leading ultimately to split-second exposure times. The first color photo—of a tartan ribbon—was taken in 1861 by

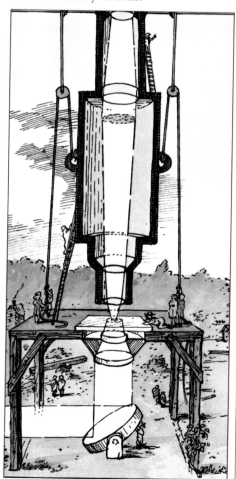

LASERS AND HOLOGRAMS

The first laser was built in 1960 by Theo Maiman of the Hughes Laboratory, USA. At the time it was scorned as the invention

MOVING PICTURES

Two French brothers, Auguste and Louis Lumière, invented the first practical movie camera and projector in 1895. At the first showings of their films, people fainted in the audience as a train appeared to come steaming straight out of the screen into the auditorium. Despite this impressive demonstration of its power, the brothers remained strangely unaware of their invention's enormous potential. When someone offered them a large sum of money for it, Auguste thought he was doing the eager buyer a great favor when he rejected his offer. How wrong he was!

PRINTING

A basic form of printing was practiced by the Romans in the third century. About the same time, Egyptian clothmakers used figures cut in blocks of wood to put marks and patterns on textiles. Block printing of books developed in isolation in both Europe and China. The Chinese produced the first block-printed book in 868 and were also the first to invent movable type in 1041. Unlike blocks, these could be used in the printing of any book, not just one, and were the vital element in Gutenberg's invention four centuries later. The Chinese made type out of baked clay. It soon became clear that only metal type could withstand repeated use. These were first made in Korea in the early fifteenth century. The letterpress method of printing is still in use today.

The press itself was adapted from existing screw presses used in trades like bookbinding and was so efficient that no significant changes were necessary until automation was introduced in the nineteenth century.

ELECTRONIC PAPER

In 1974, American engineer Nicholas Sheridon developed the Gyricon—a computer screen that could be read in bright light. It was filled with millions of tiny spheres suspended in oil-filled capsules. The spheres were dark on one side and light on the other, and could be turned on by electrical signals sent by the computer. Fifteen years later, Sheridon began developing his idea into an alternative to paper. The first electronic book reader to incorporate the idea was Sony's Librie, released in 2004.

THE RECORD PLAYER

The problems of recording sound and playing it back were solved by one of the greatest inventors of all time, the American Thomas Edison. Using a tinfoil cylinder as his "record," he recorded and then reproduced the nursery rhyme "Mary Had a Little Lamb" on December 6, 1877. He called his invention a phonograph. Ten years later Émile Berliner, a German immigrant then living in Washington, invented the flat-disc record player or gramophone.

TELECOMMUNICATIONS

Modern telecommunications has effectively solved the problem of sending messages rapidly over immense distances. Before the electronic age, people had to use whatever methods their ingenuity could devise, such as flashing mirrors and smoke signals. The Greek historian Polybius is reported to have devised a system of alphabetical smoke signals in the 100s BCE, but no Polybius code is known today to rival the Morse code, invented by the American Samuel Morse in 1838. Morse went on to construct the first electric telegraph, which carried his code over wires similar to telephone wires.

In 1844, he sent the first message, "What hath God wrought?"

PAPER

Before paper was invented, people wrote on anything they could lay their hands on: silk and bamboo in China, palm leaves in India, clay tablets in Babylon, and wax tablets in Greece. Between 3000 and 2000 BCE the Egyptians started using papyrus, a type of sedge dried into strips and then glued together in two layers to form a sheet. Paper was invented in China by Tsai Lun in 105 CE. In 751, the Arabs captured some Chinese papermakers at Samarkand and so the invention set out on its 400-year journey to the West. Today, paper is made from fibers produced by trees.

THE PRINTING PRESS

The printing press was invented by Johan Gutenberg in Germany about 1450. It was one of several elements in the printing process (including movable metal type) that Gutenberg was the first to perfect.

SOUND AND MUSIC

If archaeological discoveries are anything to go by, the first musical instruments were hollow bones used as whistles in prehistoric times. Pottery drums have been found dating back 6,000 years. The lyre was a stringed instrument played 4,500 years ago in the ancient city of Ur; it later developed into the harp. Brass instruments have their beginning in hollowed animal horns used to sound fanfares and calls. Straight trumpets over 3,000 years old were found in Tutankhamun's tomb, but the modern valve trumpet dates only from 1801. Probably the first man to give his name to a musical instrument was Adolphe Sax, the inventor of the saxophone in 1846.

THE TELEPHONE

During the great days of early sound engineering, inventors were often at a loss to think of things to say during their experiments and demonstrations. Alexander Graham Bell, however, had no difficulty when he used his newly invented telephone for the first time in 1876: "Mr. Watson. Come at once. I want you" were his first words. He had spilled acid from a battery down his trousers and needed help from his assistant urgently. In inventing the telephone, Bell had also invented two important devices—the microphone and the loudspeaker. The mobile telephone was developed from two-way radio. The first mobile telephone call was made in 1973 by American engineer Martin Cooper—although the first mobile networks were not commercially available until the 1980s. Apple's iPhone, introduced in 2007, was the first popular smartphone.

RADIO

The introduction of the telegraph in 1844 solved the problem of sending messages using electricity. But the new machine had one big drawback: it depended on a physical wire link. Other scientists immediately began working on wireless communications. A breakthrough came in 1888 when the German scientist Heinrich Hertz discovered the existence of radio waves. Seven years later, Guglielmo Marconi, the 21-year-old son of a wealthy Italian landowner, made the first successful transmission using radio waves.

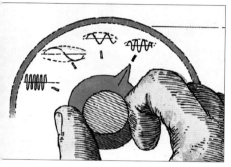

In 1901 he created an even bigger sensation when his radio sent a signal all the way across the Atlantic. Broadcasting began in 1906, when the Canadian inventor Reginald Fessenden first transmitted sound. But the invention of the electronic valve or tube in the same year by the American Lee de Forest was the major factor in the development of broadcasting.

TELEVISION

Considering that television is the most powerful tool of mass communication known to man, it was conceived in remarkably humble circumstances. John Logie Baird was a British amateur scientist who sold shoe polish and razor blades to finance his spare-time research. In 1925,

after years of work, he successfully transmitted the first television picture in his attic workshop, using a boy from the office downstairs as his subject. Because Baird's system was mechanical and gave low picture quality, it was only a matter of time before someone came along with a superior electronic product. That someone was Vladimir Zworykin, a Russian emigrant to America, who built the first electronic television in 1929. The world's first public broadcast was in 1936.

COMMUNICATIONS SATELLITES

The US government was responsible for developing the idea of communications satellites in the 1950s. In July 1962 the American Telephone and Telegraph Company launched Telstar, the first communications satellite to transmit telephone and television signals. It could operate for only a few hours each day, because its low orbit took it out of range of its transmitting and receiving stations for most of the time. Early Bird, launched in 1965, was the first satellite to solve this problem by keeping exact pace with the rotation of the Earth, maintaining an apparently stationary position.

RADIO TELESCOPE

The inventor of the radio telescope, and so of radio astronomy, was the amateur American astronomer Grote Reber. He built his first receiving dish in 1937, having heard about Karl Jansky's 1931 discovery that the Earth is constantly being bombarded with cosmic radio waves. Reber set out to focus these waves with his dish and thereby map where they came from. In 1942 he made the first radio map of the Milky Way galaxy.

SPACE PROBES

The first successful space probe was the Russian Luna 3, which sent back the first picture of the moon's unseen far side in 1959. Probing the planets became a reality in December 1962 when the US spacecraft Mariner 2 reached Venus after a 290-million-kilometer (180-million-mile) journey lasting nearly four months.

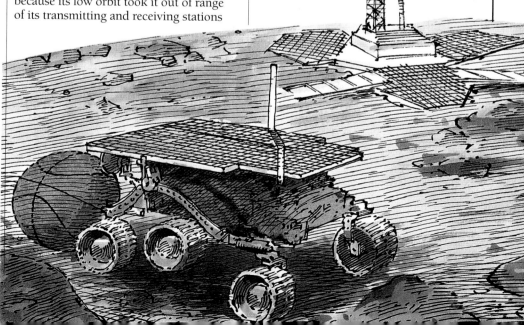

ELECTRICITY

In about 600 BCE the Greek philosopher Thales noticed that amber rubbed with wool somehow acquires the power to attract light objects such as straw and feathers. Over 2,000 years later, in 1600, William Gilbert, physician to Queen Elizabeth I, called this power electricity after the Greek word for amber. It was not until the 1700s that scientists began to learn more about the nature of electricity, and one of the pioneers in the field was the American statesman Benjamin Franklin, also an intrepid investigator. In 1752, Franklin daringly flew a kite in a thunderstorm to prove that lightning is electrical in nature. This famous experiment, in which he was lucky not to have been killed, led Franklin to invent the lightning conductor. Franklin postulated that electricity consists of two varieties of "fluid," one positive and one negative. We now know that the fluid is a stream of negative electrons, which were discovered by the British scientist J.J. Thomson in 1897.

THE BATTERY

In 1780 an Italian anatomist, Luigi Galvani, noticed that the severed leg of a dead frog could be made to twitch when touched by pieces of metal. Galvani concluded rightly that electricity was producing the reaction, but it was another Italian, Alessandro Volta, who found that the electricity came not from the frog, as Galvani had thought, but from the metals. Eventually Volta found that copper and zinc together produce a strong charge and that if he built a pile of metal discs, alternately copper and zinc separated by pads soaked in salty water, he could produce a continuous electric current. Perfected in 1800, the Voltaic pile, as it is called, was the first electric battery. Since then, a great range of different types of battery has been developed.

THE PHOTOCOPIER

In the 1930s Chester Carlson was working for the patents department of a large electronics firm in New York. He was happy enough in his work except for one thing—the time and expense involved in getting patents copied. Eventually he became so frustrated that he decided to invent a whole new process himself. The result was the first xerographic copy, taken on October 22, 1938. Dispensing with the messy wet chemicals used in existing copiers, Carlson had invented a dry process based on the ability of an electrostatically charged plate to attract powder in the image of the original document. Several years later the rights to the process were acquired by a small family firm that later grew into the mighty Xerox corporation, making Chester Carlson a very wealthy man in the process.

MAGNETISM

Legend has it that the phenomenon of magnetism was first observed by a Greek shepherd called Magnes when he noticed that his iron-tipped crook picked up pieces of black rock lying around on the ground. This black rock was a kind of iron ore called magnetite. Queen Elizabeth I's physician, William Gilbert, was the first man to formulate some of the basic laws of magnetism and to speculate that the Earth itself is one big magnet. In 1644 René Descartes showed how magnetic fields could be made visible by scattering iron filings on a sheet of paper. Apart from the compass, however, no practical use for magnets was found until the invention of the electric motor—although Franz Anton Mesmer, the original mesmerizer, did manage to persuade eighteenth-

century Parisians for a few years that magnetism was a cure for certain illnesses.

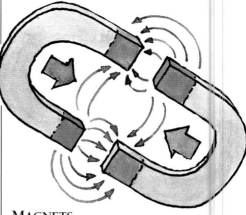

MAGNETS

The earliest magnets were made from naturally occurring magnetic rock called magnetite. Later, when magnetite's directional properties were recognized, the name lodestone, meaning leading stone, was coined and it was used to make magnetic compasses. Magnets did not really come into their own until 1820 when the Danish physicist Hans Oersted made his sensational discovery of the link between magnetism and electricity. This event changed the course of human history by making possible the great electrical inventions of the nineteenth century such as the motor, the dynamo, and, in the field of telecommunications, the telegraph.

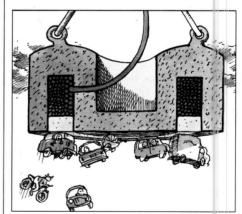

ELECTROMAGNETS

The electromagnet was one of the discoveries made possible by Oersted's great breakthrough. Shortly after it was announced, a French scientist, André-Marie Ampère, proved that wires could be made to behave exactly like magnets when a current was passed through them and that the polarity of the magnetism depended on the direction of the current. So the electromagnet—a magnet whose field is produced by an electric current—was born. Later the American inventor Joseph Henry found that wrapping several layers of